mistakes on the Path

madhuri

MJ PRESS
HEBDEN BRIDGE, UK.

This is the story of one woman's experience in a remarkable milieu.
It is wholly subjective, and is not meant to be a definitive history. This is the way it was for me; for someone else, any particular event might have been seen differently. Everyone has her/his own commune.
Any factual errors are mine.
Some names and identifying details have been changed to protect privacy.
Other, brave people have allowed me to use their names.

I want my people to understand it absolutely that unless you become blissful on your own accord, unless your rose opens within your own being, you are just a commodity, just a thing, an object. Meditation reveals your subjectivity. Subjectivity is your consciousness, and your consciousness and its experience makes your life significant, meaningful, eternal, immortal, without any beginning and without any end. A celebration, moment-to-moment a dance.
~Osho, Yahoo! The Mystic Rose, CH 30, Q1

To become a wise old person, you must first be a foolish young one.
~traditional saying

All other photos are from author's collection.

Osho's words spoken directly to me are written from memory.

"Not I, but the wind" is a phrase from the first line of
Song of a Man Who Has Come Through, by D.H. Lawrence

Cover and interior design by Peggy Sands, Indigo Disegno
Cover photo and painting by author
Author photo on cover by Lucy Cartwright

ISBN 978-0-244-47169-9

Table of Contents

Introduction *ix*

A Mysterious Summons *3*

Interlude: San Francisco *51*

Soul Garden *71*

Bouncy Castle *263*

Cowboy Planet *271*

Dipped in the World like a Frosty Cone *355*

Soul Garden in Bloom *389*

A Carnival Decade *437*

Chaos *523*

Healing *543*

Not I, but the Wind *595*

Appendix of Treasures *609*

Books by Madhuri Z K Ewing
madhurijewel.com/books

Impassioned Cows By Moonlight (1975, as Katy Akin)

Love at Dancing Leaves: a Tantra Memoir (2010, as M. K. MacCrae)

More about the Moon (2014)

A Colorful Dessert of Flowers (2016)

The Poona Poems (2017)

To all of us, and all of Him.

Introduction

I have heard Osho say, "Enlightenment isn't of the Unknown. It is of the Unknowable." He added that it is helpful for people to try to describe it, even though they cannot succeed.

This, then, is my impossible task: to describe the atmosphere in which I spent thirty years of my life. In retrospect, I would say that the sometimes-grumpy mundanities of daily existence inevitably shrink things in memory: and so retrospection can't really be accurate.

At the time, magic was the rule, the umbrella over us, the very air we breathed.

Sitting with Osho, or dancing in a great hall where he sat in a chair – we were in a different dimension than the usual. We were suddenly in a place where it was clearly obvious that Love is what things are really formed from; we were subsumed in a greater miracle, a harmonious, healed vibrancy not arrangeable by mere man. It was like being in a room where the whole vast range of the Himalaya had somehow managed to fit itself – impossibly tall, impossibly vast – and we were being shone on – poured through – by a lofty grace rich with joy.

We could only lift up our arms – .

I was a callow, scrawny, rather cynical child of twenty-one when I first went to India, in 1973. This is the story of how I faltered, and erred, and could not hear; and how, eventually, at long last, I stumbled on one or two understandings – with a bit more help, and in a very small way; particular ones Osho had tried to give me, decades before.

This book is a celebration of that most peculiar phenomenon: the-being-who-is-beyond-the-small-self; written by someone very wrapped up in her own world.

Osho told me to write this book; and gave me the title. It's about the mistakes I made – in the light of a clear sharp empty love-sun; an elegant, spare, sophisticated and luxuriant Zen star.

It's a bumpy ride.

1

A Mysterious Summons

A Mysterious Summons

1973 – 1974

An Aerogram Arrives

On a foggy spring morning I was downstairs on the sidewalk in front of the house, fishing in the mailbox, which was bolted to the wall beside the front steps.

There was a thin blue aerogram. I took it out, noting the squiggly, unfamiliar script printed on it. Carefully, I tore it open along the side, using my fingernail. Something fell out and down to the sidewalk. I bent over and picked it up – turned it right-side-up; looked at it.

It was a small photograph in black and white. A man, bearded, laughing, his mouth open, head back a little. His round head was partly bald, the hair that remained was long and dark.

Something happened inside my body. It was as if some energy entered through my middle and kept going till it touched my spine. Then it fell down into some deep, resonating area inside me. There was no escape from this picture. It had got to me, already. There it was. And my mind said: Why, he's *laughing!* I haven't laughed in… *how long?*

I took the aerogram back upstairs to show it to my mother. I enjoyed clopping up the two sets of stairs in my dramatic shoes, which made me feel agreeably leggy: I was dressed in thigh-hugging bell-bottom jeans (the bells much-widened by my own denim inserts), a snug, cropped t-shirt with horizontal stripes layered over a long-sleeved, scoop-necked t-shirt, and high platforms with ankle straps, in red and yellow leather, with stars sewn across the toe.

Our apartment was at the top of a stout, plain stucco house set right up close to its neighbors, on Missouri Street, on steep Potrero Hill in San Francisco.

For $165 a month, my mother Virginia, little brother Andy and I, had each a room (the living room being one of them, allocated to Andy). There was a light, airy kitchen, and a little wooden back porch set on tall spindly legs, with a fabulous view over the bay, the Bay Bridge with its great swooping supports and spans, and an ever-shifting panoply of ships, sailboats, barges, tugs… the whole ponderous festivity of a busy port.

The letter was from my younger sister in India. She was not quite eighteen. She told us that she had been sitting waiting for the man in the picture to come into a room; he was going to give a talk. Then, she said, he walked through the door… and, "I fell forward onto the floor… totally surrendering to him."

She said he had given her a new name: Ma Ananda Sarita, meaning 'River of Bliss.'

What did this mean? *Surrender?* I could not fathom it, so I quickly put the whole notion aside. This did not sound like my stubborn, decisive, vulnerable, determined little sister. Or did it? I did not know. There were, I perceived, things *I could not know* about all this.

Sannyas magazines followed. Our mother read them with the interest born of her life's desperation. I did not read them, after a glance or two.

Letters from Sarita

August 16, 1973

Dear Araminta,*

Okay, it doesn't matter how you approach India. Nothing can be known – only the coming – and this is good. Just being open to let India approach is good – it is enough.

As to differences between Tantra and EST – any comment I might make would either be too long or too short. I have not experienced EST and you have not known Bhagwan so there is no sameness and no difference, nothing to comment on.

I used to have a goal to live – that is why I ever did anything – to find life – to experience – something I could call, "This is life," so I could say, "Now I am alive." It was in tension I searched. It was as if a thorn was in my foot and in the blindness of pain I kept running over the earth – hoping the intensity of

* A family name – my maternal grandmother's – I coveted but had not been given.

my run would release the thorn. It was driven further & further in, till finally I am forced to stop still and examine myself.

Now the world I was running through is spinning around like a hazy dream. And the goal also, and the search also. I feel a subtle goallessness kind of like delirious honey seeping through me. I don't know. There is nothing to be known, just the emergence of all the hidden – the spring.

This thinking that you have to come to India, is a door also to nowness. Maybe now it is the right time to come if the thinking is intense. If it wants to be done then just do it totally and it is the ultimate now. Blocking is not totally flowing with what wants to be done, or needs to be done. Don't listen to me. I'm just picking up words from the evening and putting them here. I don't know what is said. But if what is said agrees with you then listening will perk up anyway.

Anyhow, I repeat these matters: Come in September – late Sept. is good. The 20th or so and make sure Mama comes in all her childishness and awe. For her it is the most important to come. Your way flows for you – she is afraid of her way. Let her take this jump. Also I might mention I don't wear prints – shades of orange but not prints. They give me the same feeling meat & eggs do – most peculiar. Just a surge which must be followed; a sensation – a declining.

[...] Just a few days back I scrawled a letter to Mama in reply to one wherein she said she felt it was best I return. What she was saying I felt is that she is afraid to come. She wants to witness my madness before she plunges in.

Mama I can't give you your own Eastern-ness. I can call you, that is all. You must plunge in to discover this in yourself. It is so wanting to be discovered. You have grown so much in this life. Your seeds have created a forest – your branches are vast and beautiful. But in the subtler depths there are so many roots – the roots of your life energy – the roots of your being – and you must discover these roots – the inner eyes. When the whole is realized then you can be at peace, just the wind passing through your branches, just your presence echoing silent existence.

Bhagwan be with you

Sarita

August 31, 1973

Dearest Katy*

Such a beautiful letter. Have mercy. My breasts are aching with love of

* The name most people called me. Our mother used to say, "A child who is much loved will have many names."

you. Please come. Let us discover each other here. Let us know one another from the depths. Please come if only for a minute. All these accumulations and pleasures which inspire your wellbeing can be washed away in a second to be overwhelmed by the ocean of you. So much is here which cannot be explained. What I meant in that previous letter was that you are strong and you will hold yourself up. You are not afraid to recreate your universe. And Mama is scared to discover her universe. Thus Mama needs to come just to discover her universe. You need to come so you can discover there is no need to recreate your universe. All the beauty all the grace of the divine is waiting to be loosed from you. Hear me again and if you hear me, remember, it is you speaking. Come to the feet of the Master and see yourself just as you are. If you feel ripe for discovery, come.

India, our mother, contains many many secrets which are the roots of our existence and yet which we know nothing about. Fairy tales become more real here than any fact of science, because fairy tales are rooted in these cosmic secrets, these currents which guide us. The West is very shallow. It is so new and has forgotten that its dust contains ancestors, it has forgotten the mystery. It is an ignorant child seeking without knowing why or where. The sourcelessness and the dissolution, the eternity and the play of cosmos is all forgotten. The West is lost in its ego and yet the soul of the original source still pulses. But India knows the secrets and guards them well. You must be a true seeker to discover.

Katy dearest, your writing is rare and your very being is even more rare. So much will flow from you if you can see yourself as you are reflected in Bhagwan. I so long to meet both you and Mama at the funky little Bombay airport & take you into this magic realm… I don't have a home but Bhagwan is here.

Bombay can appear funky like the Date St. House.* In fact, India and Indians are like the Date St. House at a deeper level. It is a good realm to go exploring in – quite significant for us especially.

So don't make any choice. Let the choicelessness make you…

Let the poet decide – let the poem of you carry you in its tide.

Sistersistersister

is it that we embrace or are we embraced?

Totally love

Sarita

---

* Our childhood house.

Dynamic Meditation

My mother and I got out of my blue Mustang convertible in front of the church. There were rust holes all around the bottom of the car, from the salt sea air. It was my first car, the only one that I would ever own. It was as scruffy as every other dented San Francisco vehicle – parking on steep crowded hills is a guarantee of dents and dings. My boyfriend Herb had helped me get financing for the $500 it cost.

It was really Herb's presence in my life that had given me courage and impetus to pretend, for a while, to be a citizen. After two years spent knocking around Europe having painful romantic and unromantic misadventures, being always broke, and writing a very great deal, I was trying to be an American. This was really just so that I could participate with Herb; to feel his warm, chuckling approval as we sat across from each other at dinner in some expensive restaurant. To sit beside him on the sofa at his house in the hills behind Berkeley, watching the Watergate trials, and derive some strange nourishment from this dry theater, just because he was warm and big and substantial next to me. Herb's family were first-generation Russian Jewish immigrants, and his patriotism was frank and clear. I was going for a ride on this exotic river of something like normalcy… My family were radicals, and then, some of us, hippies. It was funny for me, diverting, to have a fashionable shag haircut, a rich, successful boyfriend. Herb had designed the computer system for the Trans-America Pyramid building, so prominent on the San Francisco skyline. He was also a professor of computer engineering at the University of California, Berkeley. We'd met at a dream workshop at his house. I was twenty then, he was thirty-nine, a tall, bluff man with a big rounded nose and prognathous jaw, tidy of habit, usually calm, often laughing.

But today brought a new experiment. My mother and I went down some steps and into the big basement of the church. (Coincidentally, it was the same church where she and my father had married, thirty-four years before.) We were greeted by Sushila, a plump, roly-poly woman with shiny cheeks and a frequent riff of rich mirth. We joined the handful of others who had come to experience Dynamic meditation. We were each given a blindfold; then Sushila explained, and demonstrated, what we were going to do.

When the music started, my blindfold was on; the world was gone, and there was only me, and this blackness. Somehow I knew that the only way to do this new thing was *totally* – and Sushila had also used that word when she was showing us what to do. So I breathed and hopped and used my elbows as a bellows. I let my body fly into an excruciating meeting with itself – all sorts of pains appearing, moving, changing. The first stage – deep, fast, chaotic breathing – seemed to last an hour; but it was only twelve minutes.

Next we were to "go completely mad," as Sushila had instructed us. Howls and screams were bouncing off the walls. I was in it, doing my best, pushing myself as hard as I could; my body flinging itself into all sorts of contortions, beating the air with my fists. I was trying to let out any rage or pain I could find in myself.

Then we jumped on our heels, arms high above our heads, pushing the sound *Hoo!* down into our sex center, feeling the energy shoot back up and out the top of the head. This too went on forever – twelve minutes. Then – a voice came out of the tape machine: *ESTOP!* and we *froze* – forever. Oh, the arms ached! Oh, I wanted to move, to relieve myself of the pain of just being, staring myself in the face, here in the dark!

But I didn't move. I stayed still, and watched as energies shot and crawled in new ways through me.

Then, the blessed music… strange plucking melodious twangs sent me dancing all over the floor, floating, turning about, leaping, not bumping into anyone – Sushila had told us not to worry, we wouldn't collide.

Then it was over.

When I came out from behind the blindfold, my life had changed. There was a Knowing in me: *If I can't face the simple fact of the inside of me, how on earth can I have the right to live on the outside? So, I must face the inside.*

It was that simple. I was stunned, silent, gawping as we went back up the stairs, got into the car.

I turned the key in the ignition. The car started. I released the parking brake, began to back up. But what was happening? I found that the steering wheel would barely turn; I needed all my force to move it even a little. And I needed to press the brake pedal down with all my force to get the car to stop. What was going on? Was it, somehow, the meditation that made the car behave so oddly?

I drove all the way across the City like this – wrenching and wrestling with my arms; pressing and straining with my feet – from near the Presidio to Potrero Hill. Parked on our street, with difficulty. Went to find the cheap-and-ready mechanic down the block, he who had already been sweetly taking most of the money I earned these days.

It turned out the power brake and steering fluid line had sprung a leak. While I was in there yelling.

This struck me as very weird!

Letter from Sarita

September 28, 1973

Dearest Katy
Beautiful Sister
Come with braces.* If I close my eyes I see a pond filled with lotus blossoms. If I close my eyes there is a deep inner falling. I call to you, weeping before existence. The memory is deeper than the West, deeper than any western conceptions because in the West there is not an enlightened master. The blind lead the blind. They search in the right direction, the path is good but not whole. Sai Baba is a miracle maker. He awes people, that is all. So many gurus are just in a power play. When you feel the love, then there can be no thoughts, then you are dissolved.

Imagine the terror of being in the presence of one who knows your very woman-essence much much more totally than you have even glimpsed. It is exalting just to see that core looked into, entered into – and exposed.

The way you are growing is a perfect preparation for Tantra. You don't have to give up the world, you just have to give up attachment for it and that can be achieved only by going through it. You have been going through it. Now, like Mama, a more total awareness is needed, a more other-world awareness.

Your preparation has been so perfect.

My love please read this not as me talking. I am not saying anything. The pen writes. It can be frightening. I can sound so self-assured, I can inspire expectation; but really I am not anything, not assured, not writing. I feel as a medium for the magnetic flow to reach you and embrace. Something greater than me wants for you to be curious as hell, so curious that you will come to India with braces on your teeth.

Totally love
Sarita

* I had written to her saying that I might not be able to come, as I needed to spend all my savings getting braces on my crooked teeth.

Late in October Sarita sent another aerogram telling us she was in hospital with malaria-like symptoms, which turned out to be typhoid. She was accommodated next to a ward of newborn babies, and shared this:

Dear Mama and Katy

And so it is I find myself ensconced in a hospital for the first time since I was born. I am right next to a ward for newborn babies. The nurses in their white saris pass by my bed with multitudes of the squirming bundles and usually pause to show me the little puckered faces. Once in the ward they seem to begin howling. I suddenly got a feeling of how it would be to hear that cry from something that was expelled from out of my body. It is a strong instinctive feeling of love & protectiveness. In the East they say life begins with a cry because life is a misery. I guess it's like saying oh shit here I am again. What did I ever do to deserve this repetition of the same old struggle? Bhagwan says to be born is to be expelled from the Garden of Eden. He says the true meaning of Adam and Eve is to be found in birth.

But anyway this hospital seems to be pretty funky but having never stayed in one within the bounds of my memory I'm not one to judge. I must simply shrug as we learn to do here and say, this is India. What will be will be... This is actually an excellent opportunity to be checked because for 1½ years I was a traveler and had not been to a doctor for two years...

And so dearest chickadees all grace be with you.

This hospital smells like food. [...] Most peculiar.

Love

Ananda Sarita

We Are Flying

My mother and I settled ourselves into our seats in the big Air India plane. A sari-clad stewardess brought boiled sweets in crackly little wrappers. This seemed to me a mean, strange offering, and I declined. The plane was airborne.

It was so very odd that we could actually find ourselves here – we who had not had even a five-dollar bill to ourselves for most of our lives. But I simply had to do this thing, this travel to the unknown. The lure was too strong to ignore. I *wanted* to ignore it; but could not. My mother had wanted to go from the beginning; it was a tragic fact that her money arrived through an insurance settlement for the burning-down of our family home in Southern California; an accident during which a life was lost – an infant I had never met; and grown-up hearts were broken.

Now it was nearly dawn, on 9th December, but still very dark. I looked out the window. There was a full moon shining on the big silver wing. Down below, strangely weak yellow lights glowed fuzzily. The countryside down there seemed ancient, poorly-powered, and yet... there was in me a huge presentiment. I knew that I was coming here to die in some way; that there was to be a cracking-open of all that I had been. I could not know what would come after. I was only full of an ominous tide, like a huge wave arching under me. I could only dive in. I opened my diary, always as close to me as a papoose to a squaw, and I wrote...

entering India

flying into the specter
of my own mystery...
moon, old woman on the wing

below, pools of silver
flash tropical,
go black.

nobody out there.
sadness; and sadness
too whored a word
for the piano keys
it plays –

there was old mrs. swain
lived down at the corner
in a yellow frame house
with the ghost of her husband

in stiff bib overalls
who'd died on the toilet.
to us she was television
and two circles of red
on wrinkled cheeks.
mrs. swain can I have some candy?
can I have a bowl of money?
can I have a bowl of god?

i was born
asking for candy
and for a long time
i will ask, and ask
till I am dead of asking,
till I am dead of asking,
and awake.

Into the Mystery

We stepped out of the plane and down the steps onto the tarmac. The air wrapped itself around my face like a wet wash-cloth smelling of old pee, spices and flowers.

My sister was right there to meet us. She was wearing orange – a short, fitted blouse and a long dirndl skirt. Her hair was long and rippling and she had a big white flower behind one ear. She was beaming and glowing, and I knew right then that the sister I had last seen in Italy in 1971 was no more. This was a new sister; she belonged to something else now, belonged altogether. She was not mine to reach, to know, to companion. Someone much, much bigger had got her. Someone as big as the sky. I was abashed, chastened.

Something in me drew back from this painful seeing, and yet moved even more strongly forward.

We were staying in a wooden house with intricate carvings in the shutters, in a narrow street in a warren of other narrow streets, in this crowded, filthy, decrepit city. Our hostess, a middle-aged Indian woman, was a disciple of Bhagwan, the man we had come to meet. There were servants, and dim rooms with smells of sandalwood and rosewater, unfamiliar spices, and the ubiquitous smells that came in from the streets; of shit, and diesel, and flowers, and unwashed bodies, and dust, and many a thing I could not name.

The city was terrifying to me. It seemed to be post-apocalyptic – as if buildings were eroded and covered with spiderweb; and grey and decaying. Five thousand years old, and looking every day of it. Little dead men lay on the sidewalks, with mucus in their facial hair, eyes staring up, thick-soled bare feet next to the traffic. I had never seen anyone dead before… I gulped. Even buildings under construction, scaffolded by uneven, skewy, skinny tree-trunks, seemed to have already gone into old age and ruin. I wanted to run away. It was all just too strange, too horrible, too *old*.

We took a bucket-bath in a well-appointed but odd bathroom. I found that such a bath was not too bad – you could get plenty of warm water over you with the big cup. It was good to get the miasma of travel off. But the toilet, in a small adjoining closet, required squatting over a porcelain hole, then washing your nether bits with water from a crusted old cup. My sister had told us how to use this. She had already taught us many things – how to make the taxi slow down – *"aahista, aahista!"* or speed up – *"jaldi, jaldi!"* That we must wash well, with non-perfumed soap, as Bhagwan's body was very sensitive. How to waggle our heads when giving instructions to the servants; when thanking our hostess.

My sister was impatient to dress us in orange. Between her and the household, we were lent garments, made of *khadi*-cloth, or handloom – soft and simple weaves in a plain orange. Then we got into another taxi and set out for Woodland Apartments, where Bhagwan lived.

We drew up in front of a tall block of flats with a few trees in front, went up stairs, and knocked at a plain door. It opened. Inside was a desk, in a hallway; an extraordinary little woman sat behind it. Her eyes were Keane-huge, like those cheesy paintings so popular in the 60's, but these were no pitiful tear-jerking orbs. They were fierce, glowing, round, dark and yet glistening. She was very thin and slightly bent; of indeterminate age – anywhere from thirty to fifty. She wore an orange cloth on her head, vaguely nurse- or nun-like; pinned to her black hair. She did not smile.

This was Laxmi.

Sarita introduced us gracefully, easily. Laxmi nodded cursorily at our mother and let her pass. Then the full gaze of those round, disapproving eyes rested on me, bored into me. I was clearly found wanting. I sensed that she did not want to let me by; but did, reluctantly, for Sarita's sake. *Sarita*… the name suited my sister much better than any name she had ever been known by.

Laxmi nodded towards the hallway, got up, walked stoopingly in front of us, hands behind her back in her orange pleated long skirt and long tailored top, down towards a closed door.

As I walked down that hall I was registering many things at once. Laxmi seemed to me like a being out of a fairy-tale our mother used to read to us; she was either the dog with eyes as big as saucers, or the dog with eyes as big as dinner-plates, which guarded the inner sanctum where the treasure lay. There was a distinct and welcome drop in temperature – it was *chilly* in this apartment. I smelt a sort of musty tropical fustiness, which I would come to know as typical air conditioning smell in a tropical clime, but which was now entirely new to me. I saw my sister walking ahead of our mother and me, in her orange robe, her thick honey-colored hair down her back; I saw her joy and confidence. I saw my mother with her red-dyed hair, her bulge of tummy from seven babies carried to term, under her borrowed clothes; and though she walked in front of me it was as if I could see too the concavity of her left chest; her worried expression, her brown eyes and the nearly, to us young 'uns, lugubrious wrinkles of anxiety and care.

I felt my body in the unaccustomed khadi, light and lissome and somehow elevated. And I felt we were approaching the Door…

Laxmi knocked, looked in, said something into the room, stepped away, turned, went back along the hall to her desk. One by one we three entered the room.

I couldn't pay attention to the others then – for all my attention was on what was happening to me – and all of my attention was incredulous, in shock.

It was as if I stepped over the threshold into a wall of fragrant *bliss*. It pushed at me, it was unlike anything I had ever known, anywhere; it smelt of a pine forest on a clear cold day. The fragrance and the bliss and the coolness were one; I could barely step into them, I wanted to sink to my knees. But I made myself continue into the room – though inside myself, I *had* fallen to my knees, was crawling.

There was a man in there, sitting in a chair. Well... he was something like a man – but he was not a man. He was a light, it was shining all around him, filling up the whole room. The light was also a penetration – it saw and knew. I was just a beetle, a deer caught in the headlights of a car, a seen-through wisp of a creature without a name; and there was only one thought in my head, clearly noticeable in the x-ray light: "Why – he's not an Indian; he's an *Everything!*"

And then I dashed forward and tried to hug him.

Darshan

In California, of course, you hugged people when you met them, like shaking hands; or like the French do double cheek-kisses. Not real hugs, not long body-and-energy-exploring let-goes, but distinct, hippie-world, we-are-all-in-the-summer-of-love-together hugs. Brotherly/sisterly.

So that was what I tried to do.

It was exactly as if I'd tried to hug a small iceberg. But it was more than an iceberg – it was a dry-ice-iceberg, vaporous and thus ever-expanding in its field. It did not want to be hugged. It froze at me, *repelled* me.

Flustered, I drew my arms back, then sat down on the floor a few feet in front of him where he sat in his lone upholstered chair, small bookshelf beside him with books in it. There was nothing else in the room; no other furniture.

My mother and sister sat on the floor nearby. We all looked up at him. He looked at us, beaming first at Sarita, talking with her a bit about where we were staying, and so on. Then he turned to my mother. She gazed at him mutely with her brown, suffering eyes. Her heart was full and her hope entire; I could see this. Bhagwan asked her a few questions – she was circumspect, it seemed to me, in her replies – then he turned and took up a clipboard from the top of the bookshelf, and with a practised motion put it on his knee. He took a pen and wrote something on a piece of paper that was on the clipboard. From somewhere he produced a *mala* – Sarita had told us about this. It was a necklace with one hundred and eight *rudrock* beads to represent the one hundred and eight methods of meditation; and hanging from it, an oval pendant with his picture in it cast in plastic. He held this necklace out in a loop using both hands. My mother bent her head and he placed the mala over it, so that now the pendant rested on her chest. He read aloud to her the name he had just written: "Ma Devadasi. Will it be easy to pronounce?"

He asked how long she was staying – six weeks. "Very good," he said. He was glowing love into her, very soft and caring; as if she was an honored veteran, deserving of all tenderness.

Then he turned to me. And he said, "So many rings?"

It was very simple sitting there in front of him. There was just *this* – as if the moment had been pumped up with a bicycle pump until it was all there was; this cool bare room, this exact position on the floor where I sat, this odd vast *being* in front of me with its absolute authority… this sense of levitation, this slowing down so that each detail was seen curiously, as if this was the first morning of the world. I don't know if my mouth was hanging open, but it certainly felt as if it was.

I looked down at my hands; there was a turquoise-and-coral ring, or a silver ring, on each finger (though not the thumbs). I looked back up at him.

"Ready for Sannyas?" he asked jovially.

I went into further gap-state, and out of it came – "Yes." Purely a polite reflex, because I didn't know what it was about at all – Sannyas, a Master, a Disciple. Sarita had been telling us many things, about both her own ecstatic surrender and the history and culture of gurus and disciples; but I didn't feel connected with these ideas. Intellectually I didn't at all know what this person had to do with me. Energetically, factually, I was agog and in shock, utterly gotten-to. It didn't matter how many dissertations you delivered over a fissure in the earth somebody had lain a stick of dynamite in. The stick of dynamite mattered, though – very, very much.

Now, Bhagwan was holding up the loop of the mala. I ducked and he placed it over my head, onto my shoulders. I sat back up. He wrote on another piece of paper on his clipboard and then held the paper out to me. I looked at what was written: *Ma Prem Madhuri*, and the date, *9.12.1973*.

He did not tell me anything about the name.

My mother and I had brought a few photos, as instructed by Sarita. They were supposed to be of people very important to us. Sarita was holding them, and now they were produced and Bhagwan looked carefully at each one: our oldest brother Garth, his wife Kathy, and their two small sons.

Bhagwan gave each of them a name and a mala, though they had not asked. I showed him a photo of Herb, big and bearded. Bhagwan said, "We will make a sannyasin out of him!" I showed him photos of one or two friends.

Then he gave me a meditation to do: every day for one hour I was to imagine I was making love. I was to invite the lover of my choice and go through the whole act, with sound and movement and all – not a masturbation, he explained, though if orgasm occurred that was fine – but an acting-out.

I sat with my hanging jaw.

Then he and Sarita discussed what we three were supposed to do until the meditation camp in Mt. Abu in January: Dynamic meditation on Chowpatty Beach in the morning. Lecture the next evening. And then, as soon as train tickets could be got, we were to travel up to Baroda and stay and work at a farm belonging to Sheela's parents. (Sheela was a young Indian disciple.)

Bhagwan and Sarita had an easy flow between them – she sat with her beautiful big eyes, her full mouth with its perfect square teeth; and she glowed trustingly, sweetly, at him. It was as though this role was more natural and more known to her than any other she had tried to inhabit in her short, rocky life.

Then we were leaving, namaste-ing as we had been shown.

As we went back down the stairs to the street Sarita was explaining to me helpfully that my name meant "Sweet Love," and that I had been given it because there was actually a really sweet interior to me (the implication was clear that this was contrary to the exterior, which was obviously a brittle, damaged mess!) She had already explained that "Ma" meant "mother of the universe," and that that is what all women are. The next word, "Prem," was a prefix. You were either on the path of love, if it was "prem," or the path of awareness, if it was "anand." The third name was Bhagwan's recognition of our personal true being.

Here was a taxi, as Sarita was explaining our mother Devadasi's name to her: "Servant of the Nature Gods," literally, but historically temple prostitutes have been called that; Sarita explained the original meaning and beauty of the custom, but Devadasi was already beginning a long upset-ness over her name! This prostitute business, temple or no, was not at all palatable to her! (I was thinking, though, of her great joy in the woods, in the mountains – to me she seemed to have a direct link with the nature gods.)

But as I sat silently there beside my mother and sister I was noticing alarming symptoms in my body, which continued and increased as the day went on. The mala weighed around my neck, and I felt mildly electrocuted by it in a rather distressing way. We went on a boat to the island of Elephanta, very close to shore, and toured some caves in the heat; Sarita seemed keen on the carvings in them, but I just felt bleak, awkward, un-enthused. Later we went back to the house, where the servants brought to a large dining table little dishes of spicy beans and vegetables and rice and chutneys. Our hostess ate with us and was chatty and solicitous. We bathed again and went to bed… And, god, how *strange,* all the while a terrific buzzing was going on in a place in the middle of my forehead, just above the eyebrows. It wouldn't let up… and simultaneously, sharp, queasy electric currents passed through the arches of my feet. It seemed I did not belong to myself any more – bad custodian though I may have been; something had taken me over, and was making life uncomfortable indeed.

Before we went to bed I gave all my rings to the servants. They looked at me reproachfully, as if disappointed. Perhaps they would rather have had something else.

In Bombay

We were roused at 5:30 a.m., hastily donned our borrowed robes in the dimly-lit room, and went out into the pre-dawn dark of the foetid-smelling street, which was already busy with humanity's to-ings and fro-ings. I was discovering that India never sleeps. A rickshaw took us to a dim, muggy beach where other people were silently gathering.

And once again I jumped into Dynamic meditation, that extraordinary, no-holds-barred, wild discipline I'd done that time in San Francisco.

Something was taking place within me; something I would have no way of describing, not yet nor for a long time to come. I was being Called Out – an invitation had been tendered, by my sister and by Bhagwan (for she had written to us that he had kept asking, "When they are coming? When they are coming?") And something in me, some deep place below conscious thought, had understood the vital importance of this beckoning to an abyss. *Something* knew there was no getting out of this and if there was no getting out, and that *recognizing* being, Bhagwan, had done the inviting… well, I'd just better go for it! I'd better go into it, whatever it was, with every particle of energy I could muster from anywhere in the Universe, hadn't I?

So that was what I did. I did not shirk; not then, nor later.

But I suffered. Lord, I suffered. Oh yes. My body did not like this waking up!

So, blindfolded, we all huffed and puffed and then yelled and jumped; and stood stock-still… and when, after dancing about on the beach-sand, we took off the blindfolds and emerged to the light of a muggy new day, there was of course a crowd gaping at us – the inescapable, ubiquitous crowd of India.

I might add here that I had had virtually no spiritual education. Our family were atheists or agnostics. I'd carefully avoided the stray bits of spiritual hectoring I'd come across in my life as a hippie. Instead, poetry was my music, my religion; the poetic state was my bliss. I had participated in a weekend seminar of EST with Werner Erhard, during which we were famously not allowed to pee except once or twice; the whole experience did not really stir my bones. As nearly as I can remember, that seminar was all about coming into the present moment – and this seemed to require a huge amount of talking on Werner's part. But I cannot claim that anything very 'spiritual' happened to me. I'd then told Werner that I was going to India. A look passed over his face… defensiveness? – just for a moment; then he recovered himself and said, "It's all the same." "I'm going," I explained, "for the *poetry*. EST doesn't feel like that to me."*

He had nothing to say to that.

When I was thirteen, a beautiful man, a family friend and a sort of mentor to me, took me to a Zen master in Los Angeles. I was shown into a curtained alcove where sat a beaming little Japanese fellow of indeterminate age. He asked me, "If you are walking down the road, where is the Buddha?" "All around, in the trees and the sky," I replied. The Roshi had then told my mentor/friend that I "had potential." I did not know what any of this meant. It had just felt like an openness, an inclusiveness, that meeting.

My sister and I had made a wonderful friend, though, when I was sixteen and she fourteen: Morris Graves, a mystic artist of the Pacific Northwest, who famously painted birds as mystical beings. He was in his sixties, very tall, with dark-ringed eyes and a cultured accent; and he was gay. He lived in a magical

* I had a notion, you see, that what I wanted out of India was to find a way to stay all the time in the state that writing a poem visited me with: a mysterious, blissful penetration of matter and form by radiant upliftedness, Knowing, and grace. But I would get much more than I'd bargained for!

Zennish house in virgin redwood forest in Northern California. My sister and I used to row a little boat around on his small tree-dark lake, trailing our silks and scarves. Morris told us of journeys to India, of an out-of-body experience he'd had. His very presence was an incitement to adventure in realms then unknown to us.

And then, just once, when I was eighteen, in Ibiza, I had smoked some pot with my then-boyfriend and various other compadres, and gone alone to a back room to lie down. I'd entered then into an experiment to trace each thought back to its roots. This effort was prompted by the agony of teenage self-consciousness and jealousy, and resulted in an interesting state where *something* was glued much further back into me, into my body-being, than usual. There was a gap at the end of things; I came to it again and again. I felt rather exalted. I think I had gotten the idea from the only spiritual book I had ever read, *The Golden Bough*. (This interesting state was immediately and bizarrely challenged when the Guardia Civil burst in and took away everyone's passports… but that's another story!) So that was the sum total of my spiritual orientation. (Devadasi had been for a while interested in Zen, turned onto it by my oldest, beatnik brother. But it was all Greek to me.)

Next we three visited Seema, the plump, odalisque-ish daughter of Greek heiress Mukta, one of Bhagwan's earliest and staunchest Western disciples. Seema had liquid eyes and satiny skin and a sumptuous figure in her loose, low-cut robe. She lounged in a white-walled room where was a bed covered in a green cotton bedspread, a couple of large-leafed green plants in pots; a few cushions on a wicker divan. Sarita explained that Bhagwan advises us to have our houses such: white walls, green bed, green plants. A Tantra room, she explained – a special room for sacred-love meditations – is to have a red circle painted on the floor, and the bed is to stand within it, in the center of the room. (She also told us that Indians generally worship curves in a woman – the plumper, the more beautiful.)

Seema and Sarita had a good gossip about people they knew, while I listened to the unfamiliar names. Then, in the course of the day, I met a few other Western sannyasins. There were not many: Kamal and Gopal, good-looking young Americans; Haridas, a tall German with glowy eyes; Sudha, a Cuban-American friend of Sarita's with short kinky hair and a bright, wiseacre humor. On hearing about the meditation Bhagwan had given me, she told of a weird experience she'd had: she was living in a room where rats crawled over her at night, and she was completely freaked out by them! Bhagwan told her to catch hold of a rat and caress it as if it was a lover's penis... (or *lingam*, which is the Hindi word) and she did this, and the rats calmed down and after that left her alone. She also referred to her own "cute li'l raisin-field pussy," a description I thought charming and daring.

Sarita had explained that when people start to meditate they crave sweets. Sweets, it seemed, were a big thing with sannyasins. Bhagwan, in his years of traveling and lecturing all over India, had been given so many boxes of *barfi* (a sort of fudge made with boiled-down milk, lots of sugar, and various flavorings – cardamom, pistachio, chocolate, rose – and artificial colors; there is silver foil on the top, spread artistically in a sort of half-shredded way) and had eaten them all, in a kind of honoring – that he had gotten diabetes; and thus, the girls said, was impotent. (To me, this news was of only passing interest; it seemed appropriate somehow; and so it remained always. Bhagwan told us many times that when you have experienced the bliss of enlightenment, sexual orgasm is about as exciting as a sneeze.)

Indians traditionally ask gurus to bless boxes of barfi, and then the sweetmeat is called *Prasad*, or Gift. Once it's blessed, people eat it and give it to each other. I tasted some at some point during this long strange day and found it disgusting – there was something odd about it, like Mexican candy is somehow odd – cloying and oddly-seasoned, not like American stuff at all.

Sarita said that the disciples longed for candies from their homelands and there was a lot of carrying of them across oceans for each other.

Sarita had earlier written to us, "Through a girl here I came in contact with a certain book called *Brighu Samhita – Saptarishi Samhita*. It means Seven Rishis. Apparently a couple of thousand or so years ago seven Rishis gathered together and decided to write down everyone's history and future and present. Such is the nature of their knowing that they can see these things. The way this book is read is by a man who is called a shadow astrologer. He will look at your shadow and make certain calculations which show your pages. Or if it is monsoon the man will measure your hand and make certain calculations which show your pages. Then the Rishis speak. This book is written in Sanskrit. ˆThere are only four of them in existence. Sometimes during a reading the Rishis tell the reader to shut up and read no further or to skip this part or to not read this unless a question is asked, etc. Anyhow, ten of us had a few days of intense madness getting readings. The stories which emerged are truly amazing. Bhagwan first said it was all true which inspired us in our madness. Then after it kind of blew over he said the general outline is true but the details are sometimes incorrect and subject to change. What is written is our destiny and when we take Sannyas we give our destiny to Bhagwan. According to the Rishis, Bhagwan is the Master of the era. Anyway yesterday Bhagwan told us – it was a nice game now forget it… "

And so we went, with a friend as translator, to the Shadow-Reader, who worked from a hot rooftop somewhere in the middle of this huge, scary, superpopulous city. The Shadow-Reader and his son greeted us solemnly and measured our shadows with measuring-sticks. We were allowed to ask questions, and then they told us our futures. I was missing Herb most awfully… him, and also the solidity he seemed to represent. So I asked about him. The senior Shadow-Reader told me I would return to Herb and we would go all over the States together starting meditation centers.

Although I liked the part about being with Herb, I felt enormously skeptical about the rest; as well I might. The projected destiny was not Herb's style at all, nor was he a biddable fellow. In fact he had insisted that I did not need to go to India, that I was fine as I was. He was so very rooted in his house and his affable know-it-all-ness.

I don't now remember what Devadasi was told… Sarita's fate was some stern yet glorious light-filled thing I forget now too. We paid the Shadow-Readers a few rupees and climbed back down the stairs to the street.

Sarita had already told us the story of Sheela's visit to the Shadow-Reader. We'd met her briefly – she was a punchy, bossy, irascible Indian girl with a tough, matronly look about her even then, in her youth. She had short hair and biggish shoulders and a small mouth. She looked, really, like a policewoman. (It was her parents we were to stay with in the North.) The Shadow-Reader had told Sheela that she had known Bhagwan in a past life but had spurned him. He had gone by in a carriage, enlightened even then, and she had turned her back. In this life she had to embrace Sannyas with him, and one day she would be the leader of his Commune.

In the evening we went to the house of an Indian disciple for the Lecture. In a large, thick-walled room, replete with draperies and alcoves, we sat in front of Bhagwan while he spoke for 1½ hours. I was completely gripped, astonished, amazed. Whatever he said was coming from some spring of complete authority; it was both as fresh as new grass, and ancient as humankind. Each sentence felt so true, so self-evident; with the simplicity of genius, he uncovered what was really going on with the human being, and said it aloud.

I closed my eyes and watched the passionate desires that had begun to surface in me. Desires for… home. For safety; to be far away from this terrible, enchanted land with its filthy streets and immaculate interiors. Desires for particular goodies from my childhood: candy corn, gumdrops, Hershey's chocolate. Tomato soup and toasted cheese sandwiches. And I desired to be at Herb's house, oh Herb's house… clean, upper-middle-class, with a deck and a view and every sort of comfort. Home, home… I really just wanted to escape what was happening to me.

I was just so uncomfortable! Everywhere I went, the damned buzzing was happening in my forehead and my feet – a kind of incessant electrocution. I felt so strange! So, the next afternoon, briefly alone in the room where we all slept, I removed my mala and put it on the chest of drawers. Instantly I felt relieved. Peace! Quiet! I was free! I stood there, and ordinary life came back to me. I took a deep breath and let it out again.

And I knew that it was wrong. In this mundane stillness, my chance was gone. I could not do it this way.

I lifted up the mala and put it back on.

From my diary:

We were in Bombay for six days in one small room at Mira's, where kittenish servants brought tea and did our laundry. We went through sister-mother spaces more honest than ever before. We did our meditations each day – arise at 4:30. Immediately on awakening, stretch like a cat and laugh for two minutes. Then down to Chowpatty Beach for the chaotic meditation. Home for showers and tea, then out into Bombay garbage-can for business, or maybe to Woodland to arrange for the camp or to see Bhagwan. Filth and beggars, decaying buildings, dark innocent faces. After lunch, twenty minutes of blindfolded gibberish. Usually we talked or argued for hours. At night each has her special meditation assigned by Bhagwan, and I was embarrassed to do mine in company, so I've done it only slightly yet. It is to totally imagine and act out making love. It is what has won me to Bhagwan at all. He is an amazing being and yet not amazing. I love the stories about him. All women sannyasins are in love with him. I am a traveler in a strange land where my old worlds and my longings fly up into my face like alarmed birds as I pass.

The Rishis said that in my last life I had a voice of incredible sweetness, and that I sang. I came to India with a band of people from "Austria or Australia," the elder Rishi said. Yogananda was translating, and all was not clear. Herb, said the Rishi, was with the group. He became tired of India and returned home. We had a great attraction for one another which was not consummated then.

Along with my enormous and almost unconscious consideration that it is wrong and frivolous to have a lover, there is the undeniable desire to create that union. In my last life I was very beautiful and loved by many men, and my sex life was most unhappy. It is for me to create the fulfilling of my desire in this life. Life is an unfulfilled desire. All desires must be fulfilled eventually.

It was with great relief that I admitted this desire to myself, and with great joy that I heard the Rishi's prediction. I will return soon to America. Bhagwan may be my guru, but not heavily. I will be with Herb again. He will make me very happy; I should stay with him. At twenty-three or twenty-four I will marry, and in a few years have two incredible children, a girl and a boy. Between twenty-eight and thirty-two I will find great joy and fulfillment in sex, almost spiritual. It will be a very happy life. I will travel much, and gain recognition in the arts…

(As we will see, psychics are sometimes amazingly right-on; and often, drifting quite askew.)

As I lay in the dark in the decaying gingerbread house in a narrow Bombay lane, in my narrow bed with its clean white sheets, I was elevated and afraid and worn out; exhausted yet energized. And then… as I was drifting towards sleep I became aware of a Presence in the room. I knew it was Bhagwan; I could feel him floating in the air not far away. I knew that he had come to check up on me, see how I was doing. He hovered there, just looking. Then he left.

In the morning, as we had our breakfast of spicy little dishes – *idli, sambar* – and small, flower-scented bananas, and *dahi*, or yogurt, and tea and toast, I told Sarita of my experience. Oh, yes, she said. He leaves his body every night and goes to visit his disciples. And when he gets back to his body he is so utterly depleted that his caretaker Vivek makes for him sixteen pieces of toast, and he eats them all. This then grounds him back in his body again.

To the North

We sat in the 3rd-class carriage among a packed mass of smelly, jostling people. The train journey took a day, a night, and half another day. Scrawny, staring men in filthy singlets, like prisoners in a cattle-car, inhabited most of the cars, but we were in the Ladies one, and it was not much better. There was no way to sleep, and we sat on hard slatted seats, just enduring. Our mother Devadasi was freaking out. It was all too hideous!

In the morning when we looked out the window we saw people squatting by the tracks, miles of them in a row, each with his cup of water beside him and his skinny bottom showing beneath his rucked-up shirt. Others squatted in the brush at a distance. The smell was everywhere – before sunrise, during, after.

Finally we arrived in Baroda. We were collected by a car and driver, and soon were on a rutted road going out of the city. After some time we saw gates off to the left, and the farmhouse beyond them. This was Tandalja Farm. There was a long low earthen building, at home in this dusty countryside, among fields of grain and tall trees. Inside, the rooms were cool and simply furnished.

Sheela's mother Ba and her father, Bapu-ji, greeted us with great warmth. They were a cozy, round-headed, middle-aged couple in homespun garments. Ba was bustling, lovingly bossy, and efficient, ordering the servants about and making sure we had everything we needed. Bapu-ji was expansive, with a booming voice and strong, farmer's arms; it quickly became clear that he loved to talk philosophy. We were shown our rooms, and then given chai and Gluco biscuits in the parlor. (These last I found dry and dull. Why, I wondered, would somebody make cookies like that?)

We were told the schedule: Dynamic at 6 a.m., then shower and breakfast, and after that, work: we would be assisting a construction project, carrying dirt away from the site in shallow metal bowls held balanced on our heads, dumping it in a certain place, then returning for more.

I felt dread. I mostly, at this stage, felt dread. It was as if the whole of my past, and that of my parents, had risen in me like gorge, and was pounding on the door of my throat to get out. The candy-cravings were one side of that sense of being plugged into childhood; the other side was all the sadness, disappointment, tragedy, anguish of my family's lives; struggling, demanding, to get out; to be felt, allowed – to overtake and kill me if it must.

First days at Tandalja Farm

December 15, 1973

Sun and breezes in bougainvillea and corn. Flies friendly as birds. Mother is happy here in the country. It is her birthday. This morning she got to ride on a train; now she is in a thick-walled farmhouse. "When I go back to America, I will live in the country."

Sodden handkerchief crumpled by the bed. A heavy cold occupies my head. Indulging, I stay here to laze and dream while the orange-clad ashram goes into town to give a taped lecture of Bhagwan and then a Kirtan, music and singing.

I am not a fan of India. My soul is terse and sad and open. I have taken Sannyas and have reserved surrender. For the hours after I took, the mala burned a warm hole in my heart and gave me an unboughtened grace. I have written much to Herb, but not exactly of these things. I see very plainly that he, my boyfriend, is also my God, my Master. And neither of us wants that. So why not surrender to a true master, and then love Herb without need? As my sister loves.

Sarita is much beloved in the universe she has created here. India is a land of gurus and disciples. The Rishis said among many other things that I will take to meditation slowly in this life, as in the last life I had an incompetent guru. I insulted him, he became angry, and I got confused, so in this life I must go slowly.

I have plunged myself deep into the soul of my contradictions. I have done it deliberately, and in some ways it is the only glory worth having. I am heavy with it now; preoccupied with the mirror of Herb which travels at my left shoulder like death and promises; a resident pain.

Bhagwan is a laughing laughing being. He seems to have no substance and to embody all substance. And yet I am not astonished.

It is a relief in this India to wear all orange; we pass through crowds and trains as religious nuns and are accepted. In Western dress there was more begging, more rupees asked. We glide as timeless pilgrims through the land. I am both proud and alarmed to go so quickly completely into this.

Evening comes over the cornfields. The air turns melted ribbons of grey blue and pink. I am offended by the treasured photographs of Bhagwan hung everywhere. This house, this ashram, feels clean and light and good.

After gibberish today I fell blindfolded asleep, and this was my dream (I can write in dimming light as Mother walks, an evening-faded Renoir in peach and white outside, hair pinned up, museful): I returned to Herb's house from a two-week journey. I had been traveling in America. He was having a small party, and he did not welcome me. A new woman sat in his house. My impression of her was very strong

– she was smaller than I, in her thirties, with a small stomach and biggish breasts. She wore a print voile dress of simple design and had two young children. Her hair was black and short. Herb was very comfortable with her. He was very cold to me and kicked me out. My reaction was total disbelief. I went back in the morning. I knew she was upstairs in his bed. He liked it that she had children. He didn't want to let me in the house, but I came in anyway. There were huge raw steaks left from the party and he gave me one to take. His house was all changed, the entryway expanded into a room, and he was in the midst of working on it. We had words. "My mind is totally, totally blown," I said. "First the traveling, now this. The Rishis can't have been wrong! You have changed so fast! Look, Herb, my mind is so blown!" What really blew my mind and threw me back on myself was that he was absolutely not interested.

"Let me have my vibrator, then!" I cried. No, he didn't want to give it. My sex center ached with desire. A hoseful of water twisted and turned in the backyard. I went outside. A poet I fancy, Steve, waited in a pickup truck. Could the Rishis have meant him? I got in with him. Every time I talked my cold made terrible noises. He was pleased to go have sex with me. I desired him, and was filled with the total devastation of Herb's rejection.

I woke completely in that world.

A star has come out. An unknown bird chirps nearby. The sound of a tractor comes from far away. There are mosquitoes.

Is it R for Rishi, or R for Ridiculous?

All I am interested in now is my immortal soul. Everything goes back to that source. And still I feel always that somebody is watching me. Always they lurk and judge.

Bhagwan said I was to do my yoga, so I will do that, plus some work, to keep my body strong. A truce from running, on this barefoot ground. And otherwise, nothing but my meditations, my inward play. This is all I really want. Not to socialize or strive, but to withdraw and give up the impression I must make (which secretly robs me?) and I give up, give up.

Perhaps the woman in the dream was me. Of course she was.

I can't get used to having it okay to laze. Bhagwan said (he is always a devil, and an infinitely tricky one), "You are on leave for two months. When you go back to San Francisco I will set you free. But for now, wear the mala, wear orange. Surrender to me, hmmmm?" In his presence, it is impossible not to. A yes or a no is surrender.

I have two more lives to go, said the Rishis, Herb only one. And he will outlive me this life by three years. Sarita's last seven lives were spent in India as a Yogini. In this life she will accomplish her aim and vanish.

December 16, 1973

It is morning. Mosquitoes must have gotten me in the night, making red spots on my face. The sun gains strength above the horizon. Sounds of running water indicate the bathings going on. Sarita and I bathe squatted on the floor in the bathroom, with two-second ecstasies of hot water poured over us.

Sarita says that when you look at Bhagwan's picture in the mala, if the picture disappears, then you no longer need to wear the mala, because you know there is no God.

I used to think I knew what I wanted to do – now I know nothing. Slowly the old order shows its face of dried mud, slowly it uglies and erodes to show no skull. Everything in my being comes into relevance here. A scream builds in me like shit and is ignorant of exit; it thinks for itself of sweet futures or even passable ones. When told it can seek the light (all this time it was buried, spreading small systems like cancers through my cells) it knows not what to do; it swallows dirt and has no throat. No wonder I thought I had no power. I'm living in my neck and head, with occasional journeys to the inner elbows for an emotion or two.

It is after Kirtan, where we sing and dance and scream if necessary. All this is done in a canvas-fenced field near the house, which is reached by walking the long way around barbed wire. Two months of this cannot fail to make a dent.

Mother has come here to start her life over. She comes in after Kirtan and flops with an ancientness of exhaustion onto the bed, and in my antipathy I see that I am afraid: she is me. If an unrelation flopped like that I would not care.

An orange-scarfed Sarita comes through the window. She sits on the bed and looks for no purpose into my eyes and I see my flinching as mirror. Sarita and Devadasi (Mama) discuss the hard labor we must do tomorrow. This is a farm. She changes clothes. Country air through window. I gloat that I am slenderer, more waisted. Tonight, Tratak meditation where we stare at Bhagwan's photograph.

"If I had a lover he would have to taste like a guava," says Sarita.

Vision: My death came through the window. She was an old woman in tattered skirts and ragged shoes. She sat near my left shoulder, and we had made an agreement, she and I, sealed by potatoes ten lives old. She carried a basket of sticks as ragged as she. She sat vigil while I made love to my lover, whom I had brought in the door: he was made of three men – one young, tall, strong, and as innocent as I; one mature of years; and one Bhagwan, the living god. This lover touched me with his hands, arousing fires so slow and deep that a single pulse of them would take an entire day. And still this lover had less form than my death.

And so we spent the weeks there working, meditating with full screaming chaos, sleeping, and… eating. For the food at Tandalja Farm was a revelation, if only I had been in a state to appreciate it. My existential misery clouded everything, but even I could taste that something wonderful was going on here. Ba explained that all the ingredients were grown on the farm, and the dishes were seasonal – this dish served only in winter, that in summer, and so on. The spices were adjusted to the seasons too, and ground in a mortar and pestle. This food had no relation to what was served in Indian restaurants. The dishes were not the same, the flavors much more rustic, yet subtle and varied. The chapatti flour was ground here from grain grown in the fields. The yogurt was from buffaloes which lived nearby, and was thick and rich and tangy. The vegetables were grown on the farm. There were many small dishes at each meal, each with its own rustic yet sophisticated tastes. You could taste the *terroir*… I was reminded more than anything of France – at eighteen, my first tastes of the food there had been like this – an incredulity that food could be so delicious through-and-through.

We were urged to eat, there was as much as we could want of everything – breakfast, lunch, dinner, and a break at 4:00 with tea and those dry biscuits.

But an ominous decision was being made within me, down where half-conscious forces lurked and seethed…

As I daily did Dynamic, tearing whole slabs and wings off my carapace, exposing the interior; as I daily labored with the others carrying dirt, and simultaneously facing myself, as-is, without distraction – as I did my lovemaking meditation every evening, alone in my little room with the window open to the cooling December night – going through a phantasmagoria of every sort of meeting with a great many sorts of men, yet never, so far, allowing any of them entry into my imagined body – as if I had to meet everything that was *not* love, was not sex either… – I was finding it all *so painful.* The sense of being broken open into a wild-windy sea was just too much for me. All that was ever known to be 'me' was now in question, and I had to feel the agonies of eons, not only my own but those of anybody who arose in me – parents, strangers, friends. I missed Herb horribly, yet I understood that this was a spurious missing, an escape from the matter at hand. I knew that I was not grown-up enough for him, certainly not as I was now… nor was I deserving to say I was *alive*, if I didn't face this fact of my own being. And I knew that Herb could wait while this vital business was being done.

But oh, it was so painful, this ripping-open that was inescapably upon me. And so, in the hurricane of my etheric meeting with Bhagwan, I felt, half-aware, that I must, *must* find some arena of control.

Writing was not control – it was just observation. Going running, as I had in my teens, was somehow impossible here; but there was one thing I *could* do… and I surreptitiously, almost instinctively, began limiting my intake of food.

Riding in the Dark

But there is one memory from this uncomfortable sojourn that stays with me bright and shining: one evening Devadasi, Sarita, Kamal (for that lovely blonde American girl we'd met in Bombay was here too) and I rode old bicycles off to Baroda city, to attend a Kirtan evening, where people sang and chanted and clapped: "*Govinda bolo hare Gopala bolo, Govinda Ramana hare Gopala bolo*," over and over again, and rang little bells and clashed little cymbals. Something about the god Krishna and the Gopis, and going to tell somebody something. I felt bored and irritated – the music did not relieve any of the burdens on my heart; it was nearly impossible for me to make myself chant. I was very glad when it was over.

It was quite dark by now, and we were riding home along dirt roads holed with pits, rutted with deep crevices. There were no street lights, or any other lights to be seen. No lights on the bikes either. The road was lined with trees. There was no moon; I don't remember starlight either, though there must have been some.

I found myself riding out in front, my heart lifting up, a fascinated adventurousness taking hold: how to get along when you can see exactly nothing? I relaxed into the darkness and went rattle bump clatter along, not slacking speed. It was *so dark everywhere*, but I didn't care, I was riding fast! What a reckless, foolhardy, glorious sensation! Wheeee! Sarita was behind me, then Kamal, then Devadasi – who kept calling out, "Wait! Wait girls, wait! *I'm going to get off and walk!*"

We survived; we didn't capsize into any holes; and finally we saw the farm, its faint lights – we stopped, opened the broad wooden gate, pushed the bikes through… and I was revived and rejuvenated, touched with a wild mystery, the feeling of being inside a state of momentum, when nothing can be seen of what is to come.

I would never forget this; it would come back to me later, and be useful then too.

Mt. Abu

We took a narrow-gauge train to a little village at the foot of the mountain, then a taxi up the hill, spiraling round and round the unlikely tor sticking up out of the plains. It was a funny sight from a distance, the hill like a child might draw it, just one precise bump in the hazy flatness. At the top was a hill-station, a favored recreation and cooling-off spot for Memsahibs during the Raj. As the taxi ascended, we passed jungle with tribes of tall grey monkeys glaring at us callously, sardonically, with their round thieves' eyes. Some even jumped up and down, yelling *Hoo! Hoo!* – which they had learned, Sarita said, from watching people do Dynamic.

The sense of storybook exoticism mounted as we went higher and finally came out into the broad, wooded hilltop. There was a fragrance of cook-fires, a rising of plumes of grey smoke, and the ancient perfume of it mixed with flitting, spicy smells of many other things: dusty earth, flowers, unknown vegetation. It was much colder here at the top. There was a little town, with a bazaar, and large villas and guesthouses spread about among the lush trees, the crannies and hummocks and canyons. A small lake rested in a flat area, and a strolling-path circumnavigated it. A bridle trail dove into a wood and ran off to a lookout point where the plains could be seen in their dusty remoteness. We discovered all this over the next few days.

We checked in to a hotel high on a rise. It had very thick walls, no glass in the narrow arched windows, which looked out over the humps and dips in the hilltop, the plumes of fragrant smoke, then the plains. The price was 8 rupees per night each. Amenities were few, and we were uncomfortable.

Mama was fussing again, asking clueless questions, complaining, traipsing from bedroom to primitive bathroom with grim bewilderment, rebellion writ upon her face. She hated the cup-and-water-and-left-hand method of bottom-washing everyone in India used. Sarita bossed her about, got exasperated. I also treated her like a child, though I too was very much ill at ease in this peculiar place, this gorgeous place. But really, I was just weirded out with the continuous earthquake that had become myself.

Soon I pampered myself, with everyone's approval, by moving alone to a different hostelry Sarita knew of: a Parsee lady took guests in her clean, secluded house and fed them, with a fair bit of ceremony, amazingly bland dinners; such as thin tomato soup with bread-and-butter sandwiches. She kept a brazier going in the sitting room, and an eternal flame in an altar. She had a very large nose and talked fiercely and at length. I liked it there – the crisp white sheets on my narrow bed, the relative comfort.

But before the meditation camp began, with its full-on, all-day-and-evening schedule, there was something we must do… I'd brought just a few clothes with me, as Sarita had said we'd get the sorts we'd need made up here. I had some money – I'd brought $300, which had become a great many rupees indeed, far too many for six weeks' living. And as I was very much afraid of the country in which I found myself, I wanted to get rid of all this money as quickly as I could; so that I would have to leave when the time came. There would then be no way for me to stay longer, even if for some crazy reason I might think I ought. Or might think I wanted to.

So we went shopping for fabric. The best kind for our purposes, it seemed, was khadi, that soft, pliable handloom cotton, pleasant under the hand. And, of course, it had to be orange; all Bhagwan's disciples wore orange, all of the time.

The cloth shops were a marvel – narrow but open to the street, stacked to the ceiling with myriad strongly-colored bolts. There was a flat cloth-covered area on the floor in front where the trader would hurl a bolt and then undo a corner with a yank, grasp the ends with two hands and then would pull the bolt over and over with a rapid *whonk whonk whonk* while it flipped and the cloth appeared, rippling then settling, to be examined while he exhorted you with its virtues. The general drabness, browns and tans of the landscapes' hues were contrasted brightly by the vivid clothes on the inhabitants – magenta, gentian, emerald, lemon, all spangled with gold borders and swathes of embroidery.

Some shops sold only sari lengths, pre-cut to five meters; as well as the matching solid-color fabrics used to make the short, very fitted *choli* blouse and the petticoat worn beneath, gathered at the waist and tied with string. Sarita explained that pregnant women need only let out the gathers a little on the cord as the months went by; no need to buy a special maternity garment. The same trick was used on the hugely gathered trousers of the *salwar kameez* ensemble – baggy pants with tight calves and ankles topped by a calf-length shirt and set off with a narrow-folded, very long shawl or scarf, the *dupatta*, worn so that the ends trailed down the back. Then there were long shirts called *kurtas*, worn by men (though Western women wore them) and *dhotis*, strange diaper-like arrangements where the legs stuck out of a single piece of white cloth draped all about the thighs and between the legs in a bundly way. We stroked *lungis*, shorter lengths of cloth men wore tied about the waist like a bath-towel; these were also useful as picnic cloths, emergency shawls, or what-have-you. We admired embroidered woolen shawls, and I bought a few for gifts.

The robes that Bhagwan wanted us to wear, loose so that the waist is never constricted, so we could enjoy ease of breath and flow of energy – had to be made up specially, since no-one sold them ready-made. (There was very little ready-made in India.) So we took our lengths of orange fabric, with drawings of the robes we wanted pinned on, to a tailor in an alley, who sat at an old Singer treadle machine on the pavement, pumping away with his feet. We were measured, and next evening returned to collect our order, which was of course not ready, so that we had to go back again and again.

We'd hedged our bets by going to a couple of tailors, and I had ordered, and eventually collected, a set of soft peach loose trousers with a short-sleeved V-neck shirt with a slanted pocket on the left breast – a classic style here – and two or three loose robes with short sleeves (in India women did not show their upper arms or, god forbid, their armpits). I bought saris that took my fancy, for gifts; papier-mâché boxes, and scarves, and a pair of sandals, called *chappals*, with a loop for the big toe, from a shop with a vivid leathery smell, full of flimsy-looking footwear with gold bits and bright turquoise and pink designs painted on. In my split-apart state I didn't really enjoy this shopping; it felt like selecting bridal finery at the edge of a cliff one is about to be tossed off. But I clung to it desperately, hopelessly, this little remembrance of enthusiasms past.

My Little Sister

I have never seen anyone transform as quickly as had my little sister. When we had traveled together, she had been a beauteous, quiet creature, troubled as with the weight of the world; she'd worn, as I did, patched velvet trousers and long empire-waist dresses I had made from Indian bedspreads; in fact, we wore each other's clothes – a red rayon crêpe cropped jacket with black frog fastenings; an orange granny dress, patched in plenty with contrasting prints; a white lace dress we both adored, long to the foot, the skirt tiered, and a ruffle at the V-buttoning neck. We both drew, and wrote long letters with multi-colors of magic marker pens, and danced jivey sassy dances whenever the opportunity arose, or flitted balletically across some hippie park while a strange young fellow played his flute. We braided our long hair in a hundred little braids, left it overnight, then combed it out in the morning to fluffy glory. We rowed that little boat together about that private bosky lake, and shared Morris's table in our youthful decorativeness. We took dance classes together, bicycled together – then hitch-hiked together across the land of our birth. We were, for those few years during our teens, a team.

But I know now that she was biding her time in her great openness, then, by reflecting me – artistic, creatively melancholic. But the dear creature really had a whole other destiny hiding in her – and she may have known it; I did not.

I was in those years involved in a troublesome relationship, and later on, an exciting affair – and she was my confidante. I protected her from the world, more or less; for she was very young. And her unexpected bouts of forthrightness and righteous rage at some stupidity or stuckness we encountered, had the effect of bolstering, bewildering, and in some way protecting me.

And then it all broke.

I still feel pain remembering, and yet how could I have done things any differently?

We'd been auditing classes at the University in Riverside, California, our home town; but it had been discovered what our ages were, and we'd been told we could no longer attend. There was nothing for us then in Riverside – in those days a smoggy place, so that it hurt the lungs to breathe; and a hot place, and pointless. So we'd had a garage sale to offload our glorious hippie tat, and taken up a Swiss Army backpack each, and then taken off with our thumbs out. We were hitch-hiking across America, looking for a good place to be.

I fell in love in San Francisco, but did not want to remain there – our destinies called, my sister and I; and we had to go on. We visited Northern California, where I experienced a Gestalt group evening, where you would *become* a character in a dream you'd had, or a certain voice in your own inner landscape; or even another person. (That technique stayed with me – and is with me still.) And we'd just climbed 14,000-ft Storm King Mountain, in the Rockies, with a young man we'd met; it had been an epic five-day adventure during which we'd finally been rescued and fed by a Methodist Youth group camping in the woods. Then we left the young man in Silverton, Colorado, and went on our way.

We'd gotten a ride in a van full of hippies somewhere in Colorado, and they'd asked us if we'd like to go to a rock concert. Yes! we said. They drove miles, way out into the country, where a broad plain of yellow grasses sloped up to the imposing serrated horizon of the blue Rocky Mountains, stretching north and south as far as the eye could see.

We were in the back of the van, but peering out the window we observed a curious sight: a *long* line of tramping people, a mile of them at least, all going in the same direction. My eye fell on one man, I don't know why – he was above medium height, shirtless, with a golden skin; his hair was cropped into a Prince Valiant bob, but light brown. He wore chamois bell-bottoms.

And then our van went on past.

When we finally parked and got out we were near the hub of the excitement. A stage had been erected in this middle of nowhere, and on it a black man played a guitar and sang into a microphone. He was, I realized with shock, B.B. King. Extremely chic haute hippies floated in a businesslike way from there to here and back again, wearing chiffon and vast floating waves of hair, like fabric buoyed in the water behind a ship. Wiry, fit Mountain Men had also come down from the Rockies and boastfully displayed their spiked chains, the rips in their skin they swore were made by bears.

My sister and I knew what we had to do. We made for the nearest sizeable thorn-bush, flitted round behind it, opened our canvas backpacks, and changed our clothes. We were wearing shorts, tank tops, and hiking boots, our hair braided up; now we took out our only dresses. It was her turn to wear the orange print granny dress, and mine for the white lace we called The-Hundred-Year-Old-Dress. I have sometimes wondered if our fates would have been different if it had been the other way around.

I came out from behind the bush, my freed hair crinkling as I ran my fingers through it. The dress felt light and feminine about me. (There was lace between the tiers of the skirt.) I'd exchanged my hiking boots for sandals.

A man was walking towards me, as if he already knew I was there. Very direct his feet came; and yet his air was goofy-spirally, if savoring. He was carrying a little rodent skull with a leather cord threaded through the eye-sockets, and whirling it round and round. There was a sort of purr coming out of him; his bare chest and shoulders glowed golden, his midriff and belly were flat yet padded just under the skin, above his low-slung chamois trousers. It was the man from the line of people I'd seen from the van.

He stood in front of me, the whole beaming amber glory of him, white teeth gleaming, and he cried, "You! Arrrrre a *devil!* And an *angel!* And a *devil!* And an *angel!*" He had some sort of European accent – a thing I am quite sure I had never heard up to then.

I did not forget my little sister – not then, and not ever, really – but just at that moment, my destiny reached out to me and gave an almighty yank, and before I'd recovered from my shock the thing was done.

What ended up happening was this: Jacques, the Chamois Prince, said he could arrange for me to join the Medicine Ball Caravan – a movie was being made with a French director and film crew, about hippies going across the USA in painted-up school buses, sleeping in tie-dyed teepees, and setting up rock concerts in location after location, with big-name performers and bands. The Caravan was then going to fly to Europe as well… Warner Bros. was picking up the tab. Did I want to go?

"But what about my sister?" I asked, my heart floating between my throat and my stomach and back again – queasy, excited, afraid.

"She ees too young," he said. "She cannot come. But I can find a place for her, to stay in Wavy Gravy's Hog Farm commune in New Mexico. She weel be safe."

And so together Jacques and I phoned my mother in California to discuss the matter, and it was agreed that my little sister would go with the Hog Farm people next day, and our mother would hitch-hike out to get her, and they two would go on together to New York – for my sister wanted to go there, to become a ballerina. She had always had some ideal of purity; of spiritual cleanliness – and at the time she saw ballet as a way to express this.

Jacques was Belgian, a professor and researcher (he did something cutting-edge about the brain) at UCLA, and had been brought along as liaison between the film crew and the hippies, as he was a friend of the lead singer in Stone Ground, the house band. He was having the time of his life.

And so it all came to pass.

I felt different things all together in my stomach, my heart, my knees. I wanted to go. I knew this was my chance, the only chance I was going to get, to breathe the air of the wider world beyond the USA... the definitive Great Adventure. My sister and I had no money at all, probably not even a quarter; we had only government food-stamps, which had stood us in good stead. How would we ever have gotten across a sea? And in a way, I *did* want to go alone, without her – a sort of streamlining, a more adult adventure. In another way, my heart was breaking. I could barely let myself perceive what must be happening within that quiet, vulnerable child, abruptly abandoned by her protector and companion. I could not let myself feel it. It would have been too horrible.

In fact, my sister and mother ended up having a magnificent adventure together that bonded them; my sister did study ballet, and worked as an au pair, and eventually abandoned that sort of dance and managed with her then-boyfriend to get to Europe, where we met again. And so we were leap-frogging over each other, for I'd turned around and leapt back to San Francisco, and she'd leapt, in the slogging weirdness of an epic Asian hitch-hike, all the way to the other side of the Earth – until here we were on a funny sticky-up piece of fragrant, jungly ground above a vast plain in India – a place my sister had been talking of visiting since she was just a tow-headed determined little kid.

My sister had become, overnight as it were, a reflection of the best of India. She was beautiful and clean and simple in her habits. She glowed, she was serene, she was absolutely assured. She knew all the several main religions here and could point out on the street who belonged to which. She was completely relaxed in the customs of food and drink. She knew where things were, what people did, and what religious traditions made them do those things. She knew of past lives – including her own – and all the ins and outs of Bhagwan's life and words and deeds. She fitted into India like a fish, thirsty for so many years, released back into the sea: it flicks its tail and is gone, back into its element.

While it took me ages to sort out, by costume and affect, who was Hindu, who Jaina; who Parsee, Sikh, Muslim… and I did not find these things *specially* interesting – they were all just part of the overwhelming impact of this strange, compelling place. But Sarita knew everything, was everything, explained everything. There was no rocking her now.

Now, so many years later, I mourn that she didn't come on the Caravan and then to Europe with me (Jacques later, in sorrow, reported that he'd found out she *could* have come); or I with her, to India, when she'd asked me. She might have saved me from some of my bumbling excesses; she was in some ways more sensible than I. And we were, really, so much more important to each other than any of the men we met along the way. But that was not a viable choice when you are young – you have to pass through the men, the men.

The last time I had seen her had been on a short visit in the summer of 1971 at a Communist farm in the countryside near Perugia, Italy. We helped a neighbor of the farm pitchfork hot golden hay onto a wagon, stopping mid-morning for a snack of huge sliced tomatoes with olive oil drizzled on them, brought to us by a strong round mama with a scarf tied under her chin. We were given lunch in a shaded patio – pasta with more tomatoes and sliced cucumbers. But that evening the communist crew had fended for itself back at the communal house. The day's cook plunked down on the table, among all the sullen young men, an enormous metal platter of scrambled egg, which we helped ourselves to, eating directly from this dish with our hands. Then there appeared a vast wheel of rock-hard Parmigiano, to be hacked at with a special stout knife, and if you were lucky you could get a few shreds away. To this day, I'm not sure how my sister ended up there. Now, I found it interesting that she would end up here in India, for since childhood she had insisted on eating with her hands. She explained to us that that insistence was due to her Indian past lives, for Indians eat that way too – the fingers of the right hand curved in a sort of scoop, getting up a quantity of dahl and rice and *bhaji* (spicy veggies), and shoveling them into the mouth as you lean close to the plate. Devadasi and I could not take to it.

At that idealistic, grumpy Italian farm the toilet seat had been a huge truck tire. I did not like that either. Then, in the evening my sister and I had gone for a short walk, and she had said to me, "I'm going to go to India. Do you want to come?" ("Go," of course, meant, "hitchhike." We both knew that.) "No," I replied, "I have that boyfriend in France. I want to go back to him."

I have wondered, since, how it would all have gone if I had said yes...

So that had been the last time we'd seen each other. The time before that had been in the previous year, during a wet summer in England, in somebody's grubby, cold little cottage in the country, where we'd gone with some acquaintances to dig muddy potatoes out of the earth and be generally wretchedly uncomfortable, in the English way. My sister had read *The Primal Scream* by Arthur Janov and had given it to me. I'd also crammed it into my maw with both hands, feeling I'd found the Holy Grail; and so we'd decided to use that country interlude as an opportunity to Scream.

To give ourselves courage and get past any inhibitions we might have, and to make the experience rounder and deeper, we took some acid beforehand. (The others at the cottage, busy with their muddy tasks, did not participate.) My sister and I were in an upstairs bedroom when we began to scream, and we let nothing get in our way. We lay on our backs on the floor, we rolled, we found in ourselves whatever volume and scope we could... We *screamed*, and *screamed*, and *screamed.*

By and by the others got fed up with the noise, and asked us to go outside. So we went out into the muddy garden, down to the bottom where the fence was, and a tree, and we rolled in the mud and shrieked as best as we could. We did not tire.

A man came up the path to the front door of the cottage, and knocked. The door opened, someone inside explained something to the man. I heard him answer, "Oi, Oi fought someone wuv bein' moidered yup 'ere!" in an accent that sounded like he was mulling over a pile of new little potatoes in his mouth. Then, puzzled and innocent, he went away.

In my memory, that act of screaming was so athletic that although we were doing our best to summon infant or childhood memories to scream at, and the fantasy of them was there, there was no room left for *feeling.* We were being perfect screamers, and that hugeness on our parts metabolized the drug almost utterly, as if we'd drunk two coffees and then sprinted up a mountain. So that experiment in releasing trauma was perhaps not ideal... But it does show some of the camaraderie we'd used to share.

The Meditation Camp

The ten-day camp was being held at the Palace Hotel, and in a huge earthen area behind the hotel, where a vast marquee, called a *mandap*, had been erected. The support posts were the same knotty, bent tree-trunks that were used as scaffolding in buildings under construction. They held up a roof made of corrugated metal faced inside with a rather pleasing ceiling of blue cloth. The same heavy blue cloth was laid out over the ground, making a sort of floor, with overlaps and gaps where the edges of the wide strips of canvas came together. There was a stage at one end near the back entrance of the hotel.

Bhagwan had arrived and taken up residence in a little suite of rooms right off the mandap. It was possible to send letters to him always, from the beginning; now I wrote asking his advice on my personal meditation – for I had not been able to bring myself to allow my lover-in-spirit to penetrate me in body-of-spirit. I could not imagine it. Instead, everything else happened – childhood traumas came up, and courtly approaches by the phantom lover, and really all sorts of things – strange ghostie-beings came, people from my past, and so on. But I could not act out a simple act of love. I received a reply (Laxmi, the grim little secretary, ferried the notes) that I should allow the phantom lover entry. I felt a bit scandalized.

Sarita had been preparing us for what would happen in such a camp. "Everybody is *total*," she explained. "Bhagwan speaks twice a day, and leads the meditations. And the Indians… of course it's mostly Indians – well, they just let loose. Body fluids everywhere! Sweat, pee, everything! Really letting go!"

The camp, oh the camp! Primal screaming notwithstanding, nothing could have prepared me for those ten days! It was by far the most complete cacophony I had ever experienced. A rock concert in San Francisco, packed to the rafters, decibels flying, was nothing compared to the cathartic meditation.

We started with Dynamic at 6 a.m., of course; those dark mornings, waking in the icy cold, throwing on a robe, grabbing a shawl – sandals on, then slipping through the narrow lanes to the hotel… people gathering silently, standing still, waiting. And then… Bhagwan on the stage, lifting up his arms gone suddenly long as waving trees, up, up – exhorting us, into the microphone, to be total in the breathing – and then – *"Go completely mad!"* Cheerleading us along the way, so that after the breathing had revved things up, broken holding patterns, prepared us – we went gaga, screaming, yelling, jumping, twisting imaginary necks, beating on imaginary enemies. It was *loud* and it was *crazy* and it was *everything*! We were blindfolded, we were in there with ourselves, with the pre-dawn. We went for it. And Sarita was right – after just that first meditation of the day, the cloth floor was awash with sweat, saliva, mucus, pee (really!) and no doubt more. There were *puddles*.

After Dynamic we went back to our lodgings, showered, had tea and buttered bread, and returned for the next festivity: Bhagwan's morning discourse.

Each discourse was for me a tearing-open, a truth revealed in sudden obviousness, perfect wave after perfect wave: "Of *course* it's like that!" I'd think. And to sit near him plunged me into searing awareness for the whole 1½ hours. I could *see* inside my mind, my body; I couldn't *not* see.

There followed two more meditations (one, I remember, involved walking to a place where one could be alone, and gazing at the empty blue sky for half an hour). In the evening there was another discourse, followed by *Tratak*: you stood facing him, arms straight up above your head, jumping up and down, eyes open, staring right into his. No blinking allowed!

All *kinds* of things happened! The jumping for thirty minutes was at first an agony, but I could feel myself piercing through layer after layer of sleep and resistance. And what could I do? I went for it. It was the only way to survive – to resist would have been pointless, impossible. The momentum was too great – I had to surrender.

So much happened. Meditation is a miracle, and Bhagwan's meditations *mean business.* You don't get out of there alive. Transformation *happens* to you – and you find yourself present, empty, blissful, quiet... so quiet.

But I was still secretly working against myself, strictly limiting how much I ate. I was slim to begin with, but now I had to tie up my new orange pajama pants tighter around my shrinking waist. I liked the feeling – it was reassuring, and somehow exciting.

After the camp most people left, but some of us stayed on for a day or two. And it was possible to book a private meeting with Bhagwan.

Sarita went first. She came out laughing, glowing. She reported, among other things, that he had said, "Even *I* was surprised at Madhuri!" (This remains one of my favorite things he has said!)

Devadasi went next. She did not afterwards share excitedly, as people were wont to do, Bhagwan's words; but kept them to herself. She had a very private way about her. She seemed abstracted, ingoing.

Then it was my turn. I stepped up from the shady courtyard through a door into a dim, cool chamber, furnished in the Raj fashion with wicker and pillows and the odd stuffed chair. He sat in one of these, one leg crossed over the other, and beamed in welcome. I knelt, scooted up to sit in front of him. A deep breath in, full of sky. The sense of occasion was overwhelming. And I was all undone, or lots of me; taken apart like a hobby-horse, limb from limb. The light of him bathed me like a forest pool.

I don't remember now the exact conversation; only that he told me that I could wear any colors I liked when I got home; I need not wear only orange, as everyone else did who had taken Sannyas (a sartorial custom that was to cause much consternation in living rooms, kitchens, boardrooms, classrooms, airports, offices; across the known world in the years to come!) I think he told me to continue Dynamic; I'm pretty sure he told me to continue my making-love meditation. But I do remember clearly two things: first, I told him that Herb and I went out to fancy restaurants, and Herb paid, and I felt guilty about this. Bhagwan gave me a piercing look – the sort where you feel he is gazing into some deeper place in your nature than you yourself currently have access to – and then said, "Money belongs to everybody. Use it!"

And, I asked him about the burning masses of desire that I was experiencing – for all sorts of things, but especially for Herb and our life together. And he answered, "All desires are innocent."

I *loved* this. I understood it; his statement came from some bigger place. I felt absolved.

Then he gave me a beaming, joyous black-and-white photo of himself, and signed it.

And I rose, and *namasted*, and went back out the way I had come.

Back in Bombay

Returning to Bombay, we stayed in a hotel someplace along the wide curving highway beside the sea. It was fairly cheap, and quite basic and ugly, if spacious; but we could then do what so many budget travelers do: treat ourselves to tea at a fancy place, in this case the Taj Mahal Hotel.

We entered this legendary hostelry through its fabulous storybook fretwork façade, the door held open by a liveried man wearing headgear with a sort of pleated napkin sticking upright at the front. He bowed, and welcomed us into the coolness of the air-conditioned interior. That familiar musty, slightly drippy coolth followed us up thickly carpeted shallow stairs past more liveried footmen, who seemed to me to be extremely adept at gauging our precise social station and adjusting their welcome in a precisely nuanced way accordingly, whilst appearing completely egalitarian, more or less (as long as we were rich, or white, and not obvious ruffians).

There was a tea room off to the side of one of the restaurants, in a sort of long porch with windows to the street, but these windows were so shaded by the carved and filigreed shutters that the hot urban chaos out there seemed remote.

We settled at a small square table in cushioned wooden chairs with straight backs, and ordered tea and cakes. It was delightful to be waited on, to look about us in the refreshing chill, to see only pretty things and silk-clad people, and to know that we could afford it well. I had a custard tart, an unaccustomed sweet thing (since I'd been tightening my belt so much – and in San Francisco too I mostly avoided them as otherwise I might binge) and a bite or two of the sickly, somehow anaemic and odd-tasting cakes the others ordered.

Then we went shopping. I was still trying to get rid of my money, and it was hard work. I bought more papier-mâché boxes, saris, and scarves for friends and even mere acquaintances. We went into an antique shop and I got a Nataraj statue: a dancing Shiva, one knee raised to the side, several arms arranged above his head, all within a ring of metal flames – dancing to create the world. It was the best one I could find, and a goodly size too. I bought myself a bracelet, a wide silver thing with semiprecious stones set into it: amethyst, rosequartz, citrine – for Rs. 20. (I have it still, and people always admire it.)

It was strange, the three of us together, traipsing about – Sarita the confident leader, chiding, instructing, organizing; myself uneasily at the side, darting off into shops and coming back again; Devadasi complaining, brow wrinkled up, insisting she couldn't or wouldn't do a thing, then being chivied on by Sarita. I was always wanting to get away from these two, yet somehow here I couldn't, we were stuck together; and I didn't in the least feel able to navigate on my own.

That night I leant over the sink that jutted from the wall in the hotel room. The tea and custard tart were coming up in great misery and crashing into the sink. I clutched the white porcelain and retched again; stood up for a moment. My eye noticed movement. And in a fog of wretchedness I saw two long, long lines protruding from the top of the small mirror above the sink. Waving back and forth…

Antennae!

There was a goddamned enormous cockroach hanging out behind the mirror, witnessing it all!

And so another lesson about India was learnt: the most expensive food is not necessarily the best, nor the safest.

Sarita managed to get us invited to a traditional Indian feast. We took a taxi to the outskirts of the city, to a big flat ground surrounded by tall hedges. I don't remember now what this place was, but there were many people there. We sat on a long cotton carpet on the ground, facing each other in two long lines. A server came and arranged a very large fresh green leaf before each person. There was a lot of head-waggling and expostulating among the diners. Then onto each leaf was plopped a big spoonful of spicy veggies. Another server plopped down a spoonful of a different veg. A big mound of white rice came next. Dahl was ladled onto that. We each got a little banana, a dollop of dahi, a tablespoon of chutney. Big puffy *puris*, fried breads, were thrown hot beside the piles of food. We ate with our right hand, scooping up the food with the puri; since the left, of course, was used when the food came out the other end.

Dessert was a little scoop of *shrikhand*, a sweet made of yogurt which has been hung in a cloth till the water is drained out, then mixed with chopped dried fruits, nuts, and sugar. It was celestial – delicious, light, rich, tart.

Walking about that afternoon, we had a sugarcane juice, pressed on a cart by a little man who ground two or three long canes through a hand-cranked machine with tall wheels, heavy and antique; you watched the gears turning the wheels with the big sweep of the *wallah's* arm while the juice dripped, green and cold, out of the open spout into a cloudy glass; a light foam on top. It was delicious, fresh and chlorophylly, and no doubt completely unsanitary. And, somehow, not *too* sweet.

I pretty well disgraced myself on our last visit to Bhagwan – though in the moment, I was too frozen with awe to realize it.

We three went to Woodland. Laxmi greeted us as suspiciously as ever, and we had to wait for some time in the nearly-bare living room. For some reason Laxmi began giving us (I suspect only me, really) a discourse about what she called "chewing and digesting." She highly disapproved of this regrettable, non-spiritual activity, and ranted on about how people just "chew and digest, chew and digest." ('Chew' rhymed with 'few.') Her voice was rich and deep, and powerful for such a tiny paper-thin woman; and her sneering and scorn were scary. The scorn hit me where I lived: the more I prevented myself from eating, the more interested I was becoming in food. I dreamed passionately about going out to eat with Herb: about huge, varietous Jewish-deli breakfasts on a Sunday morning – about my own colorful and enthusiastic cooking.

I had with me a paper-wrapped box of barfi for Bhagwan to bless so that I could share it with people in San Francisco. (Although even in my food-demented state I could not love barfi, it seemed an agreeable curiosity to take back.) When I held it out to him and made my request he looked at it briefly, an expression on his face – cold? Annoyed? Distracted tinily by this unimportant thing, and not liking what I was doing to myself in setting store by this archaic tradition? But then he held the box for a moment and gave it back to me. I don't remember what we all spoke of then, except that Devadasi complained about her name, and he said kindly, "You will come to love your name."

Sarita had explained to us that an enlightened person is no longer really connected to his body. In order to keep it from simply dying, and he himself wafting away into the Infinite, he will sometimes adopt a sort of fetish, a focus for some vague remnant of desire or worldly interest, to keep body and soul in the same vicinity. Krishnamurti read detective novels: Bhagwan at that time was into watches. He would ask wealthy Westerners to bring him a certain expensive watch, and this was somehow a spiritual Task for them as well. And usually he'd soon give that watch to someone else.

Now, he showed me an advertisement for a certain watch, cut from a magazine, and asked me to bring it for him next time I came. I said okay – though in the midst of healthy misgivings about Herb's fitting in with the plan!

Then he gave some sort of instruction to Sarita about her next step, and we all went out.

For an extravagant treat on our last night, we three stayed at the Oberoi Hotel. This great tower, gleaming black and silver, was almost the equivalent of the Taj in luxury and glamour (though not quite, because the Taj is dripping with history, in the shadow of the Gateway of India, where the Raj disembarked from its ships for so long), but in a modern style. It was however set down in a shanty-town. As often happens (explained Sarita), the workers who erect a building and live in poor shabby huts next to it, had just stayed on once the building was completed. The hotel had floor-to-ceiling windows, so we looked down on roofs made of plastic tarpaulins, truck doors, corrugated metal, woven bamboo. We saw little brown kids running through mire, and thin wisps of smoke from cooking fires. Men washing themselves with a bucket and a cup, wearing a lungi tied round their waists. Women bathing, somehow, while clad in a sari. From here we could not hear the guttural bitchings and roars and imprecations of people driven past bearing, or smell the excrement or cooking food. But by now I knew that they were there.

I was horribly moved by all this; had given money to beggars on the street; but Sarita had explained to us that beggars were usually run by pimps who took the money. These pimps also maimed children to make them more pitiful and thus profitable as beggars. There seemed nothing I could do about this situation so I just followed what I felt in the moment I was accosted by one.

That night I wrote a poem:

heart

heart
you are more lost
than a divorcee's
broken red fingernail
fallen onto the floor
of the hotel elevator
into deep carpet

let night vacuum you

Devadasi and I left Sarita serene and joyful in her forever home, soon to go back to Tandalja Farm in Baroda. And we flew back to San Francisco.

On the plane I wrote this (because I also write silly nonsense):

Blessed Barfi Song

Oh my god
It's more prasad
What'll we do with it this time
It attracts the ants
I'd feed it to my plants
But I did and they got all covered with slime.

It's chini and doodh,** just ordinary food,*
But blessed by the hand of Bhagwan
Make it into portions
Dole it out at darshan
For everybody to make themselves a hogwan.

I took some back
In a paper sack
To Ma and Pa in 'Frisco
They sniffed at it
And nibbled a bit
And said, "Son, this ain't Nabisco!"

---

* Sugar.
** Milk.

2

Interlude: San Francisco

Interlude: San Francisco

January – July 1974

The Golden Gate Fleshpots, Kind of

Herb met Devadasi and me at the airport. I was wearing one of my new outfits, the orange top and drawstring trousers. I was proud of how loosely everything fitted me, how skinny I had become. But Herb looked at me strangely, and later, when we were alone in his bedroom, he reached out and lifted one of my bare breasts, so very small and modest now, and said, "This is not good." He touched my ribs, showing through the skin. "You look like a concentration camp victim."

When I showed him the finery I had bought or had had tailored, he said, "Look at the cloth. Look at the workmanship. Everything is shoddy. It's all so cheap, such bad quality. Everything from India is like that."

And I embarked on a strange new adventure: how to live in the comforts of San Francisco, whilst being full, full to the brim, of the New and Inescapable. How to be in the world whilst having just begun a terrifying love affair with the Sacred.

Not knowing, then, if I would ever go back to India.

I was still escaping her, that country.

But of course she had come with me.

All the things I'd longed for so desperately while I was away were available to me now – the foods, the colorful clothes, my big staunch cautiously generous sugar daddy. Riding in his quiet car across the Bay Bridge, having lovely hot showers at his house, reading the newspaper together on a Sunday morning with coffee and bagels and cream cheese, while he told me what was what politically.

But nothing was even remotely the same.

I was lost – so lost that extremes seemed to come out of me in different ways as I slewed from side to side. I was eating only once a day, but that meal was gigantic, and left me with a greatly swollen belly I was ashamed of. Herb laughed appreciatively as he watched me eat. I started cooking even more passionately, making dinners: a complicated aubergine parmesan, crusty on top and velvety-rich within; delicious cold next day with mayonnaise. A sauerbraten, marinated overnight, I accidentally dropped on the floor and picked up again to roast as if nothing had happened – but then I told my guests that it had fallen. Cakes I myself didn't eat, elaborate with added dried fruits, liqueur, jam filling, honey icing.

I'd stopped working in porno movies the previous summer – I'd done them for nine months – because Herb did not approve of them. (I strangely didn't write about it in my diary at the time... it was so uneventful; the banal boringness of meeting the biggest prick in the 50 states, the sexless stupidity of it all, the obligation to fuck the directors, the times spent lounging about waiting and eating catered lunch.) I enjoyed the surprise of different filming locations; I enjoyed the money – most of which I put in savings. Herb thought he might want to run for political office one day, and the association would not look good on his resumé (though he was fine with a couple of threesomes we gamely tried. I don't know what the women experienced, nor Herb either; but for me it was all dry and cool and empty and embarrassing – as empty as sex usually was, but with the added weirdness of this other lavish silkiness of humanity there, full of hips and bosoms. Herb, it turned out, liked round hips.)

Not doing the films, money was a problem for me. I was basically pissed off about this: Jacques, still a friend, also didn't approve of my doing the movies – but how did these men expect me to survive? I'd tried minimum-wage jobs in a taqueria and a dime store, in each case lasting just a few days – the boredom was so excruciating I simply could not make myself stay. Capitalizing on sex didn't consciously bother me – quite the contrary; I'd found the whole range of experiences I'd had up to then so disappointing that I'd thought I might as well get paid.

I still lived with Devadasi and my brother Andy; Herb did not support me, but only indulged me. I had spent my blue-movie savings to go to India.

(I remember I had saved $1200; $900 went for the ticket, and, as noted, I had spent the rest as hard as I could).

Herb hired me to stain his deck, and then corrected my work incessantly – he was a perfectionist. I got a job delivering pizzas for a new restaurant. One of the perks was being able to build and roast your own pizza and then consume it – so that would be my one meal, cheese piled in a mountain that amazed my co-workers. I had to use the old car that belonged to the shop, and the San Francisco hills were really scary when the clutch slipped, up under a stop sign, the crossroad right in front of me invisible on the steep grade – and I began to slide back down. I started having nightmares about this.

I got a bee in my bonnet that I should move out of the shared flat and get my own place; that this would be Independence, and I must do it. There was no reason for it precisely – Devadasi did not bother me with any parental advice whatsoever, and had not done since I was fifteen and she had announced that she was no longer anybody's mother. I loved her and my younger brother. And finding, renting, furnishing, paying for, one's own place was a great challenge. I was by then fueled by frequent glasses of Tab, a diet cola, which made me nervous, antsy, busy all the time, and paranoid. I kept a very tall bottle of it in the fridge.

I found a little cabin in a grassy yard behind another house on Day Street, in Noe Valley, a very Gay area. I painted the interior myself, a luscious light sunny yellow. I put on the bed a beautiful mirrored bedspread I'd brought back from India, brick-red with sage-green and other colors in the threads around the mirror-work. It looked wonderful with the walls. Another wall I painted a creamy terracotta. The place was beautiful! Then I hired a carpenter to build a loft in the living room so I could get a lodger. Unwise in the ways of the world (or anything else really), I didn't ask the landlord, who, when he next visited, was very cross indeed, saying that the loft wasn't secured and would just fall down.

I rented the loft to a young man. I gave a party, borrowing Bhagwan's slippers and robe from Sushila to display. People stared at them uncomprehendingly. I barely knew anyone I'd invited. They ate my laboriously-prepared food (three days in the making, a month's-worth of food stamps gone into it) and went away. I felt empty.

There was no insulation in the cottage. Mark Twain once said, "The coldest winter I ever spent was a summer in San Francisco." I stood in front of the heater, or sat on it, the other side of me freezing. I posted an ad saying I did alterations on clothing. A man brought me cuffed pants to take up. I said I knew how, but I didn't. I botched them. He was angry, gave me the $6 anyway. I made skirts out of jeans to sell and ended up giving them to Devadasi.

I rented another flat too, because I liked it – it was so big. But it was in a bad part of town. I never went there. The owner re-rented it out from under me without telling me and I discovered the other people's stuff when I went in one night. I got a free lawyer and served the landlord papers.

In my little house I had a wardrobe with some beautiful clothes in it – clothes had always been an art-form for me, and I had been making, altering, and buying them cheap in rummage sales and Goodwills since I was thirteen. I wore rust-colored leather platform boots that zipped up to the knee, a peach lace blouse with a peplum, brown velvet knickerbockers. Herb took me to Minnie's Can-Do Club, in the Mission, where Minnie reigned on her stool, bottom overflowing the round seat, and I danced up a joyous storm, doing backbends all the way down to the floor from my platform shoes, shakin' it up among the colorful mix of people, and Herb shifted from foot to foot like a white man, vastly amused at finding himself in a situation so foreign to his habits.

I found a job as an interviewer for a survey company. They'd been hired by the government to find out how military families liked their health care. To get this job I said that I had finished high school, when in fact I had never gone even for a day. I worked both on the phone in a big pleasant office in Berkeley, where I made friends; and out in the field, on an aircraft carrier, and the like. (I was struck by the size of the sailors' bottoms, the stodginess of the lunches, and the patrician, condescending air of the officers.) It was an education of sorts, but I was crazed, drinking Tab or coffee with fake creamer in it all day and having crying jags. Herb was cooling towards me. He hated it when I cried. He said we were going to have to break up. I was disconsolate.

The survey company said I was the best interviewer they had ever had. They were amazed at how I could transcribe an entire conversation in lickety-split time, as I was conversing, with no machine. I had had so much practice recording conversations in my diary, overheard on buses, in shops, on the street. I'd always loved that.

But what was all this for? I was lost. I did not feel really that I was getting my teeth into the world – that was Herb's thing, I was just trying to borrow it. Yet I was determined – sort of. I slewed about.

I was still doing Dynamic every day, breathing, growling, jumping in my skinny body. I was still doing my Making Love meditation. I was as total as I could be, but in the neutral atmosphere of the World, these were rather lonely exercises. I remembered a dream I had had when Mama and I had first moved into the Potrero Hill flat; it was about a spider, a small spider which nevertheless weighed as much as an entire planet. Its round little body gave off an emanation of such potent density and heaviness that just to look at it was to feel a fathomless menace. In a poem I called it "the spider made of Jupiter-stone." I'd gone into the dream, and discovered that the spider was all the unlived darknesses, the repressed emotions, of my life, and anyone else's I had collected along the way. I was now committed to digging them out; so perhaps something was lightening... Or only beginning to slide into the heaviness.

Letter from Sarita

March 18, 1974

Gloriously Exalted One
Madhuri
Just this moment awaking from a long sleep to be embraced rapturously by your letter.

Probably about the time you got your flat he was asking me about you and I said, "She drives around all day looking for a place to live," and he said "What! She still hasn't found?!" "No," I answered, laughing. "Hmmmm," he said.

Things have turned upside down here in these areas. Bhagwan is moving to Poona on the 21st. Apparently there will be an ashram and a guest house. All kinds of rumors float around – lectures every day – 13-day meditation camps – etc. For those on the outside it may be more difficult to see him also. Poona is supposedly hotter than hell and I've already been getting slight sunstroke in Baroda!

This Baroda ashram which never did make it as an ashram has now collapsed from nervous strain. Men can't get on with Sheela no-how. There was all kinds of mutiny going on so a delegation went to see Bhagwan. He said simply that work cannot happen where there is conflict so whoever is not happy here should leave. An explosion of freedom happened. All these new disillusioned sannyasins – five all together – took off for adventures into the unknown – four men and one woman.

I was also strangely affected. So I went to see Bhagwan and to make a long story short he told me to come to Poona on the 25th and a place will be found for me either in the ashram or the guest house working at cleaning, cooking, or gardening.

Afterwards Laxmi gave me a big heavy lecture on the strictness of the ashram, how there will be no rock music allowed – no freaking out except in morning meditation – to live in the ashram everyone must pay 2000 rupees a month and they won't have servants so if you work it must be full time blah blah blah

Bhagwan is purely love

Laxmi is purely business *{drawing of heart skewered with arrow, dripping blood}*

So I am here in Baroda until the 24th, then I take off to Poona. Instead of being blissful as one might expect from this new adventure, I have been going through heavy inner catharsis.

I think Laxmi's lecture was so heavy that it really brought me down quickly and I've been wandering around inside lost saying – Who am I? Where am I? What purpose? The climax was yesterday afternoon when I threw my hair down in front of the three framed pictures of him. It's done.

I shaved my head, my eyebrows, my armpits and my sex center.

It is fantastic. I am a Kewpie doll. I am a nonentity. When I look at that dead hair to which I have clung my whole life I feel liberated in a multi-dimensional way. So many illusions which have bound me with invisible silken threads are cut.

It is not a sacrifice – it is a prayer – and prayer is gratitude. I am completely naked like a child. I can see him more clearly – I have given him a very big block – the strength of my illusion – my hair – . You would adore this cute little pube eyebrowlessness from another planet and egg shaped head alarmed by its perfect nakedness. It's just beautiful.

I did it without asking Bhagwan but it is inspired in his grace for sure.

It seems there will not be another meditation camp until August because of moving and all that. I will be on the scene so I can give you the news as it happens. The address to which you can send mail for now will be Woodland because they will still maintain a center there. Poona is only three hours by train from Bombay.

Somehow receiving such a glowing letter from you really put everything in perspective. It all feels whole and divine when you send his grace from that side also…

Totally love

*Ananda Sarita ben**

Edifying Developments

One day, somewhere in the middle of this six months of lost time, lost soul, lost heart, lost flesh – all this floundering – Herb took me to a psychic. He loved psychics, and went to any he heard about.

We drove to a leafy suburb in Walnut Creek, in the Back Bay, and parked in front of a ranch house like any other. A big woman in a big dress, ordinary-looking as any housewife, greeted us and led us into a side-room. She sat behind a desk and we sat in chairs facing her. I looked about me and saw a cluttered home office. A cat appeared, leapt up and positioned himself above and behind her on a shelf, and stared at the proceedings the while. A large window looked out onto the shady street.

I was wearing belled jeans, a turtleneck, and my mala. The woman looked over at the mala, and then at me. I had said nothing yet at all.

"If you don't go back to your Master," she advised sternly, "you will fall back to where you were before." Then she turned to Herb, and he had his consultation. I was stunned.

My evening pizza delivery job was now very dangerous. Since the car kept falling back down the hill, I'd started shooting stop signs. I'd just drive up, accelerate across the intersection, and on up the next incline, without knowing what might meet me. I knew I could not last long, doing that.

Herb had long ago bought me a vibrator, a big heavy plug-in Hitachi Magic Wand. He'd laughed about it. He was a big man all over, and I loved

* Ben: a mild female honorific.

him, but I could not respond to him sexually – nor to anyone. I'd made blue movies out of bitterness, having found sex not as advertised; and it was of course my fault, something was wrong with me; this was known between Herb and me. And in my emaciation I had further discarded any sensuousness I might have had. The vibrator provoked some semblance of orgasm, but my embarrassment was so great, and also my feeling of disconnection from my lover when the thing was on, that the machine was a very mixed blessing. Herb had said it was the only thing he missed with me – sex.

He sent me to a sex therapist, a nice dark-haired sober young woman, rounded and calm. We lay spooning, fully clothed, while she asked me gentle questions about how sex was for me. Then she just spoke to me, relaxingly. She advised me to be glad that I could have any orgasms at all. It wasn't necessary to get them from a penis. So many women don't.

I didn't believe her.

I went to a Betty Dodson workshop, in a Victorian house somewhere in the middle of the City, upstairs in a huge carpeted room. Betty Dodson had extremely short hair, like a convict. She handed out specula and dental mirrors so that we could look at our own cervices. Mine looked to me like a poor naked chicken neck, chopped off in a supermarket butcher's corner. It was sweet and sad and so vulnerable I could not bear to look at it for long. Also it looked much like the end of a penis, with the little entrance in it. Uncanny. Betty gave us vibrators and said, "I socialize my sex." I did not want to socialize my sex. That sounded like what I'd been trying to do all along. I just wanted to have some sex at all, somewhere, somehow, that felt like what I thought it was supposed to feel like. I was stuck there. (The whole gift and power and mystery and femininity of the body I was born to, with its hundred levels each more etheric and mysterious than the last, the heart and sacredness and tenderness and confiding, the arcane and risky discoveries of what I am really made of and where I most thrive – none of this was mentioned by anyone I encountered in the West; no mentor appeared, my traumas were not addressed, and certainly nobody, especially not myself, understood that what I needed was endless time and endless permission to be exactly where I found myself; accompanied by the right admiring, supportive, loving words… an encouragement towards unconditional tenderness. That is all. I thought there was some mechanical failure in me. It was the mechanical outlook that was all wrong.)

I thought sex was supposed to be big, hot, noisy, the sort of thing that makes a splash and shows the man that he is important and that you yourself are wonderful. Bragging sex, I wanted. And it had to be real and convincing. This never even remotely began to occur, or, maybe just once or twice, by accident, when I'd drunk a little red wine and lay in a roofless barn on a spread of hay in the middle of France with a patient man. But that was about it for that thing called Pleasure, in the seven years of gripping, banging, stroking, giving, receiving, straddling, infections, showing off, parched inconclusiveness; I'd endured so far.

Meanwhile, something disturbing and strange had occurred back in our flat on Potrero Hill.

Devadasi said later that she too had had a strong impetus to leave India and return to San Francisco; but it was because she was worried about Andy. (He had stayed with family friends while we were away.) He was twelve and very tall for his age; well over six feet. But it was the way his chin began to grow, his elbows and knees and feet to enlarge, that told her something must be wrong. So she took him to a University medical teaching hospital nearby.

A painful lumbar puncture was done. Afterwards, he was admitted to the hospital, and underwent surgery to remove a benign tumor from his pituitary gland. This growth had been getting ready to blind him – and he was an artist, who drew comic books all night and slept all day.

I went to see him after the operation. He was folded into a child-size bed, quiet as always, his huge feet sticking out, his thick elbow-length hair pulled back in a ponytail. They'd lifted up his nose to get at the thing, so there was a bandage on his face. He'd be okay now, though would still grow a little taller while the remaining hormone worked its way through his blood. But he would keep his sight.

My good and sweet and funny and bright little brother. I stared at him with my heart all swelling.

I was too thin to really matter to myself any more. Only my spirit held life with a fierce fire, close and close… though so far away. I had no periods. My hipbones and elbows were sharp. I weighed myself: eighty-nine pounds. I thought I looked great. I went to a hairdresser and had my brown shagged hair permed into a fizzing mass around my face. I loved it. I looked like somebody else, somebody with fat hair. Herb didn't see why I'd had to do it.

I'd been getting poems published in small magazines since I was sixteen. Early in 1973 my main publishers had asked me to submit a manuscript for a book. They were a long-running literary magazine in New York, *Hanging Loose*, about to branch out into books; they wanted mine to be the first. I was honored. It was a simple matter to assemble the poems and short stories I wanted in it, spanning seven years of writing. They had accepted it immediately and pronounced it word-perfect. It would be published late in 1974.

Excerpt: Aerogram from Sarita

June 27, 1974

Beloved Madhuri,

Bhagwan? ...On one hand he will be here. On another hand he may disappear any moment.

One thing is certain. He will not be the same.

You will not be the same. Yearn for him and he is there also. The situation is a constant turmoil and flux for us around him. We have no idea what is happening. We don't know what he is or who he is and finally we just follow the heart, over hill & dale it leads us towards the unknown of him. Herb is a good vehicle for Bhagwan. Do it totally. Don't worry.

As he says you have no control over the situation. Where you are is His doing.

Have faith is all I can say. It seems as if Bhagwan will be here for you when you come. I don't think any of us are ready for his exit and as he says he is here only for us. Terror has arisen... as lately he has entered a new phase... a more intimate phase – being with those who are true seekers with heart and soul – dispersing ... the multitude. We are all afraid we are not chosen ones. It seems to me you have nothing to fear. Just relax and make plenty of money, come when you are ready – come when you are at the peak of readiness.

Love & kisses

Sarita

A Party

At the pizza place I had met a man, Robert, who had become a friend. I was not sexually attracted to him, but we had fun talking and writing each other silly notes. He seemed to be some sort of goofy revolutionary, a writer who loved to embroider his words with wild absurdities. There was a freedom in our correspondence – he was not strait-laced like Herb was. Robert was of above-medium height with tilted cat-green eyes, dark wavy hair, and white teeth with one sharp, prominent canine. His grin was shy and beamy and he had red cheeks and a long nose with a flattish tip.

One night he took me to a party. There was red punch with fruit in it, in a huge bowl, and I drank some. I did not know that it was spiked with LSD. I lay back in the big living room and laughed… I laughed all night! As the drug wore off in the dusky dawning, I drove slowly back through the thick fog to my cottage.

I knew that I was going back to India.

The Call Comes Again

Two or three days later my phone rang. The caller was Joy Phipps – a wiry little blonde with a small, angular face and long thin lips. As we spoke I could see her in my mind's eye: the funny, insouciant air about her, as if her whole life was happening in an ironic comedy on a stage. The way she tended to dart about, a sort of *experienced* little sprite, enunciating all her words carefully, speaking a bit too loudly. She was, somehow, very camp.

I had met her in the all-woman guerrilla theater group I belonged to, Les Nickelettes. I much enjoyed belonging to this troupe – the dressing-up, the writing of my own solo acts; and the strange things we all got up to, such as crashing The Top of the Mark bar, high in the swank of Pacific Heights, at midnight one New Year's Eve, taking over the stage and doing our own ironic can-can while wearing flannel pajamas and granny nightgowns. Or, taking over the stage at the Carol Doda Condor Club, the first topless bar in San Francisco; wearing Girl Scout uniforms with large hollow plastic breasts added on the outside (*while* we were stoned on mescaline… ahem!) We also had a regular slot at a downtown fringe theater, and we had a lot of fun. The other women were savvy, hip, pretty, and politically aware – which I was not. The politics were not even slightly interesting to me – I just liked the loopy, creative fun.

Joy Phipps had become, in an offhand way, a friend. I had shown her photo to Bhagwan, during that first meeting: child-sized, she was sitting on a suitcase with a ventriloquist's doll on her upraised hand. Bhagwan had said, "She is very worldly!" and had given her the name Shobha. When I had later handed her the name-paper and mala she'd responded in her usual camp superlatives; but no doubt it was all very strange for her, and she had not been using the name.

Now, she said in her dry, emphatic way, "You know my father died recently? I just inherited $12,000. I want to go to India. I don't want to go alone. I'll pay half your ticket if you'll come with me."

Three days later, on 7th July 1974, we boarded our flight. I wore jeans with an orange turtleneck in a fine ribbed cotton, and my fluffy perm. I had no check-in luggage – just a tote-bag with a couple of other garments in it, my pens and notebook, mascara and face cream, unscented soap, and a loaf of San Francisco sourdough French bread for my sister. I had not told her I was coming.

We took a taxi to Woodland (although Sarita had written to us about Bhagwan's imminent move to Poona, it had not sunk in at all) in the muggy monsoon warmth. The smells were all about us. Those smells… It was all a bit less alarming this time.

We got out, went up the stairs and knocked at the door of Bhagwan's erstwhile apartment. Nobody answered.

A man came out of the apartment next door. "He has gone to Pune!" he announced, waggling his head. It sounded like "Poony."

Very well. I had no notion at all of where Poony was, but there we would go. We took a taxi to Victoria Railway Station, an enormous, Gothic thing, encrusted with a hundred years of pollution and grime, and inside, entire tribes of Indians sleeping on the floor at night (we'd seen this on our trip north to Baroda). But now, as the morning grew later, they were all milling around, begging or sitting on bundles. Porters ran about, red armbands on their scrawny biceps. There were long queues before several murky-looking little windows. I went up and stood in one of them, motioning Shobha to come with me.

Visits to three windows were required, but eventually I had procured two tickets and reservations for the Deccan Queen to Poony.

We sat on the crowded train on the hard slick blue seats, gazing out the window. At first there was Bombay's urban greyness; then a semi-urban otherworld, with factories and acres of hutments looking squashed in the rain. Then the train began to climb. Deep jungle was out there now, with waterfalls pouring down from mist-obscured heights through huge trees and tangled creepers. It was beautiful.

Cresting a slope, we pulled into Lonavala, where the whole town was given over to the manufacture of a sweet called *chikki*, made of boiled *gur*, or raw sugar, with sesame seeds thickly embedded in it. The station was full of sellers with little stalls, and small boys shoved newspaper-wrapped slabs in the windows at us. The humid, ancient, smelly air was all around, all through us. The town was a has-been, down-at-heel hill station, on the lip of the Deccan Plateau – through the jungly vegetation we could see generous Raj architecture on some of the rotting buildings.

The train moved on. The damp magic of this enchanted, peculiar land was on me. I knew nothing; but I was here. I took out my notebook and pens…

Excerpt from my diary:

On the train. Book, book, it is monsoon. It is monsoon. Warm dampness, rain. Soft warm rain. Peace in the vagrant anonymity of the city. I love, and it spills red to the ground. The sensation is housed in my breasts again.

India is the walls of the vagina…

Thick drops thud to the pave

I am a sensor-receptor, vacant and holy I am meant only to steam in the rain

I needed to go to the dark side of the moon

The I

It is so good to love two men and to worship Bhagwan*

It is so good

The steaming rain is harder and harder down

We slept enough. Shobha doesn't sleep.

Perhaps it's better if their chocolate-desire is never awakened, these little beggars. I fed them a whole barf-bag full of stuff off the plane we didn't eat – a fancy pear-chocolate dessert, cheese and rolls and butter and tomatoes and candy.

The rain sounds like a spray-paint can being shaken up.

* Apparently I knew Robert fancied me, and I liked him – but we'd not been to bed.

Begging crow begging child   I am a beggar this is why beggars are known here, and allowed. My whole body begs. I am small, it says. A tiny girl. Care me. Care me.

A sweeper sweeps with long broom the debris between the rails   I long for nothing except Bhagwan except soft arms ever ever no interior workings there are no interior workings

Herb, my lover, is the jewel in my forehead   I adore him like the moth adores the flame – suicide

Bhagwan will see that, when I show him the picture   Bhagwan will see that celestial nose

To be in India in love   to be in India alone in love

This train this train to Poona is delaying forever I   keep feeling like I shouldn't talk

– It is like home, India – it is so funky

Mostly they wear their sandals half off their feet in front

What are they doing, these trudgers

– What will happen what will happen

How I love the soft damp

It is all so easy this time   Shobha is writing a letter across from me

Delicious gloom

The feeling is like waking up on a Sunday morning with nothing to disturb the day but the delicious prospect of the Sunday paper

Bhagwan has made my life a treat these months the freedom to worship

I do myself out of a lot of nice things because I am not ready for niceness

In the metal rafters of the train station half-roof the monkeys are walking like huge obnoxious toms

Bhagwan – transform me to a joyful noise

They walk with toes spread wide from birth to death   they walk with clip clops of sandal

Crow walks streaky-wet train roof

Crows just like monkeys same raunchy sass

It was the easiest journey I ever made We hardly spoke we just got here

Later

Train goes mooing into the void

Never has there been such unutterable beauty   monsoon

Jungle valleys size of Africa mountains squeezing waterfalls out like squeezed sponges blue green of murderous grass all deadly all murderous in beauty

I am alone I want only to know the loneliness this jungle. Too beautiful for one man's perception ever

Through black curving tunnel train halts and jerks yellow light aheadwater running alongside

In one tunnel stops completely fumes fill space Shobha laughs in the black

Strange electrical works tended by two silences perched canyonside

Station – funk purveyors alight with moldy wares

India bows to monsoon like a woman to menstruation

Rejoices and dies to the scalp-tingle eeriness I am in eeriness

Waterfall comes in the moving train Shobha laughs her thin mouth curled in a deep ageless sphinx pleasure and satisfaction she is home

I find I am holding my breast under the shawl

We went to A-1 Woodland at 8 a.m. and a shorts-dark man answered with the sideways nod and it was all, all bare

I smelled His scent oh curse that we didn't think to go into His room

A pond quivers with rain radio with western music in next car

To make love in India with either lover oh

It is getting deeper, the gloom

It will have taken from 9 a.m. to about 7:30 or 8 p.m. to go 100 miles

Into pooled and puddle-drenched flatlands

I caress the holy-piece Herb gave me a book mark from The Cannery where we had dinner night before departure it has auras on it flowers saying love comes in all colors a yellow tassel I will hold it now he says playfully

The silly man he even held it against his penis and it got very warm

I hold it and a deep tidy peace flows into me an easy love it is very warm I drank out the warmth now it must recharge I have a desire to have Bhagwan bless it too

Letter to Bhagwan:

Bhagwan
I just want you
You know the total woman I discover layer by layer

I am so pale, so barely discovering
I know nothing I am nothing
I just want
That endless sudden poetry
The monsoon wind to truly shake me
So seldom am I truly shaken
To adore adore to adore idiotic and utterly
Forever to love and adore

To love with my lover and be adored
Forever
With no threat of tomorrow
I long for it with all my being
I postpone everything
I look and look
In possible places and in impossible places
I look and do not see

Love, Madhuri

Poony

Later, much later, after many stops, we drew in to Poona Station. We disembarked, fighting off porters who tried to grab our shoulder bags from us. We walked through the dim and the crowds, emerged into a parking area where motor-rickshaws waited. We got into one. "Ashram," I said, having no better idea what to call a place where Bhagwan might be.

The driver accepted this directive without question and drove us putt-putting through puddles, bouncing in and out of pot-holes, down long wide roads lined by huge banyan trees with their multi-stemmed trunks like stretched-out sentient beings, or like elephant trunks descending from the high tree to the earth. The city was much less crowded than Bombay.

Just at dusk we swung into a narrow road much overhung by very tall trees. All seemed to be a rain-smelly jungle, with large houses in it which sat back from the road, melting into the mist and gloom. We stopped before a huge wooden double gate. "Asram," the driver said. We paid him and got out. He putt-putted away.

We had no idea where we were really; it could have been anybody's ashram. We went unchallenged through the gates.

A large house loomed in front of us and to the right. Nobody was about. The house had a scruffy, unkempt garden, a bit of low hedge, weeds. We walked to the right along the front of the house and turned left at the end.

And there they were.

In a pool of light on a narrow covered porch was a big easy-chair, and in it sat Bhagwan, beaming happily. Sarita sat next to him on the stone floor, and Vivek next to her. Shobha and I walked up to them – but in that moment I completely forgot my traveling companion, having eyes only for my sister's huge, serene smile, and for Bhagwan's big beam, his twinkling acknowledgment. I had arrived into the most beguiling quicksand of bliss in the world. All was silent in me, just for that moment.

None of them seemed the least bit surprised to see us.

Shobha and I had intended to stay a month. But after a week I knew that this was my chance to save my life, and I was never going to leave. Shobha too knew that she would stay on, though she was of course in her own trajectory; very different than mine.

3

Soul Garden

Soul Garden

1974 – 1981

From Slum to Boat Club Road

I stayed a few nights at the flat where Sarita was living (Shobha had gone to a hotel). The building was in a true slum, some distance from the ashram – the only place Sarita could afford. The flat was completely bare except for a pallet on the floor with a sheet on it. A peg stuck out of the wall to hang clothes on. The place was not, in itself, so horrible – it was clean – but just outside, the slum raged in all its sullen viciousness. The vibe of it was indescribable – feral, dark, scant, starved, sneaky, ancient in its desperation. Dark deeds had been done there, were being done there daily. I had nightmares where I could see and feel the starved and nasty doings going on outside. I told Sarita that she had to move. She was weak from a bout of hepatitis, and had no energy to try to find anything better. She had just parted from an ex, and was shattered, though serene. We planned to get a place together.

From a letter to Devadasi:

July 26, 1974

Dear Devadasi,

I'm in exactly the mood to write to you. Sarita and Kamal were saying yesterday how when you get around Bhagwan for very long everything falls apart… and it is true. I feel exactly like a fly in a huge spider's web, with no way out through the known… all is the unknown. Devadasi, it is good you are not here – we are having horrible troubles about houses and money. You would not like to see the slum where Sarita lives. The people are horrible and spend the whole day scrabbling in filth. It is weird, we are looking for a place and have an excellent possibility but no money. If my *car sold and the money came soon we could snap it up. Meanwhile the rent here is paid until the 15th, I hate the place, and I have a little over $10 left.*

Shobha is very happy in her place and I don't blame her. Devadasi, you see... everything is trying to get equalized. And these sannyasis and relatives of sannyasis are part of it – bringing some of America here. When you get into meditation you feel that you are catharsing for the world... and that it sort of owes you some of its superabundance. Devadasi, there is something bottomless happening – I am becoming part of the whole, part of humanity, and I ache for it and see that I have always ached for it, and in this slum it is particularly horrible. There is no way out but down. And it is time to do this. I have no choice.

Oh Devadasi. Whenever I think of you I think of your beautiful barefoot self in Levi skirt padding about a house full of plants. Oh my Devadasi. That you **are** *is one of the greatest miracles that ever was. And I want so much for you to still be, in your own way, the mama, to take care of your daughters who are taking care of themselves.*

Your Madhuri is much more adaptable than one might have thought from her bitchy ways – I am whatever the situation demands, I absorb the vibes, and here money belongs to all, Sarita is my blood, meditation is my sole activity besides and including living.

Many strange intangible things are happening. Food here is such a weird hell, no matter how you work it. I just had some fruit salad and yogurt, and the convolutions, complications, and time that went into getting it and making it are absolutely incredible. And yet, in America we pay in other ways. By being blinded, by working, by being tyrannized by the lie of time.

Twirling (meditation) is extremely powerful. After the 1½ hours I lie on the earth and ants, centipedes** and mosquitoes roam me and it rains and I am at peace.*

My darling Sarita... developed a sore on her toe from her sandal and in two days her whole foot and ankle swelled up and turned blue and red. I took her first to the emergency clinic and they were like gas station attendants, idiotic, they gave her aspirin and cortisone and sent her away without a bandage. I took her to a homeopathic doctor in a gorgeous stone mansion and he was a miracle man, she said his vibes were like Goenka's, he passed a magnet over her foot and I, forgetting to think, felt the vibrations and he gave her some natural medicines to correct toxicity imbalance and it was free, it cost nothing – and he measured her vibrations with a needle stuck through the skin of his finger. His office was very clean. He said that by night it would be better and by morning almost healed and

* Sufi whirling meditation, which we did in bare feet out in the garden, having as yet no meditation hall.

** Actually they were millipedes.

in one month her afflictions would be over. She couldn't have antibiotics anyway because of her jaundice. Today her foot is almost well. It was amazing. He said a normal person had a spiritual vibration of 800, that Sarita's was 1000...

Good news: In the Dynamic meditation... in the third stage you don't have to jump up and down – you just do whatever the body wants to do, making certain to repeat hoo! Hoo! Loudly and constantly. Sarita said she often gets in the fetal position. I have enjoyed the meditation since this news, and it is doing me more good...

In twirling meditation I keep my eyes closed for 1½ hours and I see many things, many spirits and angels, and Herb came, the most serious part of him, and stood and watched. My meditation is going very well.

Devadasi, where are letters for us? We are pitiful, checking mail every day! If Herb comes... SEND FOOD!! love love MUD[*]

I stayed then for a week at Mobos Hotel – some distance from the ashram, on a busy road – in a tiny partitioned cubicle with a bed in it. The walls did not reach the ceiling, which stretched high above us with great old beams looming into the blackness. It had been a fine house once, but now it was dim and grim, and did a brisk business in grotty beds for seekers.

Sarita introduced me to her friends, many of them Indian. Pratibha Lal and her very tall friendly husband lived in a cool flat in Boat Club Road,[**] a leafy, L-shaped avenue not far from Mobos. They occasionally gave us good dinners. The ashram did not yet have a proper canteen (though one was coming very soon) so we had to scrounge for meals. Next door to Mobos was the terrible Café Delite, where one ended up by default much more often than one might have wished. It had leaning metal card-tables outside in the dirt, next to the bustling road. What one ate there was toast-butter accompanied by tea or milky Nescafé.

Sarita and I sat there one morning having breakfast. "This isn't a nutritious breakfast!" I pointed out. "We need something fresh, and some protein!" "But," argued my lofty little sibling, "if you are *really spiritual*, you can live on tea and toast-butter and be *perfectly healthy!*"

I felt that certainly I was not very spiritual; or, not *that* spiritual – and also that in fact people *do* need other foods than toast-butter. But it wasn't in me to argue further. There were to be rounds of boils in our lives in the not-too-distant,

* By this time I had been given a nickname, Mudpie.

** There was an old Raj boat club on that road, beside the Mula-Mutha river; it had gone to wrack and ruin.

and I often darkly thought of Café Delite when the roars of misery were at their worst.

We had another Indian friend, The Colonel, Raj Kapoor. He was a tall, jolly, jokey man with a big mustache who did his Colonelling at a nearby military base. He and his gracious and lovely wife Usha lived with their children in a happy house in a military encampment outside the city. They welcomed and fed us and were very kind. Thank you, Raj and Usha (she now sadly out of her body) – I am still grateful. They loved to attend Bhagwan's discourses, and were I believe considered rather raffish and bohemian in their milieu because of this.

Pratibha's husband Prem knew of a flat for rent in Boat Club Road, in a tree-shaded, relatively private building. Might we want it? It was on the second floor, bare as all flats are in India; squat toilet, three bedrooms, large kitchen/ dining room. Every window looked out onto trees. 550 rupees a month, to be divided three ways. Sarita and I took it.

Col. Raj Kapoor brought to us, our first night there, boxes of groceries. That was a warm and happy moment.

Much later Sarita told me I had saved her life, arranging for this flat, getting her out of the slum. I had not remembered it as that. I only remember the pleasure, the functionality, of living in our new place. We had Mary and Rita, Christian *ayahs*, to cook and clean for us. We each had our cotton pallet, which seemed to get flatter and more spread-out by the day. We each had a peg with a few robes; an alarm clock (kept well away from the window, as anyone who could climb up that far could put a stick through the bars and drag it back to where he could reach in and get it). A book or two. Two sheets, a flattish, lumpy cotton pillow and a towel. Perhaps a potted plant. Perhaps, in winter, a green bedspread. A shawl, folded on a shelf. And that was it.

Mary and Rita were wonderful. They were from South India, very dark, and had beautiful melodious voices and ways of rolling their words. They used to bring a child or two with them – I remember a round-eyed little fellow named Innocent – and they squatted before the little portable stove and patted out chapattis onto a convex metal plate and roasted them. They swept from a squatting position with a long sheaf of straw for a broom. They washed the floors daily with a big, wet rag, swishing it back and forth, back and forth. They poured buckets of water scented with Dettol down the toilet. Sarita knew the proper way for things to be done, and Mary and Rita were part of this rightness. Their presence was not a luxury – if we had tried to do our own cooking and cleaning we could not have also plunged into our meditation as we were here to do.

Together, they got 60 rupees a month.

We rented bicycles, and rode them in the chill of pre-dawn dark to do Dynamic – each and every morning. Every day I met every demon I could find. Every day I danced at the end to the lovely trebling of dawn birdsong, as well as the music on the tape. I did Dynamic, then, daily for 1½ years, including my time in San Francisco. It transformed my respiratory system, strengthening it. It made me loose as a goose; and it transformed my inner world. Dynamic is a non-negotiable, irreplaceable, ultra-valuable resource the whole world needs.

Bhagwan lived in Lao Tzu House, another large tree-shaded mansion behind the first house I'd seen on arriving (that one was called Krishna House). These mansions were in an area of the city called Koregaon Park – previously a very posh suburb; most of the houses were owned by Maharajahs and their ilk. These grandees would come to town for the horse racing season, and the rest of the time the huge houses, set in lovely gardens, were the province of a few care-taking folk and their families. They lived in servants' quarters at the back; you could see them going about their business, sweeping, cooking, calling to each other, when you walked by.

The overshadowing trees were enormously tall – much taller than trees I was used to. Some were all a-bloom in purple or red.

So much happened. There was nothing slow about India, about Bhagwan, about our ashram. Everything happened so fast, so richly, so densely. There was no down-time, no time off, time out. No lazing, no musing, no lollygagging. This was full-on, hands-on, full-bore, no-holds-barred, get off your ass and bring it all to the table, lay it all on the line. Our days were completely scheduled. I didn't mind. I was saving my life here. I did not want to waste a moment. (My teen years of hippie drifting had often been for me consumed with restless ambition that had no place to go. I'd missed University when we'd had to leave it. The structure now was a godsend. I was in the best university on the planet – the one that brought a person to her full, streaming, rollicking aliveness.)

From my diary:

Everybody is saying that He says my name in the Hindi lectures continually just since I came

The top of his head fascinates me   it is domed and smooth   his strange ineffable presence

A week later. In Silence,   In disgust at the babbling that has been.

It has been so easy not to talk.

Last night the twirling   oh   1½ hours   then on the stomach for one half hour smooth ecstasy of rain and ant-bites

He's given Herb a name – just like that – outta the blue –

Swami Anand Madhur

Sweet Bliss.

I want to go backwards into the flower

(Note: Meditators could "go into silence" whenever they liked – the practice was called *maun,* and could be very helpful for deepening meditation. One wore a button, like a political button, which said on it *In Silence*. People knew then not to try to converse with you. Very restful.)

A Letter to Devadasi:

July 1974

I saw Bhagwan this morning. It was good there weren't too many people and I got to sit by his toe. I told him I wanted to stay and he smiled "I know" and he asked if Anand Madhur was coming, had I written him and I said yes and B. nodded with his archy eyes. He told me to eat no meat-fish-eggs-chilis-cheese. There was some discussion with Chinmaya also and I think no cheese because of the rennet, so rennetless cheese would be okay since curd is okay. B. said the above foods were "very destructive…" He said eat more fruits and vegetables. So please look in my big cookbooks under Cheese and write me a list of rennetless cheeses. Food is such a hassle here! I'm gonna try to see if I can pay for one meal a day at Prem and Pratibha's. Any soya protein you can send would be appreciated but not something disgusting.

Bhagwan told me – make no effort for catharsis, that it was coming along very naturally – the only effort I am to make is to meditate every day, which I am doing.

Bhagwan made love to me in my dream the other night. Oh wow – after August camp for twenty days there will be lectures in English about Jesus Christ. I am ecstatic. I love the lectures.

Twirling is incredible. After it all cares have simply gone and I could sit forever just sitting. I can even ride around in rickshaws in the pitchblack – Poona has no streetlights except in the rich section – and at night the rickshaw drivers drive like drunken fourteen-year-olds – yet I'm not worried.

*Shobha and I were at the Lalvani's and were persuaded to do Nickelettes songs and then she did a strip from Prem's ENORMOUS clothes and there was live music and everybody in stitches.**

Please send wheat germ, my sheets, some miso…

Bliss to Be Here

I was in love with the ashram and all we did there.

– I loved the monsoon rain plopping onto the huge leaves of the Elephant Ear plant. I loved the smells of rain and earth and even traffic, all combining. I loved the luminous, breath-caught waiting as we all lined up for Discourse each morning outside Lao Tzu Gate. I never wanted to be anywhere else any more – there *was* nothing anywhere else.

I cleaved unto my precise circumstance with an astonished wonder that I could have been so lucky. I often thought of a childhood vow I'd made, looking around at the worried, miserable grown-ups: "When I grow up I'm going to be *happy*."

Here was both Romance and Bliss, all showered upon she who did not avoid her pain, but faced it. And here was Beauty, all for free – everyone became lovely here, with secret graces and elegances falling over their moving forms or their still, meditating ones. We had not earned the radiance falling from the sky into our hearts, issuing up from under our feet and buoying us. We did not even know, really, what was happening – only that it was the most wonderful, astonishing thing in the world.

* Another time, in my compulsive show-offiness, I did a can-can on a table-top in the canteen during a spontaneous Kirtan where people played spoons and drummed on the metal tabletops. Forty-four years later, someone on Facebook still remembered this!

I was in love with the robes we wore, soft and easy on our bodies. I was in love with the feeling of a shawl wrapped gently round me while I waited for him to appear before us. I was in love with chai and brown bread with butter for breakfast after discourse; I was in love with slipping around within the walls of the ashram, step by step in the light.

Shobha – she who had delivered me here – had meanwhile begun finding her own peculiar way; I didn't see her much. She tended to wander out of meditations in the middle, a huge no-no as it is very disruptive to one's whole system. Soon she slipped off to Goa, there to stay for quite a while.

Baby Food

Sarita now had short hair, for, as she had previously written to us, she had shaved her head. I was attracted to the idea, and so I went to Darshan – where Bhagwan sat with a small group. We could request to go; and, when we were called, we could scoot up right in front and ask him a question.

"Bhagwan, should I shave my head?" I asked.

"That will be good. Save it in the morning," he said. ('Save' was his pronunciation of 'shave.')

So after Dynamic next day I sat in the flat while Sarita cut off the frizzing growing-out curls, then shaved the rest with a safety razor. I then took the razor to my eyebrows, armpits, pubic area, and legs.

Now I was a very skinny bald thing, smooth and whitey-beige all over.

I was a baby. I did not want to be a woman, of any age. I wanted to regress in every way I could.

Sarita arranged a Mother Meditation: a sannyasin woman to come to the flat and be my mother for fifteen minutes every afternoon. I lay in her lap, being a baby, while she nursed me and cooed over me. As it happened, I did not feel this woman was quite sincere enough, quite effusive enough. I hungered for a more complete welcome. But she would have to do.

I dreamt of baby food – the pureed apricots my mother had fed me with a teaspoon from a little jar... their apricotty taste. I wanted candy and alphabet soup and toasted cheese sandwiches and roasted marshmallows, swollen and black outside, sticky and hot within.

During cathartic meditations, at the ashram or at home, I screamed and railed and was so enthusiastic that I began to be famous for it.

I was eating one meal a day, at Pratibha Lal's house. I ate this lunch alone at a big table; the servants brought more chapattis, or whatever else I wanted. I was so hungry I sometimes ate a whole package of butter on my chapattis – so many chapattis. I would have been anticipating the meal all morning, but when it was over I would go into a slump. My belly swelled up hugely, and I became sleepy and sad, reeling almost as if drugged. The world seemed then a dreadful, sorrowing place. I felt *ashamed.* (It would be another thirty years before I found out that I was allergic to wheat. Every chapatti was a bloatacious sleeping-pill!)

But I loved my new naked babyhood. I went to see Bhagwan and explained to him that I was afraid of being fat, and that I had sworn off sugar, and that I knew I was neurotic. (The word 'anorexia' had never yet met my ears.) I explained that I wanted to eat sweets, but I didn't eat them.

"You will never be fat," he said. And, (as I'd recounted in my letter to Devadasi): "Eat more fruits and wegetables." But he also said that some ice cream was okay, and barfi. And he cautioned me, "No casual sex." That admonition was unnecessary – I was a baby! I had no curiosity towards men at all. I was busy screaming out my guts, screaming out the porno movies, the stupid sexual encounters, the yuck and disappointments. It was all coming out – and my iron will in the matter of food was breaking too.

This was the permission I had been waiting for. I threw my diet to the winds. Next day I went, quite ceremoniously, to the Blue Diamond Hotel – where Sarita had taken me once before for a toasted vegetable sandwich, which was made, she explained, in a special metal holder held over a fire. (Hers, quite scarily, had contained a piece of broken glass.)

The Blue Diamond was located one big block away from the ashram, on a busy road at the edge of Koregaon Park. It was a tall blue plain-looking building set in gardens, with a pool at the back, and a pavilion. It was a favorite venue for weddings, the merry noises of which could be heard in all directions – monsoon was wedding season. When I went in through the glass doors I savored the air conditioning. A liveried doorman greeted me with the usual chilly assessment. Off the lobby were two restaurants – coffee shop on the left, main formal restaurant on the right. A Chinese place (always a dodgy proposition, Chinese food in India) was upstairs. I went into the coffee shop and ordered, momentously, a banana split. It might well have been the first sugar to pass my lips since the tainted custard tart at the Taj, and the shrikhand at the feast – for many months I had been very, very controlled about food.

I ate the sundae slowly. It was not very good – not the orgasmic catharsis I'd planned. When it was over, the last melted soup scooped up with the cold metal spoon, I sat there, feeling strange. In my history with sugar – my chequered history – I would normally then look around for more. A packet of cookies? Something from the pastry-shop, that I knew already would be disappointing too? But now I let the sundae be enough.

I cycled back to the flat. Soon I felt even more strange – then very ill. I threw up, again and again. (Not that I wanted to – bulimia was never my thing – but it just happened.) I felt feverish. I lay down on my pallet and closed my eyes. I floated, glided, rose and fell into a peaceful monsoon slumber.

Sarita went off to Darshan. Sometime in the evening I was woken by the sound of laughter – Bhagwan's and Sarita's. I heard them as if they were in the room.

Later Sarita came home.

All over this end of Poona, after Darshan each night, groups of people were gathering, wide-awake, to hear the news. What did he say? What did he tell you to do, or stop doing? This was gossip of the best caliber, gossip from the Buddha's table – sparkly, fresh, very personal, and entirely unpredictable. We were all, always, entirely agog.

Sarita reported that Bhagwan had asked her, "And how is Madhuri doing with her barfi?"

And they had laughed…

Sarita later remarked to me sagely, regarding barfi: "Mother's milk!"

Victorian California

The town where my sister and I grew up, Riverside, was, perhaps, to many of its denizens, a paradise: always sunny, lots of flowers, orange groves, the white snows of the many mountains visible right around the town. If you'd come from the East Coast, and could buy yourself a nice house, and hire a Mexican gardener, it must have seemed heavenly.

But that was not how it was for two small girls stuck on the wrong side of the tracks, in a little flat-roofed stucco house set in a dry, if fruiting, yard. We felt oppressed by the relentless sun, by the mess and squalor of our house, by the way the sidewalk burned our feet if we walked on it barefoot. By the irritable desperation of poverty all about us in the house; and then, by the time I was five, by the grey, lung-hurting smog that came oozing over the Cajon Pass from Los Angeles and made it impossible to see to the end of the block. Mountains vanished, orange groves fell, tract houses rose; dry winds blew, and our feet were pierced by puncture vine thorns on our hikes with our patient father.

And there was another layer to the oppression. As the English often remark, Americans are *prudish*. Chilly Victorian moralities were grafted onto the desert heat.

I remember having a very strong perception as a child that there were two of me: a good, public one, and a private, bad one. The bad part was inevitable, because there were so many things you were not supposed to do: light little fires behind the house, put the boy rabbit in with the girl rabbit, wave the snake at the cat, look at or, worse, touch, other kids' privates (this was never said because even to say it would have been unimaginably shocking – but we just understood that this was really really bad). So there was no choice but to cut oneself in two – the waist was a logical dividing line. (When I began meditating, I was very conscious of this: that now the challenge was to let energy flow, in my loose robe, between these two parts. This did begin to happen.)

I was sent home from school once when I was fourteen for *wearing boots* – "too sexy," was the verdict. Our butch phys-ed teacher, Mrs. Tillery, was forced by law to show us sex-education films full of cautionary images of syphilitic chancres. She told us she hated the duty; she thought that if someone got a venereal disease they should not be given treatment, because it was their own badness that had made them get the disease in the first place, and the sickness was fit punishment.

In my family sex did not exist, and if you thought it did, you were a really really congenitally bad *thing*. *Shame* on you!

Our father's parenting style was to teach us geology, astronomy, and entomology, and to be a very jolly Santa at Christmas, handing out the presents with a childlike joy. All the rest of the parenting he left to our mother, who enforced a strict moral code, handed down from her own mother, who had at one time been a nurse in a syphilis ward, and had never recovered from the experience. Our mother was joyous and laughing when she was 'up,' and very fond – she loved our quirks and eccentricities – but any hint of a child thinking about excreta or sex and the daggers came out in her brown eyes. This was a double standard – she was by all accounts a passionate woman, who experienced lovemaking as deeply spiritual – and in fact she herself was allowed to swear a blue streak, and did so regularly; but we were not. (The strongest thing our father ever said was, "Gosh darn the luck!" when he hit his thumb with a hammer.)

The raunchiest thing I ever saw as a child was a small magazine that Jimmy Haffter, a chortling family friend, brought over, and left behind. My mother found it and burned it, but not before I'd looked into it. I was uneasily struck by a black-and-white photo of a woman stepping out of a shower cubicle, her mouth a big O of surprise and shock. She was clutching a bath-towel around her from armpit to mid-thigh; nothing was on display but arms and legs and face. The caption said, "*'Don't take my picture now!' – But we did!*" (This was a really risqué photo!)

I read a book not long ago called *Full Service* by a gas station attendant who had pimped for the stars, just over the hills in Hollywood during the 40's-50's-60's. The high-jinks those Silver Screen heroes and heroines got up to were of astonishing breadth, if not depth – and I had to almost pinch myself to imagine that the set of realities I was reading about existed such a short distance from the set of realities I grew up with... worlds apart!

When I was thirteen someone told my mother that I had been *looking men in the eyes.*

I had recently discovered that I had a power to get attention – energy – by engaging men in this *looking* thing. This was a heady intoxicant for me; my brothers had mostly tormented and derided me, as brothers can; and my father had much more important things to do than paying attention to a little girl. And now suddenly, I could get attention! I cinched in my belt to make my hand-me-down dresses look small-waisted, and I gazed into eyes in passing...

Mama gave me a very serious talking-to: Men, she said, could not control themselves after a certain point of arousal, so it was up to the girl to remain cool. If you looked at men, it might provoke their lusts past enduring. This idea I found rather thrilling. I felt annoyed at my mother, but I obediently then did the opposite: I kept my eyes cast down, and looked at nobody for a year.

I got the biggest brunt of my mother's fear about the troubles girls could get themselves into. My four older siblings were boys and thus exempt; sexuality was still not allowed them until they were grown, but there seemed less stigma on their behavior. My mother proceeded to wear her disapprovals out on me, so that by the time my sister was coming into puberty the steam had entirely gone out of them.

And then the 60's arrived. This earth-shaking decade really only began, in Riverside, in 1966 (it had taken a while for the news to trickle down from San Francisco).

I was fourteen when I met Jared at a meeting of the Students for a Democratic Society at the University – I'd gone there with my older brother Jack. Jarrie became my first boyfriend. He was a cherubic little eighteen-year-old college kid with brown curls and a bee-stung mouth. Mama, I think, took one look at him and decided that he was harmless. So she let me go on dates with him as long as my brother Jack was with us; but Jack would obligingly slope away as soon as we were all around the corner.

Jarrie and I spent six months making out, which was mostly very pleasant and exciting, if you didn't count the part he called "dry-humping," which made him climax but just abraded me with jeans-toughness. We would often smoke joints (my friends and I had discovered pot that year too) in his dorm-room, and I remember sensuous explorations; mostly just lovely, endless kissing. In all our petting, though, I had very little idea of where things were or what was going on – I'd never seen a vulva or a photo of one, nor my own in a mirror; just the innocent v-shaped view from above. I did not know how to ask Jarrie to do things for me; nor what those things might be. And he assumed that what we did was as conclusive for me as it was for him.

We planned carefully and lost our virginities together, when I was making a weekend visit to his liberal Jewish Unitarian family in Los Angeles. In our paranoia about pregnancy, we employed the Pill, contraceptive foam, and condoms – all at once.

And it was *awful* for me. The strong new miracle drug, the Pill, had bloated and nauseated me. The deflowering proved to be bloody, painful, difficult –

my frightened, cautious hymen did not give in without a fight. And in any case my shy though eager libido had been firmly quashed by the Pill – a common side-effect the press didn't let on about, as that news would not have sold newspapers (I'm not sure the libido ever really recovered). And poor Jared promptly became a slave to his penis, in that suddenly no other aspect of lovemaking seemed to hold the same appeal as just putting it in there. So petting and slow explorations vanished *just like that.*

I felt so sad... but we could not actually *discuss* the issue. Soon after this I gave him back his enameled Peace pendant – the 60's version of a going-steady pin – and struck out on my own.

When I was fifteen, my mother discovered that she herself had really been a nature-child all along, and she gave up her own mother's puritanical teachings, and embraced the 60's with serious joy.

Only when I was eighteen, roaming through an outdoor market in Amsterdam, did I finally see a photo of female genitalia, in a magazine opened out on display. I was profoundly shocked; it looked to me like some sort of *wild animal.* (Women still wore plenty of hair in those days.) So this is what men like? I thought to myself in wonder. It seemed so strange, like something in a butcher's shop window. (I later heard Bhagwan say that pornography is ugly because the female first chakra, like the roots of trees, is supposed to remain hidden. It is just a hidey sort of place, apparently. So vulnerable, deep, endlessly deep energetically... *private.* {Like the second, emotional chakra of the male – but I am getting ahead of myself here.})

Letter to Bodhi

Meanwhile, Robert from the pizza parlor had taken Sannyas (I don't remember if he sent in by post, or received initiation via Sushila in San Francisco). He had been given the name Swami Anand Bodhisattva.

So... I now had occasion to write:

August 6, 1974

Dear Swami Anand Bodhisattva,

Hear ye, hear ye. I am not writing this letter; Bhagwan is. And I am very pleased to be in between.

I saw him this morning. I did not bring you up; he did.

"And what of this... actor? Swami Bodhisattva?"

I was spaced out into his eyes. I could say nothing; what happened was that you were right between us, suspended in our gaze for a moment.

"He is – " said Bhagwan... "He will go very deep. He is coming?"

"He says he does not feel the need to come," I said.

"He does not feel need there – he is very deep in with me – he feels me deeply," said Bhagwan. "But to come here – everything changes. Tell him to come. He can?"

"He has no money, and he has two children," I said by way of non-explanation.

"No matter. He will not have to worry about the money. It will be okay. Write to him and tell him to come as soon as possible. He is good."

So. you have your orders.

And them's orders.

I won't speak of the me this time. Yecchhh.

*Love, Honey**

(ps tell me when you're gonna come so I can give you a list of junk to bring to India's greedy fingers – chocolates etc. impossible to get here and much craved by we in orange.)

Morning Discourse

Bhagwan's body, as Sarita had advised us, was very sensitive. He couldn't stand strong smells; even a little perfume made him ill. So, for Discourse or Darshan, we got a sniff test as we passed by the two sniffers at the gate to Lao Tzu. If our hair had a smell we had to wear a scarf tied firmly over it. A very strong smell meant banishment from Discourse that day. I have seen many a person turned away, indignant and bitterly disappointed. (A result is that in every photograph you see from that era, everyone had acres of hair – of course, it was the 70's – but it was also always very, very shiny and clean-looking!)

There was a table set up before the gate where someone sat, selling tickets for five rupees each. I quickly realized that it was very easy to use the same ticket again and again. I did this for a few days – sitting, then, in front of this

* 'Madhu' means honey.

Being who peeled you open, took your heart out whole, and turned it in his hands with his words, as if describing the loveliest thing in the universe. This did not add up. I sent him a letter telling him that I was cheating with the passes.

Next day someone gently apprehended me as I was about to pass and asked me to buy a ticket. Relieved, I did so. (Still when I look back I am amazed at my behavior. Larceny has never been my poison. Many another fault I might have; but not that.) The matter was never mentioned again.

Discourses happened upstairs on a deep, covered veranda – almost like a room, with two walls open, which had ornate iron railings a few feet high, climbing with vines. Vines crawled up the pillars that supported the roof, echoing the rich and verdant greens of the skyscraping trees. It was a lovely place – the floor was marble, like those in all Indian houses where prosperous people live. Now, in monsoon, there was a wonderful gloom, a jungly atmosphere. Big potted plants sat at the periphery.

We were packed in for discourse – the place wasn't big enough. We scooted up to let more people in. We sat on *assans*, a sort of thick soft little cotton rug with fringes. These were available in many colors and several sizes. I had a small green one, which I treasured. Some people also brought a cushion to sit on – it's helpful for meditation to keep the spine straight, and a cushion props up your tailbone and keeps your thighs from overbalancing you.

Bhagwan was speaking about Jesus, in a series called *The Mustard Seed.* I will swear now (and he has said it himself) that he was giving Jesus more than Jesus really had… making him make sense; to many of us for the first time.

Bhagwan spoke with love and exquisite understanding. He illuminated Jesus's sayings in the context of meditation and consciousness – in the light, therefore, of the East – where, he said, Jesus spent his 'lost years' from age eighteen to thirty. This was not a light the normal Christian had any notion of. Taking Jesus' sayings literally gives rise to absurd tragedies; Bhagwan was showing the parables, allegories, metaphors, for what they are: *sutras*, a Sanskrit word meaning 'thread.' A sutra is a very condensed way of saying a very large and spread-out truth. A sutra can be handed down through generations when people cannot write, but can remember a sentence of poetic words. The sutra is like a paper flower that, placed in a glass of water, swells and blooms. You have to pay attention to it, look at it in your own life, over time; decode the imagery through your own experience.

As Bhagwan spoke, to my amazement I was crying and crying. Nobody prevented me. I whuffled into my perm (this was just before I shaved my head), then opened up my mouth and wailed aloud. Something was broken open in me – my skinny body rocked itself and keened. Old griefs came piling out, blinking in the grey daylight. They belonged to my parents, and their parents – but I had to cry for them, that was my job, one of my jobs. That is the way it works.

Mommy and Glen

Much time and many tears were spent over my parents' lives. It seemed that I was absolutely obliged to feel for them whatever they were suppressing or had ever suppressed. Their lives seemed to me horribly tragic. During meditations I was torn open again and again by gouts of weeping.

They had married when my mother was twenty and pregnant, and my father twenty-four. His name was Glen, and he never wanted to be called Daddy, so Glen was how we knew him. (When I was very small I couldn't say the name rightly, and, because he was always leaving to go off to work, I called him Genny Bye-bye.) I adored my father, with his kindly remoteness, his brittle attentiveness if I courted his brief focus. He had black hair, blue eyes, and white skin. In a photo taken around the time of his marriage, he looked like a matinee idol.

Mommy – named Virginia (which she hated) and called, by my father, once in a long, long while, Ginny – had auburn hair tending towards the red, full lips, and short-lashed unassuming brown eyes. She had a lovely round behind and a very small bosom, and her nose was Roman in its proud, bumpy length. She thought that she was very plain.

They'd met at a party in Berkeley, where they both attended the University. Glen never talked about the past to us – except for nostalgic reminiscences about the natural wonders of the New Mexico of his boyhood, if we demanded them – so that left us at the mercy of Mommy's version. She loved telling stories, and so we heard a very great deal about all that had happened; colored with her romance, her rage, her interpreting, her editing and fantasizing (I have to use that word). And, of course she had a right to her indignations and even her viciousnesses – it would have been better, though, if she'd had a girlfriend to tell, instead of us kids! We did love, though, to hear the romantic tales of the beautiful Northern California of her childhood, about her beloved doctor father and his funny patients, and the camping trips the family took into the wilderness. It just wasn't nice to hear how dreadful had been her marriage, and her mother-in-law.

Mama's upbringing had been Victorian in the extreme, and Glen would have had to be forgiven not to realize that the naive and innocent nymph he thought he was courting (with hopes to turn into a help-meet in his hoped-for career) was a red-headed firebrand, with her own poetic passions and intense strength and power – for he was color-blind, and her red locks looked pacifically green to him! (I recently read that people with red hair actually have lower pain thresholds than other people. They feel discomforts more acutely, which is perhaps why they are famous for flying off the handle.)

The pair dated for some time, and then Virginia decided that they were not suited. She told Glen she wanted to break off the relationship. But then, as she put it angrily (and we heard this story again and again): "He got me pregnant!" (All requests for details, and what might have been her part in it, were met by a grim thinning of the lips and a shake of the head.) He was a chemistry major, hers was English, with a minor in Spanish. She graduated; he did not. He went stoically to work to support wife and baby instead.

But he lived for Science. That was it for him; that and nothing else. There was no God but Science. So that, knowing his young wife loved flowers, he bought her a botany book for Christmas. She recounted this perfidy to me with rage and heartbreak, all those many years after… She was Romantic, he Logical. That was the division in our family ever after.

Seven babies came along, spread out over twenty-two years. Glen worked for the U.S. Dept. of Agriculture in a job far below his capacity – for all were agreed he was a genius. He was the go-to guy for any insoluble problem at his job. His salary, commensurate with his education, was wildly insufficient for a large family. Our mother was exhausted, downtrodden, bitter. Never was there any money for clothes, shoes, housewares. The kids destroyed the house, which had been bought cheap because it was unfinished (and so it stayed). It took Glen thirty years to pay off the $7,000 it cost.

Our mother, when she wasn't angry, was poetic, sometimes rhapsodic. She adored us kids and praised us often. She wrote short stories, and, through an agent, sold them to women's magazines. The money went for taxes, the birth of children, or for one or another child to have a new garment – she never once in all the marriage, bought any new clothes for herself, not once. She had the same tube of red lipstick she'd had in college, and the same pair of black pumps. Mostly she went barefoot, and her heels were always cracked and often bled. I only knew her to acquire one pair of shoes, in all my childhood – hiking boots, $1 at the Goodwill. She was perfectly delighted with them.

Our father (according to our mother), thought romance was sex and that fiction was just worthless imagination… okay for entertainment, but not valuable. (He did occasionally read Perry Mason novels though.) Most of Mama's complaints were about the chronic, and truly dire, lack of money for necessities; but she didn't hold back on expressing her irritation with other things about him. She used to say (in his hearing), "Never marry a man if you don't like his mother, the way he walks, the back of his neck, or his accent!" And then she'd always add, "And I don't like any of those things about your father!" I remember one guileless event that turned her sneering and smoking with contempt: we were on one of our camping trips out to the Mojave desert. It was winter, and the morning was cold. Glen was full of joyful excitement because he was going to be looking for 'specimens,' as he called them: spiders, insects. (We kids loved lifting rocks and seeing what darted away underneath, and our dad would educate us about the creatures we saw.) Glen carried a ladies' square-built handbag he'd acquired at the Goodwill, and had filled it with carefully-folded vials he'd made out of paper, since he couldn't afford to buy glass ones. This was his specimen case. Then, because his ears were cold, he'd found in the VW van a pink baby blanket, placed it, folded, over his head, and tied it under his chin. And that's the way he sallied forth to do his beloved science.* Mama could not forgive his utter lack of worldly acumen.

At home, each night our mild father sat wreathed in smoke, doing equations with a very sharp pencil, on a piece of paper on a clipboard on his knee. (The pencil sharpener was the only machine in the house not broken.) Child wars and creativities raged around him, but he was neatly oblivious. Our mother labored to produce a meal, usually with very little, in the filthy kitchen. As we all sat around the newspaper-spread table and ate, she mocked him viciously, railed and bitched. He never, even once, answered back… except to say, "Now, now, Virginia." It was horrible for us kids – just horrible. Our stomachs would sink, we'd go stoical – trying to eat, with poison being slung at our Dad.

* And he did discover a spider nobody had identified before; and it ended up in the Smithsonian.

There were many very good things about my childhood. A vegetable garden, grown by an older brother, Robbie (who was a talented cook, but angry, pervy, and dreadfully shy); the smell of cucumber vines, tomato vines. Watching beans sprout and grow. Our mother's fond hilarity at things the children said, things the cats did, the geese. Being read aloud to in the living room each night by Mama, kids' books, grown-up books, poetry – she was a genius reader, taking on the different voices with full, rich drama. It was good hearing our praises sung: "Every mother crow thinks her little crows are the blackest!" she used to say. And then she'd laugh... Hearing her laugh when we were in the back bedroom and she was in the living room with company at night. We had a lot of visitors – people with conventional upbringings found our family refreshing, liberating.

And there was one more wonderful thing: our father taking us for hikes and teaching us about the natural world. His tenderness and love for that world. Camping trips to the desert, to the mountains. The cats. Our father's gentleness. Mama's joy on the very rare days when it rained. Being taken care of by her when we were ill – coming from a medical family, she had a gift for healing; she knew just what to do, and was alert and applied and caring.

For many years, Glen was working on an invention. He had wrapped all his hopes up in it. At first he was doing the equations; then he bought an old washing machine from an auction and took the motor out to power the device. The body was made with plywood. Perhaps the rest of the interior was waiting for funds. The papers were ready for the patent office; the fee – $2,000, a fortune – put up by scientist family friends as an investment. It was a Continuous Chromatography Device, and apparently the world needed it and people had been trying to invent it for some time.

Glen was dutiful, punctual, punctilious. He had not taken time off work to be with my mother during any of her childbirths – though he did take off a few days afterwards while she was still in the hospital. (Being cared for by him was funny. We loved it... he let us do anything we liked. He feared nakedness so he bathed us fully clothed, using the hose in the back yard. He fed us cornflakes out of paper bowls. He washed all the trodden-in layers of dirty clothes in the half-finished laundry porch, all the colors together, and the dyes ran, so that we had a cheerful pile of interesting new garments to claim – most of them pink. He sent me to school in denim overalls, so that I was sent home again, since girls had to wear dresses.)

He didn't want to take a day off to take the application to Los Angeles to the patent office. Instead, he trusted the job to a weird young hanger-on named Jim Petty who looked like Alley Oop the cartoon cave-man, and spoke in hare-lip grunts. (I found out later the young man's parents had asked Glen to find something useful for Jim to do, since he was feckless and all-at-sea.)

I am sure Glen had intuition, and deep feelings, but he tried to avoid them in favor of Reason. Certainly, in the worlds of Glen and his sons, Mama's intuition was to be ignored. So when Jim Petty had gone home that night, and Mama started yelling that he was not to be trusted (she wouldn't have said it while the young man was still there – she was terribly polite in person) neither Glen nor the older brothers paid her the attention you'd give a flea.

A week later the boys, grim-faced, got in the VW combi and drove to Laguna Beach, about seventy miles away. I was eleven at the time, and I was brought along – though I had no idea what was going on. We stopped outside a small cottage and the brothers went up the walk and knocked on the door.

Jim Petty answered. I was still in the car, and through the window I saw this scene: the tall, bronzed fellow, all a-muscle, wearing only swimming trunks; standing in the open doorway; leaning casually against the jamb. His bearded chin was lifted and he was saying something, and then shaking his head. I could not hear what he said, but it was easy to see that he was lying. He was casually defensive, swelled-up, chin-jut. I could see.

Behind him a bikini-clad young woman moved about in the room, and at his side could be seen stacks and stacks of crates of beer…

This all was his celebration of his windfall.

The brothers came back to the car and we drove home. The atmosphere around this whole business was so heavy – so very very grim – that to this day the boys cannot speak about it. My oldest brother Garth (later Rudra), who felt responsible for the young man's appearance in the family circle, stayed particularly mute. I can only imagine what must be taking place in the masculine stews of their inner worlds about it all.

Mama went to Jim's parents. They said that there was nothing they could do.

Nothing further was ever done. Glen folded within himself in the weight of his loss. He refused an offer of more money to complete the patent filing.

Perhaps he felt too ashamed. He was crushed… an innocent man, with eyes of something more than a child; for a child can be canny, clever. He just folded, and something in him fell down and away forever. My father. This is still the saddest tale I know.

The next year, Mama found a lump in her breast. Diagnosis, mis-diagnosis, confusion. Radical mastectomy. They said it was cancer, then that it wasn't, then that there was just one bad cell. Mama lay in bed with her arm elevated above her head, tied to the bedstead with an old scarf. Lymph nodes gone, arm swollen forever, infection never far away. We kids stood around her bed, in shock. Right then, Mama took physically against our father. She could not stand for him to touch her. Her health recovered, slowly.

She waited till the youngest, Andy, was seven, and then she left. I was fifteen. Glen was completely devastated. He just fell apart. He stopped smoking overnight (he'd always chain-smoked) and became very nervous, rattling the change in his pockets. He kept hoping she'd come back.

She tried several times to go back to him, over the next few years… but she would get so depressed she knew she'd die if she stayed. Glen kept hoping.

Together with my brother Rory and some friends, that year, 1967, my mother started an alternative school called the Free School. We were all flush with 60's idealism then – University professors donated their time. A large rambling Victorian was rented for $165 a month, a last holdout in a factory district. It was a wonderful house, with a backyard all gone to creeping vines. Mama slept in a sort of private attic-space under the eaves. I shared a room with my curly-headed artist boyfriend J.C., who hung the walls with fishnets and the ceilings with silk scarves tacked at the corners to create a billowing Aladdin feeling. J.C. turned out to be determinedly unfaithful, and I did a good bit of wailing and shrieking. But someone gave me a blank book for Christmas that year, and I began to keep a diary. This habit, a more and more passionate one as time went on, saved my life through all the rigors that were to come.

My sister and I began studying ballet at the Free School with a wonderfully dedicated teacher named Shirley Stirling. We had Encounter groups there too, led by the charismatic Unitarian minister, Phil Smith; we were supposed to "give each other the gift of our anger." I found, embarrassed, that I had no gift for screaming at others – but boy, I was good at screaming all on my own!

'The gift of people's anger' caused the school to dissolve after just one year – one of the founders absconded with another one's fiancee and there was much planting of black widow spiders in beds, and axes taken to bedroom doors, and the like – but it was a good year, and I am grateful for it. Ballet got me into my body, a place it is good to know how to be.

So J.C. and I and Mama loaded up J.C.'s VW bus with all our worldly goods (very little really), loaded in my sister and Andy, and took off for the North. We rented a colorful apartment on the restored Victorian main street of Ferndale, California, and proceeded to have Northern adventures; tulgy woods, banana slugs, foggy days, Morris Graves the artist and his outsized Zen aerie... and for me, much cooking over a wood stove, and much poetry.

And my little sister was bullied at school for being weird and so very much too smart; and her lovely little kitten Shaisohnnie, a bundle of fluff and purrs and action, was killed by a car in the road outside the cabin we lived in next. My sister's grief was terrible.

Mama again tried going back to Glen, who'd come up north to fetch her. It didn't last (the poor man had a satori, a fugue state, when she told him it was really over and she was going for good: for half an hour he was in bliss, on a mysterious island of light, until he came back to earth and had to face his loss all over again... Apparently this sometimes happens. Mama was fascinated – she loved mystical pop-psych.) She felt for him though, tenderly, painfully. Eventually Glen gave up and turned away from her. By then she had remarried.

He retired from his decades of government service and went to live in a trailer in the desert he loved, near Keeler, in the lee of the Sierras, where he did experiments and equations and continued to buy obscure machinery cheap from government auctions for some unspecified future use. His son Robbie lived in his own trailer nearby.

Much later, a wealthy woman wanted to marry Glen and set him up in a lab of his own (he'd always been trying to create his own lab, without funds or time; now he had time, but not, somehow, the muscle to deal with whatever it would require. He always did have a lab of sorts, but rudimentary, desert-dusty, full of antique bits of equipment more available-at-the-time than strictly useful.) He refused the woman because she was a Christian, and that went against his principles: science did not allow for that kind of myth-based superstitious nonsense. (But that was much later, when Sarita and I were well-ensconced in Bhagwan's universe.)

Glen's and Mama's thirty years together was characterized by a spectacular lack of communication. (A family friend once observed that they were the most gender-polarized couple she had ever seen.)

So much life – so much hope – so much duty – so much dirt and chaos and rotted teeth and shrieking and endurance and nothing to feed the kids. So much blocked drains and ants in the jam and the kitchen on fire and an old stove never cleaned so that it was encrusted with black so thickly the door could not close and you could see the fire down in it. So many golden crusty chewy delicious toasted cheese sandwiches, apricot crumbles with fresh apricots, from that oven. So much rage in that kitchen – our mother standing in the doorway, clutching her forehead: "I'd rather BE SHOT than go in that kitchen and cook supper!" Our mother with no shoes, ragged old dress held together with safety pins. The way my parents tried, sometimes, to love each other – shyly, with just a momentary gesture – and then gave up, defeated. We almost never saw them touch each other.

I cried the tears they must have longed to cry.

Letters to Devadasi

August 1974

Dearest Devadasi,

Rub a dub dub, thanks for the grub!... Oh yummy yummy how we gorged on goodies! I think they all got here... Thank you for my turtleneck and I've got 4 compliments on it in ½ hour. Tonight Sarita is making an intimate (6 people) dinner for me after Twirling... Thanks for vitamins and everything, what treasures! And money! ... Beautiful letter from Herb, who gives no indication of coming.

Just as some people were complaining about the noise from our flat and Devananda assured them that only two quiet sisters lived here, Krishna Das, who was in the shower before his appointment with Bhagwan, sang out in loud German accents – "Rock-a my soul in the bosom of Abraham!" and then let loose with a long scream.*

Love love

us

* Devananda was a jovial, short young red-haired man who lived upstairs from us in Boat Club Road.

My mood flip-flopped between wild enthusiasm and terrible doldrums. Here's one full of optimism – .

maybe August 1974

So much happens that is rich, astounding and amazing that the pen quails at the prospect of trying to write it. You must be here. I feel a sense of urgency, a hopeless loving one, to all loved beings in America – Bhagwan is a supercatalyst to each person's secret self. I want Jacques here, Beverly, Richard, Steve, Jack, Andy – all to bathe in his incredible light. My room is so beautiful now – green bed, palm-tree, a low shelf for clothes, an altar – that's all. Green tile floor. Please share my letters freely – I feel a sense of embracing without closing the arms, a wide embrace to all… We all have no secrets; we seem to share minds and dreams in the night. Since Madness meditation started we are all very hugging and physical together. Bhagwan prescribes Madness constantly now – it is incredible to watch people transformed through it. Every time I see him he reminds me to do it every day. I bought a beautiful hexagonal mirror. Bhagwan told me it is good to pay attention to appearance – "To be ugly is to be aggressive to other people." He refused to let me make a problem out of it. "It is not you – it is the collective unconscious of women. It is the desire to be loved. It is good. Be beautiful," he said. "Accept whatsoever is happening and watch it. Say yes to everything."*

all my love to you and everybody especially Herb.

MUDPIE

(A bit about the above: I now had very short, growing-out hair. I'd gone to Darshan wearing a home-sewn garment I'd brought with me from San Francisco: a stretchy nubbly cotton jumpsuit with a very low back and cross-over sashes that came back around my tiny waist to tie at the front; cap sleeves, and palazzo-pant-legs, loose and long. I had told Bhagwan that I loved clothes, that I wanted to be beautiful, that I loved to dress up. Is this unspiritual? I'd asked him. And the above wise carte-blanche he gave me in reply, I took to heart always. Some people are just born to decorate. Thank you, Bhagwan.)

And then down again….

I'm lying in bed sick
I tried to kill myself meditating

* More on this later.

now i'm just hopeless

I will never get through the garbage (crossed out garbage, added shit instead)

I have to keep stopping to cry

I just want some real food like you used to give – only hershey bars and crackers and cheese and some baby food and meatloaf and salad. I hate Indian stuff. No… India.

I'm home sick

You are all around

and I'm all alone too

did I sin so much, that I have this much to suffer

the fanatic voice has ruined my lives

if there were some way I could simply step off the wheel I would

the food trip is no more except for sharp spines of fear

dear mama

love

Katy (crossed out)

me (crossed out)

A Letter to My Father

My father enclosed pencil-scribbled little notes – often on bits of torn envelope – in the international money orders he sent each month – the $60 I lived on. He addressed me as Baby-Doll, or Katy Zelle (my middle name). He wrote bits of news I could hardly decipher, regarding goings-on in Keeler, which sat baking beside its dry lake (Los Angeles had long ago stolen the water). He was always an ache in my heart.

August 5, 1974

Dear Papa, I feel so close to you these days! Childhood rising like a mesa of brilliant-flowering cactuses out of desert where rain drowns the mirages – new beetles bursting with color like traveling garnets. My birthday was on the twelfth, and I felt myself six years old.

I dreamed you were feeding me chocolate-covered jelly rings under a piñon tree on top of a desert-mountain hill.

August 20

Dearest Desert-Papa. I feel that my letters to you can only be poems. The last few days I have been dwelling in childhood. So many easy memories coming and going. I was very sick for two days – stomachache and all that awful stuff.

When I write to you I have the same feeling as when I write to Bhagwan – that the letter is being dropped into a bottomless lake, like the marvelous ones in New Mexico you used to tell us about. You see, my Papa, when we were little you used to tell us that God was everywhere. In the leaves and the grass. I loved that, but I always felt a helplessness, an envy about it, as though I would never know it. And that meanwhile, you were certainly God. And when, later, as part of maturing, I came to let you be very human also, I knew that it was truly just a case of mistaken identity – that you really were God, but that my vision was what needed expanding, so I could let God be all of human-ness. I simply do not know how much of any of this you relate to. Like Bhagwan, you answer in riddles. I suspect that you are like a tree or grass – that your riddle will be unlocked for me only when I am totally open and at one with the riddle and not before. You have been with me as a constant shadow, like death over the desert mountains, a very beautiful thing. You are like a bird who has flown from my mouth but who still forms my vision with the invisible brush of its wings. I love you as wildly as the wind loves the tumbleweed, as the tumbleweed loves the wind. There is no hope for this love – it is its own answer, or this is what I have heard. – Does the wind hope in its wildness? But I still hope – and thus I have walked clumsily through the world, too much of the world, my Papa – my younger sister came to rest earlier and so well. I have been so restless and so blind.

Do you remember, my Sugar Papa, you and I shared such a sweet tooth? For twenty-six months I ate no sugar, no honey, no sweets. It was in that time that Bhagwan named me Madhuri, which means "sweet" – literally, "honey." Somehow the abstention has passed, and the other day I ate a triple sundae – the first sugar of over two years – and got violently ill – but I think the sundae was only part of it, I also danced, sang, and jumped up and down for three hours and later twirled for an hour, after having not had enough sleep (the seventh ceaseless day of such activity), and I guess my body revolted. Anyway, I don't even know why I told you about it all, except as a ripple in my life. Oh, yes – somehow it connects deeply with childhood – it all comes back so softly and clearly, the innocent love-sharing of hot chocolate on Christmas, marshmallows at weenie-roast, the time you walked with us to the big tree by the railroad tracks and we ate lemon-cake from the Day-Old Bakery and drank*

* I seemed to have forgotten the Gluco biscuits at Tandalja Farm and the custard tart at the Taj!

lemonade. For a long time only the uncomfortable memories were there, but now it is as if a silent dam had burst and I am flooded softly with a beautiful ocean of loving everydaynesses, and the little sweet pleasures of food and cuddlings.

Papa? Your Sarita – she really is the Jewel of the East, as you said in your letter. I won't let her read this, she will laugh and sputter – but she is recognized in her beauty here, her total beauty, and it is very great. She has come very far, Papa, and I will tell you – you have great reason to be proud of her. What she is, is of far more brilliance and depth than any actress or dancer, artist or writer – though she could do any of those things.

Bhagwan has told her that she no longer has to meditate unless the mood takes her. He looked at her and said, "I am completely satisfied with you." The essence of Papa in you rejoices. I feel it.

I wear beads around my neck that are from our desert, and the stars always make me think of you.*

You may have wondered how I managed to get here – a close friend of mine, Shobha, a recent heiress, simply gave me the ticket to come with her. She says one day I can pay back half of it. I am trying to have my car sold to pay our rent here – Sarita and I, by great good fortune, found a flat – and those are my only means and plans. I left all my possessions and my house and job as they were, simply kissed a few people goodbye, and left.

By and by, by and by, I will see you. All my love.

Forever,
Madhuri
Katy
Zelle

Going to Darshan

Darshans were amazing. We tended to go approximately once a month, though it could vary. The whole scene was so clean, so pure – a dozen people sitting in clean robes and clean hair, on clean marble. The elegant decorum of all of us, in the circle of light before him, rapt and inward-looking, excited as heck. Potted plants all leafy and tropical at the edges of the porch. And the Magus sitting before us in his winged chair… Bhagwan, beaming and

* I'd changed my mala beads for smaller, mesquite-seed ones while in San Francisco.

luminous in his white robe, full of mischief and power and compassion and laughter and above all, penetrating Mystery. And then, there was the thrill of suspense, because you just never knew what was going to happen – what questions people might bring; but most of all, what he would answer. He answered the person, not the question; he'd say radically different things on the same issues, depending on who sat before him.

I remember once early in my first year, an Australian woman sat there. He asked what work she did, and she said she ran a brothel. Bhagwan suggested, "If you can find something else to do, it would be better. That is...." and he didn't finish, but the feeling I got was that the woman's job wasn't exactly healthy for her spirit. Since I had done blue movies I pondered this... In the 60's it had suddenly been expected that we should all have as much sexual experience as we could, and that we should drop all inhibitions. (Men, I'd noticed, often traded on this ideology, hectoring girls not to be so uptight.) So I was curious to hear Bhagwan suggesting that a place where lots of free (if paid for) sex was happening was not good.

(Too, a few pretty Western women were known to be making money by sleeping with Arabs – you could sometimes see groups of men at the Blue Diamond, in white djellabas and long white headgear with a braided headband scootched down around the brow. Apparently there were plenty of these guys in Bombay just waiting for loose Western girls. This was generally frowned on in the ashram, because it meant the girls were acting out something that was really false for their spirits – they did not love the men.)

I pondered all of this... and began to sense out something of the sensitivity I'd denied myself; or that life had apparently ignored in me.

In that same darshan a young American woman with curly blonde hair sat before Bhagwan, and they were starting a conversation – "How long you will stay?" "Six weeks." "Very good... " And she had asked a question... when suddenly Bhagwan got a rather ferocious expression on his face and said loudly, "You have been a *thief!* You have been a thief!" The girl shrank back. I never heard what the story was. Nor did I see her around after that.

Another time I heard him remarking that a certain wispy, quiet, bearded young American man was "a hungry ghost." This gave me the shudders – was I a hungry ghost too? And I wondered what it meant. (I still wonder.)

Another time a French girl sat there. This was after therapy groups had begun – Awareness Intensive, Primal, Encounter, and more. Bhagwan looked at her, and said, "Much is not happening! Much is not happening!"

Then he suggested the girl do Awareness Intensive – the Who Am I? koan work – and she replied in a high, accented voice, disconsolately, "I don't want!"

"Then do Dynamic every day!" he counseled.

"I don't want!"

His tone still kindly, he suggested one or two more things.

"I don't want!"

Suddenly his face changed, and I had the feeling I was watching a mask being put into place, but it was all over the front of his body. He was projecting a certain person out in front of him – much the same way I've watched the actress Meryl Streep project a character, create a chimera. He became angry, and told the girl, forcefully, to leave the ashram.

A young Irishwoman, pale and puffy, sat before him, weeping. I had regarded her with a sort of anxious curiosity when I'd seen her about – she didn't seem to do the meditations, or participate much in the doings inside the gates. (To me, this was unthinkable.) She lived near the ashram in an old wooden house, with a young Indian man; she had given birth to a baby with spina bifida, and it had died.

"I tell you not to have children, and you don't listen!" scolded Bhagwan – not just to her, but to all of us. *"You don't know whom you are inviting!"*

Whenever someone asked him if they should have a child, he always said no. (I know of only one exception to this: Wadud and Waduda, an esoteric therapist couple from California. He blessed their conception.) But, if someone came to him already pregnant, he was very loving and supportive towards the new life; in every case cautioning the mother that for the next nine months she *should not get angry.* Be peaceful and quiet and restful, he would say. Enjoy the sunshine and flowers, take it easy.

In Darshan once I told Bhagwan that I was purposely accentuating all my uncomfortable sensations to try to make them total, so that they would be finished faster and go away.

He told me not to do that.

Another time, I told him I was trying to follow each thought back to its origin.

He told me not to do that either. He said it would exhaust me, and there was no need.

Another time I told him that, at least for me, it was intolerable to have any mind at all.

He smiled slightly.

Another time he told me, "Just participate totally – and awareness will come by itself."

I went for many darshans that first year. I was kind of nuts, but very sincere; Bhagwan sat there serenely and took my questions and answered them. And I misunderstood the answers, and went away all wobbly with the significance of it all, until the next time.

Once I sat in front of him, recounting some emotional pain I was immersed in; I began to weep. He let me go on for a bit, and then he said, "Good, Madhuri! Now, *loff!*"

And I did – midstream, the whole thing changed, and I was laughing! Then he told us all how the two are really very close together – laughter and tears..

Another time I remember him saying to me, "There are two things: One is a block about sex. It will go, and when it does, it will go all at once. The second is a deep jealousy of Sarita."

Another time he was praising me for my great dedication to some meditation he'd asked me to do – and he said, "Good, Madhuri! Soon you will defeat Sarita!" ...But I knew he was joking.

Primal Memories

I'm two years, eight months old. I had screamed a very great deal in my first two years, so that nobody got much sleep. I was just recovering from this (though I still itched and bled with eczema in the folds of my elbows and knees) and had calmed down at last, becoming a confiding, chatty toddler. My mother was my friend, my beloved, my safety – the only person who cuddled me, in a houseful of males; the person I could go to. She was always open, to some degree, to listen to me.

On this day I am sitting in my crib in a long narrow room that connects the two rooms at the front of the house with the two bedrooms at the back. The room is dim and cluttered. There's a window near my crib; through it I can see the tall green hedge, like a leafy wall.

A door opens and my mother comes in. I must have not seen her for a few days, but although I can conclude that now, I don't remember missing her. It is as though that time before was asleep, and this new time, now, is awake.

For my mother is glowing. I can see her aura – she has a halo all around her, and it is made of love – gold and pink and heart-feeling. She moves in a mist of bliss.

She is carrying something, a pink bundle, in her arms. I do not know what it is but my senses go into alert. *Danger!*

She comes up to the side of my crib. Even in her blissed-out state she is authoritative and in command. She lifts the pink bundle over the side of the crib and places it down beside me. "Here's your little sister!" she says. "Now don't be jealous!"

A kind of horror engulfs me; I am in shock. Life as I've known it is over. My mommy, my very sustenance, is deserting me, utterly without warning or preparation of any kind. But more than that, I have been instructed *not to feel what I feel.* Not, then, to be who I am. I have, in that one sentence, that breath of time, been ordered to sacrifice myself – for my mother, who cannot cope with too many demands on her energy, and for the little stranger who is now living in my very own space, my bed.

I have been told that I matter less than either of them.

That whatever my reality is, it is not worth anybody's attention.

And I have no choice but to receive this and live by it – for my mother is powerful. I do not protest – instead I take it very seriously indeed. I do not fight or struggle, that is not my way – but I take the injunction in like a knife made of ice, which freezes my inside everywhere it touches. A large portion of my spirit turns into a frozen steak, that I will then drag behind me from a sort of umbilicus, on throughout my life.

Then, to add insult to injury, the interloper, the tiny angel with its wide mouth and pale little fizzle of hair on top of its round pink head – has been installed right beside me, for the rest of my life – not only in my crib, but in my very destiny, my fate. There is no escape.

After that I feel that I am allowed to stay here in the family, but only just; and it is not okay for me to be what I am, take up space with myself. This is not wanted. I am just supposed to be Good.

Much much later, in the 90's, I was visiting my friend Lotus in Mill Valley, and she told me of a recent birth within her extended sannyasin family. Deepa, the mother, gave birth to her second daughter at home. The elder daughter, just a few years old, clung to Lotus, her little body trembling all over. When the baby was born and Deepa lay cuddling it, she also called for her firstborn to come into the room. The child held back, clinging to Lotus... but finally she went.

Deepa cradled the new baby, and beckoned the firstborn to lie in the crook of her other arm.

"I have love enough for both of you," she said.

What touches me about this story was that Deepa understood that the first child might be freaked out, and she did not judge this. She understood.

That was what I missed.

I am sure my mother was simply exhausted – she also had her four sons needing her attention – and so we all always knew this: there is not enough to go around. There just isn't. So don't expect it. And it is wrong of you to hope. It's not happening. And fathers, obviously, don't nurture. So that's out of the question. (The poor little pink creature who had landed in my crib, of course, had to put up with a horrid welcome – an energetic freeze-out – a heartbroken, angry sister giving her bad vibes. At two days old... and she told me much later that yes, this was just *horrible.)*

I now thank the lord and all providence that this sister came to me; and I suspect we planned it all before we were born. She has been the opening of so many doors, as well as the dark pathway into the forest that would most challenge me.

But I still think my mother could have done the introduction better.

And regarding the other detail of Bhagwan's diagnosis, this memory comes: I'm two years old. It's a bright warm morning, and Mommy is hanging wet clothes out to dry on the clothesline at the back of the backyard. It must be spring, for there is green grass on the ground, rather than the dust of summer. And all around the edges of the yard there are evening primroses, and a pomegranate bush, and wisteria, and a passion vine on a fence; and there is a greengage plum tree, a fig tree, a pecan tree, and an elm. I'm sitting on the grass, and for some reason I have no panties on. I can feel the cool grass on my bare flesh, and it feels absolutely delicious – a cool, tickling, sweet pleasure there where vulva and grass meet. I'm just sort of being there, feeling this; and somehow I know very well that Mommy should not realize what I am experiencing.

But she does realize – she always knows.

She looks up sharply. "Katy, *what are you doing?*" she demands. Her voice cuts into my tummy. She knows, she can see – I've been found out. This deliciousness is bad. I am bad. Her energy is pouncing on me like an ogre.

I say, "Nothing, Mommy!"

But that doesn't fool her. She goes back to the laundry-hanging, but I have been warned. Pleasure leads to shame and fury – *absolutely not allowed.*

A Teenage Memory

I am fourteen, and have come home briefly in between visits to my friend Taffy's house (I am there a great deal these days). I am in the dim, dirty, poor back bedroom I've always shared with my little sister. She is there – standing in the light of the window, where it looks out onto the wall of hedge. She asks if she can also come to Taffy's. She doesn't want to stay in our sad, falling-apart family any more than I do. I say No – for I want that escape all to myself.

My twelve-year-old sister stands there – and my eye falls on her full lips, her large eyes, her short, square chin; her long thick fall of honey-colored hair. And suddenly I understand that she is beautiful. I had not known, before, what that meant; even though I'd heard my mother use the word so many times. But now, as if my eyes had just opened, I see it.

A kind of refusal rises up in me. I cannot let her beauty in.

I do not suspect the utter determination my sister carries like a gift from a warrior past life. I don't know how far it will take her. I only know that all that beauty has to be balanced somehow – if she is beautiful, then I will have to be... sexy. I will have to get started on that.

And so, over time, I cultivated a smoky presence in my pelvis, and began to broadcast it silently; and to aim it when some interesting man was about; while my face stayed moodily still. It all took a while, interspersed with periods when I turned it off and kept to myself. But in the end it was an effective method to get into the sorts of trouble I sought.

Clouds

September 1974

My beautiful exquisite compassionate delicate Bhagwan, (your back, descending the stairs, is so beautiful I can't stand it –).

This morning's Cloud lecture put me back to childhood, when often I would gaze and gaze at the clouds forever, wondering about infinity, how it could go on and on and on and on.

I love it that the mind is like clouds. This center that you speak of – I think it is very much here in me, it was always there, but I have ignored it more and more in these last years in my desperate exterior searching. It is simple, a child-thing.

I guess what I am wondering – is it that simple? It seems too good to be true. Just that closing-the-eyes place? It is okay to let the snags and pains and compulsion just drift by, in and out of themselves?

Then I want to go alone to a cloudy hilltop for many days and just be and watch.

Thank you for the lovely little hairless head. Only please take it, too.

Love, Madhuri

More Meetings with the Master

During one darshan Bhagwan described a meditation to me, and told me to go home, try it out, and then report to him what happened. He detailed the stages: fifteen minutes each of shaking, dancing, sitting, and lying down. I followed these instructions, reported to him, and soon afterwards we were all doing the delightful, welcome, relaxing Kundalini meditation in the afternoons.

I had been using to capacity the privilege that allowed us to write letters to Bhagwan. I wrote about every pain and breakthrough; every mourning, pessimism, or optimism. I sent him my new book of poems, which had just come out. I sent him just-written poems (including a manuscript for a new book of them, which he okayed. My publisher then rejected the new manuscript, finding the references to meditation incomprehensible.) And the sense of poetry was strong in me – sometimes stronger than whatever sense the words might make. It just sounded good, so I sent it in – and, of course, it was much meant as it was coming out of me.

I generally got the response, "Follow your feeling." But one day Greek Mukta (the middle-aged Greek heiress who lived in Lao Tzu and these days relayed messages between Bhagwan and us)* brought one of my letters back with the message, "Go back to the West. Now you are ready."

Well, hell. I was NOT ready, and I knew it. I asked for Darshan.

When I sat in front of Bhagwan he looked like he'd been expecting me. "Hmmm, Madhuri? You go back to the West," he said.

"NO!" I blurted.

"No? Oh, okay!" And he turned to Vivek, his caretaker, and murmured something sotto voce. She disappeared through the double doors behind his chair, and returned a moment later carrying before her, laid across her arms, something made of cloth. In her modest way she was smiling with her long slender lips, eyes downcast as usual.

She handed the flat white bundle to Bhagwan, who handed it to me. I could see from the high folded collar on top that it was one of his robes.

My mouth was hanging open. I was in a Gap. I stared at him.

"Oh, so, you want the lungi, too?" he asked genially, and turned to nod to Vivek, who went again into the house and returned, as before, carrying something.

Now I had a luminous white stack in my lap, and as I stared at him he instructed me: "Dye them orange. And whenever you need me – but only if you *really* need me – put them on, and lie down and wait. And I will be there. And remember – never let anybody else see them."

And I never have.

Around the Flat

Although the ashram was the center of everything, there were opportunities for exploration in one's own flat too – Bhagwan gave us meditations to do, or we explored in our own ways; and, in those very early days, there was Madness meditation, held just around the corner from Boat Club Road in a huge old wooden house, where lived a woman who had once studied with Krishnamurti.

* As well as working in the Lao Tzu garden, where, incidentally, she had instructions not to prune anything!

A group of us gathered in a circle in a huge room every afternoon, and, for fifteen minutes we made terrible faces. Then we sat still with closed eyes for another fifteen minutes. The terrible faces – what I believe is called in English 'gurning' – were accompanied by spontaneous movements of the hands and arms.

I loved this! Breaking apart all convention with a simple grimace and horrid arching of eyebrow! Enjoying the freedom of spontaneous misbehavior, while structures in the body were cracked open and new life rushed in. I felt it doing me all kinds of good.

In our flat the third person was Ma Hari Chetna, always known as Ma Hari, a wide-eyed, urbane, beautiful German woman with long blonde hair and a thick fringe. She had a way of waving her hands about when she talked, and a kind of been-there-done-that laugh where she stood forthright and raised her eyebrows, her beautiful full lips parting to show her nice healthy teeth. She had been a model or actress or something – she was quite tall and slim, though strongly-built. (Nobody was very interested in what somebody had done before they came here – *here* was so utterly arresting, there wasn't room for all that past stuff.) Her voice was beautiful, round and mature.

Her boyfriend was a musician, Chaitanya Hari (known professionally by his legal surname: Deuter). He was tall and slender with a high domed head with long, receding hair, and soft pale skin. He was every inch the musician – he lived for nothing else, and everyone knew this and respected it. He and Ma Hari had some companionship, some resonance together.

Another person often at our flat was Devananda, who lived in the flat upstairs. I mentioned him before – red-headed, high forehead, full lips, white teeth, and a slightly toed-in gait. His arms were covered in red down, and he had freckles. He laughed a lot and was very friendly. He was Sarita's new boyfriend, but he became, somehow, my new girlfriend – my confidante, my buddy. It was he who started calling me Mudpie. Soon a few more people called me that. I was not altogether sure how I felt about it. (Perhaps I had told him this story: I was about six years old, sitting out on the front porch of our house making mudpies. My father came home from work. When I saw him striding with his quick bow-legged gait up towards the house, a seductive languor stole over me. I adored him, and I wanted to marry him when I grew up. So I lay back on the porch with my long hair tossed casually behind me… right in a mudpie! Glen stopped for a minute and, uncharacteristically noticing and uncharacteristically critical, he said sharply, "You're lying in the mud!" Ooooooh I was sad and embarrassed…)

One day I was looking for Sarita, and I opened the door to her room. She was in there with Devananda, and they were doing something strange – or, rather, *not* doing something – and so it was strange. I saw her shapely ankle with a decorative or holy string tied around it, raised over Devananda's bare back. But they were not moving, not breathing hard. They were just kind of being there, yet the air was full of intimate alertness. They looked up at me. I backed away quickly and closed the door.

Sarita gave me something someone had given to her: a painting Bhagwan had made, on a large, thin piece of paper, folded into four. I unfolded it… a design of circles in greens and yellows, diffuse, water-colory, yet possibly done with inks as the colors were strong in some places. It looked like ripples in a pond, and yet more like ripples in the Universe – a springtime universe. I kept it with my few treasures on a shelf.*

Meditation Camp

Every month there was a ten-day meditation camp, with five meditations a day plus a discourse. For 1½ years I did every meditation in every camp – only once I missed Dynamic, whereupon I seemed to feel Dynamic was happening to me as I lay in bed; and I immediately reported this to Bhagwan. He told me not to miss the meditation.

We did Nataraj, a dancing meditation. We did humming, called Nadabrahma. And at night, Gourishankar – gazing into a pulsing blue light, after long deep slow breathing. Then the next stage was Latihan, where we stood and let the body move itself. Then came lying down, still.

It was a full-on program of unloading old stuff and becoming more and more deeply present into the moment at hand. There was only This. It was gorgeous. It was real life. A sort of fog I had carried within me for years –

* Much later, very unfortunately, the Word went out that all such treasures had to be given in to the office. With reluctance, I surrendered it.

ever since, I must say, my first joint-smoking with my girlfriends at fourteen – had lifted away, leaving air as clean and sharp as that you'd find on a piney mountain in autumn. I could see far away. I could see inside. I could see.

One night during Gourishankar a strange thing happened... During the Latihan stage, as my body was in its prescribed let-go, discovering, or trying to discover, its own way to move – I found that I had become a wolf, was prowling to the edge of the hall, pouncing on some sacks of cement lying there; as if they were prey. When I reported this to Bhagwan in Darshan he told me I had been a wolf in a past life.

One meditation included a stage where you sat loose-jawed, perfectly still... Flies crawled on my face, into my open mouth – but, obedient, watchful, rapt – I allowed them and just watched the sensations.

I'd found a book someplace – *Alive*, by Piers Paul Ried, about a plane crash in the Andes (the poor survivors ate the poor non-survivors). I had never enjoyed a book so much since I was a child – my cleaned brain reveled in each sharp detail. I was amazed. For years I'd been unable to read anything but cookbooks. I chatted about this, as about everything else, with Devananda. He laughed delightedly when I shared.

Bhagwan was speaking about Patanjali, a master from 5,000 years ago. He described a certain meditative process called *Prati Prasav*. I was much intrigued, and knew that I wanted to try it. It worked like this: before going to bed at night, you re-live what you have just done – brushing teeth, undressing, folding up your shawl and putting it on the shelf... whatever you have been doing for the hour before bed – you re-live it. I did not do this in my imagination only; I stood and re-enacted the actions I had moved through; and I did it to re-live the entire day, back to when I'd risen for Dynamic in the early morning. I did this for four months.

I noticed that there were many things I now saw about the day that had escaped me when I'd actually been living it. Little moods, atmospheres of people around me; things seen from the corner of the eye but not remarked upon. I began to follow these threads, going into the unlived, unseen image or energy – a person over here, a suggestion of a memory from my past over there. I would jump into the image and become it, and let it reveal to me what it was. This would lead to more trails as those characters or memories revealed their own half-seen threads. Without having intended to do so, I had embarked on a project to re-identify with and thus dis-identify with (through the magic of awareness, which frees whatever it totally embraces) every memory of my life.

I noticed too that when I woke up next day, the previous day was gone – exactly like a tape that had been erased. It was the strangest feeling!

I began to practise Prati Prasav more and more – going from thoroughness to compulsion – stopping many times during the day to sit down and quickly re-live the hours just passed. I told this to Bhagwan, and he advised me to do the meditation only once a day, and said it would be stronger that way. And so I did.

When I lay down on my pallet finally after a day of meditations and then my own meditation (I'd stopped the Making Love meditation, but there was always a current one to do: Prayer, Compulsion meditation – more about that soon – and now Prati Prasav), I tended to float into the air and feel myself as a humming-all-over. This was wonderful and strange. Once I found myself right up under the ceiling... And when I woke next morning, my body would be in exactly the same position I'd gone to sleep in the night before: prone, on my back, straightly-aligned, hands at my sides.

From a Letter to Devadasi:

October 28, 1974

Dear Mama,

neurosis – that which entangles so many so madly for so long – is simply a tightly-knit sweater of woolworth's nylon far too small and hurting. If you find the right thread and pull it, the whole, by and by, unravels. And the ribs breathe...

...There is a horrible dun-colored claustrophobia which comes over me in the afternoon every day which feels exactly like the smog of Riverside mixed with all of your and Glen's anguish, oozing out of my bones. It is awful – it is at that time a dreadful thing to be inside myself. It feels too vague for catharsis, but I guess it will come.

The dearest most secret things are a seed inside me which cannot be said.

I was very very sick a few days ago, and have mostly recovered except for chronic dysentery and an occasional weakness. The sickness was total hell but I sure felt fabulous when it was over! My stomach is a godawful mess – it is weird to be 'unhealthy' – I have been craving real food – real wholewheat bread and creamcheese and apples. And what keeps happening is nasty toast and oh, I dunno, just junk. Even

Rita's good cooking sits like a sagebrush in my stomach. My stomach wants mama and/or nothingness. I'm taking some homeopathic medicine which seems to help a lot.

I feel kind of sad that when I write I leave out all the best stuff, or put it in very dry tones, but there is a kind of music in me that I cannot write and can only just barely hear myself and so many things tie in with it…

Dots, and Some Correspondence

Once when I was six I was coloring a drawing of a little girl in a coloring book. She was wearing a dress with a full skirt. I felt that this dress might like to have polka-dots on it, so I started drawing them in. I made big round dots, and more dots, and more dots… until there were pretty much only dots, and almost no space left between them. I looked at this and felt sad. I concluded that something was wrong with me; that that was not the right kind of person to be.

Another time I was looking at a comic book, and I noticed that the fields of color were actually composed of little dots. I thought about this, feeling quite afraid: suppose that everything really is just made of dots, with lots of space around them? Then everything I think is real and solid, is not solid at all! I began to feel dizzy and upset. What if it *really is like that?* I wondered.

From an Aerogram to Devadasi:

…watched the deep ecstatic rose of the twilight seep and melt over the huge trees, and the enormous deepgold moon come up, so quickly and so silently. Now that my body is more open I feel the moon as a huge pull, at my womb and my heart. Bhagwan said it acts as a gravity on the fluids in the body, of which we are 97%, and which is made exactly out of seawater. He said that the baby in the seawater womb goes through all the stages of evolution. The fluids in the brain must lean too.

Shobha has come from Goa and is beautiful and very good, very high (to use an obnoxious word for an indescribable phenomenon). She saw a beautiful naked girl die, who had fallen from a cliff to the sea in Goa, and she had a very transforming silent experience with this – she kept wondering why she didn't feel sorry or sad or guilty like everybody else – she just felt incredibly peaceful and aware and like she had witnessed a natural miracle.

"Whatsoever a master says is not out of his knowledge; it is out of his innocence." "A master never gives you answers. He just destroys your questions." He said this today.

My native anxiety, creative bent, and general obsessiveness came together in this letter to Bhagwan. If the poor beleaguered man ever answered it, I don't remember the reply…

November 1974

Beloved Bhagwan,

In this annihilation of the past, something still is struggling. It manifests thus: when I cook, the agony and anxiety I put myself through I recognize as the other side of the desire and pleasure I feel for cooking. When I cook it cannot be otherwise than total; it is an ego dance. It is always incredible, tasty, original, and even witty – I find I make things harmonize and play together, colors and nationalities, and I write menus full of nuances and inter-lingual puns, and I dress up like an airline stewardess and trot things out like Shakespeare or Mae West. I feel when cooking like when writing poetry, or like speaking with a lover might feel.

The agony is that it is compulsive and I get into almost unbearable states of anxiety. I let it take me over. It is much more conscious now but I guess I still feel somehow that it will lead me somewhere; like going on stage… I worry as well as delight in the planning; I feel martyred angry possessive etc and the worst of it is the PEOPLE. Ah, India, where a thousand people ring the doorbell as I am up to my wrists in a sensuous goo of beans and onions to go in the enchiladas, and any other time I would love them or at least accept them but in this matter I exude hatred and unwelcome and feel like a broken butterfly and juggle pots pans and anxieties etc etc. If I plan to cook for 5 people (Sarita and Path Construction company) always 3 more or 5 more show up and I feel everything out of control and then when everybody praises my ingenuity and cookingness I feel wry and I know what are the fruits of success. All fruits are in the moment. But Jeesus, like today I had 2 shaking fits and took a cold shower and lay down on the bed with your robe over my head. Whenever I get with your robe I am filled with a soft fire and understanding seeps through me like my own blood. There is really nothing to ask you. But I want to tell you everything. I love you with all that is free in me to love, and far more with the part I don't know about.

Love, Madhuri

A poem by Devadasi, rediscovered much later in an old letter to me:

Afterbirth

unhealing wound
that never will be healed;
when you hurt, I hurt,
I bleed, deep, deep inside.
I can not spare you pain
nor keep you safe
but the black shadow –
dark bruise on your young days –
how can I bear
thinking I put it there?

He Answers a Question

We could send in questions for discourse whenever we liked; he might or might not answer them. Here he answered one of mine:

Osho, please, what are you doing to me?

This is from Madhuri.

I am killing you, Madhuri. I am a murderer, and you are trapped. You cannot escape me now because once you have tasted a little death, you cannot escape. Because now you know much more is going to come. Once you have tasted a little death of the ego, you know, you can imagine now, you can dream of what a beautiful space is going to be there when the whole ego disappears: when you look within yourself and you don't find anybody there, just emptiness, vast emptiness. If you have found a little empty corner in your being, then you cannot move away now. You have tasted.

Now, you cannot go back to the ordinary world. Unless you die, there is no going back. Once you die, I will send you back to the ordinary world, because then nothing can corrupt you. Who can corrupt an emptiness? How can an emptiness be corrupted? It is open, absolutely vulnerable, and yet invulnerable, because nobody can corrupt it. It is incorruptible, it is virgin.

Come Follow to You, Vol. 4, Ch. 10, Q. 7

Jokes

There was that famous day in 1974 when we were listening to Bhagwan talk, resting in a space that was beautiful... blissful, delicate and yet firm, strong as knives, tigery, pouncing, then spun out like the Milky Way across the sky, or like gossamer cloud-cover, or spinning as with daisies in a meadow. He was telling us truths of the spirit each of us needed to know – and we were sitting, going inside, watching ourselves whilst drinking him in.

Things were sacred and holy indeed.

And then he told a joke – a terrible, horrible, unspeakably bad joke. It was the first time he had ever told one, and it was a doozy: Two tigers are walking single-file through the jungle, when one of them comes up behind the other and begins licking his anus. "What are you doing?" demands the first tiger. The other replies, "I just ate a... (here you can put in any detested Other), and I want to get the taste out of my mouth!"*

We certainly woke up! Sat up straighter! Some people laughed! Some people didn't laugh! At all! There was a sense of something murmurous passing across the auditorium – people were consulting within themselves, with each other by osmosis, whether Bhagwan was really allowed to do this?

I was shocked, but delighted by the absurdity of it all. This man was so utterly without fear – but this began in me too the uneasy apprehension that somebody sometime was going to kill him – he was just so outrageous! I never imagined not trusting him – he must know what he was doing.

Many, many people left the next day.

Bhagwan congratulated himself, out loud to all of us, on getting rid of the "dead, serious people"! And then he never stopped telling jokes. Every day he told them, often explaining them afterwards at length, which made them even funnier. He was often deadpan in his delivery, but just as often he cracked up himself! His peaked eyebrows went up and down!

* My editor said that if I included here the word Bhagwan used, she would not allow her name to be associated with this project.

And wild silly crazy jokes became part of our life. There was religion-bashing, nationality-bashing, gender-bashing, anything-bashing. We were invited to send jokes in, and he told some of mine too.

We could also send in stories, anecdotes, as well as our questions. I sent him this anecdote: When my mother was in the hospital giving birth to me, there was a woman in the next bed also having a daughter; and neighborliness arose. The other woman said that during the war she got a job at a gas station, since the men were away being soldiers. She had quite a flat chest, and wore falsies. One day a customer was staring and staring at her chest while she filled up his tank with the hose, and also while he gave her payment for the fuel. So long and hard did he stare that she offered forthrightly, *"Like* 'em? *Have* 'em!" and pulled the rubber mounds out of her bra and thrust them at him.

Bhagwan recounted this but changed the story around to suit himself, making Devadasi the protagonist! I have sometimes wondered if this was a long-distance message to her, to make light and bring comfort to her for the loss of her breast... for when she had sat in front of him, she later told me, she was asking him silently about that particular anguish she had suffered.

Much much later, Sarita discovered some research which showed that optimal learning is accomplished when two helpful adjuncts are used: baroque music, and dirty jokes. If you read or hear a dirty joke after a study period, your retention of the material goes way up. Not just any joke will do; it must be raunchy.

Perhaps this is a good place to add a bit of explanation about something people often ask me: "What did Bhagwan really teach? What were his beliefs?" And the answer is, Nothing. Exactly that.

This, I know, bewilders people even more. Bhagwan explained again and again that he was going to say everything, and contradict himself daily, just to lead our minds to a cliff-edge where the mind would then stop of its own accord. The mind can't hold contradictions; it can only choose between two apparent opposites. So contradiction makes it stop.

That was his aim... to lead us to the Great Nothing.

The thing beyond thing.

A joke, he explained, does something similar – you are led along in suspense, and then the punchline is unexpected, and you go into a tiny gap – and then, tension relieved, you laugh. (Or not!)

Certainly there was no question of bias, racial, religious, national, or otherwise, in him or in his Commune. I dislike even having to explain this; the very idea is so heartless and unpleasant – but I must: I once read that in an emergency, for example a hijacked airliner where people are being held hostage onboard – they naturally gather into national groups.

This was not how it was in our Commune. Any person was seen and embraced for her uniqueness as a being. The skin color, the racial or religious background, even the past profession or country of origin – were so uninteresting to us that they were seldom remarked on or referred to. All we saw was the lovely being in the robe, sitting with us at lunch. Her shining, and her depth.

As well, everyone who came to the Commune and donned a robe became very beautiful. It didn't matter if they were plump or thin, grey-haired or blond, tall or short, old or young. It didn't matter what their costumes had been in their own country, or their ideas had been of their own attractiveness or not. Beauty arrived and glowed out of them, and there it stayed. This was so wonderful. A kind of grace.

Because what we see on the surface – the curly hair, the religious costume, the slant of the eyes, the skin tone – is never, ever, the deepest core of the being. We were interested in that. The deepest core is that which never changes; and all those outward things change. Yes, the conditioning goes very deep – but it is exactly that conditioning that we are obliged to offload, to see through, in order to come to that deepest interior – the face we had before we were born.

And so a joke such as the one above, in all its revolting viciousness, is not about anyone's real being. It is just about exteriors. That is why it can even be made at all; no joke can be made about the real depth and beauty of the being; no words have ever been found even to speak of this naked beauty. But here, here was a safe place to search for it.

I love a story Bhagwan told us about when he was a teenager, going on a school outing with a number of other boys who were all Hindus. The young Rajneesh was the only Jaina; and in his religion it was not permitted to eat after dark, in case you accidentally consumed innocent insects.

The boys spent a happy day clambering about some ruins, and only after dark settled down to prepare food. The one Jaina boy was very hungry from all the exercise – but dark had fallen and he wasn't allowed to eat! The Hindus were meanwhile merrily cooking over a little fire.

The young Rajneesh decided to eat anyway – the food smelled so good. So he ate… and then, helplessly, spent most of the night vomiting until every bit of food was out of his stomach. Only then could he sleep.

He told us that that was when he really understood the power of conditioning.

We were there to find what was deeper than cultural hypnosis.

Cleaning in Lao Tzu

In December 1974, Bhagwan sent a message that I was to start cleaning in his house.

This was my first work in the Commune. I was honored. Sarita had been cleaning there for some time – mysterious rooms I'd never seen, might never see. I was set to cleaning all the bathrooms except for Bhagwan's; and I was also to clean the floor of the long corridor that divided the house.

My relationship with cleaning had been late-starting, sporadic, but passionate. Our mother did not clean – "It's like sweeping back the tides," she'd say – nor did she make us clean a thing, ever. (She was suited to be a mother, but not a housekeeper. There is apparently a difference!) I remember only one time that we cleaned anything: she'd been reading Pippi Longstocking to us, and Pippi scrubbed the kitchen floor by tying scrub-brushes to her feet and pouring soapy water all over the floor, then going skating. So Mama splurged on scrub-brushes and we tried it. The edges of the room were cluttered with dirty dishes and junk, and the floor had actual little *hills* of black gunk on it, so there was only so much we could accomplish – but we had fun! (As a small child I had once decided to clean the kitchen floor myself, and had creatively mixed together in a measuring cup: water, powdered laundry detergent, instant coffee, and sugar. Since the floor was as above-described, this jolly concoction simply melded into the spirit of things. {Apropos of nothing: I have all my life loved to mix things together that others find to be, in combination, unlikely, peculiar, and sometimes distressing. I attribute this to a chemist gene I must have gotten from my father. Once, at six or seven, I tried to make soap by mixing egg white with powdered charcoal, and rubbing it on my arms. I was very much allergic to eggs, so the result was a crop of itchy black welts. Mama was not amused. I still think it was worth it for the thrill of experimentation.})

So when as a teenager I discovered cleaning it was a brand-new revelation for me – something that could belong to me alone, without my family's hand in it.

Starting at sixteen I would sometimes have an attack of cleaning-itis, and spend a day or two scrubbing burnt-on gunk off whatever stove belonged to wherever I was staying. At seventeen I once staged a guerrilla cleaning party for Richard Lyons, an absent and unknowing college boy I loved hopelessly and unrequitedly. The cleaners were Self; my sister, age fifteen; and our sister-in-law, who was eighteen. (The sister-in-law's infant participated by sleeping on the couch.) We tidied the happy bachelor detritus, cleaned the bathroom, and, in a stroke of genius, spray-painted the toilet green. Then we baked and iced a cake, using whatever we could find; and hid in the shower, giggling, to await Richard's coming home.

The first thing the young man saw, in his erstwhile comfortably casual, if summer-hot attic apartment, was a strange infant asleep on his settee. We heard the questioning murmur of his mild voice (he was a very calm and stately young man) and, behind the shower curtain, clutched each other, trying to suppress the howls of glee threatening to get out.

When all was revealed and the cake breached, he asked us, "Why? Why?" and I got the strong feeling – as I would on several other occasions – that a young man in necessary rebellion to his parents does not want his chaos disturbed by tidying.

Whereas to me, cleaning was an exotic joy.

Now, in 1974, I set about cleaning in a completely different milieu. There was no chaos. There was nothing hideous and ancient to scrape away. There were very few possessions of anybody's, anywhere. Everything was already clean; one was just going to keep it that way.

I was given a run-through by someone, I forget now who; and then it was up to me. I was to clean Laxmi's bathroom, Greek Mukta's as well, a small toilet-only room beside the stairs going up to the veranda; Maitreya-ji's bathroom (Maitreya was a lovely old man, courtly and diffident, who lived in Lao Tzu), two toilets at the far end of the corridor, squat-type, with a huge sink nearby; and one more, outside the main house and around the corner, along the path that led to Chuang Tzu auditorium.

I found it very challenging to be in Lao Tzu house, but at the same time delicious and uplifting. The challenges were two: I had a high standard to live up to; and then there was Bhagwan's force-field to contend with – an indescribable, intense aura of bliss and cleanliness and just plain awesome wide-awake clear penetrating awareness that filled the house, cool and definite. I sometimes lay on Mukta's bathroom floor, right above Bhagwan's room, and quaked there, feeling like a huge pulsating sort of cosmic vulva. (I always thought, on these occasions, that I should be *utterly* disappearing into things, but I never quite did.) But it was strong enough… to lie there on the cool marble, vortexed and broadcast through, watching things whirl around inside. I loved the winter cold and how it made my toes and fingers thrill, my heart leap in the morning. It was lovely to clean in that freshness.

Once I heard Bhagwan talking to Vivek, his caretaker. He was sitting out on his own porch, just below where I was in the aforementioned bathroom, and his voice carried, though his words were muffled. There was an intimate grumbling in it, a sort of boundary-less querulousness. I don't know what it was about; but I remembered it later when he told us in discourse that Indians don't value politeness because it assumes distance; and if you are close to someone you don't require it.

To clean in, I wore my oldest robe. I had been eating normally for some time by then, after the bouts of barfi slacked off and there were regular meals at home. I was addicted to chikkus for a while – furry little brown fruits with a grainy, sweet interior and a few shiny flat black seeds – I'd eat six or seven at once. But they seemed harmless. I'd gone from eighty-nine pounds at my thinnest to about one hundred and thirty pounds. So, at just under 5'4", I was a little bit plump. My hair was growing out, wavy and dark brown. I was entirely celibate, and thought only of my process, with my still-difficult compulsiveness haunting me.

The first bathroom I cleaned was Laxmi's. It was marble, palatial, with a big thick bathmat and a large tub, huge mirror, everything posh and lush and sparkling. I somehow managed to pour a bucket of water over the floor and drench the bathmat, and that was that – I was banned from that particular bathroom.

But there were the others; and eventually I cleaned Mukta's large bedroom as well as her bathroom. (Once, dusting her vanity table, I broke a bottle of Listerine. All bottles there had to sit with the labels to the back so they didn't show. This annoyed me a bit – and I picked up the mouthwash to dust it –

and – *Crash!* She made me pay for it – eight rupees – which I resented.) And once, when I was cleaning for the affable, adorable Maitreya-ji, I badgered him to tell me why he kept a red rubber glove in his bathroom.

"I require it," he said.

"But why?" I persisted.

"I *require* it," was all he would say, uncomfortably.

So I now salute Maitreya-ji for being the only person I ever heard of who kept things sanitary by wiping himself with a gloved hand.

Over the year and a half that I cleaned in that house, those bathrooms: I had mystical experiences in them, and horrendous ones (Indian laborers used the outside one and, due perhaps to a diet of flyblown samosas and so on, it could be really smelly and… well, *loose)*. I plodded and scrubbed and sloshed, and I was at peace insofar as I was ever at peace; which was not greatly, it must be said. I felt that I was cleaning, grounding, exercising, something in myself. Even the repetition was good.

I loved cleaning the corridor – as I remember, I did it twice a day, the bathrooms once a day – especially the application of a very thick dark red paste called Mansion Polish. This was applied with a cotton chamois cloth, and then the cloth was used to buff and rub the stuff into the stone. It smelt good, made of beeswax and other natural things – a Raj leftover – and I loved the down-on-hands-and-knees thing – I don't know why. I still love that. Floors are my favorite thing to clean. I love a good rag and a floor that needs cleaning but isn't stuckity-yucky… On my hands and knees. Something very simple about it; and in my childhood house, it would have been impossible – the floor was never clear of trash, not in any room. So this new activity was a luxury par excellence.

Later too I used a very, very tall broom to clean cobwebs out of the Chuang Tzu ceiling, when that auditorium was built. Such a silent place.

A Few Lao Tzu Bits

A few interesting incidents from around this time: Sarita and Kamal had written, illustrated and bound a slender book to give to Bhagwan. It was a fairy tale, and when they showed it to me I thought it beautiful indeed – delicate, luminous drawings, simple yet graceful text. It was sent in to him; and that is the last the two girls heard about it. For whatever reason, Bhagwan never acknowledged it or commented.

I had, since I was a teenager, been making envelopes. I made them out of old calendars, out of maps, out of wrapping paper; whatever I could find. I found great joy in this; and had once bailed myself out of a tight situation in Barcelona by making envelopes from my well-used Eurail map, lining them with tissue paper; decorating the flaps with paper 'button' and 'buttonhole' pencil-shaded to life-likeness. I sold them in a coffee-shop full of backpackers and made enough for a ferry ticket.

But aside from any usefulness they might have, I just loved the scrounging of paper and cutting and glueing and lining (sometimes with silk or other fabric). At that time in history, kitsch was fashionable, and I enjoyed its ironic-retro aesthetic as much as anyone. (I don't like it any more.) So, one day when I had a free couple of hours, I cut up a gaudy calendar full of splashy Hindu gods and goddesses – I remember particularly a blue Krishna and attendant *gopis*, or girlfriends – and made envelopes out of it. I was so excited by their colorful, funky peculiarness that I sent a little pile in to Bhagwan.

They were returned to me next day, with no comment; however, the flat colorful bits of paper seemed to me to glow with an ominous, palpable sense of having been gazed upon and *not liked at all.* Found wanting in every respect. Found to be silly and not beautiful in any meaningful way.

Maybe I was mistaken – but it seemed to me that I saw those little bits of fun through his deep and ancient eyes, and they just weren't worth bothering him with.

I was shocked and ashamed and... *I knew that I was an idiot.*

Another thing that happened was hearsay, but I loved it: shortly after Bhagwan had moved to Poona, boxes of his books that had been shipped from Bombay were being opened, and many cockroaches had run out and dashed off on all sides into cracks.

The unpackers sent a message to Bhagwan, asking what to do – was it okay to kill the insects, or not? (Jaina monks and nuns, of course, wear masks so that they will not inadvertently inhale and thus kill any wee flying creatures.)

"Any cockroach that you see," came back the reply, "liberate it from its body immediately!"

Pushing, Wrestling, and Mangling the River

I mentioned being compulsive. And that's quite a subject. My hell for many years.

I don't know where my OCD came from. Perhaps it was adolescence itself; perhaps hormonal imbalances brought on by taking those first, very strong, birth control pills when I was only fourteen. Or maybe some recessive gene – our mother used to rail against her mother-in-law's supposed mental problems. Or perhaps it was a backlash against my own attempts to grow a willpower, itself a backlash against the slovenliness of my childhood home. Maybe a past life as a nun was in there. (I think so.)

But somewhere in my eighteenth year I developed something like Obsessive-Compulsive Disorder – though I had never heard a name for it. And oh, I suffered… unremitting identification with the thoughts that pushed and tormented me; and shame, and loneliness.

Obsessive-Compulsive Disorder can have different manifestations – in 1971, in London, I'd worked for an aristocratic family which had, as was so common for some reason, one member in an Institution. They'd let her out periodically and she would come visit. She was a pale, soft-looking young woman, and she had the cleanest, shiniest straight, bobbed hair you could imagine, because she felt compelled to wash it *all the time.* She'd wash it… and then, not long afterwards, she'd excuse herself ever-so-politely, go and wash it again. And so on.

I found this a peculiar marvel – and I never exactly equated what began to happen to me, with that. My own obsessions seemed to make some sort of reasonable sense – though of course they didn't at all. They were a kind of self-invasion, a seeking for control on some level.

When I look back, there was a strangely spiritual aspect to these fevered attempts to bring order to the universe: I was trying to make myself a more courageous, alive person, by forcing myself to do things I did not want to do. I was trying to combat sleep. I was trying, with extreme psychic self-violence, to plunge myself into an icy lake so that I did not turn into a lazy, dope-headed Riversideian – that town of my birth. And, later, when my compulsions moved on to sex, I was trying to both avoid emptiness (that was the craven bit) and make some sort of cosmic bridge to everybody – lose my own limiting boundaries in the flush of new territory, as experienced through a temporary lover. This seemed very important. I didn't want to come here to this earth just to end up small.

One form of OCD is characterized by insistent, unwelcome thoughts, often instructing the victim to do a certain thing they would otherwise not dream of doing. Postpartum depression can contain this ingredient, when the new mother seems to receive an instruction to, for example, toss her baby out a window. The thoughts repeat and hammer loudly. The more one tries to get rid of them the stronger they become. The victim is also ashamed of the irrational, generally destructive nature of the thoughts (though in my case they seemed perversely reasonable, as I said), adding to the pain of the situation.

The fact that we are all taught to trust the intellect is one main key to the power this disorder has: if not our thoughts (we suppose), what are we going to believe in? So I think OCD is a dearth of meditation, coupled with as-yet-mysterious chemical signals between brain and body.

When I'd gone to Europe with the Medicine Ball Caravan, in 1970, and the film wrapped soon, I'd stayed on. The man I'd fallen in love with in San Francisco, David, flew to London with his brother to meet me. I traveled Europe with them and a small band of young people, in a VW bus, for a winter and a spring. I admired David; I ached over him. He was twenty-seven, an accomplished musician, linguist, writer, and raconteur, who moonlighted as a taxi driver. He steeped himself in cigarettes, wine, and whatever drugs he could score day-by-day – not the hard stuff, but each and everything else. He fed these things to me, and though my body told me it had no interest in them (a bit of experimenting at fourteen had satisfied my curiosity) I overruled that in order to keep company with my lover.

Through a difficult few months in Ibiza I struggled to be the girl I thought he wanted – cool, 'together,' in the parlance of the day: not jealous. But I was uncool, my nervous system ragged from the depleting effect of the psychedelics, jealous of his affair with a cool German drugs-mogul teenager, and so untogether that bits of me were flying about the room and out the windows, with no center to gather round. As I failed more and more pitifully (he had had high hopes, because I was such a precocious poet) he withdrew from me. We'd started out as apparent equals (maybe) but as he grew and I shrank I projected a sort of boss-leader-godhood onto him.

…And if he was a god, then, somehow, perhaps he held the key to my salvation.

We were ejected from Ibiza by the Guardia Civil, and went with our little band of friends to Switzerland, to a borrowed chalet in the Appenzell. It was early spring, with thick snow melting from the eaves and the trees, whumping, trickling, dripping down. And it was here that the full rigors of my madness came upon me.

My mind reasoned that if I could bring myself to confess to David everything I was ashamed of in myself, the burden would be gone from me and I would be free. The fact that I really, really did not want to do this just made the idea stronger: if there is anything you fear (it reasoned) you must face that thing and also express it. Nothing can be hidden. Only then are you worthy. ...This seemed obvious.

But this hard notion left out everything else of me: my heart, my belly, my privacy, my right to my own world, my own timing.

It left out the Other too: his choice, his natural boundaries. It revoked the idea of boundaries completely: the fact is that my childhood had had almost no privacy in it; and afterwards, some severe extremist in me then denied me boundaries on principle: a boundary is small! How can that be good? Aren't we all here to strip them away?

And thus does ideology create madness.

This view pretended that my world was not my own but belonged to the god-figure who ruled it, who could turn me inside-out of myself and yank on my precious inner bits roughly whenever it liked. As if a god was outside, who owned me, who was cruel and capricious and cared nothing at all for the feminine preciousness of my inner sanctum of subtle receptivity (which I did not value at this stage) – or my self-responsibility.

But the reasoning made sense to my mind: confess and you will be free.

And, as I've said, the other person was not taken into account by this authoritarian voice. That other person might not like to be used in such a way, a way that didn't see him at all, just a cardboard construction of some sort of Authority. (Curiously, I had once, later, compulsively tried to tell Herb about all this. We were driving in his car, I remember, and he just said simply, and forbiddingly, "That sounds horrible." I understood from his vibe that he was not going to have anything to do with the whole business whatsoever. So I dropped it – with him. His clear boundaries functioned.)

This miserable compulsion to confess commandeered me for perhaps seven years. I was always so happy when I forgot about it for a while, but the moment it came back I was lost into wretched captivity again. Much of my time was spent divided and in hell.

One snowy day in the Alps David and the others and I drove in the VW bus along wet black roads from one village to another. We had taken mescaline – once again I had thought that a drug might make a hard thing easier; which it however did not do. I was going over and over in my mind what I would say to David when we stopped, and I could get him alone... rehearsing, rehearsing; my stomach clenched up under my ribs, sick with apprehension. (When I write about this now I realize how much simple happiness I've had since all this left me – and I am full of gratitude.)

We stopped beside a sloping field of snow and got out. I told David that there was something I wanted to tell him. He looked at me askance – by this time he no longer loved me – and we trudged up the hill and sat down in the snow at some distance from the others.

The sins I had to confess were interchangeable; the main criterion was that I should feel acute shame when relating them. I had had to search about for shame-worthy things to say – whether they were even true or not did not matter; only that they were humiliating, and thus nearly impossible to associate myself with in the public eye, so to speak. And, they should be made even more diabolically sharp and shame-worthy by their very silliness and banality.

I told him I wanted to make a confession to him. He stared at me in disgust. I gulped air in and, with every particle of will-power I could muster, I told him that I was in the habit of squeezing the pores on my nose. Not even pimples – I had none – but just some pores atop the nose.

"So what?" he said, shrinking further away from me. "Sometimes I have masturbated with warm water from the faucet in the bathtub!" I continued. His lip curled – not about the content, but the fact of my confessing.

And that was it – I couldn't think of anything more.

And then I waited to feel much, much better.

But that is not what happened.

Instead, that same mind-machine looked around for something else to chew on; some further transgression of aesthetics (it thought) to torment me with. And I saw that it was similar to how I'd felt after climbing Storm King

Mountain in the Rockies – when I'd reached the peak, there was only a gap of a moment before I started looking for the next one to climb.

David, poor David… afterwards when I thought about this scene, my heart ached at what came next: somewhere in between the cardboard constructs I wielded, a stripe of humanity got to me – as he started to cry a little, looked up at me, and said, "But I only wanted to be your friend!"

I took this OCD into my next relationship, an often-happy companionship with an Englishman named Paul. We each lived in Islington in basement flats and spent a lot of time together writing, and making love, and visiting his friends. But he was Depressive and I was OCD-which-at-that-time-had-no-name, and we upset each other quite a lot with these things. He would sometimes curl up in fetal position and simply wail, despite the pills he took; I would force myself to talk about squeezing blackheads, all the while shriveling with shame.

Finally, after many adventures in many countries, I returned alone to California, thinking that what I needed was the ultimate Encounter group – a thing, however, that I never found there.

Finally I was summoned to India.

Compulsion was a sort of beat of intensity through my body, carrying the message, *"Do! Do! Do!"* It wrapped around my muscles and nerves, much, I imagine, as a person with cerebral palsy must feel the rush of muscle-contracting electricity, forcing her to thrash and open and close her jaws. In meditation now I watched it, felt its exhausting power. In choosing to pour myself into the meditations, I was both subverting the disorder and feeding it – "I have to" being one of its mantras, as in "I have to do Dynamic" – and yet the format of the meditations themselves tended quite hugely to create space and peace and mindlessness, heart vibrancy and relaxation in the muscles.

During that first monsoon, before the winter when I began to clean, we had been doing Sufi whirling in the garden beside Krishna House. We turned in the mud and the rain, one hand raised at an angle, one hand down at the opposite side, and we turned and turned and turned… One was supposed to find a still place at the center of the motion, and one was supposed to fall down naturally, all by oneself, whenever one simply fell; and then lie on one's belly on the earth till the end of the meditation.

Only I never fell. It never happened. I turned until the last moment, when the signal came that the 1½ hour whirling stage was over – and then I would make myself drop to the ground. Then I lay and felt the funny black millipedes crawling over my bare skin, felt the cold mud and the warm rain; and watched...

Bhagwan said to me, quite crossly, "You have so much villpower, two hours would be nothing for you!" And I heard in his voice that this was not a good thing at all. This puzzled me.

And so I was cleaning toilets, and I got an Idea: what is a thing I *really don't want to do*, and so I *must do it?* To prove I am worthy, to prove I am alive and will do *anything* to stake my claim to a right to be on this earth as a courageous soul?

Answer: Put shit in my mouth.

Well, whose shit do I specially not want to put in my mouth?

Answer: Anybody's... but especially Indian laborers'! (I had seen the pools of loose wet yellow stool left on roadsides, just about everywhere one went in India. I knew about worms, and typhoid, and the myriad other hitchhikers that throve here. I knew that the very dust of India is made of dried shit. Loose, yellow, runny shit.)

I pondered this for some excruciating days. Then I finally decided on a compromise: since Indian laborers' shit might make me very ill indeed (not that anyone else's would be much better) – and somehow my poor masochism didn't extend that far – and since illness was not the point – terrible courage was the point...

Well. Okay.

So: my own shit. That would have to do.

But I had to quake and churn and gasp to myself and then gather myself sternly. And I did it – kneeling over the Indian laborers' toilet, into which I had just defecated, I reached down and got a bit onto my fingers – it was grey and slimy and greasy and rather loosely-formed – and put some in my mouth.

It was strange – eerily bland really – it tasted grey, like nothing much; like clay, really. Then I spat it out, and rinsed my mouth in the sink after washing my hands.

Then I wrote a note to Bhagwan and told him.

He did not reply. But soon after that I requested a darshan, telling him that I wanted to confess to him everything I was ashamed of. My reasoning here was that he really *was* a god-being and so the purge might finally be effective.

The familiar dread went with me for the preceding days, and all the way into that sublime arena, the gathering of a handful of disciples and new arrivals in that covered porch in Lao Tzu where he sat in a tall cushioned chair – and where a machine sat at the periphery, that lit up blue every time it zapped a mosquito. A little bit of the smell of roasted protein and see-through wing eddied into the air. (This smell so disturbed Bhagwan that the device was soon retired.) The pool of light. (In the very beginning of the ashram, he had given darshan during the daytime, in a grassy little lawn near the house; he sat in a chair there and we sat at his feet. But this was dropped because the disciples would idly yank and rip grass-blades, and Bhagwan found this painful. So Darshan had been moved to night-time, and on the porch; until it was later moved to Chuang Tzu.)

And so I staged it – sat before him, bowed, did my confession – the same one I'd foisted on David, with maybe an addition or two I'd managed to dredge up out of my hell. And he listened – perhaps a bit impatiently – and then said, "Good, Madhuri. Now this is finished. You will never do this again, hmmm?"

I would like to report that that did the trick – but it did not; though I never again gave in to that precise directive from the self-righteous, dictatorial mind. I still suffered, but did not act out. It would be many years before I understood the nature of addiction – its job being to give us something to grab onto, in order to avoid any abyss of emptiness that is yawning before our feet at any given moment – and many more years before I had an epiphany about compulsion that effectively freed me from the worst of it.

The epiphany, which came sometime in the 80's, went like this: "I am not enjoying this. And I have some rights here too."

That's all it finally took – putting me, my ease and happiness and well-being – my central existence, if you will – before some bossy disembodied voice, however persuasive. The litmus test was the feeling in my body – do what feels good, don't do what feels bad. (What rebellion! What risk of sloth and couch-potato-hood!)

Transferring the authority from the outside to the inside.

That was an immense risk, an immense simplicity.

And so finally the voice shut up.

Throughout my various madnesses Bhagwan sat calm and serene, alert to everything, labeling nothing. He never used the words Anorexia or OCD or Sex Addiction. (Now there are words for these syndromes, but at the time I had never heard them. I supposed I was alone, and just so very faulty.) He did not dramatize these things, he did not have me hospitalized, he never suggested I take psychiatric drugs. No – he simply trusted me, and sat there being Health and Beyondness himself – a luminous ovoid aura plunked down among us, sitting there as an example, so that we could see irrefutably that *it could be done.*

He did once give me a meditation to do when I felt compulsive: Imagine that all the energy in the body has flown over to the left side. When it is all on the left, then let it all flow over to the right.

Repeat this seven times.

I did it a lot, and found it very centering.

Therapy too was to be enormously helpful – but I can't imagine that therapy without his living example and without his meditations would have been even remotely sufficient. I believe that without his simple presence I could not have come through. I needed someone nonjudgmental and unrattled to just sit there and beam at me. Someone unfazed and unimpressed by the extremes into which my mind led me. And so I came through inch by inch, year by year, always unable to claim any useful progress until some relaxation in my state had revealed itself to me, all by surprise, in my own inner laboratory.

An Afterword About 'Bad Thoughts'

Just this morning, as I was walking under a freezing, bright January sun to the post office, and then doing laundry in a warm house – something clicked into place about this whole sorry history: compulsion, sexual repression, and… sexual invasion. Oh my god, I thought.

Any powerful misery tends to be like a river which has many tributaries; and so all the pieces of my recollection about that grueling Obsession story are definitely true. But I think I just found the final clicking piece.

I had to go on compulsively drawing attention to my own self, invading my own privacy; forcing myself to turn inside out and expose things that people usually keep private – because *that was what was done to me*, one hot summer night when I was eleven. We revisit trauma in an acting-out way to try to resolve it; here I was now acting as both invader and invaded – a neat, if torturous equation, to try to resolve something I had never been able to digest… for it was indigestible.

I used often to stay the night at the house of my best friend Taffy Bartley. She was a big platinum-haired girl with a brilliant mind and two great loves: animals and music. She was an only child, who lived across town in a one-story wooden bungalow on a shady street.

Taffy once showed me that she had tied her father's neckties, knotted together, around her doorknob and then around the handle on a bureau – in an attempt to keep him from coming into her room at night. I heard her say this; but I had no idea of its implications.* We hated Bill Bartley – everybody hated him – he looked like G.W Bush but with juggier ears, and he liked to roughhouse with us girls (Taffy and me and our two best friends), and to then use the opportunity to plant a hand on the inside of someone's thigh. He liked to take us for rides on his motorbike, and smirk and smirk and smirk… while the vibrations of the motor aroused him, as his awareness of the presence of the girl-child behind him aroused him too. I could feel this happening, but I had no frame for it – I had never heard of adults being sexual with children. I only knew that his vibe was creepy and disgusting, and I tried to avoid him as much as possible.

One time he blew his nose really really hugely – a mountain of mucus into an aluminum pie plate – and then came and showed it to us girls – laughing evilly. That's the kind of character he was – a level of crudeness and ickiness completely absent at my house. Taffy detested him.

He was a night-guard at a hospital, so kept strange hours. He and Taffy's mother had separate bedrooms, and lived separate lives.

That night Taffy and I slept next to each other, in Taffy's mother's bed (the Mom had gone out on a date). There was just a sheet over us. I was wearing a pale blue nylon baby-doll nightie set, a top and puffy panties – Taffy and I had gotten the same ones, a gift from her mother.

During a sound sleep, I became aware of an extraordinary sensation, *down there.* It felt, in a way, precisely and acutely pleasurable – but in some other way, completely wrong. I had a thought: "If somebody I loved was touching me this way it would probably feel very good." Then I opened my eyes and sat up.

* On his deathbed, from cancer, decades later, he summoned Taffy and apologized for abusing her. Somehow this didn't make her feel any better.

Bill drew his hand out of my panties and stepped back from the bed. He was smirking. Then he lifted the flashlight he carried in his other hand and turned it on, shining it directly into my eyes. Keeping the powerful beam of light (it must have been his night-watchman flashlight) in a blinding stream right into my eyes, he stepped back to the doorway and then stood there. He stood there for a long time, just shining the light at me while his lips did that weird up-and-down thing that expresses such a complexity of generally reprehensible emotings. There was a steady purposefulness in him.

I could not move. I just sat, stunned, frozen.

Then he was gone.

Next morning, a Saturday, I was afraid to get out of bed. I lay there, having to go to the toilet, but too afraid. Eventually I got up and went home. I did not tell anybody what had happened. I knew that Taffy would shoot the messenger and be angry at *me*; and I knew that my mother would forbid me to visit Taffy – and Taffy was my bestie, and she was escape from the poverty and pitifulness of my own house (that house where Taffy loved to come, because there was freedom, and kindliness, and my mother didn't yell when guests were there, so Taffy didn't see that part. And there was No Menacing Dad, only a kindly, abstracted one).

I managed to avoid Bill after that – and when I was fifteen, another girl told of his abusing her, and so then I thought it safe to tell. My mother and Taffy's mother Della – a feisty blonde beauty who looked like the 50's movie star June Allyson – listened carefully and respectfully to my story, and then Della announced, "I'm filing for divorce tomorrow!" And she did.

That was an empowering outcome for me – just far too late. And much, much too late for Taffy. (When Taffy was forty-two her mother finally told her that Bill was not her real father. Della had deliberately had an affair when she wanted to conceive.)

But now I think that that moment of invasion set in me like a crack in a tooth that stays broken, inviting your tongue to go back to it again and again. I eventually became a self-invader, compulsive and repetitive.

Later, in my early 60's, I had hypnotherapy and in the session returned to the scene as an adult, yelling and beating the bastard over the head with Della's spike-heeled shoes, then shouting from the windows into the night neighborhood, "**Pedophile here! Pedophile here!**"

But a child is a child. And I had never been warned about perverts. Our mother had cautioned us, "Don't ever accept candy from a stranger!" And she had warned us not to get in a stranger's car in case they kidnapped us. Both of these scenarios seemed absurd to us; why not take candy? What could be the harm in it? And, why on earth would anyone want to *take a child?* We knew that grown-ups found children maddening, irritating and exhausting. Children were *nuisances*. Why would a grown-up *steal* such an undesirable sort of creature? (Once, a middle-aged couple down the street did offer my brother and me some candy. We did not know the couple really, so they *were* strangers. But candy is candy, so we said yes and went into their house. They gave us jelly-beans from a glass dish. The jelly-beans smelt and tasted stale, as if they had been there for a very long time. They were not very nice to eat. I could not imagine a household where jelly beans lasted long enough to get elderly; but here they were; and so I decided that that must have been the reason we were not supposed to accept candy from strangers. It might be unwholesome.)

Discipline is a Double-Edged Sword

In my childhood, nobody stressed discipline in any form – except in school, which was quite easy, if boring and socially fraught. Our mother badgered us into getting ready each day – that was discipline. But when most of us eventually dropped out, we were not criticized; the school was. Nothing else was asked of us (except when my mother was sick, which happened quite a bit – then I had to babysit and make sure there was dinner and the table was cleared and spread with newspapers and some plates and spoons laid on it. My irascible brother Robbie often cooked.) My parents agreed on this one thing: that a child should have its childhood. Both felt they had been denied theirs.

During my teens I discovered that I could Do a thing – push myself and get rewards. This ran exactly counter to my implicit conditioning, which was quite slipshod regarding ambition. Our mother assumed we were all madly talented and ought to become famous; our father secretly wanted us all to become scientists, but never said so. But specifically, we were never challenged to any goal.

So, like cleaning, discipline was something I discovered for myself. I found it heady.

I had begun to develop the "If it's unpleasant and arduous, do it, and it will save your life," idea when I was fifteen. A young UCR faculty wife named

Sandy (the couple were friends of my boyfriend J.C.) took me jogging – my first time. I had loved running at school, for it was a lovely lonely endeavor, and I seemed to have a slight talent for it. (I hated team sports – waiting for a ball to come sailing along while everyone ran about and shouted, was so boring for me I would nearly topple over asleep.)

Sandy and I set off into the autumn afternoon, on dry paths through eroded gullies and up and down hills into the Box Springs Mountains, up behind the University. Sandy was a slim wiry woman with long hair and a thick brown bang, in khaki shorts and a t-shirt, and good running shoes. I ran just a mile that day (in sandals) but the suffering of stitch-in-the-side, wanta-stop-now gave over into the endorphin rush at the end; and I was hooked. Running seemed a worthwhile thing that I could do, a thing that took me out of the increasingly pointless feeling I had about life in Riverside. I ended up running for a total of sixteen years (with a big gap for most of Poona One).

The discipline of running became a sort of scaffolding for other disciplines to come – including Dynamic meditation. I loved running, and I loved Dynamic – it was just the getting started that required pushing myself.

...Discipline has to belong to passion, not compulsion. And it can be difficult to tell the difference, if you are not much aware of your inner workings. One is a determined application arising out of love. The other is a determined application arising out of fear.

And then, there are all the reasons one gives oneself – and the way that life is not a symphony in black and white (to mix metaphors), but in all colors and shadings. You can have love one minute and fear the next.

But this attitude – do it if you don't want to – could have very unfortunate consequences; as I found out during a visit to Rome.

At nineteen I had sold a story to *Men Only* magazine in London – a very innocent, wholly fictional, girl-on-girl story, written when I was dieting madly to get as slim and boy-like as I could, and thus became strangely if rather remotely attracted, for a little while, to round, soft females. (I thought boys had more fun, as they seemed to be permanently slender, and also easily orgasmic. Confusedly, I thought I wanted to be one.)

The magazine paid me £285, which seemed a fortune in 1971. I bought a Eurail pass with some of it – more because I thought I ought to than because I really longed to roam about the Continent by myself. I manfully left my then-boyfriend in France on a construction job, and took off like a soldier to meet what life might throw at me. In Italy I dutifully inspected cathedrals and works of art and walked miles through cobbled streets trying to shake off packs of youths who would croon importunings at me in six languages.

In Rome I was walking along a crowded avenue near the Coliseum, thinking about where I would spend the night. I had enough money for a youth hostel, but going to one just seemed too easy. I thought that what would be bracingly difficult, what I really didn't want to do, was to approach a stranger and ask if they knew of a place where I could sleep. This seemed a risk-takey hippie sort of thing I ought to do, while a Youth Hostel was… bourgeois. So; I'd have to collar some passerby.

A couple was walking by and I stopped them and asked them. They said I could stay where they were staying. They took me up some stairs in a nearby building, into a large flat, nearly unfurnished. Many people were milling about. Someone showed me a room at the back where I could put my sleeping bag on the floor, beside a woman's bed.

Then suddenly everyone left, clattering down the stairs one after the other. I was left alone.

I stood in the large living room with its white-tiled floor.

Suddenly a door to my right opened, and a young man came in. He had dark curly hair and looked just like all the other young Italian men who murmured at me in the streets: *Sprechen Sie deutsch? Parla italiano? Parlez-vous français?* Do you speek-a Eeengleeesh?

But this one said nothing. His expression was severe, even angry. He did not pause in his movements – he simply walked up to me, took hold of my arm, pulled me to a recessed cushioned window seat, pushed me down on my back. I was so surprised, I was in shock – but I began to cry out – "No! No! I have a boyfriend! NO!" The man unzipped his flies, knelt over me, raped me for ten seconds or so, finished, zipped up, and clattered off down the stairs, a look of disdain on his face.

Rape is a kind of murder. The rapist is saying to the other, "You don't exist. You have no rights. You are not important, you are negated, blanked out. I am going to use your inmost privacy for my own ends, and that's how it is. You are not here. Just your body, as useful to me as a wastebasket." It is a kind of butchery, a crippling.

I did not know that I was allowed to fight, make noise, try to hurt his body in order to escape. As a child I had been taught that little girls are not to do those things. In fact, when once I had been driven to distraction by an older brother's sadistic teasing – he had waggled his fingers in my face, on and on, chanting, "Brat-ling, brat-ling!" in a nasal voice – I had finally exploded and scratched his back with my fingernails. I drew blood.

The reaction of the family (except Glen, who never noticed anything) was instantaneous and intense. I was just plain demonized: I was an evil being, shame-worthy and diabolical, beyond the pale. I could feel the energy of this: the fact that I was female was feeding the disopprobrium – I was somehow an unnatural little girl, a bad witch.

The awful feeling of having my family see me in that way – and the fact that I'd been provoked was not given any weight at all – really spooked me. This, I realized, was a thing one must never show anyone. This vivid self-defense.

Nobody ever explained that that same energy might some day have its uses, and it would be best not to lose contact with it altogether.

...But I should not have been in that flat at all; because I did not want to collar that couple. But I'd *made* myself.

And so there is good, healthy self-discipline – getting up to do Dynamic (thank god for Dynamic, when all the witches in the world could come out of me unhindered, and only help everything get better!) – and foolish self-discipline. By the time the OCD, or whatever it was, set in, I could not tell the difference.

Prayer Meditation

A Letter to Devadasi:

Boat Club Rd, March 1, 1975

Dear Devadasi,

lying on wonderful green sheets & green satin pillow... Many things happening in the body – feels like inside is made of brick and mortar which is cracking in a most unsettling way. Minutely another vanity cracks. I saw last night in meditation: Guilt is Innocence – same energy. When I saw this a Comet came out the top of my head... and I rushed into Sarita's room – she lay naked eyes closed hands raised moaning upcurved lips – abashed, I almost left – then the two spirits joined and we started talking glossolalia together – seemed she had always been there – Words would go in head but didn't come out english... The nature of doubt evaporated for that time.

Huge ants seek across the bed – that is how the energy seeks. Loved your letters – hope you are better now – Bhagwan says he is here so that we can hope... otherwise we would just give up – body is getting fatter and I just have to watch and not interfere with any of its doings – in great weeping discovered whole new being... muscles in back and sides who had been sucked in all this time, coming awake with tingling and fear –

Prayer meditation is getting incredible – when it's over I am a totally drained vessel of energy – just a watcher of exhausted light – lying in the dark unable even to lift my hand if an ant walks on me – Ah mama. Thy daughters are engaged in being human, under the eye of God.*

In the morning all nice gossipy things come bubbling up to write – but now night and only soft warm energy tingling towards sleep. Wish you were here. Amazing what is stored asleep in the body – my toes ... like turtle legs. Write to your greedy little birdies

love

Madhuri

Two Strange Nights

During this first year, when so much pain was coming up, and I was head-shorn, and every bit of energy was going into my process – I didn't even notice the opposite sex. I was clearing all that out of me – the unrewarding tumbles, the heartbreak, the porno movies – and I needed full clear space in which to do that. I was a little child, for gosh sakes – not even a teenager yet, or so it felt to me. Even though new people were arriving – more each day, from West and East alike – I simply regarded them resentfully as interlopers, getting in the way of the first few of us being able to hog Bhagwan for ourselves. I just wished they wouldn't come!

I did not inspect them for possible romantic opportunities. That was the last thing I wanted right then.

* Prayer meditation was given to me by Bhagwan to do at night just before sleep. It involves kneeling up on the knees, arms raised above the head; allowing cosmic energy to come down into the body till the body is filled. This will often involve shaking and sounds. Then, one flops over with arms and head on the floor, allowing all that energy to pour out into the earth. This is repeated seven times.
Then one lies down for sleep.

But one of them had noticed me. He was an older man, partly bald, with a British accent so privileged that he lisped. Apparently in some world or other he was something important – he ponced about, so it seemed to me, with a supercilious know-it-all air. I was completely incurious about any of it, and I had no use for him at all.

His name was Somendra.

He kept asking me for a date, and so I supposed that something was really wrong with him – what on earth did he want with a primal-retrospecting, boy-haired, plumpish, asexual, immature creature? I went on saying No.

Also, he was seeing Paras, a lovely square-jawed young British woman with big lashy eyes and a wonderful head of big glossy brown curls – a no-nonsense, toes-turned-out, practical girl who lived in the room directly above mine in another flat, there on Boat Club Road. So what did the deluded idiot think he was doing, chasing me? Perhaps my refusal intrigued him. But eventually he wore me down, and I said that he could come over, if he accepted that there would be no sex.

So that night he came over at bed-time, and was grudgingly allowed into my room. He lay down on the pallet beside me.

Nothing happened of course; after some brusquely polite little conversings we didn't even talk. I turned the light out, and we lay there. I felt really uncomfortable. My body had peculiar electrical disturbances going on in it, edgy and disagreeable. They were not like the sort of electricities evoked by my Master. They were just weird, jarring and dissonant frettings of my nervous system – yet with a particular bizarre quality I wasn't used to. I was twitching there, unable to sleep…

Finally a thought occurred to me: I could just ask him to leave!

So I did, and he got up obediently and went.

I looked at the clock. It was 2:08 a.m.

As soon as he'd gone, a great relief whoooshed out all around me! Whew! I could rest! The room was relaxed again. I fell asleep.

In the morning I was having breakfast in the kitchen with Sarita and Ma Hari while Mary pottered around. "I had the strangest dream last night!" said Sarita, turning to me. "I dreamt a ghost came through the wall from your room! It felt really weird, and it hung around and hung around… Finally I realized I could just ask it to leave! So I did, and it left; and I opened my eyes and looked at the clock. It was 2:08, and I went to sleep."

There was a knock on the door, and Paras came in to have breakfast with us, as she often did. "I had a weird night last night," she offered. "I was waiting for Somendra, and he didn't come, and he didn't come… I waited and waited, and I couldn't sleep and I couldn't sleep… Finally I looked at the clock, and it was 2:08 a.m., and then I fell right to sleep."

So then I told them about his visit to me, and we marveled and laughed.*

It was around this time that Sarita and Devananda went to Goa for a week. People often wanted to go to Goa, and would ask Bhagwan; and usually he would say no. But he must have okayed it this time, and off they went.

The idea arose in me one night that if I put Sarita's mattress underneath my own, my bed would be softer. So I took the sheets off hers, folded them and left them in her room, and dragged the pallet into mine; lifted my own mattress up, put hers beneath it, straightened it all out, and dressed the bed again.

Then I did my Prati Prasav, which involved acting out things all over the room; and then, in my usual gapped-out, floating, gotten-to state, I went to bed and, lying down on my back, to sleep.

In the middle of the night I was awakened by the strangest feeling! The mattress was wiggling a little under me. At first this was pleasant and I didn't mind. Then it began to wave like a gentle sea, and I tried to call for Sarita but my voice wouldn't work! Finally she came in and I said, "Sarita, did you ever notice your mattress acting funny?"

And she replied, "Well, yes, I did notice it acting a little funny sometimes."

I got up because it was really pitching and heaving now, and then it stopped, and as we stood gazing at it the bedspread lifted and two hands, severed in mid-bloody-forearm, spotted with a couple of bloody sores, came slowly out from under the cloth; took hold of the bedspread and pulled it down.

More disgusted than frightened, I woke up – and took her mattress back into her room, immediately!

I felt strongly that my sister was saying, Don't mess with my stuff!

* The beautiful Paras, in 2017, in Corfu, told me that Osho had, back then, told her to teach Tantra to Somendra. But when Somendra had discovered that this meant that he had to slow way down, he'd lost interest and just wanted to do the usual.

From a Letter to Devadasi

March 1975

In meditation, my lifelong fear is evaporating. It is such a miracle that… so astounded, I evaporate too. Such a simple thing, right under my nose all this time. But it felt like death, so I kept it down. After morning meditation my fingers felt like huge swollen tingling knobs,

Bhagwan,

Bhagwan,

just from the awareness of the energy that has been there all along. There are early feelings of sex and terrified embarrassment locked in it. I am expanding past all remembered bounds, and it is just so mind-boggling. I did not do it, I did not deserve it, and blessings are showering on me. Many times in the day my heart opens to thank Bhagwan.

March 13

I've been doing the fear meditation and feeling all spaced out and empty. I got a message yesterday from B. saying I didn't have to do meditations except working and prayer. It scared me absolutely shitless; I was trembling and cowering so I did the fear thing and murdered a pillow totally. It's really good – good to try it when you're feeling awful. It feels like that what happens after a while is you still feel fear, but when you feel it the energy goes up and disappears instead of brewing inside forever. And I had all these fear dreams last night – snake crawling all over me and I had to sit absolutely still; it was a meditation. The flavor of fear I enjoy when I recognize it – a sort of existential moment – all I am looking at is somehow not real, is dead and alive at once.*

I dreamed of you, you were very close when I woke up. Wow, my gold silk pants won't hardly tie anymore. Praise the lord. I am here, I am here, can be only here. And Herb's ghost lingers, and I am at a loss as to how to vanquish it.

This is a Hindi camp with a very good high vibe. (He speaks Hindi one month, English the next.) Still I am careful not to put my head on the big rugs in the meditation area – cooties. And the blessed Indians still sit all over one's feet in the lecture. It's fun to write to you like this in little pieces when the love & gossip energy swells in me. Oh, maybe there'll be a letter from Devadasi today says the hungry little birdie. Out into the cool morning the beautiful cold-jeweled morning to wait for lecture.

* I don't now remember what this meditation was!

My mother at 16

Herb in the backyard

Me at 4 years old

Top Left: Cluelessly dressed for blue movie, 1972

Middle Left: San Francisco, early 1973

Below: Drawing of me by cartoonist Gary King, 1973

Akin family, 1952; me on Mama's lap

At Lao Tzu Gate, 1976

Osho as I first saw him

The Gateless Gate

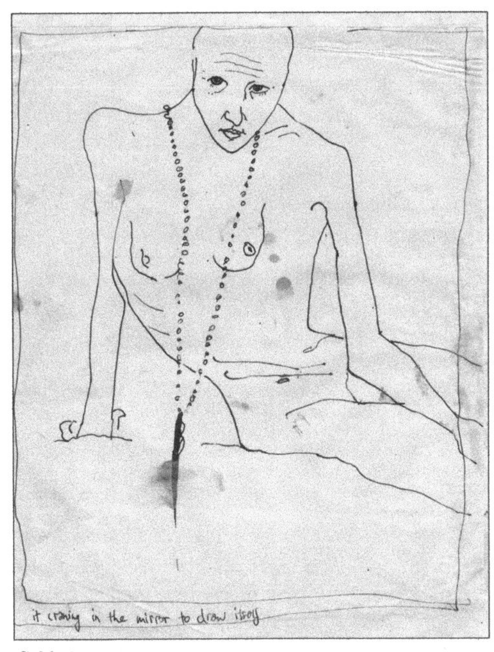

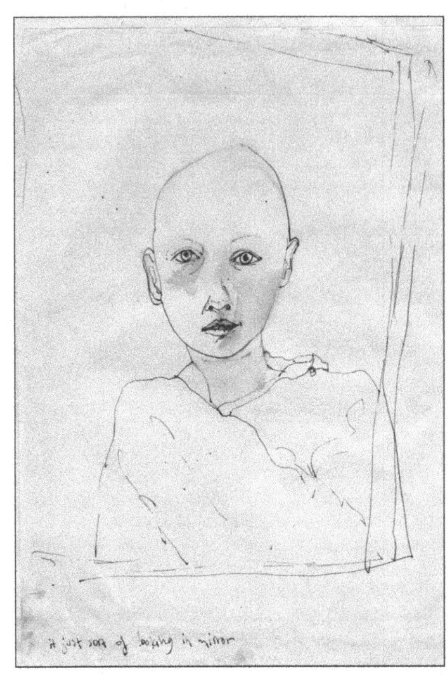

Self Portraits, 1971

My sister and I at gathering, Riverside 1968

My sister and I, Riverside 1969

Nickelettes performance, 1973

Sarita in Latihan, 1974

Kundalini meditation, 1978

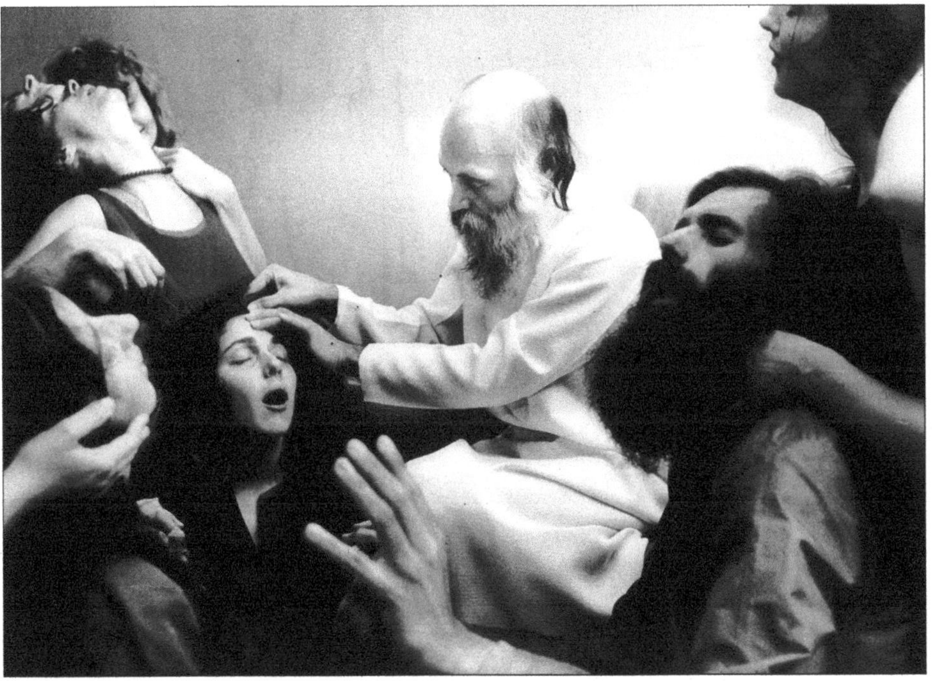

Energy Darshan

Music Group Darshan

Vipassana meditation

Sufi Dance Darshan

Waiting in line for Discourse in Buddha Hall

Darshan, November 4, 1977

Glen's retirement party, 1976 or so

T.Z. and me, 1977

Osho in Mt. Abu

Osho, 1973

rajneesh

ma prem madhuri

मा प्रेम माधुरी

9.12.1973

Sannyas Certificate

On California beach, 1973

Chuang Tzu Auditorium

Construction was proceeding on a new auditorium for discourses and darshans; behind Lao Tzu House and attached to it, so that a new roof was taking shape jutting out from the house. This was held up by pillars – there would be no walls except the ones at the back. Construction occurred in the Indian way: an army of little brown men wearing dhotis – we called these men *malis* (though strictly speaking a mali is a gardener) moved about at no great pace, carrying pans of dirt from here to there, banging on stone with mallets, hoisting things in baskets on ropes, and so on.

One day, the men all stopped working at once. There was a pause, an indrawn breath – and suddenly all the malis were running away from the structure at top speed! Off into the garden they hared!

And then… the pillars began to kneel down like camels… and the roof went FLUMP, down all over the place.

After the dust had settled, and the cool of the evening approached, Bhagwan came out to have a look. He stood there, hands on hips, gazing at the scene.

"What a *beautiful ruin!*" he said. (He pronounced it "reeewn.")

Then the debris was cleared away, construction was started again… and by-and-by we had a beautiful new auditorium, with a marble floor that extended out into the lucky jungle that was what Bhagwan saw from his room. It was roofed stoutly, and was all curves; it seemed to exude a sort of pale green peace while being washed in a luminous white vibrancy.

Many were the adventures we would have there, of the most delicate, challengingly high-voltage, and inward kind.

Darshans in Chuang Tzu

Oh, Darshan. The luck, the privilege. Now the meetings were happening in Chuang Tzu, so there was more space, and instead of a dozen, there might be two dozen people there. As always, just sitting there, so close to Bhagwan, threw one inwards, so that each thought, feeling, energy, was caught in a bright light, visible. I was sure he could see them too.

And it was of course juicy, fascinating, to watch what was going on in the front of the space, where he sat, people coming in front of him one by one. People brought all manner of questions to Bhagwan, and you never knew what he was going to say or do – though whatever he did – like, turn to Vivek to ask her something – or throw back his head and laugh – was always decorous and clean, as if any static, extra fluff, or dust had been unable to even settle upon it.

One night a Buddhist monk sat before him, dressed in his ochre robes. Bhagwan asked him when he'd arrived; but the monk just sat, saying nothing. Bhagwan asked from where he had come – and the monk sat frozen. "How long will you be here?" asked Bhagwan, and still the monk sat unmoving, just staring at the Being in the white robe.

Bhagwan turned to us, and to the translator who had come with the monk. "His conscious and his unconscious are so far apart," he explained, "that when he sits in front of me, and they come together, he goes into shock. He cannot say anything." And, very kindly, the monk was led back to his seat.

Another time an Indian man of middle age sat before Bhagwan and said that he was often angry, and did not know what to do about it. It was really a problem for him, coming up again and again. Bhagwan looked at him, that brief, careful, penetrating look that told you he was sampling the interior of just this soul, right now.

"Go home," he instructed. "Get a mattress, and fold it in three. Then... kill it." He leaned forward. "And do one thing... *use a knife.*"

Birthdays and Celebrations

We celebrated our sannyas birthdays just like our body birthdays, so we each had two birthdays a year, which was very nice. As a worker in Lao Tzu I had the chance to cook now and then for special occasions – I remember once making a wonderful mango cheesecake using a ginger-biscuit crumb crust, yogurt that I'd hung in a cloth overnight till it became cheese, honey (the inferior, sugary honey of India), and mangoes... just incredibly good.

Once, someone else who lived there was having his eighth sannyas birthday. So I ordered a cake from a bakery on Mahatma Gandhi Road (always known as M.G. Road). Indian bakeries were mysterious to me – none looked as if it had been painted or in any way renovated since 1925; they were dark holes with Mustard or Lead-Blue walls. There would be glass-fronted cases with strange flaky pastries in them, of indeterminate age; there were shelves with trays behind the counter on which would be cream puffs with colored 'cream' in them. The cakes were of only a few varieties – no matter which bakery you attended they were always the same: fruitcake, and a very eggy, dry sponge; and chocolate which did not taste chocolately. The fruitcake was also very dry indeed, and tasted like... well, a construction material, more or less. It was difficult to imagine how such a reliable thing as a cake – made with flour, sugar, eggs, milk – could contrive to be so very unpleasant. One could only imagine that chemicals had been substituted for honest ingredients; or the raw materials themselves were shockingly inferior. But even then... But, too, these were British-template cakes – and British confectioneries were not then known for their refinement and excellence.

The bakeries smelt good though, and I went to collect the cake – a fruitcake – and, out of general mischievousness, asked for special writing on the top icing (you had to order the icing as an add-on). I wanted it to say, 8 YEAR OLD CAKE. I thought this was a very funny joke, and hoped that the baker would not 'get it' – but unfortunately he did, and was pretty cross.

We also celebrated Bhagwan's birthday on 11th December; his Enlightenment Day – another kind of birthday – on 21st March; Guru Purnima – a kind of general hallelujah for all Enlightened Ones – on 8th July. Later Mahaparinirvana Day was added, in September, when Bhagwan's father died in samadhi. (The parents and other family members lived in the ashram, in Francis House near the book warehouse Godown.)

Festivals lasted a few days, with Indians streaming in from far and wide, and special food, and more and different meditations, and sometimes a concert; and Bhagwan would sit out on a big chair near his house and give people the opportunity to line up and have a moment's contact with him – perhaps bowing down, or touching his feet (he soon put a stop to this last as he did not like thousands of people pawing at his feet – and nor would you! And, we understood that it was difficult for his body to bear all the crud we all carried.) He explained that the Grace of the Master flows down into the disciple, and that is why the disciple bows. We loved those times – to receive that little bolt of love-lightning was thrilling.

The crowds of Indians were a bit much though, for us Westerners, as they were conditioned to have no sense of personal space. It was deeply offensive to have someone sit on your feet during discourse, or butt forward in a queue, even cutting in front of you, baldly. If you protested, the shameless culprit would just waggle his hands at you cheerfully, saying, "Don't be worried! No problem!" even as he slid in further to back right up onto your very lap, as the crush in the auditorium grew. (Bhagwan had said that it took ten Indian egos to make one Western ego. So Indians didn't demand as much room.)

The conditioning also allowed Indians, if they got a chance, to ask you questions a Westerner would find impossibly nosy (this was an especially popular pastime on trains): "What is your good name? From what country you are from? How much you are earning there? Are you married? Why you are not married? What is your education?" ...But what really worried we women was the threat of being groped by passionate but repressed fellows of all ages – during Music Group (regular meditative improv involving any musicians who felt like playing), or a dance that might be held during a festival; or any large gathering where they hoped they could get away with it. You had to hiss at them pretty fiercely and get away as best you could. Indians were also not allowed in therapy groups or sessions (which were coming to us very soon). Bhagwan said their minds were different than Western minds and therapy was not appropriate; you could not invite an Indian (or a Japanese either, come to think of it) to do therapy in which he had to beat a pillow he was imagining to be his mother.

This last rule was also very helpful for Western women as it prevented much groping which would surely have been tried on; and it allowed nudity in the groups to flourish safely.

(I am very happy to report that, as of 2017, this repressive conditioning, which had been universal, is now relenting enough that the younger generation in India can be freewheeling, joyful, and take their place among frisky and life-affirmative therapees and group participants/leaders the world over. It is so wonderful to relate with people who are unique and wild and exploring, in all their lovely skins and flowy garments, in whatever land. This is the task for all of us: how to disrobe from the grim past and join the party. Welcome to us all!)

Bodywork

So… groups and sessions were coming to the ashram. Bhagwan quite naturally wanted to furnish us with opportunities to free up our aliveness, so that meditation could happen with more of ourselves. I was hugely attracted, as well as scared; I waited to be told to do whatever Bhagwan thought was needed.

But I also had my own opinions of things, and when I heard about Rolfing, I thought, That's for me! Bhagwan okayed my receiving sessions from Prageet, from the States, a tall, dark man with a very straight spine and quite a hairiness about him. He had a stern, know-it-all air (I felt), and kept his strong nose a little above the level. I was still living on my tiny stipend, so I can't now remember how I paid for this, but I must have done; for I embarked on a series of ten sessions.

As bodywork, it was pretty amazing – not like a massage, but more like being dismantled piece by piece – Prageet's long strong fingers finding the knots and bits and bound-up places and literally smashing them, so that I screamed and screamed – but let go, too, and relaxed… and came out beaming and flying and undone. I was good at pain – recognizing the beneficial kind, using it to coast inwards on, letting the breath find its way with the sensation, roaring out the releasing holdings as they crumbled and took to the air.

During about session six or seven, however, Prageet, without any warning or preparation beyond the Rolfing of other parts of me, started to push one of those long strong dark-haired fingers into my vagina. Now, I think there might be such a thing as vaginal Rolfing – certainly there are healing methods, called collectively Yoni Healing, where there is such insertion – but it is done with proper preparation and consent – the client has booked for precisely that, and much time is spent making sure that the vagina and the client both are willing for the practitioner to proceed. The client can then potentially release old abuse, stresses, griefs, or whatever is there. These days, this falls under the aegis of Tantra.

This was not like that. My sense was that it was a power activity: "Let's do this because we are yang and want to impose ourself here. *You* don't matter."

I drew myself up and protested. He stood back and stared at me balefully, not saying anything. I fled, and wrote to Bhagwan.

I received a reply, "It is better for both you and Prageet if the sessions are discontinued and you find another Rolfer."

Later that Rolfer turned up – Canadian Rakesh, a very tall beanpole with a beard and a benign, sweet and funny, completely harmless air about him. And so I had Rolfing all over again, from 1-10, and loved it, and it was nicely safe. There is, in Rolfing, a very interesting move where the practitioner puts on a little-finger condom and goes up your nose, millimeter by millimeter… I had that, it was curiously erotic, and I'm sure it did me good.

Around this time a few different Western massage teachers taught some classes off-campus – campus not yet having space for everything. I took a course in Polarity massage, another in Shiatsu, another, Swedish. I enjoyed them, but I could never really get comfortable giving massages of any sort. My breathing would back up, getting stuck in the top of my chest, and I would feel both barely competent, and somehow overwhelmed.

But then… I heard about a woman who did something called Psychic Massage. I don't remember her name (it was not Sagarpriya, who later taught something of that title). This woman came to my room in Boat Club Road and, while I lay on my belly, she moved her fingers above my vertebrae, not touching them at all.

And so much happened! I felt all these energies shifting and releasing... so powerfully! So much space was created, and I felt the resonances all through myself, finely and surely. I was delighted, and I felt so intrigued by this style of working!

Maun Sadhana

In late spring of 1975 I embarked on a new adventure in meditation: a long period in Silence (I'd done short stints of it only). …So all my focus could go on my own inner, my awareness. It was wonderful, such a relief.

Mid-way, I wrote this:

In Silence

10 days she did not talk
but once,
burned thumb in tea –
the body talked

Yes, I wrote a bit, but I didn't talk. I just moved about in my loose robes, feeling my feet on the ground, navigating between people, having my tea, minding my own business. So enjoying the sense of protection, of restfulness, of freedom! Things got all quiet… and it was so… soft and happy. You forgot why you'd ever blabbed so much.

This continued for thirty days. It seemed that I might never want to talk again.

But one evening in Darshan Bhagwan told me that it was enough. "A lover is coming for you," he said, "and lovers don't like silent people."

I flinched; and then felt all coy and giggly. And then I drew back again. I had no idea what man he might be talking about, but he said incredible, shocking things every day, so I just let this peculiar news bob around inside me with everything else.

The Lover

I had of course been writing to Devadasi frequently and at length throughout all these months. Often I asked for things – underwear, ballpoint pens (amazingly unavailable in India), candy, shampoo, etc etc. She rarely sent them – she had her own troubles, and so little money. (She'd gotten a job at a home for delinquent boys, where she made the queenly sum of five dollars an hour, and had many edifying experiences, which she took in her stride.) Also, sending packages necessitated connecting with someone who was flying from San Francisco to Bombay and could, and would, bring them. She did know a few sannyasins there, and did manage to send a few things – but the number I asked for would fill a book. (In 2010 I had lunch with {still adorable} Herb in Mill Valley, and he was chortling at how he'd asked me what I wanted for my twenty-first birthday, and I'd given him a list two pages long – I think he said there were thirty items on it. That's how it was with me then.) (And, as someone has said, "The purpose of a list is to get as long as possible.")

Devadasi always answered my letters though – caringly, lovingly, warmly, consideringly. Literarily. She was seeing a man she had met at a left-wing political group, Bob. (Not to be confused with Robert of the pizza parlor, now Sw. Anand Bodhisattva.) She still lived on Potrero Hill.

One of the things we'd corresponded about was the problem of my abandoned flats and car and clothes. When I told her I knew I was not leaving Poona ever, she and Herb got together and disposed of the little house, the flat; they had a sale for the clothes; Herb saw to the repossessing of the car by the bank. They may have implied that this was all rather a lot of work; but they were good about it, and I was able to just forget the stuff and the responsibilities altogether. Thank you, Devadasi and Herb! (In about 1998 I came across a box in Devadasi's garage in Oregon, where she lived then. In it were old utility bills in my name from that little cottage on Day Street, and the like. It was like being bitten by your grandmother while swimming in some remote foreign lake, or something. Very odd.)

And then there was that other major correspondent, Robert/Bodhisattva. He wrote funny, self-deprecating letters in a beautiful cursive hand, decorated with skillful cartoonish drawings. He often signed himself "Idiot." He seemed besotted with me, I could not think why; I did not take any of it seriously. I knew he was hoping, then planning, to come to Poona. To me, he was a friend, a rather silly San Francisco relic, full of the stylization and buffoonery of the uninitiated. And yet he seemed besotted with Bhagwan, too; and it was all fine with me, all that besotment; I just didn't think it concerned me.

But he must have been writing to Bhagwan too.

One day there he was, wearing overalls like a grandpa, but orange; and a ridiculous, unsuitable, real coon-skin cap with the ringed tail hanging down his neck. Well, that was Bodhi. It just looked hot and itchy and non-tropical and… furry, that's all.

Mukta summoned me to come along when Bodhi had his arrival darshan. So I showered and put on a fresh robe, and was there in the circle of light when Bodhi was welcomed to the Commune. He bowed reverently, and glowed with his grin showing the pointed canine, and looked for all the world like a devotee of long duration; and maybe he was. Then he opened his mouth and said, as if he'd been rehearsing it, "I want Madhuri to be my girlfriend."

"That will be very good," said Bhagwan, who had an air of having known all of this ahead of time. (Bhagwan did all kinds of things – you never knew – so being put together with somebody was not weird or unthinkable at all – though I don't think it happened terribly often. At any rate, it was all very lively! I never dreamed of refusing – in fact I felt honored – even though nobody had asked me!)

Bodhi was staying in the flat in Boat Club Road, in the room Ma Hari had vacated. For three nights he knocked on my door and I would not let him in.

On the fourth day I finally let him enter… though I felt all giggly and freaked out and distinctly like a virgin.

Here's the thing about Bodhi: he was besotted, and he was a devotee. I was not besotted with him – I just found him easy to talk to, and fun – so I could experiment with what was happening to me in bed with him without my ego muscling in with performance anxiety, and without trying to please him at all! This proved to be a godsend, all told. Instead of having a terrible crush on a man and pining for his touch whilst simultaneously trying to please him so he'd love me – and never asking a thing for myself – or, being used by somebody unscrupulous for his own ends, mine ignored – or instead of dry one-night stands – I had a willing servant. This, I began to discover, had possibilities…

Bodhi said, "I love your new arms" – prodding one rounded one gently. He loved my curves, my new plumpness. He loved my greenish eyes, my bottom, my little plump up-tilted breasts. And he was ready to do whatever it took… and it took a lot.

Bodhi. Such a willing lover. His wavy dark hair to his shoulders when it was out of its accustomed ponytail. His broad, shiny cheeks, green cat-eyes with curling dark lashes – and some background of bewilderment always in them; even hurt. His habitual grin, whether he was happy or not. The slack muscles of his upper arms, used to banging away at a typewriter but not harder labor. His long legs, his small turned-under bottom, his slight tendency to a paunch. The way he would stand up, put his fists in his lower back, and sway from side to side, freeing himself from the typewriter's orderings. Bodhi with glasses on, Bodhi with a cup of coffee, with a little tot of some dire Indian rum in it, five rupees a bottle.

What had I said okay to, when I'd opened that door?

He was quite willing to spend a very long time indeed "down there." I discovered that if I wore a blindfold, and stopped my ears with pillows on either side of my head, and lay completely still with nothing expected of me, not a sound, not even a groan of pleasure, and he took both my nipples between thumb and forefinger and squeezed them rhythmically, and licked away gently… I could eventually, perhaps, at very long last, become undistracted enough, focused enough on the sensation, put my mind aside enough, to be taken over by an orgasm. Then, with great relief and a sense of achievement, I'd lie back and he would hover over me, enter; and I'd look up at his face, and it would be open and maybe scared, his broad cheeks and thin lips and his teeth… and he was my buddy, but he was a stranger then too, and I didn't feel any romantic reaching towards him, I didn't long for him as one wants the faraway. But now I had to let him in because my body had gotten into wanting that, to be penetrated and moved all about from inside, stirring up the organs with a welcome, long-handled spoon. Everything wet demanded it – and then his face would quiet as if in serious contemplation, his grin disappear, his chin go up; and more wet would be added to the first.

Within three days I had a menstrual period – the first in many years. (That had all gone to sleep with the Pill – though I'd stopped the blasted things at sixteen – and with the starving.) Once again I felt the shuttering of my eyes, the crawling back inside myself, the achey pillow inside my loins, the goosh, the mess, the heat, the sleep.

But Bodhi was fun. We laughed together. We had our literary oddness in common. We could talk.

Quite soon, Bodhi and I were in Darshan when he asked Bhagwan if he could take me to Goa. I was uneasy at the idea, since I did not want to leave the Buddhafield at all – why come so far, and find so much, only to go out into the clueless world again?

Although, as I've said, Bhagwan was known to forbid people going to Goa, he said it was okay if I went.

We took the train, all night and much of the next day, creaking along slowly, stopping often and inexplicably. Finally we were in a new atmosphere, jungly and humid, and the smell of a breathless sea came from somewhere nearby.

We took a taxi to Candolim beach and looked for a place to stay, finding finally a room in a 400-year-old house which was half a ruin. There was no electricity, and we lay on a pallet in the dark, vines whispering around the windows. Two ancient sisters who owned the place lived in the kitchen and one other room looking towards the beach.

Goa was strange; a European province eroded and decayed by India.

People ate fish, but also spicy foods – all of it very cheap indeed. We walked barefoot under coconut palms, Bodhi sampled coconut toddy. We walked a long way up the beach to the luxurious Taj Hotel, and I ate, for I think the second time in my life (the first was with Herb), – a lobster. It was delicious, very fresh, served with melted butter (and a shocking non-veg thing to do – for of course in Poona we were all vegetarians). We sat in a restaurant with open sides, from which we could see the sea; it was up high here, the restaurant and hotel having been built onto an old fort. You could walk out onto a circular grassy area atop rough brown stone blocks all built up into a tower. I wondered what labor had built it...

Then we hiked back up the beach towards our lodgings – the by-now familiar transition from luxury to funk that Westerners in India walk so often. On the way we stopped and went into the warm, opaque sea – but this did not suffice to refresh me – my belly felt like I had eaten a block of concrete. The waves seemed to tumble a stone.

I was in those days uncompassionate towards men with skin that reacted to insect bites, or with soft and tender feet – and poor Bodhi suffered from the latter, and found clambering over beach-rocks terribly painful. I sneered a bit – he was no match for my family's hardihood! I thought, in a rare fit of tribal pride. (In Goa, though, you could get hookworm – at least that's where I think I got it. It stayed undiscovered till 2000.)

It was beautiful to see the sea; but I missed Poona terribly – my real life.

After ten days we left, traveling in a boat along the coast to Bombay. This was magical... a full moon shone, we sat out on the deck all night, watching the coast go by, fort after fort climbing the cliffs like lizards with long stone tails. The water lit by the moon and very calm, the air so soft. The boat was ancient; all of it like something from a bygone time.

Then, from Bombay, we took the Deccan Queen to Poona.

Groups

There was one group that nearly everyone who came through the gates was asked to do. The Awareness Intensive – also known as 'that Koan group ' – or 'Who Am I?' lasted three days and was residential, starting with a 5:30 a.m. rising for Dynamic at 6:00. We got to sleep about 10:30 p.m.; and all the hours in between, except for the few spent going to Discourse, doing Kundalini at 4:00, a short lunch, and an hour of sweeping the path or some other simple work – were spent sitting opposite a partner, asking each other, five minutes at a time, "Who are you?"

The askee would then respond with whatever arose in her to say. At first this might be, "I'm a girl with yellow hair from Stuttgart." "I'm a Norwegian man age forty-three." "I'm a doctor." "I'm a hungry person with pain in my knee." But as the layers fall away, the responses venture into absolutely anything that arises: "I'm a giraffe with purple spots." "I'm a broom that swept the path." "I'm a fusty old fart with a soft heart." "I'm a nothing with a hole in the middle." "I'm a tree, a swimming pool, a sky."

And deeper still, experiences of mindlessness come along, yet one still has to say something, and who knows what comes out... For me, that first group (and for many years, this was the first group Bhagwan would suggest most people do) was physically demanding, difficult, painful. So much came up, and lots of it hurt; twenty-two years of gathered and transplanted sorrows and aches and suppressions, springing from their trap, and I had to feel them as they went by. But I found the energy for this, I could hang in, the short sleep did not matter, we got high on awareness and it pulled us through.

I came out feeling like my eyes had widened up so that they were as round and big as an owl's. I didn't know who I was, just that I was not only the pages and leaves of the zillion things I had assumed. And it didn't matter; I was an ongoing Mystery; that was it! Scalding, excoriating, the group had been; but Wow.

Bhagwan also told me to do Encounter, and another group called Tao which involved people being in a room and just seeing what happened, while the group leader held space. ...But first there was Primal.

Primal was led by an American therapist, Divya, a tall, curvaceous Latinate woman with wavy soft dark hair and a slight curving overbite. She had deep-set brown eyes with a lot of sympathy in them, yet a privacy about her that one respected. She walked in an abstracted, Princessy way, her hips and shoulders broad under her robe.

Warning: fashion digression coming!

Divya wore the kinds of robes I called, to myself, 'nursey dresses' – they had high round necks and short sleeves, and darts to define bust and waist. They were often made of terry-cot, the cotton-poly blend many of Bhagwan's robes were made from, that didn't wrinkle. I hated nursey-dresses. The style would have looked terrible on me, with my mound of belly, tiny shoulders, and wee bosom – but it was more than that; to me they looked prim, not at all wild and free. Lovely English Vivek wore them and others copied, I suppose; but Vivek was so pretty and self-effacingly modest, with her bangs and her long eyes and pretty slender-lipped smile – something elfin about her, somehow – she could carry off the prim look. Perhaps she felt something more revealing and self-expressive would have called too much attention to herself, and Bhagwan was the main show. Or maybe she was just being proper for the Indians.

My favorite robes had cap sleeves, a scoop neck, and a wide, tent-like effect, falling to the top of the instep; pockets in the side-seams were a must. Such a robe made me feel breezy, naked, yet covered-up; but with my heart-chakra not all trapped like a higher-necked robe would seem to do. And no stiff terry-cot – plain cotton or handloom felt fluid and light.

Okay, back to Primal.

During those two weeks, I suffered a lot. You are supposed to suffer during Primal, so I guess I did all right. I insisted on tormenting myself with the Obsession, making myself talk about private grooming rituals I didn't even do, trying to rip off my own carapace, even the layers that are supposed to be there. Divya, together with Vidya – a South African blonde with linebacker shoulders and narrow hips, thin lips, a shiny-glowy face, and pale lashes – did their best to inveigle me to come down into my body. Sometimes this would happen, and my mind would be blown, and that would be scary too. I missed Bodhi terribly and there were some secret signalings between us – since I was in isolation with the rest of the group, he and I weren't supposed to talk. When I look back at my Primal diaries I see a lot of cynicism. That wore off by and by. (It is famously though a province of the young.)

Just *being* was hell, until in some moments after a true scream, it was heaven.

I was shown what Divya wrote to Bhagwan about me – I seem to remember we all saw what she'd said, as part of our process. She told him that one had to be careful what one told me to do, because I would do it exactly.

I did the two other groups. First was Encounter, with Sw. Anand Teertha. This one was famously raw and confrontive, and I was scared, but I knew I couldn't escape it. It was a rite of passage in the ashram.

Sw. Anand Teertha was (in my opinion), as the Brits say, "a piece of work." As if the Creator, or Evolver, or his mum and dad, or whoever was responsible, were having a rather strange day when he was made.

He was very tall, thin from back to front as a slat, but very broad-shouldered. His hair was brown/grey and fine, and swept back from a widow's peak down to his bony shoulders, thinning as it went. He must have been in his forties, but his face was smooth as a girl's; and yet the long beard he wore made him seem like a man in his sixties. His eyes were exceptionally small – like little blue spiders with their spiky grey lashes. His lowering grey brows bristled softly with gravitas. His nose was long and thin, with narrow nostrils. His mouth was hidden in the silky beard and mustache, but one knew that it was thin too. In his long, long robe and sandals, he glided and loomed about, giving off an air of qualified light – he was the sort of almost-enlightened person who finds it correct to appear very stern, and almost absurdly dignified. His accent (I am told) was working-class Birmingham, his voice very soft and careful. He looked, in short, like an Old Testament prophet, who would love to harangue small multitudes. His mien was lordly in the extreme.

I began to observe, in this group, that he was predatory towards beautiful girls whilst appearing to be granting them an enormous favor. What does it matter if I look like a strand of cold cooked spaghetti, if I am so illumined? one could hear him asking himself.

There was power in that spaghetti – the arms were big, if unexercised. To me, there was an air of potential menace.

But there was light coming off him – oh, yes there was – like the silvery, cold light off an old mercury-backed mirror, all mottled and not really clear. A straight, tall, cold mirror, telling you that whatever you see in it is all your fault.

He had, one might conjecture, a sense of humor; he is known to have said, "The proper place for a woman is not on a pedestal, but in your bed." If you find that funny, you're more broad-minded than I am.

I don't suppose anyone actually liked him, but he was a force of nature in his own sinister, whispery way, and got the respect he demanded. (He had a very nice brother, also tall, but humbler and solider. Maybe his brother liked him.)

I had at this time only a tiny bit of history with him: someone had given Bhagwan a waterbed, which had been duly installed in his room, and then filled up with water. Bhagwan came into the room, sat down on the edge of this bed (if you can call it an edge – waterbeds are maritimely rocking-chairish) – stood up abruptly, said, "This is not good!" and went out.

So, what to do with the waterbed? Word went out, and I thought that I might like to have it. Teertha was in charge of off-loading it, so I had to talk to him. But installing the thing seemed to carry troubles: was the floor going to hold under the weight of the water? Was one going to be able to get a hose to fill it with? Would the landlord okay the project?

I postponed and avoided finding these things out, and Teertha said to me sharply, "You don't take responsibility!"

This was true; and he was not to be the last person to remind me of it.

I don't remember now what happened to the dratted thing – I seem to remember it did make it to my room, but did not last long.

Teertha's group-leading style, as far as I remember, was like this: get everyone into a room; get them to take their clothes off; then provoke them in a nasal, pronouncing, quiet way with insults, until they blew their tops and started whomping pillows and, frequently, each other. He himself seldom showed any emotion but condescension; sometimes there was an almost-genuine laugh. Everything about him was still and cold and slidey. He was like a bitch-princess who will never be Queen, but who is kept smooth with unguents just in case; he was like a corpse with a steely, yet drifting locomotion; like something hanging from a clothes-hanger. (I am wondering now at my own freedom in mocking this fellow. Where does it come from? I look inside myself… and see a simple rebellion against a self-styled authority. I was, I guess, really feeling hurt by my own willingness to give my power away. But I was young… I can be mean, though, and I do try to curb it. I even sometimes regret this meanness for its unreality: that is, when I am in my heart, meanness seems just sadly misapprehending of how things really are. …But it is a bit too much fun to stop, when someone seems, with a really overweening pomposity, to ask for it! …I shall probably suffer for this indulgence somehow.)

There was one person in the group though whom he did not insult: the most beautiful woman there. I'd seen him taking quick note at the beginning: who is prettiest, most buxom? Here, she was a quiet Slavic beauty with high cheekbones and bobbed hair, and a figure like Jayne Mansfield. Teertha had parked her at his side, and went on tormenting everyone else with smooth authority whilst she sat by, enduring I-know-not-what mixture of feelings.

At lunchtime, he whisked her off to one-can-guess-where.

What he said to me was, "You *were* too thin, but now you're too *fat!*" And, "Your sister is addicted to *happiness*, and you're addicted to *misery!* But you're *both addicted!*" His entire mien told me that I was an absolute non-starter as female prey. Not even remotely a contender. And that this state was beneath contempt.

I survived the group with just a broken left ring-finger, whammed by some ringlet-headed studious-seeming Dutch fellow trying to do the right thing. I never got the bone splinted, and it healed over time with only the barest bulge in the top joint. It was the first broken bone I'd ever had. And I also brought out with me a sense of being an ugly, awkward, stupid, embarrassing creature; not even very good at yelling and attacking people.

Our mother visited the ashram at the height of the Encounter group craze. She came with her man, Bob, who was now Vedant Prem. This was the first time I'd met him; I saw a big, slightly tubby fellow with a beard and an affable yet canny air about him. He had a strong Georgia accent. He'd retired from working for Coca-Cola, become a lefty radical, and he and politically-minded Mama had hooked up. It was lovely to see them – and I liked Vedant Prem. (He was obviously rather hornswoggled by all the goings-on, but not saying anything that might seem impolite – he'd taken Sannyas just to please Mama, and still very much thought of himself as Bob.) But I was distracted, into my own challenging pursuits, and didn't do as much schmoozing as perhaps I ought. However, Sarita was right on the case, and exhorted Mama to do the Encounter group. Mama did not want to do it, but Sarita badgered and harassed, and finally, with ill grace, Mama gave in. (Sarita now regrets her own zeal in this matter.)

Devadasi emerged five days later hissing with rage. She'd hated the group – "It was a *nest of snakes,*" she growled venomously, "and that Teertha is the *biggest snake of them all!*" (Devadasi really specially and particularly hated snakes. California is quite a snake-rich place.) From what she said, Teertha had called her evil names relating to her age, etc. Mama, as far as I could tell, never had any concept of a difference between 'identifying' and 'not-identifying,' so it was then *war.*

Then I did the group called Tao, led by a completely different sort of man. Amitabh was a grown-up – a warm, brilliant therapist with dark hair and a very long and somehow beautiful nose. He had a low forehead, a nice assortment of creases in his face, and humorous, bright brown eyes. He was host to enough self-doubts that he was honest and non-arrogant. He had a paternal goodness and integrity – daddyish really, an older man who looked kindlily on people. He wasn't the least bit predatory – he had a beautiful blonde wife, Anupam, who looked Scandinavian, with very full lips and broad cheekbones and straight soft hair – a lovely being. And Amitabh was a very experienced therapist when he came to the ashram; he led groups rather with an air of been-there-done-that. I had seen Bhagwan speak with the couple in darshan, lovingly, familiarly.

I relaxed with Amitabh and was enjoying the group a lot – until right in the middle, he was suddenly called back to California for a family emergency. Satlok, a therapist in his forties, took over. He was a rather awkward guy with a wiry build and a rough-and-ready face, dry brown hair sticking up stiffly here and there, and a sort of prowling restlessness about him. He was sincere, but himself a newbie in the Commune. I think he was a bit at a loss, taking over the group in the middle. I took against him right away, basically because I missed Amitabh.

The group consisted of lounging around not doing much of anything except whatever arose. The therapist might present challenges if he felt like it.

During an evening session the subject of my sexual backwardness came up, and Satlok suggested I have sex with someone, there in the group, on the floor; and he would watch and advise. I went into a horrified puritanical snit, pulling my shoulders up about me, protesting that I had a boyfriend and wasn't going to be unfaithful. Satlok shrugged and turned to work with someone else. (There was nothing voyeuristic about him. In all the years I spent in the Commune, I never saw sexual ickiness in any man – save one or two repressively-conditioned Brits and some repressively-conditioned Indians. It was not even remotely like the outside world in this way. With no repression, there was no need to be slimy, voyeuristic, and all the rest of it. As a woman, I found it a long holiday from being preyed upon.)

Then, in the after-group darshan, Bhagwan said to me, "You missed! When Amitabh left the group, you also left. It is best to trust everybody, but if you can't do that, at least trust the therapist."

'Missing' was a terrible thing to be accused of. It meant you had missed the opportunity. Something could have happened – some movement, some opening, some release of old identities – and you had stood in the way of that, stupidly, blindly, clinging on… and now you would never know, till your dying day and beyond, what might have happened had you said yes. It was a very bad thing – the only sin. For sin, Bhagwan often told us, originally meant 'missing the mark.' It was not a morality, but a tragedy.

My next assignment was to be the ten-day Vipassana group. This is classic sitting meditation, where forty-minute periods of sitting straight-spined, watching the breath, alternate with twenty-minute periods of slow and mindful walking.

This group was led by Pradeepa, a tall, pretty British woman with curly hair, an aquiline nose, and a lofty accent. Her co-leader was Gopal, a soft-spoken blond Canadian with black-lashed, smiley eyes, a set of black furry brows, and a chipped front tooth. Pradeepa was vivid and quick, whilst Gopal had an air of goodness and a sort of mysterious, taciturn simplicity.

I was looking forward to the group with apprehension and a deep excitement. How would it be, to do nothing, gaze at nothing? With someone roaming about carrying a stick to tap your shoulder with if you lost awareness? Someone who just knew, somehow, when you did go unaware?

Café Delite

Letter to Devadasi:

…I'm sitting in the scungy little Café Delite, (which is exactly like one of the cafés we went to for masala dosa when we were in Mt. Abu), having fresh lime soda, waiting for my bicycle tire to be patched. It's a hot midday… mornings and evenings now are crisp and delicious and noons, sweaty and infernal and dull – and I move in all of it like in a storm, between the drops, guided by the everpresent, eternal… surprised to be okay, okay, okay. Bodhisattva is observing and note-taking at the Primal group all day for his book. He is so open, so affectionate. Every bit more that I open, he is there with open arms to love me. So… neurosis doesn't seem to have a place in our relationship, yet there is no lack of ardor, no limit to prayer. And no end of laughter. And there has never been anything "wrong" with me sexually – I was simply always meant for Tantra, for totality, for the primal, and not for somebody's definition of sex.*

* Looking back, I didn't really know what this might mean.

Be Ordinary

After I'd been in Poona for about a year – and had thus been doing Dynamic for about a year and a half – Greek Mukta came and notified me that Bhagwan wanted me to come to Darshan. I was very excited – normally one booked a darshan when one felt like it. It was extraordinary to be called; but it did happen.

When I sat in front of him he said, "Mmm, Madhuri? Tonight will be very significant for you. From tonight you drop all effort. You just float like a cloud. No more 'Madhuri needs Rolfing, Madhuri needs Dynamic.' Just do if you feel, but you need not push yourself. Mmmm?

"Be ordinary. From tonight you
Be completely ordinary.
You are not going anywhere. You will not achieve anything.
Do exactly as you feel.
If you feel to meditate, meditate; if you don't, don't
Even think of feeling guilty. Move as you feel.
Enjoy. Be happy.
No shoulds.
From tonight you drop all control. Be an animal.
Drop all effort.
You just float like a cloud.
There is no future for you. Be in the moment and enjoy.
Do not think you will go anywhere or grow. No need.
What I am saying to you is, relax. Just relax.
No more problems. Do not have any more problems.
Never bring me a problem again."

I sat there in my usual gobsmacked way, ears open wide, but what I heard inside myself was, "Wow, what a cool thing to be able to report to all my friends! Does this make me sound cool, or what?"

I guess I liked the idea of floating like a cloud – but it seemed so alien that I could not really comprehend it. Drop all effort? How bizarre! Surely I would get fat/slovenly/lazy/stupid! Ordinary… Ordinary? What a weird, hideous idea! Dull! Boring! Nobody seeing me!

Next morning I did not go to Dynamic – but I can't say I enjoyed this. It was all, actually, quite frightening. Effort seemed to cling to me, to be stuck inside me, here, there… It was not in my power to drop it, nor did I really want to, then. It just shifted focus: here, there…

A Letter to Devadasi:

December 1975

A couple other things I really want, if somebody comes who can bring – a soft orange (or white or pink, dyeable) terry or velour bathrobe. And a pair of those chinese slippers but with thick foam platforms – My chinese slippers just broke again. I constantly crave after 'em. {drawing} Anyway, to relieve our grief at no panties having been brought, Sushila stuffed a big hunk of chocolate in our mouth…

Everybody in the 3 flats around here, almost, is in this current Encounter group and they're all going around blown out and hoarse-voiced and gooey with love and amazement and wonder and done-for-ness… Doing meditation seems to have almost dropped – I keep sort of thinking i'll do the kundalini, and yet hardly ever do, and anytime I close my eyes for meditation it's upon me in full swelling power, and a few minutes seems enough…

Living in the Ashram

Before I could do Vipassana, though, Bodhi and I were invited to move into the ashram. In those days if you lived in you were a full-time worker, and could not participate in groups; so I had to let go of doing this one. I was upset! I brooded and obsessed about it quite a bit, with an achey fear I'd missed something precious. But being invited to live in was wonderful, a privilege; the choice was clear. Bodhi and I moved into the newly-completed Eckhart House, a series of rooms-with-ensuite-bathroom in a long flat-roofed building around a courtyard. Big trees overhung it; it was bordered by a broad marble path everyone walked down to get from Krishna and Lao Tzu houses to Jesus House, another mansion full of porches and wings, recently acquired.

And so we set up housekeeping within the blessed Garden of His Love; showered day and night with the ineffable driftings of His Light.

We had a double bed – an actual wooden bed, not a mattress on a floor – with a green bedspread and a mosquito net. A bedside table. A desk for Bodhi's typewriter – he would work with Osho's books as well as with publicity materials. A bathroom with shower, real toilet, bucket and toilet cup. All the walls were white.

We took our meals, of course, at the ever-expanding canteen – delicious Indian vegetarian fare – so we didn't need a kitchen. What freedom! (It would be many a long year before I had to cook again.) There was a long covered porch outside where we often sat, enjoying the shade and a bit of leisure. I was still cleaning in Lao Tzu, and it was convenient for me to clean our bathroom, then walk over to Lao Tzu in my oldest robe and clean there; watching, watching my inner life the while.

Bodhi and I got along well – we were buddies – but as man and woman, as lovers… well, I soon discovered in myself a persona I'd not suspected I possessed: The Awful Bitch. (Ahem – it is true that once, in San Francisco, I'd thrown my shoes at the wall to protest the eating of my jade plant by a toddler niece and nephew. But normally, in any altercation, I was much too frozen with shock to find anger in myself, or even disapproval.) Perhaps it was the relentless proximity – perhaps it was the fact that I didn't yearn for him romantically – but I began to find fault with him. He spent my poor father's meagre-enough support money on that awful rum. He was sort of foolish. He had that stupid grin. And so on. I got quite carpish, and was alarmed. My mother had been viciously hideous to my father, and I did not want to repeat her ways. I wrote to Bhagwan, who had just been talking to us about Socrates.

Crocodile Discourse

I asked a question for discourse:

You spoke of Socrates' wife Xanthippe being a crocodile, and Socrates becoming more and more of a philosopher because of it. I am afraid I am a crocodile… Bodhi is certainly becoming a philosopher; and that's fine for him – but what of the consciousness of the wretched crocodile?

Bhagwan responded:

[…] Just the other day I was reading a book called Bitching, written of course by a woman.

Something has gone very, very wrong. It is not a question of one woman, it is a question of womanhood. But by bitching and nagging and constant quarreling, it cannot be remedied. That is not a remedy for it. Understanding is needed.

The question is certainly right. Madhuri is a crocodile, and she is doing much nagging and quarreling with Bodhi. Of course, Bodhi is growing out of it. He has changed a lot. The whole credit goes to Madhuri. When you have to live with a woman continuously fighting and nagging, either you escape or you become a philosopher, that is certain. Only two ways are available: either you escape, or you start thinking that this is just maya, dream, illusion: "This Madhuri is nothing but a dream... " You become detached. That is also a way of escaping. You remain there physically, but spiritually you go far away. You create a distance. You hear the sounds Madhuri is making, but as if on some other planet. Let her do; by and by, you become detached; by and by, you become indifferent. For Bodhi it has been good.

Now, Madhuri is asking, "That's fine for Bodhi, but what of the consciousness of the wretched crocodile?" Do the same as Bodhi is doing. What is he doing? He's becoming more and more of a watcher. He is not offended at what you are saying and doing. Even if you are hitting him, he will watch it, as if something natural is happening: old leaves are falling from the trees - what to do? A dog is barking - what to do? It is night and it is dark - what to do? One accepts, and in that acceptance one watches whatsoever is happening. Do the same. Just as Bodhi is watching you, you also watch yourself. Because that crocodile is not your inner essence. No, it is nobody's inner essence. That crocodile is just out of the wounds that you are carrying in your mind, and those wounds have nothing to do with Bodhi. Those wounds may have been done by somebody else or may not have been done by anybody in particular, but just by society.

Watch when you start behaving in a neurotic way, in a neurotic style. Watch it!

Just as Bodhi is watching you, you also watch yourself.

And a distance will arise, and you will be able to see your own mind creating unnecessary trouble. You will gather an awareness. Continuously watching things, one gets out of the mind, because the watcher is beyond the mind.

If you don't do that, the possibility is that as Bodhi grows more and more philosophical and understanding, you will become more and more of a bitch - because you will think that he is becoming cold, you will think he is getting far away, and you will start hitting him harder, you will start fighting harder. Seeing that he is going somewhere else, leaving you, you will take more and more revenge. Before it happens, become alert.

I have heard: A man arranged to pay for his wife's funeral arrangements by installments, but after a few months he ran into financial difficulties and was unable to keep up the payments. Finally, the undertaker rang up one morning and said, "Look, either I get some money from you at once, or up she comes!"

Don't create such a situation that one who loves you starts thinking of your death, one who would have liked you to be immortal starts hoping that you die, that it is better that you die.

The wife of one of the club's oldest and more revered members had recently passed away. His fellow members were offering their condolences, and one said, "It is hard to lose one's wife... " Another member muttered bitterly, "Hard? It is damned near impossible!"

Nobody says this, but this is what people create – a very ugly situation. And I know that you are creating it unknowingly, and I know that you are creating it in the hope of just the opposite. Sometimes it happens that the woman starts hitting the man just to break his coolness, just to break the ice. She wants him to at least be warm: "At least be angry, but be warm. Hit me back, but do something! Don't stand there so aloof." But the more you create such a situation, the more the man has to protect himself and go far away. By and by, he has to learn space travel, so that the body remains here and he goes off far away – astral travel.

These are vicious circles. You want him to be close and warm and hugging you, but you create such a situation in which it becomes more and more impossible. Just watch what you are doing. And this man has not done anything in particular to you. He has not harmed you. I know there are situations where two persons don't agree, but that is part of growth. You cannot find a person who is going to agree totally with you. Particularly men and women don't agree because they have different minds, they have totally different attitudes about things. They function from different centers. So it is absolutely natural that they don't agree easily, but nothing is wrong with it. And when you accept a person and you love a person, you also love his or her disagreements. You don't start fighting, you don't start manipulating; you try to understand the other's point of view. And even if you cannot agree, you can agree to disagree. But still, a deep, subtle agreement remains that, "Okay, we agree to disagree. On this point we will not be coming to an agreement – right – but there is no need to fight." The fight is not going to bring you closer; it will create more distance. And much, almost ninety-five per cent of your quarreling, is absolutely baseless; it is mostly misunderstanding. And we are so much fogged in our own heads that we don't give an opportunity to the other to show his mind.

In this too women have become very, very afraid. The problem, again, is of the male and female mind. Man is more argumentative. This much women have learned: that if you go through argumentation, he will win. So they don't argue, they fight. They get angry, and what they cannot do through logic, they do through anger. They substitute with anger, and of course, the man, thinking, "Why create so much trouble for such a small thing?" agrees. But this is not an agreement, and it will function as a block between the two.

Listen to his argument. There are possibilities that he may be right - because half of the world, the outer world, the objective world, has to be approached through reason. So whenever it is a question of the outer world, there is more possibility that the man may be right. But whenever it is a question of the inner world, it is more possible that the woman may be right because there, reason is not needed. So if you are going to purchase a car listen to the man, and if you are going to choose a church, listen to the woman. But it is almost impossible. If you have a wife you cannot choose your car – almost impossible. She will choose it. Not only that, she will sit at the back and drive it.

Man and woman have to come to a certain understanding that as far as the world of objects and things is concerned, man is more prone to be right and accurate. He functions through logic; he is more scientific; he is more Western. When a woman functions intuitively she is more Eastern, more religious. It is more possible that her intuition will lead her to the right path. So if you are going to a church, follow your woman. She has a more accurate feeling for things which are of the inner world. And if you love a person, by and by, you come to this understanding, and a tacit agreement arises between two lovers: who's going to be right in what.

And love is always understanding.

[...] The feminine mind can reveal many mysteries, as the male mind can reveal many mysteries; but as there is a conflict between science and religion, so is the conflict between man and woman. One day it is hoped that man and woman will come to complement each other rather than conflict with each other, but that day will be the same day as when science and religion also complement each other. Science will listen with understanding to what religion is saying, and religion will listen with understanding to what science is saying. And there is no trespass, because the fields are absolutely different. Science moves outward, religion moves inward.

Women are more meditative, men are more contemplative. They can think better. Good; when thinking is needed, listen to the man. Women can feel better. When feeling is needed, listen to the woman. And both feeling and thinking make a life whole. So if you are really in love, you will become a yin/yang symbol. Have you seen the Chinese yin/yang symbol? Two fish are almost meeting and merging into each other in a deep movement, completing the circle of energy. Man and woman, female and male, day and night, work and rest, thinking and feeling: these are not antagonistic to each other, they are complementary. And if you love a woman or a man, you both are enhanced tremendously in your beings. You become complete.

[...] Let love be your prayer also. Watch! Watch the crocodile in you and drop it, because that crocodile will not allow you to flower in deep love. That will destroy you, and destruction never fulfills anybody. Destruction frustrates. Fulfillment is only out of deep creativity.

[...] And help each other. We are together to help each other, to make each other happy and blissful, and finally, to give an opportunity through the meeting of man and woman for God to happen. Love is fulfilled only when it becomes samadhi. If it is not samadhi yet and the nagging and conflict and bitching continues, and fighting and anger, and this and that, then your love will never become a harmonious whole. You will never find God, which can be found only in love.

Yoga: The Alpha and the Omega, Vol. 10, Ch. 4, Q. 3

I quickly wrote a surreal short story about a crocodile, who cleans with buckets and mops; and sent it to my publishers, who loved it and published it in their magazine right away! (But did I learn anything? No... not until much later, when, in the Mystery School of the 90's, I really took in the transmission about men's emotional vulnerability, and women's emotional power; and possible abuse of that power – and the ways that that power can also go *right*. I really got it then.)

I'd sacrificed Vipassana; Bodhi also had had to make a sacrifice. I'd noticed he was very interested in the word 'surrender,' and sometimes he looked blissful about the idea, and sometimes not so much. He had been writing a book, working on it a lot while we'd lived in Boat Club Road. It was on the theme, Who Killed Kennedy? (Perhaps Bodhi's Texas boyhood attracted him to studying that awful event.)

Recently he'd felt the book was at a place where he could show it to Bhagwan and get his feedback. He'd given me a stack of paper to read while we'd been at the flat. I'd read as much as I could; but I'd had to abandon the thing, queasy with horror. I could not exactly explain to him how I knew that the project was wrong and unhealthy – I just felt it. In the manuscript, there was much about specific Presidents and Kings and Dictators, and their secret lives. I don't know where he got his information – this was of course pre-internet – and I supposed that he imagined a lot of it and yet somehow believed it to be true. His focus was intent, obscene, and vicious. I would be willing, most likely, to believe all sorts of perfidy of any number of power-mongers; but *this?* A president's wife deliberately infected some other politician's wife with breast-cancer via oral sex? The whole book was like that – conspiracies, shot through with improbable, and possibly impossible, sexual evil. Bodhi, I reminded myself, was a Scorpio; but still I wanted nothing to do with this stuff. The tone was just ick-making. It was the sort of book that if you were on a desert island with absolutely nothing else to read, you'd still use it to start your fire with.

And that was just what Bhagwan told him to do: "Burn it immediately."

And so, sadly, resignedly, Bodhi had burnt the stack of papers, outside our block of flats. But he did not forget; no, he never forgot that beloved project.

Meanwhile the ashram was a construction site, and would remain so always – as soon as one project was done another was begun. This was the liveliness of things. Peaceful shady buildings where one could sink deep into meditation sat hard by places of dust and methodical laboring where malis moved with shallow bowls of dirt or bricks on their heads, wearing their dhotis, pausing to smoke a beedi under a tree. Chuang Tzu Auditorium was complete, Radha Hall was being prepared between Krishna House and Lao Tzu, for doing meditations in; and Veggie Villas was under construction: behind Krishna House, in the vegetable garden, a row of rooms for residents – four people to a room. And soon the huge expanse of Vrindavan, the cafeteria, was being built, with a broad outdoor kitchen and nearby dining area under a shade, and store-rooms and offices indoors – this all next to Lao Tzu's tall hedge and behind a row of offices opposite Radha Hall.

Food and Laundry

And as to some practicalities. There were no washing machines in the ashram. Scrawny men called *dhobis*, or washermen, went around flats, houses, and also our rooms in the ashram, collecting dirty laundry. (The dhobi who came for years to the ashram smelt fiercely of rum, and was little and wheedling.) Then they took it down to the Mula-Mutha River two long blocks away and beat it senseless on rocks and rinsed it out in the brackish waters. Then they stretched it out on the none-too-clean grass to dry. (In monsoon, it never really dried.)

Then they took the clean(ish) laundry to wherever they had their iron – perhaps a tiny shack the size of a closet along North Main Road; perhaps their home, if they had a different home than such a closet. And they pressed each garment with a huge, ancient, extremely heavy iron left over from the Raj, heated on a brazier. Then they folded the clothes very nicely – they were often grass-stained too, but at least all folded and pressed – and wrapped each stack in paper and tied it up with string, so that you felt almost like you were getting new clothes. (You always had to count the garments you were sending, and keep a list, and count the ones that came back. It was amazing so many did come back.)

And so all that time I lived in the Commune I never had to wash a robe myself, nor iron one; that way, for each of us, the work we were doing, and our meditation, could take center stage. I was, and am, wholly grateful for this.

Nor, as I've mentioned, did I have to cook for myself or anyone else. Delicious Indian food appeared twice a day, lunch and dinner; and for breakfast there was brown bread, peanut butter, and chai. When I think of how much time and energy goes into shopping and preparing food, and cleaning up, every day 'out in the world…' I still feel my great good fortune – for all those years when cooking was not my role! As the Master once said, not every woman (or man) is a great cook, and it is wasteful to have so many private kitchens; why not just have the cooking done in a few big kitchens, by the people who love to do it?

Diary of a Day of Work, Monsoon 1976

Eckhart House, 5:30 a.m.

The alarm rings. I sleep again, wake, and arise in the dark. Light comes through the window from the shadeless bulb swinging from a tree. A moment after I'm up Bodhi rises too, and I unhook the shadowy mosquito net from its moorings and fold it into a cloth bag. I make the bed nicely, with fresh sheets. Lift our one creaking chair and set it outside the tiny door. Fold the rugs and mats and put them on it; sweep the room and mop it with an old red mop.

In the bright bathroom light, while Bodhi stands at the mirror, I come behind him with a new sense of something unspoken; feeling, aware, patient; not heated. Feeling – scared, and exploratory. We haven't touched for days, and I place my arms around his chest and stomach and feel also his private place, which is like embracing a flower: too harsh an action. So I move my hands up and watch them in the mirror there on his chest, white and small and padded, with pointed nails. He is cool too, and awake, and we feel the energies moving from his backbone into me.

I take the hands away, go back to lift my work dress from its shelf and put it over my head, and twist onto my hair the elastic to keep it out of my face.

I step out into the darkness and the wetness of rain and slip my feet into rubber sandals. Walk in graveled puddles to the path to Lao Tzu House. Unhook chain on fence, go past the wakeful guard who sits in his Indian mind like a piece of the house, un-separate, and I go in and dismantle my buckets and gloves and brushes from the cupboard with its banging doors. Here is disinfectant, Vim, a cloth; I'm balancing one thing and then another, turning a tap, scooting a rug out of the way, squatting with the scrub brush near the hole-death mouth of a toilet, again as ever, watching myself firmly or blearily, the energy ever enthusiastic, the mind perplexed at repetition. Scrub, duck, move, squat, wipe, shove buckets, Vim, put gloved hand with wire-scrubber into toilet to scrub away shit particles… Always somewhere inside I retch; then I wipe the wall with a cloth, rise, move, fill bucket, douse the long red floor of the little room with water.

Out in the dark to the side of the house, to scrub the worst toilet, mud of workers, wash the door and walls. Back to the doorway to scrub the garbage-can place and big concrete sink. Then back, bucketed and Vim-handed, into the warm house; put things away, un-glove, then walk back relieved and too expectant through the wet paling morning dark, Dynamic meditation beginning in the hall nearby. I hear thumping gasping sounds of the first stage.

I think of my mending, which I love now, I don't know why. I go back to our clean neat room. Bodhi's put the shaken rugs back on the floors. I shower. He's put yerba mate tea to steep for me. I slurp from his coffee and it's black and hot and sweet and cutting and bitter. I powder my armpits with scentless talc and dress in a dark red robe of soft heavy drapey stuff, and then sit to sew with my tidy tin sewing box and a torn work-dress; I patch it so lovingly, with such care and virginal joy, sitting neat and clean.

Suddenly a frowsy orange-and-white cat, with the used-up look of a recent mother, comes out of the clothes shelf and sits fussily on the bed. I want to accuse Bodhi of letting her in and not noticing, and so I say hysterical things I don't feel, but I do feel the hysteria itself, and when I put the cat out my face itches allergically. I watch the feeling and it is gone.

Now I can watch an emotion in its seed stage and see it through and through like a crystal; and then it is dissolved and gone. But again I sneak out from under myself like a barbed wire fence and am passionate and forget myself, and then again I watch.

We share a banana, and I have a piece of bread with miso and peanut butter, and we have thick sweet ashram tea. Then I hasten out after Bodhi, who has already gone to the line for the lecture.

7:30 a.m.

I'm wearing my high plastic clog-shoes, stepping over puddles and making sure I watch myself. My heart has a slight fullness, swollen, which fades as I forget that Purna just told me I got a postcard from Geetesh from England, which is yet in the hands of a sleeping newly-arrived friend. We take off our shoes and go barefoot on the rain-mud walk beside the house, Bodhi just behind me, to the clean vast auditorium, and I forget my heart and sit against the wall snug and tight feeling the rain so near, oozing and seeping out of the sky, and watching everybody file in. Watching myself watch them, and watch my own perennial morning fantasy of breasts; I always, I suddenly realize, look at the breasts of the women and imagine mine swelling and growing and people squeezing them spontaneously, and then I realize I want to nurse the men I want, want them to be helpless at my all-pervasive incredible breast, pointed like a hot soft torpedo, and Geetesh especially I want to own like a baby, and feed and cherish erotically in eternity this way. I imagine Bodhi there, but this seems irrelevant; we are a yin and yang, not any sort of erotic hierarchy.*

It is in these mornings, with my body clear and fresh, and a little caffeine or sugar just hitting my veins, that nostalgia comes abruptly, as obvious as a black cat on snow, so that I can watch it, and my heart's love of it. For a moment I smell ham frying, distinctly, through the window. Or a chintz-curtained pie-and-coffee shop in some Northwestern town leaps before my eyes, with its safety, its lumpen proprietress, innocent and wholesome. Or black coffee with a lover in a lakeside lounge in forested British Columbia, with a newspaper, and holding hands under the table... and nobody worried about the bill. Each flash is momentary, viscous, and then gone – and I know

* A man I had a crush on.

so well in all of me that here is the end of it all, the place to end all places, the morning coffee to inherit all other morning coffees forever.

8 a.m.

Then He is talking of power, of people wanting power, and I watch and feel Him instead, and I become empty and roaring, feeling him being me. He is speaking on the Buddha. How to speak of words, I no longer want to speak of them. It is futile. He says the same things over and over; it is exactly as if I tried to speak of a tree having leaves, and all the while I am sitting with the leaves, and my heart is a leaf too, fat and red and beating; to speak of him to you is futile because there is too much of him. We have all had rhinestones and dime-store glass so much, you will not be able to believe that I, one of you, have known, has found in the mulch of the jungle a pile of rubies, amethysts, emeralds and diamonds; whole and healthy and gleaming in my hands, all the more beautiful for the mud. I don't expect you to believe me because I can put no effort out for belief or you or anything. My ambition has gone and only my impetus remains and that is going; each time it digs deeper its hole in my heart so that it can vanish more.

His voice has a cadence to it, a special kind of music found in Krishnamurti too, a connectedness with Nature, yet different from the direct issuing-from-Nature I feel in Walt Whitman or Bob Dylan, whom I consider on the deep verge interior of Nature. His voice has not their passion, no, nor their concern, their belief and wild love. Bhagwan celebrates, but from the cool heart of non-doing. From non-being he brings his words like camp-fires on ice-floes, wild natives against a background of clear white sky.

He speaks and I nod and Be and watch and hold and feel and drown in Satsang... the presence of the Master; a despair and a waiting and a bliss so great it is not pointed but is rather the very air, the breath of the auditorium.

I sit, back against the wall, eyes closed. I feel the power of the presence that comes through him, surrounding everything, permeating me magically. It is magical, and yet so natural, the way the energy rises black and blossoms yellow in my skull, pressing out with all its might on the whole front of my brow, like white blooming hands smashing to get out. Each swell, when it reaches throat level, before the ascent to the brain, carries me in a moment of suspended, washing bliss, dis-attached and rivering upwards like fat black up-surged honey. I sit, and my hands fold into one another and in my stillness become one hand, and that vanishes; I am suspended. Then, later, I listen to my bottom hurting and, instead of letting the pain feed into the upwards energy, I shift position, and sigh, and relax again.

9:45 a.m.

When he is gone again hands folded, smiling, throwing his towel over his shoulder, precisely at the door to the house, and I have looked at the back of his head with its poignant bald energy white and clean and sword-like, I go quickly and up-end myself at his altar and feel again the non-happening, or indifference to happening, that my inner world is made of right now. Then I go out, and around to the driveway and a different door. Into the hallway, the red corridor, and suddenly I'm in hush; the screaming gasping Indian, casualty of all that Satsang, heard still; but my feet are bare as a nun's on cool tile, my red robe flows around a body that is always happy here in this walk down his dim hallway. I feel elegant and spine-straight and voluptuating. Devananda is in the store-room and I see his narrow t-shirted waist and go in and put my arms around him and hold him lightly with my head against him, and he says, "Mudpie," with calm affection; and continues his work. I rest my head against his shoulder and then go out again, feeling some sadness I do not know. Maybe it is the way his body was, so small and broad-shouldered and narrow, and his ponytail, and the grey rain out the window, and the workingness of him in there fiddling with wood and screwdrivers, and my own emptiness and never-be-filledness. And that I needed, and that I've been with God for an hour and a half and never saw him.

Sadness continues through the light work of the morning, which is really heavy but feels light now because I don't care anymore. Some intense madnesses come over me and I write him questions and plan many letters to him; all feel so important. But this morning I scarcely see my work, I have to keep remembering to relax my shoulders, which try all day long to hunch up and keep my mind company. In the mirror in the guest room I relax them, like them better; despair that they won't stay that way, give a purposely hazy look at my body in its knee-length work dress; I don't like to look at it open-eyed. Looking at the drab, thick-bellied creature standing there, unbelieving that it houses immortal divinity, I turn back to work. Cleaning is today fairly painless... Then it's time for lunch.

12 noon

At the canteen, Bodhi greets me with chapattis and cabbage salad and bean-sprout soup and bread and butter and yogurt. He sets these on a table and hugs me with his smiling sweet body. For those with rupees, which means not us, there is coconut banana cake and fruit curd. The canteen is a tiny sadhana for awareness while ingesting; crowded, inconvenient, six chairs for two hundred people. But the food is delicious and healthy. We eat together, Bodhi and me, and talk.

12:40 p.m.

Home: our small green room in the jungly couples' compound of Eckhart House. I would wash the yellow bathroom rug out but it's so raining. Usually I mend. Today I fold myself into a Newsweek, somewhat happily. Then it's time to rest. I blindfold myself with a folded silk scarf because I can't find my proper blindfold, and I watch myself wanting to blame poor Bodhi for that too. I put a lungi over the rest of me, face too, and pad my ears with pillows and sink to some depths; sea-lulling, rocking, sinking, oblivious until the alarm rings.

2:40 p.m.

I rise, shower, put on the same red robe, and go to work.

3 p.m.

I work. Yes I work, yes I work… in the afternoons I clean bathroom taps and shine them, clean the same downstairs bathroom again, take buckets and broom and clean the messy store-room, wash rags in Dettol water and wring them, then take them to hang on the broad airy white-tiled roof on lines. And up here I celebrate the tiles, lilac-flowered vines, clouds, grey rain seep, and I sweep and then take a broom, the tallest of brooms, thin-handled like a young palm tree, and I go into the white upstairs corridor with its green ceiling so high up under the eaves. I scrape and crane my neck back and squint to keep it out of my eyes, the debris of web and spider which showers down on me, so I am a mess of white running spider bloblets and grey web. A long pole comes out of me swinging with descending transparent spiders, so many of them, never have I seen so many, and the floor dotted with grey stuff, leaving a satisfactory mess to clean up. Then I swing the broom far out over the descending stairs, clearing the webs from the rafters, and a huge black hand-sized moth flies about like a bat and perches, flat against green wood. I am alive with wonder at what I am doing here, a long pole with a small life on the end, pushing and moving aside my days in the act of cleaning. I am moved by my spiders and webs.

When all are gone I take the long broom out on the roof and lay it waterproof on the big pipe under the overhanging ledge. As I step away from the overhang I slip in a spot of perennial slime from the damp… it's almost but not quite a fall. So often I nearly slip and break, and then I wake – and see that I have been dreaming and will awake only at danger, quick and slicing.

Then I go back down the stairs and use the smaller broom, still a ceiling tall, for the downstairs corridor. Then it's the big upstairs auditorium, plants and things, brooming and washing marble edges compulsively; scooting around on my bottom with a damp rag, and sweepings and moppings of corridor and stairs, thinking madly now to write, holding it inside me.

I see that what I am doing here is watching: watching me, seeing me, as much as possible, and it is the whole purpose of the work. The agonized primal screamings of people getting Rolfed come from Jesus House across the garden, and my mind is going on about Him and writing and me and who I am and energy and what I'm doing and what it's like to lose me.

5:30 p.m.

Kundalini meditation has started. I hear from afar its snake-charm music for the shaking, dancing, sitting, and still, passive rest which takes the day of the meditators and brings it into evening. Here we walk so many different levels and paths; I feel more elemental and almost more afraid, though quietly, featurelessly, since my life has become only work and no meditations, no love, no writing, no anything but work and the sleep between the work, which is so full of energy it is not even a sleep, for I am not heavy or involved.

5:45 p.m.

I go down into the womb-red corridor with its hanging yellow lights, and prepare my mops and rags and buckets, empty the trash, wash towels, which is my favorite thing – I have affinity with cloth, especially old raggy cloth, it is like me, and I feel always a surge of joy while standing there, in one place for once, scrubbing the cloths with laundry soap and brush, and then going up and hanging the rinsed, wrung-out, many-colored towels and glass-cloths and dusters on the roof-line, feeling like my mother in a clean good mood. I put the washed mops up on the roof too, standing against the waist-high wall.

I go down the winding aluminum-painted stairs to pick up the broom again, and start the long sweep of the red corridor, complicated by bookshelves, shoes, rugs, and striding feet and beings. I sweep and bend, think and bend and sweep, I am full of writing and cannot see. And then it's the mopping, long and arduous, down the same long turning cornered corridor, with later feet now, and the Darshan being prepared, and people waiting outside crowding at the gate to be in Satsang, intensely present with the Master, where he hits you open with whoever you are and leaves you there. Where he chuckles and wears his hundred faces. I need to see him. I am so scared for days before seeing him that it is like being in a dentist's drill the whole time. God, really.

When, one day, I am finished mopping, to my surprise... I wash the mop out, filled with evening grey heart, expectation of freedom. I go up on the roof one last time to place the mop there with the few last rags. The expected peace is settling over me, the deliciousness of the evening, my evening... He has owned me all day and still owns me and I am confused, but I go downstairs, change, wash hands, and take my warm body into the grey wet evening in my red robe again.

7 p.m.

They've already gone into Darshan, and I talk to beloved Asheesh {the carpenter} again about the robes I am mending for him because I love mending and because he put a wooden protection around my mala to keep it from shattering as I bend and bump against the bathtubs in the morning. I go towards home, aching for the pen and the fat paper, wanting so much to pour myself on it, which rarely happens now. But tonight I betrayed it; instead of my evening of mending and singing Bob Dylan to myself, an invitation to dinner has come from Deepesh and Kaveesha, and Bodhi's going to miss Music Group, which he doesn't like any better than I like not writing, but for some unknown reason a dinner invitation is ultimately compelling.

I go, in haste and wrong-feeling, high with the need to write, knowing I am wasting my heart, destroying the moment of opening, the door to the writing which has been building and stating itself in me all afternoon, beautiful as parrot-green, quick and sudden in the air. So I sacrifice, and watch the high energy, and watch the people and my own built-up nothing self, and wish to be home, and even ice cream isn't worth it, and just makes me want more; and Kaveesha is reading my poetry and says, "New Yorker," which hurts the veins in my hand and wrists, which no longer want to aspire. And I melt and melt like butter on Sambo's pancakes away from all that.

We come back in a three-legged rickshaw and I clean our narrow white-tiled bathroom... so gratefully, happily.

9:30 p.m.

I clean naked on my hands and knees, in rubber gloves, Vim and scrubbers, smashing a tiny baby of the Tribe of Cockroach with the heel of a gloved hand. I wash out the rug and hang it on the towel rack, scrub the toilet with long-handled brush, and love the fight and pull and struggle of the cleaning so late into the night, my native activity, cleaning, though I am totally indifferent to it, really, I think. It is so clean, though, such an endless clean thing to do, so awake, so active, so cleansing, so purifying. Nothing of the sleep or the grave, the meat or the wine or the decadence, the tiredness or pillows, no.

And now finally I am writing... belatedly, tiredly, but wholly and as if possessed. This, too, is my native place, or illusion; no doubt illusion.

10:30 p.m.

We are under the mosquito net, and Bodhi is reading a good simpatico mystery, and soon he'll turn the light off. Sleep will come, black and gone. This is my day every day, cleaning, deepening, listening, cleaning, and thinking too much sometimes, or getting moody and fuming, but always holding on to the work for dear life, though loudly I grumble and moan.

He is here all around us, and I sleep.

Zen Stick

A Zen stick is the long piece of polished wood employed by a Vipassana meditation teacher – traditionally a Zen master – to lightly clobber a meditator on the shoulder if the meditator's attention wavers, she daydreams, or is falling asleep. The stick intrudes sharply on the dream and one straightens, abashed, and goes back to the task at hand: watching. Awareness.

The term is now used to denote any uncomfortable event which brings a sudden vividness back to one's presence, one's focus on the moment.

I had read a biography of Bob Dylan I'd found around somewhere. The words of many of his songs were in it – and they got under my skin, like the music that they are. People thought Dylan was a prophet, but he was just a poet, just a musician; he always made that very clear. For me, the melancholic wonder of his rhymes and phrasings, the mysteriousness of his imagery, was enough – I went about singing inside myself, blissful with the achey blues.

I wrote him a letter, telling him about the magic of this walled garden in Poona, India. I have no idea if he ever got it. Still infected with the music, the often-nonsensical-seeming wording, my own rhymes and phrasings began to emerge, and the sounds felt like they were bulging, wanting to come out. I wrote a handful of discourse questions from this space, mixing up my and Dylan's words. I remember one in which I quoted, "Tears of rage, / tears of grief… / Why must I always / be the thief?" I don't really know why that bit stuck with me, it didn't really make sense, but I loved it, it just sang to me – something like, Yes, I am an idiot, and not as pretty and wise as my sister, but I'm here too and I want to be seen and get energy and love unconditionally.

That is what I was really saying, and my child self was saying it to my grown-up self – . But at the time I hadn't figured it out that far.

But far more than that, I was in love with the sound of my own voice, and with Dylan's voice, like the voice of the crows over the railroad tracks on a desert morning when the world is as lonely as the underside of a shoe.

Nothing happened for a few days, and then: someone had asked a question in discourse, which concluded like this:

[...] Sometimes I know I am a fool and in those moments can hear the birds and see the sky.

I have written questions for months and not handed them in because they all seemed foolish when the moment passes.

And Bhagwan answered:

First, all questions are foolish. I have never come across a question which is wise. How can there be a wise question? Questions are foolish. All questions are childish.

One of the very important therapists in the West was Fritz Perls. He used to say to his friends, patients and disciples, that only children ask questions. That seems to be perfectly true. Only children ask questions.

Have you ever walked with a child - just a morning walk? And see - he will not allow you to walk at all. A thousand and one questions... each step brings questions. "Why is this tree green papa?" Now who knows why this tree is green? Everything becomes a question for a child. Put anything in a child's mind and out comes a question. The whole mechanism is question-producing. Anything, any small thing - and the child immediately makes it a question.

Questioning is childish. The more your maturity comes, the more you grow in maturity, the more questions disappear. And when there are no questions, there is a possibility to see. Otherwise questions are clouding the eyes and the mind so much.

This is my experience – answering so many and their questions, I have come to observe that it almost always happens that the person who asked the question never listens to my answer. Everybody else listens. He is so much concerned with his question, he is so much worried with his question.

Others listen and understand better, because they are not involved at all. This is not their question so they can listen silently. There is no worry about it. Their ego is not involved at all. But the questioner becomes very much involved. His ego is involved. He goes on looking from the corner of his eyes – what am I saying? He has asked the question to be appreciated. He has asked the question in search – not of the answer – but in search that people will think he is very knowledgeable – look, what a beautiful question he has asked! If I don't answer questions... A few people go on asking. For example, Madhuri. She goes on asking every day, and I go on throwing her questions. She is more interested in asking than in listening to the answers. Because it is not a question that it has to be your question. Anybody's question is your question also. Any question that has happened to any human mind is part of you. If you listen rightly, it will solve many problems for you.

It will give you insight, clarity.

But there are people who are interested only in their questions. If I am answering their questions they cannot listen because I am answering their questions, and they get into excitement and fever. If I don't answer their questions they are sitting there limp and dead – "Again this man is not answering my question." Questioners are in trouble. The very effort to question is a little immature. In the old days it was the custom, it was the tradition to go to a master and to be with him – not to ask anything, just to be with him. Because what is there to ask? Even to ask, one has to know something, and one knows nothing. So what to ask? One has to be just with the Master, to imbibe his being... just to be soaked by his presence. One has to be like a sponge. One has to be open and receptive.

[...] The answer is in your inner illumination. The answer cannot come from the outside. I cannot answer you. The answer is in your certain state of centering.

So the questioner has felt rightly – all questions are foolish. But I am not saying, "don't ask," because I know the modern mind is not the old mind. Great changes have happened.

Now if you say to somebody to wait for years, then nobody can wait. The modern mind is in such a hurry that it is not in a state of patience, and the modern mind has been trained to ask. The modern mind has not been trained to be.

That's why I go on answering your questions. Not that your questions are worth answering, or that answers are needed, or that I can answer your questions. No, nothing of the sort. I go on answering you questions because questioning has become part of the contemporary mind. Only by and by will you become able not to ask...

The Discipline of Transcendence, Vol. 2, Ch. 6, Q. 2

Such a stick... it hit me right inside my torso, deep as anything. I sat and let the shock, the ache of it move through me. Certainly I felt more awake! I felt embarrassed as hell, and hurt too... misunderstood. My question had been meaningless – and yet not. And he was right: I liked the music of my question, and can be quite, quite deaf to answers. That is something for my own pleasure; my mistake was to bother him with it!

Zen sticks were a privilege we all lived with, hoped for, dreaded, expected, did not expect. One day, sitting in Chuang Tzu, listening to him, I heard him chide a pretty blonde American girl for being the girlfriend of Yogi, a much older doctor from Hollywood (a gnomish little man with buggy round eyes and a very polished air). Bhagwan said the young woman was just with Yogi for his money, and that this was ugly. She rose up from her seat shrieking a great wail – *"Ooooohhhhhhhh!!!!"* and ran out. (But that was not what he had said to me, about Herb and money, in Mt. Abu. Perhaps he could see that I loved Herb? Or that my way was somehow different? I don't know.)

There was another Zen Stick blow I got which was really funny, and merely bewildered me instead of freaking me out (or at least, not too much!)

Someone asked a question:

Beloved Master,

I am seventy now, but still the sexual urge is there. What should I do?

Narayandas, you should not do anything. Enough is enough. Just the other day I have received from the great Madhuri a beautiful Christmas card. I must have received thousands of Christmas cards, but this is the most beautiful. And particularly for you, Narayandas.

From twenty to thirty,
if you are feeling right
it is once in the morning
and once at night.

From thirty to forty, if you are still living right,
you skip the morning
but continue at night!

From forty to fifty, it is now and then...
and from fifty to sixty, it is God knows when!

From sixty on, if you are still inclined,
believe me, fella -
it is all in your mind!

Happy Christmas!
The Dhammapada: The Way of the Buddha, Vol. 8, Ch. 6, Q. 6

I was, to put it mildly, flummoxed. I had not sent him a Christmas card! Why would I send somebody a Christmas card? I was not a Christian! And to send such a tacky thing to my Master!? Then, I certainly had not sent him the poem. I didn't truck with such rubbishy poems; nor did the sentiments mean anything to me – I was still in the first stage of things, as described in the poem! All the rest of it was a foreign country I had no interest in!

So why had he pretended I had sent it?

I didn't trouble myself about it over-much though – he was just mysterious, he was no doubt taking the mickey out, and that was okay!

But when I was in my sixties myself, and Subhuti resurrected this gem and sent it to me on Facebook, then I had to laugh – because it was all true. At sixty, the whole rumbustious business of sex was neither in my body, nor my mind, any longer.

What did Bhagwan know, so long ago?

Another time, someone asked him about his own sex life! And he replied, "I bathe wearing my lungi, because I hate to gaze upon the unemployed!"

Big Black Birds

We sat in Chuang Tzu Auditorium on a winter's morning, rapt and still. He spoke, and the vibrant magnific wonder wove itself in the air all about us, and penetrated as deeply as it could go into our interiors. All caught as one, we tried to let it in as best we could, that freedom borne on sound; that freedom massaging us without sound too – and to notice its path – first down in; and all about; then pushing or gliding up through our chakras till it touched the blue sky high above the auditorium roof. Our hearts gaping open for the passing.

Suddenly another sound came shrieking through the space! A huge black bird, beak pointed yet open, wings flapping like witches' rags first, then held tight to his body, an unearthly screech coming out of him, flew like a missile right in over our heads and hit the wall beside Osho's chair. Then the creature fell to the floor, and did not move again.

This happened again on a day not long after – another kamikaze crow, or raven, or whatever he was – screaming and blasting through above us and then dying against the wall... And again.

Someone asked Osho why the birds were doing this. He said that they were dying there deliberately so that they would be born again in a higher form.

Sometimes we got from him these esoteric nuggets – this one like a strange rainbow-coal jewel. What a thing to ponder!

Once somebody asked him, "Are there beings we cannot see at these discourses too?" And he replied, "If I said no, it would not be true. If I said yes, you would not understand." And he went on to the next question.

Tribes of monkeys with cynical eyes sometimes swung through the treetops above the auditorium; and they might peer down at us before moving on. Flocks of chartreuse parrots came through too, pausing in the treetops like a few dozen peridots all communing, while we sat below, joyful in our lit-up jungle. This was the mystery and the color of our Chuang Tzu mornings.

Music Group Darshan

One night there was a singular event: a Music Group at which Bhagwan was present. It was the only time this occurred. Here is what I wrote after:

The musicians sit cross-legged in a circle on the marble floor under the colored lights, heads bowed over instruments or thrown back meditatively. The first tamboura notes, drumbeats, and they are in tune and it has begun. I have emptied out my brains; he has caught them and I am free.

Bhagwan sits in white on a black chair under white lights, and as the music rises, he becomes just a suffused light, power source, there at the end of the open hall – thick, heavy, powerful, an explosion of light. Silent, a man illumined, he sits in flame.

I feel my body stir, and I know that my mind is gone and willing, and my body wants to move... I want to begin now – though everyone is still silent, and only one or two others have begun to sway or stand...

I rise and open myself to the music. I sway, then begin to twirl. Twirling takes over. I'm not listening to the music now; I'm just dancing, letting it move me without separating the sound from anything else. I'm very much concentrated within myself, and every awareness of the outside opens the more I twirl; I'm a vortex, in-focused, out-whirling. Faster. Others are up and moving but I see them only as shapes to not bump into, dancers in my dance who magically weave aside when I'm there.

Inside the twirling I feel his energy as a vastness, a sort of endless twirling galaxy of truth; of the way things are. My rapid rotation is to penetrate this. The speed of my body roars to the speed of matter, as matter dissolves and I am here, the penetrator, penetrated. I whirl and steam.

I am joyful but without flavor. I am movement. Red shapes spin by. We are all confused by him, so confused that we are shaken and rearranged into vapor bodies, and we think they are real, and the thoughts keep intruding, trying to make sense out of the movement-by-movement opening. He is the sun, the earth is music; we are three dozen red eccentric moons.

We are supposed to move round and round the circle: it helps the musicians. Usually I want to stay in one place, but tonight with this twirling, I feel as if in a dream of flying, where all is powerful and awake and here. I'm a sensate toy, a top, a-whirl, around and round the huge circle on and on.

Again and again I approach the area at one side of the circle where his light shines. He is sitting over there in his chair, and hot bright light is shining from him, far too bright to bear. Nobody wants to be in that area in front of him, in his direct gaze; the dancers stay away from it, as though thrown backwards by a strong and blasting wind.

I find myself magnetized by that open yellow white space, and I let my breath out and twirl right out into it, as on a stage. I'm invisible in my whirling, and naked too. Even my brain is naked, thoughts blown into a fountain which shoots out the top of my head. Every time I pass him, I'm changed. Every time I pass him, another place in me, a terror, is exploded upwards and eaten by the brilliance of the present before my eyes, in my eyes, behind them in my skull, and up out the top of my head. And somewhere I am embarrassed; are people watching me?

But even in my loose robe I'm naked. I twirl. And again I find I'm drawn, compulsion, or is it him? – to that certain spot somewhere to the right of him, near the edge of the curved hall where the dark garden waits beyond, leaf on leaf; and I can see beside my turning feet the low edge of marble, dropping off into the black. Afraid, I tear myself away, hurl across that white space, into the safety and momentum of the other dancers. Wondering if I've missed his challenge. I'm caught now in the small spaces between the liquid mixing of the others, and I am of them, and they of me, red and flowing. And then again I'm compelled in front of him.

Each time I pass him the twirl grows mad in a different way, as if a different layer is igniting. My ears open to the music, my hands suddenly respond to it, opening and closing, giving character to the river of sound-lilt out my fingers.

Thoughts nudge and urge me, and when I throw one away, I'm released for a moment, bigger, more made of music. In front of him each thought is bare as a fly on a light-bulb. Light invades my brain, utterly knowing it. The release upwards of each thought gives energy to the whirling. Faces pass, suddenly clear, then blurred again. Padma passes with Yuthika holding her waist, running at incredible flowing speed, with ordinary expressions on their faces. I bump into a soft breast somewhere and the dancer just smiles, and I smile out of the side of my head as I go on: Each of us is alone here, and understood.

...I feel us bending to the mid-space of now, faster, trusting utterly in speed and darkness, disturbed by the penetrating light, exalted beyond bearing. We are twirling on top of his flame. I am huge. I am as big as the auditorium. I twirl infinitely as though aloft, taking the huge space. I am fast and high as death.

My hands leap into exact vision, held out in front of my blurred gone body. The hands are still and precisely detailed against the indistinct flesh of sound. Something peaceful exudes from them; they are so still even if gesturing to the music; that peace flows up into me. I am me and my hands in a twirling world. Only I am still, and I can twirl forever.

Sometimes a thought comes that I'll be glad when this is over, that I'm not in need, I'm just doing, just letting dance happen through me, not caring, and I won't mind a bit when it's over; I'll be glad. The thought relaxes and I go on spinning.

The music is getting older. Once it fades down in unison, almost stops; then starts again in different time and different tone. New steps come out of me. The rotation of my body loosens and I'm here, not a bit dizzy, just here suddenly in this stepping body, as though my whole form is a foot, stepping, lifted from above. I step with me. It steps me. I step here, there, here; forwards, sideways, unified as a foot. I am one. The thought spills forward out of the front of me, forward I step as me into me. I am way off the ground but the marble is up under me, too. I step with my hands, they are feet. Hunky motions sway me here, backwards there, funky as a stepping train, low as high, hands as feet. I step by holding the air with my feet and hands.

He is watching me. I see each dark-lit leaf nearby. Now instead of wondering at each movement – Do I really need to go that way or not? – I see with light pleasure and huge joy that everywhere I go is right. Everywhere I go I step into myself. I shake with upwards energy, move out again, stepping and high – very familiar and very rare. Thoughts transparent, back of the brain still rumbling like a superstitious cave, front of me pouring out the front of me into the step.

When the music drops, I'm slowly closing too; we all drop together, red figures graceful down into the music. Silent and heaping form.

At the end he's white and blinding and he nods and says very good, very good, his hands folded to us; we don't need to look but we watch our bodies sit up with folded hands to him, and he's gone and I'm grateful, what I am of me, and part of my body, the left side, is knowing that Bodhi is over to the left on his drum, and my peace spreads from that side.

They are laughing, some of them, rolling in young black-bearded faces, others plain, lying there, some crying, some hugging now, of a heap. Stillness huge and swollen with we small flies who live within. We jerk a little sometimes.

I think I should be laughing or letting the tremendous energy out, but I don't feel laughter. I feel like just lying here, suddenly curled fetal, letting be, light; then it's solved for me, for at the moment of passive rest a jerk comes, knocking the back of my spine forward through my skull, leaving me more passive; thoughts come, relax, and the JERK of everything comes through me, without me doing anything. It's so easy, as easy as lying here, because that's what it wants to do, and utterly does the jerk come, of itself and totally beyond. I am made of Whole, and released and reborn, silly where I have thoughts, otherwise I am a JERK of spine upwards. Spasms like an infant with an electric ankle, passage like a tunnel.

Finally we're getting up to go, and then laughter laughs, looking full at Bodhi, who is so there that JERK jerks me from buttocks forward with surprised face! ...and laughing follows in the thinking mind, and then comes relaxation, and then JERK!

We go out into the shoes, up the dark path, hungry, high, talking words, forward into the still and moving dark, others before and behind us, blurred, and inside we are still, and in the blur, talking.

Can Women be Poets and Artists?

One day in discourse Bhagwan said, "Madhuri writes very good poetry, but it is not real poetry, because only men can write real poetry." And he went on to say that because men can't give birth to children, they have to seek some other way to be creative, and in their desperation it goes straight to the sky, in some urgent spiritual manner (I don't have the transcript now but that's what I remember). And so they do great things. Women, he said, are already at home in their love and can be fulfilled just cooking and caring for a man and children.

Now, I want to note right away that another time he said, "What amazing poetry women might write, what great paintings they might make, if they didn't have to take care of kids and men all day," or words to that effect.

But there we all were, sitting in that sacred space, and he'd mentioned me, so I was electrified, and mildly embarrassed. But in some very clear way, what he had said didn't register as important or relevant: because whether the poetry was 'real' or not, it was simply necessary for me (and he had told me once, "You have to write. It relaxes you.") Poetry is an intimate conversation with oneself, and nobody else can interfere; a sacrosanct inner celebration, a communion with the moment and what is in it. It doesn't have anything to do with anybody's standards of greatness. Whatever anyone said, made no difference – I wrote because writing was breathing. Whether it was 'real' or not just didn't matter a bit.

And, I'd like to comment as to men and kids: I had already cooked for a man during my teens, and had found it diverting not so much because of the man but because I got to mix unlikely ingredients together for my own curiosity. (Which sometimes upset the man.) I can say in hindsight, after more cooking-for-men, that if you have to compare, poetry lasts longer (my teenage poems are still in my life, trotting alongside me like a musical lynx, faithful and cavorting), is more fun and has much less cleanup after. I have enjoyed cooking – but it tends to become a servitude, quite quickly. As to kids… seeing my mother freaking out, at the end of her frayed rope, and scarred with childbirths and operations; looked like too high a price for that particular creativity, no thank you. In fact, the anorexia I'd suffered had been born partly from a disinclination to grow up into a rounded woman: women got babies, and husbands, and their bodies got distorted, and they hollered and screamed, yelled and mourned and cursed. That was their life.

So, maybe I missed… or maybe I'm an unnatural woman. But at the time, what he was saying felt maybe like some sort of horse ca-ca, though I didn't know just what kind. He did play tricks on us.

I Get Restless

Bodhi and I had been together for more than a year. Bhagwan seemed to like us as a couple, saying at one point that we were made for each other. But the more comfortable and at home I became with Bodhi, the more some restless part of me began to stick its head up above ground. If I could have successful sex with Bodhi, it said, what about other men? Life is long, life is rich, I didn't want to miss any of it… Could I possibly start to branch out?

I asked Bhagwan and he said, "Follow your feeling." Then, to Bodhi in a separate darshan, he said that Bodhi must never, ever let me know if he was jealous. (But I didn't hear about this till later.)

I wasn't quite sure what "follow your feeling" meant. What was my feeling? And what was my mind? I didn't know; but I wasn't going to let this confusion hold me back.

I began to chase men. Men didn't say no – not usually – though they were very often bemused. But I didn't let that stop me either.

And so I began a long career as a sex maniac.

I remember this: There were weeks and months of prowling and staying up most of the night, coming back to Bodhi at 4 or 5 a.m… then going back out next night, with ashram guys of so many stripes… anybody who caught my eye, to whom I felt drawn, who looked cute, who had a headful of curly hair, or seemed difficult to catch. I had adventures with them all. I loved the sense of expansion this gave me – as if I didn't have to be confined to my normal self any more – I could become bigger, lose boundaries; trespass in somebody else's universe. It felt so daring, so free – and I quickly became addicted to this high.

Finally one day I lay down in our room for a nap, and hardly woke up again for four days! Someone had brought a package for us from the States, full of large chocolate bars, and there was cake in our room too for some reason – and I'd wake up and eat cake and chocolate, and go back to sleep. After four days I emerged and, worried, sent a message to

Bhagwan asking what was going on? He replied that I was just tired!

(And then, of course, I had to go to the dentist, with new cavities!)

Since I'd begun dieting at sixteen in reaction to BC pill bloat, I'd had a sort of knot in the area of my diaphragm. It was an effort to keep the muscles taut so that, I hoped, my belly wouldn't stick out so much. This knot had become so habitual that it was impossible to relax it. Robes were a challenge: they didn't girdle me, hold me in. We were supposed to enjoy the flow of energy, but I felt much more secure and relaxed in jeans which zipped me in! Drawstring trousers just added to the puffy blobby feeling. (What I didn't know was that it was wheat – chapattis and toast-butter – that were now bloating me.) I hated feeling like a freak with a pregged-out belly! I'd start the day slimmish but by evening I looked pregnant. I tried in meditation to allow the belly to relax – but it was deeply scary.

But all this interesting sexual activity was having an effect on my shape. I lost weight without trying to. I still bloated, but I acquired some skirts which held my tummy in, and knit tops which made the most of my small bosom. I even got hold of some orange bell-bottom jeans, which I wore for years, under a robe; they acted like a girdle, and helped me to relax – though other people were apt to think they were an eccentric affectation.

We were now wearing a whole spectrum of orangish shades, some of which suited my coloring better than others. The deepest dark reddishest orange was best.

There was a disco now, that somebody had started, with a bar, about half a mile from the ashram. I was there every night, cutting loose, dancing up several storms at once; drinking fresh lime sodas, for I've never liked alcohol. And always, always, I went home with somebody. (...And was I orgasmic with any of these shy, cute, cautious fellows?

Lord have mercy. Certainly not.)

During this time there were many couples in the ashram, and it was a given that newly-formed pairs would go to Bhagwan to consult about their relationship. There was a certain prim seriousness in the way we approached these liaisons: we were trying to be spiritually correct to the best of our ability, without knowing what that would really look like. So people sometimes grew very earnest indeed. It was called "Moving with": "So-and-so is moving with Such-and-such."

So – Bodhi and I were an official couple, as were Sarita and Yatri, a jovial Brit much her senior who worked in the editing department and made wicked, clever cartoons. (They'd been together for some time, and during my celibate year I used sometimes to visit their room and make Yatri nervous because, he said, I always looked around as if I wanted something. Guilty as charged… Some nameless thing, yes, or even a nameful one – I always wanted.) They made a stately, laughing couple. Haridas, a tall glow-eyed German, was with Krishna Priya, a perky little blonde Canadian with a back-and-forth Africannish derrière. Veena, a South African beauty, also in editing but soon to make Bhagwan's robes, was with Naresh. And so on. I remember once being in Darshan while Govind and Gayatri sat in front of Bhagwan. They were an American couple, very good-looking, who lived next door to Bodhi and me in Eckhart House. Bhagwan said to the darshan group at large, "Now *this* is a permanent couple." (The only time I heard him say that about any two people! And, yes, they are still together.)

Then there were Satya Bharti and Christ Chaitanya, also American – he slim and pale and jokey and kind, with round blue eyes; she petite and brilliant, with a sloping chin, and the hugest eyes in the place, all fringed with dark lashes. One day, she began spontaneously to laugh, up in their room in Krishna House; she laughed for days, we could all hear it, and we glanced up at their balcony sometimes in wonder. Bhagwan said not to worry, it was fine. Eventually the laughter tapered off and stopped.

Bhagwan, as we have noted, was apt to tell people startling things. For example, if a couple wanted to separate, he might tell them to stay together; or, he might tell them to continue to live together, be freely moving with others, and not give each other trouble. He often did this – there was the sense that some valuable growth would be occurring during this non-traditional setup.

Bodhi was suffering, and he never said a word to me about it. I could see by the looks he gave me, sort of worried and fearful, that something was going on; but I was mostly interested in my own activities, and took for granted his non-interference. This unsettled period went on for months. Eventually he found a new girlfriend – a pretty, quiet young musician named Chhaya. I was slightly nonplussed, but not so very; and eventually I was moved out of Eckhart House and into a very large room, at the back of Jesus house, on the ground floor. Four women lived there. The beds were in the four corners, quite far apart. It was all fine with me.

Here though I suffered a spate of boils, on my rear, which eventually cleared up and did not return. That was an education... What a weird, painful, and disgusting ailment! By that time we had a medical center (at No. 70 Koregaon Park, in a street behind the ashram) and our own doctors, and I was treated there by a nice funny kindly Brit named Dr. Amrit, whom I remember very fondly. He was impervious to my flirtations, but warm-hearted just the same, and thus felt to me trustworthy. (At least, he was impervious then. Do I remember, later, a sweet skinny naked torso, a shaggy head, a plug-ugly/beautiful face... embarrassed to find itself there – in my arms? Oh Lord, I don't exactly remember...)

Somewhere along in here, I met an amazing man. We were friends as much as lovers, for an all-too-brief time – he was soon to return to England. He'd been with Bapak Subud in Indonesia: a Master whose chief technique was Latihan, that spontaneous movement of the body in the moment, finding its own flow. The two of us did crazy all-over-the-room Latihan together, and then made love – but he never ejaculated; and there was something just *epic* about his energy – when he touched me, energy began to rush through my body skywards; when he was inside me, energy poured like a reverse waterfall up out the top of my head, so that I was screaming and shaking. I just went out of my mind...

I was also receiving Shiatsu sessions from a Japanese guy at Mobos Hotel, and this too was a dismantling. He went in between my tendons and muscles and bones so far that I was screaming blue murder, and loving it – and afterwards I felt completely taken apart. It was wonderful.

The Englishman, blond, stocky, good, and wild – with a huge booming voice – went back to England. I never met anyone like him again – and later I heard he had gone into a mental institution. This seemed... all wrong.

And so I continued my wild social life. But one day Bhagwan mentioned me (to Sarita, or Bodhi? I don't remember now) during Darshan, saying that I was immature.

So I sent a question for Discourse:

You tell me to follow my feelings, and when I finally dare to and am feeling much freer and simpler and happier, you say I am immature. What does it mean?

It is from Madhuri.

It means exactly what it says: you are immature. What is immaturity? Whatsoever you are doing, you are doing almost unconsciously. Yes, I say be spontaneous, but I don't mean be unconscious. I mean be alert and spontaneous. By 'being spontaneous' you immediately understand to become a driftwood; so whatsoever happens, whatsoever and wheresoever the mind leads you, you are led by it. You become accidental. Immaturity makes a man accidental; maturity gives man a direction.

Maturity comes from a Latin root, maturas, which means: to be ripe. A fruit is mature when the fruit is ripe, when it has become sweet and is ready to be digested, can be eaten, can become part of anybody's life. A mature person is one who has come to know what love is, and love has made him sweet.

Now what Madhuri is doing is not love, it is just sexual fantasy – so one day moving with one man, another day moving with another man. This can be very destructive. Remember, what I say has to be understood very accurately, otherwise my sayings will not be helpful. They will become harmful.

It happened:

Mulla Nasrudin came home. His wife asked him, "What happened, Nasrudin, when you asked your boss for a raise today?"

"He was like a lamb," said Mulla Nasrudin.

"Really? What did he say?"

"Bah!"

Please listen to what I say carefully, and don't give it your own interpretation. Don't distort its meaning. Be spontaneous, but you can be spontaneous only when you are very aware. Otherwise you will become an accident – one moment going to the north, another moment going to the south. You will lose all direction. A spontaneous man is ready to respond to each moment. Sometimes some may see that he is moving to the north, and sometimes others may see that he is moving to the south, but his inner direction remains absolutely certain. His inner direction remains arrowed. He may have to adjust to circumstances, but once adjusted, he again gains energy, momentum, and starts moving towards his direction. He has a feel for the direction, but that feel comes only when you are very, very alert. Otherwise, just spontaneity will reduce you to being animals.

Animals are spontaneous, but they are not Buddhas. So just spontaneity cannot make one a Buddha – something more, something plus is needed: spontaneity plus awareness. Then you are not a mechanism, and you are not a driftwood either.

[...] I mean: listen to your feelings, but your feelings have to become a garland. Your feelings should not be like a heap of flowers. Your feelings should be like a garland, a thread running inside the flowers. Maybe nobody is able to see it, but a thread is joining them in a continuity: that continuity is the direction. Unless your feelings are a garland, you will disperse into fragments, you will fall into pieces, you will lose your togetherness.

Yes, I had told Madhuri to be spontaneous, to move according to her feelings. But I have been insisting continuously to do everything, but always remember that awareness is a requirement, a basic requirement – then do whatsoever you want to do. If there is something you are doing for which awareness becomes a hindrance, then don't do it. If there is something you are doing and awareness does not become a hindrance to it but on the contrary helps it, do it.

That is the whole definition of the right and the wrong. The wrong is that which cannot be done with awareness, for which unawareness is a must. The right is that which can be done only with awareness, for which unawareness has to be dropped; otherwise it cannot be done. Awareness is a must. The right is that for which awareness is a must, the wrong is that for which unawareness is a must. That is my definition of sin and virtue. And you are to decide; the responsibility is yours.

It happened:

A worried woman went to see her doctor and told him that her husband appeared to have no virility, and had no interest in her whatsoever.

He gave her a prescription, saying "These will help him. Next time you and your husband are having a quiet meal together, just slip a couple of these pills into his coffee and they will make him spontaneous. And then come and see me again."

Two weeks later she went to see her doctor again, and he asked her if his remedy had been successful.

"Oh yes, doctor," she said. "Absolutely marvelous. I slipped the pills into my husband's coffee and after two sips he began making love to me."

The doctor smiled. "Fine. No complaints then?"

She said, "Well, there is one. My husband and I can't ever show ourselves in that restaurant again."

Now remember, Madhuri, what I say has to be understood, because finally, you will decide where to slip those pills. I cannot follow you. You will decide where to be spontaneous, how to be spontaneous – and unconsciousness is not spontaneity. Spontaneity is very alert, very responsible, very caring. You are simply fooling around.

You tell me to follow my feelings and when I finally dare to and am feeling much freer and simpler and happier, you say I am immature. What does it mean?

I give you a certain rope to see what you do with my assertions, with my statements. I give you a certain rope, but when I see you are going crazy, then I have to pull you back. I have been watching, waiting to see what Madhuri is doing, but enough is enough.

[...] Oh yes, I told you to be free with your feelings; now I tell you to be aware. It will be more arduous, but if you can be aware, then you will really become simple. This simplicity is nothing: this is just regression into childhood, or regression into animality. The simplicity I want you to attain is the simplicity of a Buddha; not a regression, but the very climax of life. This simplicity is not going to help much. It has not helped anybody. This simplicity is very primitive, childish, immature.

But I wanted to see what you do, and I have seen what you are doing. Now become more alert. Bring a discipline to your life, a direction. Become more caring, more loving, more responsible. Your body has to be respected; it is the very shrine of God. You are not to treat it the way you are treating it; it is disrespectful. But it will be hard, I know. But I create situations in which hard things have to be done, because that is the only way to grow.

The Beloved, Vol. 2, Ch. 2, Q. 3

I felt very sorry and shaky to have been singled out for such a scolding. To me it seemed almost arbitrary, random; I didn't really know what I'd done wrong. The garland was missing? What did that mean? I didn't know that I didn't have the contact with my center that makes everything worthwhile. I was floundering around, whapping my arms every which way, in a sort of wild inconsistency. The only consistent thing was that I felt driven.

Another time I wrote to him asking, "You had previously told me to participate, and awareness would come by itself; but now you are instructing me to be aware. What is going on?" And he replied, "Now is the time for awareness."

I cannot say that I understood what this meant.

Amongst His Books

I was still cleaning, and had also been doing some occasional proof-reading of his books, sitting on a balcony in Lao Tzu or in No. 35 next door. Some months previously, I'd told Bhagwan that I was fed up with cleaning and would like a new job. He had said that he would not change my job as long as I was fed up, but would wait until I wasn't fed up any more! So I forgot about my disenchantment and carried on – and then one day I got the message to go to work in Bhagwan's library.

I spent a year there. The library was a large room at the front of Lao Tzu House – once, no doubt, a spacious sitting room. It had a light marble floor, and French doors opening onto a narrow porch with an ornate railing, and a good number of windows, with shutters on them, all shaded with the tall trees outside, and bracketed by the jungly plants that grew up close to the house. Bookshelves had been built on all the walls and also on the walls of the corridor which bisected the house. When you went out of the library door you could either turn left, to the stairs up to the veranda or the main house door, or right, into the corridor which was here greenish marble – always clean as a dinner-plate fresh out of a dishwasher – then, at a doorway, changed into the red tile I had cleaned daily for so long.

Right across the greenish marble corridor from the library were two recessed doors: the left was Bhagwan's room, the right his caretaker's.

So the vibes were as cool and pale-green and clean as the marble.

My boss was an earnest, studious-looking Italian (we'll call her H.L.) She wore glasses, had ever-so-slightly prominent front teeth, and was sedate, serious, and secretly bosomy, like any good librarian. Her boyfriend, a famously-endowed, brown-skinned, skinny fellow, a kind of drifty California-esque flautist – had many Gopis to play his flute to, and often did not come home to her at night. The next morning H.L. would be repressedly unhappy, and, in her difficult fashion, would confide in me. I could see her softness, her devotedness, her open vulnerability… but I felt disconnected from these beautiful qualities. I was in a gung-ho sort of mood.

And mostly she didn't much like me. I did many things in a way that did not suit her:

o Every morning, when I took a rickshaw to M.G. or Laxmi Rd. and went around the bookshops searching for religious or philosophical books for Bhagwan, I also darted into my tailor's shop and ordered clothes. H.L. instructed me not to take these side-trips, but it was like telling the wind not to blow.

o I wore fabulating outfits: I remember one strapless dress with a huge frill at the hem and a tie above the bosom, worn with a matching turban. The cloth draped in such a way as to emphasize my plentiful behind, and I enjoyed incidents such as the time Scottish Pramod came up behind me as I was walking through the Gateless Gate and remarked sotto voce into my ear, "It's sa nace an' rrrooooond!" I had a backless jumpsuit with an empire waist and spaghetti straps which I wore with gold high-heeled sandals. And so on. H.L. wore strictly nursey-dresses, high-necked, short-sleeved, and tailored.

o Every tea break and lunch break I would dash out of the rarified bliss of Lao Tzu to the big world of the rest of the Commune, and flirt with boys. I was very often late back to work. This did not set well. H.L. would grit her teeth and finally overflow with vexed complaint against me. (Perhaps all my flagrant wantonness reminded her of her wandering boyfriend!)

o Despite my best efforts, she was not satisfied with my filing skills, my fumbling in the card catalogs housed in cabinets in the main room. I was so annoyed and flustered at being disliked – yet so determined to plow my course regardless – that I no doubt messed up out of nerves. Lack of sleep due to nocturnal celebratings can't have helped.

Here was my weirdest sin (and it would freak me out too, the other way around): as I've said, I was obsessive-compulsive – my extremes of behavior were as much addictive as exuberant. I was subject to terrors and goading inner incitements. Meditation was slowly sorting me out, but it was a long road back to natural ease. So at this time I was still very much in the grip of the notion that If I did not want to do a thing, I must do it – just to make myself; just to know that I was not a half-dead coward.

I did not like my boss as much as she did not like me; somehow we had nothing to say to each other. Therefore I would insist on hugging her.

I would ask first: "Can I hug you?" She would snort annoyedly through her nose, but how could she say no to such a spiritually-correct request? So she would say yes, and I would step forward and wrap my bare, sexy, outlaw arms around her, and we would have a silly, uncomfortable hug. And she would snort in embarrassment and we would pull apart.

I often did this when she was really irritated at me, which made it particularly strange.

Working in the library was, of course, an aesthetic delight, discomfortable boss-relatings notwithstanding. The silent, watchful, bliss-drenched vibe… the thick walls, cool interiors of the house – that covered porch, where large-leafed foliage pressed against the railings. The doors were always open onto this porch and I would sit out there on my haunches cleaning the huge stacks of books I'd brought home from town. With a wet cloth I'd swipe the top of the book – around the sides and bottom where the page-edges were; then the front and back covers. Open book at front – wipe inner pages where, for some reason, dust tended to collect – then the last pages. Flip through pages quickly to dislodge dust. Place book upright and open to dry. (I still clean books this way; it makes them fresh and vibe-free, ready to be mine until I'm done with them.)

I enjoyed this work, alone out on the balcony, with rain dripping down nearby, or with summer sweat, or in lovely cold winter. I was out of H.L.'s line of sight, it was peaceful, satisfying work, and I could ponder the strangeness of Bhagwan's book choices: he actually wanted books from the Christian bookstores full of stuff about Jesus! I supposed that this was a desperate measure, H.L. sending me to those places; it was for backup books, when nothing better had shown up.

Bhagwan went through an enormous stack of books every day, reading fifteen or twenty and marking them all up in felt-tipped pen, underlining this and that, so he really did read them. He always needed more. It was understood that this was one of the ways he managed to stay in his body.

The piles and piles of dusty Christian books, and the philosophy books I'd manage to find at Manneys' Bookstore, which filled the floor, and half the seat, and behind the seat, of the rickshaw I'd taken, all had to be lugged in, cleaned, then allowed to dry. Then they were put outside the door of his room. Next day the piles would be back, with just a few books chosen to be kept. I'd return the rejects to the shops, and search, like a good hunter-gatherer, for more.

Meanwhile. disciples from English-speaking countries shipped to us boxes and boxes of much better books – shiny and new, colorful and weighty and worthy and cutting-edge. Books about new therapies, about social issues, women's rights, Zen, mysticism in all its expressions. These books were not dusty but they stank of newness – printers' ink, colored inks in the jackets, paper, glue. They too had to be cleaned, then left to dry. Sometimes a book would still stink even when it had aired for a week or two. Sometimes a particularly desirable book just couldn't be sent in to him at all because the smell never came out. H.L. and I spent a lot of time sniffing books.

And the books which passed muster would go in to him, he'd read them with the speed of light, and back out they'd come, to have a card made for them and then be put on the shelves. Though there was the card system, the placing of the books had no logical order; they were, at his instructions, placed in such a way as to have their tops make a wavy line. So all up and down the corridor the books surged and subsided like gentle movements of the sea.

When I first began working in the library Bhagwan was still painting magical, astonishing designs on the frontispieces of certain volumes. It was like caressing jewels to find them, to gaze at them – it was like falling into outer space/inner space, where the patternless flow of stars seduced you. It was like looking at a thousand different kinds of flower, or like glimpsing the inner machinery of some fabulous robot tall as a skyscraper. Gears, crosshatches, supernovae, marchings of brilliantly-colored creatures over a sea floor – things that tugged at the observer and brought her into unexplainable awe. The grace – the sureness – the finality, totality of those paintings – their color-drenched impact – was a constant accompaniment to my work.

But he stopped doing them when he became allergic to the smell of the magic markers he used.

Sometimes I bumped into him in the corridor – his tall white flame suddenly right here – and I would be flustered and agog and joyful all at once – most of all I would be, somehow, completely disarranged in my existence as to what I had heretofore assumed was 'me' – and I'd stand in hasty namaste until he'd passed. Then I'd be shaking for half an hour, uplifted, disarmed.

One night, in July 1977, I was in Darshan when there were important visitors: Werner Erhard, founder of EST; a friend of his, the friend's new wife, and Diana Ross of the Supremes. Bhagwan was gracious and welcoming, suggesting the visitors stay a little longer than the two or three days they'd allotted. Werner's friend said proudly that he and the woman with him had just been married by Muktananda at his ashram, and asked for Bhagwan's blessing.

"When you want to get married, go to Muktananda," pronounced Bhagwan genially, "and when you want to get divorced, come to me!" (He pronounced it 'die-vorced.')

The visitors sat there all freaked out! All the rest of us laughed!

Next day as part of their Commune tour the party traipsed through the library. Diana Ross was at the back, and she drifted her fingers across things – piles of books on tables, the filing cabinets, whatever. (She must be a tactile lady.) When they'd gone, H.L. fussily attacked all the touched surfaces with soap and water and a cloth, to get the unenlightened vibes out.

It was good job, the library; full of beauty, a job done in clean and hallowed rooms. I am so happy I had that year there – the high priestess's disapproval being another matter!

Head librarian, I'm sorry I was compulsive, and importuned you! Sorry for any incompetence or inattention I displayed.

I'm not sorry I was so wild.

I loved the shopping part, too.

He Answers Another Question

Right away, I sent a (pretty stupid) question in for discourse. I guess I was kind of interested because I had been to EST, and Werner Erhard went about with such an air of knowing important things. (Though when he sat in front of Bhagwan he seemed just as gatless as the rest of us!)

Is Werner Erhard anywhere near to being enlightened?

This is from Madhuri. Erhard is as near as Madhuri. Everybody is as near as Erhard. In fact enlightenment is a jump, not a gradual phenomenon – in just a single step the journey is complete. It is as if you are sitting with closed eyes and you open the eyes and the sun is there; the whole world is filled with light. Somebody is sitting with closed eyes: even then the world is filled with light and the sun is there, only he is sitting with closed eyes. And if he is enjoying it nothing is wrong in it, perfectly okay: but if he is miserable then I say why don't you open the eyes? The difference between ignorance and enlightenment is just that of opening the eyes. It is not much of a difference, if you are ready to open. If you are not ready to open, it is a tremendous difference.

Erhard is as near as anybody else, but intellect seems to be the barrier for him - as it is a barrier for you, most of you. He has understood the point - exactly he has understood it - but intellectually. When I talked about his few sentences last time, I okayed them all. They are all perfectly true, but I have not said anything about the person. Whatsoever he has said is perfectly true; but you can study Lao Tzu - intellectually you can understand and you can say the same things. As far as the words go they are true, but the man seems to be much too intellectually in it, not totally in it. And that's the problem.

And that is the greatest problem one can encounter: you understand everything I say, you can even explain it to others, but enlightenment will be as far away as ever. It is not a question of intellectually understanding. It is a question of total understanding - your total being understands it, not only your mind. Your heart understands it. Not only your heart - your blood and your bones, your marrow understands it. Nothing is left behind - our whole being understands it, is bathed in that understanding. Then the fragrance comes, then the dance happens, then you flower.

And there is only one step and the journey is complete. Between you and me the distance is only of one step - not more than that. Not even two steps are needed.

But forget about Erhard. Just think about yourself, because Erhard is a problem to himself; it is none of your business to be bothered about. Just think about yourself. Have you not many times felt that you understand me perfectly, and again and again you miss? Why? If you understand me, why do you miss? You understand me intellectually, verbally, theoretically, but your being does not participate in it. So while you are near me you understand; when you have moved away, the understanding simply disappears: you are again back to your old standpoint, to your old world and the pattern. While with me you forget yourself and everything is clear, crystal clear. Away from me you are again into your hole, and everything is confused and nothing is clear.

Only one step exists. And the step has to be taken with the total being. You are just sitting and imagining that you have taken the step. You can go on sitting and you can go on imagining a great journey. If you do it for long, the journey becomes so real, appears so real, that you can start talking like an enlightened man - but that won't help.

You have to be enlightened. It is not imagination; it is not thinking. It is being.

Yoga: The Alpha and the Omega, Vol. 5, Ch. 2, Q 8

Falling in Love

During this time I had two main lovers – an Australian named Ketan and an Englishman, whom we'll call T.Z.. I'd met Ketan first; he was an exceedingly quiet, satin-skinned, tan young man with nice quiet kisses and a languid air so pronounced you wondered if he was quite all there… but he had a sensitive, incisive intelligence when he did deign to speak. I loved him on those tropic nights we spent together, lounging in each other's arms… his eyes were private with some old sadness, his smile hesitant and half-way. He was not your typical Aussie, being Russian by heredity. I felt close to him, yet I was kept somewhere away.

But T.Z. was my sweetie, my chum, my delicious, bright-as-new-pebbles lover. He was an English guitarist and psychotherapist, with dirty-honey curls, a wiry, compact body and a saucy, elfin face. His eyes were blue and very round, his buttocks pert, and his mouth full and laughing. I adored him, and so enjoyed his quick warm presence and his sharp yet soft brilliance. He was sweet and happy and wonderful in bed; present, and applied, and as strong as I could want. We'd met like this: I'd gone to a concert in the ashram, seen him onstage playing his guitar – and, like girls everywhere who see a musician in action, I determined to get near enough to get my hands into those curls. He'd just emerged from a long relationship, so he wasn't sure he was ready to get involved. But we really clicked, and soon a lot of lively, sweet and satisfying nights had been spent together.

I was in love… and it was scary. I sent in a question for Discourse:

I am in love, and I feel like a moth dying into a flame. Should I try to somehow separate myself and become alone and aware, or should I die into the flame?

Madhuri, die! because to die in love is to be reborn. It is not death, it is the beginning of true life. To die without love is death. To live without love is death. To be in love is to know something of God, because as Jesus says, "God is love." I have even improved upon it: I say love is God.

Die, Madhuri, die. Utterly. Abandon yourself. Be lost.

There is no need to protect yourself against love, because love is not the enemy. Love is the only friend. Don't protect yourself. Don't hide from love. Don't be afraid of love. When love calls, go with it. Wherever it leads, go with it, go in trust.

Yes, there will be moments of agony, because they are always there when there are moments of ecstasy. They come together, it is one package; just like day and night, summer and winter, they come together. But when there is ecstasy of love, one is ready to pay whatsoever agony it brings, one is happy to pay.

And remember, nothing is free. We have to pay for everything. The more you can pay, the more you will get. If you want to move to the higher peaks of the Himalayas, you take the risk of falling into the valleys. Those who cannot take the risk of falling into the deep abysses surrounding Himalayan peaks will never know the joy of rising higher and higher.

Love is the highest peak of consciousness, the Everest of consciousness, and sometimes one slips and falls. And naturally, when you are moving on a height, you fall very deep. It hurts. When you know light and you fall into deep darkness, it hurts. But once you have known those peaks, you are ready to go into any valleys for those peaks. A single moment of ecstasy is enough: one can suffer for it in hell for eternity, then too it is worth having.

Meditate on these words of Kahlil Gibran: When love beckons to you, follow him, though his ways are hard and steep.

And when his wings enfold you yield to him, though the sword hidden among his pinions may wound you.

And when he speaks to you believe in him, though his voice may shatter your dreams as the north wind lays waste the garden. But if in your fear you would seek only love's peace and love's pleasure, then it is better for you that you cover your nakedness and pass out of love's threshing-floor, into the seasonless world where you shall laugh, but not all of your laughter, and weep, but not all of your tears.

Love gives naught but itself and takes naught but from itself. Love possesses not nor would it be possessed: for love is sufficient unto love.

When love beckons to you, follow him, follow to the very end, follow to the point where you disappear completely. Become a moth. Yes, love is a flame... and the lover is a moth. Learn much from the moth: it has the secret, it knows how to die. And to know how to die in love, in ecstasy, dancing, is to know how to be reborn on a higher plane. And each time you die a higher plane is reached.

When you can die ultimately and utterly, not holding back even a little bit of yourself, then that very death takes you into God. That is resurrection.

The Secret of Secrets, Vol. 2, Ch. 2

T.Z., when he wasn't making music, worked in the woodworking shop, making surrounds for the new, round malas. After the Moth discourse, he made for me a gift, which I kept and treasured. It was (and is – it sits on my desk as I type) a square rosewood pen-holder with a weighted bottom. Inlaid on the side is a mother-of-pearl moth hovering above a lifelike candle flame. It's quite big, and has four sections. It was, and still remains, one of the most beautiful things anyone has ever given me.

Under His Roof

One day in 1976, while I was in the library, Vivek came to me. "Bhagwan asks if you would like to move into Lao Tzu House," she said. "There's a condition – you would have to be in the house, alone, by 11:00 every night."

Here is what leapt out of my mouth: "But I have this really active social life!"

"Just let me know within twenty-four hours," she said comfortably, and glided away.

Of course, I knew within minutes what my answer had to be, and I ran to find her. Soon after that I went to darshan.

"Hmmm, Madhuri?" said the Glowing Pool of Light before my gape-jawed gaze. "Choose one man, and be only with him for the next six months. And remember your curfew!"

And so I chose T.Z., putting Ketan aside, not without regret (and not forever).

Here was the new routine: we had hot dates every night at his place and then I would creep, at one or two or three minutes past 11:00, back through the side door of Lao Tzu, and scuttle down the hall to the room I shared with Veena, the South African beauty with the mature air.

Great seismic waves went through the ashram at the news of my installation in Lao Tzu, for I was known as unorthodox and colorful, I guess; and I have long supposed this was why he moved me in there – to confound everybody!

The first thing that happened was, when I had put my things in the room I was to share with Veena, and had come out into a sort of utilities space back at that end of the house – ready to go outside – Shiva the Samurai* was lurking there. He was in a relationship with Gayan, and they lived in the room next to Veena and me. He had always ignored me – my man-radar told me he saw me as an insignificant little squirt, not glamourous enough for him – but now he backed me into a corner and bent down and pressed his thin mouth to mine, hard; and ground it about a bit.

It was a power move, a power kiss. It had no warmth or tenderness or friendliness in it. It was some sort of challenge, or a possessing of the status I had just gotten. I felt this immediately, and drew back and said, "That was a power kiss!"

He said nothing, just stared at me for a moment with his stern blue eyes, then moved away, job done – he'd lifted his leg and peed where it counted.

But T.Z. and I were much enjoying our times together. Soon I had a darshan. This is the unpublished transcript, with a preface by Maneesha, the lovely Australian who edited the Darshan Diaries.

Madhuri, one of Bhagwan's librarians, had recently moved into Bhagwan's residence, Lao Tzu House, to live with the seventeen other sannyasins there. For the past year or so she has been moving freely with many people, and the one stipulation that was given her when she was invited to live in Lao Tzu House was that she be in each night by 11 p.m.

Some days later she received a further directive - that she settle with one partner for six months.

In a state of considerable consternation at the curbing of her nightlife, Madhuri now comes forward.

* More on Samurais later.

What about you? asks Bhagwan, with much warmth in his voice. I watch Madhuri with affectionate amusement as she begins to try and explain herself to Bhagwan. She is a poet and has almost a compulsion to say exactly what she feels, thinks, fantasizes, without leaving anything to the imagination. Without any censoring. Her hands move this way and that. She pauses and sighs, then tries again, her face screwed up in concentration...

Madhuri: There's been just so much energy always going on. I've been puzzling so much since I moved in... wondering if I love life or was afraid of emptiness. I'm always running after men and I'm always doing all kinds of things, and sometimes I feel... When I feel that nothing's happening I become absolutely desperate and terrified.

I'm having this incredibly crazy relationship with T.Z. which is just complete chaos. I feel like pushing him away part of the time or being with him part of the time.

Just sitting there I was feeling my question vanish and vanish, and yet I want something from you. I feel constantly at a turning point.

Bhagwan: Mm mm! Come close! Just raise your hands this way. Go into it.

Madhuri has her arms up now, palms facing Bhagwan. Immediately the right hand goes into a kind of claw-like spasm, the left hand quite floppy. Her mouth drops open, her head is lolling back and then is suddenly jerked forward. Then she has bent forwards, her head at Bhagwan's feet.

Shiva makes to motion her back lest Bhagwan is disturbed by her proximity, but Bhagwan indicates that she should be left as she is. He is shining his small torch on her back now, on the knobbles of her spine. After a few moments he calls Madhuri back to earth...

Bhagwan: Mm! good Madhuri! You are at a turning point. And this moment can be used very very creatively. I have been watching you: you have been running after men desperately. It has nothing to do with men, it has nothing to do with sex; it has nothing to do with all that. It is just that you are avoiding yourself through occupation, and sex is very occupying because it brings all kinds of misery. Sex is just the engine and the train is of so many things, mm?

All types of compartments are there: jealousy and misery and pain and fight and anger and hatred. The whole train is loaded and sex is just the engine. It is not much; it just keeps the train running...

Mm mm, that will stop automatically once you stop chasing people. That is part of the chasing. If you want to chase people you have to remain young and beautiful and this and that. And in fact, just the opposite happens: the more you chase people, the older you will be, and sooner.

Have you heard the story? that a king had many wives. Outside the town he had made a special place for them. He had one man who had to go to fetch one wife every night for him. The king lived up to seventy and by that time at least seven persons who had to go and bring the wife had died. So it is not women that kill it is the chasing! *(laughter)*

Madhuri: I was thinking that that was what was keeping me awake and alive. But when I moved in you told me to come in at eleven every night. I was really threatened. I started feeling my energy was going to move. No matter what you told me, what boundaries you gave me, the energy moves any way.

Bhagwan: Mm mm, let it move! In your room let it move. Nothing to be worried about. Stop chasing and then you won't be worried about the body. And you will remain younger and beautiful longer. In fact if a person drops all kinds of chasing and desiring, even in the old days he remains beautiful. In fact the older you become, the more beautiful, because age has a grace which youth cannot have.

Youth is a little foolish... bound to be so, it is natural. Youth is shallow. It can't have depth because depth needs experience of life, many experiences - sweet and bitter and all. When one has passed through many experiences and one has seen all that life makes available, then a grace, a silence, a dignity arises. One becomes luminous from within.

And that is the criterion for whether the life has really been lived or not. If in your old age you become more and more beautiful every day, that means you have lived rightly. You lived; it has not been a sheer wastage. The last day has to be the most beautiful day in your whole life. And the last moment, when one is dying, has to be the most graceful.

And it happens! One just has to stop hankering, chasing, desiring, lusting, because those things create turmoil; they are destructive. So stop chasing. Be friendly with T.Z.

Madhuri: I often want to ask you about sex because I feel so puzzled about it; I keep feeling that there's something in it that I'm not finding. I'm afraid about not having orgasms or not what I think are orgasms. I feel inferior about it, and all that junk keeps continuing — that I feel inferior and left out and things.

Bhagwan: You have the western attitude about sex; that is creating trouble. The western attitude is always about making things happen, doing something!

And there are a few things which cannot be done. There the West becomes very very crazy!

For example, sleep, sex. These are things you cannot do, so the West suffers very much from lack of sleep also, insomnia, and also from sex. Everybody is worried that he is not experiencing it as it should be. The orgasm is not coming or it is very local or it is very lukewarm or it is not total. And sleep is not good: there are too many dreams. Many times one wakes or one has to wait hours for it to come. People are trying all kinds of things to bring sleep: the tranquilizers, the tricks, the mantras and TM.

And about sex also people are very very worried. That very worry and that very effort to do something is the problem. Sex happens; it is not a thing that you have to do. So you have to learn the eastern attitude.

It has a thrill but that thrill is tiring. The valley orgasm has no thrill but it has silence, and that silence is far more valuable, far more transforming. That will remain with you for twenty-four hours. Once you have been in a valley that valley will follow you. The peak will be lost and you will be exhausted and will fall in sleep. The valley will continue; for days it can have a kind of effect on you. You will feel relaxed, together.

Both are good, but nothing can be done. One has simply to allow. So love is a kind of relaxation in which things have to be allowed. Drop the western mind...

Madhuri: Once in a while I've got very deeply turned on and then also feel very frustrated afterwards. Sometimes the energy was really deep and it would rise when I came in the house. Other times it would just stay in my genitals, and I could tell that I was feeding it there and I would feel very frustrated.

Bhagwan: That frustration comes from your attitude, mm? It will go.

Madhuri: I know I have a fear of cessation and death and things going away, and I also have a fear of having too much energy. I've been using my energy in a really outward way, and if it happens that I come home and I feel I haven't used my energy up, I just feel somehow very threatened by that. I can't stand to have all that energy in me.

Bhagwan: Just do these things that I have told and then...

Madhuri: Okay... okay!

Bhagwan: Good, Madhuri!

I went home and reported to T.Z. We tried "staying in the Valley" – moving only enough to keep the man's erection; relaxing as much as possible, as Bhagwan had directed in a discourse we remembered. Neither of us understood the point at all. The whole direction just seemed absurd!

T.Z. requested a darshan. We both went.

"This kind of lovemaking seems like having a Rolls Royce and keeping it in the garage!" reported T.Z. in perplexity.

Bhagwan suggested that he persist, and that later he would understand.

But we never did make sense of that experiment. Not then, not with each other…

No, I never understood until twenty-eight more years had passed. But then I did.

Another time, in Darshan, Bhagwan said to me quite crossly: "Why you go on with all this *doing?* You are just *wasting time!*"

"But" – I protested, "I feel *stuck!*"

"So?" he said, "if you are stuck, just be stuck! What is the problem in it?"

This blew my mind. Surely, stuckness was the worst sort of mistake imaginable? Dynamite was surely needed?! But… he said it was okay to be stuck.

How could this be?

But it was relaxing – or would have been, had I allowed the sensations of stuckness and just observed them. But I was too afraid to do that; it would have felt like laziness, fatness, and Riverside.

Another time he said to me, about lovemaking: "And remember, it doesn't have to be *grrrreat!*"

Another time he'd said, "Sex is the holiest of the holies." I'd gaped at him, feeling the caution in his tone. But I didn't really understand. I was like somebody who had decided to climb Mt. Everest, whatever the cost, and was blindly struggling away, no matter the frostbite and the nearby precipices. I wanted to perform as the sexual being I thought everyone had to be – whether in a relationship or with different people. The evidence was that this attitude didn't suit my nature at all – but I just kept trying anyway. Only much later would I put the higher before the lower; I had supposed this was not allowed. But I now think that for me it is, in fact, the right way about.

So. Here was what I did with the opportunity of my new home: I had this Idea – that being in a relationship meant fighting – I thought that *really alive* people yelled, screamed, catharted, etc etc. Wasn't that what Encounter groups told us? So even though T.Z. was purely adorable and confiding, and kissed so plumply and nicely, and I did not at all feel like yelling at him, I *made* myself. I would consciously act angry – just because it was difficult. I would not feel it, but I would try; yell! Argue! Oh yes, I tried so intensely to be a good Encounter groupie sort!

Uh-Oh

One day T.Z. and I were making love when he suddenly cried, "Ouch!"

A trip to Dr. Amrit showed that my copper coil, the intrauterine device I'd had for six years (you weren't supposed to keep them nearly that long) had come partly out of the neck of the womb. It had to go.

When the device had been extracted, my whole body took a deep breath and let it out – whooosh! I relaxed all over. Wow! I felt so much better with it out! I could not bear to put in another.

Not long before, I'd been talking with another girl, who had had an abortion at Shree Clinic, a gynaecology center run by Dr. Saraswati, a sannyasin. This girl worked in the ashram kitchen under the famous Deeksha, a very wide-hipped Italian Mama with a long thin hooked nose, very soft pale skin and a wave of soft black hair. She seemed at least forty, but was probably thirty. She ran Vrindavan: the large enterprise of all the food-making in the ashram, in the big kitchens next to Lao Tzu (separated from it by a tall hedge) and behind Radha Hall. Deeksha worked her people hard, was irrational yet firm, but also generous – a true Godmother. This girl told me that Deeksha had paid for the abortion and laid on a car and flowers. The girl had only good things to say about all of it, even the procedure itself.

Somewhere in the experimental, furtive half-conscious of my foolish mind, I thought this sounded like a good experience to have. I wanted to try it too.

Not too long after the IUD was removed, I started to feel kind of… different. Tired, and my breasts grew sore and began to get quite astonishingly bigger, with straight-forward, pointy tips. I began to be sick in the mornings. Uh-oh. Was I getting hepatitis?

Dr. Amrit said, "You don't have hep. But you do have a baby!"

I went away and thought about things.

Then I asked Abhiyana, the acupuncturist, if he could cause a miscarriage by stimulating certain points with his needles. He said that he was willing to try.

During the session, he said, "We're trying to do an odd thing here – because when a woman is pregnant, the energy goes up; and we're trying to make it head in the opposite direction: down, and out. So I don't know what will happen." I lay with closed eyes on the treatment table and tuned in to my womb. I saw the little creature – definitely a boy – and he was not going anywhere. He had decided to come and stay – very firmly rooted, he was.

So acupuncture did not work.

I booked at Shree Clinic for a termination.

I screwed up my courage and asked Deeksha for help. Normally she was someone I avoided – who knew what she might do? (But once I *had* asked her for advice: again and again I'd let T.Z. come close, but then push him away – an unconscious ploy to keep him interested, I know now. But it was so painful to watch him eagerly bobbing outside my window, hoping to catch a glimpse of me; while I hid! And *made* myself keep away! What did Deeksha think about it? She'd stared at me for a moment, with her customary disapproval; and then she'd scolded, "You 'ave-a to geeve-a, you geeve-a!" – *if you have something to give, give it!* was how I'd translated this.)

Now she stared at me again. Then she said, "You don't-a work-a in-a the kitchen! But-a I 'elp-a."

Arup (later Garimo), who had some power position I never quite knew what it was, was very angry at me. She stopped me at the back door of Lao Tzu and berated me for being so stupid as to get pregnant. I hung my head, my bra-less new breasts* quivering high and lush. "Don't you get $60 a month from your father?" she asked.

"Yes."

"Then don't ask for help! Don't you ever do such a thing again!"

As I waited for the date of the termination my breasts swelled further, and sickness consumed all my days. It wasn't just morning sickness – it went on and on, day and night. I remember throwing up palak paneer, and being unable to look at that dish again for many years. Saltine crackers were the only thing

* I don't think any of us owned much underwear – what we'd brought with us would have died, and the Indian stuff was unwearable – 50's cotton cone-bras with weirdly close-together cups. We liked our naked-beneath-robe feeling. And undies cost money.

I could keep down. I watched how my mind altered too – in the evenings the tiny infant dictated what I did: No disco! Stay home! T.Z. isn't your lover any more; he's my Daddy! I was shocked at the power the tiny thing could wield. I saw that Nature favors the new life, and sacrifices the old: it didn't matter what *I* wanted to do; the baby came first.

Bhagwan, on the other hand, wanted us to live out the potential of a lifetime we could call our own – devoting ourselves to our own being, our own growth into becoming truly ourselves. Traditionally this search for one's own life stops with the first child and does not resume until all the children are grown – if ever. What a waste of generations!

I knew – had known for a long time – that I would never actually have a child.

T.Z. was his beautiful, sensitive self with all this – supportive and pragmatic. He was there for me, and he agreed that we could not have a child. In those days, and in that place… it was so very much not the thing to do. We needed all our energies for saving our own lives.

When I was coming out of the anesthetic I asked to see the foetus. The shocked nurses refused.

Later, much later, I gave myself a session where I could talk to the little man; apologize to him. "I could not have had you," I told him. "I did not want to leave the ashram. And I would have had to. That would have been impossible for me. I would not have been a good mother."

He replied, "But... I would have *loved* you!"

(Sometimes I have thought about him – how he would have been – tall, I think, like my brothers, but with T.Z.'s curls – always with T.Z.'s curls. But I had to live with Bhagwan for as long as I did; not a day less. I could not have spared an hour away. I was no grown-up, to give birth to a child. I'm sorry, little one. I hope you went to a good place – maybe to Australia, like many other children who wanted sannyasins as parents.)

T.Z. and I were really very compatible, but I couldn't leave it at that. I had to create difficulties, in order to avoid the dreaded complacency I feared so much. I was always feeding bees to my own bottom, so to speak – stinging my own tail to make myself lively. Here is a terrible thing I did: T.Z. had lovingly made a gift for me in the woodworking shop where he loved to play: two turned wooden goblets with stems, and copper rings embedded on the outside of the bowl, below the rim.

One evening, when I was in a self-invented, cranked-up snit, I challenged myself to be an enraged sort of woman who Takes Great Steps in Her Rage. This went against the grain, so I pushed even harder towards Doing Something. Unless I Did Something, nobody would see that I was a Good Sannyasin, Exploring Her Scary Feelings. Which is all very well, except that they were feelings I did not actually have. This scared me – that I might be calm and pacific. Then, thought I, was I dead?

So on that wave of pretend anger, I took up the goblets and hastened to the empty woodworking shop. There I found a vise, fastened to a workbench; and I duly squashed a goblet in it, turning the crank by hand while the black screw moved slowly to compress and finally burst the bowl of the thing like a skull… and then I did the same to the other. I left them there, like murdered children, for him to find. I'll never forget his face when I saw him next – perplexed, hurt, surprised – his light brown curls, his full mouth, his round blue eyes – his elf-beard – all looking at me, unable to understand.

I continued to pour out my relationship troubles to Bhagwan in letters. After one particularly agonized missive went in to him, I received this classic reply: *Either drop it or continue, but don't write again and again!*

Then I sent in a question for Discourse:

Please help me to understand what is happening in this relationship. I am so attached and so resisting, so ecstatic and so wretched and hidden. I see no way beyond the contradictions. Your guidances to me remain a seemingly impossible mystery. Osho, what is it, a depth I'm not falling in?

P. S. Is a relationship a sort of koan?

The question is from Madhuri.

Yes, Madhuri, the best koan there is is love, is relationship. That's how it is being used here. A relationship is a puzzle with no clue to it. Howsoever you try to manage it, you will never be able to manage it. Nobody has ever been able to manage it. It is made in such a way that it simply remains puzzling. The more you try to demystify it, the more mysterious it becomes. The more you try to understand it, the more elusive it is.

It is a greater koan than any koan that Zen masters give to their disciples, because their koans are meditative - one is alone. When I give you the koan of relationship it is far more complicated, because you are two - differently made, differently conditioned, polar opposites to each other, pulling in different directions, manipulating each other, trying to possess, dominate... there are a thousand and one problems.

While meditating, the only problem is how to be silent, how not to be caught in thoughts. In relationship there are a thousand and one problems. If you are silent, there is a problem. Just sit silently by the side of your wife and you will see - she will immediately jump upon you: "Why are you silent? What do you mean?" Or speak, and you will be in trouble - whatsoever you say, you are always misunderstood.

No relationship can ever come to a point where it is not a problem. Or if sometimes you see a relationship coming to a point where it is no more a problem, that simply means it is not a relationship any more. The relationship has disappeared - the fighters are tired, they have started accepting things as they are. They are bored; they don't want to fight any more. They have accepted it, they don't want to improve upon it.

Or, in the past, people tried to create a kind of harmony forcibly. That's why, down the ages, women were repressed - that was one way of sorting things out. Just force the woman to follow the man, then there is no problem. But it is not a relationship either. When the woman is no more an independent person the problem disappears. But the woman has also disappeared. Then she is just a thing to be used; then there is no joy, and the man starts looking for some other woman.

If you ever come across a happy marriage, don't trust it on the surface. Just go a little deeper and you will be surprised...

[...] A relationship is a koan. And unless you have solved a more fundamental thing about yourself, you cannot solve it. The problem of love can be solved only when the problem of meditation has been solved, not before it. Because it is really two non-meditative persons who are creating the problem. Two persons who are in confusion, who don't know who they are - naturally they multiply each other's confusion, they magnify it.

Unless meditation is achieved, love remains a misery. Once you have learnt how to live alone, once you have learnt how to enjoy your simple existence, for no reason at all, then there is a possibility of solving the second, more complicated problem of two persons being together. Only two meditators can live in love – and then love will not be a koan. But then it will not be a relationship either, in the sense that you understand it. It will be simply a state of love, not a state of relationship.

So, Madhuri, I understand your trouble. But I tell people to go into these troubles because these troubles will make you aware of the fundamental problem, that you, deep inside your being, are a riddle. And the other simply is a mirror. It is difficult to know your own troubles directly, it is very easy to know them in a relationship. A mirror becomes available: you can see your face in the mirror, and the other can see his face in your mirror. And both are angry, because both see ugly faces. And naturally both shout at each other, because their natural logic is, "It is YOU, this mirror, which is making me look so ugly. Otherwise I am such a beautiful person."

That's the problem that lovers go on trying to solve, and cannot solve. What they are saying again and again is this: "I am such a beautiful person, but you make me look so ugly."

Nobody is making you look ugly – you are ugly. Sorry, but that's how it is. Be thankful to the other, be grateful to the other, because he helps you to see your face. Don't be angry.

And go deeper into yourself, go deeper into meditation. But what happens is that whenever a person is in love he forgets all about meditation. I go on looking at you – whenever I see a few persons missing, I know what has happened to them. Love has happened to them. Now they don't think that they are needed here. They will come only when love creates much trouble and it becomes impossible for them to solve it. Then they will come and ask, "Osho, what to do?"

When you are in love, don't forget meditation. Love is not going to solve anything. Love is only going to show you who you are, where you are. And it is good that love makes you alert – alert of the whole confusion and the chaos within you. Now is the time to meditate! If love and meditation go together, you will have both the wings, you will have a balance.

And the vice versa also happens. Whenever a person starts moving deep in meditation, he starts avoiding love, because he thinks if he goes into love his meditation will be disturbed.

That too is wrong. Meditation will not be disturbed, Meditation will be helped.

Why will it be helped? Because love will go on showing you where there are still problems, where they are. Without love, you will become unconscious of your problems. But becoming unconscious does not mean that you have solved them. If there is no mirror, that does not mean that you don't have any face.

Love and meditation should go hand in hand. That is one of the most essential messages that I would like to share with you: Love and meditation should go hand in hand. Love and meditate, meditate and love - and slowly slowly you will see a new harmony arising in you. Only that harmony will make you contented.

Take It Easy, Vol. 2, Ch. 13, Q. 7

Jaundice

During this tumultuous time – tumultuous because I courted and created tumult – one day I noticed that I felt very heavy in my gut. That day at lunchtime T.Z. and I were on Lao Tzu roof and I doggedly shouted at him a whole bunch. (The Master must have heard!)

After T.Z. had gone back to work, I did something so foolish that I've never forgotten the lesson. I'd thought that the stuck feeling might be remedied by a dose of slippery elm bark powder somebody had given me, and which I'd not tried before. Western nostrums were highly valued, and I like little jars and tins of things generally, so I didn't want it to go to waste.

I remember standing in the dim coolness of the space by the big sinks at the end of the red corridor, near my and Veena's room. I took a spoon and stuck it in the tub of the powder, then put the heaping spoonful directly into my mouth.

Instantly the powder absorbed all the moisture in my mouth and throat. There was no way to swallow – the powder expanded and became a mass of substance, a kind of hard glue sealing my throat and blocking off my airway. It was too far back in, and too glued, to be spat out and there was no way to draw air in to help with spitting. Unusually, nobody was around. I couldn't breathe at all. I was going to choke to death.

I leaned over the sink, turned on the water, and began clawing the cement-like stuff out of my mouth and throat, splashing water in at the same time. I managed to get out enough so that I could breathe… and eventually got all of it out. But it was a close call.

Many people were feeling ill. Then everyone's eyes went yellow, their pee brown, their poo white. An epidemic of hepatitis A had hit the ashram!

I had two blissful weeks in a hastily-fitted-out hospital room in Krishna House, during which I was far too weak to Do. It was wonderful! I just lay there completely limp and at peace! We were brought simple meals of white rice and boiled vegetables, which tasted delicious.

When I got out – still very weak but no longer infectious – I found that Deeksha had sent her minions into my room and they'd taken away my beautiful fuchsia velvet skirt, my clingy t-shirt, my hippie-raggy lungis, my sexy strappy robes. They had also taken all the gifts the Master had given me (satin pillowcases, a really well-used hand-towel, a painted hollow egg with a Japanese girl on it reading a book; a pen). And my passport.

I went out of the room and staggered weakly along behind the canteen, and there I spied it – a pile of my clothes on the ground, like a heap of emaciated gypsies. I bent down and seized as many garments as I could hold and began, with the last of my ravaged strength, to drag them away with me. Venu, a petite Canadian who was the formidable Deeksha's right-hand woman, came out of a door in her nursey-dress, and stood there, admonishing sternly, "Madhuri, this is not the way!"

Ha ha, I thought angrily, What does *she* know? (I got the passport back later, with an apology of sorts.)

Soon after that Arup came and found me where I was sunbathing* on Jesus House roof and told me that Bhagwan had said I was to move out of Lao Tzu.

There was this Moment… where it all hit me, but sweetly, truly; tears went down my cheeks… but nothing felt wrong about the message. I just accepted it as it came to me. My mind did not become involved really; it just Was.

Next day Bhagwan spoke about me in discourse: "I have moved Madhuri out from my house. Just to live with me does not mean that you are close to me. But see did not become angry. See cried – but see was not angry. And now many more blessings will be sowering on her." (That's the way he said "she" and "showering.") His voice was loving!

* This was a popular sport. The white tiles, huge blowing trees, empty sky, peace and quiet… bliss. I did it for vanity's sake, though I only turned gently yellowish and never tan. Eventually the Indian Air Force discovered us and began to buzz the roof with their planes.

T. Z. and I Set up Housekeeping

T.Z. and I were moved into a funny 'room' on Jesus House roof – really just a sort of cubicle with cloth walls, made by dividing up an area of upstairs veranda which had been roofed over with corrugated tin. I remember that room with laughter in my heart! Vasumati and Aneesha, who were each other's close friends, lived next door to us, and of course we could all hear everything each other said. T.Z. and I had a bed, and a set of shelves, and that was it. And we were happy; so busy with our jobs that there was no time to feel discontented with anything, and so cranked-open from meditation that there was no inclination for disgruntlement anyway. It was fun to live together, to come and go in a sort of privacy which had, however, an inadvertent audience!

It was winter, and in winter we all got colds. I still think that all that milky chai that we, and the whole country, drank every day, had something to do with it – because every winter the whole of India starts blowing its nose all the time. On the street, people hold the nose between thumb and forefinger and blow first one side, then the other; then snap the hand at the ground and hope the snot flies off tidily to land down there (instead of on a foot or on some passer-by). I've seen Westerners in India do this too, but I didn't favor the method; my mother had always made it very clear that you didn't even put a finger in your nose without a Kleenex on it. And indeed, the puddles of mucus and sputum on Indian streets were a trial to us Westerners. The glop had a way of getting inside your sandals and was then often flung onto your ankles by your gait. (That is why I always advise people to bring closed shoes to India! – tai chi slippers will do.) I have been much struck by accounts of how the dreadful human suffering caused by tuberculosis was finally stopped – in the USA at least – by the simple expedient of outlawing spittoons and public spitting. And some things are just disgusting, T.B. or no. (I've also read that beedis, the ubiquitous little cheap Indian cigarettes, rolled in a dry leaf – are made by people too ill for any other labor; ill from T.B.)

But I digress. We didn't have Kleenex in India then (it was the time of Indira Gandhi's Emergency, and all imports were banned; paper was relatively precious). So I had taken an old worn-out bedspread I had unwisely dyed green – it had red stripes in it, and came out strange – and torn it up into a great many hanky-sized squares. These were folded on one of the shelves.

Now, this is going to sound strange, and I don't understand it myself.

But that set of shelves had no back, and it sat against a mere curtain standing in for a wall. And all those piled hankies toppled out of the open back, down behind, and poked out under the 'wall.' And there was something about the absolute let-go of this – things just toppling and giving way, when normally they would be bounded hard and fast – that struck me as incredibly funny. So funny that I started to laugh… and just didn't stop – new waves of hilarity kept arising. On and on and on! It was like, another time, in my years of mass dating (which were not over yet), when I found myself with a guy in a tree-house in somebody's garden, some distance from the ashram; a tree-platform really, with a tent on it, quite high up in a tree. And we were fooling about in the tent – ah, youth – and various belongings that were arrayed at the edge of the platform – water bottle, comb, whatever – began to fall off the edge and down to the lawn below. And that made me laugh like a nincompoop too – helplessly, in waves, on and on. Something about helpless, unexpected let-go.

It reminds me of cat vids on YouTube: a dignified kitty, finding himself in a fluffy heap on the floor after trying to leap atop a door – but even more, a picture I saw of a flat blue-and-green world and a cat shoving a bottle of wine off the edge of it – with the caption: If the world was flat, cats would long ago have pushed everything off the edge.

Later this theme would recur…

During this joyful interlude, one night I wrote in my diary:

Tonight my lover has Darshan and I am in our roof-room eating dinner and feeling the pen loving the paper.

My nature seems more than ever erotic, more than ever, more than ever. During the morning lecture Bhagwan's energy rises me into a swoon of sensuality. The new thing is, feeling more and more joy in it – that somehow this is my path: melting. He said Die, die into the flame. The moth is to die into the flame, to not keep its individuality.

To my lover, this is a strange world, and he loves it that I am that. And I marvel that it is not his world.

I worship. I fall on the floor and worship when he comes in the room. When I wake up in the morning he is there and I am in such a wonder – he is there! God is in my bed! The king wakes beside me! His curly hair seems to hold every mystery the earth has ever known. All this, after a recent series of fights, during which I thought the thing would be to overcome my worship, outgrow it – I thought it was awful, that he would *despise me for it – after the explosions, the it's-all-over, the But-I-can't-change, and the But-**I**-can't-change! And the rage and jealousy and crying alone for days at work, at lunchtime, waiting waiting waiting for him – (so many times have I waited for a man's step, on so many different stairs!) (...And each man the vital man, each man the gentleman, each man the pirate and the god.)*

...I fell deeper into worship, and accepting, and we laughed and fell into days of lovemaking and meeting again.

Dusk has absorbed the day. Electric light glows. He is down there waiting for Darshan to start, his energy falling deep inside himself, the awareness of his energies rising in waves on waves; my stranger, my friend, who is never mine. No matter how many times I wake with him, he is never mine. He always puts a pang in my heart when he goes by. He is always unreachable, un-final. Whenever he goes by I feel, I want that man! ...And we might have moved deep in each other, surrendered to each other, been in bodysoulmeeting joy just an hour before;

and because we have made love a thousand times and I have still not become him, I sometimes look at other men and think, half-consciously, Maybe he would satisfy, at least for moments. I could sup him, he looks delicious. And my lover looks at blondes with cat faces who eye him, power-eye him in Sufi dancing while he sings with his curly hair and rock-star body and Pan face with all its seriousness and heart worn in it, and he power-eyes them back and his genitals stir and he wants to crush them, scoop them to his mouth and bruise and take them. And he remembers me and feels sad and trapped, afraid of losing that frightening deep thing we share.

And we have both experimented and shrieked, and then rejected, and tried to overcome, and we have discussed, and connected more profoundly, and hated, and lain alone nights in trembling black. And still we choose again, again to wake up together. To live here. And watch the dreams break and mend and new ones form, never the ones you expected.

And he won't let me tell him my dreams in the morning. "Just words," he says. And I remember all my indulgent lovers who loved my dreams, and their old part-grey heads, and I shriek and pounce on his head and shake it by its youthful curls.

And he remains the best man in bed in the Universe. And I am still not whole.

And lately he confessed that he's not total with me, and I yelled and mourned and then a light came inside: My totality is mine, my dying is mine. In the moment it seems most his, it is mine too. And a luxury came into me. And I can total all over him. And he is total with me – I can feel it now. In his own way which is always at an angle from my way, he ***is*** *total. He only thinks he's not because he is.*

Now dinner is finished and his is hot in the big thermos and I stop writing and get up to wash the dishes, not knowing who this letter is to but wanting it to be to many, or at least a many few.

I think I will mend his robe and then go down and work in my office (more on this job-change later) *waiting for Darshan to be out. He is in there now and Osho must have come out to sit and be. White blur of greatness and delight.*

We Move Again

After we'd lived in the cloth room for a while we were moved to a newly-built room behind the Godown (the long, solid half-underground storage building where Bhagwan's books were warehoused). There was a row of rooms there with plywood walls separating them. The spaces were just big enough for a double pallet and a bamboo mat on the floor. On the wall were a few hooks for our robes. There was one screened window, and a door opening onto a narrow concrete runnel where water could drain when it rained, and we could make our way back and forth to the end of the row and the bigger walkway. On the other side of this runnel-path there was a wire mesh fence, that we could look through to the next back garden – a generously-sized, dusty place with a tall flame tree exhibiting lush red blooms in season. Servants of that big house moved about back there on their tasks, and sometimes a quarrelsome-looking lady in a silk sari was seen having a drink at a table under the trees. Chickens pecked about.

T.Z. and I were very happy in our little room. It was cool and private and here we had our lovemaking, our understandings and misunderstandings... And, one night in his sleep he turned his head towards me on his pillow and sang!

Bhagwan's birthday was approaching, and T.Z. was to be one of the musicians playing at the celebration on the night itself – 11th December. He was going to sing a solo, and was fretting, trying to write a song; he needed, in fact, a few new songs for the evening. So I got helpful and gave him some lyric ideas, which, I'm afraid, were not very good.

And so he sang, on the night... *"Who – ooo – oo am I? / God only knowwww wwww wwww wws... "*

No, it was pretty bad songwriting, and yet his ardent, sincere voice lifted even that poor and silly thing. But he was disconsolate after, and couldn't stop beating himself up, curling into a ball on our mattress and groaning. Finally he wrote Bhagwan a letter, apologizing for having ruined his birthday, and gave it to Mukta.

Next day the letter came back, and with it a prezzie – a huge, grand, expensive watch.

Bhagwan was speaking on the chakras, describing and commenting on each in depth; one per day. I was fascinated! I drank it all in, and each day when T.Z. and I went back to our room and lay down to lounge around for a bit before it was time to go to work, I hovered my hand above the day's chakra, or I'd lay my hand lightly on it, on his body – for I just felt like being with the chakra in the light of Bhagwan's words.

So, with my hand above T.Z.'s solar plexus, there I sat... and images were coming out of his stomach, his diaphragm. I saw a little boy with a red wagon... so I told him about these things.

Then I asked, "Now it's *my* turn! Look at my chakra!" And he said, "I can't do that."

"Of course you can!" I insisted. And I yearned to lie down and have my tummy read. But he said he couldn't! But I knew that, of course, everyone could!

The more I looked, the more interesting and subtle things I saw. I felt like I was entering into a new world. I liked it very much – a sense of welcoming mystery buoyed me. I discovered that chakras have three layers – the surface; the deeper wild power, often made of suppressed material; and the deepest: the most true and fundamental quality that person has there. It was all so beautiful, I was awestruck.

One day I was walking on the red corridor through Lao Tzu house when I bumped into Teertha. Since he was considered guru-like, people sometimes asked him questions about themselves. I stopped and told him what I'd been doing with these chakra explorations. Was it, I wondered, okay? (I was afraid to write to Bhagwan about it in case he said don't do it! I think now that he would not have said that... but who knows?)

Teertha looked down his long cold white nose at me. *"This,"* he pronounced, "is *your energy*... and you are *doubting* it!"

Okay. So I stopped doubting it. So much.

T.Z. was very nice in bed. He was a wiry little guy, but he was strong and warm and plenty big enough where I wanted it. He was bright and sweet, and he laughed, and he gave me what I liked… I usually had two orgasms; in the relaxation of the trust that was at least partly there between us; in the relaxation that only grows over time. I was in the full flood of my twenties' hormonal ascension. I'd hold him within me and press myself on the outside… The crescendo drove me in to where my cervix met him, and I would howl and then lie still and replete until the energy rose again and I crested a second wave. Or I rubbed him on myself, in a fever with the gorgeousness of his hardness. And then he filled me again, and sometimes I went completely out of my mind, and stars showered all through me and I forgot my own name and where I was. Or he would lie patiently beside me, bent over, touching my sensitive place with his giving tongue. All of it was good.

I found though that after such orgasms I "went off him" for a couple of days – just as I hear men lose interest in a lover after they've climaxed. I just wanted to be alone then – but I was never alone, we lived together. Amongst, too, a mass of people! So this could be uncomfortable and strange.

Although I adored T.Z., I worried that life would leave me behind if I didn't also go with other men. My six months' monogamy injunction was over. T.Z. too wanted to experiment. We felt obliged to follow our impulses and let the chips fall where they may.

T.Z. was having an affair with L., a tawny fox of a California girl with a long slender sway-back and a pointed bob of dark gold hair. She had long grey eyes and a certain candid honesty about her;* she glided about the ashram in her robe, her pretty behind swaying. T.Z. loved to have sex with her, and described to me her orgasms when he kissed her 'down there.' I was horribly jealous, but I did my best to somehow get along with the freedom of it all. But whenever I saw her around, my stomach lurched and my teeth heated up.

Later he had an affair with S.V., a beamy, sumptuous Monégasque with "plenty of these and those," as my mother would say. She had straight platinum-blonde hair down to her very-indented waist; a Shylock nose, white teeth, small bright eyes, and a confident laugh. T.Z. told me how very wet she was. I didn't really like to hear this.

* She later, in California, married well and became a pilot.

Looking back, all of this was wonderful and good. (T.Z. reports that he also has no regrets.) We were not trying to find permanent partners; we were living the energies given by Nature – the lusts and the joys, in all their compellingness; and the jealousies in all their awfulness and doom. Only by not suppressing, Bhagwan had told us, would we eventually be able to go beyond sex. You must know what it is you are transcending before you can transcend it; you must know it fully, wall-to-wall. And then, by itself, it will find different forms: a more silent, Tantric meeting; or a freedom just to fly in the inner skies as yourself, alone.

It was like an apprenticeship to become a master sailor. You try out all sorts of boats, of so many sizes and shapes and makes and models and seaworthinesses; you capsize, and storms tear you up and calms beset you (not so many of those). And eventually the wind itself becomes your lover.

One night I was at Darshan, and so was S.V., the buxom, glow-eyed Monégasque. Bhagwan had, that other time, told me to "stay in the Valley" with sex. Another time he'd said to just play with the lover's body, goalless.

But to S.V. he said, to make sure to have an orgasm every time she made love, even if she had to do it herself.

That was one of those interesting illustrations of how different people are, and what is right for one might not be right for another.

A Change of Job

One day Vivek found me in the corridor outside the library and told me that I was to have a job-change. I was excited and nervous, and, when I found out what it was, I felt sorry to be leaving Lao Tzu… back into the hurly-burly of the world.

But very soon I was enjoying the new situation very much!

I was boss of the newsletter subscription office. I cleaned it up – it was a mess – and reorganized everything. A few people worked there. We started out in a funny round house beside the front gate but thence were moved to a spacious, tidy office in Radha Hall. I liked the fiddly precision of the filing system. I liked checking for mistakes. I liked my kindly directorial role – soon there were five people working under me. I was very happy! It was lovely to be busy at something I found so pleasurable.

I loved chai and bread and peanut butter after discourse, sitting in front of the office, the chai coming around in great clanking urns wheeled on a cart. I loved the peculiar letters we received requesting subscriptions, the same name spelt differently on the return address, in the body of the letter, in the signature. All these people writing from villages, towns, cities; all over India.

In my next darshan Bhagwan told me how happy he was with my work. It felt novel to be getting praise for a change! I felt, though, somewhere in me, like I would like to be valued for something else… Why just *work?* was what I thought.

He gave a discourse about a Sufi mystic named Mojud, who worked at one job after another, moving about his country; each of these moves directed by a mysterious Guide. Mojud eventually became very silent and wise; after simply letting himself be moved, he knew not why, again and again over many years. Bhagwan said, "This is what is happening here. Madhuri works in the library. Suddenly one day she receives the message, 'Leave the library. Go to some other work.' If trust is there, there will be no anger, no disturbance, because here you are not to be in the library or to be in the kitchen, or to be in this or that. All those are devices! You are here to learn the ways of trust."

The transcription was made into a tall thin book: *Mojud: The Man with the Inexplicable Life.* On the inside of the jacket, there is a quote from Bhagwan: "The heart is an adventurer, the explorer of the mysteries, the discoverer of all that is hidden. The heart is always on a pilgrimage. It is never satisfied, it has an innermost discontent, a spiritual discontent. It never settles anywhere. It is very much in love with movement, with dynamism.

"When you go deep into meditation it will happen again and again. A moment will come when your circumference and center are very close, and there is no barrier between them – not even a curtain – and you will hear the center loudly, clearly."

(Nearly forty years later, at a time in my life when I was out in the world and seemed to myself to have no power, and in fact had no home either; this book would become a light for me, a joy, a transformation – for it gave me courage to let go and wait for life to find me, show me what the next little eddy of the flow would be. Thank you, beloved Master.)

Denouement

But now T.Z. was seeing S.T., a stocky, pretty Schweizerette with well-turned ankles, an up-tilted nose, and a shiny black pageboy. We were at odds, T.Z. and I, though still doing our best. Hot passion does that – it includes separation in its very DNA – though I didn't understand that then.

One afternoon I went back to our room and T.Z. wasn't there. Suspicious, I went up to S.T.'s room, on top of the tree-shaded Godown. I heard murmurs from inside. I pushed the door open and entered.

T.Z. and she were on the pallet bed under the mosquito net, making love. I saw a bottle of water on a shelf – lifted it up above the net, and upended it – all in a moment, all over them! Ha ha! *Drenched!* As they sputtered and rolled apart I dashed, glaring and cursing, out of the room.

The next day, in my full frenzy of jealousy and pain, I followed him around that end of the ashram, near our room, scratching my own face with my nails and wailing.

This certainly did not make him love me again!

T.Z. was such a good man, courageous and sincere. But I was much more neurotic than he was, and eventually this would break us up. It happened like this: one night I went to the disco by myself. I've always been a dancing freak, ready to boogie night or day. But what happened there that night was different – a departure even for me. There was a man, a non-sannyasin, good-looking and dark-haired, perhaps in his forties. We danced, and somehow or other I agreed to go home with him – even though I could sense that he was somehow strange. Even though it was, socially, really, really not okay to "move with" non-sannyasins; they were… dark. Clueless. Unclean. Off. Ungraced. They smelt of the World.

But I was compulsive. So I walked with him as he wheeled his bicycle, back to his dark lodgings somewhere in the jungly town.

And he was indeed strange, and somehow sick. I don't remember now what exactly his fetish was, but he had one; I think it had to do with panties. I only know that when I was going home afterwards, I felt unclean and as if I'd been out on a scarily dim and deluded edge. I fled back to the ashram, scarcely daring to hope that I'd find everything as before… my beautiful home in the Land of Grace. I could hardly breathe for guilt and relief.

In the interests of Total Honesty, I told T.Z. about my escapade. He thought about it for a day, then announced that we were finished – "What really did it," he said, "is that he wasn't even a sannyasin!"

And I knew that I'd destroyed something beautiful and good for the sake of a sick compulsion. But I didn't know how I could have done otherwise.

T.Z. was moved into another room. We still met sometimes. But I was mourning him.

Immediately, a tall American man, Krishna Deva, was moved into my room. (Two single pallets, one on each side of the tiny space, had been substituted for the one double one.) He was on a night shift, so he slept all day on his pallet. When I looked over at him all shrouded there in his sheet, I could not but think I was looking at the corpse of my love.

We Get Ailments

Until that first bout of hepatitis I had been quite healthy in Poona, as if some leftover Western robustness lasted out that long. But hep had really knocked the stuffing out of me. I was exhausted for weeks afterwards, and I came down with an attack of herpes, which I'd gotten in San Francisco when I was twenty, doing blue movies. I'd had one bad attack then, but none since; and I'd forgotten all about it. But at twenty-four it returned when my liver was unwell.

When it had first returned, with its nerve pain in the vulva, its ache down the leg, its blisters which opened into painful, raw sores – I had still been with T.Z. We'd been lying in bed together on the roof of Krishna House for some reason I don't remember… and I had told him I had herpes. "Any herp of yours is a friend of mine!" he'd said lovingly, recklessly; and I took him at his word. And so he'd gotten it too. (He said later that if he'd known what he was getting himself into… !)

So that was herpes, wrecker of dates. The official medical advice was that it was contagious only during an actual breakout. I was always having dates; and so beforehand, how I hovered over every ache and twinge, praying for it not to surface as a sore! But it nearly always did. (Later it was discovered that the virus could be transmitted when dormant. Or just in the aching stage. Or after it had healed. There was really no escape. The virus was so tiny, it could even get through the pores in a condom!) I know I gave it to several people –

five that I can think of, though one was untroubled, having had only one small attack and then no more. It can be like that. But I am very sorry about all of it, whatever the effect on anyone – and usually it was not good.

This joke says it all:

Q: What's the difference between true love and herpes?

A: Herpes is forever.

Then there were amoebas, which most of us got. There was boiled water available in huge metal pots, where we could fill metal cups. But all tap water was bad. I have read that more Brits died during the Raj from amoebas than from all the battles and mutinies put together. It was thought that anyone who did service in India could be expected to live twenty years less than someone who'd never gone.

You knew you had them when you felt a sort of dull ache in your stomach. Then you started feeling tired, heavy in the gut and foggy in the head. It was miserable. Some people got dysentery – I generally didn't. You would go get a shit test at a lab not far away, costing very little; but the results were not conclusive because the amoebas didn't always show. The doctor would give you a prescription for a dreaded big flat yellow pill, sold in foil packs, called Flagyl. It was a terrible drug – you felt like yellow death when you were taking it. Just truly horrible all over. Then, when you stopped taking it, soon you felt all better. Until the next time. I had plenty of bouts of amoebas.

Curiously, there was no malaria in Poona – or at least I never heard of anyone having it. But there was dengue fever.

We all had mosquito nets, but of course mosquitoes bit us while we were having dinner, or sitting in the garden. Sometimes they'd get in under the net with you – the smallest hole and they were in; or they'd lurk about waiting for you to have a pee in the night and slip in while you were hastily sliding back under the net. Later many dwellings were mosquito-netted at the windows, which helped a lot; but it only took one feisty, hungry little bastard to keep you up half the night trying to get a swat at it while it danced about adroitly. Mosquitoes that carry dengue are large and have striped legs, as if they are wearing pajamas. One in a hundred of these fellows is a carrier. Dengue's life-cycle has to pass through the intestines of a dog. There are lots of dogs in India – street dogs, mangy, starving, abused. Sometimes foaming at the mouth, twitching in a coma in a monsoon-green ditch… I've seen that.

Dengue hits you like a flu – you're achey and tired – but it's much, much more than that. You have a headache like steel blocks are being smashed on your head. The virus was known during the Raj as "bonebreak fever," because you feel like your bones are breaking, there is so much pain all over your body. You have a high fever, and can be delirious. You might throw up. I had it three or four times, always during monsoon. It was hell, and left me as droopy as hepatitis did. Some people got very very sick indeed and had to go to the hospital. It was bad enough anyway.

And there were worms. It was supposed we all had them; you were supposed to take a dose of worm medicine whenever you went to the West. There was no point while in India, as you'd just get them again.

The yearly winter cold got everybody. It wasn't fun to get this, because, as well as the wretchedness, we couldn't go to discourse or darshan. Sufferers could, however, sit in a prescribed place in a building or plaza where there was a way to hear the live streaming audio.

Then there were the by-products of our sexual experimentation, our untrammeled life-force: cystitis. Kidney infection. Gonorrhoea. Chlamydia. Trichomonas. Yeast infection. And so on. So many invisible critters were happily privileged to hitch-hike on our sense of freedom and exploration. There is nothing to judge here; invasions of exuberant microscopic life were all about and through us – gut, genitals, or wherever. This was an inevitable side-effect of being in India, and of sexual freedom. At least, then, there was nothing in the venereal infections that was going to kill us.

But just the things that went wrong with our tummies were enough to keep us busy.

My health had deteriorated so much that Dr. Amrit sent me to an old Indian doctor who had once been physician to Bhagwan. He did many tests, which showed that I was anaemic and also deficient in B-12. He prescribed a supplement called Complan, full of vitamins and minerals, which came in a big metal tin with a press-down lid. I chose chocolate flavor, and added a scoop of the brown powder to my chai every morning, stirring it in well. It tasted a little strange, but was certainly robust. Over time it seemed to work, and I grew a little stronger. I was also given occasional injections of B-12, which were a revelation. For a day or two my nerves would be marvelously calm and I would feel grounded and serene. Then this happy state would pass and I'd be back to feeling strung out and airborne.

Mental Illness

There were other sorts of ailments one could come up with too. Meditation is a hard master; it forces you to face all sorts of anguishes. Sometimes, once in a long while, a person would break… at least for the time being; at least until some future healing might arrive.

Early in my time in Poona, one day I had sat at a lunch table with some people, and there had been with us a tall young American with a very hooked nose. He was very thin, and had tight dark curls; his bare arms were hairy. I noticed something odd about his affect – as if part of him was looking backward, or inward; or someplace that the rest of us could not go. He was humble, and rather distracted, and yet he said something observant and precise, I don't recall what; and still it was as if some big part of him was looking elsewhere. A few days later he jumped to his death from the roof of the Blue Diamond hotel.

Once I was traveling in a rickshaw from the ashram to M.G. Road to buy books for Bhagwan. It was mid-morning, and I chanced to look out to my right, and what I saw was so surprising I could not really believe it. At the back of a parking area beside one of the two petrol pumps flanking the entrance to North Main Road, a beautiful and elegant Swedish sannyasin with great ringlets of pretty light-brown hair on her head and great round blue eyes with long lashes – I'd of course seen her around and thought her very chic – was standing, wearing striped pajamas that looked like cartoon prison garb. She was in the process of removing the bottoms of them, so that her own round bottom, and most of her white legs, shone to the smelly tooting and blatting street. She was looking back over her shoulder with an expression on her face like that of a little girl who knew she was being naughty, but just couldn't resist – quite delighted really.

After that she disappeared… sent back to Sweden. Bhagwan encouraged us to go mad, but consciously, in meditation; so that, devils jettisoned, we could regain sanity more surely. But the ashram was not a hospital for people who really couldn't function. (Later Sarita asked Bhagwan what had happened, for, like all of us, she was disturbed by the fate of the lovely Swede. Bhagwan replied that the woman had been doing the meditations wrongly, contrary to instructions in some way. The meditations were scientifically designed and you were not to meddle with them, or leave something out, or go out of the hall in the middle. This would be very disruptive to your whole system.) Many people who were having an episode of instability were banned from coming in the Gates, and were sent back to the West to recover.

An astrologer once told me that I would never really go mad – something about Moon exalted in Taurus. This consoled me more than once.

Death in Our Midst

A tall young Dutchwoman named Vipassana had a brain tumor and quite quickly died. Hers was the first Death Celebration in the ashram. Bhagwan gave us very specific instructions: dance and sing and give her a good send-off! Take her body to the Burning Ghats, still celebrating. Stay while the fire is lit… Then, Bhagwan told us, go home and have a shower and wash your hair. Wash the clothes you'd worn, and put on fresh ones. This was very important!

And so we all went to the hall together and danced while musicians played and Vipassana's body, flower-couched and flower-strewn, lay on the stretcher on a table. Energy flew high, our arms were raised, as we looked with little inner gulps of alarm at this one among us who had abruptly flown. Most of us were young, and this thing called death seemed very far away; yet here it was in our midst. We gawped at the mystery of it and sang away.

Then we made a parade down the empty ashram road, crossed the more-trafficked North Main Road, then proceeded further on under the trees and down to the dirt area around a shallow concrete rectangle now piled with wood, where Vipassana was lain, and drizzled with ghee from a can; and then her brother held the lighted branch out to the wood and set it alight. And we watched while the empty body burned, and we were touched by the Mystery.

And then, after an hour or so, we traipsed home in little groups or alone, and had our good long showers, and hair-washes, and piled up our dirty robes for the dhobi.

Because of the climate, bodies had to be cremated very soon after the spirit had left them. There were no refrigerated morgues. Then, once the body was burnt (or once the wood ran out – for poorer families that was the cut-off point, so that a body might not be burnt all the way –) the ashes and whatever bits of bone remained would be thrown onto the river, just beside the ghats; and float away downstream, often with flowers cast on to the river with them.

If the body was of a Realized Being, these ashes and bones are in fact known as 'flowers.'

When Welf Prinz von Hannover fell down during warm-up for his martial arts practice, and was taken to the hospital and diagnosed with a brain aneurysm, the whole ashram went quiet. I had known him only as a taciturn blond German, tall and slim, who had a therapist wife (who looked like a blond Jackie O, but smarter) and a little daughter, Tania. Vimalkirti – his sannyas name – was a Samurai, one of the elite coterie of men charged with protecting Bhagwan; they stood calmly in their maroon karate clothes wherever he was: Discourse, Darshan. (This band of knights had been gathered together after a Hindu fundamentalist had thrown a dull knife at Bhagwan during a discourse. The knife had clattered to the marble floor at least ten feet before the dais where he sat – and the guards, at that point just a few men – hustled the would-be assassin out. Samurais arose soon after.)

I had heard that Vimalkirti was a prince, a cousin of Prince Charles; but this did not mean anything much to me. He was just a tall blond guy who was around the place. People generally didn't care if someone was a celebrity; we had a few of these coming and going – Terence Stamp, Vinod Khanna – and we treated them much like everyone else.

Vimalkirti was a very retiring sort of prince; not in the least snobby or vain. I think that people liked him a lot. He seemed genuine, and also introspective – as if he had a burden on his shoulders and was doing his best to examine it and examine himself to find out what was true.

But everybody went quiet when he fell… and then we were waiting.

Bhagwan did something unprecedented – he went to the hospital to see Vimalkirti where he lay in a coma, on life-support machines. He gave instructions that the machines should be left running, though it was clear that Vimalkirti would not recover.

For five days the Prince was kept alive. Members of his family were mustering to fly in.

Then, on the fifth day, Bhagwan said that the machines could be turned off. And he gave a beautiful discourse, telling us what had happened to Vimalkirti – that at last he had stepped beyond the ego and gone into his true nature. He had become enlightened as he died.

"Give him a good send-off!" …And so we did.

I was much struck by this – that something could proceed in the realm of consciousness, something important and vital – even if you were in a coma.

Bhagwan very much wanted us to be healthy. He spoke again and again of a 'New Commune' he wanted for us all, where we would not be bothered by anyone and could build our meditation life in peace. This place would have vegetable gardens, and clean water, and whatever we needed... He dreamt aloud about it, time and time again.

Still Clueless

After the breakup with T.Z. I went back to as much moving-with-men as I could. Sometimes I had experiences that were fun, juicy, expanding, rewarding. Sometimes meetings were almost cosmic, mysteries touching, depths vibrating together, for that little time. Sometimes the contact seemed meaningless and stupid. But I persisted.

I was seeing Ketan again, the low-key Aussie with the soft voice. I felt at home in his languid arms.

I had a date with a nice Scotsman, Pari. We had a good time. The next day he met me on the path and said, "This morning I bumped into a friend of mine. I told him, 'I had such a nice date last night!' 'Who with?' my friend asked. 'Madhuri!' I said. 'But – *I* had a date with Madhuri last night!' said my friend."

Pari was laughing, but after that he didn't want to go out with me again. I found this sad and puzzling.

Irish Mukta had a boyfriend, muscular, with wavy dark hair. We had a hug on the path. He was only wearing a lungi, and it tented up in front. We went back to my room and went to bed.

One day I counted: twenty-eight men in thirty days – some of them more than once.

I even had terrible, creepy, wet-noodly sex with Teertha. He was like a flexible cadaver, pale and clammy. Why did I do that? Because I could. Leaving no stone, or noodle, unturned, sort of thing. I don't remember any animation occurring, of any sort.

Someone complained to me that when I hugged, in the long drowning-in-unique-expanding-vibes hugs we all fell into many times during a day – hugs that came from Bhagwan's huge space and our own heart-endlessness – I laid my *full weight* on the other person. This, it seemed, was not liked. But that was how I'd always done it.

Embarrassed, I stopped doing that, and tried to remain in myself when hugging.

I had a different roommate now, in my little room: Ma Anando, one of Deeksha's kitchen bosses. She never did anything but work and sleep. We talked a little, and I felt vaguely chid. I didn't understand her. How could somebody want to work so much? I felt guilty. Something, I supposed, was probably wrong with me.

A Tense but Provocative Affair

A man came to work in the newsletter office, Shantideep, a dentist from England. He had blond hair and a Goa-style tan; very blue, crystalline eyes, and an air of tense propriety. His square jaw, his clipped accent, his reserved but jokey, glinty surface – his handsome figure but rather hurried stride... I vowed to get through his reserve and get him into my bed. There was something about Englishmen...

But Shanti was in a long-term relationship, with a quiet, blonde English girl with bee-stung lips, limpid, accepting eyes, and a slightly falling-away chin. She had beautiful skin, and her pale hair fell straight on either side of her soft face. In my preposterous blindness, I dismissed her as unimportant. They had been together for seven years.

Shanti and I chatted and flirted over tea, and during work. He loathed dentistry, was subject to migraines, loved his girlfriend. I think he found the filing work he did to be beneath him, but he gave it his best anyway.

It didn't take a very long time – days? weeks? – before he came back to my little room with me.

We discovered that the sex was compelling. I always had two orgasms with him, too – though it took weeks of lovemaking before my body relaxed just enough for the first one to occur... and then I got into a rather demanding rhythm with them. As always I supposed something was wrong with me because orgasms didn't happen solely through penetration; it was always such a production, all that licking and twiddling and squeezing of muscles until finally my mind was tricked for a moment out of its supremacy by a confusion of concurrent pleasurable sensations… and everything welled up and went bang. I was aware of many levels of energy during a meeting with a man; I felt his mysterious being, I knew if the heart was involved and if it wasn't – but the idea that something was difficult or missing in the mechanics obsessed me, and I didn't appreciate the other elements enough. Too, I was a bit allergic to nice, heartful men, and liked 'baddish boys' who would give me some kind of hard time. (Young women often suffer like this.)

Poor Shanti entered a hellish period. He loved and respected his girlfriend, yet he couldn't stay away from my bed. Periodically he'd get into a state, hissing at me about my perfidious, inferior nature, and then erupting in a rage, telling me I was just *glass* and his girlfriend was *diamonds!*

I'd sit gazing at him, traumatized by his anger, and yet implacable. As always when somebody shouts at me I simply go into moveless shock.

His woman accepted the situation passively, philosophically, seeming to be barely upset, where in her position I would have been stalking about the place howling and spying.

Shanti (I called him, fondly, Shanti-Beast) got those terrible headaches – I could see the gathering-up of his facial muscles, the storm pulling itself together in his head. His shoulders were very tightly held, his eyes glinted more in their sockets, the outer corners of them crow's-footed with strain and suffering. I didn't know what to do, except give him shoulder massages, and more sex. He'd give in reluctantly, groaning as the erotic took over. What hid in his pants was unusually beautiful – strong and sheathed and weighty. In a conversation I can't now imagine how we got into, his girlfriend said to me, "Yes, he's *got something in his pants,*" in a mild, equable, ladylike tone. By now they were living apart.

I became concerned about Shanti's uptightness, as I saw it – he seemed to me prudish and old-school, despite his loose khadi trousers and open orange vest, his golden tan – as if he was bearing the burden of all sorts of societal repression. I lay awake at night (we did not live together – Shanti was not an ashramite), trying to dream up some gift I could give him to bring some wild joy to his soul.

And I found it…

At that time there was working in the newsletter office a tall young American girl with a more-than-hourglass figure, W. I took her aside and explained my idea. She agreed in a friendly way. A day was set; a time – very soon. On the appointed day Shanti was waiting in my room, where there were clean sheets and an expectant air.

I went to fetch W., but when I leaned over to whisper to her, I happened to see into her hair… It was extremely thick hair on a cushiony-looking scalp, very very curly; blond-brown, fanning out about her pretty face and down past her shoulders. And at the base of every hair, and on higher reaches of each hair too, I could see a little egg, the same color as the hair itself; clinging fast…

Oops! Change of plan!

So instead of the festive occasion I'd prepared for, I was helping W. wash her hair with lice shampoo!

Next day we were on again. A lice-check showed the little buggers were gone! She'd need to do the treatment again in a week, but for now we were fine.

And so, behind the Godown in that shady little room, an experiment occurred.

This turned out to be the first, and last, time I enjoyed being in bed with a woman. W. was lovely! Young, alive, tensile, present, surprised – even in her laconic California way she was vervesome; firm and cushioned to the touch. She too was acting entirely in the spirit of exploration – as if we three were the first young people to have done this thing. I can't exactly tell you what we did – just whatever came along – in a romping yet sensitive sort of way. Shanti was amazed and applied in equal measure. W. (who was in a relationship we deduced was a bit lackluster) praised him unstintingly.

After a few hours we all emerged into the evening blinking in re-acclimatization with the world outside. All of us were flying. We felt so released from normal parameters that we gazed about us in astonished wonder. Our hearts had flown open, and everything was new. We'd pierced the forbidden, and found space and great permission. We loved everybody because of it. For me, this space lasted days. And I felt that I had truly given a gift to Shanti, a gift of value and consequence. And he'd received it.

This was very fulfilling.

Then… a week later, the thought arose (I love it when Bhagwan says, telling some story: '…And then an idea came to him…' and you know that something *really silly* is about to happen): that the threesome event was such a breakthrough, such a positive experience, why not do it again, with a different woman?

And I looked around for one, settling soon on D., a soft, blushing, quiet, big-eyed, stocky-ish English girl with a beautiful voice, who somehow seemed about forty-five, though she must have been not more than twenty-five – it was her air of settled seriousness. She agreed; and so we three duly met in my room.

And it was all quite horrible. This was not poor, brave D.'s fault; the chemistry was just strange and unworking, all of us were shy, and D. was so feminine that I could find nothing to engage with – no tensile strength – just a wetlands, swampy and abysmal; and I sprang up within myself like a cat that someone is trying to drop into a full bathtub, alive with shock and aversion.

And so I never tried *that* sort of thing again.

(And as to Shanti: forty years later he told me that when he and I met, his relationship with his partner was really over, and it had been time to move on. Thus relieving me of four decades-worth of guilt. Thank you, Shanti.)

Teeth

One day Devageet, Bhagwan's dentist, a busy, brilliant man – sort of a vivacious leprechaun – stopped me just outside the ashram dental surgery, opposite the newsletter office. "I have to go to London for something to do with Bhagwan's teeth," he said. "I'll only be there for two days. I could also get two crowns made for you. It would not be expensive – I can get them at cost. Would you like me to do that? If so, I'll have to grind the teeth down and make castings of them right away."

I stood there all amazed, and then said Yes, I would like it.

When I told Shanti that evening he was disapproving. "Crowns always cause trouble," he said. "They weaken the teeth, and decay gets under them." I did not want to hear this – for the prospect of being able to smile without shame was just heady. I can think of only one photo taken before the Great Teeth Update where I smiled: I'm beside T.Z., we're both beaming – and you can see the one sharp, sideways-on canine – like an open door – protruding on the left; an indented tooth beside it. I was just very much afraid to smile, since I'd been a child and a nasty little boy at school had called me 'Dracula's Daughter.' I couldn't imagine what it would be like to grin freely. At fourteen I'd suddenly paid attention to a large free-range tooth that had come down through the roof of my mouth – there was no room where it should have gone. A boy kissed me and put his tongue between it and the rest of my teeth; and I'd known shame. So I'd taken myself to the super-cheap family dentist, and paid him $10 to pull the tooth out. Too, my incisors were spotted from measles and a little jaggedy on the bottom, as if the enamelling wasn't finished. My family had not owned toothbrushes till I was eleven, so my teeth had been green till then. My mother always said, "You were behind the door when the teeth were handed out."

When I was deciding whether to use my porno movie fortune to go to India or to get braces on my teeth, the dentist I consulted said that my bite was too bad (on two teeth only), and my tongue had a habit of swallowing with an outward push. (This habit is acquired in infancy when the baby is bottle-fed – in my case my mother's breast-milk had dried up very early – the baby pushes the tongue out to keep from drowning.) He said braces wouldn't work on me, I would have to have surgery to cut out sections of my jaw. Subsequent dentists have diagnosed, "bad architecture;" and they would always ask, "But how do you *chew?*" *Very slowly,* was the answer.

But I didn't like the sound of jaw surgery. I went to India, and had every-goddamn-thing-etheric-surgery instead.

This wonky teeth business was accompanied by a mashed-about cartilage in my nose: a deviated septum. (This sounds like something worn by a pervert priest!) If I take thumb and forefinger and, grasping the outside of my nose, straighten it – very difficult, as cartilage is tough stuff – my whole life changes. Suddenly there is silence in my head – there is nothing much to think or do – I am not driven. The back of my neck gives a satisfying little crack, and life streams upwards coolly and emptily.

But as soon as I release the nose, I am again driven on the bent flow of the energy, out to the sides: shopping! Do artwork! Pay attention to this, that and the other thing on the periphery! Doctors have refused to operate – the risks, they say, are greater than any possible rewards. And so I accept my karma – forever harried into side-roads. I'm in thrall to a particular system – Human Design* – and so here are some sad words on a detriment on my Gate of

* See Appendix of Treasures.

Intuitive Clarity: "The tendency to keep on keeping on, that can end up as a misguided missile. When in action, the intuition may become overwhelmed and unable to assess and evaluate its progress." So it's not just the nose that sends me into batty overdrive – the nose just steers it all awry.

Eventually this wonky-streaming energy would contribute to a crisis that was very serious indeed – but that was much later.

And, none of this is about the country of the heart. The heart does not know or care what is wonky; she only loves, and welcomes, and throws back her head when the Master is about, and drinks with wondering and vasty awe. Expansion lives there, and love; and it doesn't matter what is crippled or uneven.

I had once written to Bhagwan about my uneasy dentition, and he had replied, "Don't worry about your crooked teeth." But I had been unable to comply.

A few days later, true to his word, Devageet was back with my new teeth. The ground-down ones had been covered with temporary plastic crowns. Now he removed these and installed the heavy porcelain ones he'd had made. I was upset by one thing – the recessed tooth, to be built up in front, still had a big bulge in back to house the root. It looked weird when my head was thrown back – as in lovemaking. Devageet said the tech people had been unable to believe that the teeth had no bite on them.

Still, as he commented, the new teeth looked much better than the old. I began to experiment with smiling. It was a huge change in my life.

I Make a Boo-Boo

I was the boss of the newsletter subscription office, but I also had a boss – the unlovely (to me) Vidya. She smiled a great deal, showing white teeth and pink gum, and her chin was sharp, her blue eyes small and bright. Her bosom was large, her toes turned out, her legs slim and covered with soft blonde hair. She roamed around looking for things to correct, and when she talked, in her rather attractive South African accent, little bubbles appeared at the corners of her mouth, and her eyes crinkled up. I could not like her – I felt that she was somehow dangerous – but she liked me, and had cajoled me into giving her private yoga and stretching sessions before work started each day. I did not enjoy this – trying to stretch this lummoxy, dangerous, grinning creature, who was showing me her friendliest, most amenable self – but I dared not refuse.

She said I had a reputation for making no errors in my office work. That is, until one day…

That lunchtime Vidya came and found me as I was leaving the canteen. She always smiled, but today there was a line between her pale brows, a set to her chin. She marched me to the newsletter office, where a few large, weathered canvas mailbags sat, stuffed full. Wordlessly she hefted one up, untied the string around its neck, and turned it upside down, so that a cascade of newsletters poured out. She picked one up, turned it over so that the address area of the paper sleeve was on top. The sleeve had been franked, over the stamp, but the address area was empty. She dropped that newsletter, picked up another – same thing. And another… I started to laugh.

"This is NOT FUNNY!" she stated sternly.

But I thought it was hilarious. Three mailbagsful, and not a single address anywhere! How on earth had this happened? I had no idea; but I was, then and there, demoted. Irish Mukta, quiet, mature, and eternally mild, was put in charge, and I was just a peon. My pride was hurt – I couldn't quite get used to the loss of glory – but there it was. I was happy that I could continue working in the newsletter office anyway. I liked it there. I often went in early or stayed late, just because I enjoyed the fiddly filing.

A Toke and an Ending

One night I tried an experiment with Shanti. He was into smoking the occasional reefer, but I had completely lost interest in that sort of thing, even before taking Sannyas. Intoxication just seemed boring and distracting. What could be better than one's own raw heart, exposed to the Master? Why fog things over? Drugs, alcohol – they've never been my thing, despite teenage experimentings.

But I was fixated on the idea that I was sexually missing the boat, and I thought a high might help – remembering pleasurable stoned gropings with my first boyfriend, Jarrie, before all the disappointing penetration started.

So, one evening when Shanti and I were at his flat in a big shady block near the Blue Diamond, I accepted his invitation for a smoke.

The result was, for me, just plain scary: we made love in a state of cotton-wool padding. I felt distanced from my emotional nature, from my heart, even, perhaps, from my soul. Sensation was expanded but nothing happened that felt like a departure, a breakthrough. I could not orgasm on the wings of dope. I was simply full of grief for being lost to myself, my precious, fresh, clear-water consciousness. And I was so spooked by this sense of distancing that I have never gone near the stuff again.

Shanti came down with a fever. We made love anyway. Then he was diagnosed with hepatitis. Soon, I noticed that I was not feeling well – my belly felt heavy, and I was tired. My pee was brown… Uh-oh. Turned out I had hepatitis A again. Shanti's lovely, patient ex took care of him at home. I was put into the ward at No. 70, where were other sufferers, some much more ill than I – I saw them, dark yellow, scarcely able to raise their heads; heard them vomiting into buckets. Dr. Amrit tended us faithfully. He was a good doctor, game and witty, and I will always be grateful to him. A male nurse tended us too, moving about among the mosquito-netted beds in the big dim room. It was monsoon, which added to the gloom. I was not unhappy – but I was sick a lot, and lay back after, sweaty and drained. It was worse than my first bout. We were brought the classic hep oil-free meals: white rice, steamed veggies.

I had been in bed for about eight days when Shanti came to see me. He was feeling better, and he wanted to go up to Mahabaleshwar, an old British Raj hill station not far from Poona. He asked me to come with him.

Although I was deep in the classic exhaustion of jaundice, I was recovering, slowly… and I said yes. We left next day, taking a taxi up and up in the rain, climbing a hill to an upland. It was my first time there.

At the top was a village. Our hotel, set in big park-like grounds, was wonderful – a vintage Rest House, with a huge bathroom approached through a spacious dressing room attached to the main bedroom; but with a door opening to the outside as well. This was so the servants could bring hot water for Memsahib's bath in the old claw-footed tub. It was wonderful to open that door and look out onto a lawn under breathing, rustling trees.

The air was much cooler up here, much fresher. To my amazement, as soon as I started walking on the path under the trees I felt quite recovered!

All the buildings had extremely steep pitched roofs with corrugated tin on them – Mahabaleshwar gets 380 inches of rain in a year. The village itself had open-fronted shops packed tightly together. Many shops sold leather goods, which had a terrible smell, so we avoided these and walked away into the landscape, sauntering on paths among huge dripping trees. We hiked quite a lot, and we both managed fine. It was wonderful to feel well again, in this fresh clean air.

We dined in the huge, nearly-empty hotel dining room, with crisp white tablecloths and white china. We had mulligatawny soup, and rice, and spicy veggies; and, for breakfast, tea and toast – the tea in a heated metal pot, the toast out of a toast-rack. There was butter, and the inferior, artificially-colored jams of India.

I loved the funny antiquity of the place, as if the Sahibs and Memsahibs had left only yesterday, and the old waiters were ready for them to come back at any moment. Everything was gently decaying, utterly habituated, and quite regal; only the food seemed thin and without much nourishment, as Indian food, grown in soils depleted by millenia of cultivation, generally does.

The affair with Shanti ended in a sordid way, due to my unreasoning addictiveness: the thing that was *my* drug. (And addiction is not the same thing as pleasure, mind you well.)

An Irishman who smoked, had a large reddish nose and viscous saliva, and little spaces between his teeth – and was nevertheless sexy – had been flirting with me for a while, though without a great deal of conviction. But I picked up on it and bore it home, that tiny advantage; the scorer's lookout for the main chance. I let him know that I would like to go to bed with him. He told me that he was on antibiotics for gonorrhoea. I told him I would just take some too.

This was the second time in my life I had done this unbelievably, unthinkably deluded and foolhardy thing, the very idea of which now sends me into near-panicked shudders of embarrassed and hypochondriacal freak-out. (The first time I'd been seventeen, in San Francisco, and the boy was just irresistibly beautiful.) Okay, you have to make mistakes to learn. But I've heard the Master say, "Just don't make the same mistake twice." My epic stupidity just beggars belief, quite frankly. Where was my sensitivity to my own precious body/soul?

Life has enough ghastly illnesses in it without deliberately getting them.

So we did, and I did, and it was all meaningless and unhappy and terrible, just bad and crappy and dry all over, and then of course I had to tell Shanti.

He railed and stormed and criticized, and then, quite wisely, broke up with me. What else could he do?

Energy Darshan

For years Bhagwan had been bringing energy work into darshan. He would ask someone in the gathering to come forward and lightly hold, in a particular way, the person he was addressing; someone else getting behind and supporting the disciple who was in the 'hot seat,' while he, Bhagwan, pressed his finger into their third eye. Sometimes he shone a small flashlight into the third eye.

When I was there, he nearly always asked me to come forward and be a support. This was unofficial, just the spontaneous happening of that evening's darshan.

Now he instituted something called Energy Darshan, which really stepped all this up.

Musicians were nearby so that when he put his finger on a third eye, drums were throbbing loudly. Lights were rigged up to flash on and off. And there were now to be certain women called Mediums to support the work, positioned by Bhagwan particular to each hot-seat occupant's energetic needs right then.

Vivek was in charge of recruiting the mediums, and I was called for the first-ever night of Energy Darshan. We had received a little coaching from her – if Bhagwan said, "Rise with the energy!" we were supposed to do Kegels, really – clench and unclench the vaginal muscles, our arms above our heads (unless we were using the arms to hold the person in some certain way). And, otherwise, we were just to let go into the energy, and hold the person as indicated by Bhagwan. Or sometimes a medium would be positioned to hold a medium to hold a medium, who was holding the hot-seat person. The general effect was of a waving garden of women swaying in some cosmic breeze, tending in a completely selfless way the usually falling-back-in-blissful-swoon person who was receiving the divine attention.

On this first night, the lights went down… I was in position as Bhagwan had placed me. There were about six of us, some standing behind others, who knelt – waiting for the hot-seat person to fall back after being touched by the magic thumb…

The drum-beat rose.

And I… well, I just sort of let go. A high ululation came out of my throat. I did not stop it, though my mind commented that perhaps I ought. But it was happening, and so I let it happen. A witchy treble wiggled its way out of me, a tremolo both effortless and yet perhaps just a little bit tortured. It went on and on. And on. Until the lights came back up and the person was helped back to his seat. The same thing happened with the next person receiving. And so on.

I was never called back to be a medium again.

On the one hand, I was embarrassed and disappointed. On the other, I was glad to have my evenings free!

During Energy Darshan the lights all over the ashram went out, and we could hear the music from Chuang Tzu bomming and bashing and rising, reaching a crescendo. Then it would stop – a gap, a silence – and then begin again. We, all over the ashram, had to stop whatever we were doing and just Be.

Receiving Energy Darshan was amazing – all that attention and energy focused into your deep being – all that music just for you. You'd be in your best robe, very clean indeed, waiting… You'd be called up, your heart beating like anything… And then… nothing to do; he would position you, and these motherly, soft-bodied, big and silent women would be behind you; and then his touch… and the mind would skitter from side to side like a rodent under glass, looking for a place to hide – and there *was* no place – and the thumb would be boring into your forehead, and then when you fell back you would be supported by all that warm/cool absent/presence of the women… And then you'd be helped back to your place and, usually, lie down, unable to even sit upright. The mind could make no sense of any of this and would be trying to find some foot-hold; but you'd be basically just kind of drowning, and have to lie there and feel the swirling/swaying abyss of things… Quite marvelous, ahhhh.

Nothing to think afterwards, either, when you were going out – . Except the usual stuff the mind liked to cleave unto, like, "Oh, I should have been able to surrender *more* – ."

A Weird Session

I had heard that Somendra, he of the Boat Club Road mini-haunting, was giving thrilling esoteric sessions. (He was now living in the ashram proper and was a Great Group Leader.) Curious, I arranged to have one. I went to his apartment; it was shady and cool, and his girlfriend, his Shakti, Bhavani, a pretty young blonde Swedish woman, moved domestically around in the background like a handmaiden.

The session went like this: we sat opposite each other on a mat on the floor. I told Somendra, no doubt in detail, various things that were going on with me. Then I waited for what might come next.

Now he was kneeling, sitting on his heels; gazing at me with his dark eyes under straggly-bushy brows. He said nothing; just stared – and then suddenly, he shot a bolt of energy out of his solar plexus, and it hit me, and I fell over backward, going "Oh!"

I picked myself up, thinking, "What the hell? What was *that* all about?"

But I *knew* what it was all about – he was showing off: "Look what I can do!" It was also some sort of punishment, I'm not sure for what; perhaps for kicking him out of my bedroom long before? But it felt like it was a punishment for being stupid, silly me.

I was so very not impressed; there was no utility in it, no love, no nothing – just a meaningless *Siddhi*, thrown about like penny candy, with a macho frown.

Bottoms

In one corner of Krishna House there had been built group showers and toilets, in a large white-tiled room. This had been designed specially for people who were doing groups in the new underground, soundproof therapy chambers beneath the house; but anyone could use them. There were no walls – you showered with everyone else. (There were other facilities around the commune, but those had curtained-off shower and toilet cubicles.) For the first time I showered with many people of both sexes, in two open rows on opposite sides of the space. These people were gregarious and conversational due to the opening-up they'd been undergoing in the groups, so it was a sociable place. This was an enjoyable thing – steaming water coming out of ten shower-heads at once, people from all over the world soaping up and rinsing off, shampooing and brushing their teeth, gossiping and chatting, laughing and grooming. So natural and easy! What is all the fuss about? People are people. (And I received a compliment there: "You look like a statue, with your clothes off!" said some woman; which stayed with me, as I still thought I was too fat.)

It was in this shower that I learned a great lesson: people wash their bottoms! I had not been taught to wash mine. A Pakistani friend tells me she was taught as a child to wash her "front bottom" and her "back bottom." But in my family, these parts of our bodies were regarded by our mother with great ambivalence. The girls' "front bottom" was called our "beauty spot" (which we could not pronounce, so called it "beauty pot.") This sounds pretty and fond, and it was; but although our mother could refer to it thus, we were not really supposed to refer to it at all – unless it hurt, in which case she would do a brisk, rather angry external examination and probably put bright-purple gentian violet on it. Our "back bottom," though, we were not supposed to refer to or think about at all. It was called variously "bottom" or "derrière," and the only thing sort-of-acceptable about it was its possible promise of having a nice shape when we grew up. The other things it did were unspeakable and unthinkable.

We girls were taught the importance of wiping from front to back, but no mention was ever made of washing anything "down there." When I began having periods at thirteen I found it necessary to wash there though, so I used normal bar soap, and got itching irritations as a result. (It was decades before I discovered Dr. Bronners Liquid Castile soap.) But the back bottom was never washed, since, of course, I was absolutely not supposed to touch it – I could hear my mother's rising shriek of horror at the very idea. (I have wondered since what my many lovers, in those many positions we twisted ourselves into, thought... smelled... saw... or even, heaven forbid, *tasted*...) So to see healthy German women busily sluicing their back bottoms with their hand under the shower was a revelation: the behind stuck out, hand back there, swishing up and down, pert female carrying on a conversation the while. They actually *do that?* I thought. *They touch their own anus? With other people watching?* They didn't seem to use soap; just the fast-flowing water. But it gave me courage, and one day I started washing mine too.

All that Indian washing-one's-bottom-by-hand-after-defecating was, of course, going on at the same time, so I'm not sure why the showering version should have been such a shock. So, in fact, my bottom *had* been getting washed since I'd come to live in India; though without soap. It was the time before that must have been dreadful. (Astronaut trainees were tested and it was found that three days of non-washing of the lower parts is all it takes for the bacteria to make their way up to your face!)

The strange thing is that my hygiene-minded mother, and father too, habitually cleaned themselves after a poo by using dampened toilet paper. They didn't teach this to us, and my one attempt at it resulted in such a mess of dissolved paper everywhere that I didn't try it again. But I always remember hearing the ferocious rattle rattle thump of the paper roll going round and round, round and round – whenever my mother was in the loo. It was all a very serious matter, like, I imagine, a cat on the litter box, its expression absorbed, private, frowning, hurried, severe. (One of my nieces, the same one I freaked out at for eating my jade plant back in San Francisco, reports that as a toddler she once shat in the {always filthy} bathtub at Date St. House. My mother shrieked blue murder, acting like the infant had set the Queen's dress on fire. Oh Lord.)

Bhagwan's doctor, Devaraj (later called Amrito) took a very dim view of all this Indian toilet cup water-washing business. He even wrote a tidy, quite readable little book on the unhygienic-ness of the practice. Apparently faeces get under the nails and is not easily dislodged even with washing (as is obvious by how easy it is to get Delhi Belly in a restaurant). Devaraj determined to change our hygiene habits. He designed and had installed, in all the toilets, little curving copper pipes, hooked up to faucets, so that we could use a little fountain of water to clean ourselves.

Unfortunately this was not really the solution. What tended to happen was that little crumbs of excreta fell into the pipes – narrow though they were – and sat there like tiny scoops of ice cream in cones. The pellets were then visited upon the next person. (The aim was to keep us from passing on amoebas – but someone else's poo up your back passage could plant them where they liked to grow.) If they went into a woman's vagina, she could be in trouble. Also, with unskilled maneuvering one's own poo could be washed into one's own vulva. This was not fun.

I have heard that Indians consider toilet paper terribly unhygienic. And it's true that it doesn't get everything off. Nor does toilet paper always save your hands; and if you then don't wash them, then we're right back with the germy germs. One reads so many things. Poo transplants can apparently save the lives of people suffering certain colon-centered diseases. (But probably not administered via copper pipe.)

But nice clean toilet paper has something comforting about it – and I'll vote for it, plus a good washing of the hands, plus a daily shower where the "back bottom" is washed with Dr. Bronners, and the hands are then washed too – five times. Yeah. Though on further reflection: if you wash your back bottom with soap and water in the shower, perhaps germs can still survive under the nails? You can't win!

But toilet paper in India is a challenge, more so back then. You *could* buy it, but the cardboard roll itself was very thick, the paper scanty; it was (and is) very expensive, India having cut down most of its trees after the Brits left; and you were quite likely to discover insects, alive and walking, or dead and husking, under the cellophane wrapper. If you are going to India, I would advise packing quite a few rolls; then, as you use them up, you'll have more room for the pretty scarves and floppy trousers and spangly blouses you will no doubt buy.

No Babies Ever

Many sannyasin women had tubal ligation at Shree Clinic. Bhagwan had told some of them to do it; others decided for themselves. (I cannot say why he did that; I am assuming he must have seen that for *that* woman, there were better fates than child-rearing.) I had been thinking about it for some time, and in 1980 or so I wrote to Bhagwan asking if I should undergo the procedure. "Follow your feeling," he replied.

Once again, I listened to somebody reporting a great experience, and was swayed… One woman told me that she had been given ketamine as an anesthetic and had had a wonderful out-of-body trip. Greed awoke in me. I wanted such an experience too! I booked the procedure.

Dr. Saraswati himself was to do the operation. He was a reserved, bespectacled man of middle height with an air of patient wisdom and boundless experience. He seemed both present, and economical with his energies.

You had to take a very long rickshaw ride across the city to get to the clinic, which was housed in a huge building in an area of tall trees, apartment buildings, and coconut-wallahs operating from wooden carts with awnings. The area was busier than Koregaon Park, but still it was leafy and green. But the traffic all the way there was a frantic pooting snarl. A woman going for a delicate operation had to cling to her wits and her center as she was flung this way and that in the putt-putting rickshaw, bouncing through puddles, falling in pot-holes, swerving at the very last second as a huge truck bore down on the tiny vehicle; the driver muttering, blaring his horn, shouting at other drivers, hands raised in gestures of disgust; all in a welter of toxic fumes.

Every patient entering an Indian hospital is asked to bring a family member. This escort – which usually expands to include most of the extended family – provides all kinds of support – food, drinks, gossip, reassurance, liaison with staff; whatever. (In fact, it has seemed to me that the family are quite capable of giving the patient a relapse – domestic squabbles are sometimes played out at top volume across the sufferer's bed.)

But I was supposed to bring somebody – so I brought the guy I was sort of dating. A very strange choice, all things considered… I'm not sure what nurturance I thought I was going to get from this young near-stranger.

He was an extremely handsome black-haired German with a deep squared-off jaw and a pale skin; he had not been around the ashram for very long. He was tall and very well-built. We had no chemistry in bed or in conversation, so I can't think what I was doing with him, or he with me; I think I was just really impressed that a man of such singular beauty would consent to be around me at all!

I was given the ketamine. This veterinary anesthetic is supposed to render you pain-free, though still conscious, for about twenty minutes. However, I vanished forthwith into deep nothingness. The operation was done, via a little slit below my navel. The young man was allowed to gaze through the instrument's viewing lens. He found the sight cosmic and yet queasy-making, he told me later – the inside of the female body where the fallopian tube comes obediently down from the ovary to the womb… *so pink*, he said.

All this did not take long. I was then wheeled to the recovery room, and Dr. Saraswati left the clinic – gone, as I remember, for the rest of the day.

At any rate, nobody told him that I simply did not regain consciousness… for twelve hours.

The young man (who looked a bit like a hairier Elvis) sat by my side, waiting. He became impatient – he wanted to move! But what could he do? He was supposed to take me safely home.

He waited and waited. After twelve hours of this he could stand it no longer, and shook me awake.

I surfaced in a terrible thick grogginess, unable to remember my own name, where I was, or what I was doing there.

"Do you want to go to a party?" asked the young fellow.

"A *party?*" I stuttered numbly. "Argh… !"

"It is midnight," he said. "I want to go!"

He took me home in a rickshaw, propping me up as we swayed. (Needless to say, I was not going to any party.) He ensconced me in my little room behind the Godown, and took off into the night.

Next morning I woke up sick as a dog, and for the next three days I hung my head out into the little rain-gutter, throwing up. The young fellow came by a few times, bringing a big supply of sugar donuts he had gotten somewhere. They looked to me as awful as the party had sounded. I threw up again.

Slowly I recovered. And I was heartbroken – not about the young man, not about losing fertility; no, not at all – but because I *hadn't gotten to have a great experience.* I had been *counting* on it! And I'd *missed* it all! I'd been *asleep*, and *missed* it! I was so pissed off that I wrote an interminable poem about it. (Mercifully I have not included it in my book, *The Poona Poems.)*

We all loved great experiences. Great experiences were (and still are) a most elemental excitement for the silly seeker. Never mind that Bhagwan said, "All experiences are of the mind." In the face of all this emptiness he was offering, Great Happenings made us feel important, at least for a little while. They made us hop up and down… cheap thrills! So I had a nauseating and disappointing experience instead of a Great one.

I was left with a tiny, curving scar below my navel, instead of a brood of babies. It's always seemed a very prudent trade.

Many years later, in 2008, I had occasion to talk to Dr. Saraswati. I told him what had happened to me back then, in 1980, and he was very much surprised. He said he had never heard of ketamine affecting anyone like that. He said I must be allergic to it.

All Change

Bhagwan very often talked to us about "the New Commune." His idea was that we would move up to Kutch, to Gujarat, and there flourish in splendid isolation from the world, building our community as we pleased. He seemed to yearn over this dream. In fact, Laxmi had found a property there, a huge place with buildings already on it; though it had a problem with insufficient water. Sheela had been going up and down, meeting with the brokers.

I didn't pay much attention to all this – I loved our ashram as-is, and didn't want to think of a huge change like that – although there was a certain heady feeling of freedom for all of us, in the dream. (I could imagine the cleanliness of the air up there.) I just lived so intensely in the present, like we all did, that pie-in-the-sky didn't get much energy.

But I did know that Bhagwan's back had been causing him lots of trouble and pain. He walked with tiny jerky steps, as if he wasn't quite in the body, as if whatever animating force the body had, it was more like a puppeteer than an inhabitant. I knew he was getting acupuncture and bodywork from various Commune practitioners. Sometimes he was ill and didn't come out to talk to us, and we drifted about, bereft and fearful, till he came out again.

One morning I'd been on an errand into Lao Tzu for some reason and when I was coming out, somebody stopped me and told me that Bhagwan had left the night before, with an entourage.

This was so shocking I felt calm.

Then many things happened very fast.

People began making plans to leave. Everything about us soon settled into a sort of peaceable uproar as people's different directions began to show themselves. I was told that I was invited to the Castle in New Jersey where Bhagwan was now staying – but I had to get my own ticket together.

Meanwhile I was moved back into Lao Tzu; but this time it was to the same upstairs veranda where in the beginning Bhagwan had given discourses. There were rows of pallets there now, with mosquito nets strung up over them. So many strings there were, tied to whatever could be found to tie them to! They criss-crossed the whole area at head or throat or chest height.

Very soon, the male English disciples started getting drunk at night. This was new; nobody had been doing that while Bhagwan was here. If one went out to dinner one sometimes had a vile, cough-syrupy port wine, or a glycerine-infused beer that induced headaches. (Imported spirits were very hard to get, and the Indian copies were famously rough.) But that's all. But now Englishmen were coming back to the veranda at all hours of the night, steeped in booze; and then, as they roamed about the rows looking for their pallets, they bumped into the strings and fell down. I would hear them crashing and thumping and falling, but it was dark; and in the morning there they'd be, not even in a bed, but just lying there between the rows like fallen soldiers.

I was shocked at this unseemly behavior in his house.

...Now I think that those Englishmen, like the rest of us, were very, very afraid. What if we never saw Bhagwan any more? The world is so big!

I wondered how I would get money for a ticket. My father had stopped sending the $60 a month when I was twenty-six. I had nothing. I wrote to my mother and told her the situation. Soon afterwards I got a letter from a wealthy friend of the family, offering to lend me the money.

So I now had a ticket to New York via London.

Many sannyasins had let their Indian visas lapse, not wanting to leave the ashram long enough to go away and get a new one – often with an obligatory six-month wait before the new application was possible. Sheela had negotiated with New Delhi for amnesty for those people, and it was granted. Everyone who had overstayed had to hand over their passport and a special stamp would be put in it and it would then be returned. A booth was set up on the Zen Walk for this handing-over. I was moved from the Newsletter Office to this booth, where I had daily chances of flirting with overstaying men. I took full advantage of this, and, liking clerical activities too, I greatly enjoyed the job.

I was of course sleeping here and there, vaguely wishing for a real boyfriend. Once, the idea arose in me that I had never experienced an orgy, and ought to. (Certainly, contrary to the hopes of the general population of India, America, or wherever, there were no orgies among us in the commune – the event about to be described notwithstanding.) I didn't *feel like* experiencing one – I don't really know what it *would* feel like to want an orgy. But I thought I'd be neglectful to leave one out altogether. I managed to find three willing guys – one very old and gangly – and went into a room with them. What followed was like something that might happen in a train station medical office in East Germany during the Cold War. I *so* don't recommend it.

Then the Great Demolition took place, and I was on the demolition crew.

The ashram was by then stuffed with temporary structures, made of bamboo, cloth, wood; even the tiled roof over the dining area was an illegal addition. All of these rattletrap little rooms, and annexes, the more solid outdoor rooves – were illegal, and had to come down before we left. A skeleton crew was to remain in Poona, and everything had to be shipshape.

And so we roamed around in a pack, with a ghetto-blaster, knocking things down.

This was hugely fun! I loved being in this crowd of mostly guys, wielding hammers and crowbars, dismantling, shoving with main force, watching things topple and collapse in a shower of detritus, plywood, bamboo, and dust. Building takes time and care; destroying requires neither. We just went for it.

I felt full of energy. We bopped to the music, we laughed and joked, and down came the rooms where we'd loved and meditated and eaten and sat… thinking things would never end.

Paraphernalia was being sold off – all sorts of equipment, tools, audio-visual machines, kitchenware, clothing from the boutique, medical equipment, books – every little thing. For the Indians all about us, it seemed, this was a bonanza of unparalleled excitingness. They descended in well-heeled packs, bargaining like the canniest housewives, trying to get each thing for as little as possible, frowning and bickering and grimacing and denigrating the coveted merchandise.

One day I was helping take tile down from the roof over the eating area beside Vrindavan. Some of the tiles were glassed in the middle, to let light through. I squatted on the roof, lifting the heavy tiles, piling them in stacks – two, four, six – then standing with the stack and handing it off to the guy who would give it down to the next guy, to put it on the pile on the ground.

I did this for hours.

Next morning when I woke, my right knee had doubled in size and would barely flex. This knee had a troubled past (and would have a troubled future). It had suffered dancing injuries, a collision with a plate-glass window… So I tailored my demolition to fit a hobbly knee, knocking things down but not squatting to lift them. And went on having fun.

Leaving

I was sorting my clothes, seeing which ones might work in the West. Robes? No… But how could I get rid of my soft, flowing robes? I kept a couple. I had somehow acquired a set of faded red knitted trousers and top, which seemed to me thick and sturdy – something good to keep warm in. By this time our range of clothes-colors had expanded into various shades of pinks, corals, reds, even violet – as long as it had red in it, it was okay. The only shoes I had were chappals, of course, so they would have to do. I did not own a coat, or a scarf, or a hat. And autumn was on the way. Someone gave me a pair of wide-wale brown corduroy trousers – somehow reddish enough to pass – and they were the warmest thing I had.

That monsoon had seen a particularly dreadful dengue fever hit us. I had had it very badly, lying on my pallet up on the veranda, listening to the rain, day after day, as I sweated and hurt all over – and I had become very thin indeed. Word was trickling back from people who had already gone to the West that they came down with the virus on their arrival there, and had to spend two or more weeks in bed, sick as dogs. So it was an epidemic.

Finally it was time to leave. I traveled alone, and by a miracle had a row of seats to myself all the way to Frankfurt, where I had a few hours' wait. The culture shock was immense. I sat in the airport, gawping at it all – the strange synthetic fabrics and building materials everywhere; in Poona things were still made of bamboo, wood, cotton, silk, stone. The fine and polished products in the shops awed and frightened me – a world I could not afford, that had moved on without me; cold and exclusive and unobtainable. I did not know if I wanted such things or not – perfect, tough handbags, a bottle of liqueur with a whole pear inside. My fingertips, for some reason, felt uncomfortably dry, making it very unpleasant to touch things. And the people… they seemed hard-edged and almost completely remote from each other. This was just *strange*, and impossible, and desperately sad.

I landed next in London and went off for a few days to the house of T.Z.'s parents, who were sannyasins. It was not a big house, but it was in the country, and stood in its own little garden. They were very kind to me (so that I had to consider, briefly, what life might have been like had I had their grandchild –) but it was soon time to go on my way, not to linger in that world which also had its shocks: I was helping dry the dishes after dinner while T.Z.'s mum washed. I was amazed to see that she submerged each dish in hot soapy water, gave it a scrub with a cloth, and lifted it right out and into the rack. "But – aren't you going to rinse them?" I asked. "Oh, it's only washing-up liquid!" she said airily. (To this day I find this British practice inexplicable and unacceptable! And I've been confronted with it many times!)

My clothes! The knit top and pants that had seemed thick in India seemed tissue-thin in England. Not only that, but everything I had looked worn and limp and old.

I landed next in New York and was collected at the airport and taken through bewildering labyrinths of urban landscape to a hill; and up, and up, and up… to a castle high on a wooded ridge in New Jersey, in sight of the New York skyline. Quite a few selected ashramites were there before me.

It was wonderful, so utterly safe-feeling, to be back among my Tribe. To be near Bhagwan, though I hadn't seen him in person quite yet.

That first night, and every night after, there was a large and delicious dinner spread out on a long table.

Such profusion!

I ate a lot.

4

Bouncy Castle

Bouncy Castle

September 1981

In a Lofty Palisade

I was to sleep on a pallet in a long room with others, in a tower. This faced onto a courtyard, on the other side of which was the large main house, where Bhagwan stayed, and the offices were.

My job was a sort of records-keeper: by now we knew that Sheela had bought a huge ranch in Oregon, and we were all going to go there; and many people were applying to come out there to live. Files were kept on them all, just an index card with a photo and a few details about their qualifications and skills; and particularly noting any amount of money they had pledged to the project. (On these cards 'money' was always euphemistically referred to as 'amount.') Many skilled people would be needed to build up the new commune's infrastructure – construction workers, architects, pilots, plumbers, mechanics, engineers, city planners, and so on.

One could feel the long arm of Sheela in all this far-looking practicality. She had already gone on to the Ranch, but there were a few women at the Castle who were her helpers, already sprouting a sort of party line. In Poona, Deeksha had been the only despot I had even obliquely encountered. I now felt the whiff of something control-freaky from afar, but as usual I took as little notice of such things as possible, being mainly interested in my own existence – if highly, constantly grateful for the presence of Bhagwan.

I enjoyed my work – more nice officey stuff.

Once I bumped into Bhagwan in a hallway, just like in Poona – only in this case I had a glass of water in my hand. I needed to namaste to him – what to do with the glass of water? Oh dear! …I simply held it between my hands and namasted around it. I felt like an idiot, embarrassed and alarmed and delighted. (Embarrassed, someone has asked me, why? Didn't you already *know* each other? ...Well, not exactly. First of all, as the Master says, you can't step in the same river twice. So this moment of meeting is acutely new, every time. That is the very soul of being awake – that nothing is old. It is a different moment.

(And then... in the presence of a Buddha – any Buddha – one's very identity is called into question, in a completely existential way: *Hunh? Um, here I am? Am I? Who is this me? WTF?* sort of thing. As if 'you' are being seen through, through and through! – and this is most disconcerting to the one-who-supposes-she-is-this-concrete-something-or-other. Because, of course, one isn't; or not in quite the way one thinks. And the being suddenly registers all this, and is flummoxed to the max. So 'embarrassed' is just as good a word as any.)

I had one date at the Castle, which was worse than terrible, but otherwise there wasn't any of that sort of action. I just kept eating big, delicious, nutritious dinners.

Right after I arrived, a few of us went to a shopping mall. Everybody needed clothes, and people bought sporty, practical anoraks and sweaters and jogging pants. I could not afford any of these things (I had $8 in my pocket, and that was all I owned), and was over-awed by the clothes all about me in the shops. I was mortified by my shabbiness when I saw myself in a mirror. This was childhood revisited: like when I'd accompanied Taffy and her mother to the Mall, and watched, mute with unshed tears, while garments were tried, and piled up, and bought – and none of them for me.

As I've been assembling this book, someone has asked me what I felt about this move. Didn't I feel betrayed to wake up and find that Bhagwan had left Poona? That many of us were stranded without money or a ticket? Why, this person asked, would I follow him when he'd left us in this way? And why did he choose America – such an expensive place?

These questions amazed me – though it's not the first time I've been asked such things.

I can only say it like this: for all that I'm a quirky, lopsided, self-absorbed soul, I still felt no distance between Bhagwan and his Commune, and myself. There *was* no 'me' to stand back and scratch its chin thoughtfully and consider its options. I was completely immersed in the romantic river in which I found myself – its every eddy and swerve and flood. It was *life* to me, and no other place was life. It wasn't possible to exist in his Communes and maintain a separate sense of yourself and your destiny. You would be so buffeted by the prevailing winds of cosmic includingness that the fight to stand upright and be separate would become far too painful. The state of surrender (and I call it a state rather than a willed Doing) was so delicious – so intriguing – that you would as soon forgo it as forgo love, and chocolate, and sunsets for the rest of your days.

I could not feel betrayed – that would require an entitled separateness. Bhagwan did not owe me anything. He was a Mystery; mysteries do not owe. As far as being stranded goes, well, that was just more adventure. That's how my life had been since I was a teenager – and would be again and again. Calculation wasn't part of it.

The question, too, presupposes that Bhagwan was a normal human being, as we understand humans that we know – neighbors, family, co-workers, even movie stars or politicians. Then, of course, you might have the normal range of emotions towards him.

But this was not the case.

I have never seen a less grossly-embodied being; a more ephemeral, a more slenderly-attached to this world. Where we have bodies and minds and clothes and feet, he had Light; it had displaced the usual equipment that homo sapiens carries. There was no weight to him anywhere. Does a laser beam have weight?

...Why would I follow him? Because he was my leaf, my branch, my tree; my roots and wings. He was not a 'he' and I was not a 'me.' I was not as small as that.

As to America: yes, an unwelcome place by and large; I did not love it. But again, wherever he was, life was. And life was not otherwhere. Even someplace in America could become a sacred place if he was there.

He did not choose it. I didn't know this at the time, but nor did I think about it in any considering sort of way. I learned later that he had wanted to go to Switzerland to get his extremely incapacitated back fixed, then return to India and create a new commune in Gujarat.

But Sheela, now his secretary, had other ideas.

But more on that later...

A Ride More Fly

Somehow Bhagwan had managed to get a driver's license right away, and someone must have given him a Rolls Royce. So he now took two drives a day, morning and evening; and for each of these rides, two people would be invited to come along. They would be notified well in advance so that they'd have time to bathe, brush teeth, and put on fresh clothes.

One evening we had all gathered under the trees outside the big steps that led down from the main house, to wait for his appearance. The big, sleek, classic car was waiting there, and Nivedano the drummer led the musicians in playing; we all clapped and sang.

Suddenly I simply *knew* that he was going to ask me to come along tonight – though I had not been notified. And I was horrified – my teeth were unbrushed after dinner, I had not bathed, my hair was a mess. And to top it off, my trousers would not zip – I'd been replenishing all the weight I'd lost from dengue. My corduroy trousers were partly open, under a T-shirt.

Bhagwan emerged from the main door, all glowing in his white robe. He teetered a little there, in his not-quite-in-a-body way, and then he said softly, almost too low to hear – "Madhuri?" And he looked at me.

So I went to the car, and was shown to the back seat next to a guy from accounting; Vivek sat on the other side of him.

Bhagwan drove, and beside him was his doctor, a cuddly-bear American whose name I forget.

Rapidly it grew dark. We drove through suburbs and then, accelerating up the on-ramp, we swung out onto the freeway. An expert foot on the accelerator kept us flying, faster now, and faster.

Nobody said a word. In fact, during that entire drive only one thing was said – and that by Bhagwan. He was accelerating again – yes, we were *speeding* – when we passed a white car with a woman driver. She glanced over at us, and did a double-take, with a look of worried surprise. Then we zoomed far ahead.

"Ha ha!!" Bhagwan chuckled naughtily. "Ve really scared that vooman!"

What went on *inside* a poor mortal in that hurtling metal can was something else! I was sitting not two feet away from him for an hour and a half, and my mind went nuts. It bounced about the inside of the car like letters in alphabet soup; noisy as hell! …And its content was mortifying: it obsessed about how my unbrushed teeth might be offending his nose. About how gross it was of me to ride with him with my trousers unzipped. About how of course he could HEAR all this crap my mind was shouting. It seemed to me he was the unwilling witness to what people do in their bathrooms when nobody is watching. Oh lord, what I felt was thorns and brambles and SHAME.

Strangely, I wasn't afraid we'd crash, though we were going way too fast! Crashing with Bhagwan just didn't seem anything worthy of fear... What a way to go!

The ride was amazing in fact. The smooth projectile force flattened us back in our seats as gravity climbed, spaceship-style. His presence... well, you know. It kind of just creams your brains like they are in a blender or melting in a saucepan ready to become sauce – whatever of them isn't resisting like mad. It was epic, it was enchanted, magic, transported. All that too.... It was... *sensual.* The speed, the transported state... immensely.

When we returned to the Castle everyone piled out. As usual the passengers were giggling, careening, high and giddy. Bhagwan, of course, stepped sedately, smiling, apparently delighted with the fun of the jaunt.

I fell out crouched over, and kind of crawled to my pallet in the turret, feeling like I'd been run over by a truck. For the next few days, any chance I got, I went up to my bed and lay down. I was totaled, smashed – I didn't know why. I was ashamed of what had come out from under rocks and paraded itself in front of him in the intimate ether of the vehicle. And most of all, scared witless of my Master. Scared of what, I cannot tell you even now – some existential ruthlessness. Something like, what Outer Space might be like, if you were to float around in it.

And Soon...

I don't know how long I spent at the Castle; not longer than a few weeks. A couple more things happened in this time: a woman in the office put out a call to all of us there, asking us to donate whatever money we could to the new commune in Oregon. In my fervor of gratefulness for being there, I handed over all my treasure: the $8, and an old Timex watch that had cost $10 new, and still worked. The office woman – we'll call her A. – laughing gently, told me how touching it was that I had contributed these things.

Then, my long-time publishers at *Hanging Loose* magazine in Brooklyn had written inviting me to lunch, which of course I was happy about. I informed A., as I'd have to take off work for a day and find a way to get into the city.

Next day I was called into the small, cluttered office, where A. greeted me. She was a genteel, virginal-looking young woman with a creamy skin, dark curls, and very white teeth. (She was not bohemian at all, a thing I always found weird – why would somebody not want to look funky and wild? Instead she somehow managed to look immensely straight, even in her red clothes.) She informed me that I was to fly to Oregon next day.

This was puzzling and disturbing. Of course I was excited about going to Oregon, but to miss the lunch with my publishers… could it be an accident? What on earth could be threatening to the office about my going to that lunch? Did someone think I'd have a big head, or have too much fun, or be too much of a separate individual?

In my non-confrontive way, I said nothing; but I had to phone *Hanging Loose* and tell them I could not come. I felt strange doing this – as if they must think I was being held captive by a cult. (It would be thirty years before I would finally meet someone from the magazine for dinner in Greenwich Village, and by that time one of the partners, my main champion, had died.)

And so I flew to Oregon the very next day, and was met at the airport and brought over the hills and through the valleys, and we drove into the Ranch in the dark with the windows open, and the crisp air smelled of sage ice cream…

5

Cowboy Planet

Cowboy Planet

1981 – 1985

Wild East Meets Wild West

So, I was at the Ranch, 164 square miles of hill and valley, river and woods, scrub and dirt and silence. Beautiful, remote, wild. The hills were very steep and high – almost mountains. One valley was broad and flat and sloping, another narrow and woodsy. There was a small wooden house in the big valley, and nearby a barn – very rustic and Wild West. There were a couple of areas where trailers had been set up for people to live in. A few people lived in tents, or had come to the Ranch with their own travel-trailers. People drove the dusty roads in pickup trucks.

There were only about fifty people here so far, and forty-seven of them, I noted, were male. (The other two women were in relationships.) We were all cowboys now. The men I'd flirted with in India in their robes and lungis now wore red jeans and t-shirts and cowboy boots and hats. I could see their behinds now, and their long skinny legs; and I liked what I saw. What were those monogamous women thinking of? thought I. The miserliness! The boring self-defense! So many cowboys. All those earnest, rugged figures, going about the labor of the land, riding pickup trucks, wearing tool-belts. All that new swagger. They had nobody to cuddle up with at night!

I had to do my best to fill the gap.

I was given a space in a trailer, and was grateful not to be in a tent. The trailers were mostly double-wides, warm and cozy, planted to stay. I worked in a little building over near Sheela's under-construction house. The office was called Hakim Sanai, and the job was a continuation of what I'd done at the Castle, vetting applicants. I enjoyed this job. So many people wanted to come! So many were German, with legal names like Irmtraut and Edeltraut. They all seemed to be social workers. But here they would be construction or kitchen workers or taxi drivers.

Hakim Sanai wasn't far from the old ranch house, the little wood-frame place under tall cottonwood trees. This house had a small yard, and a porch; food was served up on the porch, and we ate at long tables on the lawn. Right away, the food was fantastic. I remember a great rectangular pan of chili rellenos – thick and rich and spicy and wonderful. There were leftovers, and I had a plate cold for breakfast with strong sweet coffee. Delicious!

Sometimes, amazingly, we all got a day off! I was taken up in a small plane on one of these days, and looked down at this vast craggy landscape we'd claimed – with the big John Day River winding along at the edge. I felt safe and belonging here – because it was us, because it was Bhagwan.

So even the Wild West was do-able. It was not a fantasy of mine, this Wild West – I grew up too close to it (related, as it happens, to both Daniel Boone the frontiersman and Wyatt Earp, the famous sheriff – turns out there's a drop of Shawnee blood too) – but many Europeans probably adored it.

Very soon after I arrived, I was directed to the clothes trailer to get some proper outdoor gear. This was tremendously exciting. It looked like an old-fashioned general store in there, with boxes of snow-boots piled to the ceiling, jackets hanging from hooks, piles of jeans. I was issued with a faux-down vest, a thick jacket, double-layered insulated boots I called Alligator Boots, because of their swampish color. There was a pair of plain rubber boots too, black with a red line on the heel. Jeans, t-shirts, sweaters, socks, knitted hat. I carried the pile out, wishing I could poke about more, find more. They were hardly sexy, these clothes, but I knew I could be creative with them.

Devadasi and Vedant Prem, her husband, had been some of the first people to come to the Ranch. But they didn't last long; in fact, they left shortly before I arrived. I was sad that they had left.

Vedant Prem had been helping to install trailers. The siding used at their base was composed of some man-made substance, the cutting of which released a sort of synthetic sawdust. Vedant Prem, it turned out, was so allergic to this that his face and head swelled up in a terrifying manner, especially one of his ears; and he had an asthma attack. He was very much affrighted. So he and Mama left, and eventually settled in Weed, California, near to Mt. Shasta, where they were very happy. It had been years since I had seen Mama, and would be a few more years before I saw her again.

I was drafted temporarily for Deer-Hunt Patrol. It was autumn, deer-hunting season, and the Ranch's neighbors were accustomed to hunting freely on this land. Naturally, we did not want them to do that. So on every road going in and out of the Ranch, sannyasins were stationed in pairs, either in campers or tents, to warn the hunters away. I was loaded into the back of a pickup truck with others and taken up a strange valley. (I felt engagingly boyish, like a ranch hand, leaping over pickup-truck sides, that sort of thing!)

I was let off in a remote hilly place with a thin blond American guy, a tent and some supplies. We pitched the tent at the edge of woods not far from the dirt road. It was just us out here; the road was normally nearly un-trafficked except during deer-hunting season.

I walked up a dry creek-bed and was amazed to see, built in between the round river-stones, many, many of the tough, conical webs I knew to belong to black widow spiders. Indeed, there was a black widow now – a shiny, bulbous arachnid with her spidery legs and red hourglass on the belly – uh-oh! So black, shiny as patent leather, and so heavy and profound-looking!

And another! And another! They were standing on rocks – I saw egg sacs, and broken egg sacs; and a zillion little babies running around. A black widow breeding ground!

A large camper rolled up to where N., my partner, was manning a chair by the road. I could see him talking to the driver. As I approached I heard the driver arguing: "…But we *always* hunt here!"

"Not now," explained N. The hunter was very cross, but he turned his vehicle around with some difficulty and went back the way he'd come.

To my disappointment, there was no chemistry between myself and N. We talked some, and then I went out into the woods to look for entertainment.

I strolled deeper into the trees. It was a thin wood, idling up a long slope to the higher hills. It was very quiet here – anything that might make noise was far far away. There was just the hushy baffle of tree-trunks and half-blown-down leaves. I could feel the cushion of leaf-mulch under my feet – yielding, thick, slightly crackling.

I knelt down. Big breath in, big breath out.

And then I got an idea. All that experimenting I'd been doing, with feeling the energy of chakras. Why not try that sensing-with-my-hand thing, on… these fallen leaves?

So I hovered my hand above the leaf-mulch, closed my eyes… waited…

By and by, I noticed that something was coming up out of the leaves; showing itself to my hand. It told me of the life-cycle of these leaves – how they grew, green, trembled in the wind, carried the sap of the tree to the air and the sun, drank the sun. How they were later released by the tree and fell gently. How they'd piled up here; and so many, so many seasons' worth, hundreds, thousands, millions of years of leaves – becoming mulch, becoming soil. Time was so much bigger than our impatient lives could comprehend. Cold, cold Winters – hot Summers – breezy Springs – chilling Autumns – all were felt and experienced by the leaves… wholly. And now they were in layers, decaying, decayed, or not yet crumbled. They told me all this.

I was amazed. I understood then that *anything* could be read – anything at all. A great world opened out before me.

I can still feel the leaves in my body. The mulch.

One morning I presented myself at 4 a.m. at the little old ranch house, as requested. A few others were gathering there too. We were fed a substantial breakfast, which felt odd at that hour. Then we split up into different vehicles to be taken to different locations for deer-hunt patrol.

I was dropped, along with a man whose name I now forget, high up the rutted road behind the house where Bhagwan lived. The Master's home too was a double-wide trailer, slightly improved in a Zennish way, with a deck added; we would catch a glimpse of it on the way down, later – but for now all was dark. We could not even see the road. The house sat in a fold in the valley just below a range of hills. There was a sense of weighty responsibility, to be guarding the land above it.

My partner and I walked up the last of the distance to a broad plateau; we crested the rise as the sun rose. We carried lunches and water. The pickup we'd arrived in had gone back to town, and would collect us later.

We two began to roam around over this strange, utterly deserted place.

It was eerily beautiful. In fact, in my memory, it was a day out of the world, out of time, out of the normal; and was to become imbued with indisputable magic – as if the wonderful Being who reigned at the base of the hill had somehow invited a transcendent realm to this hilltop too. The plateau rolled and stretched as far as we could see; it had irregular edges, like a doily. There'd been rain, and the grass shone luminously green. There were no trees, but crevices cut down through the plateau; also green. Behind us the valley dipped down, but from here we could not see our little civilization.

We simply ambled about, watching out for people; but we saw nobody.

What we did see, though, was something extraordinary – something I've never seen before, or since. There were little rainbows everywhere! All about us, like stripey etheric fairies, rainbow segments marched and shone. As we moved, they moved – it was as if the plateau was the home of a secret, enchanted race, and we were privileged to see it. They hovered, moved, here, there, everywhere we turned. And it all felt somehow so appropriate – that the hills above the house of such a One, someone so exploded into the All and the Mystery, should be watched over by such a cadre.

I spent two months or so sleeping with as many men as came along… quite a few! It was difficult to fit them in. I had to work in the office all day, and then eat dinner at the temporary cafeteria. (A proper one was being built lickety-split, up the valley; a great thing with huge ceiling beams, solid, and huge of window.) If I was really exhausted and needed to be alone, I could not go to dinner, I had to creep home without eating, for if I was there amongst people someone would catch hold of me, and I would not say no. Those solo nights were rare.

There was S. – tall, Canadian, thick light-brown wavy hair, laughed in a diffident, big-as-the-woods Canadian way, was unreadable, was wonderful to lie in the arms of… so tall, such strong arms, such big silently articulate hands. At some point he turned his back, I didn't know why. Was it the other men? He wouldn't say.

There was an Aussie mechanic, with a thick James Dean upswing of hair, not tall but ever so rugged, with something of the depressive about him, yet, as a lover, so sweet and willing and grateful.

There was a skinny speechless cowboy, American, the real thing, rough and glinty-eyed, drawling… vulnerable as heck. I loved 'em and moved on… there was something in everybody to love.

But, right away, more women started showing up. I didn't approve of this at all – lovely blonde Vibha, German Gatha with her strong jaw and deep fringe and air of innocent wisdom, very attractive to boys. Not fair! They were cutting into my monopoly.

I had an orgasm with tall S., just from petting and caressing, and I was very impressed. It didn't happen with the others, nor did I expect it. And I must say that when I look back on this time – which seemed to last much, much longer than the two months or so that it did – I feel a pure joy, a laughter, a delight. What a project! What a silly person I was! But – what richness, what freedom!

I was extremely interested in what happened in bed. Within the Buddhafield, this often seemed to be some high-flown amazingness – some mystery impacting me, spinning me around. Deep caverns opened around me. I fell off tall buildings and spun to earth. I flew in star-struck night skies, without a map of any kind. ...My breathing, though, never felt quite right. Nothing was ever slow enough for me – yet I myself was so often the one to speed things up – as if I couldn't bear the meeting to last longer, go deeper. I knew that I was inadequate. Whatever passion I felt would subside in the middle somewhere, go into a gap, a coolness. Other energies rose and peaked, but not 'down there.' But I so loved the weird adventure of meeting.

Fool for Love

Husky Vidya was still my boss. This was creepy, though in a way comfortingly known.

One day she sent me out to get some background information from a certain English person, for the records... Ah. But I get ahead of myself.

In the midst of all this running around with all those men, one day a strange idea came to me. It seemed that now I would like to get into a real relationship. I wanted to fall in love.

To prepare for this, I stopped going to bed with anyone. And to do this, I had to stay away from the cafeteria at night. This went on for three days, which felt like three months. Surely I would have to have supper again sometime?

Then Vidya sent me on the bus (we had old school buses making frequent, regular runs up and down the valley) to interview this guy, a construction worker called Anand Subuddha. I found him at the bottom of the short road up to where Magdalena Cafeteria was under construction.

As he answered my questions, I watched his face. He had a long slender mouth that moved through many expressions. One of his front teeth was slightly uneven at the bottom, and just a trifle beige. His hair was dirty blond and very straight and fine. He was of just above medium height with extremely broad and mobile shoulders – he used them when he talked, moving them about – and very narrow hips – these also all shot through with fluidity.

But it was his eyes that really got me; they were the most profoundly guileless, blue, crystalline eyes I had ever seen. (Only later I reflected how very like my father's they were. Glen too had that guileless blue, peering at you mildly, abstractedly, when you slid yourself into his world and asked him something.)

Subuddha seemed completely present when he talked to me – absolutely *here.* He answered thoroughly, seriously. Yet – there was also something about him that seemed to be answering the woman in me. When he laughed he was both wicked and sidelong, and yet frankly guileless. His eyes sparkled, his mouth curved all over the place, then he threw back his head and laughed. His shoulders moved, making commentary.

That night we were together, in his trailer on the other side of the valley from Magdalena. We were alone; his roommate had gone to be with a lover. Towards morning we slept, and I had a dream…

This dream was so powerful, so all-consuming, that I remember it even now as if it were yesterday; an event of such significance in my life that even now I can see things as 'before that dream,' and 'after that dream.'

The dream was full of music. My body was saturated with the swells of it, exactly as if I was in the sea, rolling in the waves, feeling them pass in and out of me. The music was a song – a particular song – rising and subsiding, filling and falling back again: *I can feel it comin' through the air toniiiiight, oh yeah… I've been waiting for this moment / for all my liiiife, oh yeah…* And there were portentous violins, and the whole Phil Collins lyricism – though at the time I didn't know whose song it was.

It was *my* song, that early morning…

That was the beginning of my symphony, my cymbal-clash, my harmony, my discord, my great swelling orchestra of obsession and love and hell and heaven – heaven snatched always just out of the teeth of hell.

It took a few meetings for the power un-balance to assert itself. (I unconsciously engineered this imbalance into every interesting relationship. I needed to be in longing and pain, so I propped the Other up onto a pedestal as best I could, until he fell in tune with the plan, like it or not. Then I had something to strive for, to pine after. Then I knew where I was.)

Subuddha was emotionally cautious and physically daring. We roamed all over the hillsides after dark, walking, walking, and if he found a pool or a puddle or a lake or stream, off would come all his clothes and in he'd get, splashing and making animal noises of reserved joy. Then out, dry himself with his sweatshirt, and on we'd go. He had the most beautiful walk – his shoulders seemed to swing along above his narrow hips, back and forth, back and forth. They had an almost Italian ability to communicate.

And he could dance – oh, he could dance. (His mother later told me that when he was a teenager, he'd danced in front of a mirror in his room – so tirelessly, for so many hours, that he wore the pile off the carpet and there was a bald spot there.) By now a disco was going, several nights a week, and there we went – . And we could dance together – like panthers, like rattlesnakes, winding and twisting, our hips never very far apart, mirroring each other's movements, looking in each other's eyes – his, guarded-but-amused, like chips off a warm glacier – mine hazel and hopeful and ready to fly into other worlds with him, or anywhere, or bed, or the desert hillsides – as long as it was with him, with him.

Those first few meetings he was respectful, honoring, enthusiastic. He was learning my body and my responses; and, in fact, learning new ways and means of pleasuring that I taught him. Once he said, "I hadn't known you could make a woman come with licking! *I'm going to have fun with this!*" he added ruminatively, and a chill went through me, because I knew he didn't mean *just with me.*

For he made no secret, not then, not later – that he had no intention of being faithful to me. *He was going to be with other women, any time he felt like it, any time it happened. He just was.* I can still feel admiration for his steadfast clarity. He never misled me, never hid, never lied. I love him for it even now – it could not have been easy, when I was so drunk on not having power, yet wanted to keep him by me with every force I could find to possess in the universe.

Those nights we were together, in his trailer or mine – somehow, though we all had roommates, I seldom remember there being anyone else in the room – were magic such as I had never experienced. It was not the magic of friends discovering each other, of twin souls spinning on the same axis (for I don't think I've ever felt that, only read about it) – but the magic of falling into a heavy-handed vortex, attended by the most romantic images, sensations, moods – his beautiful body at twilight, seen in silhouette against the dying desert light. The way the night woke with us as we played and tangled and breathed. The way we wended our way through the dazzling thickets of dark till morning sent us scurrying to work, bleary with lack of sleep, but soon exhilarated on coffee and remembered wetnesses and flesh-drunk dissolutions.

I think he loved me – or at least wanted me – at first – in his calm, considering way – but soon my need outstripped his, my mania showed. It was as if I'd just been waiting for a chance to fall, and now I was falling, farther than I'd ever done before or ever could do again. He could not help me – nobody could help me – I was *going* to drown, and find out, once and for all, what that was all about – to lose oneself, forsake one's center, go off spinning into the pit of madness – over an Other, a beautiful stranger, lovelier than imagining could ever bring.

That was Subuddha for me – my intoxication was not only lust though oh lord god it was that – it was also Beauty, and Distance – my own tragedy, that Distance; from my father whom I adored but could not meet in language or in touch. I had to be in love with that tragedy; that is how things work.

One thing I must say about Lust here though... that man had the most beautiful male equipage in the world. Sensitive as a sea anemone – quivering with its own aliveness – unsheathed, it stood and glowed like a luminous mushroom with a tall veined stem. I had never met, nor ever would again, such a whole and entire baby-sensate creature – as sensitive as a Buddha – and there he was, trying to Buddhafy it altogether. For he was alive to it – oh yes he was – with a kind of respect for its properties, a careful attentiveness to its apprehensions and sensitivities, its pleasures and its habits and, most of all, its possible transcendences.

For he was an experimenter, and he wanted to experiment more or less endlessly, without loss of energy – and he did his best at this, and studied Mantak Chia in a book – while I tripped him up as best I could, taking him further than he wanted to go – out there in the desert behind a sagebrush at lunchtime, or in an abandoned school bus or a festival tent – because the only time I could see him out of control, and, therefore, a tiny bit, in my thrall – was at his moment of orgasm. Dear Subuddha. You never blamed me. I must have been a test for you. I don't know what you learned from me – but later you found a real Tantric lover, who was in collusion with your longlastingness, and you loved her, and by all accounts you stayed conjoined for six or seven hours at a time… or so the story goes.

And, Beauty – all of it was Beauty. The Ranch, with its sharp clear air and cleanliness and junipery fragrances – your face, your swinging stride, the way you'd raise the heel of your hand to your face to wipe away sweat, your long smile, your careful diction (which now that I think of it was kind of neutral Brit Midlands); your neat behind, your long feet, the way that you only sometimes, so rarely, let me see anything of your vulnerable soul; let alone your heart – though it was probably shining around you all the time, if only I'd been relaxed enough to see. And I don't blame you for not trusting me with it – for I was as rapacious as any winged dinosaur out of pre-antiquity.

This obsession lasted all the rest of the Ranch time. It saved me from lots of bothersome things that might otherwise have tried to get to me – too much involvement in anybody's politics for example.

By and by my lover was running away mostly. And I just didn't give up.

He was a challenging quarry. I'd hurtle out the door from work, find him at Magdalena, bolt my food, leaving half of it, so that I could go out the door with him, hoping for a tryst at his place (he'd moved just up the hill). If I darted into the toilet on the way out, I would emerge and invariably find him gone: off with somebody else. Anybody else, it seemed! He found beauty in most women – didn't care about age, size, looks. He was there, ready and experimental. He wasn't scoring, adding notches to his belt – nothing like that. He was *checking things out.* Finding what it was all about being in a male body, with sexuality. He was an earnest seeker in that way.

I got very fit, running after him.

He'd worked as a handyman in the cafeteria for a bit and I once heard a jolly female boss there say, laughing, not in the least judgmental, that Subuddha was the only male whore she'd ever known.

Now, during all those years, as we all know, a great deal happened…

Our Utopian Experiment

The Ranch lasted from September 1981 to about the end of 1985. It started out as a jolly-if-perplexed, open-handed, permissive, friendly, outdoorsy Buddhafield, and proceeded very gradually to a peculiar showdown: our sort of people, enmeshed in an ever-tightening grip by a posse of power-hungry (if possibly well-meaning), drugged-out-on-over-the-counter-meds, possibly-infiltrated-by-evil-forces, fascistic, paranoid, scheming, even murderous, possibly-greedy people – many of them 'Moms,' the rather cloying and sinister (eventually) word we used for the female bosses. Some of these turned out to be the exceptional sort of woman in whom steel and coldness take over heart and love – and can even turn monstrous. It does happen.

But this is not a 'history of the Ranch' – others have done that much better than I. It's just my story. And while I was sniffed out for the corridors of power, I resisted whole-heartedly, and devolved eventually to an ever-more-lowly foot-soldier. Thank god, thank god – and what amuses me now to write down are just impressions that remain of that time – not attempting even to know *quite* where they fell in the general climb and fall of things. I was like a child, knee-high, gazing up in awe and often fear, and busying myself with my own world, playing with what had meaning for me. Of course the two worlds intersected – the Moms fed, housed, disciplined, transported me about the place in school buses – but I was really only interested in what I was interested in: the passion and the poetry of things. Clothes. Love. Dancing. Going running in the gorgeous wilderness. Surviving the work-day. Meditation? It fell by the wayside, except insofar as how the whole experience, for all of us, was a hugely educational thing. For Bhagwan has said, "Spirituality is the same thing as maturity." Through the power-chaos that was to come, we had a chance to learn what not to do; how not to do it. And to trust our own bellies instead. It was part of our getting ripe.

From the time I'd come to Poona in 1974 and knelt down before the luminous Being in the chair behind Krishna House, I was no longer granular, but syrup – I flowed and was part of. To be on my own in the world would be lonely, and terrible, and small. And He would have searched me out and found me, right away... and invited me back into love. So that everything that happened at the Ranch was just part of this great whirlpool of involuntary surrender. I just was *of* this place – because here was courage, and all-things-Beyond. Oh god, how lovely. How lucky I was. And am.

So I could not exactly question what was happening – just gaze at it in wonder and sometimes confusion, and eventually begin to trust the deft movements of my body as it *got out of the way* of forces that felt unhealthy to it. That was really all I needed – not to question, debate, or second-guess; but just to get out of the way.

That is easier for a foot-soldier.

I had a long trip to get back down to that position, though. And at first the upswing seemed harmless. At first I could still be myself.

After some enjoyable months in Hakim Sanai, peering just a bit uneasily into people's private business, I was abruptly sent to a new job: co-coordinator of Edison, a department which lived in a narrow old trailer in the middle of 'town,' where benches ran down each side and a half dozen men bent over toasters and drills and so on, trying to fix them. Small machines, wires, soldering irons, etc. hung about overhead, like artifacts in a pub.

The men were all very nice. They sat, focusing on gears and ratchets in the dim, each somehow mature, serious, calm – and utterly sweet. These were older men who had had businesses, families, careers – and now found themselves in a funny trailer out in the back of beyond, fixing toasters. They gave it their best.

I am a very hands-off, egalitarian boss, and I simply left them to get on with it. I was very happy gossiping with curly-headed Deva, my co-boss, who sat in an office at the end of the trailer with his cowboy-booted feet up on his desk, listening to Country music on cassettes. We had a high old time – he was a good buddy, and also an easy-style boss. My other favorite thing was running errands, which I tried to do as much of as possible. I was given a bicycle, and I dashed about all over the Ranch doing this and that, but basically looking for Subuddha. Deva was not the least bit interested in improving me, so he didn't mind.

The repairmen talked to me. One had been in Vietnam and had terrible nightmares, from which, he said, he regularly woke screaming. Helplessly, I felt for him. Another was big and calm and handsome and married and I fancied him, though not realistically.

In the summer I wore short shorts, and bicycled madly about everywhere.

When I came back to the office, there were little work-order slips to organize. The ones for jobs which had been finished went onto a metal spike. I took phone calls about more things that needed fixing. I could have been happy like that for a long time.

...Well, as happy as one can be who is searching for a lost love, who hasn't exactly said he's lost, but it's hard to find him.

That first winter was shockingly cold. I needed my alligator boots, and two knit hats, and two pairs of gloves. The snow was deep. I have a memory-byte of going on an errand to the garage where trucks and buses were repaired; I saw my Aussie friend scooting around under a school bus, on his back on a little wheeled board, in a mixture of ice and mire. Snowdrifts piled high around the garage. I had never seen such snow! We saluted each other. He was another man who had had to stop seeing me when Subuddha came along...

We all worked hard, and the trailers were warm. I was getting so much exercise that I wasn't really cold even when it was freezing. I liked stomping about in a puffy vest but no jacket.

Everything felt so lively – never a dull moment.

The seasons went on changing. As in Poona, festivals happened several times a year and were a very big thing. (The first one at the Ranch was in July 1982.) Here, they were dramatic and enormously labor-intensive events. Hundreds of tent platforms and tents to be erected and furnished! Huge meals to be made, served, and cleaned up after! Crews of workers to be organized! People coming from all over the world! I tried to keep out of all the commotion, finding so much excitement and hard work annoying. I watched people preparing food, outside, under stretched-out awnings, for thousands – and I thanked my lucky stars I didn't have to do that. The magnitude was scary – 20,000 people came to the first festival! I like hiding away.

But those empty tents, waiting for occupants... how handy for a lunchtime tryst!

Bhagwan finally came out and there was Satsang every day – we sat with him; he was still in Silence, as he had been since we all came here.

One night there was a talent show on an outdoor stage. I got up and sang a Motown song – I forget now which one – just for Subuddha. I looked out over the audience, so that I could sing it directly to him.

But he was in the very back – I saw him – he was on the linoleum floor that had been laid there, and he was rolling around with a certain matronly woman.

That was Subuddha.

From time to time Sheela gathered all the workers together in Magdalena after dinner, for a meeting – basically to badger and harangue us; exhort and caution and nudge and chide us, like a schoolmistress. I wanted to be invisible and certainly not get asked to do something; but in my own peculiar psychology, there was also a tortured compulsion to perform. So I waved my hand around and when I was called upon, I told jokes. I didn't know why I did this. If I knew, I was sure I would not do it – why stick your head in the hyena's mouth? But I would stand up, and with full theatrical intonation, perform:

(Strident, Black-American, female voice): "Raaaaastus? Whatchoo doon up thar?"

(Deep male voice) "I'ze layin' linoleum."

(Strident, Black-American, female voice): "Ah didn' know Linoleum was up thar!"

Or,

Rastus meets Liza walkin' down the street, and says, (deep Black-American male voice) "Hello, Jello!"

(Strident Black-American female voice): "Why fo' you callin' me Jello?"

(Deep Black-American male voice): "Cause you so *easy to make!*"

Next day Rastus meets Liza again on the street. And Liza says, "Hello, Cream-o-Wheat!"

"Why fo' you callin' me Cream-o-Wheat?"

"Cause you's *done* in *three minutes!*"

This would likely sound really racist now. We didn't think of that then. There were probably only a handful of American Black people there (this would one day change), though eventually in the Master's communes there were people from a hundred countries: many styles of human, many accents, all shapes and sizes and hues – and all beautiful, beautiful; in that unlikely, crazy, graceful milieu.

Sheela never gave me a hard time about these joke interruptions. In fact, she never gave me a hard time in person – even later, when she really *was* giving me a hard time, she just did it through her minions, by sending me to miserable jobs.

Bhagwan, as I've said, was not speaking. We had no daily dose of sanity, of transcendence. Our work, we were told, was our worship. In Poona we'd worked six hours a day; here it was more like twelve. And Rajneeshpuram (the name our settlement took after it incorporated as a city; before that it was just The Big Muddy Ranch) grew: truck farm, down by the John Day River, which bordered the property. Cafeteria. More trailers, grouped in threes usually, in niches up and down the valley. Sheela's large modern house. A proper downtown was growing, with office buildings, restaurants, boutique; modern buildings in wood and glass. The large garage. And, sooner or later, the townhouses… by 1983 these were under construction.

Every day, though, Bhagwan went for a drive in his Rolls Royce, up through the valley on its main road; then out of the Ranch onto the country roads round about. We stood by the main road, if we happened to be near, and namasted as he went by; and got a blast from the Cosmic which left us giddy and maybe silent, maybe giggling. But quite soon Drive-By became a big thing, with musicians and disciples lining the road for miles, singing and swaying.

Edison Moves

It was a bitter day when Edison was removed from that funky old trailer, that was like some scruffy old guy's workshop, and relocated to the second floor of Zarathustra, an enormous new warehouse not far away. It was all state-of-the-art inside, with huge work tables, and carpeting, and big windows, and proper desks with ergonomic chairs. I had my own desk, and a phone – but what was missing was Deva! He'd been moved elsewhere, and Julian was now my co-boss. I was sad. I'd really liked Deva – he was relaxed and casual, though wide-awake. We spoke the same language, at least enough of the time. Whereas I felt that Julian was just *sinister!* His nostrils looked like the holes in abandoned snail shells; his skin was golden-olive. His hair was black, thick, lank. His teeth were white and square and widely-spaced. He chortled falsely, had an entourage of other people's children, in particular a boisterous thirteen-year-old girl. He was neither short nor tall – more on the short side. He had a British accent and a nodding way of telling you things, as if all authority in the world was his, and he was going to visit it on you with a sure confidence. He was so avuncular, with one and all, that it was like a parody. It seems to me that there was just nothing real about his façade – he was an artificial man, driven by some unseen and peculiar ambition (or perversion?) He gave me the holy creeps, and he chid me, and in his nasal snail-hole voice did his righteous best to boss everybody around by making snide allusions, side-comments, declarations – whilst chortling fakely, and blinking his big heavy-lidded eyes. And he apparently found all this so easy – this bossing a big department (for he didn't really let me boss anything, but in case I ever did, he wanted me to be hard on the fellows – which was purely against my nature!)

My errand-running intensified. So much more fun to be out on my bike!

Once, after lunch (I was almost invariably late, due to exquisitely interesting meetings with Subuddha in a particular dead school bus out in the boonies), Julian bitched about one of the repairmen he'd seen windsurfing on Krishnamurti Lake: "*Wind*surfing," he said, rolling his large eyes. "He's got to learn – we're not here to have *fun!*" (chortle snorf) "Ha ha, what does he think we're *doing* here? We're *working! Wind*surfing! Hunh!"

And I thought, "Sounds wonderful to me. What the hell am I missing here? Is there something wrong with me for thinking windsurfing sounds quite heavenly, and work, well, not that much?" But I just stared at him, too afraid to argue, but certainly unable to agree.

Anyway, Julian had so much energy left from his duties that eventually he got into spying. I saw Rajesh, a young blond slender fellow with a southern drawl and a laid-back air, coming in with spy-equipment magazines – and I couldn't figure out what the hell; so I just, like, *didn't think about it.* And I was not party to the discussions in the back room – thank god. (If you haven't read it yet, do, please, read *The Day We Got Guns,* by the late Rajesh. All about this spying thing. It is just brilliant. One of the best thrillers I've ever read. And all true. And so well-written!) (Just a side-note: Rajesh, along with French-Canadian Michel, his sidekick – used, at the beginning of the Ranch, to play a game that was so silly that it kept them in stitches. All you have to do is point at some object – say, a Bobcat ditch-digger, or a soldering iron, or a picnic table – and say {or better yet, write on the object with a black magic marker}, **Not a toaster. Not a rosebush. Not a double bed,** or whatever else it isn't. I can't tell you why this is funny, and maybe it isn't funny, but in Rajesh's dry way {which Michel never quite got}, he made it so droll that when he told me about it I was *falling about laughing*…)

But anyway – if you go to sit at the feet of an enlightened master, why also bug his room? Why spy on him? That's just *weird*. (I think that Sheela, in her increasing speed-fuelled paranoia, was worried what he might be saying about her.)

A year or so after we met, Subuddha had to leave the Ranch for some months to sort out some official business. He went to stay with a woman in California.

This was of course a terrible wrench.

In a way it was a relief to have him gone – that awful tension, of how to catch hold of him, had left with him. The dear man was not a letter-writer, so I didn't know what was going on down there; but I could guess – I knew he liked his hostess. So I felt it my duty to let no grass grow under my feet while he was away.

There was Guru, a stunningly handsome young American who looked like a teenage girl's rock star dream. He was tall and had fine soft light-brown hair in a Beatle-ish cut, and was so equable of temperament that it was almost unreal. This mild exterior covered a Shiva-stamina of epic duration. He could make love all night, defeating me again and again. He had a crush on me, but I found him too agreeable, young fool that I was. (Much later he told me that when Subuddha returned he took one look at him and realized all was lost… for Guru.)

I remember, during that free time, a snowy night. I'd just left someone's trailer after making love for hours. I walked inside the brilliant full moon's light, the lit-up snow ploughed high at the roadsides. All was still. I went to another group of trailers, entered one, knocked softly on a door. My second lover of the night.

Another time, I had no date. I wanted one. I didn't quite exist till one was there. What to do? I went in the late blackness to someone's trailer, his room. I got in bed with him. He acquiesced.

I had a date with a Spanish bodyworker. It did not go as I might have wished. He said, "Your body is strange! Stand up! Let me see you." I stood on my unstable feet, with my curved-out behind, flat upper back. "I've been with many women," he said. "And you are strange – it's like you're holding your sex *away* from the man. Like a little girl."

I felt sad. I wanted to be a sexpot, but he'd seen through me.

I had a strange spooky date with a much-older guy, an engineer, who had his own trailer. It was a very peculiar night. He was a wonderful being – dark and deep and labyrinthine; made of some private inner landscapes such as I'd never met before. He was patient and present, but I felt whatever chemistry there might be was all askew, like stars wheeling out of orbit. In the morning I fled, running down the hill through the junipers in the dawn light, desperate to be gone.

Later I slept with his teenage son – a beautiful, unformed young boy. I salute them both, oh uniquenesses! I was a fool, trolling for almost anything; ignoring so much. Going where I had no business to be.

But ah – I remember Narayanadeva, privileged son of some California dynasty, whom I really loved – hair in gold waves, soft voice, big hands. He of the kidney belt, master of the great earth-movers, the scrapers being used to create Krishnamurti dam and lake – we'd started our affair early in the life of the lake, then. We managed to get sent together to Antelope, the little town ten miles from the Ranch's border, to guard, which didn't really mean anything except that we had to answer the phone in the little wooden house where we stayed, and keep our eyes open for what might be going on. (Antelope was all in an uproar about the Rajneeshees, but Sheela had bought property there anyway. She liked uproars – or maybe Bhagwan did. It was never quite clear which.) Narayanadeva and I wallowed about making love, and the phone only rang once in a while, some pesky Mom, while we sniggered to ourselves that we managed to talk even *in flagrante* – like teenagers conversing with Mom while stoned. We really liked each other… but gentle Narayana eventually broke it off when he realized Subuddha was there to stay.

One memorable September day in 1982, after Sheela had instituted three-hour lunch breaks so that we could go swimming – the summer was as hot as the winter was cold – I was at the John Day River with Samaya, a tall, gorgeously handsome Canadian. He had a very soft tenor voice and a great mane of tawny crinkly hair; long curly eyelashes around hazel eyes, full lips, strong white teeth. We felt like buddies more than lovers, though we tried. (One hears so much about the beauty of sannyasin women – and it is so true – but right now, looking back, I'd like to say that Bhagwan attracted an amazing number of gorgeous, sweet, good, and wonderfully long-haired men! Vulnerable, strong, patient…)

It was very hot. We were beside a stream that emptied into the fast-moving river. The John Day was maybe forty feet across there. On the far side were a shallow bank and bluffs; on our side, a more gradual slope leading up to the truck farm. But this place, here, was deserted save for us; drowsing in the sun. I was lying on my back in some very shallow rapids, feeling the cooling water ripple beneath me, and the smooth stones just below the cushion of the water. Samaya was sitting beside me. I closed my eyes; he must have closed his too…

When I opened mine again a few minutes later, I was out in the middle of the river, still floating on my back, advancing rapidly downstream. I hurriedly put my feet down, but there was no bottom. The water was green and swift around me, carrying me off towards unknown territory. It was a terrifying moment, to find that the water was so much deeper than I'd guessed. I couldn't really swim – childhood lessons had never really taken. I looked at the banks of the river, sandy, quite flat; but heading towards steep bluffs. I struck out dog-paddling as hard as I could to my left, angling towards the shore as the current took me. It was a tough fight, but I made it, and, crawling out, flopped down on the shore, breathing hard, staring at the sand… grateful, so grateful, to be alive. Such a vivid sense of sweetness, being here in a body! (Samaya hadn't noticed I was gone! His eyes were still closed.)

The John Day River. When we'd all first arrived here, a few roistering cut-ups had gone down to the river one evening and tried to get across on a raft. They'd made it – but only three of them made it back. The fourth, a young American man, had drowned. The survivors were very quiet for a while.

I decided I needed help. I knew that I was an addict – that the way I approached getting dates was compulsive, born out of some nameless fear.

Some of the Moms had recently been appointed counselors. Sheela had instituted a service whereby troubled workers could consult one of these women. I wonder now about their creds – I wonder a lot. These were not trained psychologists or any such thing. (Now, I am imagining that these women were supposed to report back to Sheela on whatever was discussed. A real counselor would have been constrained by confidentiality.) But I was feeling kind of desperate, so I requested a session, and was assigned to one whose name I forget. I explained to her that if I didn't have sex with some man or other, I felt like I was wasting my life – so I kept making sure I got into bed with this, that, or the other one. But I thought that something was wrong.

She was affable and kindly. "If everyone were truly themselves," she said, "everyone would be completely eccentric." This sounded very good; but I did not actually feel heard. I knew something was wrong. I was acting out of fear, not confident eccentricity (well, okay, some of that too).

Now, I'm going to posit a very strange thing. It's been hovering at the edges of consciousness, not quite permitted to come in; but today, in 2018, as I strolled across a large, close-cropped English meadow, under a vast and soft grey sky – it came home to me, and I will say it.

Besides an Avoidance of the Howling Void, maybe my sex addiction had another ingredient. I have noticed that the same energy that is used in creativity is used in shopping (at least for me!) It's something about interacting with color, with exciting new beauty; with not knowing what will happen next. Something is twinkling at me, tickling at me; if I make it or if I buy it or scavenge it, it is all part of a similar joy – perhaps not *precisely* the same, but related.

And both, in some way, are a kind of work – an action/activity, in a state of aesthetic pleasure.

In the Commune, up to that point, my working time had been spent at various jobs given me to do – jobs which helped the community, which added my two cents to the general running of things. In no way was I invited to "do my own thing" – for 'my own thing' is not community-oriented. I doubt if anyone even noticed any of this or gave it a thought – each of us was to contribute our labor to the whole, and that was that. And certainly this challenged us, opened up new energy-pathways, expanded us, gave us a bigger scope in which to live and breathe.

But in fact I experience myself to be a soul who is here to create her own little things, in her own way, pretty much all the time; no other person is relevant to this. There is nothing market-driven about it; nothing helpful to others in any practical way. Nevertheless, this is who I am and must be; and to stay away from my nature for very long is to court trouble.

I was spending my days on a bicycle or with repair orders, and later in pickup trucks, on building sites, in foundation holes; it was lots of *fun.* But I was also bored – for there were no free-wheeling *words* in it, and no playful art. I wrote the odd poem, but that was all – there was no time for anything else. We were *building a city,* for all our sake!

I needed this bigger world – it expanded my universe and let my individual creativity rest within a vaster womb – but if it was meant to be a meditation, a Zensome watching-of-myself whilst doing these jobs – this wasn't much with me; though of course in Poona I'd been so imbued with Watching that it was certainly there, no doubt much huger than I knew.

Meanwhile, my creative energy had to do *something*. It amused itself greatly by dressing me each day; each night I fell asleep with soothing leafings-through of my wardrobe in my mind, planning the next day's outfit. I couldn't paint or cook or write or bind my own books – and so I *went shopping*. I could not buy anything as I had no money; scavenging clothes from mud-rooms/lost-property boxes (!) took only a few minutes now and then.

And so I shopped for men.

It wasn't perhaps the best use of my creative energy, but it was fun and twinkling and tugging at me, and best of all it could be done *all day long* – everywhere I went, I could watch out for men; and, shopping-like, try to sense out how to get hold of them.

Eventually Subuddha returned. We slipped right back into our relationship, such as it was. Subuddha didn't really talk – he was a man of action. Nor did he exactly want to be in a thing called a relationship. But I used to pray to be with him for the rest of our lives.

He liked to tell me about his other lovers. I listened, because I wanted to know; but I hated what I heard. I tried to be enlightened about it. And, I also made sure to keep having other lovers myself, just not to be left behind. When I told him about these other guys, he shifted uncomfortably and said he did not want to know.

As it turned out, my apprehensions about what he might have gotten up to in California were realized. He regaled me with his revelations about the value of making love to a woman who'd been much-stretched through several childbirths! He'd had to let go of his expectation of friction and excitement; and instead he'd found a new joy in 'being with' the energy without being pulled towards a goal. He was filled with a sort of creative appreciation of his discovery.

While I… was filled again with the bliss of feeling that blood-boned umbrella opening inside me, pressing beguilingly on my close and stretchy walls… (Now, as I write, all this relentless focus on people's *'bits'*, as the Brits call them, seems narrow and regrettable. But that was then, and I've always had a *dogged* sort of mind.)

In Subuddha's arms was neither shelter nor comfort, but only the Edge. He was not a port in a storm; he was the storm.

Coordinators' Meetings

By this time a sense of oppression, of being controlled by a regime, was growing. I felt it most keenly when I went, at regular intervals, to the Coordinators' meetings in Sheela's big roomy house. There I observed the women, focused and conspiring, privileged and insanely hard-working; who ran the whole show. They'd be telling us whatever the new rules were about this and that; I was supposed to report back on all this to my department. But during the meetings I hid behind the couch as much as I could, as close to the door as possible, so that as soon as the meeting was over I could bolt for my bicycle and rush off to find Subuddha, and *get naked* behind a sage bush. That's when I could feel real – and I craved to feel real – not a dressed-up coordinator, wielding a notebook and ready to lay down the law… oh god no! I wondered what satisfaction those Moms felt in their work that could compare with what I felt, naked with my lover. There could *be* no comparison; I had Lust and they had Dust. That's how it seemed to me.

One day the rule we were to pass on was this: there were to be no private phone calls from work phones.

This was devastating! Because of course all phones were work phones! And I had been wont, every day, to phone Subuddha (at that time he was working someplace where there was a phone), and make lunch dates. Arrgh! If I didn't do that, he'd wander off with whoever!

I was so angry and freaked out that I refused to pass on the information at the after-Coordinators'-meeting Workers'-meeting, and Julian had to do it.

So I found a ploy: I'd phone Subuddha and say, "We've got a box here that needs fixing!" And he might say, "I'll be able to fix that box at lunchtime," or, "No, I'm busy, I can't fix the box today." Once he said, "I'm fixing someone else's box." (I could see the devilish glint in his eye!) (Tragedy! Trembling!)

People who worked at Edison of course realized all this was going on, and one day a helpful woman, on whose shoulder I'd been sobbing, gave me a lecture about finding my own center. "I DON'T HAAAVE A CENTER!" I wailed.

I cried a lot in those years. Most days, I cried. Often onto some poor innocent bystander.

One day, one of these Moms came to sniff out how things were at Edison. She was a Canadian woman with a very hefty overbite and a straight bob of black hair. A few prominent moles starred her white face.

Now, in my faithfulness to my job – my various jobs – as I've said, creativity did not much come into things. I'm a good organizer – that was useful – and I like paperwork. But that's not the same as *making things.* So, I had discovered potted plants. I'd found out that I could take cuttings and put them in a jar of water, and they would miraculously, after a week or two, make thready little roots. When they looked nice and rooty, I could plant them in a pot, and thus have more! (Particularly coleus likes this method; and many other plants too.) So I'd really gone for it, and the office was teetering with potted plants of many sizes and a few different types; on windowsills, desks – anywhere I could fit a pot or a jar. These plants made me very happy. I loved watching the roots appear and grow hairy, I loved watching the potted new baby get its grip in the soil and start to flourish.

Of course, these plants were mostly not huge yet, not filled-out. They were just doing their best.

The bucktoothed Mom stood looking around, hands on her hips. Then she went around gathering up potted plants in a businesslike way and taking them out to her pickup truck, sticking them peremptorily in the bed.

I was grief-stricken! *My babies!* How *could* she? So I protested. "What are you going to do with them? I *grew* them!"

"I'm throwing them out."

"But – but – but –!" I cried sadly, "that's not right!"

"Madhuri," said the Boss-person in her slightly nasal voice, "they're not *beautiful!*"

Oh. Grrrr. And neither are you! I should have shouted. *Shall we throw you out too?*

But I didn't shout that, or anything else. I watched my babies go off to be dumped somewhere.

Vidya confided in me that she had had a dream – she was lifting up the edge of her carpet, looking for bus drivers. More bus drivers were needed!

Soon afterwards I was advised that I was to get a driver's license.

Nightmare visions assailed me: trying to back up a school bus full of tired workers on an icy road. The bus slips down a bank into a deep ditch… and so on.

A driving teacher was sent to give me refresher lessons so that I could take the test in Bend (a city some distance away). She had a placid face, straight brown-blonde hair, wide hips, and a cool, no-nonsense air. We had many, many lessons, where I drove all over the Ranch with her beside me in the passenger seat, telling me what I was doing wrong. Which was an amazing number of things.

For example, if we drove on the road up above Krishnamurti Lake, and I looked to see if the windsurfer over there was Subuddha – that was an inexcusable lack of attention to the road.

I could not imagine *not* looking over there to see who the windsurfer was. How could a person manage that?

Eventually the teacher said, "Some people are just not meant to do this."

The project was dropped.

I was so glad.

A *Really* Weird Afternoon

One of my duties at Edison was to liaise between the Ranch and the County phone company. This job did not suit me; I am not by nature a diplomat/schmoozer. But we were not there to find what suited us; we were there to be disarranged, disturbed, and upended.

I present the following scene as a tableau, to be gazed at in, perhaps, some awe; I present it in a painterly way – this figure here, that there; each doing their thing, however strange: Sheela was giving a luncheon party for two representatives of the telephone company; a number of Ranchites were invited as well. I, as liaison, had to be there (though what good I could have done in what was to come, I cannot tell you even now). *Some* sort of smiley arbiter was needed in the relationship, because nearly every day since I had gone to work at Edison two years before, some sweet red-jeaned cowboy on a backhoe had dug up the only phone cable between the Ranch and the rest of the world. The phone company then had to send someone to repair it. This happened fully as often as border incidents in the Middle East – truly, it was daily.

And now that we were to have many more phone lines installed, even more PR was needed. ...If I had been invited to read aloud Walt Whitman's poem about the Body Electric to those phone guys, I could have done so with alacrity and aplomb. Instead, I now hung uselessly about Sheela's house – Jesus Grove – like an ocelot in a business suit, with a bubble of permed hair and lots of makeup on, itching to get out of there.

Sheela had recruited an extremely tall and lanky Russian named Veeren, who had a marvelous gloom about him and a guttural, accusatory wit, to act as some sort of barking dog to the hapless phone fellows. I am still not sure why she did this, except that Veeren and the sidekick she brought in for him were tech geniuses, so that the nastiness could claim that it was scientific somehow? The cohort was German Bodhi Garbha – known, inevitably, as Bodhi Garbage. He was a stocky little badger of a guy, obnoxious in best Teutonic tradition.

These two then, in their unpierceable accents, advanced like earth-moving equipment to surround and verbally bludgeon the two skinny phone dudes who dodged about Sheela's gracious living room, still trying to be polite. Thick, sneering insults were lobbed like grenades, one after another. Perhaps Sheela thought that the warlike histories of Veeren's and Bodhi Garbage's collective conditionings would make them amenable to such an assignment. Whatever grudges they had against anybody since time began they could now turn into punishment. Who knows what Sheela thought?

The poor duo from Outside were outnumbered, flanked, bitten – and they tried so hard to be cheerful and friendly! The *whole weird afternoon!* I felt so sorry for them that I could barely stand it. I was so embarrassed I could hardly move. (It's true that I am usually a disempowered female, a scrawny coyote who cannot fight back even when confronted by someone's flouncing bossiness – so perhaps my allergy to what I witnessed has roots in my own dispossessed awfulness. It's worth considering.)

Lunch was announced and we all went into the dining room – there must have been twenty of us. Though Sheela was hostess, she made a late appearance at her own party; we'd all been milling around without her up to then. She now appeared, standing in her bedroom doorway wearing a long white lace wedding dress. The middle finger of her right hand was elaborately bandaged in white as well; and, of course, it stuck straight up whenever she raised the hand. Which she did immediately, to show everyone and explain: "I was cleaning out a cupboard, and a spider bit me. My finger got so big – !" Her huge round eyes blinked – the heavy flat voice seeming to come from a glossy, cynical brown toad. "So it had to be bandaged."

She sat down at the long table, we all sat, and soup was placed before each diner. Sheela went on, "I'm wearing this dress because Jayananda and I are going to get married again. Last time we got married it was on an airplane. So we wanted to get married on the ground, too." Jayananda, her big, solid American husband, as ever giving nothing away, sat near her; he neither spoke nor nodded nor shook his head. His eyes held… what? Not nothing. But what sort of something was it? I could not fathom him at all.

Then there was that Filipina nurse Sheela kept near her, who dispensed pills from a sort of plastic lunchbox she always carried. Round face, pocked skin, always beaming. Disappeared without a trace when it was all over… (I have since heard that she had had a troubled childhood, which had turned her into a devotee rather than a meditator; and she was devoted to Sheela. A tragic life, apparently. And somewhere a soft heart in her… soft and helpless. Ah well…)

Well, whatever pills she had given her patient to cope with the pain caused by the mighty spider's mandibles, their effect was accelerating as we watched. Sheela went on discoursing, blinking those sanpaku orbs, her small mouth in her broad face slackening, her fuck-you finger on the table, pointing at whoever. She was, quite frankly, maundering, with sentimental slurrings coming in amongst the matter-of-fact words.

Then she toppled forward into her soup.

The table held its breath and scraped its chairs back. The phone company guys, I saw with a quick glance, were in shock, and still trying to put a brave face on it. Someone helped Sheela sit upright and mopped her off. As I remember it, another pill was administered – presumably to wake her up. It worked; some dreadful eternity later we were all gathered in her bedroom, phone guys included, and many more Moms arrived to crowd in and watch the ceremony. Sheela and Jay stood near their bed while someone – I don't remember who – married them again. The bandage really did look fetching with the dress, in lieu of a posy. Many gifts were given and unwrapped – they all seemed to be large enameled or pottery plates – and then the bride subsided again. I seem to remember that she found some energy to nag at the poor wretched innocents first though, before turning them back over to the Growling Garglers, who let fly with more pointing abuse. None of it made any sense to me. The phone company was not evil, it was just a rural phone company. (Maybe the abuse was to distract from its being our fault that the lines kept getting dug up?)

At last the afternoon was over and it was time to get ready for the evening; the Oregonians were allowed to escape, and they drove off in their jeep. I do not know what tales they told their wives that night. Whatever it was, I had no part in it, despite my title – in my coral PR suit, there was no way I could explain to them (or to myself) what had happened to them; no way to comfort them.

How I Got Fired

One day the dreaded Vidya, accompanied by Julian, walked me around a windowless chamber behind the main large, light Edison work-room/office. This main area, huge as an airport waiting lounge, had views of wild hills and big sky, of the busy comings-and-goings to RBG, the garage not far away. But the back room was in constant twilight. There were counters back there on which were lined up these alien things called "computers." They had just arrived.

The pair told me I was now going to be in charge of these machines. That it would be a lot of work. That I would often have to be here till 2 a.m.

I stood there, watching my sought-after, hard-won nights with Subuddha vanishing like a desert mirage. Watched him wandering insouciantly away with that teenage blonde with the aerodynamic breasts and blushing cheeks. With the wasp-waisted little Irish girl. Or whoever!

WAAAANNNNNHHHHHH! I burst into noisy tears.

I could not stop crying; didn't even try. I collapsed in a small back room (the one where Julian went to have his spy consultations with Rajesh and the pure-hearted, adorable Michel). I howled out my grief of projected lost love. *WAAAANNNNHHH!*

How disgusted Vidya and Julian were! Finally they left me in a pool of mucus and went away, full of chiding. I wept there for four hours.

Next day I was demoted and sent to a laundry trailer, somewhere between downtown and Magdalena Cafeteria.

FREEDOM!!!!!

I only hated having to give back my bicycle.

Happy Foot-Soldier

Now I was a laundress, doing sheets from the trailers in big machines, alongside the disaffected and angry Divya, she of Primal fame, probably also sent there as punishment. She wasn't happy – she cursed powers-that-were, and I was shocked. (Later, much later, though, on FB, she said she had loved that job!)

I was blissed out. I loved clothes! Loved washing them! Folding them when they came out of the dryer! I got to work normal (i.e. very long) hours, but not half the night! Nobody peered in and gave me a hard time! I think that when it was realized Up Above how much I was enjoying myself (I'm sure I unwisely told somebody), it became necessary for punishment purposes that I got sent to all *sorts* of other works, one right after the other, possibly in hopes of finding something I'd really hate!

Probably not in precise order, here are some I remember:

Standing in a hole that was to be filled with foundation pilings. Beautiful, aristocratic German Sadhana is in the next pit. We use big coffee cans to scoop the dirt out and deposit it up beside the hole. The earth smells… earthy. We are gossiping joyfully every time we both rise at once, like groundhogs. She is wearing a pair of wonderful overalls, like farmers wear, but orange; and a little t-shirt. She has such a slim, flat figure, so lithe, the ensemble looks cute as heck on her.

Later that night I ride around with the tall skinny narrow-eyed cowboy who drove the foundation-digging truck, and give him a BJ in the cab.

Traipsing around in a crew, over the hills, doing something with fencing. I am so bored – it is perhaps the single worst day of work I spend at the Ranch, my mind just *hungering* for stimulation, entertainment, occupation – that I am miserable. I don't revel in the meadows and hills and trees and rough up-and-down land. I trail behind, trudging as if nearly asleep.

Sheet-rock crew. Lifting big white slabs into place on the inside walls of the new townhouses that are just going up, at a smart pace, in a large area under the hills on the left side of the valley as you drive towards Magdalena. Guys come with screw-guns and secure the sheetrock to the joists. Then I'm spackling the screw-holes, the broad putty-knife scraping and scraping the excess goo away. This is quite fun. Then I'm asked if I want to learn how to use the guns, so that I can hang the sheetrock myself. I assure the male team leader that I do not want to learn this. He won't give up, and keeps haranguing me. I stick to my (non-)guns.

Insulation crew. I'm afraid of getting fibers in my lungs, even though we wear masks, and paper suits over our clothes. We climb around in attics, it is too hot, not fun. Also only one day.

Deck crew. Also just a day. Heaving posts and boards about while the men hammer and measure like they were born to it. Also intensely boring, but I like hefting things about – always have.

Cleaning Walt Whitman A-Frames, the cute pointy houses built for workers, up the valley beyond the airport.

Moving Crew – a rowdy bunch of guys who cruise around moving people's belongings while the people are at work; if the Moms so decree. (You didn't have any say about where you lived – though I have known of people who complained about a roommate and were quietly moved. Sarita was assigned a room once with Sheela's abovementioned nurse. Sarita, true to form, fell down on the floor screaming, and a new roommate was hastily arranged. I myself once shared a room for one night with a young Californian who was going through a Gay phase. I put plants down the middle between our beds, but I was so disturbed by the energy of the goings-on just nearby – extremely aggressive and fast – that I asked to be moved, and was, without complaint. Other people's sex can be strange... bad-smelling, or educational. I'd even heard some intriguing breathing-styles, for example.) Anyway, I ride with the Moving Crew, a maverick lot, and it's tons of fun.

Then I'm on night duty during a festival, riding with the taxi guys, taking snacks around to night workers: brownies, cinnamon rolls, thermoses of coffee, sandwiches, fruit; in satisfying paper boxes. We drive out to the far-flung guard-huts, to the special auxiliary kitchen, the taxi dispatch, etc. Hungry, lonely workers are glad to see us. The unfathomableness of Night! I enjoy this a lot, except at 3 a.m. when the body *really* wants to be asleep.

Once I am sent to look after a bunch of little girls for the night. This is a rotating duty among almost everyone; the kids live in their own building, somewhere at the edgy middle of things. For some reason it's just girls tonight, all sleeping in a room with bunk-beds lining the walls. They've already had their suppers, so it's my job just to sleep in the room, and be there in case I'm needed.

I find it a strange business. Here are these little people, with decided opinions about things. They don't smell very good at all – I don't know why. I end up giving them all palmreadings, which they get very excited about. I am amazed to see how each little person, who has barely been here in life for seven or eight years, is not only completely unique, but has hands that tell of much gnarled history… These are old souls, with much in their pasts that is intricate and convoluted, much that is time-worn, weary and wise.

What also strikes me is that they want to know, more than anything, how many children they are going to have! That seems very odd to me. I don't really do futures, so although there is a place on the hand where you can supposedly look to see the number of kids you're destined to have, I find I am much more interested in reading energies than lines. But I tell them what the kid-lines say.

I am very glad to leave them next morning, and go back to my sort-of grown-up world.

Summer

I loved Subuddha so achingly. While I was still at Edison he'd become involved with that lovely blushing California blonde teen; he spent a lot of lunchtimes with her, and many nights. I was soon crazed. I stalked him – following him onto the bus when he was going to see her, sitting behind him, staring at him, refusing to get off.

One night – and this is one of the most extreme things I ever did in my life; never before or since did I do such a thing – I sat alone in my room and put a transparent plastic bag over my head and held it around my throat and breathed in. The plastic was drawn into my mouth. My body said, "Hell's bells! This is bizarre! We're not doing this!" and my body simply took the bag off its head. I also, I am very sorry to report, did some voodoo. (I had forgotten all about this but much later Subuddha reminded me, chidingly. I still feel awful about it.) I don't remember what exactly I did – something with an effigy. But the poor young girl got a cough, and it didn't go away. When I bumped into her in Ashland, Oregon in early 2003 she still had it. She was not well, inside or out. (Nor was I, come to that… but more on that anon.) I hesitate to think I caused any of that. I have, with whatever white magic I've learnt since, done my best, during meditation, to un-voodoo it.

So sorry, Blushing Maiden!

It was summer. One day we had a Day Off. Subuddha and I took the special bus for Patanjali Lake, a natural lake quite far from town. We sat in the back of the bus and kissed and stroked and fumbled with each other. It was a long ride, and I had him all to myself – he couldn't get away, now, this day, this ride. We were all tangled up together in easy summer bareleggedness. I was in a plateau of excitement, brimming there.

When we got to the lake, there were people swimming, sunbathing, picknicking, all over the place. (The isolation made it possible to swim nude.) There was a log raft out on the water for people to swim to and lie out upon. It was gorgeous, and the place was all surrounded by trees so it felt quite private. We spread a cloth out behind a bush and rolled around. He slipped his fingers under my shorts, and I went over the brink. I was so impressed! So much focus was always needed, so much tuning out of extraneous sounds and thoughts. So it was an unlikely achievement.

Later he said, "And you wonder why I keep coming back to *you?*" The teen, he hinted, never could let go. (When I was a teen, I couldn't either.)

Subuddha was on the Fire Crew. One day they had a training: a fire was set on hills outside the town and the crew had to contain it, and then put it out; as practice. But the fire got away from them. It became a real grass-fire, leaping and traveling, much faster than they'd expected. They battled it for many hours.

Subuddha came home late in the dusky evening, exhausted, smoky, sooty. I had never seen him so upset. He took a shower, then came to bed and told me about it. He was so moved, so traumatized, that he wept. I had never seen him cry. I held him. I felt his openness, his vulnerability. I felt it through my whole body, my heart. I had never felt these things in him before. My heart opened like a split summer peach. Nectar poured out onto him. I was ecstatic. It was like loving a baby – just tenderness, tenderness. Pouring out of the front of my body, all over him. A profound experience. So exquisite, overwhemingly sweet.

He made himself stop crying. Went to the bathroom and blew his nose. Washed his face. When he came back and got in bed he said scathingly, *"You* like *negativity."*

I never saw him like that again (though I did, much later, see him vulnerable, open; though for someone else). But I never forgot it – I seemed to have caught a glimpse of what love could feel like. The heart, cascading all over someone's being.

Sagarpriya, a well-known therapist who had published a book on Psychic Massage, somehow ended up giving me a reading. I went to her trailer after work one day, and she sat and gazed at me for a few minutes. (I'm sure I first unloaded my various worries to her.) Then she said, in a concerned tone perhaps not devoid of loftiness, that she did not see Bhagwan anywhere about me. The general gist was that I was a lost and probably unredeemable soul, mired in error so thoroughly that my very aura was barren.

I limped away in shock. I knew that it was not true – the way one simply *knows* things – but still it was an ugly blow. I don't think it helped anything.

She would reappear much later, at an inopportune moment, too…

Teertha, the tall, wisp-bearded quasi-guru, was giving darshans of a sort – people could ask him questions, and he gave Sannyas – sitting in a Bhagwan-like chair in the middle of the Mandir (the big hall that had finally been built where we could gather with Bhagwan again for Satsangs or discourses). He had not changed – still transparently ethereal, still snooty and pointy-nosed – but for some reason I went once, and sat in front of him. I don't remember what I asked, but he said, "I've seen you, *running along the roads.* You certainly aren't doing it for *pleasure.*" His tone implied that all spiritual correctness was being violated by my dogged pursuit of some wayward discipline.

I was annoyed. How could he know the bliss, the endorphins? The *necessary* joy of fleeing the Tribe, the boring yet threatening pressures from the Moms, to taste free air, go the long free road down towards the river, ka-thump ka-thump in my yellow Kangaroos? The sense of wonderful fleetness, just me and the planet, wild together, *surviving?*

Once, in Antelope, I'd gone for a run and a thunderstorm had rolled in. I was way out on some long road on a great plateau, and the crash and grumble of the storm was upon me.

And what did my body do?

It *ran by itself* – I was not 'doing' it – it just picked up and *flew* over the ground, powered by holy adrenaline, not at my will but at the will of the ancient-most law of beings on Earth: *Git yo' ass to shelter! Now!!…* in order to survive.

I have never forgotten the feeling of that flight – no effort at all, it was as if some invisible outboard motor was revved up and shoving me along out of the water at top speed – and I was simply pushed along by it. Wonderful. (This was, in a way, a precursor of when, much later, finally, finally, very very late, laughably overdue – I discovered non-doing in meditation.)

Throughout those years, we were encouraged to see work as our meditation – in fact, we had to call it 'worship.' Okay. I get it. But I can't say I ever *really* got it. Still, if I look back I see that whatever work ('worship') I did in the Commune, did not belong to any sort of work-reward bargain the world might adhere to. This was because the work was actually being thrown into a great pit of divinity – we gave ourselves to something greater. Not just the Commune itself, and each other – though that was the practical evidence and application of it – but some unseen, reasonless bliss-and-beyondness sump that accepted all our giving and gave back to us a thousandfold. We got to fly in the very sky of bliss, we were included in it, beautified by it. Beatified.

So I guess it *was* worship.

Like many of us, I'm sure, I often thought I was woefully secular and profane. I remember once at the Castle, where Bhagwan wasn't giving discourses, being brought into a room with a bunch of other people, a video machine and a TV. We were going to watch an old discourse; but somehow before this started we were inadvertently shown a few minutes of some movie – a thriller I think, somebody trying to find somebody else in the snow, something like that – and this mundane drama struck me like a joyful stream of water for the thirsty, like candy after a fast, like shopping when you've been poor for ages. My very body lusted after the movie greedily! But then they turned it off; and how could I complain?

The word came down that workers had to start the day with something called "Gachchhamis." We would gather together, kneel down and bow, and recite all together:

Buddham … sharanam … gachchhami … I bow to the feet of the enlightened one

Sangham … sharanam … gachchhami … I bow to the feet of the commune

Dhammam … sharanam … gachchhami … I bow to… (Hmmm… I don't remember what!)

But I hated chanting the Gachchhamis, whatever wonderful things they meant. I generally loathe mantras – somebody trying to put words in my mouth! Reciting mantras all together: nah. Too much like the military, individuality sacrificed. I felt like an idiot, kneeling and droning. I could barely bring myself to do it… like the Pledge of Allegiance to the Flag at school, which I wouldn't do, and they had to let me get away with it, because America is a Free Country, so they could only glare at me like I was some sort of religious heretic, beyond the pale.

That being said… all those kneeling people, in their hearts, saying Gachchhamis together… probably sent some nice acreage of vibes upwards into the cosmos, from our little Planet Earth. Who am I to argue?

One day, a confluence of events occurred which was to have both ominous and creative repercussions in my personal life. There was some sort of meeting I had to go to – I don't remember now what it was about – and Subuddha also had to go. This was new – we'd never sat at a meeting together before. Then, for some reason Subuddha was feeling unusually affectionate that day. So we sat side by side on cushions on the floor in some big office room, I forget in what building; and he brushed his welcome hand across my shoulder, and then leant over and nuzzled me with his wicked lips and rounded nose, and glinted his cautious, sparkly eyes at me. Rubbed his head on my shoulder and purred in his insolent, guarded, yet innocent way.

Right then Sheela walked into the room.

I saw her see us.

And I Knew.

With sinking stomach, I knew what was going to happen next.

Sure enough, next day I was told that I was going to go work at the hotel in Portland. The Commune had bought and renovated a medium-sized hotel in that city so that people arriving from all over the world would have a place to stay the night before embarking on the long bus journey to the Ranch. I had no interest in the hotel, not feeling the least bit connected with the outside world. The idea of going there to work was horrible, terrifying… for I *knew what Subuddha would get up to while I was gone.* The very *minute* I was on the bus he'd be off with another woman – most likely, these days, the pretty little Scotswoman with the ginger-blonde hair, teensy waist, and very hot box (we'd hugged once and I was astonished at the temperature though her skirt. *Why couldn't I be more like that?* There had been the evening when I'd come to his townhouse and seen outside his door his own big floppy running shoes and a pair of little bitty slip-on shoes… Oh yes, I knew they belonged to Ginger Lady! And so I'd pressed my ear to the door, and when nothing was heard, I'd lurked outside the house for a while, staring balefully at his window… till I finally gave up and crept away.)

It was intolerable. Sheela had seen Subuds and me cuddling and just *had* to break it up! The sour old !"£$%^&*! thought I. Breaking attachments? Good for the Path? Having too much fun? …Whatever.

Oh lord! It sent me near-crazy. What could I do? Nothing… you weren't allowed to fight your assignments, and I was not, to my knowledge, allergic to hotels; so could not plead health reasons.

The hotel turned out to be a very nice place. Manned and womanned with lively, sweet, and youthful folks, it had a very good restaurant, a disco, and sizeable, fresh-smelling rooms, scrupulously clean, of course. There was a feeling of constant flow and movement, and the excitement of the Master's nearness, relatively speaking. Portland was a benign-seeming city, and in our brief free times we workers could wander and explore.

I was a chambermaid, cleaning guest rooms. Oh, how my helplessness burned! To be so far away from Subuddha! So I decided to *get into* my rage. I imagined that the buckets I carried (for cleaning bathrooms) were filled with blood and you-know-whose severed heads. I *really* imagined it, till I felt the delight of mayhem and carnage to my toes. I did this sort of thing all day, for two weeks.

To my surprise, lots of fears of all sorts vanished. In fact, an interesting after-effect of this self-administered therapy was this: after that ride with Bhagwan in his Rolls in New Jersey, I had stayed afraid of him for about four years. And at the Ranch I had not been able to look at his eyes during Drive-By. Nor could I wave my arms around and go ga-ga. I stood behind others, waiting for it to be over. I didn't know what I feared; just some state of abyssal annihilation.

You can imagine that I carried this too as a secret shame!

But after two weeks of Enraged Cleaning Lady Deep Livings-Out, this fear of Bhagwan vanished! When I then went back to the Ranch I could look him in the eye again, and when I had a wonderful dance with him at Jesus Grove (more on that later), he twinkled at me in the most mischievous fashion… as if he knew.

At the hotel there was that disco – and it was *wizard,* with a strobe light, a disco ball, and fellows to dance with, so I had opportunities like crazy to show off my moves. I had a wicked little twirl I'd learnt in long-ago ballet class, that segued well into rock'n'roll flights of funky fancy. I could do the splits (still can). So my time there was not actually misery. And the food was great as always.

Another thing happened, that would not have found space, back on the Ranch.

The chakra reading I'd experimented with in Poona back when I'd been with T.Z., had grown into something larger. It had started with that deer-hunt patrol where I'd 'read' the fallen leaves. I'd been experimenting with reading things with my hand, and by the time I got to Portland I was ready to experiment in a bigger way. Being so far from Sheela made it feel safer – I knew that Waduda (later Leela), a well-known Intuitive from California, had been asked by Sheela to use her psychic abilities to some political end. Waduda refused. I did not want to be asked in the first place! Instinctively, I kept these experiments secret.

I began giving chakra readings to other workers at the hotel. They lasted ninety minutes or more, because once I started, a great thoroughness came over me, and I couldn't leave the person's aura, or their interior body, until I'd looked at *everything* – whatever arose, I had to investigate. And describe aloud.

This was an incredible experience. Suddenly I was in a realm where I was utterly at home. Not only at home – I was in the very path of creation – for as I read I was participating in life, in energy. And its description, as I gave it, changed things – illuminated, lifted, whatever was there – childhood images, past lives, physical ills… moved and changed; and somehow that material was transformed into light. I entered the universe of another being, so very different from myself; and in awe I traversed it, dove within it, opened it out. I felt that I could fly.

I would walk out after the reading feeling transformed myself. I had flown! I could do this! This… sublime, unearthly, *gifted* thing! I could! I could see behind leaves, through walls, underneath stones, between fingers and toes, up noses, inside livers, behind, and then behind again, something the thickness of a hair.

I could.

I was so happy.

Whatever the mundane world around me was, the nuts and bolts of daily living, was sent into the sky.

I hugged the knowledge to me as a secret joy. A scarce-credible, yet actual, secret key.

I came back from Portland and sure enough, Subuddha had been with the wee-waisted Scotswoman. But he welcomed me back into his bed.

An amazing thing happened: Subuddha and I were sent on Fire Watch together. There was a National Forest not far away where there was a watch tower, and all summer it had to be manned. I myself was on fire with hopeful, possessive excitement. We were driven up to the place in a jeep, along with a lot of supplies. The forest was dry and piney, with a sandy floor. It stretched over hills into the far distance.

The incumbent couple greeted us – a handsome pair, in their thirties, absolutely reeking of garlic. The garlic smelt both old and new – as if it had been mulling inside them for days, but also just for hours. We went up inner wooden stairs to the living and watching area – a big open-plan place with windows all around. This too reeked; the whole room was in an advanced Mediterranean funk. The couple explained that they had been eating garlic for five days, for their health.

What struck me was how these two separate human beings, man and woman, had decided, together, to do this (stinky) thing, together, almost as if they were one person. There was a settled, mature air to it all. I marveled.

It was wonderful to gaze out at the far-flung forest, looking for smoke, or just looking. There were instruments which the couple taught Subuddha how to use, and he took his duties very seriously. I had come here hoping for intimacy, but I was sorely disappointed. Subuddha spent almost every minute gazing out the windows and fiddling with the instruments. He was exactly as forthcoming about his inner states and emotional details as he was down at the Ranch – which meant, not at all.

Just to add a garish fillip and furbelow to my frustration, I had my period. I didn't have any thingies for it, so I just bled and wiped, bled and wiped. There was a curious freedom in this. It was as if Nature was just allowed to weep unchecked. My pelvis was breathing, open… if grieving.

There were no fires on our watch.

Dusty main street, Rancho Rajneesh 1981

Building bridges

Truck Farm

Musicians at Drive-By

Festival tents

Cleaning the Mandir

Osho in Discourse

Biking on the Ranch

Celebration in the Mandir

The townhouses

The Mall, 1982

Bathing at Krishnamurti Lake

In the A-Frame factory, 1982

Repairing one of the many check dams

Lunch at Magdalena Cafeteria

Celebration, Rajneeshpuram; Satsang with the Master, 1982

Coach leaves for Portland

Winter in Rajneeshpuram

Me and Subuddha in California

Strip-o-gram costume, California 1987

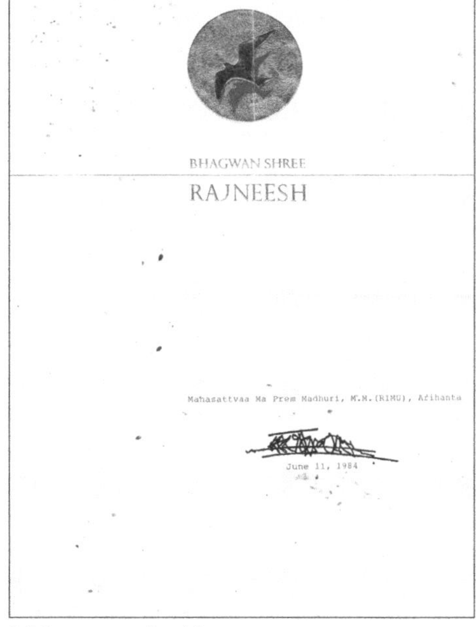

BHAGWAN SHREE

RAJNEESH

Mahasattvaa Ma Prem Madhuri, M.M.(RIMU), Arihanta

June 11, 1984

Mahasattvaa Certificate

AIDS is Declared

I know, that's an odd way to put it, but that's how I always think of this earth-shaking event: the day, in March 1984, that AIDS was declared. (Now, apparently, it is correct to refer to this dread disease as AIDS-HIV. Simple AIDS is felt to be somehow derogatory. But at the time we just said AIDS.)

It was like a declaration of war. There was a general meeting in the Mandir – absolutely everyone had to come. Sheela stood up on the stage and told us about this new disease; Bhagwan had predicted it would kill huge numbers of people, and had handed down the rules of engagement for us.

All of us were gobsmacked.

And how wise and prescient Bhagwan was… how practical.

As everyone now knows (but it was news to us then) a new disease had surfaced in the early 80's, mostly among promiscuous gay males. Nobody really knew where it came from (a conspiracy theory held it had been engineered to kill off gays) but it now seems sure that it leapt the wild-primate-to-human gap like a little spark of malign electricity, and had then gone on from there. Monkeys carry it in the Congo; and people kill them for dinner. Monkey blood makes contact with open cuts on human skin. That's all it takes.

Anyway, Bhagwan realized there was no earthly reason why the infection should stay with gays; they are not a separate species! And he moved quickly to protect his people – by 'moved' I mean, 'spoke' – and also called for protective measures in the population at large… if people would only listen. (Instead, they laughed at him in the newspapers; of course. Only later did the medical establishment finally suggest, for all sexually active, non-monogamous people, the same sorts of preventive measures Bhagwan had outlined.)

From that day thence, Sheela told us, we were to use condoms during every sexual encounter. And surgical gloves for foreplay. And we were to stop kissing. Best to be celibate, Bhagwan had said. (Everybody snapped to attention.) If that wasn't possible, monogamy was best. If you'd been monogamous for two years, no need for condoms. Otherwise, everybody had to use them.

This injunction actually came to me in a right moment. My whole being had become fed up with my addictiveness. It was a good time to stop. Or…

I didn't mean *stop;* I was still Subuddha-obsessed – but somehow I'd gotten over the need to be with somebody *every single night.* I was productively tired. Sometimes tired is a good thing.

People took it different ways. Some did become celibate for a time. Others clove unto one person. I remember there was only one couple who qualified for the no-condoms exemption – a handsome middle-aged American couple. Everyone looked at them with envy.

We were asked to report people who broke the rules. Slackers would have been easy to suss out since we all shared rooms (though I'm not sure anyone ever actually reported anybody). And as far as I could tell, people really did religiously adhere to the condom rule. You'd hear the squeaky stretch and snap of them, before the (somewhat diluted) sighs.

Subuddha and I had no choice, so we condom'd. And he condom'd with the teenager. (In fact, once I was visiting him at his house and there was a string, like a washing-line, stretched across the kitchen with condoms on it, hung up to dry. He'd been washing them! Somehow the supply had run low, and he'd washed a batch with soapy water in the sink to make sure he had enough. That was Subuddha! Always eccentrically enterprising.) What was much tougher for people was the surgical gloves. These were hated by everyone. Like, *loathed and detested.* It seemed worse to lose sensitivity in your hands than in your genitals. You felt like a doctor, not a lover.

People came up with ways to cheat the system – the most common, I believe, being to "just sort of keep a sheet between your hands and your lover's whatsit – " and go gloveless. Of course, moisture still traveled through the weave. But it was better than gloves in every way except hygienically... while still being achingly unsatisfactory.

The gynaecologist at the medical center reported that her work had been cut in half. So people must have been actually using the condoms – they weren't getting diseases anymore.

Everyone was tested for AIDS. A scant few men tested positive – and one woman – Zeno – was told she had, except that in fact she was some sort of strange scapegoat, because she didn't really have it – which she knew, and somehow everybody else did too. But things had gotten so weird by that time that you never knew what was going on: and it was dangerous to speak up. And who would you speak up to? (What I later heard was that Bhagwan had scolded Sheela during an evening talk he gave at his own house, with a few invited people attending. Sheela then caused that talk's recording to be 'lost.' Zeno was working in audio-visual and she knew this, and told people. That was her capital crime.)

There was an area of trailers called Desiderata, up on a hillside on the way to Krishnamurti Lake, quite a ways off the County road, and invisible behind a stand of junipers. The men, and Zeno, were sent to live there. They were very well taken care of, with meals brought in, and medical care provided. A grand crematorium with a copper roof was constructed in a valley that had been sacred to the local Indians. And Lazarus, an affable, mustachioed American, and the others had their time up there, waiting to leave their bodies. Except Zeno, who was very, very careful the whole time she was there… (She only died many years later, falling down a cliff in the Himalayas. Goodbye, funny, smart, friendly Zeno!)

When Lazarus died – that gentle soul, with his round glasses, short stubbly haircut, and ready laugh – we had a celebration for him, streaming up the path to the crematorium in the gathering dusk…

Somewhere in all this time – it was summer, I remember – my old boyfriend Herb came to visit, flying in in his own small plane and landing at the airstrip. He wanted to take me up for a spin, but I was afraid, and would not go. It was good to see him again, but I'm afraid he didn't have a very good time – I used him as a weeping-shoulder for my relationship woes. I was also pining for my surrendered bicycle, and wished that he would buy me a new one – and I must have hinted that – but that is not the sort of man Herb is; you can't just use him for an uncle. He gazed about him at our desert project, and I don't know what he thought; and in late afternoon he went away again, and I didn't see him any more until about 2001.

I used, when I couldn't help it, to ask Subuddha how he was feeling, wanting him to share with me. And he would invariably answer, "I think… " and then say something dry and factual and quite impersonal. It drove me nuts. So once I cast my psychic vision inside his chest – of course I did – and saw his heart all bunched up in there with itself, giving nothing away, brown as a walnut.

How could this be? It made me doubt myself – though it is perhaps the only time I ever really did; for while the process of intuitive reading is in one way beset by doubts every moment – I check each morsel of impression again and again, just to make sure; and it is always the same as the first time I looked – in another way it is my greatest security. The way my body just knows something, with the resounding clunk of accuracy.

But *this?* How could this be? Ah… I know now: if someone is chasing you, and harassing you, and wanting after you as if you are God and a chocolate-dipped frosty cone rolled into one, and they must eat you up – your heart goes inside like a mollusk into its shell and protects itself against the onslaught. It cannot afford to come out and bask in the sun – someone might eat it. It was my own crafty desperation, shriveling his fourth chakra at that moment. (I saw him many years later once when he was grieving, and his heart glowed with peachy, tender aching like a tentative sunrise.)

In 2017, I was at a party in Corfu, and got to talking with someone who was at the Ranch during those years. He asked me if Subuddha had been the love of my life. "Why, yes, he was!" I replied, surprised that anyone had noticed.

"I used to see you guys," said the man, an electrician from London. "You looked so… *right* together. You don't often see that – something that looks that good. I used to like to watch you."

I was amazed. I'd thought it was all only neurotic, when you got right down to it. But an onlooker had seen some validity there.

Guarding

I was given a new job: I joined the ranks of the Guards. There were guard huts dotted about: Top of the Ranch, on the County road where our property began; then, five miles down the hill towards town there was another guard hut; then, five miles further and you were in town, where there was another. There was also a hut at the turnoff to Desiderata, the enclave housing the AIDS patients; and one or two in more remote places.

The guard huts were there because anybody from outside could drive on the County road coming in from Antelope, and we wanted to see who they were. Some trucks had rifles in them, in gun-racks mounted up in the back window. If we saw something worthy of note we'd radio down to the next hut, and so on; and the Peace Force might be notified.

Guard huts were wood-built, hexagonal, and big enough for two people to sit in comfortably. They had a counter, and were windowed all round above counter-height, including a sliding window so you could talk to people. There were a couple of chairs. The huts were warm and snug and quite pleasant to be in.

We guarded in twos, in eight-hour shifts, as I remember. We all took turns for the different shifts and locations.

The uniform was vile. For women, it was polyester/cotton all over: purply gathered culottes – not flattering for anybody, ever, anywhere – they made you look like a lumpy eggplant. Then, a lighter mauve man-style tailored shirt with collar and cuffs; and a purply knitted vest for cold weather. We wore *pantyhose* with this, and running shoes. So of course I unbuttoned the neck and cuffs, rolled up the sleeves. (I cannot stand closed necks and constrained wrists!) And of course I was given grief for this – "Button it all up again!" So I'd do it, sullenly, till the Mom was out of sight, and then unbutton again. Very much like a girl in a Catholic school, rolling up her skirt.

Of course, looking back, I am just feeling how wonderful it all was – a bunch of lively, agreeable young people, and older people too, thrown into the crazy workings of an attempt to start a… civilization. We were in our own protected biosphere, or cosmosphere, here; gliding about in our blushing, ruddy clothes, happy in the very heart of happiness.

And truly I reveled in being moved about, and not knowing what would come next.

And the Moms, bless their cotton-poly socks, worked *very* hard to make it all happen.

Guarding was a good job. Not much happened. We were supposed to be very watchful, report things. Who knew when rednecks might try to invade? But somehow not much ever went on on my watch. Instead it was all about telling your guarding partner your life story and listening to his, all night long. And eating big fat cinnamon rolls and drinking coffee! Then, in the morning, I would run – ninety minutes was the norm after sitting still all night. That was wonderful… down to the river, up the road behind the hills into a secret verdant valley full of wildflowers, with a stream and an old rundown cabin in it. Then back home, shower, and such a good sleep…! Or, if I was guarding at Top of the Ranch, or the hut five miles downhill from it, I might run *up* the hill before my shift, in the lumpy purple clothes and my yellow sneakers, to my post. Even in a snowstorm! I loved it! (Running uphill is great – there can come a state where your body is running, but the inside of you feels as relaxed as if it is sitting back in an easy chair.) Then I'd arrive, full of blissful endorphins, and get into the warm, and settle in for yummy snacks and a good gossip. (I didn't sweat in those days, so didn't need a shower.)

(I remember enjoying a Canadian's story about going camping with his girlfriend in some wild woods in his homeland. A bear trundled into the campsite – lay down on its back and, whuffling and grunting, began to roll onto the tent – and its breath was just intensely disgustingly bad! …I heard lots of good stories.)

Once, when I was guarding at Desiderata, under the trees, on a winter night where snow was piled in drifts all about, there came a terrific banging at the door. We looked out the window and saw an enormous cat circling the hut, stopping sometimes to hammer with his fists to be let in. It would not have been humanly possible to refuse him… Then, in the morning, he did something so funny – a school bus came down the County road, ferrying people to work, and stopped opposite the hut. Mr. Huge Tomcat strolled over to the bus, leapt in, and went off to town.

My guarding career lasted quite a few months, and was mostly a joy – all that space to gaze at, all those far-flung little cozy housies, all those caffeinated conversations. Not knowing which part of this beautiful high, brushy desert I'd be going to next.

But then something happened… One summer night I had a date with M., a musician from Mexico. We sat on a terrace at the bar in town and I had a Tequila Sunrise. It was the only time I ever went to that bar, and the only Tequila Sunrise I have ever drunk. (My entire history with hard liquor wouldn't fill a teacup.)

The drink was tall and cold and had stripes of reds and oranges in it. It tasted fruit-juicy. I don't remember anything about that night except that afterwards I developed a crush on M. It had not even been a great night, I do know that – I just crushed at the slightest provocation, and, strangely, sometimes I crushed on men where there really wasn't anything interesting happening energetically.

Next day I had a bonafide hangover – the only one I remember ever having. And I had to go to some godawful department meeting for the guards, led by Su and another Mom. Su was Australian, of medium height, slender, short dark hair, maybe forty. She looked like a pretty gay lady, but I think she wasn't – I seem to remember a lanky, pale-eyelashed, mild-seeming cowboy consort in the background. Su was *tough,* and the cowboy's choice seemed odd to me (but maybe it wasn't his choice?) She did have a raucous sense of humor though, and was sometimes funny and laughing.

I also could not imagine when these tough women found time for lovemaking. The Moms worked all the hours of the day and half the hours of the night. (Perhaps they were doing all that hard bossy work because they really loved Bhagwan and wanted to make a Commune for us all. I don't know.)

We all sat in a big room at Sheela's house and were badgered and harangued. There were a lot of us – twenty or thirty, it seems to me, sitting on chairs. At one point Su told us that if we were guarding at Top of the Ranch and a nearby car with people in it caught fire, we had to call Su and her co-boss on our Motorolas *before we went and helped the people.*

I raised my hand. Su called on me.

"I would help the people first," I said. "There's not time to waste, trying to call on the Motorola. I'd try to get the people out." I felt annoyed, and it showed. This new rule seemed to me like the egregious, meddling stupidity of fanatics.

"See me after," glared Su. So I did. She told me to come to a private meeting with her in two days' time.

I grew sick with worry. A cold sore appeared on my lip – my first. I expected to be kicked out of the Ranch – it had happened to other people. Sometimes somebody would just disappear… either fled, or ejected. The increasing pressure to conform to rigid discipline and even rhetoric, was intolerable to some; others ran afoul of the Moms. (Sheela had printed a little booklet called *Rajneeshism: an Introduction to Bhagwan Shree Rajneesh and his Religion,* to which I felt righteously allergic without ever having opened it. Others might have voiced these same allergies.) The threat of being thrown out of the Garden was the most terrifying thing in the world. I *was* the Garden. The outside world was boring, bovine, dull, pointless, full of grey and twisted ciphers. It would be like ripping out my guts, my very bones, to leave.

I sat in a small room with Su.

She told me I had to leave the Ranch: "I can't trust you to protect our Master."

I gaped at her. Then, "That is not an option," I stated firmly.

"You might not have any choice!" she snapped.

I explained about the hangover, and how it had made me grumpy and reckless. Then I just sat there, obstinate.

But then, somehow, she softened. "You are a perpetual teenager!" she said, almost affectionately.

I felt pleased enough with that.

She relented and let me stay. But I could no longer be a guard. I felt a little sad… it's always a shock to be kicked out of something. But then I realized that the horrible uniform was no longer necessary.

I was sent into another parade of jobs…

Donuts

I was now the sole donut-maker in the Commune! The old house, where we used to eat at the very beginning, was now my kitchen. This job, which lasted several months, I remember with joy. I loved the isolation, and the way that the early start – 4:30 a.m. – gave me a sense of privacy. I could escape the notice of the Moms!

I rose every morning just before 4:00, dressed quickly, and ran in the dark the two miles to work. I'd load the oil into the square basin in the huge donut-making machine, turn it on to heat it; mix the batter, and start birthing big round donuts with holes in the middle. While they were frying, I'd mix the glazes – chocolate, vanilla. At around 10 a.m., while the finished, glossy donuts were sitting waiting for the taxi drivers to come and take them round to the various venues, Subuddha would also drop by, in his wordless way, to enjoy any imperfectly-formed chocolate donuts I had set aside for him. (I was hoping to trap his feet in the sticky glaze.)

I generally knocked off work about 4 p.m., after a laborious cleaning of the machine: I had to take it all apart and clean each gear and widget in hot soapy water, then lay them to dry on a cloth; then re-assemble it all before I could go home.

One afternoon I got a bright idea – why not mix up the batter now, so that in the morning I could just start frying the cakes immediately? – So I mixed the flour, sugar, eggs, milk, and so on, and left the big bowl covered when I went off home for the night. In the morning, I measured the batter as usual and dropped it into the hot fat.

But what weirdness was this? The donuts were *crawling* up onto the slanted moving metal conveyor-thing that brought them out of the oil, struggling like dying soldiers swarming a beach! How heavy they looked! How bloated! These were not the light, puffy donuts so popular with the Commune workers – they would not hold their shape! They looked odd, kind of like sci-fi Blobs, or undersea sponges.

Hastily I mixed up a new batch and cooked them. When Subuddha came around, I gave him the bloated, misshapen ones. He accepted them eagerly, ate a couple right there, and said he would take some home. He said they didn't taste too bad; just a bit… heavy. Sodden. But, a bunch of free donuts!

Next day when he returned he reported the effects of the gift. He had eaten several, and fed many to his roommate.

The whole night the room was alive with sound! And smell! Both guys were afflicted, and the walls resounded. Unpredictable rhythms, explosions, and fragrance-bombs! Exciting! Unrelenting!

…Someone in whom I confided told me that the sugars in the batter must have melted into the rest of the mixture and created a porosity into which the hot grease just… poured. Who would have thought?

Voila!

Backfiring donuts.

There are a few more things I remember about that job – how much I loved the solitude, for one thing – the way that being the sole proprietor allowed my happiness to come up and play. The way I one day devised a great many new icings for the donuts and showed them to Vidya, who said Oh yes, but did not adopt any. The way I frequently used Mop & Glo on the linoleum floor and made it shine, shine, shine. You just poured some goop from the bottle onto the floor, and then wiped it all over the place with a sponge mop;

then cleaned out the mop and left the floor to dry. The stuff both cleaned the floor and waxed it. Kind of a miracle.

One morning, something rather hairs-stand-up-on-the-back-of-the-neck happened. I set out from the Townhouses, where I lived then, in a pitch-dark pre-dawn, to run to the donut-making house. There had been a lot of rain – but that morning there was none; just black, black sky. I was running at a good clip – I liked this shivery early-morning dark – when all of a sudden my body *just stopped.* It would go no further.

I thought I heard... water. I stepped forward very gingerly, inch by inch. Right in front of my feet I discovered... nothing! There was a chasm where there had been a road. And at the bottom of the chasm, a swollen rushing stream ran.

I found out later that a storm-runoff culvert had been washed away and taken the section of road with it. The crevasse was ten feet deep. If my body had not had the sense to stop...

One day a Mom, Rikta, a hard-bodied rather truck-like Texan with a laugh like a mean Janis Joplin, came round to the donut kitchen and wanted to take a bagful of the treats on a day-trip. (She was homely, and bossy, and pudgy; and she blew hot and cold. You never knew where you were with her. I tended to avoid her as much as I could.)

I had been expressly forbidden to give donuts away, so I refused. She clucked her tongue admiringly.

Unfortunately, the donut kitchen's days were numbered. During a festival, a worker was sent over in the early morning; she was supposed to help me clean up. But she'd already been working all night, and was exhausted. She dropped the heavy motor and it broke.

The Moms decreed that a new one was too expensive. No more donuts. I was devastated – I was losing my hermitage!

Another benefit of the job had been that I hadn't had to wear a uniform. Oh well... now I would; I was being sent to the Ice Cream Parlor.

Ice Cream Parlor and Restaurant

In one of the fine new modern buildings comprising the Mall on the main street, there was a spacious restaurant. The ice cream parlor, my next (and fun!) workplace, was right next to it – a small, duck-in shop, with a wrap-around counter and a great many tubs of ice cream in a waist-height freezer. The uniform was a pair of red jeans with a red t-shirt; I wore these snug, and rolled the t-shirt's sleeves up, and tucked it into the jeans. I played with the look, adding a scarf, earrings, narrow belt, pumps with little heels; worn, as was then the fashion, with short socks with lace round the ankle. When I leaned over a freezer with my metal scoop, my behind hoisted by the heels, and all the cowboys stood there waiting for their cones… well, life was good. I was lavish with my helpings – great heaping mounds of ice cream scootched down on top of each other – triple cones, each scoop a different flavor, were the most fun.

And of course some pesky Mom told me I had to cut the scoop sizes down, or we wouldn't make any profit. But little miserly scoops just weren't 'me.' I tried for a minute or two to minimize them, but reckless nature reasserted herself, and the cones teetered and bulged once more.

This was a cheerful job – easy, physical, dancey, and full of boys. I was happy.

Then I was transferred to the restaurant, to wait tables.

The uniform gave some scope for sexiness – narrow red skirt and t-shirt. (I remember some guy complimenting me on my hip-shot slouch as I leant back against the wall in a slow moment.) But the restaurant was full of cigarette smoke. This was horrible for me! My throat soon felt raspy and my face sort of swelled up and turned red. Weird hot energies coursed through me in waves. Any exposed skin began to itch. My lungs hurt.

It was dangerous to complain about anything, but this was just… not okay. I told the coordinator I was allergic to the smoke. She regarded me with cold suspicion. Word went back to Sheela, who ordered an actual doctor's edict, nothing less. I was sent to a really stellar doctor – an allergy specialist who happened to be there. Bless his soul! For he became an ally… In this instance, he wrote a note attesting to my allergy to cigarette smoke, and this was duly presented to the coordinator.

This note made powerful people very cross, and I was given a stern lecture about Surrender. I was sent to the kitchen.

But first, an adventurous, romantic interlude… and other things.

Hiking in the Dark

One spring night Subuddha and I left Magdalena Cafeteria after dinner, and went up to his house, on the slope above. Then, on the spur of the moment, we decided to hike up into the high peaky hills that went on and on behind that… into we-knew-not-what. At that time I lived way out in the farthest outpost of housing: if you took the school bus down the valley past the Mall and then on for many more miles, a rough road curved up to the left. After a goodly distance there were, on the left, two trailers. This place was called Subhuti. Subuddha and I had a vague, crazy notion of heading over the hills to my house.

The night was moonless. A trail ascended the hill for a short stretch only, then petered out. We climbed through a fence, bending over and flattening our backs, and then stood upright and continued. As we crested the first hill and went down the other side, the lights of Magdalena vanished and we were in the dark.

I cannot overemphasize how unknown to most of us were the hills around the settled part of the Ranch. We worked so hard, and partied too, and generally went exploring only as part of crews sent out to fence or build a lake or dig a foundation. We had no weekends in which to roam around in the out-of-doors. This particular part of the terrain was unused, untraveled. Subuddha and I did not know how far the hills went on jutting up all jumbledy in the rugged landscape. We could have ended up in Yellowknife, Canada, for all we knew…

Right away we were on our hands and knees climbing a steep incline. We could see our pale hands, and we could see rocks, lighter than the surrounding earth – but all else was blackness. I was exhilarated – I was in love with this guy, and now I had him all to myself, and I just didn't *care* that all was dark and blind. I just went on. Soon I was in the lead, and flying by the seat of my pants – scrabbling, reaching a peak, sliding down the other side, and then encountering a new steep rise to go up, hands in the dirt, on the grasses, on the stone. I hadn't any idea where I was leading us; I just went.

After a while I perceived, with my paranoid-lover's sensitivity, that Subuddha was feeling admiration for me, for my daring, for my certainty. This was heady stuff, as by this time in our relating he was the one in charge. I flew on the lift of it, on and on into the deep hours of the wilderness night unfolding.

There is something fabulous, ecstatic, freeing, about hurtling forward when you cannot see a thing – it is just you and darkness, and maybe something else is guiding, or maybe nothing is. You just go. I'd had that night bicycle ride on that road near Baroda, in December 1973 – and so I knew it could be done. There's something weightless about being on the move when the sun is not oppressing. I just let go, and kept going.

We never knew how high any particular hill was going to be; we never knew if the next shuffling step would send us off a cliff or tumbling into a ravine. But we neither tumbled nor crashed; hour after timeless hour we crawled and leapt and walked and slid, and when dawn came gently hoisting the sky on its long arms, inching it towards the deep purple of the upper reaches, we were standing on a hillock looking down… at a sandy road! We ran down to that stripe cut through the sagebrush; we ran with the flying feet of the young who have just popped the lid off some old forbiddenness. And as we walked up to a curve and turned to the right, there, crouching in the junipers, were the little pair of trailers where I lived.

…Just like that.

The last stanzas of a poem I later wrote about that adventure:

By the time we got home to amazing civilization,
Warm kitchen; bedroom; and lay dreamless for another hour
Loving and tangled in covers
You said you felt yourself opening to me
You said that the way I, knowing nothing,
Had led us home…
You said I would take too much from that opening
And that you must decline.
I said I had no designs on you –
But I lied
In the flush of new morning light
Which struck the curtains aside –
I wanted to devour you, entrails to eyes, so clean
And strong you are, so separate
And milky-clean.
And so we never met

Though for a year
We swam in lilied snakebit pools
And sipped each other open-eyed
In tall grasses that cut like knives –

My breasts sensate in waves of rippled sweetness,
As a snake ripples, silent as near-extinction.

A Few Fashion Notes

In my endless enthusiasm for happy adornments, although I had no time to sew and no needle and thread to contrive alterations with, I made do. You see, each townhouse and trailer had a mudroom, necessary in Big Muddy (in certain seasons the valley was really very muddy indeed). And each mudroom had a Lost-and-Found or maybe Free Box. (Which were they? Hmmm… not quite sure. Probably lost-and-found.) So here's how I shopped: many an evening I'd hop off the bus at my stop and make a quick furtive dash along the row of houses, nipping into each back door and having a quick rummage through the box. This was great! I scored great stuff! These were *art* supplies. I needed to own plenty to choose from.

Once there was a meeting in Magdalena where Sheela held forth about proper dress. She kept going on, with great relish, about glimpsing a cettain woman's "tangle of jungle" while that woman, wearing loose cut-offs, was pumping gas at the gas station. I was called to task for wearing short shorts on my bicycle and was then issued with some stupid culotte things in a peachy color which didn't suit me. But they were nice crackly brand new, and I thought if I had *lots more new stuff* some of it might be interesting; so I asked. The relevant Mom frowned at me. Apparently a person should be satisfied with just a few outfits to wear again and again! What bosh!

When the Moms had appointed me liaison between Ranch and Outside Telephone Company, I'd been supposed to dress all proper and businesslike. I'd been optimistic; but I was issued with a number of ghastly suits with padded shoulders, and high necked blouses in no-iron, staticky fabrics, as well as a pair of really fab high-heeled Italian suede shoes. Always game for dress-up, I had my hair permed so that I looked like Little Orphan Annie Goes Corporate. But I felt *weird* in those clothes, like a squirrel wearing a diaper, and it must have showed.

One day I was informed that I was going to be moved to another house. The moving crew came while I was at work and they somehow managed, between the old house and the new, to lose one of my boots. It was a very fine short boot, maroon with a wedge heel. I asked after that boot and the rowdy bunch who did the moving had no sympathy whatsoever. For *years* I felt burned about that boot! The power of that feeling of loss was a startling thing to see. It was, I felt sure, a sign of a really recalcitrant spiritual state.

Lots of women wore velour tracksuits in jewely purples or garnets. And the cowboys probably liked their jeans and tough-looking jackets and their hats.

One day Prabha, a beautiful therapist who'd befriended me, told me that violets and pinks, but never corals or beiges, suited my complexion. This proved to be very good and lasting advice.

The Presence of the Master

So where was Bhagwan in all this? I love something I heard him say in a discourse, when he began speaking to us again in the Mandir – "Here are so many people, doing all kinds of things… things that should be done, things that should not be done… " And his voice was so equanimitous, I smiled all through my tummy. Yes. Exactly so.

We were all driving, dashing, laboring, creating – and what we were *not* doing was meditating or getting therapy. These things were available, but only festival-goers seemed to avail themselves of them. Therapy cost money – meditations took time – and work was oh-so-full-on. There was a general sense that Sheela only wanted us to work. (My own opinion, if anybody wants it, is that one deletes meditation and therapy at one's peril. My various anguishes with my love affair could, I'm sure, have been productively addressed.)

Bhagwan was, for the first few years, visible only in Drive-By – when each afternoon he drove one of the fleet of Rolls Royces down the now-tarmac'd main road while we all stood on the left side dancing and swaying and generally having a good hoo-ha – and, when you got to see his face, he *might* beam at you, or look at you… and you'd sort of almost fall down, and sway about dizzily with the impact of his gaze. Musicians played somewhere in this line-up, banging drums, tooting flutes – and he always gave them special attention.

He had begun, in late 1984, after the extended silence, to give evening talks to a small group at his house. These were recorded, and played to us the following night in the Mandir – late at night, though, when we were exhausted. One had been hefting, trudging, stirring, hammering, for twelve hours... it was so easy to just lie down and go to sleep. The discourses might have been censored by Sheela's people, too. It felt like she did not really want us to hear them. Bhagwan was too incendiary; we might get rebellious ideas.

I never attended any of those talks at his house. But then, in 1985, a new thing started happening: journalists were allowed to come, stay in the new 100-room hotel in the downtown, tour the Ranch, and then ask Bhagwan questions at evening gatherings held in Sheela's big house, Jesus Grove. Workers attended by invitation, in some rotating order.*

Bhagwan had a lot of fun with the journalists – teasing, flirting, haranguing, provoking, and in general flummoxing them utterly. He would address each one as a real, present, urgently viable *soul* – rather than as an employee of whatever newspaper or news service. They'd be unmanned, trying to cling to their professionalism in the face of this beaming, glowing, incredibly penetrating Wild Being with the big ocean-deep eyes.

On the way in and out of these meetings – a few of which I attended – musicians played skirling, lilting, rising-to-wild-heights gypsy music – and people lined the path, dancing. (Some of these were invited only to line the path, and would listen to the interview in a large entrance room of the house. Others sat inside and also lined the path.) And, as Bhagwan walked from his car to the house, he would dance with us...

One evening he stopped right in front of me – his hands first together in namaste, then brought apart, going up and down in time to the music – while he looked right into my eyes.

I was jumping like a pogo stick – and my eyes would close, I couldn't stand the intensity any more, while my body bounded high on invisible springs, higher and higher! – then I'd open my eyes, and he'd still be there! Staring right into me, digging down deep as deep, beyond all my daily consciousness, into the Abyss! – and I'd close my eyes, and bound higher, mouth wide open, *AGGGHHHH heeheeheeheeheeheehee agh!!!* Then my eyes would open, and he was *still there!* My head went back, trying to fall off my body, as I leapt higher and higher again!

* Once I was first into the room, and saw Jayananda and Sheela sitting in front of Bhagwan for a personal meeting. Bhagwan was saying to Jay, "And remember – you don't owe anything to anybody – not even the truth!" I marveled at this, and felt threatened by what it might mean for Subuddha and me!

Eyes close! Open! There he still was, beaming with joyful beams, relentless, staring right down into my soul while an unknown energy bounced me up into the sky!

Finally he moved on… and, years later, somebody who had worked on this particular video, in the audio-video room in Krishna House in Poona, told me that it was a movie of… orgasm! Some sort of orgasm. (I've never seen it.)

We heard that he liked to swim – a swimming pool had been made for him, in the garden of his house. We knew that Sheela consulted with him – but only later it came out that he was scolding her for many of her actions and attitudes. This she did not tell us. Others were in the room, and they (later) did…

When the Mandir was built, and he began coming out for Satsang, we could all meditate together in silence. It was festival time; there were thousands of visitors, and during the silence, people were restless and moving about. So he decided to start speaking again, the very next day – and he did. He would roil us up, soothe us, lift us, exhort us, use his rapier vision on "the Priests and the Politicians," – the twin evils of the world, in his opinion – and who can argue with that? – including very specific politicians in the USA. He was fearless, but we were not… and it was scary to hear him. I was always afraid somebody would shoot him.

And so he was there, but rarely seen; rarely seen, but oh-so-there. Sheela was his messenger, and a rotten one she was – pushy, censorious, in-your-face, and doctoring what he said whenever it didn't suit her own logic. People ask me again and again, "Why didn't he fire her? Why did he put up with her?" – as if Bhagwan was the CEO of a company, hiring and firing, steering the corporation towards a logical profitability.

No. It was not like that. He was not that.

I love this story about George Gurdjieff, the mystic from the Caucasus who later lived near Paris and had many notable English disciples. He used to host dinner parties and gatherings in his flat. There was a tea-merchant who used to attend, and people wondered what he was doing there – he was not interested in 'waking up,' and spoke only of banal and tedious things. Nobody liked him – he was completely out of place – a traditional, hidebound man. But still he attended.

Only after Gurdjieff's death was it discovered that Gurdjieff had been paying him to be there!

I think too of when Bhagwan began wearing hats. Just for photo shoots –

but all sorts of different headgear appeared on his head – a big sun hat, like a Lady would wear; a turban, a fez-like thing, a Tibetan woolen construction with wings – and many other sorts. Somebody asked him why he was modeling them, and he said, "They just came along, and so I wore them."

If a Sheela comes along, and insinuates herself, and takes power by muscling out another secretary – then kidnaps you to a hostile country, and installs you – and you can barely walk, and are not inclined to try to control life or reality or existence in any way, because it is all so orgasmically marvelous, and unfolds itself in its own way – and you do not fear death, or soldiers, or anything – and a spectacular drama is playing itself out, full of the lightness and darkness of human beings – and your disciples depend on you, but they have to grow up too, you are not going to protect them – they have to use their own discernment, their own intuition – and even if you wanted to control things, which you surely don't, you have no gun or whatever it would take to seize control – because she has you sequestered, bugged (yes, bugged), and effectively muzzled, since she can censor your words – well, what a party! And you *do* say things to her and to others, you speak your truth – but you do not, cannot, 'do' something.

It is not about correcting. It is about watching – being the witness, and only the witness, of all that is – the witness does not choose, or limit, or divide. It is not dualistic. It is a wholeness.

That is what it means to have the mind stop – the constant dualistic choosing of the mind falls away and the great space of watching comes instead; whole, embracing all the opposites.

The mind can't do that.

This is one of my favorite of all the stories he told us: A Zen master at a temple in a little town was accused by a teenage girl of fathering her out-of-wedlock child.

"Is that so?" said the Master.

The townspeople were very angry. They brought the baby to him and insisted that he raise it at the temple. "Is that so?" he said. And he did – he raised the little boy and fed and educated him.

Years later, the girl, now grown up, married the real father of the child, and came and, with many apologies, asked to have the child back again.

"Is that so?" said the Master, and gave the child back.

Bhagwan also, he told us, *did* make mistakes – just being a Buddha didn't mean you were immune to them. "For example," he said, "just look at me and this Big Muddy Ranch... !"

The Homeless People

When Sheela occasionally called us to big meetings, she would often harangue us about political matters – things having to do with zoning, regulations, the stupidity of Rajneeshpuram's neighbors (who were not near at all but out here they were still seen as neighbors). Who was running for what office and what that might mean for us. And so on. Increasingly she was flying around, whisked aloft by a craggy little pilot named Cliff, appearing on television or in the offices of local government. Her negotiation style was pure obnoxiousness: that was her calling card, her stock-in-trade. She insulted people, attacked them verbally. Then she'd report to us whatever she wanted us to hear, and exhorted us to work harder, or whatever.

I found all this stuff wholly unpalatable, and simply shut it out. Just insufferable tedium, I thought, full of uncomfortable dissension and embarrassing encounters with benighted Americans. Why did we even have to talk to those people? They were living in a different century. I wanted nothing to do with them, but certainly didn't wish them ill. Sheela' s confrontational style worried and upset me – even if, as she claimed, Bhagwan had instructed her to be like that! There were news bulletins posted on boards here and there, and I never read them. I couldn't bear the tension, the controversy. Newspapers reported things sensationally and incorrectly, often being nasty to us. And, too, if the non-sannyasins Sheela was berating were sweet and well-mannered, like those telephone company guys... it was even more excruciating to watch her be a hideous beast to them. Just made me sick. Too much beastliness all round. I just didn't want anything to do with it.

But then, in September 1984, political unsavoriness – for that was what it smelt like, though it masqueraded as philanthropy – came to us. Right to our own hidden, glorious, and rather fraught Utopia. Sheela told us that we were going to be hosting a great many homeless people, in a program called Share-a-Home.

Whatever she was cooking up with these homeless people, I didn't want to know. She said it was charity; that we had so much, we were going to share it. I knew this was bullshit – she was not a charitable soul. I didn't like the sound of it, but what to do? The homeless people were coming to live with us. We'd see what happened.

And so scouts were sent out to big cities – Portland, Seattle, even Chicago and New York – and they brought back homeless people by the dozen!

Suddenly the outdoor disco (which had replaced the indoor one) bobbed and swayed – while *Sexual Healing* played with its melodious, creamy flow – with a lot of young black men! And cleaned-up white ones with sly, reckless looks on their faces! And a few shuffling older ones! Suddenly, a lot of our women who hadn't had a date in years… had not only dates but full-on love affairs! The supply of spinsters dwindled! The Share-a-Homers were housed separately from us – issued with clean new clothes – fed separately. Rumors went around. The homeless guys were being given tranqs and saltpeter in their food to keep them tame! Some of them wanted to rebel!

What the hell was going on?

The likely explanation was that they were brought in to vote. Don't ask me for who, or what – my memory of those things is a pasta-draining colander. Whoever Sheela thought they should vote for. I think some of our people even ran for office. The City of Rajneeshpuram had been incorporated, and disincorporated again. (Even the word 'incorporated' makes a grey veil come down over my eyes and sends me sleepwards.)

I think those homeless guys were weirded out by the whole business. There they were, happily miserable, slouching about whatever city, and all of a sudden they're in this strange place where everybody wears red, and the women take them to bed, and they get fed? It all rhymes. They must have wondered what the cost was – I saw their wary eyes.

But a few took Sannyas, and stayed, when it was all over… and that did warm the heart. Some lives were turned around.

It was during the last festival that we were ever to have in Rajneeshpuram – though we could not know that it would be the last – that Rudra, Sarita's and my oldest brother, came to visit. Bhagwan had given him a name that first day Devadasi and I were in Bombay, but he'd never met Bhagwan. He rode his motorcycle down from British Columbia, where he lived on an island; he didn't announce his impending arrival, so it was a big surprise when some Mom or other told me that my brother was here and wanted to sleep in a field and that this wasn't allowed! Of course he had no money; sleeping in a hotel would never have occurred to him anyway. I guess he thought it was going to be a wide-open hippie situation… Anyway, he was somehow housed for the few days of his visit, and so finally he saw Bhagwan – speaking in the Mandir.

He loved seeing the Master, promptly became a devotee, and left to drive back to B.C. so that he could wind things up there and come to stay at the Ranch.

We just didn't know then how short the time was to be. Meanwhile, life and work went on…

A Joke, and a Hidden Document

One day in June 1984, a very peculiar thing happened. Bhagwan gave a list to Sheela – twenty-one people he said had become enlightened. She announced to us the names, and of course there was a big kerfuffle. People stared at each other – *You? Enlightened?* People looked at themselves – *Moi!? Enlightened?* What have I been missing here?

And it was *weird!* Because who *were* these people? Just generally hard-working, sometimes obnoxious folks, for the most part… no signs of enlightenment that I could see: grinning, beaming, dancing in the street. Not even an especial serenity. Except for one: Maitreya, the elderly, kindly Indian gentleman whose bathroom I had cleaned in Lao Tzu. (And he said, when he heard about the list: "Oh, Bhagwan is a *rascal!*")

Basically, the whole thing registered on me almost instantly as a device, or joke, a thing that the Master did for some reason I would not be able to guess; so why try? I dismissed it right away as something I need not grapple with; and then just ignored it... Because I knew and they knew and everybody knew that those people were just idiots, like the rest of us.

Then, many months later, early in 1985, he told us it had all been a joke. Certainly the announcement had had the desired and salubrious effect, of shaking people up like crazy! I mean, that's what we were all doing there, wasn't it? Getting enlightened? (Though I'd given up on that dream pretty much instantaneously upon being apprised of its possibility in human life… realizing that I was a hard-core doofus-goofus, I was settling for whatever else I could get instead.) But enlightenment drives you crazy if you want it. The two things – enlightenment and wanting – don't go together.*

Much later still – about nine months after he'd said it was all a joke – a strange thing happened. I was sliding along the Mall on Main Street one evening, under the roof that covered the walkway. Work was over for the day, I was on my way somewhere… and, as always, I was hoping not to encounter any Moms. There emerged from a doorway a certain round, pleasant little American woman I knew slightly (she'd been very ill indeed in the same ward in Poona where I'd lain with my second bout of hepatitis). Her name was Priya and she was Sheela's secretary (an unenviable job!) and she labored in an office in the same complex where the restaurant was. She was short, with a strong forehead, shoulder-length dark hair with a fringe, and a neat, curvy body. She worked hard, had a very sweet, rather hidden nature, and always looked as if she was conserving energy for unforgiving duties. She had a special quality – something soft, feminine, quiet – and a beautiful, melodious laugh. Without knowing her, I liked her. She seemed to spend most of her time at a word processor.

Now, she beckoned me into the office, where lights still burned, though everyone else had gone home. We two were alone.

"There's something I want to show you," she said in a low voice, almost whispering. "Come on back here." And she led me into the depths of the open-plan office, past many desks, to the one where she worked. "Have a seat," she said, indicating an empty chair.

"Bhagwan sent this for you, back when he was declaring those 'enlightenments.'" she said, handing me two pieces of paper. "But Sheela didn't want you to see

* In Poona, enlightenment had seemed a viable, if unknowable, puzzle – the thing he said was 'beyond experience.' The way that beauty contestants examine themselves in the mirror for flaws or winning features, we'd examined our inner worlds incessantly for laudable (we hoped) or disqualifying (we feared) symptoms. Bhagwan had once said, "The only way to know if you are growing spiritually is if you are feeling more and more loving to people." Ah. Hmmm.
In Oregon, this whole concern and competition had gone by the wayside as we worked and slept and ate and worked again, in our cowboy clothing. But now we suddenly thought of it again… I would like to add my own opinion: the futility of aspiration aside, it is my contention that if you lay eyes on an enlightened person – if you apprehend him in your vision, grok him even just for a moment – at some profound and final level, the work is already done. You might not know it for lives to come; but somewhere in you, you have seen what is possible. You have participated, with your witnessing, to something utterly Beyond – beyond the mind, beyond the mundane, the known. You too are in some way freed.

it. But I thought you should. Please don't tell anybody. Here, you can read this paper – " she indicated one of the sheets – "but then you have to give it back to me. And this is your certificate," she said, indicating the other piece of paper.

I sat back, agog. I was just an invisible, 'wayward cog in a great, complicated wheel. What was this? For a moment I was transported back to Lao Tzu House, where I would sometimes meet him in the corridor by accident – and be all a-flutter – and yes, at that time he surely knew I was there; for better or for worse. But now? I'd had no personal contact with him since the Castle; that crazy ride in the Rolls. I wasn't even writing letters to him.

I looked down at the papers.

One was printed with text, covering most of the sheet. The other was a certificate much like the one I was given when I (accidentally) took Sannyas – just a few words, top and bottom, and his signature. The Rajneeshpuram logo was at the top, a gold circle with two birds flying in it, one silver and one dark orange.

Then, the words **Bhagwan Shree Rajneesh.**

A big space, then, about two-thirds of the way down the page:

Mahasattvaa Ma Prem Madhuri, M.M. (RIMU), Arihanta

Then his wonderful, angular signature, a work of art in itself.

Then the date: *June 11, 1984.*

Oh.

Ah.

Hmmm.

Then I read the other piece of paper.

Since I could not keep it, and was also not allowed to copy it, I remember very little that was in it. But a few things I do remember: that I would get enlightened either when he left his body or when I left mine. That I should stay in the Commune as much as possible. And that I was "the esoteric roots of His teaching that would never be known to the world." Sarita told me later that an Arihanta was a type of enlightened person who would dearly love to communicate enlightenment; but doesn't really offer a path to people – just likes to talk about it.

The 'enlightened' people had titles that included the word Bodhisattva. The Mahasatvaas were different. Not enlightened, but, apparently, enlightenable.

(There was something in the document about Mahasattvaas being able to do birth and death ceremonies, but not marriage ones. Sarita told me that bit too. I found out later she is also a Mahasattvaa Arihanta.) Then I had to give the paper back.

Here was the effect it had on me: as if he had reached through the morass of the bullies who were tightening their grip on his Commune, and said to me: "I see you. I acknowledge your esoteric gift. I trust and support you. I see your nature – what is possible for you, even if now you are romantically obsessed and whatever else. There's you and me here; we see each other; in this beauty, in this secret wonder. You are okay."

Something in me relaxed right then. I was full of amazement. I so often thought that Bhagwan belonged to other people; not to me. But now he had given me a nod, right where I lived. I no longer had to care about the fascists and why they did what they did – or wonder what I might be doing wrong, that I was not like them. The Jungle had spoken to me in a secret voice, in a language just for us. Behind the scenes, behind the backs of the usurpers.

Of course, I don't know if he meant all this. But that was the effect it had on me – I felt trusted again. Connected.

I have the certificate still; that I was allowed to keep. And I love the *M.M.* – he had said that anyone who lived in the Commune for ten years got a Masters in Meditation. And it was then ten years and a bit... I keep the certificate with my sannyas one, in a plastic sleeve. They are the most luminous, important documents of my life – more empowering than my passport by far. Shinier than my body-birth certificate, with its little inked footprint, and an ad for Borden's canned milk on it, with a smiling cow wearing a 50's flowered house-dress.

So my own conclusion about the enlightenment joke is that it *was* a joke; it came at a time when we were all full of serious exoteric labors; it shook us and shocked us and had the wonderful silliness of a koan. But maybe there were other messages hiding in it. Because Maitreya-ji really *was* enlightened. Maybe if that had been declared all by itself, people would have hurt him, as, in Zen stories, disciples are often depicted as doing to others who 'make it.' And maybe other people also got secret messages with their certificates. Maybe I'm not the only one who got a sort of telegraphic boost to her belonging, her confidence. Maybe real messages were couched among the false.

Just maybe.

Tomatoes and Tumbleweeds

At Magdalena Cafeteria I was a sort of floating dogsbody, being sent to do this or that as the need arose – bakery, cleaning, freezer. Sometimes too I'd be sent off on strange jobs. For example, I worked one day down at the Truck Farm. (This was the impressive, ambitious veggie farm down on the flats by the river, at the eastern edge of the property.) I picked cherry tomatoes and ate them as I went along, squatting down and pulling the warm baubles off the fragrant bushes. I did not feel very good after this (turns out I am allergic to tomatoes). I felt all weak.

Suddenly there was a shout from ten feet away, and my head jerked up – "SNAKE! RATTLESNAKE!" someone was shouting. And there indeed, coiled around a tomato bush, was a huge thick snake! We all stood back, and then fled! – and soon the reptile slithered away.

Next came carrots. I ate some as I pulled them up by their frondy green tops, and felt much better and stronger.

It was a beautiful farm, and gave beautiful veggies, and we had great food at the Ranch – much variety, creatively rendered, and plenty for us all.

One day I was sent out with the tumbleweed crew. I was happy – there were four or five of us with a long flatbed truck, and we were gathering up the ubiquitous prickly dried-out bushes that roll across American deserts, strewing seeds wherever they go. They are unlovely (though some people spray them silver and use them for Christmas trees, I always found that a tragic idea). It hurts to touch them as they are so sharp and stickery. During the Santa Ana winds of my childhood, 1500 miles to the south, these bushes were one of the poxes of those cold dry blows that lasted days and days: those high, skirling, dry, shrieking gales, sucking moisture from lips and fingers, whipping your hair across your face in a crackling staticky irritating awfulness – and then, if you were walking somewhere (we had no car then), the spherical bushes would come rolling out of the horizon, flung along at a great pace, and bang against your shins, while dust blew into your eyes and mouth.

But now, this job was actually a lot of fun, because we weren't just hurling the light prickly balls up onto the truck – we were then climbing up onto the roof of the cab and jumping down onto the weeds, to flatten them so that we could put more on top.

I don't know whose idea this was – somebody with lots of uncomplaining free labor, of course – but what nobody seems to have thought of was that if you smash up dry prickly things, lots and lots of dust is generated. And it's sort of... *prickly* dust. And this gets breathed in to your lungs. Nobody'd thought that we'd need to wear masks.

So for the first couple of days I was having a great time, leaping down onto those great grey piles of unloved botanical lace-work, feeling them crush and compress beneath my weight; joking with the others, stopping for a delicious and welcome lunch, drinking fruit juice, brought to us by the taxi; then more leaping and crushing, like our whole bodies were feet in a vat of grapes. (Dry, sepulchral grapes. Ghost-grapes.)

But on the third day my throat closed up and my breath went shallow and wheezed in my lungs. I was having the first, and so far only, asthma attack of my life. I sat under a juniper, gasping for breath, bemused; then someone took me home, where I lay in my bed, perplexed at this new sensation of breathlessness. Next day I was sent back to my friend, the allergy doctor.

This worthy man taught me, with every evidence of delight in his subject, about allergies (which I'd suffered from great numbers of, since I was born).

It seems that it's not so much that one is allergic to certain things, but that a general *amount* of allergic reaction takes place in the body until one day, like water rising behind a dam, it overflows; and then there are symptoms. So the thing is to keep the water level low enough that it doesn't overflow. The best way to do that is to cut out dairy.

Most substances that you ingest take five days to make their way out of the body again – four really, but the fifth day is your insurance – and therefore there are many allergens that won't react if you leave a five-day gap in between ingestions. (I've employed this principle with eggs ever since, to good effect: I eat them once a week. More often, and I get a heavy headache. But eaten once a week, they are exciting, nourishing, and substantial, and don't make me sick.) However, the doctor said, dairy products are different – they take thirty days to leave the body. So a good experiment is to cut them out totally for thirty days and then see how all your other allergic symptoms are. Do they go away? Usually they do.

I was thrilled with the lucid information, and with the way that he treated me with respect! Like I was a viable grown-up! He said that I was allergic to both junipers – they were flowering – and tumbleweed dander, and cutting out dairy should bring the allergy burden in my body down enough to keep the reactions away.

And it did. I carefully avoided all milk products after that (to the occasional disgust of some powerful person, who didn't like the specialness this seemed to confer). I lost about five pounds in a month, which was quite nice really, and I felt better all over. Apparently allergies bring water-weight to the tissues – and removing such allergens lets that water get peed out (the water is felt by the body to be some sort of protection against the toxin) so removing milk from a diet makes weight-loss inevitable. Nice.

I didn't really miss it – the brownies we so enjoyed, made in our bakery, were non-dairy. So was the fresh bread.

Another Stint in Portland

I was sent to Portland to be a chambermaid again. It was weird to be in an American city after all our sequestered etheric richness. The streets seemed grey and shut-off from warmth and intimacy; yet the shops had beguiling goodies in them, and this could be seductive.

I had absolutely no money. One didn't really need it on the Ranch – everything was provided – but sometimes I pined for little luxuries. Eventually every resident was given a card once a month with $10 credit on it, marked out in $1 boxes. It could be used for things like brownies and donuts. This was mildly exciting. There was nothing else to spend it on, though, if you didn't drink or smoke. The boutique was completely out of my league. What I wanted: earrings! Makeup! Magazines! Chocolates! Lacy undies!

It seemed wrong that I could not, ever, buy a pair of earrings. I must have written to Devadasi, complaining about this. One day I received a little package from her. In it was a pair of silver earrings, the painful screw-on kind – but I have pierced ears. The earrings were beautiful though – acorns, light, hollow, gracefully crafted; with a leaf curling around each. There was a loving note enclosed, telling me that they had belonged to my grandmother, Araminta Harvey. I could feel the grace and beautiful workmanship of the trinkets; but to my taste they seemed clunky, too short. I plotted what I might do.

I took them along to Portland, and one day I flitted out onto the streets during my lunch hour and found a jewelry shop. Rather reluctantly they bought the earrings from me for $6. I took this money to a dime store and bought many pairs of fake gold earrings with fake stones. I felt ashamed and didn't tell Devadasi what I had done. (I still feel bad about this. In India, later, I could have had those silver acorns made into piercey ones. They were lovely. *So* sorry, Mom! And Granny Araminta!)

So now I had a bunch of glinty little things to hang in my ears. I took what pleasure in this I could.

A few of us went to the movies, to see Prince's *Purple Rain.* How wonderful it was! To sit again in a big theater, and see on the screen some sassy musician (Larry Blackmon I think) twanging his suspenders with his thumbs and singing "Wave your hands in the air like you don't ca-a-a-are!" and then Prince, leaping and melancholic and purple and singing about his childhood… I loved it.

Ah yes. And M. the guitarist was at the hotel. My Mexican crush. I badgered him and he agreed to a date, and then didn't show up. So I went looking, and found his room, and he didn't answer my knock, but the door was ajar, and when I peeked my head around it I saw… the back of a naked woman, the color and shape of a fine, polished violin. Languid and resting. I ducked out again, shocked, queasy and chagrined, and went and wrote a hot-blooded poem in Spanish.

I was at the hotel for two weeks. And I went on reading chakras, secretly, in a wholly different kind of passion. I'd stagger out after, woozy with cosmic overload. I was exploring… finding out more about the Layers of the being, and about how, if I saw an energy that felt loaded, unresolved, I could 'become' it and live it out for the person, right then, right there – leaping and groaning and howling and stomping, *being* the thing until it had transformed. I also fidgeted with surgeries – moving things about, delicately slicing them away; though I always asked the Forces I perceived nearby, in some other dimension, to do this work. They have such clever little tools – lights, colors, shells, leaves, pine-cones, or anything at all that exists anywhere, or never existed before; and might want to come to hand. I'd continue the session till everything felt solved, no matter how long it took.

And I was witness, too, to the particular unique god or goddess energies the person had at her or his core – I got to bathe in their glorious cosmic characteristics, feeling the fountain of life celebrate itself up through my own spine and middle; and out the top of my head.

Last Stint in Portland

Not long after this, I was sent to the hotel again. It was right after a festival (Bhagwan had decided that it was better for people who were leaving after a festival, to leave immediately it was over, and not wait; that way they would take the high with them). It was early evening when I boarded the bus for Portland along with a host of other people. It was a nice big clean bus, one of our own Rajneesh Buddhafield Transport coaches, and the route passed through woods and hills and flatlands, and we stopped midway by a river for snacks and a bathroom break. Thoroughly pleasant really… a mini-holiday. The trip took four hours.

Sitting next to me was a handsome, sloe-eyed, slender young Brazilian I had been noticing around from time to time. He was *really* handsome; sort of louche and lazy, in a quiet, watchful way; and he had what my mother used to call Bedroom Eyes. And so we made out in the dark all the way to Portland. It was quite *thorough* making-out; and then, shortly afterwards, while I was at work cleaning rooms in the hotel, I realized I had cystitis (unwashed fingers are just *never* a good idea. Girls! Make him wash his hands! Men! Wash them without being asked!)

There was a doctor at the hotel who gave me antibiotics. (Back then I didn't know about D-Mannose, if in fact it existed yet. Girls! You don't have to take those rotten antibiotics! D-Mannose really works! It is a nice white powder extracted from cranberries, and it keeps bacteria from adhering to the bladder walls!) But next thing I knew I had a kidney infection, and was sent back to the Ranch to the hospital.

It was not approved of to be ill. Most of us were healthy – the sun, exercise, good food – and good hygiene. But sometimes things happened. A woman named Saki, for example, got rubella – German measles – and lost all her hair. Then I got it – even though I'd had it as a child – and my tummy was covered with a red rash. I was quarantined in a little trailer. Vidya, my boss then, was annoyed. I lay about reading books, not feeling unwell at all, until I was pronounced healthy again.

The kidney infection resulted in a rest too, though in a ward with others. Nobody could visit me – you weren't supposed to have a very good time – and soon I had recovered. But I never forgot the lesson… about the hand-washing.

The Kitchen as Punishment

Magdalena Cafeteria was a popular punishment destination, I'm not sure just why. It was a vast and pleasing building, all huge metal beams and glass, and there were long tables where at mealtimes there were wealths of wonderful veggie dishes and farm-fresh salads laid out lushly. There were lots of comfort foods – soups, veggie burgers, oven fries… and Indian, or Mexican, or Italian specialties. Feeding everyone was a colossal undertaking.

Now I was sent to the bakery, where I was mixing bread dough in a big machine and forming it into loaves. Other punishees (I remember Crazy Harideva, a famous, well-meaning rogue, gamely making apple pies and crimping the edges, while wearing a shower-cap thing) labored about me, making chocolate chip cookies and icing cakes and so on.

The desert air made my already-dry skin very sere indeed, and all the hand-washing with strong liquid soap dried them further, so that soon the fingers cracked open and bled into the bread dough. Since everyone was panicked about AIDS by this time, the very idea of blood in food was terrible. I showed my bleeding fingers to the Mom-in-charge, who reluctantly agreed that baking might not be the best job for me. So I asked if I could deep-clean forgotten things – the little notches and bevels in machines, for example; or go outside to collect litter from the surrounding areas. For some reason I wanted to pay attention to that-which-nobody-else-paid-attention-to. I like edges of things. I told the mom that the center of the operations would be greatly helped if the periphery were not ignored.

The Mom was suspicious – I could see her wondering if I might find a way to enjoy myself too much doing these obscure things – but she finally agreed. And I did enjoy myself, cleaning gunk out of machine-interstices and, most especially, wandering around the grounds with a plastic bag, picking up flotsam, which I'm sorry to say was plentiful. It was so nice to be outside! – out there on the scrubby land under the junipers; and I would feel rather better.

What I also did was to go on a long run during break-time each day, all the way down to the truck farm, in the beaten-up running shoes I'd found somewhere. This was wonderful! Escape! Fleeing, straight off the mark, dashing through the clear air on the hilly curving road, on and on! I'd run for half an hour, and feel quite restored.

I worked in the freezer for a while, in a padded suit, hefting trays of brownies around, and eating them. (They were quite good frozen.) I injured a place in my upper back that way – lifting boxes of things, in the extreme cold – my only back injury during that handful of years when many messed up their backs pretty badly, and we had occasional tutorials on how to lift right. But it wasn't too bad, and I enjoyed the solitude of the freezer.

Another time, I was cleaning machines with a toothbrush and q-tips, and feeling vacant, humble, bored... time stretching out. It was Sheela's birthday, and a big sheet-cake had been made for her; she already had a cake, so, as a special treat, she sent the sheet-cake back up to Magdalena for the workers. Everybody was excited – the previously-abundant afternoon tea snacks had been completely cut out a while back for the sake of economy, and people were feeling the pinch.

However, I couldn't eat cake due to my allergies. Timidly I approached the big snobbish-lumpen Mom-in-charge, with her straight dark hair, pointed head, and skin like peanut-brittle smoothie; and asked if I could have a piece of bread instead? She looked at me for a long moment, then stuck her nose up in the air and announced loftily, *"No substitutions!"*

I was hungry; but I was also bewildered. What had I done to deserve to be treated like... well, like a crawly little rat-breathed mangey doggy? With bad karma? Why on *earth? No substitutions,* indeed.

One day while I was picking up trash outside, I was wearing my uniform – red jeans and t-shirt – duded up thusly: little leather peep-toe pumps with low, narrow stacked heels – the leather holed all over, like polka-dots. Red, of course. Short socks with a turned-down cuff with lace on it – pale pink. And a red bandanna round my neck, tied jauntily at the side. T-shirt tucked in – if you've got a bottom worth showing off, why hide it? Then a narrow belt. And a pony-tail.

Rikta was coming up the path when I was going down it. (She was the bulky Texan Mom who'd wanted to co-opt free donuts.) She stopped, and, looking at me pointedly, did a slow once-over, head-to-toe, toe to head; inspecting, assessing, her eyes narrowing to slits in her puffy face. (I'd seen warring ghetto girls eye each other like that back in Riverside.) Then she ordered me to remove anything that wasn't part of the uniform: scarf, socks – and to roll my jeans-legs down (I'd rolled them up a bit for the sake of the cute li'l ruffle on the socks and for the general proportion of things on my petite frame.)

Then she marched away.

I went and sat under a tree and thought about things.

I had believed that since Bhagwan was benign, the Moms must be benign too, and so if anything went wrong – if they were mad at me – it must somehow be my fault. They were connected with him, weren't they? I was accustomed to being chided by him; so if the Moms chided me, did it mean I needed to be chid – like a Zen hit?

I contemplated long my sin of decorating and improving my uniform – and I just *couldn't find anything wrong with my actions*... I just couldn't. I *knew* that I was not wrong.

But I was sad... oh yes. This was my place, but I was being sneered at. (It did occur to me, not for the first time, that sexual jealousy might be at work here. I was just too cute in my red britches. But I dismissed that thought as too arrogant, and too obvious. But it was no doubt true; how could it not be?)

Scary Weird

Now we come to a rocky patch of history.

As a foot soldier, I only heard rumors, then listened in horror and disbelief as they were confirmed. Shrank back even further towards the woodwork. Saw peculiar things with my own eyes: a host of workers were about to tuck into a boxed supper after a Festival event in the Mandir, and suddenly word went round that we must toss out the fruit salad as it had gone bad. This was just strange; it smelt fine, and everything we cooked was freshly prepared from the freshest ingredients.

Quite soon rumors circulated that this had had something to do with a salmonella poisoning visited upon hapless people in a salad bar in Bend... by Sheela's gang! This simply made no sense, and was ridiculous, embarrassing, impossible. Or was it? Apparently the culprits were afraid that our fruit salad had been accidentally contaminated by the salmonella. One guard had eaten some and gotten ill.

It seemed that Sheela's cohorts, no doubt madly paranoid by now on speed, so that they could keep working like superhumans, were persuaded (or maybe it was their idea, in some brainstorming session indulged in while the innocent Ranch slept), to drop that salmonella juice into the salad-bar in Bend. Many people were made ill, though nobody died. The police figured out who'd done it. Charges were being brought.

I was so embarrassed. What kind of pitiful shit was this? *Salmonella?* Jeeezus wept!

Then, Dr. Amrito (then still called Devaraj) fell down at the end of a discourse – I saw this – and was surrounded by people and carried out.

It turned out that one of Sheela's gang had injected him in his hip – with something meant to poison him.

Why would anybody want to kill Devaraj? I had no idea. He was a tall, kindly, distant, elegant, utterly goofy absent-minded-professor sort of doctor whose peculiarly oblique sidestepping conversational style reminded me of my own father. He smoked like six chimneys and had a posh accent. He'd been Bhagwan's doctor for a while.

He recovered, but things were cracking up all over the place.

Sheela called us to a big meeting where she said that the National Guard were massed on the perimeter waiting to rush us and create a firestorm. We had to be very careful to *only be positive.* No negativity allowed! If we heard anybody being negative, we were to report them.

Argh. I didn't know what to make of the National Guard story, but later it was confirmed: they were waiting for the word to charge. That would have been ugly – so ugly. Later it emerged that the powers in Washington had said that if Bhagwan just happened to be caught in the crossfire, that would be okay.

A couple of days after the incident where Rikta glared at my uniform improvements, I got ready for work in the morning and came out into the living room of the town house where I lived. An excited housemate informed me that Sheela and all her gang had absconded during the night.

I stood there, utterly gobsmacked. Could this be *true?* Then, a rush of pure joy filled me. I was exonerated! Absolved! It was *they* who were fucked up! Not me! I clapped my hands, danced up and down, waved my hands in the air. HALLELUJAH!!!

And it was true. Sheela, Vidya, Su, Rikta – who'd been running for office – and more… all gone! In the night, like thieves! And maybe they were thieves! Rumor said they'd escaped with a lot of money.

Bhagwan immediately started talking about the whole situation. He invited the Feds in to investigate. Offered hospitality. (He'd said a lot of nice things about the U.S. Constitution over the years. But those stars would soon go out of his eyes…) He denounced Sheela and her crimes. He was free now to speak whenever he wanted, say whatever he liked – no more censorship or late-night exhausted workers falling asleep. And he ran with it… They were riveting discourses.

And what did the Feds do? Took the invitation, oh yes; but came in all frowning and secretive as if they owned the place. Dragged people into rooms for questioning. Didn't crack a smile. You could tell, seeing them about, those men in their suits and ties and sunglasses, that they were not here to appreciate Bhagwan in any way shape or form. You could tell they had their own deadly-serious agenda, dictated by their bosses.

I was so glad I was invisible. I never even had to pass one of them on the sidewalk.

Nor did I have to worry about bumping into obnoxious Moms anymore. It was scarcely believable – they *were* the Commune, and now they were gone!

Wow.

People floundered around – many didn't go to work – infrastructures suffered. Bhagwan blasted us for this irresponsibility. Very quickly order was restored, though the feeling of giddy looseness remained. Hasya, a beautiful woman in her forties from Hollywood – she'd been married to the man who made *The Godfather* – was now in charge. She looked a bit shell-shocked, but was competent and very private and calm.

Things were happening very fast.

There was such a short time of feeling free. We were all still working – bouncing around, stunned – and then – :

"Bhagwan's gone! He flew away this morning!"

A great pit opened in my stomach. *Him? Gone?* For… he really *was* the Commune.

Without him… what was there?

Just a bunch of kids in silly red clothes, moving about cluelessly. Glued together by hope and trust and… well, Him. His light.

So he still *was* here.

We waited breathlessly.

Very soon: "He's been arrested! In North Carolina!"

Oh, *shiiiiiiit…*

Tummies churning. *Now what?*

We all went into some reality-disconnect then. How can one reconcile the two most disparate forces on the planet – the lightest light that ever was; a sane, guffawing, brilliant, incisive light – sucked into the maw of the deepest darkness – the governing machinations of the U.S. so-called legal system? Owned, bought, sold, by largely unseen wheelers and dealers, somewhere or other – twiddling and tickling and slicing along on their own sort of tightrope? Dealing great blows whenever they felt like it – .

These two, in the same cage?

We were accustomed to the delicious freedom of being far away from all that rot – governments and handcuffs and pounding gavels. We were accustomed to jungly leaves and monsoon shelter; satiny bodies in our arms; striding free-legged under boundless skies. And here was all the hardness of courthouses and hard-jawed FBI-wallahs. Yack.

So we crowded round and watched the news, shown us on screens in the Mandir… And we felt even worse.

The newscasters could not, it seemed to me, imbue their serious voices with any *real* sense that Bhagwan had done anything wrong… All these counts of whatever crimes they could cook up that were charged against him. (I can't even remember what any of them were. They just didn't seem to have anything to do with him. Now if they'd charged him with *speeding in his car,* that would have made sense maybe! But nothing else.) They dragged him from one jail to another, twelve in twelve days – trying to elude the newshounds. He was angry – you could see this in one of the vids, where he was in prison garb and chains, his usual hat missing – denouncing his captors.

It was so scary to see him like that – such an impossibly frail body, more sensitive than any other I have ever seen – even more sensitive than a baby – chained! How could those monsters be so blind? ...But monsters *are* blind.

We all went about our work, our hearts in our mouths.

It was a great relief when he came back to the Ranch; looking, however, much the worse for wear. He stayed just a few days, and then, somewhat restored, re-hatted, he took off again in the small plane for the arraignment in Portland. At least he was nearby.

The proceedings were speedy – a whole long list of absurd charges was read, and a plea bargain reached – he'd pled guilty to Immigration Fraud (disciples marrying each other for green cards – though why they'd charge *him* for something his *disciples* might or might not have done, is a valid question). The agreement was that if he left the country immediately the rest of the charges would be dropped.

Some huge fine was also levied – $400,000 I think it was.

The moment the proceedings were over he was, as formally agreed, flown directly out of the country. We did not know then where he was going.

The people who were left at the Ranch were mild, bewildered, and friendly. It was clear that we were all leaving. Many people wanted to go wherever Bhagwan was going. Some were disillusioned – they'd loved a Utopian dream, poured much labor into it, and when it shattered, something in them did too. Some felt so guilty at their own part in the fascistic goings-on that, even though they'd not been legally incriminated, they crept away to deal with their shame as best they could. Some went back to their own countries, to work and save for whatever might come next. Some went to countries not their own, exercising their freedom as Citizens of the Universe. Some went off in couples to found nests, or empires.

But it was a strange time. When it was learnt that the National Guard *had* been gathered in Bend, ready to plunge in and start shooting, it was clear to me that Bhagwan had drawn the fire. By leaving right when he had, he'd averted a bloodbath. The whole history of our crazy experiment would have been so very different had he not got in that little plane that morning and headed off for the eastern USA. The government is not averse to massacres, as has been proven often enough. We got away, all of us... through his getting away.

It was a miracle really.

And the fact that the National Guard didn't invade, meant that it had been him they were gunning for.

And they got him – oh, yes, they got him. It just took much longer than they expected.

People were leaving in droves. As our numbers shrank we got jollier, if a bit more ghost-like. We were selling off equipment, eating luxuriously in the restaurant, scavenging the leavings, having little parties of our own. Probably some people got drunk, like the last time, though I didn't see it. One German artist from a wealthy family sat in his room in the hotel giving away his new inheritance to whomsoever might need some.

And we were all tuned to Bhagwan, winging off to parts unknown...

I had a choice: stay on as a caretaker, and, when he settled somewhere, go to him. A ticket would be provided. Or, go to California with Subuddha and a little crew of people: Saki, Azad, Satyamurti, Sundaryo, Peter from England, Indian Vairagya and his girlfriend. We'd rent a big house, go to work and save money.

I chose Subuddha. I guess I had to... but right now I feel sorry enough about it! What a blast that would have been – to go where the Master was.

Though no place Bhagwan went would last. He left in November; after many adventures and expulsions, in the Spring he was in Greece. It took only eighteen days on Crete before he was kicked out for "destroying the culture." As he pointed out, any 2,000-year-old culture that could be destroyed by one man in two weeks might not be worth saving.

6

Dipped in the World like a Frosty Cone

Dipped in the World like a Frosty Cone

1986 – 1987

California, Here We Come

Meanwhile, I was running around gathering box-loads of red clothes people had abandoned! Bhagwan had said we could now wear any color, and that we also didn't need to wear malas. But this felt so strange to me! To wear blue, or black, after all these years? I knew I'd probably get used to it (and I certainly have), but it was sad. I couldn't let all those clothes go to waste! So when the Saki-and-Azad crew finally left, in one of the school buses we'd bought (or *they'd* bought – I hadn't a dime) we loaded it up: washer, dryer, tools, bedding; and boxes and boxes of clothes – the others thinking them unnecessary; I insisting.

Saki was basically the boss. She wore a shiny bobbed light-brown wig – her hair was starting to grow again after the rubella, and she had short fuzz. She kept meticulous notes, budgets, records. I let myself be carried along on whatever wave all this was.

My mother, Devadasi, had been ill. She was still living in Weed, in the lee of Mt. Shasta, with Vedant Prem, and taking classes in silk-screening and photography at the local community college. They lived in subsidized retiree housing and were very comfortable there. But some strange ailment had befallen her – the doctors didn't know what was wrong – and she was very weak.

The loaded-up bus left one morning, with the previously mentioned crew; Peter was driving. We headed out over the Top of the Ranch, through Antelope, and thence towards a freeway and the south… And of course I wanted to stop and see Mama on the way down to Laguna Beach, where we were going. Peter the driver, a blond, stocky, short Englishman, driven and (I thought) cold, refused to stop.

This was unthinkable to me – it was as if he refuted the whole idea of mothers. (And I think he did. He'd been adopted, and didn't like his adoptive parents.) After much argument, and pestering from me, he finally, angrily, agreed to stop near Weed *at a coffee shop only* and *only for half an hour* (he timed it).

It was shocking to see my mother shuffling and thin, as she came through the crowded coffee shop towards me! Stout Bob (as he was still called by everybody) was beside her – that was good – but oh, she looked wan and brave and tragic! She'd suffered many bouts of ill health in her life – giving birth to seven children is hard on a small body – as is the backbreaking labor of bringing them up – if you aren't designed for all that work, all that servitude (she wasn't). I felt like crying. We hugged and held hands and talked, and then Peter peremptorily insisted that time was up and we had to go. (Note: I am so happy to report that Mama lived another thirty-and-a-half years!)

We were looking for the house Saki had rented in Laguna Beach. The long bus went up and down hills on the tree-lined streets, past little wooden cottages and big modern houses… and at the bottom of one hill, on the way up the next, the weight of the washer and dryer at the rear caused the chassis to crunch alarmingly on the steeply graded asphalt. *CRUNCHHHHHCRRKKKGGGGRK!*

That first house we lived in was a big modern thing with sea views, a few blocks from the beach. Subuddha and Peter shared the huge master bedroom and bath on the ground floor, Satyamurti and the rest had rooms on the top floor (which was street level as the house was on a hillside) and I had a little den in the garage, fenced off with packing boxes and things. There was a huge kitchen-dining-room with lots of light from floor-to-ceiling windows.

Everyone immediately started looking for work, coming back with sad tales of carpet-laying and restaurant hostessing at $5 an hour. Subuddha had a skill: concrete driveways – and he made much better money than the others. Saki started a house-cleaning business, Columbine Cleaning, and had flyers made up. All the girls in the house participated in this, though Sundaryo was also a restaurant hostess, looking very sharp in black velvet, with her long blonde hair.

All of our earnings went into one pot, and Saki was the book-keeper.

Right away I had three jobs, and started making money hand over fist: I cleaned houses with the crew, did chakra readings for Hollywood third-tier people (the support system of the support system of movie stars: clothing moguls, personal trainers, would-be scriptwriters, and whatnot –) and, in many of the evenings, I did Strip-o-Grams.

A Funny Employment

Someone had suggested doing strip-o-grams, and I'd been intrigued. So I'd phoned up an agency out of the Yellow Pages, and Saki drove me out to the weedy-gardened, toy-strewn-yarded, foliage-obscured, unbelievably dirty tract house where the agent, Sally, lived and worked and had her family life. She watched me dance for a minute, and hired me.

I got half, she got half. I did my own costumes, wrote my own material. Sally would supply me with personal information on each client, given by the wife, co-worker, etc., who'd ordered the 'gram. She got good feedback on my work, and she never interfered. She was a gravel-voiced Southerner with a few bad habits which left her organizational capacities sketchy at best. She was beautiful, and smart, but in pretty bad shape – I'd guess pills of some sort.

Soon after I'd signed up, my first gig was almost upon me. And this diverting job was almost derailed right then! The directive was to come out of a huge wooden cake at an outdoor wedding reception; pulling the legs, figuratively speaking, of the marrying couple – by telling jokes about their lives – and dancing with fewer and fewer clothes on.

But a couple of days before this was supposed to happen, I went for a long hike with Subuddha. We parked, that afternoon, in a rutted dirt area at a dusty trailhead, up in a range of hills ten miles or so from home. We took off walking into the scrubby hills, where soon an oak forest swallowed us up into relative coolness, and we found a nice location to have carnal knowledge alfresco (of course). Then we hiked some more, had a little picnic, and, with dusk gathering, we were hurrying along an eroded trail, trying to get back to Subuddha's truck before dark. The mountains were fragrant with sun-warmed herbiage, the thickets were thorny with manzanita, the view was beautiful, out to the sea.

There was a steep hill to come down, and the trail seemed to be taking too long. So I slid right down the slope on my behind, getting scratched a bit, but there was a nice cushion of something green – some low-growing vine. I was wearing short-shorts; Subuddha had on long trousers. He came down in his running shoes, grabbing onto manzanita trees.

Two days later, I lay in bed with my lower quarters all covered with huge watery blisters, itching and inflamed… poison oak! But I was supposed to go out and do this strip-o-gram performance! Oh god… I felt awful, feverish, exhausted, and unwashed as well – the blisters encroached on very private sectors, and bathing them was just too painful! (Subuddha complained about this smelly non-bathedness. He also caught poison oak from me, on his arms.)

Anyway, I staggered out of bed and started dressing in my costume. I pulled the black fishnet tights up my legs – secured them with garters to my garter belt. Blisters bulged out the openings in the fishnet… all up and down my legs.

I *wanted* to do the show – though I was nervous with stage-fright, it's true – but I wanted the job, and I didn't want to piss Sally off.

But those *blisters… !*

Nah. It would not do. At the very least, I might somehow give the bridal pair poison oak.

So I phoned Sally, who railed at me, "Naow wha did y'all go an' dew *thayut?*"

When I'd recovered, I did go to work, and did pretty well…

So now I had my *really* first gig – and, under my influence, Subuddha was participating in it too – a double strip. It was at a huge hotel in Los Angeles, for a convention of Filipinos. I thought that Filipinos were colorful people, and might appreciate a little let-go. I was wrong, as it turns out (perhaps I'd confused them with Puerto Ricans), but it was an amazing night for me.

Three days before that first job, my knees dissolved, and I couldn't walk without holding onto the furniture. I'm not joking – old dancing injuries, plus sixteen years of running on often-very-hard surfaces, plus lifting heavy things during the Poona demolition – had made huge holes in the cartilage. I went to a chiropractor (an eccentric sannyasin of Italian extraction, who during the consultation picked up the phone, dialed, and said to someone "I'm in bed with your wife! I'm in bed with your wife! It's wonderful!" and hung up). He dramatically asserted that I would be lucky ever to walk again, should have complete rest, never lift anything heavier than a bread-roll, etc. etc. I walked out (in my high heels, of course) and bought a long rubber knee-brace, black, with a fetching little hole for the kneecap. I filled the hole with black lace, sewed a black lace ruffle top and bottom, and added a red bow.

On the way to the hotel on the big night I made up my song. I was wearing a clingy long dress, a velvet cape, and various other hippyish clutter. I don't know who exactly I was being – it was just what I'd found to put on. I'd never sung in public except once in a pub in England on talent (or no-talent) night, which had scared me a lot. I often didn't know how I'd got myself into things.

Well. In my high heels, on a knee so crippled I'd had to lean on Subuddha to walk from the car to the building, in my knee brace and smoky stockings and lace undergear and velvet cape and makeup, I just stepped out there onto the floor of the vast ballroom, took the mike, and sang as soulfully as I could:

I'm just a crippled stripper
Tryin' to support my kid
I'm just a crippled stripper
Doin' what I always did
I might not mooooove so fancy
But I can still move nice
I'm just a crippled stripper
But I think I'm worth the price
I'll bet you've never seen one
Bet this is a first for you
Go home and tell your family
You watched a cripple do the boogaloo…

The Filipinos, each and every one in a stiffly-pressed grey suit and starched white shirt, stared uncomprehendingly. I don't know what they expected at their convention, but I certainly wasn't it!

Subuddha then came out as a policeman and arrested me, and we had a duet tussle, and then our duet strip. He'd been hiding in the kitchen, where all the Mexican workers thought he was a real policeman, and hid behind the huge refrigerators. (Subuddha, though the sexiest dancer imaginable, had a very short stripping career as, by Bhagwan's definition, he is immensely intelligent and therefore has not much memory at all. {I have heard Bhagwan say that to be in the present, without memory, is true intelligence.} Subuds never remembered a single person's name, or any of their personal foibles; so people complained and he was fired. But we had a few good dances together first.)

I learned something that night: adrenaline forgives all sins and all bad knees temporarily. I had flown about the dance floor doing pirouettes and splits and Arabian things with my hips and it had worked perfectly. I learned too that Bhagwan was with me all the time including (or especially) in really ridiculous situations; that one could jump into something utterly absurd, not knowing anything and crippled to boot, and come out feeling absolutely wonderful.

Next day I couldn't walk again but I didn't care.

My next job was impersonating Madonna for a birthday party full of nine-year-old girls. I had no idea who Madonna was, so I just sort of winged it – listened to *Like a Virgin* once, and put on various bustier/fishnetty things and lip-synched to that stupid song. One of the little girls asked me in her piping voice, "Are you Madonna's sister?" – so that was okay. I found out once again that you can just sort of hurl yourself in at the deep end, and it might just turn out fine.

The smiling receptionist showed me into the lawyer's office. I was wearing a maroon wool suit left over from PR at the Ranch, maroon suede heels, and carried a large totebag. Sitting in the chair the youngish lawyer indicated, I poured out my story. I wanted to get a mortgage on my house – but something had happened with my credit rating – I'd been wronged, etc. The lawyer listened, interrupting once in awhile to ask questions.

"Where do you work?"

"Oh – me – I work for Gucci," I said.

"*Gucci?*" he exclaimed.

"Goochy – goochy– goochy!" I cried, leaning over and chucking him under the chin.

"Uh" – he said, and sat back abruptly in his chair. In a moment he went on as if nothing had happened.

"I'm sorry, but it's so hot in here," I said a few moments later. "Do you mind if I take off my jacket?"

"No, no, go ahead," he said absently. The discussion continued. A few minutes later –

"I'm really sorry, but it's still awfully hot. Do you mind if I take off my blouse?"

That got his attention!

He was flustered!

"Happy Birthday!" I cried and pressed the button on the tape recorder in my tote bag. Funky music blasted out and I rose into dancing – all over the room – casting clothing here and there, telling jokes which showed an amazing knowledge of his personal habits and proclivities, making him take off my stockings one by one, and in general blasting a huge hole in his day, in the orderly, pedantic vibe of the office, the building, the banal, sleepwalking, sun-shiny city world. The women working in other offices crowded merrily to the door to see.

Twenty minutes later I was out the door, putting my suit hastily back on over the bra and g-string I'd kept on, stuffing the other six layers of undies in my bag. The receptionist, who'd hired me through the agency, beamed and thanked me and pressed a tip into my hand.

It was a summer night in a little beach town in Southern California. I rang the bell of a stucco house in a row of little stucco houses within scent of the sea. I was wearing a red-and-white pizza-delivery-girl costume: short flared skirt, puffy short sleeves, white lace-up front – over the inflated balloons underneath (which said on them *ha-ha* {left}, *fooled ya* {right}). White fishnet tights and white high heels and a pizza-delivery box in my upraised hand completed the effect. The tape player I hid beside the door.

The door opened on a party – neighbors gathered, drinks in hand; blonde hostess greeting me, pulling me in. Her husband – it was his birthday – took one bleary-eyed look at me and simply removed all of his clothing (even in the shock of the moment I noticed that he looked like a goldfish hanging from a barrel). Seizing my arm, he tried to pull me down the hall towards the back of the house. Since I was an entertainer, I was determined to entertain, no matter what the mood of the entertainee; fighting him off, I pushed the play button on the machine that someone, pre-arranged, had brought in. Prince: "Strip right down to your *underwear…* " – a song about dancing, about letting go. I love to dance!

Niftily evading the barrel's grasp, I managed to tease him wordily, sing a song, take some clothes off, and leave some on, and in general entertain all the neighbors and the wife, though the man himself was too drunk to get any of it.

At one point when he tried again to singlemindedly haul me off down the hallway, his wife stepped up and very calmly and disinterestedly slapped him across the face.

After four songs – Prince was the last too, with *Kiss* on a mix cassette Subuddha had just made for me that day – I wound up my act. I was down to the g-string and the gold sequinned cones with black tassels in the center, glued over my nipples. There was a moment of silence, and then Bhagwan's voice boomed out through the room. Everybody went blank, including me for a moment! Then – I was cracking up laughing! I don't remember what he was talking about, but it was just so wonderful.

"That's what happens when you let your boyfriend do the tape!" I said. (But now when I think of it, I could have chosen *quotes*, appropriate *quotes*, and played them!) They tipped me $40 above the normal fee. I went off into the night, holding my sides!

Newport Beach, a big fancy hotel. I was supposed to go to a certain room for a stag party. I was wearing a black evening costume decorated with black lace. I knocked on the door. Someone opened it and, cringing, holding my breath, I stepped inside…

There were at least sixty large black football players in there. They were sitting on chairs, tops of chairs, chair-arms, bed, floor; they were lining the walls; hanging out of the bathroom. They looked defensive, sophisticated, wanting to be cool. There was a TV on with body parts on it going monotonously in and out of each other. I glanced at it in dread, ignored it, and got on with doing my thing. Somehow I could kind of get under the room, feel the vibe, do what was needed. Then I got out of there. I felt very small and very white! (But all stag parties were the same: dismal. The guy didn't want to get married, and somebody was leaning on him. I teased the guys unmercifully. I told Bhagwan's jokes. And I'd ask them, "What do you want to get married for?" "The family's pressuring me," they'd say gloomily, and go back to their tenth beer, while the video did its boring thing.)

Doing party entertainment surely got me out of my post-Ranch, grumpy-to-be-in-the-stupid-world doldrums. Holy crap – the *adrenaline* – to be thrown into a roomful of strangers and have to entertain them nonstop, and take off clothes to boot! And it made me *laugh* – I felt like a roving messenger, some kind of beyond-society starburst, springing through the paper of the walls and bearing news of some completely other world – a world outside the humdrum, certain-rules-apply society. I could say anything – the more shocking the better. On someone's fortieth birthday I'd sit on his lap and say, "I knew a guy once, who on his fortieth birthday decided to get a medical checkup… and the doctor told him he had only a few hours to live! He rushed home, grabbed his wife, pulled her into bed, and they made passionate, tender, wild love until three o'clock in the morning…" (Here I'd always glance at the guys' faces. Invariably, exactly like eight-year-old boys', their faces would *eccchhh* up at the romantic words.) "… and then they fell asleep. An hour later the guy woke his wife up and they made love again. The man lay there afterward thinking, My god, I don't have much time, it's my last chance… so he shook his wife. 'Darling? Darling?'

"Wearily she turned her head. 'It's alright for you! You don't have to get up in the morning!'"

Or to a young guy – "I knew a guy like you once. Pussy on the brain – every month he'd get a nosebleed."

I know it's coming out of the usual sex-obsessed, male-chauvinist mind to even *do* strip-o-grams – but is that all of it? To me it was an explosion – a real energy event – I lit up when I danced, and came from my *own* space. It never felt sleazy. Just the very fact of leaping in, saying terribly personal things, dancing, leaping out again – *broke* something in some structures of the way-things-are. This was wonderful fun. (A friend of Saki's remarked, "Madhuri is the only woman I know who could do this work and not get corrupted.")

It was also great to just be utterly silly. I'd deliver a pizza, open the box, and cry, "Oh, my god, they sent the wrong kind! This is a *crocodile* pizza!" And out would leap a toy crocodile on wheels and scoot across the floor.

Sometimes it was touching too. Sometimes I felt sad.

One night, Officer MacBust, with the huge balloons under her police jacket and shirt, hid her tape player behind a bush and stalked up to the brightly-lit baseball field. The team was playing hard; one guy in particular, young and black, was just up to bat. I showed my badge to the spectators, asking for a certain name. The people edged away from me at the fence. Someone went to fetch Robert. Dropping his bat, he came towards me. "It's about your car," I snapped. "Did you know the registration was out of date? Do you want to lose your license?"

I watched beads of pure sweat – the sweat of terror – break out on his face.

My heart, under the balloons, swelled with compassion. I grew up in a black neighborhood, damn it! I was scared of cops too! That open, childlike face… I got that one over with quickly, punched the button, and got everybody to boogie. That was much better.

Saki drove me to a gig once and came in to watch. She told me afterwards, "It's not the dancing that people love so much – though that's fine – it's the way that this big *light* comes on in you when you dance, and it just lights up the room."

The worst part of that job wasn't the stage fright, or changing my costume in the car, or fear of homicidal maniacs. It was driving the soulless freeways (actually I was paying a very grumpy Peter to drive) often for hours, to find a gig. That's what took it out of me.

That Zen Roshi I'd been taken to when I was thirteen… who'd asked, "If you are walking on the road, where is the Buddha?" He didn't say, "When you are driving on the freeway, where is the Buddha?"

I didn't know where the Buddha was on the freeway. I couldn't find him except in my longings – the spontaneity of my dances – the rough-and-tumble inventiveness of my costumes. In my own heart, which felt ever, ever so vulnerable and somehow endangered in all that concrete and metal. I was only waiting for Bhagwan to stop somewhere on his world tour…

I gave up doing strip-o-grams after nine months. But I had one last gig. Sally told me I'd be a pie saleslady, going to a hotel kitchen to offer a fabulous bargain on pie sales and delivery. She said she'd acquire the pie (or "pah" as she pronounced it). So I made up a fancy name for myself, donned my only suit, and Saki drove me to Sally's house. Sally was so spaced out that she'd gotten the pie just moments before, from the day-old bakery section in the supermarket. It was a very ugly pie. It was in a flat cardboard box with a cellophane top, sporting a lot of small print about chemicals and artificial this's and that's, and it looked like someone had sat on it.

I was already late for the pie-assessing appointment. Sally hastily wrapped some aluminum foil around the box, "tew decorate it," and off Saki and I went.

It was yet another huge hotel in the Behemoth of the South – the vast toxic spread of L.A. The desk man told me where the kitchen was. (Saki stayed in the lobby.) I tripped in on my high heels carrying my pie, asking for the head cook. This was an extremely fat, slovenly, dissipated-looking Latino in his 50's or so – chin melted onto chin. He took me behind the kitchen into a sort of little hallway with a tiny table, and two chairs facing each other across it. I saw him staring me up and down.

I put the pie on the table and went into my spiel, praising that pie; I told of the great deal he'd get; the free delivery if he ordered such and such number of pies per week. (The deal was designed to be ridiculously good, which awoke his greed but, strangely, not his suspicion.) I offered him the pie, to have a slice. He fetched a plate and a fork and a knife, cut a piece of the poor flat thing with its garish red cherry-goop coming out where he sliced it. He sat down. I sat down. He put his fork into the thing, lifted it to his sagging lips. He chewed.

"Mmmmmm! Good!" he said, and ate it all.

"Oh, it's really hot in here!" I said, "Do you mind if I take off my jacket?" (Sound familiar?)

"Mmmmffff?" he said, mouth full of pie, "Unhhh – "

I took it off. A couple of minutes later – "I'm really sorry, it is *so* hot – do you mind if I take off my blouse?"

I will never forget what happened to that man's face.

It slowly, millisecond by millisecond, underwent a transmogrification. Like a California seacliff after a heavy rain, when all the houses come sliding down, his face slid down into his chins. It crumpled, dissolved. Broke into a shower of muddy, sludgy, wet lumps. The sweat of lust broke out on his cheeks. A dull and hideous light shone behind his eye. He leered.

He couldn't believe his luck… nothing like this had ever happened in his life before, and he'd been waiting for it every day! He had not, after all, been forgotten! His tongue lolled into view. His eyes came open. An intensity came from somewhere behind his face; a languid, grasping, *slobber* emanated like a trapped thing finally freed to burble its way to the surface.

I wouldn't do it now… and, thank all the goddesses, I'm too old – but I took off my blouse. He sagged in his chair, the breath struggling up out of his massive flesh. He was in heaven.

I punched the button. All the Mexican workers rushed gleefully from the kitchen and crowded at the end of the hall to watch. I danced.

The man was angry. "You really *tricked* me, you – !" he cried.

That slow motion frame-by-frame breakdown of his turgid awakening of lust stayed with me – it was a glimpse into a very specific hell. I could see the worlds of that man's inner life playing out upon his features. A life unlived – a spirit unknown; even the flesh unknown. Not known at all – just gobbled, like that cheap pie… If even that.

An Intuitive Reader in the World

The readings came about because I offered a local sannyasin a free one, so that if he liked it, he could tell people about it. He had his reading, was blown away, and told his girlfriend, a go-getting Hollywood personal trainer for stars' makeup artists and suchlike. She sent a great many people over the next two years, taking a cut. I had no idea how much to charge, so I told people to pay whatever they felt like. Typically they would give me a check for $200. (This was of course mind-blowing, though I could see their point. I left no etheric stone unturned.)

I also did palmreadings in psychic fairs, and there were lines out the door.

It took me nine months to realize that community money-sharing – communism, so to speak – wasn't really paying. So I pulled out of the all-into-one-pot thing, as did Subuddha; and then everyone pulled out. Now we were all capitalists. Very soon I had saved enough money to not only pay back the family friend who'd lent the money for my India-New York ticket, but enough also to go back to India and see Bhagwan, who was now in Bombay after his crazy journey all over the world being kicked out of many countries.

But all that took some time. Meanwhile, there was daily life in Laguna Beach.

Subuddha and I went to the Sunday morning gatherings at the Laguna Beach meditation center, and he'd hug women, and I'd feel jealous (though I don't think he was straying). It was because of this that I gave up drinking coffee. We'd had a ritual to stop at a coffee place on the way to the Center (which was in a canyon outside of town). By the time we got there I'd be flying, three feet off the ground. But an hour later, when the Sitting had finished and people got up and went around hugging each other, I would have hit the nerve-jangling skids of the caffeine high/low, and I'd be paranoid – seeing mistresses, or potential ones, where there were none. So it became obvious to me that coffee wasn't helpful, out here in the world.

My great treat during this time was, once a week, to walk down the leafy streets into town, buy an 8-oz. carton of chocolate Tofutti, sit down on a bench someplace green and peaceful, and consume it all slowly with a spoon I'd brought with me... my tongue enjoying spreading out and feeling itself met by all that bowl-shaped concavity of metal, all robed in ice-cold sweet creaminess. That was caffeine enough. It was delicious! The last few spoonfuls were hard going – I would have had enough by then – but I'd manfully shovel them in, unwilling to waste a brown sticky melted drop. Sugar junkies are sugar junkies, and high fructose corn syrup is just the same.

The woman who was sending me all the clients was tall and hairy (she was getting electrolysis on her bottom), and had a long heavy mop of straight dark locks. She owned a large boa constrictor that lived in a screened cage in her small, cluttered flat at the edge of Hollywood. I used to ride in on the bus and stay for a few days giving sessions. (I gave her one, and during a very intense moment a tall plastic T-square leapt off the table and crashed onto the floor. We stared at each other. This happened sometimes.) I had no sense then of conserving energy, and did not protect myself from exhaustion. I felt deeply obliged to heal utterly, right then, everyone I worked on. This meant that I myself 'lived out,' there in the room (it wasn't the snake's room, though) *all* the repressed or unlived energies I could perceive in the person. Which was a *lot.* As the energies found their way out through my body, I leapt and howled and hollered and cursed and wept and laughed, shuddered and sighed and raged – as I *became* each energy that I encountered; as I penetrated the etheric body with my hand. (I used to use the middle finger as a laser for the initial penetration. Then I'd jump in and let go into the stuff I found in there.) I'd go up through all the chakras this way, each three layers deep except the seventh, which doesn't do that layer thing. So in the course of a ninety-minute or two-hour session – or often, god help me, longer – I would sense and become a hundred locations. I never left a single thing unexplored... integrity seemed to demand this. Once I was going, I was in it, and had to continue, to resolve everything I found – by letting it all move and have voice.

Every session was an incredible journey into unknown realms, into totality, into planes and dimensions that were not me, not my own daily life. This vacation from 'me' was a side-benefit of the work. (I remember though one fat man, dark and big, on whom I worked for five hours, with a break in the middle. I just kept experiencing un-metabolized fried chicken and ice cream, and I was trying to process it all for him. Agh!)

People *loved* it. They told each other. I was very busy.

This empath method was to nearly kill me in the long run – but it would take almost twenty years.

Dheeraj, the founder of Tibetan Pulsing (a kind of energy-healing work in which the practitioner uses his whole body, in different positions, to effect changes in energy-flow in the client) lived with his English girlfriend Prabhuta in Venice Beach. They invited me to go and work under their umbrella. They too had a wealthy clientele, and the $200 checks kept on coming. I was saving money, watching it grow. (But I did go clothes-shopping in Venice one day. A hugely thrilling expedition! I got a soft furry sweater striped in jewel colors, a black straight skirt, a big grey sweater. A ribbed cotton undershirt and knickers that said Crocodile Undee on them, after the movie popular at the time. Some black silk undies too. A pair of French-heeled lace-up ankle-boots... which would soon figure in further adventure.)

Dheeraj used to smoke pot and then lie on his back on his kitchen floor with his feet up on the wall way above his head; thinking out new Pulsing moves. He said he got his best ideas this way.

Once he gave me a session. He pressed his fingers down into my pelvis, got them around my poor little right ovary, and crunched it painfully! It hurt for weeks after. He said it was releasing stuck energy. Why did I let him do that? Feels horrible, just thinking about it! I heard from someone else that she had a session with him and was lying there afterwards with her mouth open and her eyes closed. Next thing she knew, there was a strange sensation in her mouth… something soft. He'd flopped his flaccid penis into it. He was not a 'behaving' sort of man.

After I'd given a session to one of his long-time clients – a session in which things felt like they'd gone into a *healed* period where she could relax and not work on herself so much – Dheeraj got extremely angry with me. I had lost him a lucrative client! He dropped me after that.

My mother came south briefly to visit family, and I ended up giving her a chakra reading. It took five-and-a-half hours, with a break in the middle. It was like putting my hands into the most transparent water. Some therapy was also included (always a dodgy proposition with family) as I asked her to express some of her rage at my father. She clammed up, her eyes darting back and forth. So I guided her into *being* my father, and expressing *his* rage at *her*. Lord, how the venom came piling out of her lips! She hissed, she spat, she ranted – *as him.*

When this felt complete, I brought her back into herself. I found myself telling her, "You're going to travel a *lot!*" "It doesn't *feel* like it!" she protested. …But it was to be true.

I was wrung out beyond belief after that session, yet uplifted too.

There was an esoteric fair at the meditation center. I gave sessions and also received a couple. A palmreader took a magnifying glass to my palm and examined it carefully. Then he looked up, a worried expression on his face. "There is no *Jew* in you," he said, "and this is a disaster!" (He then added that he himself was Jewish.) Much later, Human Design would say basically the same thing: the marketplace is not, in any degree, my native universe.

Lemon Tarts

From a letter to Devadasi:

Laguna Beach House, October 1986

Each night that I cook – a few of us take turns – is like entering a beneficent battlefield with a thousand cohorts and a thousand foes, with a deadline of twenty minutes ago. I clean all day and never have time to be leisurely at cooking – and if I don't get the dinner on the table, huge sweaty paint-covered boys come in and lean all over the place talking business and grabbing things out of my artistic creations with their huge paws.

Last night I cooked for company – fifteen people, including Sundaryo's relatives – and was totally lost in it. Concocted dish after dish, directing three people and innumerable pots and sauces. The dessert is always the favorite thing to make and in the headlong rush of it, I mistook a container of sea salt for sugar as the container was similar and it had been put in the wrong place.

I had been working like a fiend, and washed the dishes while everyone was eating, and then assembled these little lemon-cranberry cakes on plates, with lemon sauce and whipped cream. When I cook these days I normally hide from the people, and as soon as it is ready I run to my room to meditate. It's the only time I have alone, with my energy risen from work, but the pressure gone. Last night though I did appear at the table to put some of the little plates out, in my sauce-covered apron – and everyone was exclaiming with delight and telling the guests about the desserts I make.

...Then Sundaryo's dad took the first bite. His expression changed. "Um – I'm afraid you used salt instead of sugar!"

I was frozen there at the table leaning over with a plate, my face just... exposed. It was as though my pride and embarrassment were both naked, and when I found out the dessert was inedible my naked face froze – as when you are a child and in a repressed house you catch sight of a naked person; and it was like a Zen stick, a shock, and I thought simultaneously that I could rush and create another dessert and that also I was finished, finished, utterly ripe to be in my room, I had for hours hustled and washed dishes and it was past my usual time to disappear; it was ***time****.*

Riding on the crest of my embarrassment and shock and a kind of incredible enjoyment of it, I grabbed my tape recorder from the kitchen (I listen to Bhagwan while cooking sometimes) and fled headlong to my room.

There as in the haste for a lover I threw off the sweaty clothes and put on cotton knits, plugged in the tape recorder to some funky woman singing and lost myself utterly in the dance, going completely into my body's electricities and watching with astonishment as the emotions flowed and passed over and through me. (I've been meditating each night and lately I've been dancing or stretching before I sit. When I sit the bliss is incredible. And I've got this new feeling growing in me, which is a seeing that where I am and who I am with has nothing to do with my growing – that the growing is all mine, and that just with the ***attention*** *to the inner – nothing particular, just the attention that way – some mysterious joy is unfolding and blooming inside, like a whole other life parallel to the outer one I am living, of cleaning and cooking.)*

I danced madly for what seemed like hours, and every cell of my limbs vibrated in unison and every particle of my flesh vibrated. And I watched the embarrassment come up and physically move all over my body and into my face and in a flash I understood a whole mass of stuff – the embarrassment, simply felt, opened my face and I saw that I am with Subuddha, my British, difficult, anti-faithful, taciturn lover, ***because*** *I feel unworthy around him. If I blame him it is just another side of the same energy. But just to* ***see:*** *– I put out something and he doesn't respond. I feel frustrated and as though what I put out must be wrong or he would have responded. So I feel unworthy again and again, a thousand times a day, and I am with him*

because *of that –* ***because*** *I feel unworthy anyway, and this is the situation which best reproduces it. If I were with someone who loved me, I would not feel unworthy, so there would be no point.*

Then I saw that I feel unworthy about Bhagwan. And memories of all the billions of times I have felt that way flashed around me and I cried and sobbed and gasped, dancing, just seeing it.

And I felt incredible. I sat on my short bench with meditation music, piano and flute, and watched the full force of the opened feeling moving inside and settling and then moving upwards.

Mama, each night Subuddha comes with a kind of mixture of confidence and hesitancy to my room and we murmur and cuddle a bit. I know that if I ask him about work his attention is engaged and he'll talk some and thus open a bit, because his heart is quite a lot in his work; so I ask him about that. And I tell him things to which he doesn't respond, but I am used to that, or am I; if I talk about my work he responds though. And he is silently tender sometimes or sometimes we lie there with the unspoken discomfort of strangers, while our bodies search lightly but deeply and surely in the airwaves for harmony with each others' resonance. If I relax and tune a certain way it comes. The harmony of strangers whose bodies seek agreement even in the face of dissonance – a rhythm deeper than the surface. Like a great current in the ocean, a pull, a tug, rather than the waves themselves. The waves are all at odds.

But last night he didn't come; if he had I would have needed to be alone, because the movement within needed all my being. But this morning when he said he'd just been "knackered" I felt unaccountably hurt – because it meant he really had no clue on this earth what was going on with me – I would have thought that if I put salt in the dessert he would have at least come to laugh with me or see if I was okay.

And of course I can't mention it to him because he gets so uptight about such things he just suggests we break up.

Anyway. Time to clean the bathrooms and then make lunch for the gnawing packs of army ants.

We Move House

After one year at the big house in Laguna Beach, some of us moved to a large tract house in an upper-middle-class neighborhood in San Juan Capistrano, a flatter town not far away. Sundaryo had gone back to Hawaii, and Satyamurti left too, but the rest of us were there. A nice woman owned the house; she'd had dogs, but had now downsized to just one cat* and had moved to an apartment in a tower near the freeway. (It was impossible to get to our neighborhood in any way except by car, because you aren't allowed to walk or bicycle on freeways. That was the only road in. How weird.)

The first night we were there, I was settling in to my small room, lying on my mattress on the floor. The entire house was carpeted save the kitchen – another unpleasant fact of American life – and soon I noticed little black specks shooting up from the carpet, then falling down again; then shooting up, curving over, and falling back to the carpet – *boing! Boing!*

Fleas.

The owner got the house fumigated. (I can't remember where we went in the meantime!) Then we moved back in. This time I slept in an erstwhile dining room. Subuddha had a room upstairs.

I bought for him a particularly wonderful teddy bear, with an expression on its face that was somehow very likeable. He took it by its arm and tossed it into his room. But it stayed in there; later I saw it sat upright on a table by the wall… and later, when once it went missing somehow, he came and asked me, "Have you seen my bear?" – and I figured out that he loved it. He just couldn't say so.

We all worked hard. I pined after Subuddha – though he was in the same house. He did strange things – for example, he made a pot of pinto bean soup without washing the beans. "But there is *dirt* on beans!" I protested. "And little *rocks* are in them!"

"Yeah, but it'll all sink to the bottom!" he countered reasonably. His stubbornness was legend.

One day for some reason I was getting something out of his scruffy little white truck, and I found a tall stack of porno magazines behind the seat. Boy, was I incensed! "What do you need *these* for?" I demanded. "You have *me!*" And I thought of my willing body… oh, so willing, for him. What a waste! I thought.

He defended his rights implacably.

* I gave her a chakra reading once and the cat, shut out, spent the whole time hurling himself at the bedroom door, yowling.

A Visit from My Father

My father, Glen, was excited that I was back in California. We'd always written to each other, if sporadically, and now he was coming to visit for an afternoon, bringing my brother. I prepared a big lunch for them. (I had earlier posted several boxes of red clothes* to Keeler, where my father lived in an old trailer when he wasn't roughing it in the even-more-desert Saline Valley. There was a tiny community of people in Keeler who had feasts together, and played poker, and so on. Glen reported that the clothes were shared out among the people very happily, and everyone was delighted. I had also bought him some new blue {his favorite color} cotton pajamas and sent them along; but he seemed happier about the castoffs – that was my dad. I got the feeling the new pajamas were a little too rich for his blood. And as far as I knew he'd never owned pajamas; he always just slept in his clothes. It was disconcerting for him to come up against too much civilization.)

Glen and my younger brother Andy arrived in an old VW van (the only sort of car my family ever had). They seemed nervous. I was nervous too. And yet they seemed to feel I was important to them in some way. I couldn't exactly fathom it – my father's letters were tiny illegible scribbles on scraps of envelope-flap; my brother Andy didn't write. I equated love with communication – can't have one without the other. I couldn't imagine how my family's men could care about me if they never really reached out.

Andy, my wonderful, adored brother – as I now think of him – followed me around talking eagerly. He was incredibly tall – 6' 9" – and seemed to me needy and freakish. I felt distant, embarrassed. (I am so sorry, Andy! That was shallow and immature of me… *so* sorry.) My father, always unable to talk about feelings, talked about… I don't remember what. But what I do remember – and still feel bad about – is what I did that awkward afternoon. Proudly, amazed at what I had managed to attract to myself, I showed Glen one of those checks someone had given me for a chakra reading. $200.

He drew back, stunned. And he seemed… *hurt.* Terribly *hurt.*

I felt like a murderer.

After he had been given a raise when I was eleven, I'd seen one of his

* The rest of the red clothes were sold very cheaply to a flea market trader, whose dubious feeling about the deal proved right: people shunned the red stall almost completely!

paychecks. For two weeks' work, all day, five days a week, he made $265. To feed a family of nine.

Now, he said something about fortune-telling – how it wasn't *scientific.*

I told him I didn't tell fortunes. Instead, I explained, I looked deeply into the person's present… layer after layer. I said that the past would emerge out of this; but I wasn't looking at futures. The future unfolds out of the present, and if that present is laid open, made conscious – including what it bears from the past – the future arising out of it would be more conscious too.

But I could see that he could not grapple with this at all. And again he said something about fortune telling. The implication was that I could not be acting in integrity if I made so much money doing something unscientific. (He remarked at one point, "There *is* nothing but matter – but matter is amazing stuff!").

And for him, integrity was all.

Which I understand. It is for me, too.

But afterwards I felt so sad – that I had selfishly gloated over my earnings when his hard and faithful work had been so poorly paid, and he had suffered so, so much because of it.

He and Andy went away. I was not to see Glen again for six years.

The Airplane Game

Subuddha always wanted to get as rich as possible as quickly as possible; and was willing to work very hard for this. But his choices were sometimes strange!

We all tried to talk him out of buying, from a concrete-driveway client of his, an entire library of out-of-date legal books. He thought he could sell them for a nice profit; we said the books would just end up stacked in the garage, teetering to the ceiling, there to stay. Subuddha, however, was deaf to influence in all things; and so the books piled and remained exactly as prophesied. Later there was the famous Exploding Beer Caper, and so on. (The latter misadventure took place in Poona a year or two later, when he decided to make beer and sell it to his fellow sannyasins. The bottles were stored under a staircase in a big house in Koregaon Park; to age. The rest you can guess.)

Saving money towards a trip to India was enough for me – getting-rich-quick ideas reminded me too much of my brothers' ever-doomed but always optimistic schemes to outwit, with their superior brains, the casinos in Vegas. These all-male discussions had animated many an evening in the chaos and squalor of my childhood home.

One day Subuddha came home very excited about a sure-fire way to make tons of money. There was, he explained, a thing called the Airplane Game, a pyramid deal where the earlier you got a 'seat' the better – you could exploit more people under you, and eventually become a (very wealthy) 'pilot,' as people under you sold 'seats' to each other. It was marketing with no product. He wanted to enlist me in this dodgy enterprise, and I resisted and resisted – my tummy told me *right away* that this was not for me!

But Subuddha was my Great Love, and so finally, just to have some time with him, I agreed to accompany him to a meeting at a big house in Los Angeles.

There a toothy hoppy shiny guy told us how rich we were going to be if only we could convince enough people to buy 'seats' from us.

Subuddha, being a Brit, wasn't used to that sort of grinny character, and believed everything the guy said! I knew this was just another Californian smiley-ass con. But to keep the peace and S.'s attention, I then *tried hard* to convince a few people they ought to join. I chose people I didn't really like, whose friendships I wouldn't mind losing. There was a red-haired prissy stripper I knew from when I'd done strip-o-grams. We'd done a couple of two-girl gigs together, and it seemed to me she undressed rather in the manner of a prim housewife folding towels. I phoned her up and hounded her, just to do my best at the pyramid job; until she became very cross and told me she *was not interested.* … But I kept up the pressure on myself to try to lasso some marks.

But then suddenly, three days later, in the afternoon, everything changed inside me. I hit a sort of wall; I could not do this anymore; could not go *out* and could *not* badger poor innocent people! I immediately gave both my 'seats' to Subuddha, went into my room, closed the door, fired up the cassette player, and did Kundalini meditation.

My god, how *good* it felt to go *in* after all that grasping and grabbing and pushing *out*wards! As soon as Kundalini was finished I rewound the tape and did the meditation again! Then I lay down on my futon on the floor and picked up a book by Ram Dass, where he mentioned something about not being the body. Then I put the book aside, lay back, and fell asleep as twilight deepened.

Sometime in the dark wee hours a very odd thing happened.

The mattress sat up!

I had to sit up with it! I was terrified by this, and I leant and leant back against it, using elbows and hands to try to make it lie down again. Finally it did.

But then it suddenly began to tremble and flop. Then…

Something came and got me and pulled me up off the mattress, so that I was floating in the air, up under the ceiling. I looked back down and in the deep darkness could just see the pale skin of my face and arms down there. Then I looked up – there was a twitch – and I passed through the roof and was outside in the foggy silent air… All around me the suburban neighborhood lay still in sleep… nothing moved at all.

I hovered there, scared out of my wits – until I had a thought about my body. And instantly I re-entered it; and then lay amazed and exalted, scared and triumphant, all at once. Because in those few minutes, my life changed – now I really knew that I was not my body; that I was free.

Next morning too I felt just… different. And, I reflected, I had quit the game, and yet I was the one who got to take to the air and be a pilot!

Back to the East

The most promising country Bhagwan had spent time in during this last, traveling year – he'd been in twenty-one countries – had been Uruguay. But soon the U.S. said it would call in all loans if he wasn't kicked out, so on he went.* We were out here in the world without him, often not knowing where he was. But I wasn't really afraid I wouldn't see him again. I was making money, I'd be able to go to him – but mostly, I was just so trained by now to be in the present… seeing what happened.

Eventually all that was left for Bhagwan was India – which could not kick him out, as that was where his passport was from. Finally, we had got word that he was in Bombay, staying with a wealthy disciple. And he was giving talks.

It was December 1987. I bought a ticket, packed a bag, and took off for a six-week trip. Subuddha wasn't ready to go yet, so I went alone.

In Bombay I stayed in a big cool room in a Hare Krishna establishment

* I heard that while he was there, his accountant, Jayesh, presented to him some seemingly insurmountable practical problem. Bhagwan said, "There are always at least twelve possible solutions to every problem. Look at it again. Always remember this."

in Juhu Beach. (Juhu is a leafy, busy neighborhood near the warm sea where little, indifferent wavelets lap the shore. If you walk there at dawn you will see – as you'll see on any other beach in India except, maybe, Goan ones – people squatting down to evacuate their bowels, trusting the ocean to flush their excreta away. It is not really a pretty sight or smell – and, to a foreigner, sits strangely with the upscale mood of the nearby streets. Bollywood stars live in Juhu.)

The Hare Krishna temple was funny. Each morning at 4:00 the faithful gamboled in a line through the courtyard below my room, clanging bells and singing, of course, *"Hare Krishna, hare Krishna, Krishna Krishna, hare hare."* One struggled to wakefulness and then fell back asleep again, while the faithful began their chores – their own worship, as I am sure it was for them – making delicious vegetarian food, keeping the place clean, and so on. It was cheap – Rs. 40 a night – and I had a roommate – an Austrian girl I'd seen around in Poona and at the Ranch, but had never spoken to. (As I write, in Corfu in 2017, I am lounging on a couch in her apartment while she goes off to the dining plaza to lunch with her Human Design group participants. We didn't become friends in Bombay, but later we did.)

To everyone's great disappointment, Bhagwan wasn't speaking; for he was ill. People milled about, waiting… and waiting… and waiting. Still he did not come out.

It was dispiriting to wait… and scary too. We didn't know what was wrong with him. There was always the fear that he would leave us – an unthinkable, terrible fear. Daily we'd take a taxi to the large house where he was staying, to see if he was coming out yet. It was always no.

One day Greek Mukta said to me, "Why don't you go to Kathmandu? There is a sannyasin guesthouse there. I stayed there and it was very nice."

Why not? If I was going to wait, I might as well have an adventure. And, go to the Himalayas! I'd never been. Bhagwan spoke so rhapsodically about those mountains. Bombay was incredibly polluted, crowded, noisy – not a fun place to hang around.

It was an epic journey. I flew to Patna, Bihar; booked a bus to Kathmandu. The bus office was a tiny wooden cubicle with a board for a counter and eight men all crammed in behind it waiting for custom. Why all of them were needed

I can't imagine – I suspect they were relations with nothing better to do. It took all of them about two hours and an enormous amount of discussion and wrangling to finally issue me a ticket.

I was staying in a hotel with dirty sheets, and, in the dining room, liveried waiters serving cornflakes in china bowls placed on white tablecloths stiff with starch. 110 rupees per night. The desk clerk demanded, "Where is your husband? You are lady, traveling *alone?*"

Well might he ask, actually. I would have liked having a husband around for what was to come!

The bus broke down six times in the first hour. We had gotten beyond the city, but not very far; it was an area of banana trees, papaya trees, huge shade-trees, and rivers where women beat clothes on rocks beside the water. I was the only woman on the bus. At one of the stops a crowd of giggling boys surrounded me and took an ominous interest in my Timex watch. They thumped my hat-top experimentally. That sort of thing.

Finally the bus was abandoned and the passengers flagged down passing trucks. I was crammed into the cab of one of these death-defying monsters along with at least fifteen men; my feet were turned sideways-on to the rest of me, pressed up against the broiling-hot motor housing.

Finally, after the pitch-dark night had arrived, we reached Nepalganj, a strange border town lit with oil lamps only. It was very cold. The next bus would leave from here. Waiting, I wandered in the black lanes looking for food. Vendors stood in the dark behind tables where piles of foodstuffs sat atop huge leaves. I watched the silhouette against the lamp-light of some inching caterpillar or worm moving over one of the mounds of comestibles. I turned and went back to the bus shack, still hungry.

A skinny, smirking man told me that the bus was boarding, and I had better come this way, this way! It was too early; I was suspicious; but I went. He led me into a field where were parked many empty buses. I became more suspicious – nothing is ever empty in India. Where were the other passengers? I got onto the bus though, carrying my stout valise. The man got in behind me, and then he grabbed my behind.

The Black Goddess flared up in me – as if I had turned on a light switch. My body of its own accord swiveled and began to use the valise as a battering-ram, pushing him off the bus, shouting and cursing.

He went – but he was laughing.

The correct bus was found. The bottom-grabber was helping on it. He smirked nastily, joyfully, each time he saw me. I was sitting next to a young Nepali boy, perhaps sixteen. His head was all a-stubble, as if it had been shaved for lice and the hair was just growing out again.

The bus took off on its midnight, careening journey, twelve hours to Kathmandu. I was thankful that it was impossible to see the depth of the gorges we skirted. The cold intensified. Men smoked, and the interior was all in fug. A pair of Brits with very brown teeth sat at the back and fetched out from a bag a bottle of vodka. This was passed around the bus, and all but I drank from it – including the boy next to me.

I opened the window. There were stars up in the sky, winking sharply, and the air was sweet and crisp. The boy mimed shivering, leant over me, closed it again. This was repeated.

Hour after hour we careened up and down unseen cliff-sides on raw roads with no guard-rails. People stretched out to sleep in the aisle, on top of each other, three deep.

When there were pee breaks, the men peed against the side of the bus. A lone woman in trousers had no way to pee, unless she walked up the road far enough to be out of the lights shining out of the bus. …And squatted, hoping her pale bare behind was not too much of a beacon in the night.

As we continued, the boy fell asleep against my shoulder. Then suddenly he woke, brought his index finger up to his throat, opened his mouth. With an air of urgency, he moved the finger from down to up again and again, making a noise, urgh, urgh!

I got the window further up (I'd surreptitiously opened it while he slept), squished myself back in my seat, and he leant across me and vomited out the window.

As we came down into the broad high valley where Kathmandu rests among areas of farmland, the sun had risen. Seeing that the end was in sight, the boy next to me, in a fit of celebration, snatched my prized Panama hat from off my head and crammed it onto his own.

I found the guesthouse, checked in, and, in my own spacious bathroom, lay in a tub of hot water… and contemplated this epiphany: happiness is a function of *contrast.* That trip had been so hideous, so wretchedly uncomfortable, so sleepless, so filthy, so miserable in so many ways – that the contrast – finding myself in a hot bath – was bliss indescribable.

I threw away the clothes I'd been traveling in – they were striped with black oil and brown with dirt. I'd left the hat with the boy.

Sojourn in Kathmandu

I ventured out to explore. That first day, I somehow found myself on a dirt road where nobody was. This is nearly impossible in most of Asia, to find yourself alone – but here I was, on a city street, with wooden buildings and painted temples, but no people.

Suddenly I felt somebody grab my behind!

My body, once again, spun about by itself, and I faced the man who had done it – an unexceptional Nepali, in brown clothes. Within myself, I pressed the button that summons the Black Goddess, Kali. My mouth opened, my tongue protruded, my knees bent, my eyes bulged, my fingers were claws, and a great *HAAAANNNNNHHHH* came out of me, like a huge fangy cat – totally ferocious! (Thank god for Dynamic meditation!)

The man backed up, a look of great alarm and then affronted injury in his face; then he turned and fled, as if the punishment had *far* outweighed the crime.

I was proud of what my body had done all by itself!

Then I went on into the busier part of town. It was amazing to walk around the Thamel area, simply gazing up over the rooftops and seeing the mountains ringing the entire horizon – an endless spread, jaggedy, like a handkerchief-hem upside down. I was hungry, so I started looking for what food might be on offer.

The lanes, muddy from recent rains, were busy with backpackers from all over the world, and there were cafés – in ramshackle open-fronted wooden buildings – to serve them. Menus were posted in hand-written scrawls offering Western comfort foods: pancakes, macaroni and cheese, oatmeal porridge, hamburgers, cookies and cakes, plus all manner of salads, smoothies, and sandwiches. Veggies were made hygienic using potassium permanganate, which gave them a lurid purple color and made them taste a trifle strange.

It also didn't work. But it took me a few days to find that out…

I met Joe, an Aussie, in the post office queue – a tall, strong young man with a thick brown beard. He told me hair-raising stories: he'd come from Tibet over a high pass in a van where a healthy young man had simply died in his sleep, presumably from the altitude.

Joe and I had a good time at first. That evening we went out to dinner, and as we strolled along the street looking for a good restaurant, it was wonderful to look up at the mountains as all the pointy length of them – a wrap-around horizon of peaks – became roseate and glowed with the pinkest light. I wore my new colorful sweater from Venice Beach with the padded shoulders (it was the 80's) and my French-heeled shoes – not really the thing in those muddy lanes! Later I did a strip-tease for him in the guesthouse; we had a nice time in bed.

But he became (justifiably, I think) cross when I *refused to tell him* why I had come to India. That's how paranoid I was about governments right then – seeing what had happened to Bhagwan, it was essential that nobody official knew that you were connected with him. On visa applications it was important just to tick the box for 'tourist.'

But with a backpacker friend? Reticence was silly of me. Joe naturally became more and more curious, and kept pestering me with guesses: drug-smuggling? Spy? What could it be?

And I wouldn't say. It kind of chilled things between us.

We planned, though, at his suggestion, to fly up to Lukla and then trek to Everest Base Camp. Plane tickets were bought. I was uneasy; I'd heard that it was cold and windy up there, and I was expecting my period… I was imagining trying to change a tampon behind a rock while the cold wind tussled me about. There's an ancient quote that I love: "Some things are just not favored by heaven. Even a Buddha has no explanation for this."

My ego wanted to go; my body might not feel the same way.

I woke while it was still dark. Rolled over, unfolded myself, got out of bed quietly, not to disturb the still-sleeping hulk of the giant Aussie. Something in the bed caught my eye. What was that? A dark pool in the bed. My period! Oh dear. Ah well – so it goes. I shook Joe gently. "Joe! Joe! Wake up! Sorry – it's my period… in the bed!" I whispered.

"Hunh?" he grunted, and rolled away.

I tugged on the sheet and got it out from under him. Took it away to the big tiled bathroom to rinse it out in the sink. Lifted it up – held the dark pool under the light.

Oh my god. No. What's this? Oh shit.

Yes. Shit.

I had never, like, *lain in an actual pool of liquid shit* before.

I rinsed it out, did not inform Joe of the true facts, and begged off going. He left, and I never saw him again.

An herbalist the guest-house recommended gave me a little paper bag full of ground-up plants. They did not help, but only backed up the problem inside somehow so that it felt like a mass of herbs and sickness was in my body, distending my belly, packed up to my ears. Giardia lamblia.

Nonetheless, since the idea of 'missing' the fabled Everest Base Camp was niggling at me, I paid $50 to ride in a small plane up, up, and around the mountains, peering down at Everest from a window. The mountains went on forever! I was then given a nice touristy certificate saying I'd done this flight and seen Everest. (I still have it somewhere.)

A few days later I flew south in another small plane, after long hours of delay; and landed first in Ahmedabad, then flew on to Bombay. I thought of all the Indian subscribers to the Rajneesh Times who'd hailed from Ahmedabad, and all the other little villages, and great grumbling messy cities, sprawled out below. How I'd enjoyed their funny letters.

Bhagwan Comes Out

In Bombay I went to a doctor and was given some horrible medicine in great yellow pills. I lay on a pallet in a flat in a high apartment-block tower, where other sannyasins stayed, and felt like clammy, hot, living death was climbing about in my body. I could barely move, so dreadful, toxified, and exhausted did I feel.

On the fifth day I decided that since *I* was almost dead, and the germs were much smaller than I was, they must be dead too. And I stopped taking the medicine.

It worked. I recovered quickly after that, though I was still very thin and quite weak.

I got to see Bhagwan once before I left. He was well again, and there was a discourse. It was wonderful to be there in the sacredness again. I sat in front of him, in the big room, with maybe thirty people... and he smiled at me, and then a peculiar thing happened: I felt a big toe made of energy come out of his foot and very precisely push me away.

I was shaken (still am when I think about it). Perhaps I just had to go out and moil around in the world some more? ...Or?

London and Home

I flew to London and stayed in a big house in St. John's Wood, belonging to parents of the boyfriend of a lovely, deeply hippie-ish, earth-mothery, elfin young girl who had been a buddy of mine at the Ranch. So this house was a surprise. The neighborhood, with its insular stone houses, winter-bare trees, and air of ancient, settled, worn-in walls, gates, fences and protections – and the humming great square-cornered taxicabs, puffing steam out behind them – evoked a sense of trepidation – an attraction to an inchoate unknown, and revulsion both. Who *were* these people? How did they live? What *was* this England, this world, anyway?

I felt so thin, so undernourished. The idea of fish and chips had been haunting me since Bombay. I'd been strictly veggie since 1974 – but the idea took hold, and so I went out in the cold, found a stall, and received my newspaper packet of hot food with vinegar shaken on it. I took it away to a bench, sat down, opened back the warm newspaper, and devoured the whole hot crispy meal.

As I was walking back to the house a new energy began to arise in my body... and it was *bliss.* My body was full of bliss. I was drunk with it... streaming with goodness and joy! I went to the room I had been given. Night came early. I went to bed, but I could not sleep – I felt too amazing. The cat came in and settled his huge fluffy self onto the bed too, and began to purr. He had one snaggly fang sticking out over his bottom lip, and he rubbed against me, purring and purring, all night long. I rolled in bliss. Oh lord, it felt so good – verve and power and energy in my body!

Feeling much better, I returned to California. Back to the sprawling house in San Juan Capistrano, my three different jobs, and my difficult relationship. I'd been writing letters home, so my house-mates already knew about most of my adventures.

Assisted Melting

People were talking about a new drug called Ecstasy, which dissolved barriers to intimacy. I thought I owed it to myself to try it. But when I asked Subuddha if he'd like to take it with me, he declined.

I acquired some, and after taking the little tablet I went for a walk. Walks in San Juan Capistrano were confined to the large suburb where we lived since, as I've said, a pedestrian could not leave it. Normally I walked round various blocks, again and again, doing, along the way, a sort of advanced Prati Prasav, where I 'became' any-and-everything I could think of or see; stars, moon, trees, dog, bush, comet (I'd already 'become' every memory of my past that I could summon, and all adjuncts that arose from them). But on this hot day, as the drug kicked in, I walked up a road where nearly-identical large houses stood behind wooden fences. On a fence behind one house I saw a vine... dry, shriveling, climbing, but parched. It was thirsty! I could feel its thirst in my own body. Oh, how deeply that vine longed for water! How I longed too, through it, empathic with it!

When I got home I went to Subuddha's room. It was dusk now, and we sat in his large room with its window out onto the yard. I yearned towards him, longed to merge into him, all my great thrust of intimacy-hunger vibrating in disappointed potential. But I would not suffer too much, I would just work with what I had, somehow. I looked at him. And that is when I saw it...

I observed, coming out of my own body, a kind of fishing-net, an auric netting which I had cast out and around this man. I had created a trap for him, was trying to contain and apprehend him.

And he? He... looked just now like a very conservative banker-type of man, timid and repressed.

I was deeply shocked to see what I was doing.

We lay down together. I could tell that he was uneasy with my openness. I heard a sound – a scritch scritch scuffle, coming from inside one of the walls.

Mice. Our house was situated at the edge of the development, there was a little hill behind the back yard, and mice came from this wilderness into the house. I could see them now, having their existence in the walls, and their whole life-force was a seeking for food – a sniffing, pointed, forward-moving, urgent and unashamed total focus on getting something to eat. That was what they were made of.

I felt a momentary pang that that was what I had to expend this precious empathy on… mice! when I wanted to merge into another human being. Subuddha. Go into some vast mystery with him.

What to do. So be it.

My breathing slowed… slowed so much that I began to be afraid I would not breathe and would die. Subuddha reassured me, not warmly.

When I was coming down from the drug I felt like my veins had broken glass in them. The stuff must have been cut with speed. I felt terrible! Everything shrank and became cold.

And for a week after that, I could not meditate properly. It was as if my subtle sensibilities had been hit with a hammer, and had to recover. I had become dull and stuck and shallow and dumb.

So I did not take it any more.

Going Away Again

Months went by. Subuddha and I took a trip to see Sarita in Aspen, Colorado. We flew from Denver over the Rockies in a small plane – bumpiest ride I ever had. Aspen was luxurious – even the airport was posh in a woodsy way. It was winter, skiers rode free on the trams, skis all standing upright in racks.

Sarita and her boyfriend Ambhoj were caretaking a big house for some rich people, on a winding road outside of town. We had an uneventful visit and then Subuddha and I and another sannyasin had a terrifying drive through the mountains back to Denver, *nearly* driving into the back of a parked truck on a dark straight road.

Subuddha and I drove to the Grand Canyon. It was his first time to see it, and an exclamation escaped him as we stood at the rim: "Oh my god..." (in an Indian accent, quietly).

I was proud that I'd succeeded in affecting him some way, even if by proxy… via a 2,000-foot-deep, russetly-colorful, baroquely-striped, cut in the landscape!

I worked hard at my jobs. I was saving money, but there wasn't yet nearly enough to get back to India. Bhagwan had by now moved back to Poona, and so that was where the center of the universe had returned to. That was now my only goal, my whole focus: get to Poona!

Then Subuddha announced that he was ready to go! I panicked! I also wanted to go! My whole being was yearning for the Commune, for the real thing. Subuddha lent me $2,000, and within weeks of one another we had flown to Bombay, gotten to Poona and rented separate spaces somewhere near the ashram.

7

Soul Garden in Bloom

Soul Garden in Bloom

1987 – 1990

Poona Two

Poona (now spelt Pune) is, I have read, the fastest-growing city in India. 100 miles south-east of Bombay (now Mumbai), it sprawls across a portion of the Deccan Plateau, at 1840 ft. elevation. From Mumbai you can get there by train, or rent a taxi, or fly; now the trip by road takes only about three-and-a-half hours – much shorter than it used to be, as the road has been improved. ...Though you still see dead trucks lying on their backs in the ditches. The air pollution on this road is stunning. When going by taxi, I eventually resorted to wearing double masks – one special pollution mask, and one surgical one.

The front gate, the Gateless Gate, of the Commune was the same... that huge heavy curvingly-carved slab of timber, rolling on wheels to open or close. Overhung by a strong, declarative sign: **Rajneeshdham Neo Sannyas Commune**. The wonderful vibe of love and depth and magic was there, as before. The eastern Mystery was fully present, underpinning everything. But I soon realized that this was a very different commune than either Poona One or the Ranch. (We were now calling the two periods here in Poona like this: Poona One and Poona Two.) Like Poona One it was leafy – in fact, much leafier, as before he left in 1981 Bhagwan had given instructions to plant many trees, and these were now tall and thriving, giving a welcome shade and breathing their healing sweetness on us all.

But the whole atmosphere was much more relaxed. With the power-trippers gone, the sense of danger was gone too. There was the feeling that we were each responsible for ourselves; that we were something resembling grown up; and it was okay if we simply participated and enjoyed and did what we loved to do. Work was something you chose, not something you were assigned. We wore whatever we liked – there was no prescribed color range or style. And, somehow, the arts we studied were gentler… therapies were softer and, to my sensibilities, deeper. There was a loving, accepting feeling in the air. We were all in this together, nobody was a big bad boss; we could continue to revel in Bhagwan's presence whilst pursuing what appealed to us. We had come of age.

I was so happy to be there that I ran about collecting jobs to do, and soon my agenda was packed hour-by-hour with duties and appointments. This was to be the pattern for the next many years; until I was forced by circumstances to examine just what I was Doing. But that was later. Now, I filled my plate and then added more, until the last morsels teetered precariously on top and threatened to topple.

I cooked in the big outdoor kitchen, creating delicious casseroles with beans and cheese and herbs, roasting a huge pan in the big oven till the top was browned and crackling. I was 'hired' by Sangeet the lawyer from California, to do interviews for a proposed book about Sheela; the idea was that Sangeet's book would counter one that Sheela was threatening to write. However, Sheela's book didn't happen, so Sangeet's project was later dropped. But before that time I learned enough to appall and delight me (in an appalled way!)

I interviewed Cliff the pilot, who had ferried Sheela about the U.S.A. and observed her being dosed up or down by the hapless nurse Puja; he had flown, at Sheela's command, veggie-burger patties to Germany so that all commune kitchens worldwide would have the same food! (Weird, weird idea!) This last trip involved a death-defying stretch over the Arctic with iced-up wings… Cliff's stories were great.*

I interviewed Sardar Gurudayal Singh, a big colorful Sikh who laughed loudest and longest of anyone when Bhagwan told jokes in discourse; Bhagwan spoke of him fondly. Sardar-ji told me that Bhagwan had really wanted the Commune to be in Gujarat, but that Sheela had queered the deal deliberately – she went on a car ride with the agent; and when they got back the deal was off. Sheela, said Sardar-ji, simply didn't want to go to Kutch; she wanted, like so many Indians, to go to America. Bhagwan had hoped to go to Switzerland for back surgery, but Sheela didn't intend that to happen either. And so to

* Cliff died in a crash of his own small plane in Australia in the 90's.

America we went. Sheela had a brother in Chicago who was in real estate, and he brokered the purchase of the Ranch, making $50,000 on the deal.

I was 'hired' by Devageet to proofread and help edit his own juicy memoir of being Bhagwan's dentist. I cleaned the group showers. I taught English to Japanese disciples, an hour at a time, sitting out in the garden. And – this was not forbidden yet – I gave sessions, lots and lots of sessions, outside the ashram structure; and kept the money, and got exhausted, and did very well. I had queues of people wanting psychic palmreadings.

Bhagwan was speaking to us, at first in the mornings (leaving our evenings free for a good promenade and romantic opportunities), and then later he switched to speaking in the evenings. I liked mornings better, when I felt more alert.

The evening discourses, though, quickly became a gorgeous focal point for the whole day. I had not been idle with the tailors, and I could show off my colorful creations every night. Then there was the flirting, the positioning of one's cushion, (or, finally, little-chair-without-legs that we could buy in the boutique, and have something to lean our backs against), the expectant hush... and then, clad in astonishing glowing velvety robes of increasingly sophisticated design, and knitted hats with sequins or chenille or velvet trim, the Master would emerge from his car and come wobbling and beaming the few paces to the semi-circular white-marble podium – stand and namaste to us all – facing each direction in the huge auditorium, acknowledging us all... then he'd lower himself, supporting himself with his hand on the arm of the big white winged chair, and sit back... cross one leg over the other – turn his upper body and pick up the perspex clipboard sitting atop the silent air-conditioning unit beside the chair – then, he would close his eyes first for a minute, just Being there. You could feel his poise, his command – a command based not on a core of power, but a core of emptiness, in its best sense. Then he would begin to speak.

In those few years we still had with him, he pulled out all the stops. Perhaps he knew he was going – perhaps he wanted to pin us down and feed us nectar as emphatically as he could before he left. But he would sometimes talk for two and a half hours... then it went up to four and a half... till we were writhing with unspent pee, wondering what the heck he was doing! During this time he began to wear sunglasses; creating an interesting Gangsta-Rock-star-Buddha effect – but he did it because his eyes were aching so badly that too much light was intolerable. We didn't, then, understand why…

One night he said something I clearly remember – but when later I tried to find the quote I could not; despite much searching. I'm going to record it anyway.

Throughout the life of the Commune, women outnumbered men. Men thus tended not to chase women; indeed, they often fled them, pleading a necessity for meditative space. When men did engage with women – which was inevitably quite a lot! – they tended to like to graze as at a smorgasbord, whereas women were seeking deep, meaningful relationships, and were generally frustrated in this! That night, I heard Bhagwan say to the men: "Don't make the women chase you. Chase them! And remember… women are on a higher level than men sexually. Don't blame me – it is not my fault! I did not design it. There are two possibilities: either the woman can go down to the man's level – which is *not possible* – or the man has to come up to the woman's level." After that discourse I saw men creeping out bowed over, and women strutting with their heads held high! Nothing, though, came of his admonishment!

Buddha Hall was quite wonderful – a vast oval floor of white marble, over-arched by a huge dome made of some strong synthetic material pulled taut on mighty swooping metal struts. There was a catwalk high above bisecting the dome, from which, for very special occasions, rose petals could be flung in profusion… fluttering down upon us then like cherry blossoms in spring. The walls were not walls, but mosquito netting only; which allowed the soft weathers to touch us, allowed us to hear the creaking of the bamboos that were planted close up against the hall here and there, the swish of the monsoon and its gurgles and patters. Dynamic meditation there in the morning was wonderfully cold until you heated up with movement. Winter evenings we wrapped in shawls and socks while we drank his revelatory lessons.

I lived in Popular Heights, down at the end of what came to be called German Bakery Lane. One entered the compound between concrete gate-posts and was confronted by several concrete apartment blocks of modest size. It was all very plain and unadorned, but it was shady with plenty of trees, and there was a sort of "Housing Society" to keep things tidy and running as well as possible. The river was not far away – I could see the burning ghats from my balcony. The ashram was just a short stroll up into Koregaon Park.

For a time I shared a flat with a young German woman who was housekeeper to Jayesh, Bhagwan's chief accountant. No doubt because of the pressures of her job, she lived in a cheerful state of chaos, her room strewn with layers of whatever. She was an affable flatmate, rarely home. I, on the other hand, kept my room fresh and clean and pretty, with lovely handloom bedspreads, colorful cushion covers, a low table with fresh jasmine in a vase. Though Subuddha didn't visit... I had to go to him. I wanted also to be open to new possibilities.

I continued to have strange out-of-body experiences, sometimes coming awake after one of them with my body paralyzed, unable to move for a while. Sometimes I allowed the disconnection from my body, and sometimes I was too frightened and held onto the mattress and prevented myself taking off into the Vastness. Sometimes, if I was snatched out of my body in the night and sent flying upwards into a strange warm wind, I would simply dissolve as 'me' – "I" would not be there any more but instead there would be a huge amazing Everythingness… and my consciousness would be clear and alert even though all substance was dispersed. This was just astonishing. Then I would be gathered back again and sent into the body once more. Those were the best times; I woke in the morning feeling wonderful, refreshed and renewed. The times when I prevented the flight would result in a disgruntled, abashed morning where I felt I had cheated myself of something valuable.

One night I was sucked out of my body upwards by a strong force, and a strange roaring that was not quite sound surrounded me. It was as though some determined, impersonal intelligence had fixed on me and *would* draw me up. I focused on Bhagwan's name, saying it over to myself; but it seemed to be just a word, a word for my own aloneness, which was all that seemed real.

I kept relaxing each time the fear and amazement mounted, and I was rushed on and on into god-knew-what.

Then I thought longingly of being in my body, and immediately I dipped down vertically and re-entered.

Soon after, I got out of bed, and walked about a bit, feeling that curious sensation all over that my body had somehow become unglued from itself and then come back together – each cell vibrating. When I returned to bed I lay pondering: all my life's small excitements seemed the utmost trivia compared to this. My relating with Subuddha seemed infantile – this naked aloneness only was true. I wondered too if there was perhaps another dimension, simultaneous to ours and mirror-image, so that when I entered it I was rushing, not outwards, as I perceived; but inwards towards my center? I felt like someone unknown had bought me a ticket to a carnival ride – some monstrous ferris-wheel or roller-coaster – and I could be snatched from my bed at any wee hour to be shoved onto the thing, and could only submit as gracefully as possible.

I had the idea that there was something I was supposed to be remembering when I went airborne – maybe just to be aware?

I wrote to Bhagwan about all this, and received a reply:

You don't have to remember anything, simply watch what. Whatever has happened to you is beautiful but don't make it a sweet memory – let it go and much more will happen.

Sometimes I flew around weirdly into Indian alleys and homes. And sometimes, on exiting the body, I would feel myself to be horridly threatened by monsters, all looming over me, ready to pounce. This would be so frightening that I would extricate myself from the experience as fast as I could.

So I wrote to Bhagwan about that too. He replied, *There are no monsters. Just be the witness.*

So next time the monsters came I told them that they did not exist. Sullenly, they withdrew to the horizon, where they lurked just out of sight like faraway thunderclouds.

From my diary:

March 10, 1988

A strange half-hour the other morning. I was asleep, dreaming that I was flying around above a park like the ones in Australia – big and spacious and clean. I was beginning to get up a little too high and couldn't easily come down again; I was getting a bit scared. I thought, "Look, kid, you know it's just trying to get out, why don't you just relax and let it?" I knew that I was asleep and dreaming. So I relaxed and next thing I knew – ***whoooosh****, I was out, and traveling with great speed somewhere. I felt detached and scientifically critical and was trying to really see what was going on. I was aware of my body being somewhere in the vicinity, breathing, but I was aware of myself not being of* **it**. *I thought that I was going inwards rather than outwards.*

The intensity was growing. I came to a sort of level-change or gear-shift place where on all sides I could 'see' a certain pattern repeated in the blackness around me, of tiny stars with squares. The velocity got more intense and I began to want to come back into my body. I was thinking constantly of Bhagwan but could see with complete certainty that He was **not** *something nicey-nice, with a name; He was this very nameless aloneness, naked and utterly vulnerable.*

Something was intruding. Something was pulling me back. What? – a sound, harsh and penetrating – . Ah – the doorbell. I staggered up out of the mosquito net and made my way groggily down the corridor in my short nightshirt, to the door.

It was the dhobi, with his cherubic smile and halo of rum-fumes, holding out the clothes I blearily remembered my flat-mate had given him the previous morning. I looked at her door and saw the bolt was shot; she was out.

"Kidna paise?" *I asked; "How much?"*

"Tree rupees,",said the dhobi, hesitating not at all.

I gave the money to him, took my flat-mate's clothes, closed the door, and put her things on her bed. Five minutes later she came in.

"I got your things from the dhobi and gave him three rupees," I said.

"You did? But I already paid him yesterday when I gave him the things, and it was only 1.50!" said she.

I lay on my bed and felt that now-familiar feeling all over my body, of having gone out and come back in again. This time for some reason there was no exhilaration in it. It was a strange few minutes.

After some time the experiences stopped, or almost; it seems they were just needed during that period, I don't know why.

Separation

Amongst all this newness and the agreeable relaxedness of the Commune, Subuddha and I were breaking up. And *that* was painful and hard. One morning this scene transpired: I slumped crumpled outside the door of his flat, whimpering. He had *hit* me! I, though, had hit him first!

I had come to visit him and had observed feminine *objets* lying freely about – clothes, a hairbrush. "What is this?" I demanded, though of course I knew. He was seeing a curvy little Indian teenager with a forthright nose and a small waist, a solemn little person, rather homely yet with a frankness and honesty about her. These were her things.

"I never said I would be faithful," Subuddha reminded me again. He had told me that this girl had asked him what an orgasm was… that she had often heard Bhagwan using the word, but she didn't know what it was… But although *our* lovemaking was always still bio-electric, now everything felt different. Our relationship as such was dying. He said he did not care if he was ever with me again.

As I lay groaning and sobbing there against the door, some sober Indian citizen of the building went by on her way down the stairs and gazed at me askance.

That was one of the low points.

I wrote to Bhagwan around this time, describing to him a pattern of behavior I'd seen in myself: during my years with Subuddha, I would try to please him by not challenging him; but when my period was on the way the inner torment and pressure would build up and build up… until finally I would chase my boyfriend around the house, back him into a corner, and demand that he *tell me how he was feeling.* He never would tell me – preferring, as I've said, the words "I think," and using oblique references in abstract ways. This was intolerable to me – I wanted to know how he was feeling about me, about us! I thought that for human development and growth, obviously people had to communicate frankly! We all must be honest and self-revealing! How could it be otherwise? Wasn't that the point of all this therapy and meditation?

Whatever I expected from Bhagwan, it was not what I got. He replied, *Do not interfere with his life. Just be a witness to the biology.*

I was shocked! *Really?* I thought. A person can get away with all that non-forthcomingness? And the Master *supports* it?

This was a huge eye-opener for me. It seemed that personal freedom was a higher value than virtuous and evolved behaviors. I have never forgotten this.

I sought help. During the Ranch we workers didn't get therapy, didn't do groups. But now the whole world of therapy was open to all of us, and thank god for it.

Subuddha and I went to Vasumati, the astute and laughing curly-headed therapist who'd lived next door to T.Z. and me on Jesus House roof in Poona One.

The session too was a shock and a revelation; it set the tone for a brave new world for me – instead of just floundering along, flailing about, bumping into things – I could take the whole enquiry inwards, *with assistance.* What a blessed thing this is! How we can benefit from it! I've heard Bhagwan say (and he has said many things) that for men it is natural to just close their eyes and go directly inwards; while for women it is helpful – he might even have said required – to have someone else there to help.

Subuddha and I sat with Vasumati. Subuddha said very little and I said a lot, my indignation spilling over, my desperation, my hunger, my passion and need. And then Vasu turned to me and said in a scolding tone, "This is *entirely* your doing! *You* are stirring this *whole pot!*"

I was shocked to be spoken to like that; but something came home in me then – a sense of responsibility. I thought of the vision I'd had on Ecstasy, of the net I'd thrown over this poor guy. The sense of responsibility was very good. A new beginning.

So, soon I met a satin-skinned Dutchman working in the kitchen, and he became my new squeeze. We had some blissful nights of tangled limbs and bedclothes, slow breaths and mysterious meeting below the level of words. (Mmmm hmm. More wordless guys.)

Subuddha and I became, in some way, friends too. Now we were really separated, and the pressure was gone, we could chat and enjoy each other's company sometimes. (I always think that if you invest so much time and energy and feeling into a lover, it is only right that they later, when the storm is over, become an excellent friend.)

New Doors Open

Subuddha had somewhere acquired a lot of strings of semiprecious stones, thinking he'd go into business with them. Changing his mind, he offered them to me to take to Amsterdam, where I was going on a visa turnaround with my new lover. I took the stones… not knowing at all then what a world this would open up for me. Thank you, Subuddha.

I found that my palmreading table in the café in the meditation center in Amsterdam was made rich and glorious by the colorful strings of gemstones.

I discovered that I loved to have them there. I discovered that I could hold a strand in my hand, close my eyes, and read its energy. That I could then place the stones in the hand of the client and read the combined energies of human and stones. Wow! I sold them all, too. (An aside: one day I was giving a reading and the energy became very intense. Suddenly a large bottle of Amaretto hopped off a glass shelf behind the bar and shattered on the floor. The bartender glared at me. I felt guilty and abashed.)

But back to jewelry, and Poona; one notable (to me) thing had happened in the wake of the breakup: the little Indian teenager had given me a present: a pair of cheap dangly earrings, made of some alloy, but in a very pretty style with tiers depending from each other and little fringey bits of metal hanging down. Later, when I was back from Amsterdam, I had them copied in real silver at Shree Jewellers, on Centre Street, a busy lane parallel to M.G. Road. They were beautiful. They now had shine and weight and gravitas. (I am wearing them as I write, in 2017, in Corfu, outside the Buddha Hall atop a tree-clad hill… Thank you, Subuddha's little girlfriend.) I learned through this an alchemy new to me – instead of just getting clothes copied and duded up at the tailor's, I could also do this with stones and jewelry. This was to become an overwhelming artistic joy, and even a very lucrative one!

But in our rich and light-lifted Commune life, there was sadness too: Bhagwan was often ill – not coming out for discourse. We'd all get a little bit quiet… worried… and then go about our business, one ear cocked towards Lao Tzu House.

I had more love affairs (the lovely Dutchman being driven away when I was senselessly, compulsively, unfaithful to him once in Amsterdam). I suffered, I gloried in motorbike rides on the back of some straight-in-the-saddle guy's Enfield. I danced at every disco and had teenage sorts of excitements and anguishes. I fell in love and it was oh, so not love… a weightlifting Berliner sauntered away with my heart, that he did not even want. I became obsessed. There were trips to Goa, there were rejections and silly happenings of many sorts.

Late one afternoon I put on the tape and did Kundalini meditation in my room.. The door was open onto the balcony, and sometimes I danced to the door and looked out into the thin thorny trees, and beyond, down to the burning ghats and the river; and on the far side of the wide, turgid, brown flow of water, more burning ghats.

As I shook my body all over, then began to dance, I had an odd feeling that all sorts of ghosties and ghoulies could get into me, flying in from the ghats. There was a decision to be made; open, or close my energy?

If I was meditating, I had to open! So I did… and welcomed the death's-heads, the masked intruders with waving antennae, the teethy fiends that might or might not exist. But I totally let them in, and oh, what a ride I had! The bad scary stuff transformed in the meditation and became pure energy, pouring up my body and out my shivery arms and thrilled spine and out the top of my head. I jogged and leapt to metabolize it, to allow it through me and out. Fear became vitality. Whoooo!*

Tamo-san, a tiny enlightened lady in her 80's, came from Japan to visit the ashram. Bhagwan formally confirmed her enlightenment and, one night in Buddha Hall, showered rose petals on her. More, a little more, about her later…

Then, I participated in a lovely group – the first for me since early Poona One; and afterwards wrote the following piece for Sannyas magazine. I was so happy to rediscover the beauty of groups! And, as I've mentioned, the groups had become so very much softer. Here I am having a glimpse of something that would later become very very important in my process; and it was, of course, the very thing Bhagwan had brought to my attention so many times: Doing vs non-Doing.

Alone and Together

Each time my eyes open, jungle hushes outside the second-story window: tall jungle, the special flavor of trees' upper branches; bamboo rustling in occasional wind. A subtle multitude of leaves and greens, and through it, just seen, His rooftop – reminding us, as the whole atmosphere reminds us, to be aware.

* I read recently this quote from George Gurdjieff: "If the devil comes when you meditate, teach the devil to meditate."

The circle of us sits. Zen stool on mattress, cushion on stool, the legs a firm-folded gravity beneath the stalk of spine. Ten of us perhaps; each in his or her focus of self, and yet one with the watching. We just sit… and watch… and, if a thing rises up and wants to be said – for whatever reason or non-reason – wants to laugh itself, or weep or merely comment – we say the thing aloud.

Nobody answers. Nobody judges. Especially, nobody judges. And what a space this leaves for each of us to see our *own* judgments!

What *is* conversation? Generally, it seems, a series of unconscious reactions in the self, sparked by the unconscious reactions of the other to what *we* have said. All of it churned out and traded in a kind of sleeping (if animated) bargain to reinforce and re-establish our ideas of what reality, and our egos, are all about.

In the context of this group, speech and response are seen in an entirely new way. To me this was a beautiful gift, a fun dismantling of the known, unconscious, and sometimes tension-ridden process of conversation. Words have been for me as easy as walking, and I enjoy them like walking – each word a step, the whole a flow – but when they come to a situation fraught with a basic energy-friction – as in a biological love-affair which can't quite figure out if it is also emotional or spiritual – they can so easily become weapons and shields, ammunition and muddy trenches of war.

Even in a conversation where both partners are relaxed and enjoying – as in a good gossip between friends – unconsciously each is seeking the signals of approval and disapproval, judgment and comparison, which define the world of the mind. How far can I go in outrageous comment about a third person not present? Will the woman I'm talking to think I'm awful? Does she mind how much I am complaining about how that guy treats me? Will she give me advice? (Lord knows I need it, even if I actually probably won't follow it!) And if I do follow it, and things still go wrong, I might talk about *her* to somebody else… And so on. A tirade of give and take – pleasurable, sometimes joyful, sometimes difficult – but generally unconscious.

In the setting of the group, speaking and meditation are seen with a new clarity, a light both raw and soft. Since nobody judges what you say, you can say anything. You can close your eyes – what you say will not be in reaction to the facial expressions of those around, but in response to your own inner urgings.

And it *is* strange in here, inside the human being! How to say it? Especially if you think in German, and are trying to express in English… Here, you can express in German, then. How to say what is so subtle, or so fleeting, or is something you have been afraid to say? In the clarity of this space it becomes possible to see… In the deep relaxation of this group – for it *is* a deep relaxation – you can see if your German past is compelling you to speak against your will, or to shut up against your will – you can see if something wants to be said because the mind temporarily thinks it is clever, or because it is a true urging of the heart, or of something unconscious which now wants to be conscious, exposed, let go of.

And nobody answers you! Nobody tells you to beat a pillow, or suggests a technique to rid you of what you are feeling, or even gives his opinion. You are left with your words fading into the air and your own experience of yourself in the echo of your words, the release of your feeling. This can be very, very beautiful – the double-edged sword of your awareness on the vanished words outside, and the fresh being within, always changing. What you have said is yours and yours alone.

I've fumed and fussed so much about the non-response of a certain lover, to things I say. Now I have a much clearer vision of how spoken and unspoken words beg, and ask, and push, and demand response, like dogs on their haunches begging biscuits. How lovely it is to watch one's words as they emerge… watch from where they come… and not expect them to be merely freight trains, conveying the desire outwards and returning with the appropriate response after a journey through the other.

With closed eyes, and the bamboo outside, felt sometimes as rustling through the transparent body in the silences… the minds of others are heard spoken, and in our relaxed quiet we see our own thoughts rising up, our feelings and associations connected with what is said. Often, too, each person seems to be living on a different planet, in a different world of thought – we are sitting together, but inside each a story continues oblivious of others. This can be comical, absurd.

And then there is Purna, who is facilitating this gathering, this opportunity, this sacred, held space. She is enjoying herself immensely. She loves to sit here and do absolutely nothing. You can feel her enjoyment of her own being, and a kind of rich laughter rolling off her from time to time.

Did I say nobody answers you? That's true… but Purna is always alert and watchful – and completely a participant too, sharing her own being as she watches, saying things sometimes – and she at times steps in and comments on where we are stumbling or caught. Identified. She goes on reminding us: Just watch it. Don't *do* anything about it. That too… watch that too. No need to *do* – that's the mind. Or… allow that. Experience it. Open your doors to it. But watch. Where is it taking you?

But all this quietly, relaxedly.

For me, this was so valuable – each time I perceived the point where the mind would normally urge me to *do* – and was able to stand aside and watch it – it was as if a dark misty energy-shape rose up in my body and, finding no womb-wall of identification in which to sink its cord, shook itself like some great sea-beast and rose towards the sky, alone and out of me. What a feeling of freedom! What miracle!

At one point many thoughts had risen and vanished and I was in an image of space, quiet starry universe, and even remembering to watch that too. Energy was rising, moving, changing, but basically a feeling of unity and bliss – when I actually saw the mind reach out its arm into this space dangling a tid-bit of thought – some thought I would normally chase after – and wave it temptingly – saying, "Don't you want this, hmmm? Nice tid-bit? Yum, yum, come and get it!"

And I didn't! So many billions of thoughts I have chased down billions of dark alleyways – and to what avail?

Each day after a light lunch, we jumped and jogged around the room for a few minutes to oxygenate the blood and wake us up for the session to come. We then lay down, heads all towards the middle of the room, feet to the periphery, and relaxed. Purna put lovely quiet music on and began slowly, relaxedly, in her deep, resonant voice, to guide us into – ideally – a state of deep relaxation with greater alertness than normal. (Some of us fell asleep sometimes. I found it generally more valuable not to!)

In this deep semi-hypnotic state – which is remarkably easy to fall into – she gave us suggestions about acceptance, non-interference, the witness… guided us into letting go and becoming the alertness… and, a few times, played sections of discourse tapes. Bhagwan's words and voice penetrate in a very direct way in this state. His voice seems both to open us – relax and soothe and part our very flesh – and to hammer our sleep into awakening. He goes right through the trappings of misunderstanding and tradition into the very core of a thing and lifts it naked to our eyes – uncompromisingly, again and again, for each thing he speaks of. In this state of deep receptivity it is *our* very core he goes to, and lifts naked before our eyes.

This is how it seems to me now, though I drifted in and out of sleep. On the day I was most alert, and came closest to really seeing the utter futility of my thought-process in a situation so inappropriate to it, my mind threw up a wall of physical pain to distract me – which vanished as soon as the exercise was over. I wept afterwards, and Purna drew me immediately back to *watch* – to watch what my mind was doing with the experience, which was already past – and very quickly I was still and relaxed, released, and felt light and lovely again, a little smile at the corners of my mouth.

Amazing, the long-running plays on the Broadway of the mind!

We also did Dynamic and Kundalini each day, and in the discourses enjoyed Bhagwan's further jelling, cooking, crystallizing, melting… and re-inforcing the witness, the watcher, the one-without-form-who-is-everywhere-and-nowhere.

With the mind, confusion. With the watcher, freedom.

This group helped reveal in me a new continuity of awareness. A new depth of seeing the machinations of the mind; a new soft, subtle joy; and even a new awareness of *watching* when things are *nice* as well as when they aren't!

I found I could simply sit for much of each day, watching… it felt like a perfectly natural thing… my body became very light, very open.

The last day, I didn't want to say anything for at least an hour while the inner flame coalesced and gathered energy from the far corners of my body and rose… until it was time for lunch!

And it was all so relaxed – and easy – and we didn't Do anything!

When I Was a Man

I'd mentioned a musclebound Berliner – we'll call him R. He'd asked me for a date; it turned out to be not a great date. In fact, nothing much interesting happened, in bed or out. We did talk about crystals – both of us liked them – so that might have been the only bond. He was pale and fussy and pumped-up and had a slender, beaky nose. He worked out religiously, and talked about this.

Right here I want to take responsibility: I went to bed with him too soon. (Who is surprised?) And I want to take responsibility further: I am sure he is a lovely being. And I, an idiot of several sorts at least.

(Anyway, two days later I realized with an awful sinking sensation that I had become hooked on him. This sometimes happened with men there was nothing really going on with; I don't know why. No doubt it had to do with my father. I've recently read, too, that this can be a symptom evidenced by people who've been sexually abused.)

R. immediately realized I'd fallen, and he backed off. (In the Commune, like in a small town, there was no escape: we all bumped into each other all the time. So whatever he felt or didn't feel, and I felt or didn't feel, it was immediately known to the other and mirrored.) So my obsession took deeper root. For the next six months I was possessed, nutty about this pedantic Berliner who didn't want me. The drama played out in Poona, in Goa, and back in Poona again.

I participated in a group led by Vasumati, Zencounter. One night, following her instructions that we were to dress in our best and go visit someone, I put on a beautiful white dress I had had made for *waltzing*, of all things – we had a waltz night once a year in Buddha Hall – and dropped in on R. at his flat on the outskirts of Koregaon Park. He was stoned, lying quietly on his mattress. I took off the big foofy-skirted off-the-shoulder dotted-swiss dress and lay down next to him.

And nothing happened, and I cried piteously, and he patted my shoulder and said, "Much slime! Much slime!" Which must be a translation of how Germans delicately phrase the phenomenon.

Next day Vasumati cried, "You *took off your dress* and lay down next to somebody who was *stoned?* You have *no boundaries!* No boundaries at all!"

This was a curious notion for me… *boundaries*. What were those? Weren't we supposed to be unbounded? Wasn't that what I had been doing here, all this time – getting rid of boundaries? (Another time Vasumati said, after I'd been doggedly sitting still in the group, determined not to do my usual thing of waving my hand in the air for attention and then blurting something: "It's so nice not to feel the air of Impending Doing!")

One night I got on my bicycle and went in search of R. He was not at home, and on my long ride back through the dark, curiously deserted streets I heard from behind me a *thruuummm thruummm* as a motorbike drew up at my right rear. Suddenly I felt a jerk at my shoulder. The motorbike, with two men on it, drew abreast and then passed me, as the tugging at the bag continued. Slowly my bike pitched sideways and the strong strap on my little bag held as I was dragged along the asphalt, first on my front, then on my back. I held fast to the strap and eventually the men gave up and released it. Their bike vanished in the dark and I picked myself and my sprawling bicycle up and made my way back to Popular Heights.

My black leggings with yellow stars on them were torn, as was my black sweater. I had bloody abrasions on knees and back both. I cleaned the abrasions and then, for some peculiar reason, went to a party I had been invited to. I danced and chatted but I was in shock – and in denial about it.

Next day I couldn't get out of bed. I stayed there for two days, grieving: where were the *men* in my life? Where were brothers, father, a vengeful and capable lover to go find those scoundrels who had assaulted me, and punish them? Where the hell were the protectors I knew I had been born to have?

I told R. about the assault when next I ran into him. He seemed uninterested, merely shrugging.

And I knew, of course, that I should not have gone desperately in search of him that night anyway. My shameful neediness and desperation…

I did not know then how to love myself for everything – all of it. The only healing is that.

One day I was sitting on the Zen Wall – a low stone wall with a flat top that runs the length of the Zen Walk from the Front Gate to Lao Tzu Gate – perfect for sitting on and watching our wonderful world go by. R. was sitting beside me. He was speaking, making a point about something, I forget what – possibly the error of some weaksome attitude of mine – and he turned to me and *thumped my skinny chest with his forefinger.* Now, his worked-out finger was fat as a sausage, heavy as stone. It thwacked on my breastbone (if I had been a bosomy girl would anyone have treated me like that?) and this was the thought that arose in me half-formed: what is *fair* about his having all that strength and power and my having none? It *cannot be that the universe would give it all to him and leave me a lesser being. There must be a secret here! And I mean to find it out.*

In order to understand and thus grasp and decode that power, I decided to do a meditation where I would *become* him. I thought I would do it for three days.

Next morning I tied back my hair, drew a tattoo on my upper arm with a ball-point pen, and pretended, as I rode to the Commune, that my bicycle was a motorcycle. I worked then in the ashram post office. When work was done at 4:00 I went off to join a gym in Boat Club Road, and began lifting weights. I found that this was marvelous: as the days went on my body felt solid, supple and pantherine. (I ended up lifting weights for six years! The benefits were amazing! Thank you, R.!)

As I continued being R., my head emptied; I was just a body, striding, sure and roll-gaited. I was enjoying myself! – so much so that when the three days were done I continued the meditation, not knowing now when I would stop.

I could not read romantic novels at night anymore so I read war stories. My period was due but it did not come. I was a man, free and silent, and I loved it. People at work, knowing nothing of my experiment, for I told nobody – complained that when I walked into the room it was as if a wall had walked in.

I enjoyed myself so very much, feeling strong and muscular… autonomous and self-contained.

On the twenty-first evening of this man-meditation, I was in Buddha Hall for the taped discourse. Normally I liked to listen whilst lying on my back on a thick cotton rug… just resting, being, imbibing. But this night as I lay on the rug on the cool floor and felt the growing summer warmth around me, I found that I could not melt, could not *feel* Bhagwan or take him in – because I was stiff, I was protected and tough. And it seemed to me that I had come into a woman's body in this life for a reason; and perhaps I'd better get back to it.

And so I shifted slightly in myself and let go… gave up the man and resumed the woman. And I melted, and sank, and was again at home drinking in Bhagwan's voice and words.

Another Group

Somewhere in here I participated in a group led by Sudha, the Cuban-American therapist with short kinky hair (whom I'd first met back in Bombay, in 1973). During this group we had a Repressed Parts Party, where we dressed up, and interacted, as parts of ourselves we normally didn't engage with. Most people came out all sexed-up-looking, in revealing clothes, and flirted with each other.

I drew hair on my legs and wore a frumpy old dress and told people, in a nasal voice, "I'm a mother," and then tried to tell them about my kids. People were of course uninterested and wandered away. I began to feel lonely and rejected. I glanced over and saw the blond Belgian I'd spent the previous night with, rolling about on a mattress with a woman. He was wearing *my pretty black panties* he had borrowed from me, and they were, shall we say, challenged to contain him. I felt resentful indeed!

But what really remained with me from that group was that somewhere I crossed a threshold: I got it that the only door to higher spiritual realities was through *being a fallible human being honestly.* This was a huge breakthrough for me; my sister's example only showed exemplary, sedately-robed, softly smiling, mature *already-arrivedness.** I had no hope of being like that. It was a huge relief to really get it that, probably for most of us, the more human, the better.

Something Icky and Gruesome

On one trip to Goa, when the weightlifter was also around, I suffered both rejection by him, and the theft of 700 rupees from my room. To console myself I made a rather peculiar feast: fruit salad with lots of mangoes in it, and a chocolate sauce concocted from un-chocolately Indian cocoa, and custard powder, and whatever else I could find. I ate a lot of it.

The mangoes and chocolate apparently didn't like each other, for my left-side-of-behind came out in a big bubbly rash. Strangely, there was no pain – but what could it have been but herpes? The disturbed area was very large, as if it found ample room to enjoy spreading out in. I covered it with cotton dressings and surgical tape, and went back to Poona, where I ended up making a date with a muffled, drinky Russian.

Why?… He was blond. He was there. I was all sorts of habitual desperate Dummkopf.

* Though she was great at human catharsis too. And, having a Divine in the family is much like having a movie star in the family. Mixed feelings are bound to arise. And… naughty Vasumati asked me to dance *as my sister* for the group! Which I did! It was… cosmic!

We went to bed. When he encountered the surgically-dressed buttock, he looked at me questioningly. "What is that?"

"Ummmm… herpes," I admitted, all clenched in embarrassment.

He stared at me.

I hope that I apologized, got dressed, and fled; but quite possibly I didn't. I don't remember now… nor do I know his name.

Sooo sorry, muffled, drinky, heavy-lidded Russian. I was as unscrupulous, in my own way, as despised Teertha in days of yore.

I remember, wincing, one awful event: I had a date with a blond German man, very quiet, sensitive and somehow grown-up too. But there was no chemistry, no meeting. Afterwards I thought I ought to say something nice to him, as we got dressed in embarrassment. I thought about what I could say that would be honest. So I said, "Thank you for fucking me so well!" He stared at me strangely but said nothing.

A little while later, a friend of his told me that the man had felt very hurt.

I puzzled and pondered over this.

Another time, I came back from a trip to Goa with a can of fish, for purposes of protein; which I put in my room in Popular Heights, waiting for the right moment to eat it. A day or two later, Bhagwan said in discourse, "Some people bring tins of fish and put them in their rooms! Don't do it!"

Goa. Whenever I returned from that sandy province – or from chaotic M.G. Road, or anywhere else I went – I would feel so lucky I could hardly believe it. The outside world seemed saturated in corruption, stinking with ignorance; while inside the gates all was clean and light and loving – and I felt, breathless with furtive relief, that I was allowed to cling to the cerulean skirts of God.

I Start Teaching

Somewhere in here – it was 1989 – I got the idea that I wanted to teach Psychic Palmreading.

Our campus was growing – more old Raj mansions and grounds were being purchased and then became part of the Commune. The Rajneesh Multiversity (this name was first used at the Ranch) was a great and gorgeous phenomenon here. Groups and sessions of many sorts took place in many dedicated spaces in most of the buildings. Although I was still happily working in the post office – a dear little cubbyhole off Radha Hall with a board for a counter, where people could collect their letters and packages – I was also giving lots of sessions off-campus, and felt I would like to do them within the Multiversity.

As well as the Center for Transformation – which was sort of mainstream psychotherapy and Reichian-based trainings, though with the Bhagwan difference of being based in meditation, not just the more superficial level of psychology – there was Healing Arts – with acupuncture, Colorpuncture, bodywork, and so on – over in Mirdad across the road. There was also a faculty devoted just to meditation; for example, Mystic Rose (three weeks, three hours a day: week one: laughing. Week two: crying. Week three: Sitting still and watching). And Born Again (playing like a child), and much more.

And then there was the Mystery School.

The Center for Transformation – the therapy faculty – turned me away. I had no formal training in psychotherapy and in any case was esoterically inclined, which was not their field – though one of the 'examiners' I had to give a practice session to was the dreaded, and decidedly esoteric, Sagarpriya, the woman who had, at the Ranch, informed me regretfully that she could see no Bhagwan anywhere about me. I was so nervous of giving her a session that I got the second cold sore of my life… and indeed, after I'd read her chakras, she opined, rather apologetically, that I ought to just go back to work in the post office.

But other people said I should enquire at the Mystery School.

This was a mysterious body, begun and overseen by a large, pillowy, extremely dignified and enigmatic, dark-haired woman named Kaveesha. I had met her many years earlier, when she was young and slim and newly arrived in Poona. Bhagwan had been very welcoming to her, as if she was an old friend he'd met again after a long gap. (And perhaps she was.) She lived with her companion/nephew David, a much younger, quiet, handsome man with dark eyes and dark curly hair, in a roomy apartment upstairs in Krishna House.

I did two practice sessions for examiners. One was Waduda, to whom I gave a chakra reading. Afterwards she said, "Usually I might get one key from a session… but from this one I got five!" (She was so happy that she gave me an introduction to a client of hers in Switzerland – Devika – that would change my fate and fortunes much to the good.)

Kaveesha gave her okay for me to give sessions in the Mystery School and also, when I later asked, to teach a group in Psychic Palmreading.

The structure of this group came to me as if it was writing itself. I designed exercises to allow people to experience for themselves the different steps and principles I could identify as being essential to this fun, deep, and powerful method. I broke the whole thing down into components, and suggested to the people to just immerse themselves experientially and totally in each one, and the palmreading would come together at the end.

I made diagrams and xeroxed them; made lists of materials I needed (watercolors, paper, cups for water, brushes). Almost every group I've led has had painting in it. Painting, and especially watery painting, unlocks the second, feeling chakra, connects us with the elements, and levitates the subconscious into view – all in a state of bliss. I had come across a soft and sprightly piece of music called *Morning Breeze*, by Anugama; I played it for the twenty-minute painting exercise. I still play it for any painting in a group.

I was sent an assistant – a vivacious blonde Austrian girl called Nisarg – the same one who'd shared a room with me at the Hare Krishna Hotel in Juhu Beach. She was just wonderful – totally onboard, joyous, capable, enthusiastic – and, quite soon, a matchless confidante and friend.

At the time of this first group, Kaveesha had gone to Los Angeles on a brief trip. But when the first day was over, I sat down and wrote a note to her, on beautiful hand-made paper on an upper corner of which I'd painted blue blossoms. It was a kind of poem – saying that I felt as if flowers were growing all over my body.

For I did. Such a wonderful feeling of expression and expansion, realized creativity and unfoldment! Such a joy to share what I had uncovered in this line of work… what had arisen in me.

Later I heard that it was that letter that decided her – for she'd had some doubts – and from then on she welcomed and supported my various ideas and endeavors. The five-day group had gone well – everyone had 'got it' – and, as I'd emphasized that each participant would find her own way of reading energy, people had each and every one discovered in themselves intuitive faculties they'd not known of before.

Somewhere along in here, at Sarita's behest (for she was now in the Commune again too) I began to study Colorpuncture (now known as Color Light Therapy), participating in many trainings and working in Healing Arts giving sessions – particularly the Transmitter Relays series, which worked via points in circles on the scalp to open up and cleanse the circuitry of the body/mind/emotions, including birth traumas and past lives.

Colorpuncture was such a magical opening – it prises out all sorts of unconscious material as you apply the correct color to an acupuncture point via a colored perspex wand held in a sort of flashlight-thing. All the treatments that we learned we also experienced, practising on each other. A core group of a dozen of us (including Sarita) went through years of training together, mastering complex and difficult techniques. We learnt Kirlian Reading too, where the aura of the fingertips and toes is photographed on a special machine and then interpreted. Peter Mandel, the huge, brooding German healer who had developed all of this, came every year to teach us. It was a thrilling time. Colorpuncture opened my energy-flesh and showed me my inner world. It sensitized my body extremely. It was wonderful.

And, as with the stones, I found that I could read the points – tune in and see colorful, astonishing movies… nuances of energy… and, being verbally-wired, I could describe them to the client; whereupon the images would change and deeper levels and Knowings would appear. It was all quite mind-blowing.

I heard that one of Bhagwan's secretaries was quite upset about all these esoteric goings-on. In the Mystery School, there were esoteric fairs, with mini-readings available. Kaveesha had gone to Brazil and returned with massive crystals, which lived in various Mystery School rooms, and a group was offered to learn about them (I participated in one). Psychics of various sorts were coming out of the woodwork, happy to read cards or hands or give crystal healings. Wasn't this nonsense, wondered Ma Anando (the same pretty, worky Aussie woman who'd shared my little room behind the Godown for a while in Poona One); wasn't it against the spare, cool spirit of Zen?

"If something makes them happy, let them do it," commanded the Master, and so we esoteric beings could expand and explore to our hearts' content.

Glen, my father, in his 70's

Osho painting his signature

Anando on his Enfield

Osho entering the hall for the evening meditation, 1988

Dancing with Osho, 1988

With Anando after Metaphysical Surgery

Mouth of the Dragon demo, 1991

Test session on last day of the Mouth of the Dragon group

More Dragon demo

Tai Chi in the early morning, Nalla Park

Shopping in Hong Kong

Devika and Devadasi

Osho in his garden

Writing in Nepal, 1992

Osho's greeting before evening meditation

Osho's pyre;
January 19, 1990

Osho's body before being taken to the burning ghats, 1990

Meditation in Osho's Samadhi

Tamo-san, Morioka 1996

In France with Sarita and Devadasi

Bindu in Copenhagen, 1998

With Sarita and Jamie, Zurich

Tromsø, 1998

The Pyramids seen from Nalla Park

Sarita and Devadasi, the Swiss Alps

His Name, Our Robes

It was still 1989. One day, Bhagwan announced that he was henceforth to be known as Osho. He'd wanted to drop 'Bhagwan,' because of the Hindu origins and connotations – he no longer wanted to be saddled with that whole past. Somebody had then suggested 'Osho,' which is an affectionate term of reverence for Zen masters in Japan. He liked the sound of it.

It's a beautiful word, and it suited him. We had used to shout *Yahoo!* all together, arms in the air, when the pre-discourse music reached a crescendo. Now we shouted *Osho!*

Also, he sent the word down that we would begin wearing robes again: maroon for daily wear, black with a white sash for therapists who were at work; white for the Evening Meeting, as Discourse was now called. After that, at night, or outside the ashram, we could wear whatever colors and styles we liked – our regular street clothes. Indeed, the robes were to be worn only inside the ashram.

Thus, a 'black-robe' was somebody facilitating groups or sessions in some way.

I bought a maroon robe in the ashram boutique and was offered a bookmark as a gift. The bookmark had Osho's beautiful signature on it – a powerful, graceful line of indecipherable squiggles and peaks – underlined most dashingly with one long streak. On the other side was this:

> *Your Meditation Robe...*
> *...has a special purpose. You will find that it gathers a certain energy the more it is used in Commune activities.*
> *The MAROON COLOR has been chosen by Osho to join people's energies. He says that when people are dressed all in one color it creates a certain atmosphere which intensifies the energy. Hence maroon robes are worn in the Commune for all daytime activities. Please change out of your robe before going home.*
> *WHITE ROBES are used only for the evening meeting of the Osho White Robe Brotherhood. Osho says: "It is to be strictly understood that these robes should not be used anywhere else or for any other purpose, as that will disturb the collection of energy." So please change out of your white robe before going to dinner.*

The result was an aesthetically delightful scene: beautiful, glowing people walking about in a rich, royal color, against the backdrop of lush green foliage. Silent white nights where we lined up to go in to Sit with him. And therapists on duty in solemn and depthful black, brightened and protected by the white belt. Garnet, obsidian, pearl; against the vivid green, with blue sky or black sky above. And robes helped us flow in our bodies as we all became one body, in a way... helping and supporting each other with our presence. (Osho once said he intended eventually that we would wear robes striped in the colors of the rainbow.)

To add to this aesthetic, money wasn't used in the Commune – you bought cards at the entrance where your canteen meals, purchases in the bookstore and so on, could be marked off. ...And on each card it said, *It is a meeting-place of friends.*

Pretty Woman and Consequences

I had now moved into a room round the back of a mansion two streets behind the ashram, where a few spaces were rented to sannyasins while the main part of the house still sheltered a wealthy woman, whom I never saw. My room was large, upstairs, with a huge Raj-style bathroom with a claw-foot tub. There was an enormous window which was covered with screen instead of glass. A narrow walkway led along in front of this window, overlooking the dusty back-yard of the mansion, where the servants moved about desultorily and great trees offered shadow. Beyond the yard were fields of cane.

Next to my entry door was a hallway, and on the other side of it lived Nisarg and her boyfriend Subhuti, in an identical room.

I paid 300 rupees a month for this room, which was quite a lot then, but worth it.

The movie *Pretty Woman* was shown in the ashram. (We had occasional movie nights, in what I'd been told was a converted elephant barn, in Meera. Only later someone insisted it had really been for huge, shiny black water-buffaloes. But somehow I can only see that beloved barn with an elephant in it.) I was utterly undone by it – the kindly gent, Richard Gere, showering the innocent prostitute, Julia Roberts, with gifts. I wanted this sort of thing for myself!

And, with no Richard Gere in sight, I decided to do the next best thing – provide a bunch of beautiful clothes for myself. I had just enough money for the upcoming rent, but I borrowed it from myself, hoping more would come along. I was told of a very good tailor, and I bought fabric, created designs.

What beautiful things I then had made! A short red jacket with white polka dots and bias-cut frills, in silk crêpe. A dress to go with it. A vermilion silk-velvet jacket with black satin-silk lining… and so on. The tailor wasn't in M.G. Road, but nearer, in verdant Boat Club Road – so it felt quite luxe to go for the fittings.

Finally the clothes were ready, and I went, on one of my usual frantically-busy, over-scheduled days, to pick them up. I *rushed* to collect them, then *rushed* on to the next thing… and somehow, by the time I'd gotten home, I didn't have the new clothes – I must have left the bag in a rickshaw.

I was *devastated* – just *devastated!* All that indulgence of the little poor girl, the neglected whore… who just wanted a nice daddy to take care of her, finally – *gone!* No indulgence after all! No rescue!

I put notes up around the Commune, in case anybody else had seen those clothes, either in a rickshaw or on some person – I drew pictures of the missing garments.

Someone took the notes down again, right away.

Somewhere I'd gotten my hands on a little book by a psychic, who gave formulas for getting back lost things. I just happened to be reading it right then. So I tried the prescribed ritual. I forget just how it went – but it was a distinct and direct plea for the return of lost items. I did it with great fervor before I went to sleep.

And then… sometime in the night, someone got into my bed behind me and lay there, putting an arm around my waist. He squeezed my body *hard* with that arm – so hard that it was as if the arm had metal in it – hard, and vicious. He yanked me back against his own body.

I woke up, brushing the hair out of my eyes, putting my hand down to try to pry the arm off me. It was very difficult, but I managed, and, completely terrified, I turned towards the other side of the bed to see who was there.

There was nobody.

Just then I saw the wavering beam of a flashlight outside the window, moving along the narrow terrace before my room, then turning down into the hallway.

I was too frightened to move, but I thought of Nisarg and Subhuti, and after a bit I forced myself to get out of the bed, go to the door, unhook the screen, go hesitantly across the hall, and knock on their door.

The flashlight had been shone right into Subhuti's face! He'd called out and the intruder had vanished. Subhuti was going to get out of bed and investigate, but Nisarg wouldn't let him!

I listened to all this, and then went back to bed.

Next day I found out that the mansion had been burgled for the first time in forty years. Silverware was taken, and a few other things; and some sannyasins' rooms downstairs had been raided.

I met Sarita in the ashram later, and told her the story, of the actual burglar and the spectral assault.

"Greed," she said simply, referring to my ritual and its purpose...

Sigh.

A Particular Silence

Just a little vignette – something that happened one night in Discourse:

Two thousand of us sat on cushions in the vast oval hall with its marble floor and walls of mosquito netting; its high arched roof. The night's tropic darkness clung closely to the structure, but we sat in soft light. Silent ourselves, we heard rustlings from thick stands of bamboo outside, and from far away the blatting of rickshaw horns and the rumble of trucks.

We were listening. We had *become* listening; and it was really more like drinking. In front of us on a low dais a man sat in a chair, and he was speaking. His words and phrases vibrated like a drum and crept down into our cells and gave us something we'd always been thirsty for. We were great hollow wells being filled from somewhere mysterious... Rain-light and love-bliss flowed into our hearts and buoyed us and expanded our auras and gave us something to sit upon, to see the stretching reaches of, to drink.

And so we ourselves did not rustle. It's like, if you are drinking water you do not simultaneously jiggle about, cough, sneeze, or snore; it would interfere with getting the life-giving stream down into you where it can spread out and do its work of rehydration. And so unlike people in audiences everywhere we did not fidget, and we made no sound. The hall was filled with the reaching of souls towards silence, for that is what the speaker's cadences contained...

Between the words, great gaps came, waking and intentional, stretching us deeper and deeper into the moment. The words too were made, somehow, of silence. That was what we were listening into.

I was in perhaps the third row, to the speaker's left. As I sat bathed in the vapors of Indian air and the stillness of all of us and the flowings of my own energies rising and the breathing of the tall trees outside, I suddenly felt a movement in my lap – a small pressure, a weight on the fabric of my clothes transferring to my skin's sensors. I opened my eyes downwards and saw looking up at me a wee grey creature with a pink flesh flower for a nose – petals like a little propeller. It stretched its neck up towards my face and the flower twitched. I looked back at it, mute. My posture stayed exactly as it was. I took in the surprise of both of us, and I watched the movement the surprise made in my inner world without reacting outwardly whatsoever. My mind quickly computed the wee thing's probable identity: mole? Shrew? Vole?... some wee mammal living underground, so that it sees via smell – thus the amazing, delicate little blossom-snout. I believe that it was blind. I don't know if the creature computed my identity.

He got down off my lap then and went along the row of meditators to the next person, an Italian woman of generous curves, and he climbed into *her* lap and gazed up at her like a cat does when it is feeling curious or confiding. I slanted my gaze sideways and watched as the woman opened her eyes, took in the situation, and moved not a muscle nor made a sound. And the little animal made his way like a mountaineer down off her lap and on to the next person. For all I know he had gone to many before me. Nobody squeaked like a rodent, nobody flailed, nobody screamed, nobody did a single thing but stay absolutely still, observe, and continue to just *be.*

I closed my eyes again and went back into my inner space.

Wrapped in Golden Arms

My love life was a shambles – despite occasional blissful nights with some sweet, rugged motorbiking Dane, or the like, I was nearly always being disappointed; was forever hungry and seeking.

Nisarg got tired of hearing about it – each work meeting we had could not proceed to business until I had moaned about my terrible times in Love.

So, when the next Psychic Palmreading group was going to have its demo in a place called The Egg – a sort of white marble low-walled enclosure opposite the bookstore, purpose-built for whatever little outdoor events – Nisarg enveigled a friend of hers to come along and watch.

I was dressed up as a gypsy – I'd had a wonderful, very full patchwork skirt made (why did I ever get rid of it later? Virtuous throwing-stuff-out often brings regrets!) and I wore a black taffeta blouse with puffed sleeves and net trim. My hair was very long then and I wore it loose. I demonstrated a bit of reading on someone's hands, told people that everyone is really psychic, it just needs to be re-claimed… And at the end, Nisarg's friend, Anando (yes, another Anando: it is a unisex name), stepped up to give me a hug. I had to stand up on the low, broad-topped Zen Wall for this, as he was so tall! I wrapped my arms around him, and he wrapped his long, strong, gold-furred arms around me… I was enfolded in this Other, this world of warm, delightfully smelly, power and magnificence. He stepped back then and caught my eyes with his. Those eyes were blue, and the lashes striking: gold as anything, spiky, surrounding his suddenly-solemn eyes – his sometimes-glinting eyes – catching the light, the sunshine of India.

He held my gaze for a very long time.

The second Psychic Palmreading group was held upstairs in Mirdad, a leaf-shaded building over near where the Pyramids would later rise. It was a fun, uproarious week (the group now lasted seven days), at the end of which everyone could do a psychic palmreading, in her own way. (For example, I tended to get more information when I lifted my fingers a bit away from the hand of the client; but I noticed that many people seemed to pick up more when they pressed the client's skin.)

On the last day, after the last hour, when everyone had hugged and chatted and was trooping out the door, tripping off down the stairs towards Kundalini meditation, Anando stayed behind. The house was an old mansion, and there was a huge bathroom next to the group room, with a claw-footed tub. Anando caught me there for another long hug – I had to stand in the tub to reach up high enough – he was 6'4"! He had obediently desisted from hugging me for the whole length of the group, which was only right and proper. A group leader is a group leader; a lover is a lover; they are different roles entirely, and it doesn't do to mix them.

We climbed onto his Enfield – a long blue couch-ponderous machine with a deep-throated smoker's roar – and took off through shady Koregaon Park, then into the grimy outskirts of the city… riding into the brown mild hills till we were hungry, then going back into town to a restaurant near the train station for *dhingri-caju-mutter* (mushroom-cashew-peas curry). The place was quite fancy, in an antique, ex-Raj, ingrained-dirt way – for all that it overlooked one of the most sordid and filthy areas in town.*

But I enjoyed the air-conditioned restaurant – conversed with the big sunny man opposite. His accent, while classically German, had an American tinge to it, from a past relationship with a Californian. He grinned a lot, laughed with his head thrown back.

We were together for the next five years.

We both felt the relationship to be very healing. We'd both suffered, and wanted to feel relaxed and welcomed at long last. The first many weeks of our association were made rocky and interesting by the fact that he was still very much attached to his previous girlfriend, who kept putting him in his place and complaining about whatever she found wanting in him, thus keeping him extremely alert and interested in *her.* That is *rarely* my relating style – to bitch and complain – though it's been known to happen – so I was the warmly accepting mistress – a position I recognized, even at the time, to be temporary and privileged. And so it proved… as long as he was seeing her too, I was a nice cool drink of water for him. I knew that if they truly separated and it was just him and me, all the chickens, as the saying goes, would come home to roost. We'd have to face ourselves, each other, the full, unruly weight of our unconsciouses. Oh lord.

– But we never lived together save on holidays – thank you Osho for that practical understanding: every human needs her/his own space.

* Later, one of my organizers, a Swedish doctor, told me that he had had the following conversation with a rickshaw driver:
Rickshawallah: "We are hearing that Western men, they are having sex for one hour. How this is possible?"
Swedish Doctor: "Ummm… What do *you* do?"
Rickshawallah: "We are going behind station. Pive, pive minutes only."
The doctor became curious and decided to see for himself. He went into an alley where were doorways each hung with a dirty old curtain. What he saw there he would neither describe nor discuss; only that when he had made his way out of the alley, in one piece as it were, he'd bent over and vomited…

The Master Beyond Body

It was mid-January 1990. For nine months, Osho had been sitting with us at night, but not speaking. He came out on 17th January, just for the first part of the evening meditation, when music pulled us skywards, and we shouted *Osho!* and then settled ourselves to go Inside. Then he left, and we watched a taped discourse. Then, on the 18th, he didn't come out at all, saying he would meditate with us from his room.

We were holding our collective breath – we knew that he was not in good health; but not exactly what was ailing him. He'd said several times that he'd been poisoned while being dragged from jail to jail in America – he thought it was one particular breakfast he'd been given, just before he was yanked out of that particular jail and whisked off to another: a piece of white bread covered with a nameless gravy. He thought the poison was in the gravy.

There had been a weird event while he'd been talking, during a fairly recent series of discourses. Suddenly, he'd stopped speaking on the topic at hand and had said loudly, fiercely, with some alarm, some anger, that some sort of ray was being aimed at him and was hurting his body.

This happened a few days in a row.

I didn't know what to think. It sounded weird, paranoid.

But much later, in 2004, in Italy, a moody, round-eyed, genius German healer, Christ Krishna, told me that he had taken a Geiger counter all over the ashram a day or two after these incidents, looking for a place from where any sort of ray could have been aimed at Osho while he sat in his chair on the podium. He found two locations: one on the roof of Krishna House, the other out on the street – at which points the Geiger counter showed greatly heightened radiation.

I heard too that Dr. Amrito had carefully taken various tissue samples from the Master and carried them to England. Making a precise list of the symptoms Osho was experiencing, he submitted all this to the best laboratory he could find. He did not use Osho's name – the patient was listed as anonymous.

The diagnosis came back: probably thallium poisoning; undetectable, at this remove in time, in the tissues (thus a favorite for political murders). But the symptoms fit.

My guess is that he was expected to die much sooner, and when he did not – somehow, in his supernatural way, hovering around his form, however much in pain it was – the CIA, or whatever self-important shady body, sent someone to zap him with radiation. That was when he roared during discourse – feeling that. And yet still he did not die, and still he roared and ranted at the Priests and the Politicians; naming names, terrifying us with his fearlessness.

There is one scene I will never forget.

I'm at Mariam Canteen, out in back, where there are a lot of empty tables sitting under a grey sky. The trees loom overhead, some big-leafed, some tiny-leafed. It is January – normally in the middle of the day it would be almost hot, though nights and mornings are very cold.

But it is raining. Not a lot – but drops are falling down.

In so many thousands of years, it has never rained in January. Rain is for the monsoon only; from June to September. It does not rain at any other time. Ever.

An Indian sannyasin is sheltering in a deep doorway. His face, half-lifted, is stricken.

And we all know that while the sky is doing something it is just not supposed to do, something else terrible, doomful, is occurring just nearby as well… in Lao Tzu House. We can feel it in the gathered silence; the way the everydayness is shot through by dread, by denial, by hope, by unspeakingness.

During mid-morning of 19th January, Anando, my beloved, and his not-quite-ex were sitting in a small plane at the Poona Airport, waiting for lift-off to Goa. It would be many hours before the news would reach them.

I was teaching a Psychic Palmreading group in the big house across the street from the front gate.

And, during the afternoon, the word came…

We gathered in Buddha Hall, but we were so stunned that we could not dance or sing. Osho lay there in front of us, clothed in flowers, piled with colorful flowers. Then we followed his bier – a sort of stretcher, held aloft in silent shock by six male disciples. We went through the streets to the burning ghats, thousands of us, in our best white robes – as if to sit with Him.

We gathered in arcs, in clumps, or stood in solitude… whilst ghee was poured onto the logs that nearly covered him. His face showed there, though, visible to us all.

His brother lit the fire with a burning torch, and first the kindling and then the logs began to burn...

His face... and his delicate, ephemeral, beleaguered body, weighted now by wood, yet still casting up so much light that the logs seemed to float – began, slowly, to catch fire too.

The musicians were playing, but we were all so stunned that the spirit could not enter the music yet. We began though to sing... *"Walk into the holy fire... Step into the holy flame..."* and we began to thaw, and crack, and tears of different sorts welled up in us, and energy began to climb towards the sky.

There was a moment – I will never forget it – there amongst the stunty thorn-trees, under the *peepul* and *neem*, near the thick-flowing river in the darkening evening – when I saw Him – some gathered spark made of mindless power, an awareness as ancient as the Himalayas or the galaxies – an awareness which has watched human life and removed from it every particle, every fraction, of self-interest or fear or manipulation, every shred of artifice or dishonesty, or custom – and taken the essence... a kind of watchful planet gazing at us from afar, yet in the near distance... a seer and describer of human life who is himself free of it.

Among us all who loved him, who were called, or stumbled, into the infinite generosity of his Commune, and knew there something bigger than they had ever known, and more gentle and subtle and complete – something where the heart is at long last king and queen, and can burst from the chest in wondering celebration – .

Among us, yet not of us, that essential vital, streaming nugget flew upwards like a bird released from captivity – and streamed into the sky. The music swelled suddenly, taking over the space, our voices rising, our lives suddenly thawed, and we swayed, and lifted our arms – and that essence that was him, which is too big to measure or to name, flew all in an instant all over the world, and entered into everyone who loved him, who had bowed down to him – and implanted itself there, in a sort of time-release capsule, to release itself gradually and in the right timing for each person... *as themselves;* as their own growing into consciousness.

"Into your hands I lay my spirit... into your hands I lay my life," we sang.

In my long-sleeved, loose-pleated white robe, I sat all night beside the heap of ash and bone as it cooled and then slowly chilled. I sat in ashes, uncaring, as if I sat in meadow-flowers... for I did.

When dawn came I walked the short distance on the dirt road to Popular Heights, and took a shower, and dressed, and went to the ashram. And along the way everything was already getting born in me: I was to teach a training; a long training incorporating all the things I knew how to do – readings, and much more… and I began to build it in my mind, this thing that I must make.

His going affected different people very differently. For in the vast out-drawing of the wave, the silence when nothing can be known yet – many stayed in a graceful waiting and presence, struck to the core and beyond.

But we humans are a fidgety lot.

Some said, "He is dead. I am leaving."

Some said, "Let us go on just as we were!"

Some said, "I will return to my country now, and become practical finally."

Some said, "I will find another guru! For I am not done."

Some said, "Let us see what happens next!"

Some said, "I will spread his word far and wide!"

Some said, "He has told us that he will really only be with us when he is gone. Shall we apply ourselves, and see if this is true?"

Some said, "I have always wanted to go to the Himalayas on a motorcycle, and now I will go!"

Some said, "Ah – Goa is so nice. The life is laid-back and easy. I am off to the beach!"

Some said, "Ah – now I can smoke as much as I like, without offending his nose!"

Some said, "Now I will keep a house where I can shelter a hundred cats!"

Some said, "I am also enlightened. Come and listen to me!"

Some said, "I will play music all day in the garden."

Some said, "I will tell everybody else what to do!"

Some said, "I am lost. There is nothing for me now. It scarcely matters what I do or where I go. But I will wait… what else to do?"

Some said, "I will marry my sweetheart and move to Australia, and maybe we can have a family of our own as well!"

Some said, "I have always wanted to become wealthy. Maybe now I will try."

Some said, "I have a great project in mind. I will move to the West and go about trying to birth it."

Some said, "I will teach all that I have learned!"
Some said, "Death is the end, and so now all is finished."
Some said, "Death is not death, and I am alive to whatsoever might come."

We heard that amongst his last words to Amrito, his doctor, he'd said, "Existence decides its timing."

8

A Carnival Decade

A Carnival Decade

1990 – 2000

Creative Explosion, and Moving In

Here is my experience and my perception of what happened next: a tidal wave of creativity moved into us. For about seven years, there was a blessed explosion of new therapies, meditations, musics, techniques for the inner work. No doubt in other countries sannyasins found themselves in some similar wave, taking some form or other – or maybe just the formless – but, a wave; and in the ashram, this became wonderful collaborations between therapists and musicians, cooks and carpenters – to create new ways for people to go In, and to also enjoy the Out.

Because there was no economic factor, therapists could get together and come up with new methods without competition or fighting over who got the rewards. (The rewards were in the work itself.) Primal, Anti-Fischer-Hoffman, Tantra, etc. – all took wings.

For me, the prize of prizes, the best inner work I had ever participated in, the most subtle, the most conducive to both heart-vastness and gimlet inner alertness, was in the Mystery School.

Quite soon I took my proposal for a training to Kaveesha, who accepted it. I began the joyful task of writing a program for a twenty-one-day process. At the same time, another big change was afoot: with my living situation.

I'd been living in Popular Heights again for a while – this time in a kitchen where a bed-platform had been laid across a stone sink. It was on the fifth floor, and the small window looked out on scrubby treetops. That was where I'd suffered the worst of the jealousy of Anando's other girlfriend; feeling pulled deep down inside myself to face my own being, because there was no place else to go. I'd found that jealousy can be an amazing spur to meditation. But his relationship with her had finally dissolved, and he was with me.

Amazingly, I was soon living in the Commune again. It happened thusly: Waduda, of the Mystery School, had, as I've mentioned, recommended me to a client in Geneva, where I'd been invited to work on my next visa turnaround. I'd duly met tall, French-Swiss Devika, an ardent, mature seeker. Somehow we clicked. I gave sessions to some of her extremely aristocratic family (part of my continuing informal education into what can be called Conditionings of the World!) Devika and I were very different, but we were friends, sharing, over the years, many visits and long conversations. (My heart goes to her still.) I often stayed a few days at her mountain chalet when I was in Switzerland for work.

Devika came to Poona once a year in the winter. She wanted a place to stay which was inside the ashram. The Pyramids were just going up, to Osho's color scheme (we heard that he had seen a Japanese coffee table book about Zen architecture, and had adopted elements from it): black buildings, blue windows, green foliage, raked gravel gardens. The buildings all had pyramid roofs and were very striking – there were four of them, two residence buildings, two for groups and sessions. Later another residential one, in the main part of the campus, and a large meditation hall were also built under pyramid roofs. People could buy apartments in the residential ones.

Devika proposed to Jayesh, the accountant, that she would buy a studio apartment in one of the pyramids, if – and only if – I could live there when she wasn't there. Jayesh said they would need to think about this, as it was unusual. People sometimes bought rooms for other people, but not as timeshares.

The next day they gave their agreement.

I was, as the Brits say, gobsmacked! Suddenly I was being asked to choose a color scheme – walls, marble for the floor, furniture. And I was being treated very respectfully! Not that I wasn't treated nicely anyway – no reason not to, I guess – but this was something more!

At first, I made mistakes in the décor – beige walls, rosy-beige floor! Awful! Like a 50's psychiatrist's waiting room. I was most impressed that nobody complained when I wanted the walls to be done over in white! The rosy-beige floor remained, and never sat quite rightly with the white, though my profusion of orange-flowering jade plants, and so on, in the deep windowsills helped a lot.

I would live here for the next ten years, and somewhat beyond…

The apartment was on the ground floor on the corner of Tilopa Pyramid. It was small, but it was mine to inhabit, and the inhabiting of it also seemed to confer the privilege of taking my working hours much more lightly: I was working very hard giving sessions and leading groups, but now I could skive off and go to the tailor a lot too. At least, I never *asked*, and nobody ever *said*… but nobody gave me a hard time about it (at least not then). I felt guilty a lot though. It just seemed *necessary* to me to go to the tailor. And, later, to design jewelry a lot. And, one stolen day, paint little pictures all day. The only time in all my commune years I ever did that… and such bliss it was I still remember… I didn't want to stop.

As soon as I moved in, I stopped doing sessions Outside. This was a relief really, though it meant I had to make enough money during forays into the World to last me all the subsequent time in Poona.

Sheets

I often visited Out of Africa, a huge house set in wide grassy grounds on the very far outskirts of Koregaon Park, to stay with Anando in the outbuilding he'd beautifully renovated. He'd put in arched doorways and marble floors and a sleeping loft – he has wonderful taste, and such an eye for spare lines and rich fabrics as complementing elements. An ayah cleaned the house but not the loft.

One morning I woke up and turned over and noticed that there was lots of dust around the bed! Too much dust, in balls and drifts! In fact, the loft was grubby! I mentioned this to Anando, who became indignant and defensive. But he did jump up then and, with a certain set of his jaw, found a cloth and dampened it and began to clean the space. I helped, and we got it spiffy and lovely and fresh.

We rode in to the Commune on his motorbike then, and during the morning I ran into Devika – she was staying in her room in the Pyramid. "I was looking for you!" she said. "I just received a present… from Osho, well, really of course from whoever decides what of Osho's things are given to whom.

And I feel embarrassed by the gift, because it is too much… I am not a great disciple, I have just donated for a room and that's why they gave it to me, I think… " She laughed self-deprecatingly. She is tall and quite royally distinguished, but very shy with it. I wondered at her excessive modesty, but I didn't interrupt. (I had been given his tall milkshake spoon. I tied a silver ribbon round its handle, and it lives in my treasure drawer even now.)

"So," she continued, "I want to give the gift to you and Anando, to use, and then when you go away to travel you can store it with your things, and you can use it in the room too. Here – " and she held out a pile of white folded cloth. I took it – and felt the weight – and lifted a corner, and looked – and saw the shining whiteness. A sheet! And a duvet cover! With lace at the top! And two pillowcases! That he had *used!* You could see that they were worn!

I held them to my face and breathed them in. "Yes! Wow!" I said in astonishment.

And then I remembered… was this why, unknowingly, it was simply time to clean the sleeping-loft that morning?

The Mouth of the Dragon

I had a job to do that was all-consuming: preparing for my first big training.

The Mouth of the Dragon was a confection the likes of which has probably never been seen before or since. The name came from an Italian astrologer, Prembodhi, who looked at my chart and said that that was my job in life: to be the Mouth of the Dragon. (At first I'd thought to call the training Spiritual Muesli, but luckily I came to my senses and adopted Prembodhi's powerful phrase.) The aim of it was to teach people some things I found that I knew how to do: read chakras and palms, dialogue with parts of ourselves, invite mysterious beings to do psychic surgeries, and even a bit of astral travel. I wrote a program comprising three weeks of esoteric experiential learning; and oh, how it was decorated, fraught, and baroque with settings, food, costumes – it was to be a sort of Broadway-Musical-Banquet all studded with witches and wizards, elves and sprites and Tibetan demons, Greek goddesses and what-have-you.

Cost was no consideration, for that brief time in our history – Kaveesha was backed by what was known as the Hollywood Crowd, a coterie of a few high-flyers from that interesting burgh. Kaveesha, as the High Priestess of the Mystery School, lived well and spent money. My group's budget seemed unlimited. The group was quite expensive for the participants – trainings always were, more so than other groups – but even so the preparation didn't seem to take into account what money might come back. Whatever I dreamt up, was caused to come into being. How lucky we were!

My friend/cohort Nisarg helped me from the beginning. I designed costumes for us two – long black dresses with lace inserts and gold trim, and long pointy medieval sleeves; conical black hats with long veils swooping down from the points. I designed a demo – a fifteen-foot dragon was made (Dwabha was in charge), fringey and whiskery and scaly and active with human feet beneath him, and a ghetto blaster hidden in his midst. Witches and wizards, carefully and colorfully costumed, danced along before, beside, behind him. We took our dragon on the road through the ashram after White Robe Brotherhood one night, and there were complaints that he disturbed the silent space of the people coming out of the video discourse; but I thought the objections sour-grape-ish and churlish. We had such fun dancing along to Soul music with our wild dragon!

The group took place in a huge room in Meera, the big old house across the street from the main gate. We decorated with a different set each week: a Tibetan temple, complete with a small, stoop-into red portal to enter through, and, once inside, warm bright primary colors, and windows with views of painted mountains.

The next week took place in a Grecian temple – the walls were hung with murals painted on cloth, with pillars and hanging grapes, olive trees and a sea-with-islands in the near distance. It was beautiful! For that week Nisarg and I had black Ancient-Grecian-style robes, with one shoulder bare, gold braid, pleats to the floor. And the group had a fabulous feast, with grapes, and a whole special menu – whatever could be concocted with the materials at hand. (For practical reasons this ended up happening at the canteen where everyone else was eating – and I heard there were jealous grumbles from those unlucky enough not to be in the group!)

The third week took place at Stonehenge, with that moody, mist-hung, cryptic temple depicted on the wall, and oak trees round about. The art director was the talented Komala, and she did such a fantastic job that I am still in awe when I think about it. Thank you, Komala!

I will say this: I heard, later, from participants, again and again, that it was the best group they'd ever done. I think this was from the sheer innocent generosity of the endeavor – the no-holds-barred colorfulness – and the sweet happiness of Nisarg and me as we sat conducting this phantasmagoria. We had invited guests – Subuddha came to talk about Tantra (he was by now in a Tantric relationship with Satya Puja, who later became a great Tantra teacher). Musicians came. Once we did Running in the Dark, inspired by my night-time bike ride in Baroda long before: blindfolded participants *ran* down a long corridor formed by the other participants, while music played; at the end they were caught by a mattress held by more people.

And we had, the very first day, a glorious mess that nearly got us shut down!

It happened like this: First, participants lay down on a long sheet of paper while a partner drew an outline around their body. Then each person painted her own chakras onto the paper – just as it arose in them, while *Morning Breeze* played. Then, they dialogued with the chakras with a partner; *becoming* each of their own chakras, in turn, and letting the chakra tell its own story. Then, the partner painted chakras directly on to the first person's naked body. Then we changed over while the second person had their turn to dialogue and be painted.

Then everyone sat in a circle with closed eyes, while the helpers cleared away the painting materials. When a gong sounded, the participants opened their eyes… to discover that behind them, all around the circle, another circle had silently formed: tall men had crept in, with spears, naked except for being painted brown all over with mud, and decorated with stripes and designs! (Later, people in neighboring buildings complained about all these naked black warriors running through the courtyard on their way to the group room!)

Everyone danced wildly together to live drums, and when all were sweaty and loosened up, buckets of ice cubes layered with rose petals were brought in, and everyone rubbed each other all over with the rosy cubes!

There was plastic sheeting on the floor, but still a great mess occurred; this had been anticipated, and there was a bathroom right next door. Anando had lovingly fashioned a waterfall in the big tiled shower, with rocks all piled atop each other – a sort of woodland ambiance. All the tall Maori warriors we'd recruited, plus the painted-up everybody-elses, got under the shower one by one to wash off the mud and paint.

Now, it later became known that Anando, who worked in the architects' office just next door to that bathroom, had *told* the powers-that-were that there was a danger that if the bathroom ever flooded, the architects' office, and all its carpet, and its papery works, would be flooded too. He had recommended building a raised little lip people would have to step over. But this idea had not been approved. And so, when the bathroom now flooded, so did the architects' office, and the powers-that-were decided to shut my group down. Anando said I-told-you-so to the powers-that-were.

But what really decided everybody on how to treat this sudden hot controversy was this: Kaveesha was in Los Angeles just then; but a fax was sent to her by a gaggle of her disciples – all of whom heavily disapproved of the colorful mayhem I had wrought: the mysteriously-processing naked painty warriors, the subsequent din of drums and hollers and squeals; and then the flood. As I've said, nobody had ever done anything like that before. Groups were minimalist in décor, streamlined in action.

I was, to put it succinctly, getting bad vibes from some people. I saw them staring and frowning when I went to lunch.

But here is the wonderful thing: I don't seem very susceptible to these censorships when it comes to my creativity. I live inside a profoundly hermetic bubble. I am so willing to share – I love to share – but there is just no interfering with me. And, blessedly, thank the providences, Nisarg strode out in front and took the flak and protected me. Through all the groups we did together, she took that job upon herself – for I would be simply unable to deal with the 'outside world' and its complaints and demands (still am) – even in this 'inside world' of the Commune. I could ignore the flak; but I couldn't answer it or negotiate with it. And Nisarg somehow intuitively knew this.

Thank you, Nisarg!

Anyway, as people glowered at me, the fax was ka-whirring its way out of a machine in Los Angeles… and a fax came back: "Madhuri needs support, not criticism."

Suddenly everyone was all smiles and supportiveness! And the group went on… at least, for a couple more days until it almost stopped again: there were twenty-seven participants, and seventeen helpers – all of them needed for the set designs and shiftings, the artwork I'd commissioned, the feast, and the bringings-in and clearings-up of paints, and so on. Many of the participants, for some reason, were French, and they took exception to the helpers' getting what they saw as a free ride into the group, when they, the participants, had had to pay. So all the French banded together and, in true Gallic tradition, went on strike.

I would have had no idea what to do. But once again, Nisarg, bless her heart, sorted it all out. I don't even know what she told the strikers, but it worked, and the group flew on, through all its days until its completion.

I had learnt a beautiful lesson during the preparation for the group: I had described my vision for the sets to Komala, and what she had produced was far more beautiful than what I had dreamed. So, you can entrust a task to someone's creativity, and let them run with it. I found this out again and again, with the food, the dragon, all of it. People created gorgeous, ambitious, unique things, all from their own wellsprings. Much better than I could have anticipated!

Thank you, everybody!

And, sorry, everybody, for the flood. I can be pretty obtuse sometimes.

Devadasi Has a Dream

I was rushing off to Kuala Lumpur for a visa turnaround. This was not necessarily a straightforward thing, because you still had to hide any association with Osho. It was never a given that you would get the visa, either. The consulate might say you'd been spending too much time in India, and refuse it. They could refuse it without telling you why. I'd heard many stories. So I was very nervous. I had picked Kuala Lumpur simply because it was the cheapest flight I could find – I'd never been there before.

I landed at midnight, and, getting in a taxi, I asked the driver to take me to a good hotel in the city. Next day I went out and began the visa process – it would take a week at least.

But I felt ill. On the street, the strange smells of durian and spices assailed me. I was too nervous to eat, too nervous to enjoy the novelty of my surroundings. The cafés had icky-sounding animal parts, even primate parts, on the menus. I only wanted to be back in Poona.

The hotel, I finally realized, was much frequented by prostitutes. I stayed in my room a lot, fretting. I was afraid to put on any makeup in case that indulgence somehow, etherically, negatively influenced my visa application. I became so spartan I barely breathed. There was a phone at the front desk that I could use, and I spent most of my money phoning people, to make myself feel better.

I phoned my mother in Oregon. When I told her where I was, she said, "Hmmm… Kuala Lumpur. Where have I heard that word recently? Kuala Lumpur… " Then she remembered… She herself had no idea where the place was, but a few months back, she had had a strange dream: an image of a snake with a crown on its head. When she woke up she didn't know what the dream meant.

Then, two or three weeks later, my brother Andy's cartoonist girlfriend, Nina Paley, had shown to Devadasi a new comic she had just made, about a trip she had taken to Kuala Lumpur, Malaysia, to visit her parents, who were living and working there. The first page of the comic had featured a large image – a snake with a crown on its head.

The coincidence was so remarkable that Mama had remembered the name Kuala Lumpur.

So now she said that she would find out the phone number of Nina's parents, if she could.

Next day I was lying in bed with a fever when there came a knock at the door. I opened it, and there stood a sturdy American couple, saying briskly, "You're coming with us!"

And so I was rescued (a thing I love), and taken out to a big villa on the outskirts of the city, where all was green and spacious. There was a huge garden, and I had my own room. Thank you, Nina's parents, wherever you are!

One night they took me out to dinner with a group of expats who met at intervals to socialize. As the lazy susan covered with little dishes full of spicy offerings went round and round, the woman next to me asked about my life, and I gave her a capsule history of my adventures. "Why, you poor thing!" she said, in her Midwestern drawl. "I grew up in Iowa, in a small town, with elm trees and sidewalks and a little school, and regular dinners and everything nice. I am so sorry that you've had such a hard time!"

I gaped at her. In my universe, my hard times qualified as adventures, learning experiences, and material for good stories. It astonished me that she saw them as negatives. I tried to see things from her perspective, but found that I could not. Had I missed something obvious and important? I wondered.

After the week of waiting was up, I collected my visa and, with tremendous relief, went shopping, flew to Madras, and took a long happy train ride back to Poona.

Poisoning

During the next high season I taught The Mouth of the Dragon again. It was sold out; everybody wanted to do it, whether they cared about giving psychic readings or not! This group turned out to be just as juicy and crazy as the first. But for me, something ominous was happening…

I had heard, in idle conversation in the canteen, that it was a good idea to get your amalgam fillings removed. They had mercury in them, and it was not doing you any good. However, (added the speaker), you needed to wear something called a Dental Dam, to protect you from the toxic gases and shards released by drilling. And, a cold drill should be used, not a hot one.

Knowing I'd be unable to afford to do this in the West, I consulted my then-dentist, who had an office next to the rather shady-vibed Chinese restaurant on East Street, parallel to M.G. Road. This dentist was affable and ready with his no-doubt antiquated set of tools – I had never had a reason to either particularly doubt or trust him. He waved his hands around – "No problem! No problem! Don't be worried! I can take them out, replace with white fillings! No problem!"

"But don't we need to use a dam?"

"No, no, no problem! Not needed!"

Mistakes indeed… I don't really have an excuse for this one. Laziness. Deafness. Lack of experience.

Little sharp flakes of amalgam flew around my mouth as the dentist drilled with a hot drill. Every few minutes I'd spit them out into the little round sink beside the chair. Eleven fillings, to come out a few at a time, over a six-week period. Eleven 1950's sugar-eating childhood fillings.

Meanwhile I was fully immersed in preparation for, and then teaching of, the second Mouth of the Dragon. (Ironic title, oh lord.)

Strange symptoms began appearing. I sat in the video discourse at night, wondering why I felt so… transparent, exhausted. Strange nerve pains in jaws, ribs. Headaches. Weird feelings all over.

Finally it was all I could do to drag myself to the group, find some spark in myself to transmit. Luckily by now the group was only a few days from ending… One memorable evening, we were all going to tell ghost stories. To set the stage for this, the whole temple had been converted into a spooky graveyard. Shredded mosquito nets had become spiderwebs – there were big creepy autumnal trees – lots of leaning gravestones. The brilliant artistic crew had outdone itself, as always.

There was even a hanged man, depended from a tree. His trousers were down around his ankles and his legs were covered with hair made with eyeliner. His big shirt hung down over his thighs. A bloated blue-painted styrofoam tongue stuck out of his open mouth. Saliva dripped from the end of it – an unforeseen complication. He had a rope around his neck with a hangman's knot in it, and the rope went up into a tree.

When the group participants came in, they looked around for the group leader, but she was nowhere to be seen. Where was she?

Well… she was the hanged man.

Because that was how she felt by then.

It was a great ghosty session – Arjuna (who wrote so many books about the prophet Nostradamus) particularly shone. The hanged man had been cut down, and pulled his pants up, took out his sodden tongue, and officiated. Lots of nice scary ghost and other esoteric stories were told.

I had an audience with Kaveesha, something about the group, I don't remember now. But all she did was, silently, lean over and press her long, manicured fingers, with their red nails, into my liver area… three pushes: press, press, press. At the time I didn't know what it was about.

A night or two later I was in Discourse and suddenly all the pieces fell into place: I had mercury poisoning!

And when the group finished I was finished too. I lay very still on my bed. Even to lift a finger was too exhausting. What was happening?

Next day I managed to get a Kirlian reading with Peter Mandel, the developer of Colorpuncture, who was again visiting the Commune. I sat on the stool at the Kirlian machine with my hands and feet on white paper on white screens while the machine buzzed loudly for a minute. Then Peter pulled the sheets of photographic paper away, developed them quickly in the nearby darkroom, and looked at them.

My toes and fingers had nearly vanished – there were only a few black blurs on the pages. (I normally had all my healthy number of fingers and toes on these readings.)

"It iss a miracle you are valking around!" glowered Peter.

Anando wanted to go to Goa with me on his Enfield. I peeled myself up off the bed with great difficulty. Barely managed to pack a little bag. Sitting on the back of the bike was torture – hour after hour, trundling along the indifferent, sun-blazing or jungly roads, willing a threatening herpes outbreak to go away.

We stayed in a little guesthouse right on the beach. I dragged about. My boyfriend was not best pleased: "I want a *cheerful* girlfriend!" I stared at him blearily.

Life was grey. Dull. Ceasing. Going away.

I thought with awe and longing of the energy I had spent so heedlessly on trips to the tailor, shopping. What luxury! Because now, all was fading... and I saw all my excesses for what they were: *love of life*, however out of balance anyone might think them to be.

I had a sort of healing crisis then, throwing up a lot.

After that I started to get better.

The Gulf War came. I canceled a work trip to Europe that I had planned. We drove back towards Poona slowly, stopping at a nice big jungly hotel along the way. Anando went out on his bike by himself to get something, and, just that once, didn't wear his helmet...

There was a knock at the door.

Two men supported Anando over the threshold and into a big chair. There was a bone sticking up in his shoulder, clearly visible under the skin. His face was bleeding, swollen. A big lump was rising on one side of his forehead. He was stricken, in shock. He said he just wanted to look at a photo of Osho. I gave him mine to gaze at. Tears welled in his eyes.

He had hit an oil slick, coming round a curve.

We hired a van and driver to take us back to Poona. I was by now feeling quite recovered. It was Anando who needed care.

He later had two surgeries, and eventually healed well.

Some months later I spent a month working in Lyon, France, in a bare, frigid flat. I kept finding my own long, long hairs lying all over the floor, carpeting the shower... too many of them. It took a while for me to realize it was from the mercury. But later my hair all grew back.

When I returned to Poona, I found out that the dentist who had removed my fillings had died.

A Partnership

Anando and I were a solid couple in those years. Creatively, we supported each other tremendously. He loved everything I did. He had a capacity to see and appreciate beauty I have never seen in another man – or woman. Any beautiful object – a plate, a painting, a flower – he held up and turned from side to side, seeing details, taking the time to tune in, to really *see,* that most people have forgotten or never had. He was *transported* when he looked at something lovely – sometimes tears came to his eyes. Time stopped for him; he stood, huge and open, reveling from head to toe. It was a deeply endearing quality.

And I loved seeing him approach me on the path through the ashram: the whole height of him would light up – he'd stretch his long arms above his head and leap up and down, making himself even taller! – He'd be grinning and aglow, sunshine seeming to pour from him. Then those same arms would reach out to me – and I would run into them – and be scooped up into a warm, smelly-in-the-right-way embrace, wrapped round and round. I was faithful to him for the five years we were together; I used often to think that this was possible because this great blond Viking was as big as one and a half normal men, so I didn't have to feel the sense of limitation monogamy can bring!

It was not a trouble-free relating. I didn't get enough time alone, because I was easily mowed down. If he wanted to be with me, I tended to cave in even if I needed alone time.

We did Tantra meditations together. As was to become something of a pattern, I'd meditate with him (and later, with other boyfriends) – for example, Goddess Gazing. It works like this: for thirty minutes the man gazes at the woman, not touching, while she sits about six feet away, naked, meditating with closed eyes. Candlelight and soft music are nice. Then they lie down together and see what happens. I loved this one! For once I didn't feel rushed, but had so much time to just feel subtle things, and watch them go by… a relaxed opening would arise, from a much deeper place than normally.

And then, all opened up, soft, and ready, I would hope for a different kind of lovemaking: the meditation should carry over into the sex.

But what would happen in every case was that the sex would remain habitual

– and I didn't know how to un-habituate it. (Recently I asked Sarita about this; she is now a world-class Tantra teacher, traveling all over the world. She said that this is a common problem and that it is needed for couples to first learn in a group setting the keys that would enable them to continue the lovemaking with presence and awareness.)

And so the lovemaking would end up being, as usual, too *concentrated* for me; I could sense so much *space* wanting to enter into it. But I didn't know how to ask for this. I loved describing aloud exactly what was happening to me in lovemaking – to Anando's dismay; he remained passionate but mute – but I couldn't find words to ask for what it was that I wanted him to do differently so that this hunger for *space* was addressed. Although the sex was mutually satisfying, explosive and orgasmic, I knew I was skipping over something in myself… and I felt remiss.

At that time, Sarita told me about a Tantric meditation she had done with Wadud (now the Great Wizard of the Mystery School) when they were lovers for a while during the Ranch. I loved the sound of it: first one partner, and then the other, spoke aloud *every thought that went through their mind* whilst making love. Sarita reported cosmically vast orgasms through this method!

I asked Anando if he would do this with me, and he agreed.

It was my turn first (generally speaking, it seems it always has to be my turn first since men will not say anything right up front). I was excited to see what would happen when I exposed the wayward mental material that inevitably arises during lovemaking. I was looking forward to the vulnerability and exposure and resulting Space! …So I spake every nuance of thought-shred that wandered into my inner view – ALL of it – and lord, it was a wandering minstrel show of mundanities, worries, greeds, poetries, judgments, questionings, etc. etc., along with fleeting impressions from the sidelines: leaves moving outside the window, alertness to noises from outside – . I think we timed it for ten minutes. At the end of my turn I felt high, emptied, lifted, incredibly bare. And then I said, "Your turn!"

But Anando was very, very angry. *"YOU THOUGHT ALL THAT WHEN YOU WERE IN BED WIZ* ***ME?"*** he demanded. And he refused to take his turn.

Oh well.

But on other fronts, beautiful things were happening…

The School of Mysticism

You might wonder what it was like, not having Osho there with us. It wasn't really any different, except that I terribly missed, sometimes, his commentary on Commune and world events. But certainly he wasn't *gone* – the energy was still here, absolutely; even, maybe, *freed* – from confines, freed to roam and clarify and penetrate. So we went about our days exactly as if he was still in the body.

And I was discovering just how beautifully his deep teachings could be transmitted in the right caring, alert, careful surroundings, with the right teachers.

The Mystery School; or, as it was soon re-named, the Osho School of Mysticism.

This faculty (which had its offices in one of the Pyramids) offered, among other groups, a series called the Stream: Co-dependency (2nd chakra), Power (3rd chakra), The Heart: The Alchemy of Acceptance (4th chakra), and Beyond Belief (5th chakra). I participated in Co-dependency and Power, and was then asked to join the Mystic Ring. This was a group of black-robes who were taught by Wadud, that premier Wizard. A short, quiet, intensely intelligent Californian, he had been married to the curvy, canny, earnest, loveably goofy part-Cherokee psychic Waduda, and they'd run an esoteric school together in Berkeley. Now Wadud was with Alvina, a tall pretty German woman with long black hair. Sitting in a group with him was wonderful – one was held to a very high standard of awareness.

The work was so subtle – so intelligible – so useful: we watched our chakras, experimented with group and partner exercises, painting and dancing, breathwork, and more. And all of this heightened awareness and opening resulted in a much-transformed daily life. One could actually see what one was doing, in all those knee-jerk reactions one usually had. And the reactions softened and changed, and space and heart and light took their place. It was incredible!

These Mystery School groups happened in a certain sort of space – always lovingly cleaned, simple; marble floor, plain mattress and cushion covers in a shade that would support the chakra we were working on (orange for the 2nd, yellow for the 3rd, green or pink for the 4th, blue for the 5th). The helpers for a group met daily with the group leader so that they too could share what was going on with them – so that not only participants could air their process, feelings, concerns; but everyone could. This made for a heartful and flowing milieu. There were potted plants (Osho had suggested that cut flowers were not happy beings, so we should switch to plants). There was music chosen to support space and heart – and the group would sit at the beginning of each day, and each re-gathering after the lunch break – sit all together with soft music and just… go deep. Before anyone spoke, there was this time of just sitting, just being. So much would bubble up then – so much would be seen – and such a deep space would happen in the heart. The stage was set for the session's very experiential exploration.

These groups were absolute revelation for me. Instead of just being thrown in at the deep end with Osho's teachings, to make the best of them as I could, I was receiving daily hands-on guidance and tools for specific areas of concern. I was able to notice what was happening within me very sharply. I participated in each group, and then went through it all again as a black-robe. In this capacity I was supporting participants – by sitting with a person during a breathing exercise, for example, and sensitively employing both hands – usually in the aura – to assist both energy movement and deepening awareness. We helped also with just our presence; holding conscious space.

And there was the revelatory fact that as a black-robe, I was not merely in service; my state mattered too. The practitioners mattered as much as the participants. The Heart groups with Waduda were a case in point. I remember a scene: I was one of several helpers. On the last day, we helpers, and the participants, were supposed to shower love all over each person in turn, wiggling our fingers above our heads and saying, "Shhhhhhhh… "

But right then I didn't *feel* like showering love. I felt Scrooge-ish, churlish, grumpy. My eyes narrowed – my lips thinned – I felt like… a cold-eyed killer cowboy! Yeah!

So I took a risk. I went over to the side of the room, lay down, and let myself sink down into the cold-eyed killer cowboy. I just *was* one – mean, bitter, pissed off, all shrunk up. My eyes were slitty, my chin stuck out, and sour vibes came off me.

And… the miracle… As I lay there in utter permission for this state, it changed… and became bliss. Love arose in the cold-eyed killer cowboy… because he was utterly accepted!

That's all it takes.

This is the lesson of the Heart; and this is the lesson for all of life. And it has, over time, changed my life.

One night, as part of one of these groups, we walked into the bar (the

Commune had a bar, open at night after White Robe). But we didn't just walk in – we entered first in the Your Meditation Robe; felt what that was like. Noted how we'd be looking out for sex, for something grounded and basic. We'd talk with someone, have a conversation. Feel what that was like. Then we'd walk out, and come back in a few minutes later in the 2nd – emotions, feeling. Then the 3rd – power. Then the 4th – the heart. That was amazing, walking into the bar vibe in the heart… soft, accepting, non-hunting. Tolerant, embracing. The heart was the best.

This was massively educational. The real thing is to be aware of what chakra you are in, rather than trying to control anything. Just be aware… So, if I am in a gathering and I feel a vibration in my solar plexus, I know to be very alert: because in that chakra I am probably going to be in judgment, comparison, and other unhelpful things – and will thus be inviting that sort of thing towards myself, too. If I'm in my heart, though, all is well. It is so wonderful, so helpful, to be aware of what is going on inside – in this little daily sort of way. (That night in the bar – I don't remember in what chakra! – I ended up sitting for a bit with an enormous, brooding young Russian, who kept his mouth almost completely closed as he mumbled, asking me for a date. "Ummmm… " I said, always hating to hurt someone's feelings. "I guess we could meet and… ummm… talk." *"DALK???"* he cried. I didn't go out with him.)

I also eventually participated in the Women's Liberation group in the School of Mysticism. And again, for three long and memorable days, I had a chance to be a man.

This time, instead of a lonely ballpoint ink tattoo and pretend motorbike, I got to be in company with other would-be men. It was a revelation – for one thing, we got to dress the part, with bulging stuffed condoms in our pants and, in my case, a hairy toupee sticking out of my shirt! I wore a cowboy hat, and became a cowboy, then a hired gun. I was a little twerp but utterly fearless, and my integrity was adamantine. I sang a cowboy song to the assembled company, and knew I could sleep under the stars rolled up in a scratchy wool blanket and be blissfully happy. I acquired a buddy, a French-Canadian fellow in combat pants, and knew the sweetness of buddy-dom with all my soul. The female fears – am I beautiful? Will I be loved? How can I improve myself, my looks, to make myself more attractive? – were gone. I was just a little squirt, but I went after the most beautiful woman in a flame-red dress, of the group of women who came in to dance with us… and I courted a princessy quiet maiden in a gauzy gown – I wanted only to serve her, bringing her a glass of water – for that was all there was!

A strange thing happened then – the princess suddenly asked me, in a soft but rather stern German accent, to take off my cowboy hat, remove my shoulder pads, and take out my hairy chest toupee! I think she felt these things were not… *natural.* I went off her immediately. I did not need improving, and any woman who thought I did was right off my list!

When we had, after three days of this glorious fun (we mostly sat around playing cards and bullshitting) to become women again… it was quite awfully painful for me. I had to let go of my best buddy, he of the combat pants, whom I knew I would never see again once he had become a she. This was *so* sad! Then, I had to start fussing again about how I looked! This seemed both craven and stupid. But there it was.

I also reveled in a women's group, taught by Karima, and was much edified by the 5th chakra group. And later, in the training I underwent as a Mystic Ringer, we learned how to read energy by resting in our own heart, or resting back in the middle of our own third eye – not sticking it out, as I had been doing. Wadud was wiser than I…

Dancing and Natural Breaks

I used often to assist in the wonderful dancing groups created by a vibrant, messy, emotive, springy American woman called Dancing Maneesha (to distinguish her from Lao Tzu Maneesha). I loved these groups! The music released me into rapturous imagery as I danced, and realizations would descend and unfold. I remember dancing a scene where I was being tried before an Inquisition, as a witch. And I danced for the Inquisitors! – danced my own being, even if it got me killed. And then… I saw blackberries assembled above my head – squeezing the sweetest, most ambrosially midnight-ecstatic juice down into my veins.

Dancing is simply one of the best meditations it is possible to do.

One day I had my period and could not come to the group. Periods always followed the same pattern for me: in the days leading up to one, I was gripped by a relentless randiness, a need to be filled by a man, jostled and provoked. A howling-at-the-moon kind of feeling… a need for orgasm to release the pressure building up. Emotions would be expansive, irritating, and deep.

But the moment the first drops of blood appeared, the world turned 180 degrees and I wanted, needed, only to shut the door, put up a Do-Not-Disturb sign, and go to bed with a blindfold over my eyes. For one-and-a-half days I would then descend into a grateful depth… a sacred depth, a wonderful private blackness where none save I could enter. The very idea of the World, work, men, expectations and bright lights – was anathema. Everything was turning in. I would feel the previous month flushing out of my body – my bowels too would flush, with the blood, and all the tensions of the month. It was marvelous, healing. There was fierce pain for a little while, but I'd discovered that one ibuprofen at first blood would take care of that nicely.

So on this occasion I'd stayed in bed, and slept and bled and poo'd, and swum deep in blessed blackness. And then I returned to the group.

Maneesha was very cross, and scolded me: "With all the work you've done on yourself, haven't you gone beyond that yet?" (I'm sure she herself felt under pressure.)

I was shaken, of course – nobody likes being berated – but there are some things that cannot be doubted; that just *are.* And that in-dipping was like that; a sort of absolute which was not a question, and so needed no answer. I could not say that then – the idea was too heretical – we did not get, or ask for, days off – so I just stared at her, or perhaps muttered some slightly defensive thing; and then glided into the next dance.

More Studies

I was, as I've mentioned, also learning and practising Colorpuncture. This tended to unearth stuck and hidden energies, often to the person's discomfort and dismay; so clients had to do Dynamic and Kundalini to process the after-effects. The treatments worked on physical, emotional, and spiritual levels. I underwent all the treatments myself, so life was very intense indeed!

I also studied Aura Soma – a beautiful method using little bottles of colored liquids applied to the hands or wrists, and then into the aura. The combination of all of this, and being in the Buddhafield, was so intense that I became acutely allergic to the color red. Just the sight of it could trigger herpes warnings in my body – little nerve-pains and uneases, settling into an ache or tingle. My body was acutely sensitive, but not very grounded; rather, nervous. A very nervous body. (This was to get worse before it got better.) India is not a very healthy place for Westerners. The immune system is under constant stress with unfamiliar pathogens; the soil is depleted so the veggies aren't nutritious enough. We must have been lacking trace minerals, vitamins. (Curiously, much much later, it was taking two supplements: Vitamin B-12 under the tongue, and Vitamin D-3 drops, that finally calmed down this aversion to red. It is still with me, but only slightly. For a long time it was quite distressing.)

Vasumati, the brilliant therapist I've mentioned before, experienced one of my chakra readings, and invited me into her Therapist Training in the Center for Transformation for the module of Voice Dialogue. So I had five days' training in this masterful, compassionate, truly effective method. I have used it extensively ever since. It gives the different parts of a person's psyche a chance to speak their own truth without being judged; with impartial and warm welcome. This is transformative – I used to feel after a session that little detonations had gone off in my aura, leaving silences where tangles of psychological/emotional Stuff had been.

Anando and I took part in a wonderful Tantra group taught by Wadud, Waduda, and Alvina. Conducted in a sacred-feeling, very clear and beautiful pyramid room, it focused on the chakras and their polarities – the way men and women have oppositely-polarized energy centers, and what this means in daily life. (I was to make use of this more and more as the years went on, eventually teaching it myself.) Then, after being a participant, I got to help in the next group. I *loved* it!

In Healing Arts, I participated in a three-day group called Beyond the Psychology of the Healer, taught by Devapath. Two things I remember: how much fun it was to sit opposite a partner and role-play as therapist and client. As therapist, you were allowed to say to the client what you really thought and felt! "Go away! Fuck off! What an idiot you are!" etc.

Then, the other thing I remember: sitting alone, you were asked to go back to the moment when you first knew you would become a healer. I immediately found myself in the dim cluttered living room of my childhood home. I was about eight years old. Everyone was out except for Mama... She was in a nearby bedroom at the front of the house, and she was *moaning* and *howling* and *wailing* with pain. An abscessed tooth had been treated by the dentist and the painkiller he had prescribed wasn't working. I stood alone in the gloom, hurting terribly along with her. It was just so awful, and somewhere inside me, below consciousness, I knew that I would one day do whatever I could… to try to heal my mother. That was how it all started.

Osho had asked Devageet, the dentist, to develop a Colorpuncture series that would help to release animal energies from the teeth. Devageet had done this, and I was a willing guinea pig. I remember having such acres of deep insights and releases as the colors were applied to the areas around the lips. One moment I remember: I was a raccoon, resting high in a tree. The energy was of *ordinariness* – a restful, happy, simplicity. I already loved raccoons but this added to it – it was just so great to be in the furry body of one!

I was finding that Healing Arts and the Osho School of Mysticism had very different atmospheres. In Healing Arts, much as I reveled in the techniques we were studying and practising, the orientation was very much towards patient care and didn't take the practitioner into account – she just had to do her bit, and if she suffered, had too much work, or had other things on her mind, it was just too bad. This seemed to me a more traditional approach – so that although we were practising Colorpuncture, Kirlian reading, Segment Massage (a powerful – and painful – method where certain areas of the back, corresponding to certain organs, were massaged very hard with fingers or elbows, in order to release stuck energies) and other things, on each other – and going through deep and often uncomfortable internal rearrangements and releases because of it – fascinating, colorful, vital, astonishing – when it came to our job of work, we just had to be there, fully functional, with little room for complaint or even commentary. Whereas in the Mystery School, the practitioner was all: her space was what would be communicated to the client. The School also had frequent faculty meetings. And our training continued throughout.

This was simply great – and seemed to me a much more mystical approach.

I underwent, in the School of Mysticism, a six-week process called Metaphysical Surgery. I was in Silence for much of this time, except when I was meeting with my two assigned therapists, Rahasya and Subodh. (Anando was also allowed to relate with me sometimes as he was felt to be a healthy influence.) The therapists found and printed out for me many pages of transcripts of my darshans; and pointed out the theme running through it all; Doing vs. Non-Doing. I spent a lot of time going for idle walks in the nearby park, meditating, and of course, attending the evening video discourses. But the great excitement of the whole process (which was basically wrenching and scary, since I was having to let go of my busy-holic-ness) were the Surgeries, done by a specially trained team working in my aura as I lay on a massage table. The atmosphere was secretive, exclusive, and very sacred: the surgery room was extremely clean and orderly, the team present and compassionate. There were three surgeries in all.

After one of these I was carried back to my room in the Pyramid and lain gently on my bed. I was floating, gapped-out, laid open; wanting only to be alone and go within myself. The carers left, and I lay there… and then I Saw, hovering above me, a tiny creature – a pink fairy or angel-being, glowing with love. She had come to see how I was doing – not to do anything, but just to monitor things. It was so lovely to see her!

For the entire six weeks, I had diarrhoea. The therapists, one of whom was a doctor, became concerned. But I was not… it felt right, somehow. And the very day the six weeks was over, the runs stopped too.

I emerged blissed out. I can't say that my Doing stopped, but who knows how much worse it might have been without the surgeries?

Dr. Amrito had initiated, in Healing Arts, something called the Healing Circle: a person with mysterious symptoms nobody had been able to figure out, would be sent round to each sort of practitioner – medical doctor, colorpuncturist, intuitive reader, acupuncturist – whoever was there. Then we would all meet with the patient and discuss our findings. This was to happen once a month.

The first patient was a German man of middle age, dark and strongly wiry in build. He had periodic attacks of malaise and generalized pain that were increasingly debilitating. In between these attacks he felt fine. Doctors in Germany hadn't been able to find the cause.

I held his feet and tuned in. What I saw was so odd – so outside my knowledge and experience – that I doubted myself. I saw, deep in the coils of his intestine, a little lump; and this lump had the power to send into his whole body, at intervals, some nasty toxin, which made him ill.

Nobody else saw this; each discipline had done its best but had not been able to pinpoint the cause of his symptoms.

Later I heard that the man had finally gotten, in Germany, a proper diagnosis: he had a rare tumor that was cytotoxic: it released, at intervals, a poison into his system. Nobody knew why.

Only much later would I have cause to remember this.

Sarita and I even taught together, and though this was in the Healing Arts faculty, my esoteric riffs were half of the substance. We taught a couple of Colorpuncture procedures with intuitive reading included. Sarita and I could finish each other's sentences in this last regard! She and I each developed sessions too that could be incorporated in Colorpuncture series, to help people metabolize the color: Past Life, Healing Journey, 7-Bodies Journey, Dancing with the Demon, Keeper of the Threshold. (The Past Life session I had experienced with another therapist and immediately made my own.)

I enjoyed receiving Rebalancing sessions, a soft, thorough sort of body work. I participated in a very meditative group called Hara Awareness Massage.* And I had a session from a star bodyworker from Portugal, who said to me, "Your body was not made to run. Look at your legs!" (Knock knees, one fallen arch.) And I continued studying with Peter Mandel – who once demonstrated on me, before a group, a strange dial he had created, a circle of Osho marble (more about this substance later!) with semiprecious stones inlaid in it in a particular geometric design. He held this to my forehead; then pronounced, "You were born to be horizontal! Not vertical!" I still don't know what he meant. But it sounded relievedly relaxing.

One day I woke up and had a strange feeling: I had been, somehow, *paying back karma* with my exhaustive psychic readings and healings. This karma had its origins in a past life. And now I had repaid it; there was no longer a true need for me to work so hard.

However, although I took note of this feeling, I went on working as before.

* Hara is the door to birth and death, the place beyond all the chakras and yet giving rise to them; the location of all centering – two inches below the navel and *in*.

A Goofy Guy

One of the principles we experimented with in the Mystery School was Projection. One evening I attended an event taken from a group called Path of Love. It was such a mind-blowing eye-opener that I would like to describe it here.

I stood in a huge room with about fifty other people – all experienced, dedicated seekers. The facilitator asked us to begin walking around the room, looking at each other; we were to notice if anyone sparked judgment in us. When we met someone we had some censorious feeling towards we were to stop in front of them.

I walked… stepping carefully, aware of my body, my inner hush with this scary assignment. My hands went behind my back, my slippered feet felt the floor beneath the thin soles. When I passed some people – a woman with a large, encompassing energy, perhaps; or a slight, friendly girl I had worked alongside – my heart felt a nice outgoing bouquet of rays, and so I did not stop. Towards a man I might feel, for example, some longing… so I didn't stop there either.

Now, here coming towards me slowly, is a fellow – I've seen him around for years. I know he's Dutch; and he is… well, disagreeably *goofy* in my opinion. He's tall and thin, has small wide-open eyes with curly star-spiders of lashes behind thick glasses; his freckled nose looks like it's being pushed up with a finger. His girl-full lips are parted perpetually and the tips of his square white teeth show. His expression, it seems to me, is startled, silly, vacuous. I feel a distinct stab of energy coming out of my 3rd chakra. I know that this means I have a judgment towards him. I slow and stop in front of him. He gazes at me with his helpless, stubborn, startled eyes.

We are now asked to tell the person opposite us what judgment we have about them. I feel a sinking in my tummy. Awful… I don't want to hurt him! But I trust the process. So I take a deep breath and say, "I see you as… goofy. Silly-looking. I think you are…*unattractive.*"

He breathes, his gaze not leaving my face. I'm standing here, and inside I am feeling my oppositeness to him: for am I not sexy, accomplished, with long lush fine brown hair and big mascara'd eyes and snakey hips, with lots of mean dance moves in them? Am I not recognized for my talents as a psychic therapist? Aren't I… *groovy?* I *mean… ?*

These self-reassurings go on at a level below conscious thought, a sort of flattening-down of the anxiety I feel facing him. A very habitual inner riff, I'd know if I were usually able to notice it.

But now the group leader is saying, "Close your eyes... look inside. Where is the judgment coming from?"

I close my eyes and it's here – right here. There just isn't a moment's gap, the picture is immediately in front of me.

I'm ten years old and I'm on the playground at Grant Elementary School. I'm an outsider, an outcast to an appreciable degree. The popular girls are over there, by the jungle gym, under the pepper tree; and each is combing the hair of the boy of her choice, with the boy's pocket comb kept ever handy for taming that lock of over-eye auburn or blond. That sexy way they have, the boys, of tossing their heads to get the hank of hair out of an eye, then whipping out the comb and swiping it through the hair so carefully carelessly... drives the girls so wild that they've taken to combing it for them.

I have no boy to comb, though I wish I had. But I am the strange girl, and many are my sins: My family are poor. That's No. 1. I wear hand-me-downs that don't suit me; while the most popular girl, Debby Pergin, has a perfect wardrobe of preppie shirts and A-line skirts, because her mother works at a clothing store. That's Sin No. 2: my old wool jumpers and baggy dresses. Then, I have long, straggly, uneven hair which crackles with static in the desert air. The other girls have coiffed flips. That's Sin No. 3. Sin No. 4: I write poetry! Ugh! I have *read it aloud* to hapless girls at recess! That is *soo* not okay! *Ick!!* How *embarrassing* to listen to Love poetry!! About some skinny little boy with a swash of shiny hair! Sin No. 5: I am too smart. This is really uncool, and deserves punishment. Sin No. 6: I bring, sometimes, *soup in a thermos* for lunch on a cold day, instead of the absolutely obligatory sandwich, apple, individual packet of chips or Fritos (a baggie of them taken from a bigger bag won't do); carrot or celery sticks, and cookie. And as I sit at the picnic table in the schoolyard with the other kids and gaze sorrowfully at that thermos (and they are all looking at it too, and making upward lines on the uncool-o-graph), I am on the verge of tears thinking of my poor workworn mother saying lovingly and anxiously, "Now, this'll be nice on such a cold day!" Sin No. 7: I have crooked teeth. Sin No. 8: When the teacher asks if anyone knows the answer to a question I *wave my hand around in the air a whole bunch!* Every time! Can't prevent it, though I try! And Sin No. 9: Once I had no clean underwear and my mother told me I'd have to wear a pair of the brothers'. I knew this was a horrible idea but she was my mother so I obeyed. Then I forgot I had them on and at recess I was merrily swinging round and round the bar with one knee (I was good at the bar) and some other kids saw! And began to sing, "Katy wears boys' underwear! Katy wears boys' underwear!" in nasty, taunting voices. That sin will last for a long, long time.

In short, I am a goofy, snaggle-toothed, unsexy-to-the-max kid. And I *suffer*... and grow up to cool/sexify myself as hard as I can! Oh yeah!

The group leader asks us to open our eyes and share with the person opposite us what we've discovered. So I tell the young man about it – how I see that I am projecting onto him that pariah status that caused me so much pain long ago, and that I therefore want to disown.

He looks quite different to me now. He looks like a... *being.* Not a status; he looks like a heart/soul/body with depth and sensitivity and richness; an alive sensate aware holy trembling ripple in the calm sea of the Beyond That Is Here. In short, he looks dignified and... *beautiful.* Here, breathing, poised, doing his best to face himself; graceful and lusty and soft and unknowing. Not a *thing,* but a process, a verb, a growingness.

And I tell him this; and thank him.

Subuddha Speaks

Somewhere in here, Subuddha returned to the Commune. (The dear man had spent three years in Japan unavoidably detained. Don't ask.) His time there, and what he'd gone through, had left him humble. He told me that I didn't need to re-pay him the $2,000 I had borrowed when we had each moved to Poona in 1988.

"But... why?" I asked. "All I ever did was chase you around and torment you!"

"You were *beautiful,"* he said fiercely. "I was just *too blind to see."*

And each of us suddenly felt a jet of tears *spurting* from our eyes – for a few seconds – and then it stopped.

And the relating had finally ended in peace.

Soon after this, one morning I saw him in the canteen, and there was a strange large red area on his forehead, where it looked like skin had been worn away. "What happened there?" I asked him.

"Oh," he said, looking away, embarrassed, "Satya Puja" (his then-girlfriend) "flew back to South Africa yesterday, and I felt so disturbed by her leaving that I… rubbed a hole in my forehead with my hand, rubbing at it all night."

I was amazed. So he *did* feel vulnerable, and gotten-to, just like me, or any other human! I felt very tender towards him.

Going to the Mountains

Anando and I sometimes traveled together. We went to Greece, Germany, Italy; and, most of all, the Himalayas. He loved these mighty mountains more than anything on Earth, and dreamt of leading tours there.

He and I tended to get along well in Poona, where we each had our own dwelling; but as soon as we were living together even for a short time, troubles cropped up. These tended to be very much a mirror of our different conditionings: East German and Californian (more about this later). Being on the road together in the Himalayas was, for me, both wonderful and terrible.

We took four motorbike trips there overall, the last being a big, glorious, scary adventure in 1992. We penetrated far into the Spiti Valley, in Himachal Pradesh, where monsoon floods had washed roads away, and there were landslides. We took a day-trek behind the Kunzum-La Pass, at 17,000 feet. I suffered in a freaked-out way from the altitude – complaining, sagging back behind the others, whining a lot, sitting down and gasping for breath, groaning in exhaustion and fear... I felt like a wobbling Ancient, joints insecure as rubber bands. I did not earn my companion's respect or pleasure – in fact, he quickly grew *really pissed off* at me.

Still, I am so glad I went – the sheer vastness of the mountains, the joy of being exposed to the skies and phenomenal landscapes on the back of the bike – remains a gorgeousness in my memory. And there was one fabulous and mysterious Rescue, when, near Kunzum-La, I was, as detailed above, staggering along at the end of my energy, and suddenly Something – I saw it as the goddess Durga, Kali's Himalayan counterpart – entered my body and filled me with a new energy that was so strong and hale I felt I could have walked to the moon and back. I had been using a stick – I'd had a knee operation four months before, and the doctor had said I'd never walk in mountains again – and suddenly I didn't need it; I used it then like a tightrope walker's pole, balancing along a narrow trail high above a gorge – or like a tap-dancer's stick, in happy horizontal play. And I understood in that moment that it was my very *complaining*, the totality of my suffering and how I had embraced it with whining and sadness and trembling aloud, that had made space for this healing current to enter me!

I felt great for days afterwards. (My annoyed companion did not!)

On that same trip we visited a monastery at 14,000 ft., Key Gompa, and had hot yak-butter tea, and talked with the monks. They told us how they chant scriptures all day. It certainly seemed to me that in Poona we had much more fun in our religiousness than they did in theirs!

And then there was an uncomfortable trip to Nepal, where we kept falling off the bike into the mud on the long slow ride from Pokhara to Kathmandu. In Kathmandu I saw a stall selling Chinese shoes, and, overcome with happy greed, bought six pairs; as Anando insisted more and more angrily that the motorbike *could not take the weight of them,* what with all our other gear. But I had to have them; and there was no place to put them but to tie them by their shoe-strings all over the bike; and that is how we went out of Kathmandu and onto the mountain roads towards India. Sure enough, some important central stalk on the bike cracked from the weight, and we had to spend hours by the side of the road waiting for stoic little guys in a roadside shack to solder it back again.

Sorry, Anando!

Later we drove through a quiet mountain hamlet at dusk, looking for a camping place. As night filled the hills we found a river, and in the dark pitched camp and went to bed. In the night I had a strange dream: a little Indian girl had died, and was lying in a sort of stone bathtub by the river while people put flowers on her body.

In the morning we looked out of the tent and saw piles of ash and ends of part-burnt wood. We had camped in the burning ghats!

The villagers stared at us as we drove out that morning, their gaze heavy with disapproval.

But I terribly missed the ashram and especially the Mystery School during these trips. It all felt futile, this mountain rambling, in comparison to the tender bliss of going inwards.

On the trip to Kunzum-La I thought often of my parents, whom I had not seen for so long. How many years might they stay around? How could I ignore them, here on the other side of the world? I wept about this; and resolved that I would somehow manage to visit each of them during the next year. I tried to persuade Anando to come with me, but this was not his enthusiasm.

Something Misguided and Harmful

There was one incident on my various travels that still fills me with remorse. I was giving sessions on the Swedish island of Gotland, in a beautiful summer full of wildflowers, sunshine, and fat trundling bees. I was working too hard, empathing souls, and I missed Anando, who was in Germany. One afternoon I gave a chakra reading to the teenage son of my sweet and kindly host (the same Swedish doctor who told me the rickshaw-driver-and-Station-brothels anecdote). The session went wonderfully well – some rapport emerged that felt rich and light. After it the boy – I think he was eighteen – lingered, and we talked heart-to-heart late into the evening. …Then I asked him if he wanted to go to bed with me.

That was the only time in all my career that I did this – or even wanted to. But I was feeling both privileged (as addicts do) and sorry for myself, going without for *two whole weeks!*

The boy drew back and said, "But you must be *forty!*"

I was shocked – I hadn't a line on my face yet. What did he mean?

And there the matter rested; we wandered off to find some food, and he was chilly towards me afterwards, as well he should have been. (He also had a girlfriend whom he loved. I never paid attention to that sort of thing.) It was a heavy betrayal of trust – and I didn't even *get* that until I was back in Poona and heard someone remarking on the six-weeks rule, which I'd not heard before myself: that if group participants and leaders felt attracted to each other they must, after the group, allow six weeks to go by before acting on it; if indeed the energy was still there. People had now begun to talk about how harmful it could be to participants if randy group leaders hit on them. And so I got to thinking about it a little more... Once, in Poona One, I'd had fun and warm-hearted consensual sex with a handsome Californian masseur, on the massage table, after a session. We both wanted it; simple; no regrets.

He was an adult.

This was not like that.

Thank god I did not touch the young man.

Later I sent him a proper snail-mail letter, apologizing profusely. Of course he did not reply; and I never worked for those people again. So so sorry, everyone. Teertha hadn't a monopoly on bad behavior. I hope that young man didn't fear therapists forever after… but he might have done.

Just Like Me

Osho told us a joke: Luigi has lost his wife. Friends, neighbors, family, are all at the funeral. But Luigi is inconsolable, sobbing and carrying on.

People pat him on the shoulder kindly, saying, "There, there, Luigi, we know it is terribly painful to lose your wife. But just think of this – in a while, a year or two, you will be feeling better. And you will eventually meet someone else and maybe fall in love and get married again!"

"Yes-a, I know-a!" sniffs Luigi. "But-a, what-a about-a *TONIGHT-A?*"

That was me. What about *tonight?*

A Visitor Comes to Healing Arts

Back in Poona, the Healing Arts faculty had a guest teacher from Japan: Kohrogi-san, a quiet, handsome man in his forties with strong, mobile features and a deep voice. He spoke only Japanese, and his translator was one of the team of Colorpuncture practitioners, Champaka. We hard-working hard-studying Colorpuncturists developed a sense of camaraderie; Champaka had become a friend of Sarita's and mine.

Kohrogi-san taught us Ito-thermie, a healing technique using special incense made from loquat leaves, among other ingredients, burning inside metal holders with vents in them so that the aromatic smoke could warm the body. It was a relaxing, heady sort of session to receive, and Kohrogi-san's application of it had a special something that made the sessions penetrating, deep, and somehow transformative. He stayed only a couple of weeks, but I would see him again… though at the time I had no idea of this.

Devadasi Comes to Poona Again

Sarita and I were delighted to welcome Mama when she came to visit (without Bob this time) in 1993. Sarita took charge and brought Mama into Colorpuncture groups, where she received a lot of treatments. Mama stayed in a nice place and generally hung out and enjoyed herself. I showed her the diary I had kept on the uncomfortable high-Himalayan trip, and in her usual Mama-style she enthused all over the place about it. She even hired an Indian girl to type it up.

Mama's hair had become very white by now, and her aura looked to me so beautiful: fine and subtle and full of soft earthy colors like the stones in streams in the clear clear air of the high mountains. We three women went to the Goddess Grove together, in the Osho Teerth Park,* where in a hidden bamboo-shielded enclave a statue of a female Buddha presides. We took a few pictures there.

There is one scene that remains with me from that visit – and still makes me laugh: at lunchtime one day, we all sat at a table together: Devadasi, Sarita, her tall, handsome, musician boyfriend Jamie (who was usually laughing anyway!) and me and my tall handsome boyfriend Anando. Sarita and I were telling stories from our childhood, and this one came up: I was four years old, and I lured my little dandelion-fluff-headed two-year-old sister into the bathroom. I had brought tools for my intended project: a package of aluminum foil and a cookie sheet. Then I told her to get onto the toilet and produce some poo. She dutifully climbed up and then went to work on the request, straining and trying her best. As each hard little ball of ca-ca emerged I caught it, wrapped it in aluminum foil, and put it on the cookie sheet. Soon there was a nice little row of shiny silver 'cookies.'

Our mother, who had a sixth sense about these things, suddenly rapped hard on the door, crying, **"What are you girls doing in there?"**

When we unlocked the door and came out, and she saw what we had been doing, she freaked and shrieked as if we'd been robbing banks or burning up perambulators.

* Also known as the *Nalla* Park. The ashram had negotiated with the City of Poona, that if we made a polluted nalla, or stream, into a park, we would after five years hand it over to the City. And so it was done; and a lovely refuge it was too, all full of bushes and trees and benches and half-hid pathways; the stream gradually becoming clearer as it passed through the area. Courting Indian couples frequented it.

Jamie and Anando were laughing, Sarita and I were laughing – but Devadasi sat there frowning. "Girls, girls!" she said, worried. *"Don't tell your boyfriends stories like that! They won't feel attracted to you any more!"*

And of course we laughed even more.

It was a nice visit – adult and relaxed. Sarita and I were so happy Mama had come.

Two Epiphanies in Relating

Over the course of my relationship with Anando, I discovered a couple of things that I have never forgotten; that have remained very valuable. Indeed, in my later life as a metaphysical therapist I have cited them many times to others.

The first was about the nature of Clinging. When we were in Poona, and he and I had spent a couple of beautiful nights together, I would then get a hunger to spend a night alone. I just wanted to empty out from all that richness; to potter around and tinker in my own space; to rest in silence. But then he would ask me to spend the night with him again. We might have had dinner out, and he'd be dropping me off at the Pyramids, and his full lower lip would stick out a bit, and he'd say, "Anando would *really like it* if you'd come to Out of Africa with him." (I think this third-person thing is a peculiarly German linguistic foible.) And I would feel both mowed down and flattered, and I would go with him – abandoning my private bliss; letting myself be carried back into his world. I didn't realize that this was setting up a toxic situation in me that would turn into addiction! Research shows that we can only become addicted to something that is intrinsically bad for us; that we are in fact allergic to. People get addicted to sugar, to nicotine, to alcohol; nobody gets addicted to kale. A spurious high attends the allergy, the toxin. We get addicted to that itchy high. So the state I was in when I was with him whilst needing alone-time, was ill-at-ease, wrong-footed; and this turned eventually, weirdly, into a neediness. My surrender came with a terrible price; but I realized it only later. At this stage the phenomenon was still developing.

The moment when I capitulated, I was going against my body. My body did not want to be there; it wanted to be at home. When it was instead with him, at his house, it was in a state of some sort of toxicity. Like a cat being rubbed the wrong way, irritated energies moved in it. But these were not "allowed"; if I had taken note of them I would have had to go home. So I suppressed them, and did the best I could to enjoy myself.

But that enjoyment was crippled, and carried a load of discomfort, like slightly-spoiled meat... and so, instead of a healthy rhythm of togetherness and aloneness, I slowly veered into a state of addiction and clinging.

When I saw this, later, it was like a clear sharp crack, like ice breaking – I saw the mechanism. And it had been my responsibility: say No when I want to be alone; or suffer the consequences of falsehood. (Once, though, I did take time off – while I had my period. I had a good rest, and then, on the last day, when the period was waning, I went early in the morning to find him at his house. And... he was in bed with a beautiful dark-haired Scandinavian! Of course, this was his right – and it might, or might not, have been the only time, I don't know – but I went away again; and my bleeding did not stop. It continued for days... which just never happened to me, so I was alarmed. Someone gave me Colorpuncture: three points across the top of the pubic bone, in blue. The bleeding stopped. But I saw while the color was going in that my body had been protesting the perceived betrayal, bleeding for it.)

The second epiphany was about something even more painful. In Germany Anando became more German, it seemed to me (I've seen the same happen to Aussie and Dutch and other nationalities of boyfriend. In the home country, the lover Reverts). I was subject to his house rules, which cramped my style (he remarked disapprovingly on my 'piles,' which meant my little stacks of books and writings which tended to accrue here and there, as they had nowhere of their own to live). Germany wasn't my favorite place, though we stayed in beautiful countryside locations where his family had property. His sense of aesthetics was much shown in the interiors he designed and built himself: spacious, with quality rustic materials; made to scale for his big frame.

Germans and Californians are poles apart. I didn't think of closing doors inside a house – in my childhood both inner and outer doors were usually open, and had no locks. It was hot, and any breeze was welcome. But in Germany you had to close doors because of the cold. Anando got cross at me for leaving them open. He got cross because when I cooked, I used every pot in the kitchen (though he loved the food I made!) He didn't like how my tampons smelled in the bathroom trash. And one day, he didn't like the way I had flushed the toilet – it had left a running of water down inside it somewhere, like postnasal drip. He brought me into the bathroom and began to explain, in a pissed-off voice, how the flush worked inside the wall.

Suddenly something rose up in me, and I declared, "No – I don't want to know this."

"But you *have* to know!" he insisted, and started again to explain it.

"But I don't *want* to know! I want it to stay *magic*, how the flush works! And it is my *right*! I don't *have* to know!" I protested.

He would not give up; he was incensed that I could willfully choose magic over practicality and responsibility! And I was incensed that he felt he had the right to interfere with my ways, however benighted they might seem to him. But apparently Germans are taught from an early age to be responsible for themselves and instructive to others. My own upbringing was a sort of indulgent semi-chaos with accents of shrieking mom.

I fled to the basement and sat by myself for a while.

There were many other things – so that I was often ambushed by criticisms when I least expected them.

One evening we were sitting in his living room, he in a chair and I on the floor; and he began to tell me, forcefully, angrily, about my faults: my lack of responsibility, my carelessness, my paper-piles. He was unleashing a mass of resentment; a volley of heavy energy was barraging me.

A thought arose in me: I want to give this a fair trial. Supposing there is something in it that I need; that will do me some good? I don't want to avoid that.

So I closed my eyes and looked inside. I wanted to see what the energy was doing.

I perceived that the barrage of bad mood and criticism coming from him was entering my body through the solar plexus – the third chakra.

It was like a bulldozer, mowing down present energies within my body.

I perceived that it was wholly destructive; that if I allowed it to continue like this, it would simply kill things, kill my own life.

In that moment I understood that verbal abuse is 100% harmful. Nobody should stick around for it. I also saw that it can be very difficult to get out of the room, as the energy pins you down, pierces into you, sticks you in place like a spear. Energy is a kind of matter.

Verbal abuse falls into the category of what I call "bad manners" in relating: something never to do. Intimate partners, I believe, need to be specially careful and respectful to each other, as the possibility of abuse is so great. I call this "chivalry," and it works from each sex to each other sex.

If one of you is angry, the first and best thing to do is Dynamic, or some other form of catharsis *not directed at the partner.*

What you must never, ever do is lay your pain and rage on your best beloved.

And, in that moment of Seeing, in that fine upstairs living room with its great wooden beams and tidy spaciousness, I came back to myself in trust: *This is what I see. It is true.* Instead of mutely and in shock allowing the tide of blame to wash into me – and then escaping; I really looked, and really saw, what is what. (I must have told him this; I don't remember how he responded. He was angry at the time so was probably not receptive.)

I've also heard that once a man stood before the Buddha and began to berate and abuse him. Buddha waited until the man stopped for breath. Then he bowed and held out his hands as if something was in them that he was giving to the man. "Thank you for your gift," he said, "but I find that I don't need it; so I am giving it back to you."

Wow. I wish I had ever had the presence of mind and being to try this. Maybe I won't always be fish jelly when under fire.

I Go See My Father

That year I did go to the States for a family visit, and saw my father. I flew into San Francisco, and took a Greyhound bus to Lone Pine, where my (peculiar) brother Robbie collected me.

Glen came striding towards me from his battered, ancient trailer, crying, "This is a *red-letter* day! This is a *red-letter* day!" And I was surprised… for I had not known he *cared* so much. (I did not know, then, how to read men's feelings when they do not show or speak them. And I still find it very hard work!)

It was a shock to see him. He'd had a bout of ill health – Valley Fever, borne on dust from the nearby dry lake-bed – and, though he was now recovered, he was thin and very, very old-looking. But he had his usual dynamic energy, and his blue, blue eyes were clear and bright. His white hair looked like a sparkling halo.

We went around together holding hands like lovers, and we talked, and talked, and talked… My heart was full and breaking, and it was the first and only time we ever conversed together like grown-ups. I aired all of my issues about him and his marriage with my mother; and he was frank with me. I asked him, "Why did you and Mama have so many kids when you couldn't afford to feed them?" And the reply burst out of him: "*I* didn't want to have all those kids!" And, "But I couldn't survive without all my kids now." I told him I'd never felt grown up enough to have any. "It sure makes you grow up fast!" he said ruefully. Then he said he'd always hoped that at least one of his children would grow up to be a scientist: "And I hoped it would be you."

I'd had no idea.

And at one point he said to me, "Why – you *beautiful person,* you!"

A few of my nephews also visited, and it was a family-fest – all conducted at the edge of a dry lake near the Sierras, in a nearly-abandoned town. Teenage nephews walked with me out onto the dusty lake-bed, amazed at my travel stories. It seems that the path my sister and I had taken was disapproved of by some brothers and so we were not discussed.

I felt that my father would have loved for me to stay and take care of him. (His second son Robbie was his caretaker.) But this idea was terrible for me, and my father didn't say it aloud. I fled after three days, and went to my mother's and Bob's house in Tucson, Arizona. This *ménage* seemed in comparison to my father's Spartan world to be bourgeois, cushioned, 'normal,' placid, and… nearly mediocre! I could not blame Mama of course, after the deprivation and squalor we'd all suffered for so long – and certainly I myself would choose 'cushioned' over 'stark.' I love to be simply comfortable. (And Osho has said, "Comfort is outer meditation.") But I felt disloyal in this – not exactly to my father, but to something I had seen in him when I had, with his permission, held his hands and 'tuned in' – a kind of nobility, a willingness to be bare, in his spirit, to the desert sky.

In fact, the beauty of my father's desert soul took my breath away. The masculinity of it: bare bones, only this, let's look into the sky and see what is really, really there… without the trimmings, without the padding. A kind of god-calling really, my old father with his white beard and incredibly alive blue eyes – his own calling of Truth, Truth as Science – that he lived every day of his life.

I bow to this vision too.

I spoke with him on the phone next time I was in Germany. First I'd spoken to my mother – she was doing fine, and was brisk and caring towards me, as always. Then I phoned my dad – this was only possible because he was temporarily in Berkeley, at my brother Jack's apartment (there was no phone in the desert where Glen lived). It was an odd conversation. First, in contrast to my mother he seemed almost childish; self-absorbed. But then, he said something so out of character that my ears opened wide – . As we were going to close the conversation, he said, "A love like ours… " and I *heard* what he didn't say: the end of the sentence: "…will survive even after death."

He was not an esoteric man – in fact, he was anti-esoteric. And he had almost never spoken of love. And here were the two together… (An exception to his diehard logical-mindedness: He had once been seeking the answer to a mathematical problem, without success, doing equation after equation. Finally, after many weeks, one night he had a dream: the answer was written in letters of fire. He tested it next day and it was correct. A scientific empiricist, he immediately began to believe in things *just like that,* if not every esoteric thing!)

Sarita had visited him in Keeler not too long after I had, and had had a similar experience of unprecedented intimacy and sharing. Later she told me this: He had asked her if I was happy in my relationships with men. She replied that it had been difficult for me for a long time, but that now things seemed to have settled. He said he was glad of that; he had worried because he knew that his parenting of us girls was lacking in physical contact. He explained it thusly: He – and his father and grandfather before him – had felt sexually attracted to little girls. He had never acted on this, knowing that it was destructive to the child. But in order to keep things safe, he had not touched his daughters at all – not even to hold their hand or hug them.

I was very much surprised when I heard this – because in all the open sensitivity of infancy and childhood, I had never felt from my father the slightest iota of threat, creepiness, sneakiness, or lust… not even a particle. I had only felt his distance, his distraction, and his hands-off caring; as well as a certain sort of romantic connection which was not spoken. I have read that a girl must have her father's grounded love and attention in order to understand her own value and be able to set healthy limits. This (obviously!) I lacked. But I felt safe with his integrity. (Another version of this story is also heard in the family: in this one, the birth of his first girl – me – showed my father that he did not in fact suffer from this family tendency to pedophilia. He felt at ease with me, and as lustless as with his sons. He just didn't touch any of us – or our mother, come to that. It just wasn't how he lived.)

And yet, my little sister, who had the same father, turned out very differently – able to sustain long, loving relationships.

Everybody's different.

More Silly Arguments

For now, though, Anando and I continued as a fairly harmonious duo. Once, in Poona, he walked behind me down the steps from the architects' office (which was now upstairs opposite Mariam Canteen). I was wearing a slim knit skirt and a loose top, and when we reached the walkway he said to me, "Madhuri, you are a *dark woman.*" (Apparently in Germany this is a compliment, meaning deep.) And I found his big solid presence so comforting and stabilizing.

But both of us did have moments when irritation with the other peaked. I am not very good at arguing (though he did once say to me quite disgustedly, *"You have an answer for everything!"* I know it was difficult for him, to have conversations with me – when English wasn't his native language. I can only imagine how frustrating that would be!) But once I complained that he didn't put any sort of cover on the pre-war down duvets he had inherited; that they must be dirty; and that when he shook them to fluff the feathers around before settling them on a bed, the feathers got out and floated around and I was horribly allergic to them. (He did the same with down sleeping-bags in the mountains – he called them "done" bags, rhyming with 'cone.' When he was shaking a done bag, he was glowing with complacent satisfaction at the goodness of the thing. In a small tent, the shook-about down was enclosed and I was even more allergic.)

He said the feathers couldn't get out, because the seam was sewn up.

I said they could, and did.

He said they couldn't. He was getting angry now.

I picked up a quilt and showed him the seam – tiny curled feathers, with pointy quills, working their way out between the stitches. He had nothing to say to this, but it pissed him off anyway.

In Poona we saw funny movies in Meera Barn – a wonderful thing to do of an evening, everyone lying on mattresses covered with fresh pink sheets, laughing, cuddling. You could buy terrible, shrunken, seedy, greasy Indian popcorn in little bags, and I loved to crunch it while watching. Anando asked me solemnly to stop doing this, as the crunching disturbed him. To me this was as preposterous as asking somebody to stop praying in church.

We had an argument about which is stronger, water or rock. I said water, because it can wear rock away. He said that was stupid: it is the tiny fragments of rock in the water that do the work. I said that water has weight, and mass, and, over a million years, it can do the job. He said it couldn't. (We were really arguing about male vs. female energy, but this wasn't said.)

In the mountains he pitched our little tent on a slight slope. I told him – what my mother always taught us – you don't pitch a tent on a slope. Because you can't sleep on a slope; you will slowly roll downhill in the night and end up in a pile by morning.

He said this was stupid. That he had always pitched tents on slopes, and it was no problem. "I *won't sleep* on a *slope!*" I insisted. "Zere is nossing wrong vis sleeping on a slope!" he insisted back. We slept in the slopey tent, and by morning everything, and us, had rolled to the bottom. But he wouldn't hear a word about it.

It seemed that our cultural realities were very different. When we'd stayed at the house of a friend of his in Bavaria, I'd found a book about the WWII concentration camps. I'd shown it to Anando, and he became angry. He said he'd been taught nothing about any of this in school (he grew up in East Germany, and escaped with full scary drama when he was twenty-four). He didn't want to know about it now.

We boarded a plane together. My carry-on bag weighed at least 20 kg (stones, books). This mighty Viking did not want to lift it into the overhead bin for me – "It is *your* responsibility!" Women also should not have doors opened for them, coats held up for them. ...But I *like* these things, within reason!

He also got angry at me, at various times, for:

○ Laughing really a lot while reading P.G. Wodehouse, reclining in an upper bunk in a 2nd-class AC train carriage traveling north through India.

○ Lying in the bathtub in Beewild, his country house in Germany, (I named it) reading magazines – for two hours.

○ While getting off the Enfield in the mountains, my bootlace widgets –

the metal thing the laces pass under – scraping across the seat of the bike and scratching it badly.

...And various other things. (It makes me laugh now. It didn't then.)

Break-Up

He fell out of love with me in 1993, when we were in Germany. One morning he wanted to make love, but I was full of a letter I wanted to write, and I took a risk: I said no to him, and went off to scribble while stretched out on the beautiful blue bathroom carpet. When the letter was done I came back to bed, ready and willing; but he had closed to me. We never made love again.

I was distraught, howling and weeping for a week while we drove, for some reason, to a hotel in Switzerland, and down into Italy; and he remained cheerful and stoic.

Driving into Italy I got a punnet of plums from a roadside stand. I briefly cheered up while we drove up, up, up a long winding road into the hills... and I amused myself by tossing the plum pits one by one out of the car window, where they could fall freely from that great height (I have always liked throwing things off of things). He asked me to stop doing this – "One might hit somebody on the head, down below."

Party pooper! Now I had *nothing.*

Back in Poona, we ended up one day doing a beautiful meditation I'd heard about, which somehow released me: in his house, with his consent, I put a large pillow on the floor. He sat nearby. Then, facing the pillow, but facing away from him, I began to hit the pillow with both hands clasped together, starting with the arms raised and bringing them down again and again – yelling, *"YOU FUCKING BASTARD – YOU WON'T FUCK ME – GOD DAMN, THIS HURTS, I HATE YOU, YOU BIG POWER-TRIPPING BULLY!!!"* etc. etc... then finally just sounds, gibberish. I really went into it, letting the feelings come up out of my belly, my feet, letting the release into the pillow feel so good – and I said whatever my truth was to that pillow, no longer afraid of being somehow mowed down – because I was facing away from him, I could have the courage.

Afterwards I lay down on my belly for a while... and I could feel that this method was brilliant – there was compassion in the room. Anando was not on the defensive. He had sat there quietly, had been present, had *heard.* And a new understanding arose in me: power does not really mean "I am bigger than you, therefore I have the power." That was how I'd been living: he had the power, he was bigger, I'd been mowed down.

Instead, I saw that power means one thing: truth. I had expressed my truth, stood in it. It might not have been spiritually correct, and it was not coming from a big body, I had no weapon either. But I had contacted my truth and had said it aloud. That was all I needed. I was at peace now. Power just means, "This is my truth." It can be spoken in a normal voice, it just has to connect with the inner.

And even if one was punished for it – which I was not – one still had the quiet power and satisfaction of truth.

Next, I had discovered the amazing beauty of *conscious and safe catharsis* in a relationship. When you take a step towards careful, conscious behavior, the universe seems to take ten steps towards you; and it was just so brilliant to see how even anger can be constructive instead of destructive, if you don't use it to abuse the other with, but own it as your intrinsic responsibility.

We all need safe, simple ways to take a good emotional poo without doing it in the other's lap. One feels so much better!

And so that day I cracked the code of that relationship. That day I was freed. I no longer needed the bond as it had been.

After that, we became really good friends. (He said later that he'd broken up with me because it was just time for the relationship to end; he felt it had run its course. But I always suspected that it was because my breasts weren't big enough to fill his huge hands!)

A Dream I Ignore

This was a wild, frolicsome time in the ashram. Festivals had taken on a new colorfulness, with costumes, stilt-walkers, and live music on every hand. But things moved fast in other ways too – many sannyasins left around this time and went to Lucknow, where a guru called Poonja-ji was giving Satsang. The attraction seemed to be that you could get enlightened just sitting with him – that's what people said. I did not go; I had a couple of dreams about him though, very clear and real, where I was flying around in the air near him, full of a loving, mysterious bliss. It was difficult to ignore the dreams, and stay with my life in Poona; the draw was very strong. But I reasoned that I had always been monogamous spiritually – there had only ever been Osho for me – and I did not want to disturb that. It might be the only time I deliberately ignored such a 'message' dream.

Three Dreams

In October 1993, I was in Hamburg, working at the Osho center, a huge, rambling place in the midst of the city. I led a sort of 'house-healing' for the whole complex, involving a parade of all the residents through the property, in costumes, some playing musical instruments. I used in the healing: epsom salts, Aura Somas, sage oil, Tibetan bells, and my personal brand of ferret-ing-the-old-bad-vibes-out by tuning in, entering and becoming, expressing… And, once the ghosts and bad vibes were transformed and satisfied, and had left of their own volition, we would move to the next room, or stairway, or hall. It was a lively, noisy process, ultimately exhausting for me; but everyone enjoyed it greatly. During that visit I also gave sessions, and there was soon to be an esoteric fair.

I was sleeping in a little room at the back of the huge building. Early one morning, I woke from a curious dream. My old schoolfriend Taffy, from whose house my father used to collect me every school-day after his work, lived in a frame bungalow on a corner in a tree-lined street. In the dream, there was a dead tree in her front yard, and in its bare branches stood a large black panther.

I have an excellent, very reliable method of deciphering dreams. There is nothing intellectual about it; no book is needed. In fact, dream-decoding books tend to be silly: there is no universal code for the imagery one finds in dreams. Each dream has its own code, and each person has her own in the moment. So each dream needs to be understood by the dreamer, in that particular instance only. This is easily done: when you wake up from a notable dream, simply get out of bed, step out of 'you,' move the consciousness over into one of the dream symbols: a wardrobe, a character, a cat, a meadow… and become it. Just experience the thing. It will unfold, give its energy back to consciousness. You will then know what it is, wholly and completely. And in the process, you will be working on the dream; finding its message to you, getting the benefit of it. The symbol dissolves, the energy is given back to you, conscious. Repeat for all the symbols, and then for the dream at large: step into a space called 'meaning of the whole dream.' Receive the Knowing. Then step back into 'you.'

But once in a very long while there will be a dream for which this doesn't work. After experiencing the symbol, you are none the wiser. In such a case, it must then be considered that this dream might belong to a different category. For there are wish-fulfilling dreams, and heavy-dinner dreams, and erotic-release dreams, and dreams with messages about how you're going wrong, or right… all of these quite decipherable. But some dreams are different: they might be psychic, future-predicting, warnings, or dreams for someone else. Or something like the equation-on-fire dream my father had, with an answer in it that comes from a mysterious place.

I could not find out what that panther meant. Or the bare tree.

The next morning, 21st October, I had another dream:

I am trying to get onto a bicycle. Spread out beside me is an enormous city square, quite deserted except for two policemen way over on the far side. I try and try to get onto the bike, but I keep falling off. Finally I have an epiphany: "It's okay to fall off the bicycle!" And I begin to laugh, in some big sense of relief; and the policemen also begin to laugh, in quite a kindly way.

This dream too I could not decipher.

The next early morning, a third dream arrived:

My father had, at long last, made a clear success of something: he'd acquired a piece of lawny property, and had had a great hole dug in it, that was to be a swimming pool. I am delighted – now I can invite my friends for a swim! It all seems so pleasant and relaxing. I am so happy that he has succeeded at something at last!

I woke from this dream, too, none the wiser.

Two days later, a message reached me, from my younger brother in California. Nobody in the family had known exactly where I was, and they'd had to track me down. My father had one afternoon been working on equations on the rotation of antimatter in galaxies. At 6 p.m. he had remarked to my brother Robbie that he was going to go take a nap.

He never woke up.

Robbie didn't know what to do, so he went and found two policemen.

They came to the trailer with him and were very kind. They all sat in the kitchen together for a long time.

I was in shock. I had not yet in my life experienced the death of someone I loved.

I was supposed to be giving sessions in the esoteric fair, but instead I sat stunned, now and then eating a spoonful of peanut butter from the jar – the only food I could manage. My father had been a great love, with whom there was almost no communication. (I was so incredibly grateful for the three days we'd spent together in Keeler, when we'd been able to talk! I can't imagine the loss without that.)

The dreams gave me peace. There is something bigger than us all, connecting us… The panther had been a warning, an announcement. Falling off the bicycle was Glen's letting go into a place beyond the body. (It turned out that I dreamt this just about the time that he was leaving his body.) The policemen, of course, were the ones my brother found. And the swimming pool… at first I thought that this must mean his patrimony, his inheritance of grace beyond death. That that was the thing he'd finally succeeded at.

There was a funeral three days later. I could not get to California that fast; I said I would come to the memorial at Thanksgiving, the month after. While the funeral was going on (a hundred people went – he was much-loved) I meditated, and saw that he had flown out of his body, very surprised to find that he still existed; that all was not simply blackness and void. He visited his own funeral and saw the people there – and he thought, "My daughters were right after all! There *is* something after death!"

The memorial was held in Saline Valley, which is separated from Death Valley by the Panamint mountain range. This was my father's favorite place; he'd had a sort of shack there, where he spent much time. There is a hot-springs in Saline Valley, where the family used to go when I was a child, and soak (wearing clothes of course) and look at the stars. My oldest brother Rudra had called this a 'star-watery mungle.' There was a spring just beside the pool hot enough to cook an egg in. Glen had told us with joy that it came from a place so deep it could not be measured.

People had streamed in to the memorial, staying in campers and tents – family, friends, kindly desert neighbors, admirers of my father. My old school friends, Taffy and Karen, were there. A couple of poor souls drank whiskey and got in the hot-springs pool and then had to get out and throw up. But mostly the crowd was sober and decorous and respectful.

Afterwards I was taken to see Glen's grave, in a small cemetery at the edge of Keeler. There was desert all round about, but the cemetery was green and grassy. A pepper tree overhung part of it. The sky was always blue. Behind us, the full mass of the Sierra Nevada raised itself skywards, topped with snow.

And I understood: *this* was the lawny place where he had bought property. It looked just the same – the hole I saw in the dream was his grave.

I sat on his grave… there was no headstone yet, just a slightly sunken area. I closed my eyes… Where was he? Was he okay?

I was shown that he had taken a great leap in consciousness at his death; just as I had seen when I meditated during his funeral-time. A surprised joy was in him. All was well… and, in a strange way, it was as if Osho, whom my father had mistrusted absolutely, had still managed to communicate something through Sarita and me. Something about the Mystery.

An Ill-Advised Liaison

I was back in Poona. One night a few months after Anando and I separated, I was roaming around the ashram and met a young man. It was dark; we were passing each other on a little path between some bushes. Something made us stop… two bug-eyed hunters in the bush. We could not really see each other, but we spent the night together.

He was a fantastic, unselfish, romantic lover… and only the next morning I realized I didn't actually *like* him, or his looks, or his conversation. But we were both hooked; we could not stay out of bed. (I don't recommend this relating style.) There followed one and a half years of unpleasantness. We spent time in his native Switzerland, experimenting with meditating together, in a borrowed house high above a lake. This was where I learnt another lesson: physical pleasure, without heart, deliberately extended to a period of forty-five minutes, becomes nausea, and a rejection of intimacy, lasting days. I don't need to elaborate…

I have heard Osho say that it is better for your spirit to be with somebody who doesn't love you than to be with somebody that you don't love. I was now going to have the chance to meditate on this at length. We'll call him S.L., for Swarmy Lover.

The School of Mysticism Relocates

The School of Mysticism, to my great sadness, left Poona and moved to Sedona, Arizona. Before leaving, Wadud and Waduda gave each of us Mystic Ringers a beautiful pendant of Osho marble*, a long narrow rectangle with a ruby on it – the ruby was for navigating the struggles of the World, particularly with money.

I didn't want to leave Poona, so didn't seriously contemplate moving to Sedona. But some of the School groups continued, led by others; so that was good. I participated in and helped in women's groups, dancing groups; heart chakra groups; I led a dream group. And I went on giving session after session, exhaustive, lengthy, deep. And somewhere in me, the *noticing* of Sedona, Arizona was there: a pull, a longing, a fear of Missing; a sense of mild betrayal. But Poona was home.

Travail in Tokyo

Sarita had been working at a healing center in Tokyo for two months a year. She wanted to discontinue this – it was a grueling place to work – so that she could instead periodically work in Europe with her then-boyfriend. She asked me if I'd like the job.

During each of the next five autumns I spent two months in Japan. For the first four of those I was at the aforementioned center, accompanied by Ma Deva Leena, a Danish Colorpuncturist and Cranio-Sacral practitioner, who also did Aura Soma. We were worked half to death, in classic Japanese style (there is a word, *karoshi*, "too-much-working-death." It is considered an honorable way to go).

Japan is like no place else on earth, and it was as if I'd found myself on the moon. The spatial sense is different – I'd kept crashing my bike into bollards and curbs till I'd gotten used to it. Taxi drivers wear white gloves and put clean white lace covers on their cab-seats. Taxi doors open by themselves. Even the man who tends the parking garage wears white gloves and bows to each customer who enters. Public toilets play woodland-stream sounds to cover the embarrassing other noises that might

* Beige-ish marble which had been dug, at Osho's orders, out of the walls of his room in order to make space for a planned renovation. He has said that marble holds the energy of the Buddha for 2000 years. Many people, including myself, ended up making jewelry out of it.

ensue. Toilet seats are heated, and toilets have computerized control panels so that you can spray water on yourself (or on your face, if you can't read Japanese). It is noble to kill yourself if you feel humiliated. Women refuse to have dishwashers because then they would not be working hard enough. (They also wear two pairs of panties at once, I discovered while applying Colorpuncture!) The English language is used for decorative purposes without its sense being comprehended. The damn Earth under you shakes almost every day, lightly, like somebody shaking dry leaves off his shoulders. It's a strange place.

We stayed in a bare-bones, dark, funky little flat nearly two hours away from the healing center. Each day we had to bicycle, then take two trains, then walk another twenty minutes to work. The flat belonged to the center's owner, and was in a poor district, where cats without tails sat about on metal porches, and fleas hopped before front doors waiting for people-ankles and cats. The bathroom was tiny, molded out of plastic; the sink right above the toilet, the bathtub deep and extremely short, so that you sat in it with your knees up under your chin, like an ancient burial. A vile sewer smell came up out of toilet and drains at all times. We used to come home exhausted after our long commute and then take turns sitting in the bathtub – I'd often prop my dinner on my knees and eat it there, unable to wait.

The center leader, whom we'll call D., was a night person, so we started late and finished late. Often we'd have to sleep over at the center as it was too late to go home. On one occasion a typhoon was going on – autumn is typhoon season, so we were often treated to exciting commutes dodging flying random umbrellas while slopping through minor floods – and I was sleeping in the upstairs session room. I woke in the night under a cold waterfall! The wind had wrested off the skylight door, and I was right under it!

This was at least refreshing; sleeping in the same room where you've given sessions all day is like bathing in your own sweat, and some stranger's sweat as well.

We didn't really have breaks – the next client was always waiting – so we'd have to shovel in a bit of food standing up and then go back to the battlefield. The clients had traveled so far to come there (Tokyo is unimaginably huge) that they wanted two-hour sessions. I was doing Colorpuncture, Kirlian readings, past life sessions, chakra readings, etc… empathing away. Japanese conditioning does not allow for honest emotional expression (if you are ill, overworked, insomniac, frustrated, and wretched with depression you have to giggle when you recount this). Therefore, clients don't give back resonance to the therapist. As a practitioner, you don't know how much you depend on facial signals and the like to reassure you that you are going in the right direction. Without this, the unfortunate tendency is to keep trying harder and harder. And still… nothing much seems to be happening. Soon, I was getting very tired. But if we wanted any days off we had to fight for them tooth and nail.

Here's how Leena and I let off steam:

○ Laughing ourselves silly, in our exhaustion, at strange signs on the subway: an ad for mushroom chewing gum: **Vits. A, B, C, D, Champignon!** On a t-shirt: **Girth of a Vagrant.** On another t-shirt: **Normative Sections of Standard.** Another: **Laughter Fills Hesitation Brightly Everywhere.** On a tissue package, with a photo of a two kittens: **Kitty's Short Life.** On a bottle of some hair product: **NUDY Hard Stiff Hair Water Milk.** An ad for something, I don't know quite what: **O.D. on bourgeoisie MILK BOY MILK**! On a drinking-straw package: *"Let's try homeparty fashionably and have joyous talk with nice fellow!"* And, on our walk from Kichijohji Station to the center, we'd pass a shop selling nice conservative clothes for matrons. Each item had a cat appliqued on it somewhere, and on many an apron or sweater it said, **What could be more purrrfect than the nicest little cat-house in Nevada?** (Somebody was having a good laugh somewhere! Or not?)

○ Eating green tea ice cream from the health food shop.

○ Shopping. There is great shopping in Japan – the artistry, delicacy, quality, refinement, imagination, of items – astonishing. I still have, and use, boots, hats, socks, etc., bought on those trips. (There was one department store I favored where I could get a cup of delicious tea in a little tea-nook after I'd rushed all over the five floors hunting and basking in variety. The sweet, trim waitress would bring the tea in a pot with a bamboo strainer beside it, and ask me in her little high voice, "Coo-kie, o der pound-o cake-u?")

And then… our sanity was saved by going to see Kohrogi-san, the healer whom Champaka had brought to Poona.

Usually we'd manage to do this twice during a tour of duty. It was a long, complicated bus trip through the labyrinthine city – but oh, when we arrived and were welcomed into the simple room where his treatment table stood, and all was aromatic from the smoke of the incense – and our friend/colleague Champaka was there to translate – we exhausted would-be healers could finally let go and receive.

We could ask a question; and Mr. Kohrogi would hold our feet for a moment, then turn to his nearby table and light the two incense sticks… the sheaths of the holders would be placed over the sticks, and then the instruments would be moved deliberately, seeingly, over the body, pausing here and there to apply a moment of pressure – shoulders, back, soles of feet. And at some point he'd say something, which Champaka would translate.

And we'd come away refreshed, relaxed, and transported, with something to ponder over.

At different times, he told me: "You are only to *play* from morning till night." And, "If you go on working like this, your body will be destroyed, and you could even die."

I understood this to mean, "If you go on working this hard… " and I kept on, for everybody knows that working too hard is laudatory, really, don't they? Only later did I understand that he had meant, "If you go on working with this technique… " (empathing). (I had myself wondered whether this technique was okay, but had been reassured when I'd seen a printout of a darshan where Osho had told a doctor, Indivar, that he could allow the client's illness to pass through his own body, harmlessly: "Just for a moment you will feel it, and then it will be gone." But he'd said that to Indivar; not to me. And I'd never asked him about it myself.)

The center leader, D., was boisterous and volatile.* The premises were dirty – D. pled bad eyesight – and the finances needed arguing over. Translators, fed up with being called at 2 a.m. for a session next day, quit in droves. It was not a relaxing place to work.

Champaka wanted to take me on a three-day holiday up to the mountains at Morioka; three hours away on the bullet train. After *much* struggle I was allowed to go. (Champaka is an impossibly handsome man, with incredibly thick hair {now, it's white and looks even more striking.} He's well-meaning and giving – he once came over to the stinky flat and made beautiful soups for me when I was briefly ill. He is a student of Kohrogi-san as well as being his translator.)

And so at the station I got a *bento* box (a rectangular box made of thin wood in which are several compartments holding delicious comestibles: rice, vegetables, pickle, a rice ball wrapped in seaweed, or what-have-you; as well as chopsticks) for a very civilized lunch onboard, and got onto the train for

* I once overheard her on the phone to her boyfriend, complaining loudly, "You say you ruv me! Then why you fuck Kolean?" (The Japanese don't like the Koreans for some reason, or no reason.)

the mountains. I enjoyed the train – it went 300 miles an hour, yet seemed almost not to move at all. Champy met me in the piney mountain town, and we walked to the house where we would stay, with some friends of his, a sweet young couple. The wife gave us rice balls – *onigiri* – for breakfast; sticky rice with a salted umeboshi plum in the center, wrapped in nori. This is a very good breakfast! We'd munch them while walking on the road among the trees.

We went to an *onsen* – hot springs. Ahhhhh…* I adorned my body with large wet leaves – they stayed on nicely – and Champaka took pictures at my behest.

But the most amazing thing happened unexpectedly…

Tamo-san

Our hosts said that Tamo-san, the tiny enlightened lady on whose head Osho had showered rose petals, was in town, and we could go and sit with her if we liked. We liked!

We walked out of the village along a narrow road to a little valley all filled with wildflowers among the long grasses. It was an Alpine heaven. There was a little wooden house set in a meadow by itself. We knocked and were welcomed in by a young woman. The house was traditional, charming – wooden beams, paper inner walls that slid back to open out rooms, or slid forward to enclose them. There were perhaps fifteen people there, sitting in a living room, and we took our places on high cushions facing the front. Everyone grew silent, going inside themselves, waiting. Tamo-san had not yet come in.

Then she entered from another room… a tiny kimono'd figure in high *geta* sandals. And the whole room changed – it was as if I had been served back to myself. Tears began coursing down my cheeks – and I understood all at once how *exhausted* I was – how *finished* – and that this was *not healthy.*

Tamo-san then began to sing. Her voice was high; the tune atonal, strange to Western ears. As she went on singing in Japanese I felt a waterfall rushing down before me, inside me… I could see it, feel it. I was looking at a waterfall, in a deep forest; and my tears poured too… I was in touch with me, and the rift healed there, for that time, with her.

* I remembered Wadud saying that these were a trial for him because the Japanese men had heard that all Western men had large penises, and so they'd kept on staring at his.

When she had stopped singing, the session was over, and the meditators rose and began to move out of the room. I told Champaka about the waterfall vision. "But – she was singing about a waterfall!" he exclaimed.

A late lunch was served at a long table in the next room – vegetables, tempura, rice, soup; many pretty and delicious dishes. Tamo-san sat next to me. I noted with interest that she had a sort of rebellious air about her. She had no English, but she spoke to me anyway in Japanese; Champaka translated. But she just said the same thing, over and over, emphatically, till Champaka was tired of translating it again and again! I had no idea what she meant, then nor now… she just went on tapping her own collarbone with her finger and looking at me quite fiercely and saying, "Your *bone* is like *mine!* Your *bone* is like *mine! Your bone is like mine!*"

After lunch we all went outside to take pictures, gathered amongst the wildflowers in the late afternoon; and as we stood there, first one and then another person snapping the group with their cameras, I saw an extraordinary thing.

There were high hills rising up a few miles away, darkening with evening. And suddenly a bright light rose up from one of them – went ZIG then ZAG – then ZIG again – up – up – then *shot* off into the sky and vanished.

I don't know what that was either – but certainly the ambiance of that uncanny afternoon seemed at the root of it, whatever it was.

Because I was selling my own jewelry designs, in semiprecious stones, my income in Japan was twice what it would otherwise have been. Of course, the selling of them was not simple – I had to tune in with each piece the person was interested in, together with the person's energy as they held it in their hands. (If it didn't feel good and appropriate, they couldn't buy it.) This required every crevice of time not spent in sessions or a very brief spate of food-shoveling. By the time my eight-week stint was done, I had made a good chunk of change, less my rent and food and shopping. This had to last many months of course, but in India that was easy. I had no bank account – and in any case I had to repay my jeweler for his work – so saving money wasn't a thing that seemed possible. (It would have felt strange anyway. We lived in the moment, not an imaginary future.)

An elderly client I loved and greatly admired, Goto-san, had been growing more and more serene over the weeks of his Colorpuncture sessions; while I, the supposed healer, had been draining and collapsing by the day. I mentioned to him the irony of this; and during my last week there he took me first to a department store and let me choose a silky, luxurious black sweater; and then out to dinner at a fancy French restaurant. There were many stately courses, each of which seemed to be some raw squidgelly morsel from under the sea, sitting lonely on an enormous plate. I reveled in the restfulness, even as I was pitching forward with exhaustion. Thank you, Goto-san.

When I was leaving finally, I was a hollowed-out husk, barely able to get myself to the airport bus. It was a depletion far deeper than that brought on by hepatitis. It seemed to be a draining of my every resource, my very soul, almost. I had actively, totally, empathed through the days and weeks without surcease (except for the blessed break in the mountains). I was *done.*

The bus wended its way to the airport through the endless city, with its streets full of box hotels with names like 'Hotel Tomato.'

I went to the toilet at the back of the bus for a pee. On the wall was a little red plastic plaque with an emergency button on it. The sign said CALL BUZZAR.

So I took out my metal nail file and scratched a 'D' at the end.

A Present for My Mother

In Bangkok I joined S.L., the young man I didn't love, and we took a bus south, riding all one long night through while loud Thai Bollywood-style wailing played over the loudspeaker. A ferry took us to the island of Koh Phi Phi, where we stayed in a pleasant, isolated guesthouse close to the beach.

Insecurity made S.L. arrogant; weariness made me intolerant; but in that place we did not squabble – the heat and damp were enervating, my exhaustion too profound. We walked on shady tracks though the jungle, dodging grass-green snakes mimicking reedy plants by standing almost on their tails, their tiny heads waving slightly; we dodged imprecations hurled from trees by monkey tribes; we swatted at the vicious no-see-ums. But mostly we hung out in the salty bath-warm surf where none of the above ventured; and it was here one evening that I saw the most incredible sunset of my life.

It was not a sunset in the normal course of such things – a molten red sky in the west, or some love-pink shadings on mountain snows. This was a whole production – a silent opera, a Northern Lights mixed with strawberries and cream; an entire wardrobe of royal finery laid out on the bed of the sky for inspection. The colors of masterpieces, the purity of altitude, the palette of cloud and flower, stream and rock, blood and jewel, night and dawn, grass and thunder, all lavished at once on one purling, changing, timeless unfolding display.

I got out of the water and lay on my back on the beach, and my companion did the same at a little distance, and for eons we were ploughed under, drowned, mesmerized like women beneath a goodly lover – challenged and sated, covered and uncovered and transformed.

There were clouds full of smoky, inky depth – edged by silver dancing-shoe light – backed by olive transparency – alongside spring leaf – nearby grape satin – laid with paths of garnet, peridot, and tourmaline crushed like wine. Lion color and brass shone in curved swoops like garden edgings. Cloaks of color were swathed slowly over us and then pulled away. The curtains of the sky went on drawing back and showing other scenes behind them – enough dancing dresses for a vanished world of lissome girls, a hue to flatter each complexion – enough colors to furnish an entire planet with everything it needs.

I had seen these same nourishments, these substances, in black Hawaiian pearls – in grey ones – in pink ones – in stones of every sort under my joyous gaze on a jeweler's back room table in India. In the bottom of a mountain stream over lucent rock at 17,000 ft. in the Himalayas, and the springy grass beside the stream as well. In the coats of the sheep there, and the rich old dyes of the shawl the shepherd wore, as well as in the new garish dyes in the wool in towns lower down. Pink like Hawaiian hibiscus rang there, and changed to sea-coral, and flame.

Night beckoned from the black core of a cloud and yet always the sky behind showed fields of clearest blue topaz, softly assertive as mid-morning, spread behind everything, fluid as water.

I think my mouth fell open – I could not absorb it all any other way. I think I drank it with my skin.

Next day I ventured through clean sea up to my shoulders out to a tiny island, perhaps the size of a large suburban house and yard. It wasn't far; and it was irresistible. Trees grew on its hillocky middle; it was composed all of white sand. I went there alone, leaving S.L. back on the beach, and I poked happily about looking at shells, rocks. (The flotsam of broken flip-flops and plastic bottles and so on that lined the high water line on Koh Phi Phi was strangely absent here.) There was a sort of shell I kept seeing pieces of – one side was a rich, deep orange, pitted like a Mediterranean wall weather-blasted over centuries; the other side smooth and pearly cream-white.

And then I saw it, just over there – and leant down and picked it up – a rectangle of this stuff but with rounded edges, about the size of a large cat pawprint but narrowed at the sides, with a proper hole worn into it at the top, just exactly right to put a gold ring in, to suspend it from.

And so I took it back to our bungalow and put it in my suitcase and carried it back to India, and there I took it to Shree Jewellers, and sat on the other side of the table from him, and showed him what I wanted done.

Later that year I flew to America and saw my mother. I gave her a small padded bag, in a tawny silk, and she opened it, saying "Oh?" hesitantly. And she held the necklace on her worn hand, her work-tired hand, the puffy hand that had always aroused my pity and my love – a hand, with cracked fingers, fed up with labors it had no true use for; thoughtful in the bliss of truthfulness it found in scrawling a poem in lyrical loops; scrubbing the top of the purring cat's head with her fist (that cat had loved her brusqueness). The hand swollen by lymph from that long-ago butchery she'd undergone. That hand wondering when, when it would ever be free.

Then she held the necklace up, and we both gazed at it in awe.

It was a long rope of pink natural pearls, irregularly shaped, each about the size of a cherry blossom bud; depended from it was a wide hasp of glossy, satiny gold with the shell swinging gently from it. The sheen of the shell's white back was… royal, glad, velvety. The terracotta of the rough front was commandingly colored so deeply orange it was like the best of the robes we'd worn in Poona One. It was the epicenter of a desert-rock star. Those pearls... they glowed beige, cream, apricot, ballerina – many shades are held in that small word 'pink.'

My mother said, "These pearls… are of course… *plastic?*" And my heart broke inside my chest as if a yolk broke inside an egg. For she had survived the Depression, and so much more subsequent want and worry and wretchedness, and she could not imagine genuine pearls – in *her* hands.

"No, Mom, they're real!" I said.

And she put the necklace on, and the pendant came to just below her breastbone. And those pagan pearls with their tameless shape glowed on her and picked up the wild love she'd always had for nature – the wildflower bunches, rocks brought home from hikes and placed on the altar she always made in every house she lived in.

And I think now of a photo of her, from when she was sixteen. It's black and white of course so you can't see that her hair was auburn, perfect for the gold and cream of the necklace; nor can you see the profile of her bold Roman nose; but you can see the innocence of her full lips and questioning eyes – and, if you know her, you can find hidden the innocence of her innate rebellion.

And how nature echoes it! – wild, bringing shells to beaches, and mosquitoes and swearing primates to jungles, and daughters to tramp the world, and bring her mangoes couched in stone.

Violence

Perhaps a year had gone by of this uneasy relating between S.L. and myself. He was a wiry little guy with a narrow face and a long black ponytail, and in one of his earlobes he wore a choice emerald set in platinum – he'd been something successful, back where he'd come from. He was esoteric-minded, clever, and the most devoted, willing, swarmy lover, who gazed at me in the night with huge flowery eyes; trying to pack me with *meaning.* He'd given me the kind of prone goddess-worship Anando hadn't liked to do, and that therefore for five years I'd done without – the kind involving a warm, wet patient tongue. He himself had had just a few lovers, but he said that each of them had agreed that he got it right.

But he was otherwise tetchy, with a spurious sense of privilege; and he could *sulk* like the veriest teenager that ever lived. If he didn't get his way, he'd withdraw outside the gates and smoke a graceless fag, drawing on it quickly, in anger, defying me to disapprove.

One night we were in bed in my room in the Pyramid. He *really* wanted to have drawn-out carnal relations, and I really did not. I turned on my side and went to sleep.

Suddenly I was wrenched into wakefulness by a terrible impact on my face – first one side, then the other – *whap, whap, whap, whap!*

The hideous little twerp was slapping me in my sleep!

I sprang up – standing on the bed, then leaping to the stuffed chair by the wall. I pointed at the door, and, summoning the Black Goddess, bellowed, *"GET OUT OF HERE! OUT! OUT!"*

He left; I heard him negotiating with the gate guard to let him out the big gates (which were always locked at night, to keep out marauding townsfolk).

In the morning I reported to Garimo what had happened – she was at that time in charge of the Multiversity. The upshot of it was that S.L. and I each had to have therapy, separately – and were not to see each other for six weeks.

I was very grateful for all of this. (Violence was absolutely not tolerated in the Commune. Thank god.) Devapath, the therapist I went to, heard my story. Then he told me that I didn't need therapy – just a different boyfriend. I felt cheated – I was all psyched up for therapy! So I went home and gave it to myself: I lined up all my brothers (on pillows) and I dialogued with each of them (meaning, I talk to them, then sit on the pillow and *become* the brother and let him talk to me). Then, in the interests of thoroughness, I had each brother talk to each of the other brothers. With five brothers, this took a long time.

Then I went back to Devapath, and told him what I'd done.

"Nobody does this," he said flatly. "Nobody has ever done this!"

S.L. did not enjoy his therapy and would not ever tell me about it. (He didn't like his mother, so I drew my own vague conclusions.) He also had no remorse for what he had done to me.

Why did I go back to him? For I did... after the required six weeks; for a further uneasy time. Well might you ask.

Later he and I were in Lugano during the summer (he was very good at conjuring up nice places) and my old school friend Taffy visited. She and I had not seen each other for thirty years, and we talked without ceasing for three days, finding great nourishment in our chatter. S.L. grew jealous, and began engineering protests – for example, he picked the resident cat up by the scruff of its neck, because he knew I hated him doing this. (Taffy said, "That guy is a *pill.")*

We three went to see *Casino* together one evening. It was a horrible movie – the climax comes when a lot of mafiosos murder a lot of other mafiosos by deftly sticking plastic bags over their heads and shooting them; the plastic containing the gore, sort of. I had to cover my eyes and retch. S.L., though, sat rapt and took it all in.

Afterwards we all stood outside. Taffy was then working as a music editor for the movies, so she wasn't so affected by the special effects. But I was just icked out to the max! The nastiness of the film was in my body. So I reproached the young man, "Ugh! That was disgusting! How could you *watch* that?"

He just stood there and *smirked*... There was a secretive look on his face, like, *This is an Italian thing, a male thing, a really pleasurable thing you have to be part of the in-crowd to understand.*

My hand, of its own accord, just hauled off and slapped his skinny chops.

And he smirked some more.

The responsibility is mine. I should never have been with him. The relationship should never have begun. And, once begun, I should not have allowed it to continue. I didn't love that young man. I was with him for the wrong reasons – just a kind of icky-sticky, situational lust – nothing beautiful in it, nothing of the heart. And the elder in a pair has I think a greater responsibility, in a relating, to be wise.

I'm sorry, young man.

Flying Clothes

I had just come back to Poona from Japan again, so was well stocked with cash. S. L. and I enrolled in a channeling group taught by the gentle Italian Dharma Jyoti, held in a room in the Pyramids.

I met a man in the group – Swiss, long pointy nose, stocky, mostly bald. Something about the back of his neck, in front of me where I sat in the group, captivated me. My mother had said, long ago, that men with thick necks were gross and unsuitable for such intellectually refined women as we. Since then I had been intrigued by wide-ish, strong necks on men and had felt repelled by slender ones. (S.L. had a thin brown throat between his wide angular shoulders and his dark narrow head.)

I drew pictures in my notebook, of the Schweizer's back and neck. He looked sort of solid. I liked this. S.L. was twitchy and slidey and delicate (if determined as a badger), always complaining about his digestion. I didn't think men ought to complain about their digestions.

After the group finished I spent half a night with the Schweizer (I'll call him W.) He undressed me. Nothing else really happened. There were no buzzy ecstasies, no slottings-in-to-home. He told me he loved a fiery Spanish lassie.

Perhaps we did not even have sex – I simply, now, cannot remember. (Am I the only one with that problem? Surely not?)

Next day I met S.L. at lunch in Mariam, and told him where I'd been the previous night.

"But-a – " exclaimed that young Italian, "He-a is-a *BALD-a!*"

"So what?" I shrugged. "That is *masculine!*"

The young man swept his oily black locks away from his slim olive face with his slender hand. I was supposed to realize… *hair* is where it's at!

The pale W., with his leading nose and abstracted air, became an inexplicable focus for my dreams of love. He dodged me, he gave me nothing but polite phrases as his eyes wandered away, but I persisted – talked to him when I could find him. Finally he agreed to meet me in Zurich, where, coincidentally, we were both headed. He even said he'd meet my flight at the airport. (The Spanish woman's presence in his life I simply ignored.)

Then I went into a flurry of creative overdrive. I was consumed with visions of *clothes!* Clothes I would wear on the plane, so that he'd meet an elegant woman at the airport. Clothes I'd wear to bed, to lounge around in, to walk in, to dine in.

And I had the cash!

So my work in the Mystery School was punctuated with intense, bullet-fast yet thorough trips to M.G. Road. I knew all the cloth merchants of course; and I'd settled on my tailor, Mirajkar, underneath Wonderland Shopping Center, years before. I recruited a sad little man in glasses with a shop next to his as well – there were so many garments to make. My trousseau!

Mirajkar was my hero – a tall, round-bodied fellow with betel-red teeth and a sharp mind, he could be counted on to make up my designs, late – oh yes, very late – but with only a few trips' worth of corrections to harass him about. He 'got' my requirements, more often than not. My drawings he wrapped in the cloth I'd brought, and stowed the bundles amongst untidy piles of similar things behind the last sewing machine, or in a cupboard overhead. He employed several foldy-legged little men who sat all day stitching by hand or operating ancient treadle machines amidst the piles of floppy off-cuts of brocaded or sequinned and embroidered fabrics left over from rich ladies' garments.

I went for silk in a big way – the best cream satin-silk for a loose poet blouse with full gathered sleeves and real cotton lace (of the kind impossible to find in the West) at neck and frilled cuffs. I had a nightgown made of the same cloth and design, but coming down to the top of the instep. Nubbly raw silk tweed trousers in black and white with a wonderful slub feel. A full three-quarter-length skirt in royal blue silk with matching nipped-waist jacket. A glorious vivid-blue dress with a huge dirndl skirt to just above the ankles; dolman sleeves and an open collar; small in the waist. A dark-pink cotton one in the same design. And so on. My little closet stuffed itself with black velvet opera coats lined with satin, and a mellow cream aviator scarf, and a long vest of the most gorgeous hot magenta raw silk with a woven-in design that would have looked right in a mosque, with its sacred geometry. And a kelly-green velvet one, the same pattern.

The day came for me to fly. I dressed so carefully for the longed-for meeting… tweed trousers, black silk jacket, white blouse. My hair washed and done in a French braid. Black flats with a red dot at the toe, that pinched my foot rather, as M.G. Road shoes are wont to do.*

And, of course, W. was not at the Zurich Flughafen to meet me.

I waited three hours – of course I did – and then, in dismal mood, took a taxi to the flat where I was renting a room. And I phoned him. No answer.

Again.

Etc.

I finally got through to him next day. He mumbled some excuse and agreed to meet me at a street corner near the flat. I was a little cross by then, but gamely, hopefully, I bathed, lotioned my body, and dressed in another version of my best.

He didn't show.

Finally, on the phone that evening, he said he was waiting for the Spanish girl, who was difficult, but that was where his energy was.

Okay.

My birthday arrived, and S.L., who was now in Sedona, managed to have flowers delivered to me in Zurich, just in time for a dinner I had cooked that W. was missing by turning his back on me. (This too I have compassionately left out of *The Poona Poems.)*

And, bit by bit, I gave many of those clothes away. Not out of bitterness – how could I feel anything but covetous of such beauty? – but because of a general sense of just *having too much* – too many luxurious gorgeous clothes (I have so often felt this way about jewels, poems, paintings, as well). So I gave

* When I was shopping for black shoes, I'd complained to the salesman that I didn't like the red dot. "Oh well, when you get out on the street they will get all covered up with dust and dirt and stuff!" he'd reassured me.

the poet blouse to someone whose complexion suited it better. And I left a negligee set in Sedona with a friend, when I went there next (and broke up finally with the rather ferocious young man, for good and all).

And the way I thought about the episode was this: "What a pitiable, preposterous, absurd idiot I am! A junkie for love, to the extent that I'll waste masses of time, energy, money, *passion* – on a non-starter, an obvious non-match, a gap in the fabric of the Universe! How could I do such mind-blowingly moronic things? Must be that my Distant Father is behind it all; his unavailability dragging me into futile attempts to engage unwilling men. Oh, woe, woe is me. Oh well! Let's get up and go do something else now."

But just the other night I was sitting in Nelson's Wine Bar in Ivybridge Mills, in the north of England, at a little round table, with two lovely women. And we got into telling stories of crazy things we'd done for love.

One had left her husband and children in India, to fly to England to be with a man she'd met once. And the other had escaped a long, moribund, abusive marriage in a highly suspenseful style, to live on her own.

So I told my little tale of the clothes that arose in me, and failed in their mission; and flew away.

"What a romantic story!" cried the Indian woman. "That is *pure romance!*"

"It *is?*" I asked, amazed.

"Yes!" she cried.

And I pondered this. And my perspective shifted. And I saw myself in an additional light, if not an altogether alternative one.

For is not this the essence of romance: to make something beautiful, *whether anyone is there to appreciate it or not;* and then cast it to the winds? Not holding – not selling – not demanding anything in return. Not preserving. Like a dance or a song or a piece of music played to the skies: a lovely blouse is born in concentration and labor and the lilt and puff of dreams. It rests on a moving form for an afternoon. It goes on elsewhere. A song sings because it must – and then it's gone.

I am thinking that when we die, and we cannot take anything with us... we might respect those gestures, those moments, greatly – more so than the things we gathered, measured, held.

...Just perhaps.

The Much-Traveling Years

The next five years were more of the same exuberant, nerve-wracking intensity as the previous had been. Twice I bought round-the-world business class tickets – $2,400 in India – and set off for a couple of months of working here and there as well as visiting family and friends. I might land in Zurich – London – New York – California – Vancouver – Maui – and then on to Japan again. (I discovered that I relished arriving in a new place; and then relished leaving it too!) As well as this, I worked in New Zealand, Australia, Scandinavia, Germany. Like most of us, I went on visa turnarounds to Sri Lanka, Bangkok. I remember taking a boat ride way up the Rogue River in Oregon, where Devadasi and Bob had moved to... seeing a mama bear and cub on the bank, and huge eagles overhead. Dancing ecstatically to live Soul Music at a bar in Sedona, pulling out all the stops, letting my hair down. A strange holiday in Scotland where I got terrible flu and had to crouch in a B&B for days. An airy flat in Zurich where I worked hard and sold splendid jewels to a man who worked in a bank (everyone worked in a bank) and wore them under his clothes.

On one trip to Japan, I was leading a group at a resort in the mountains not far from Tokyo. I knew that Kaveesha was ill, that she had cancer in her spine. On the morning of 22nd October 1998, we were all lined up for a lavish buffet (D., the bumptious center-leader, was a great cook) including (I remember) black noodles made with squid-ink. And suddenly a wave of energy passed through my body, with a strange feeling around it... and I knew that Kaveesha had died. Later that day a fax arrived – it was true. This was the end of an era. She had some very worthy (and some not-so-worthy) people to carry on the particularly subtle, wise and heartful work she had done. But there was only one Kaveesha.

I managed at last to break up with S.L. We'd gone to visit the mystic artist Morris Graves in Northern California, and S.L. had been sulking and wouldn't get out of the car. Tall, owlish Morris had a way with young men, so he went and spoke with S.L., who finally came into the magical Zennish house, and sat and gloomed at nothing while Morris and my brother and I visited. I'd had enough, and when S.L. and I got to Sedona I managed to get away for good.

Sedona was beautiful, light and fine in vibration. I found the School well established, and enjoyed going to White Robe evenings there. I next embarked on a nonsensical relationship with a tall, troubled American with stiff black lashes and green eyes. He had no money, and after my next tour of duty in Japan I paid for him to come to Poona – he'd never been. When he arrived he right away went off me, and dived into Primal, which was just the thing. He said the fact that I'd paid his ticket meant I'd become his mother, so he wasn't attracted to me any more.*

Someone suggested that I look for my next boyfriend from my belly. So I sat in the Multiversity Plaza, a large, roofed circle of marble where were desks and posterboards, where you could find out about, and sign up for, groups and sessions; and I watched the guys. People moved through fast, or meandered, stopped, talked, hugged, moved on. Finally I noticed a rather hulking man, not very tall, with strong features and beautiful silky blond hair. My belly seemed to relax. I bent my right eyebrow at him just a tiny bit, and we ended up going to sit on a bench overlooking the park and talking. I read much later, in *The Male Brain*, that men are wired to spend the first few weeks of a new relationship bragging. It can take some time before they start to reveal their deeper insecurities. Fool that I am, I tended to believe the brags. This very sweet, expansive young Dutchman, C.B. (for Conan the Barbarian, whom he resembled), said, among other things, that he "had a house in Amsterdam." Good, I thought, I won't have to buy him any tickets! He's a solid guy. I liked his meaty hugs, his willingness to please, his grave childlike goodness. But my critical eye was also already finding fault: he ate cookies with his mouth open. His shape was not quite in the proportion that I wanted it to be. Things like that. I'm a finicky, nit-picky sort.

But soon I flew off to the North Island of New Zealand to work. It was my first time there, and I was shocked by how provincial it all was. The island was sparsely populated, and the people seemed very hard up for entertainment – that seemed to be why I was there. As a wandering therapist, I tended to see the underbelly of a country right away. In New Zealand it seemed that leftover Victorianisms still governed people's lives – sexual repressions and perversions, desperate ambitions and stiff lonelinesses. What also disturbed me was that, at least where I was staying, everywhere was private property, meaning

* He much later, in California, summoned epic willpower, worked very hard, and became wealthy.

that you couldn't go on lovely walks. I just walked beside the narrow highway. (I'm guessing the South Island is much more walkable.)

C.B., who was in Poona, fell into a funk, and sent me many faxes about it, which tended to be signed, *This Little Elvis.* This made my ears jiggle and a sneer come to the corners of my mouth.

An odd thing happened in New Zealand: I was staying in Auckland with some sannyasin women, in an unassuming little house on a suburban street. The women were talking about going to a Satsang with a sannyasin guy who had become enlightened. They told me his story: he was an awkward, grumpy man nobody liked. One day, he went to the beach… was sitting there… and, as he later put it, "My head fell off."

I had no intention of going.

But that night I had a dream: this fellow, whom I'd never met as far as I knew, was saying to me, "You've got a date with me!"

"No I don't!" I replied smartly.

"Yes you do! You've got a date with me!"

"No I don't!"

"Yes you do!"

So I went. The car drove way out into the dark countryside to a big house, where a large circle of people sat on the floor in the big living room. We joined them.

The enlightened guy (whose name I don't recall) sat with us for a while. The vibe was… real. Simple, but real.

Then we all stood in a circle and he said things to each person in turn. He scolded, reminded, admonished. When he got to me he said nothing – paused – and then continued on.

I felt that that was somehow good. For once I wasn't being admonished! I thought I must be doing okay. And New Zealand can feel excessively sleepy – it gave me the heebie-jeebies – so this peculiar interlude was tonic.

But actually I'd been going against myself again: before leaving Poona for this trip, I had been receiving Colorpuncture weight-loss points (done on the ears) as part of my education – experiencing what I was giving. I didn't need to lose weight – I was just trying out the treatment. But now I found that I was super-sensitive, couldn't stand most foods, and became weirdly transparent and very nervous. It was scary and uncomfortable. Eventually I had to use the opposite color (purple instead of yellow) on the points to block and reverse the treatment. I went around in that green North Island wearing green Colorpuncture glasses to try to calm things down. The color-reversal worked; but I was still very delicate and strung-out. It was a wake-up: don't do treatments you don't need!

What is Tantra?

I rendezvoused with C. B. in Goa, and we stayed in a shady, quiet guesthouse near the beach. We tried meditating together, but again it wasn't working. Meditating together was fine, but sex was same-old same-old. There wasn't any meeting happening in it that I found worth having. I didn't know what to do. C. B. had no idea either. He just kind of stared at me, eyes narrowed, mouth a little open, his red lips and cheeks full of health.

I both liked and sort of didn't like this guy – he was such a kindly soul, affable, moody, unsophisticated, given to hyperbole. Again, he was just too young for me, really. But he cheerfully slung my suitcases about wherever they needed to go – no complaining that they were my responsibility! In fact, he loved showing off his impressive muscles! I gave him sessions, a really silly thing to do – you don't therapise your lovers – and they seemed to have no effect. I thought he was just as clueless after as before.

One day he came back from picking up a fax, and great clouds of dejection were swimming around him. He got onto the bed, under the sheet, and pulled it over his head. Then he stayed there, crouched over like a great kneeling beast, mourning under the shroud. He wouldn't tell me what was wrong.

Finally, hours later, he emerged and told his tale: it turned out that when he'd informed me, at our first meeting in the ashram months before, that he "had a house in Amsterdam," he wasn't being entirely revealing of the truth. It had sounded to me as if he owned some nice skinny little stone pile by a canal, safe and sound as such a thing can be. But the fax (from C. B.'s angry father) had apprised C. B. of the fact that the Council flat he'd illegally sublet to an African chef, was now taken away from him. The chef had done a voodoo ritual in the kitchen, so that animal blood and bad smells had come out from under the door, and the neighbors had called the police. So now

C. B's income had gone, and he was freaked out. What was he going to do?

I didn't have much patience with all this. His behavior seemed to me unmanly. I should have bowed out with as much warmth as I could muster, right then. My heart wasn't big enough to embrace all this youthful folly – I had enough of my own. Instead, I hung in, ambivalently. I had an idea that I should be more like my sister, who tended to love a boyfriend well for years before changing to another one.

It's a bad idea to compare ourselves with other people.

And in this case, things would get much, much worse before they got better.

But back to Tantra. There was a man in the ashram who had studied the Barry Long method in Australia, and he was willing to practise with different women. He had a waiting list. I couldn't quite imagine what it was all about: you just lay still, joined; and verbally shared with each other what you were experiencing? Hmmm… ! I thought sex was for pleasure; pleasure was elusive; also not conclusive really; but what else *was* there? The Barry Long idea seemed both flat and mysterious.

But I felt a need to find out, somehow or other, what this different way of approaching sex might have to offer.

I gave a cassette of Osho speaking about Tantra – basically, it was about the Barry Long method – to C.B., who had often used to chortle boastingly about great Tantric (as he termed them) fantasies starring himself. These often involved a stage, and great erectness.

He listened to the tape. Became very quiet. "That is the death of sex," he said dolefully. And he never brought up the subject again.

Back in Poona, my beautiful, serene sister invited C.B. and me to have dinner with herself and her handsome French lover Geho. They lived in a quiet, thick-walled house in Koregaon Park, shaded by many trees. The house, as are my sister's houses always, was pristinely clean and orderly. We sat out on a large terrace as twilight fell, talking and eating veggie sushi lovingly prepared by Sarita. C.B. asked if he could have the last piece; it sat on a plate on a ledge half-under a bush. Everyone said yes. He put it in his mouth… and, a moment later, said, *"It's… really chewy."* Then, "Ummmm – uh – " …and then he rushed off to the bathroom to gag and wash out his mouth for many minutes! He had eaten a slug!

But Sarita liked him, approved of him, and when, a few days later, I confessed my ambivalence and asked her advice, she said she thought I should stay with him. And so I did.

Under the Midnight Sun

C.B. accompanied me to the far north of Norway, where we spent six enchanted weeks working, at the invitation of a professional palmreader who had done one of my groups in Poona. I adored the North! The fjords, the slanting light! Hiking at midnight! Heading onto the snowfields like the reindeer do, to avoid the horseflies! Feasts of strawberries at 2 a.m.! C.B. frying and eating smelly reindeer! (Ewwww… I didn't eat any.) And, at my behest, C. B. organizing a hilarious male striptease for an after-group party – really funny, guys sporting auto-mechanic tools and tighty-whities. C.B. was in his element!

C.B. was at that time giving sessions in Tibetan Pulsing Healing, the method pioneered by Dheeraj, that handsome Texan scoundrel whom I'd known in California. Although I've always loved therapies generally, I didn't like TPH – to me it smelt of something skeevy and icksome – and I thought it was probably about as Tibetan as supermarket lemon meringue pie, though I didn't say that to C.B. I had participated in a group once, during which a woman had to sit with her bare big toe sticking into my belly for twenty minutes. Afterwards my belly came out in a weird rash, which lasted for days. (One of the group leaders had predictably told me that this meant that toxins were being released.) Then, at one point Dheeraj told his many pupils that humans have a parasite in their sinus cavity, that causes all their problems and needs to be banished, and that TPH could do it. So everybody was sticking their toes and elbows into each other's backs, fronts, etc. even more, in an effort to get rid of the coiled worm-thing. It seemed to me Dheeraj had just felt the many aficionados needed some further drama to keep them engaged, and had concocted the Parasite to suit. Anyway, it's not so good when your boyfriend does work that you don't respect. I never said it, but the unease was there in me, adding to my tendency to be judgmental.

Expeditions in the North were great. One day we went to a zoo where arctic foxes and wolverines and brown bears lived in huge outdoor enclosures where they could roam about. The wolverine vibe was *wonderfully* ruthless and ferocious. Another day, hiking, we found a bed of arctic moss twenty feet deep, where you could bounce while the tender sun bathed your face. C.B. peeled off his clothes and jumped into an iceberg-strewn, incredibly blue little lake, grinning and shouting while I took his picture; then he clambered hurriedly out again.

Dear C. B., bless his heart, went out to a bar one night and ended up having a meaningless quickie with some woman, then confessing to me in maudlin self-flagellating misery, on and on. I was happy to have an excuse to sleep in a different room.

An odd thing happened: our host took us to Tromsø for a few days of work. When we returned to his large wooden house outside of little Finnsness (the furthest-north town on the mainland), we saw that the front door was hanging open. Thieves had been, and had stolen many of his knick-knacks and decorations, his music system, and some of my clothes... and all of my personal jewelry (I had a good collection by that time. My selling jewelry had been with me for work). My host was stricken. He sat staring morosely at his cold fireplace. Suddenly he turned and asked me, "Can you tune in and see what color of car the thieves were driving?"

I can't do that! I thought. *That's not the kind of gift I have.* But I didn't dare say that to him; I didn't want to upset him further. So I closed my eyes and asked the universe to show me what color the car was.

I saw a blue-green station wagon. My host immediately phoned the chief of police, who was a friend of his. Next day, the police in Tromsø found a green station wagon – and in it were some of my clothes; nearly every piece of my personal jewelry; and nearly all of my host's treasured artifacts; as well as his music system.

He was so delighted that he told everybody. It was a very small town, and soon people were wanting me to find lost things for them. I tried without success to locate a lost pair of glasses on the beach, for a little girl; and was very glad that it was soon time to leave... apparently the Gift only cared right then about my own stuff! (My stolen clothes, though, ended up earning an insurance rebate chez my host; and with it I had tailor-made a gorgeous enormous quilted bedspread with mirror-work on it, off-white... that I kept and used for many years.)

I had done so well in Norway (people in that tiny, lonely place were so hard up for entertainment, like people in New Zealand, that *everybody* came for sessions and groups) that I asked my eldest brother, Rudra, if he would like to come to Poona.

I had had an Idea, whilst fueled on green tea during a long-haul flight: why not, in the Commune, have a sort of work-study program whereby people without funds could work, and get entry and lodging and a group or two in exchange? (The Commune was by now almost completely non-residential – only some few important workers, and people who had bought rooms, lived in; everyone else rented flats nearby.) I'd proposed this to Garimo, who was in charge of various things, and she'd liked the idea. (In fact, she suggested I organize it. This sounded so horrifying to me that I promptly acquired a lasting suspicion of the tricky effects of caffeine. Things can seem like *such a good idea* when you are high on it – and then you are stuck with the consequences!)

Rudra never had any money; he was living then on an island off the coast of Vancouver, rationing his food to half a sandwich a day (though he always had enough of beer, wine, and tobacco – that was what was important to him!) I had enjoyed visiting him there.

So I bought his ticket, and he came for that work-study program. He had a wonderful time, fell in love here and there, usually with women he met in the Smoking Temple (there were several of these dotted about, both inside and outside the gates, where smokers could, it was hoped, smoke very consciously, aware of each motion and breath and sensation. And the rest of us needn't have smoke in our midst.) He did various kinds of work, and meditated, and had a high old time. I was so glad I'd invited him.

And I would be even more glad later… but more of that anon.

Stones

Back in Poona, I again gathered work and did sessions. But I was also indulging in my great love of stones. (It had been, all along, a Thing in the Mystery School to wear, and perhaps work with, beautiful minerals. I was delighted to participate.)

Once on M.G. Road I wandered into a rather grungy jewelry shop, attracted by a chunky jasper choker-necklace in the window. The shapes of the greenyearth-toned stones were pagan and irregular; the thick metallic string was knotted in between each. The large catch too looked archaic, a silver bar which fitted through a loop. The piece was striking – it had a heathen weightiness.

I held it in my hand and closed my eyes. Its character flowed through my body… the rich, happy 'groundingness' of the agate family; a feeling like a country walk in autumn, with a nip in the air and plenty of big rocks along the path, among the trees. The irregularity of the shapes gave it a kind of wild freedom.

"How much?" I asked the shop-girl.

"I was going to ask two hundred rupees, but when I saw you *praying to the god,* I decided to charge you only one hundred!" she replied with a waggle of the head. So I bought it, and soon someone bought it from me.

I was deeply in love with geology – with rocks, those earth-made, weather-made wonders. I spent a lot of money and a lot of time playing with them, reading them, designing pieces, cleaning, charging in moonlight or starlight, getting fancy bags made, and then getting them to the West and selling them. In the back of this book there is a section called *Appendix of Treasures,* in which, if you like, you can read more about stones: their characters, uses; and the cleaning and charging of them.

More, soon, about one special sort of stone…

Griddle-Dancing

By this time I'd been burning the candle at both ends for a long, long time. (We were all burning thus.) And so I lived in a little apartment very close to the center of a very hot soup. I often had an image in my mind of a little device my father and brothers had once engineered: they took an offcut from a 2x4 piece of lumber; hammered six large nails through it so that the points stuck out several inches on the other side; then wired the heads of the nails with copper wire, and fixed a plug on one end. If you stuck hot dogs onto the nails, and plugged the thing in, soon you'd hear sizzling, smell roasting flesh, and the hot dogs would split open and steam would come out. They'd been cooked from the inside.

I was one of those hot dogs. My body couldn't keep up with the demands I placed on it. My nervous system was often just on the edge of collapsing into some debilitated, wrung-out state. Yet here, in this amazing place, this intensity was inescapable. I'd try to find coolness and silence in visits to Osho's beautiful Samadhi – the big marble room with a donut-shaped crystal chandelier hovering above the meditators like some uber-glitzy UFO; and through the wall of window, a waterfall. I loved sitting there on a cold winter morning, all wrapped in a velvet robe, eyes closed, going In; feeling the Vibe, the eternal Vibe, of the Beyond cradling me. There was a marble bier at the front with a plaque that said, *Never Born – Never Died, Only visited this planet Earth between December 11, 1931 and January 19, 1990.* It was so good to go there, like the cool center of the storm. But still I'd get wrung-out again, quite soon after coming out of Lao Tzu Gate.

I supposed that I just wanted to go on like that, albeit with a more satisfactory boyfriend... in other words, something even more intense! But one day in my room I sat down and wrote a yearning little poem, a fantasy of living all alone in the flat, flat lands of the American Midwest (of all places!) with short foofy hair and bare feet on the grass... the only drama coming from the thunderheads piled above.

To me, this was a shocking fantasy – it went wildly against all that I had been trying to be. That I saw myself as.

And yet the picture was... *Ordinary.* A word that Osho loved, and that he used as praise.

Moldavites

Old Sam, as he was known – tall, white-haired, beaming Sufi-whirling Sam, ex-CIA Sam – lived upstairs in Tilopa Pyramid. One day he offered me a fat little baggie full of moldavites someone had brought him from Czechoslovakia, where he had worked in his younger, CIA years (before he became a radiant old lovebody with trains of girlfriends and a joyful job leading Sufi Whirling). He said he'd give me the whole lot for $200. I'd never heard of moldavite, and gazed surprised at the pile of dark-green stones that spilled from the baggie. They were pocked and bubbly, bumpy and irregular, as if they'd had acne, long ago, and then healed and petrified. Apparently they are desirable in this natural state, as well as when polished. Eighteen million years ago a meteor struck a rare glancing blow to Earth, careening along a path across what would one day be Czechoslovakia (now Czechia). The soil along the way was cooked instantly into these glassy pebbles, which are found only there… tektites, geologically speaking. Moldavite is called, in New Age parlance, The Starborne Stone of Transformation.

I bought them, and took them to my room; tipped them onto the bed. One especially large piece I placed on the flat-topped headboard. Then I put the others away and lay down for a much-needed nap. …And I had a dream; of the sort that is not just a dream. The kind that's so real that when you wake up, you can't feel a disconnect from it.

I was lying on my bed taking a nap, and there was a knock on the door. I got up and opened it, and an E.T. was standing there, with another E.T. behind him. Wadud was behind both of the E.T.s, with his characteristic half-scowl.

The first E.T. said to me, "We've come to remove the worry gland from your neck!"

Then I was shown a scene – green, peaceful – just a green place, with nothing much going on in it. My belly pulled me towards this place. Oh, peace! Quiet! Calm!

What heretical ideas these seemed to be! We were supposed to cook *all the time*, so we would be done faster! Osho had joked about the 'camels' who are happy to live sleepy lives in peaceful places, like Santa Fe, New Mexico, where a group of sannyasins lived. They were not lions. They were not living 100%.

But my body ached and yearned towards the green vision.

I played with the moldavites. When I held a piece in my hand, closed my eyes, tuned in, I saw it like this: the extraterrestrial vibration of the meteorite had communicated itself to the tektite; so that the effect of the stone was as if you were resting in Outer Space looking down at Earth; looking at the person wearing or holding the stone. From that perspective, you could look right into the person – to their purpose here on Earth, to their true nature.

Then, everything that was in the way between that true nature and the outside world, would start to vibrate and crack.

A moldavite can have very strong effects. I've seen it cure constipation, instigate divorce.

And when I think back on what was to come, it all seemed to begin with that moldavite.

Panic

After another Japan tour, I was back in Poona, collecting jobs, loading my plate. I was always so incredibly grateful to be home again! In the love-field, in the innumerable hugs (it could take the whole first day just to get from the Gateless Gate back to Lao Tzu Gate – so many long heartful cosmic-spacious melting hugs there were with all and sundry, men and women alike!) I wanted to show my earnest by working hard.

But this time I kept feeling odd… wrong and weird. As if I were in a vortex – spinning, falling. Each job I set out to do, I fell sick and had to cancel. I morosely munched *neem* leaves from a tree near my Pyramid, hoping their bitterness would bring me health. Garimo had asked me if I would lead another Mouth of the Dragon training, and I'd said yes; that was to be in six months' time, but now I found that the idea weighed on me. I didn't, it seemed, really want to know what was going to happen in six months. But this reluctance seemed unacceptable – of *course* I wanted to lead the training… didn't I? And yet… somewhere in me I knew that creatively, I was finished with that training. It wasn't new any more; for *me*. But that selfishness seemed not allowable. My stomach felt churning or knotted. Something heavy lay on the back of my neck, like a succubus.

I had been trying to break it off with C. B.. But he would not go – he would become deaf when I would tell him it was over, and then he'd present himself at my door in the evening as usual. We had a session with Devapath, who supported the splitting; and yet, again, C. B. turned up at my door that night, wide and blond and boulder-shouldered, as if nothing had happened.

Somewhere in all this I bumped into Bindu – I'd seen him around, but now we connected and clicked. He was a very attractive man, a Dane with an Eskimo look about his broad brown face and slanted eyes, and very urbane. He was my age, a well-known commune musician. We laughed together, and there was a juicy, humming yumminess to his touch that lit me up with warm electricity. He finally told me he had a girlfriend who was arriving that same night – so our meeting was cut short. But we both knew the other was there.

I had a bladder infection. Oh, lord. The prospect of a course of antibiotics was hideous – they made me feel *so* bad. And even if you took them, the infection could come back later; the story could go on and on. I knew it too well! At the medical center I asked the doctor (I think it was Dr. Pragitam, a soft-voiced American with round glasses) if there was a shorter treatment – I'd heard of a two-pill cure. Did he have that kind? Yes, he said, that was a possible way to treat it – "but it can be… intense."

And with that warning ringing in my ears I took the two pills home.

I was afraid to take them, so I kept postponing. Finally, after midnight, I thought I had better just get it over with. Normally I never stayed up that late; but I couldn't really go to bed without taking the pills – what if the infection crawled up to my kidneys in the night?

Still I postponed. I'd started reading a thriller by Michael Crichton, *Airframe,* so I read a bit more… then, around 2 a.m., standing up between bed and window, I poured a glass of filtered water, threw back my head, popped the two pills in, and swallowed.

Almost immediately, a dreadful sensation took over my body. I saw an explosion of light – but not a *nice* light – and then my soul, or my 'me,' or my 'self,' or whatever the point of reference is for this… passenger in the vehicle – exited the vehicle about half. It was the most horrid feeling – like having something stuck halfway down your gullet – or like being temporarily blinded in one eye – or like… entering a world of grey smog, where every nerve-ending is nevertheless raw and exposed to whatever comes along, and you are stuck halfway out a window, with the sill pressing into your middle.

There was, simultaneously, a kind of heat all over, and yet a coldness in the throat; and a *sound* – a sort of silent roaring.

This state lasted all night. I could not sleep; I phoned my avuncular friend Devageet, who said a few calm, kindly things. Later I phoned Dr. Pragitam. He suggested I take a Valium. I had a few around that I occasionally took to help myself sleep while jet-lagged (I wouldn't take them now). I took one; but the effect was dreadful – as if a sort of extra speediness I was suffering as my heart raced, reversed itself and became extra *sloooow*… my breathing *sloooowed*… but I was acutely conscious, and this plummeting into the slow-zone felt like death. I phoned Dr. Pragitam again and told him I felt like I was dying.

"You're not dying," he said. "Your voice sounds strong. This is a panic attack. It's connected with menopause. And if you get it once, you'll get it again and again."

I was not menopausal then at all – and as to getting it again and again… over my dead body! But I was happy to be reminded that I wasn't dying!

I tried to distract myself by continuing to read *Airframe.* It was a bad choice. Terrible scary things go on with a huge airplane wobbling around and falling to bits in high flight. It felt like exactly what was going on with me.

In the morning I felt a bit more grounded. But it *still hurt to pee!* The pills hadn't worked! Oh, shit! So I sat down and gave myself a Colorpuncture treatment in the ear, for bladder infections. The color used in most of the points is red.

When the first hit of red flooded my nervous system, there was a flush of heat, my heart started racing, and I careened out of my body again. And that was it – I was stuck there, half out, in terror. This wretched and anguished state was to persist for three months. It was by far the most horrible thing that had ever happened to me.

I cowered in my apartment, afraid to consume anything except papaya and fresh coconut water. Yogurt was too heavy, too animal – it made a bad smell in the back of my nose. It was as though each food I might try could be seen in its transparency by my body; my body knew all about it, and mostly wanted nothing to do with its earthy qualities – its spice, or its oils, or anything else. It all just felt heinous, it all just *freaked me out.* I lost weight fast.

Words are inadequate to express the misery of this mad state. It was, moment by moment, an irredeemable hell.

My friends were all healers, and they came and went, giving me sessions. Nothing worked. I went to a hypnotist, but I felt his own fear at what was happening to me, and he could do me no good at all. Tibetan pulsing simply moved the weirdness from one place to another in my body… and that weirdness was not a mild thing, in an intrinsically protected organism; it was a raw and excruciating weirdness. Each session I received was like being dragged through a field of electrified metal spikes, so keenly did I feel each moment of it.

C. B. visited sometimes, but his presence upset me. He was so helpless. He'd get all nonplussed, and then defensive, and just didn't know what to do.

There was really only one thing, in those days and weeks, that I wanted to say to any human: *"Help me!"* …But nobody could.

I got the idea that going to Goa might help – I thought of how going up to Mahabaleshwar had brought me out of hepatitis that time in Poona One. So C. B. and I went to Goa; and to hell. Sitting on the beach, all was grey, and I was floating above the sand. There was only dullness on sea and sky. The food scared me, so again it was papaya and coconut water. And I was convinced I now had a kidney infection – my back ached, it hurt when I peed, I felt feverish. I was frightened and despairing. C. B. would go out and eat big greasy meals by himself and then come back to the room. I could see the grease popping out of his pores, smell it on his body. It nauseated me, grossed me out, scared me. I spent my days lying on the bed, white and thin, picking at my skin, trembling, heart racing.

We took the night-bus back to Poona. I had read that apples were calming; I ate one and observed the amazing way a temporary quiet came over my nerves. But it didn't last.

Back in the ashram, I went to the medical center for a urine test… and it was fine; I didn't have an infection.

Within half an hour of getting this result, the kidney and bladder symptoms disappeared! This was great! But – the panic remained. I existed in a sped-up anguish.

Finally, two things happened: someone did an astrology transit reading for me, and said, "Wow, everything is in the toilet!" That was an incredible relief – an objective explanation! It really helped.

The other thing was this: I started getting sessions with Madita, the NLP (Neuro-Linguistic Programming) goddess, with her short thick henna'd hair and big glowing smile, her air of maturity and poise – like a fun and pretty auntie.

Madita wasn't the least bit spooked by what was happening to me. Indeed, she seemed delighted about the way my mind worked – she said she enjoyed it a lot! And so the knots and clenchings in my mind started to come unraveled in these sessions – and the fact that she *liked* my mind, was *having a good time* working with me, was the kick-start my healing needed. Nothing less would have done… As the man says, Love is the only healer.

It turned out to be very simple really. I'd said Yes to leading another Mouth of the Dragon – but my unconscious didn't want to do it. It wasn't interested. It was now turned, like a daisy to the sun, to a vision of a green silent place where I could just rest and be. And because such a dream seemed wholly spiritually incorrect, there was a division in me. Division creates shock, and then panic… part of you is going one way, part the other; and you can only freeze, and shake.

I wasn't in love with C. B., and I needed to break up with him. I'd gone against this knowing, getting him to take me to Goa. (Very sorry, C. B.!) And still he wouldn't leave me, despite how obvious it must have been that I didn't welcome his presence. I was trying to be nice – though I could only show him my panic, so that's not very nice anyway. The panic was the division between my politeness and my real feeling.

So during the sessions, I tried out a new word: No.

This was amazing! Every time I said it, I came back into my body a little bit more.

After five days of three-hour sessions (oh, thank you, Madita!) I was back in my body and the panic was gone. It had just been the fierce division between what I thought I ought to do, and what my body wanted to do. Add a suggestion: "This can be really *intense!*" (the pills) and there it was: panic on wheels.

And, up to now, I've never gotten a panic attack again, despite what Dr. Pragitam had said. This is because I consciously saw the path into it that I had taken, and now knew what to avoid. I'd been *feeding* it really – and I saw how not to feed it. It could still happen I guess – but the only times I've come close were when I had to take antibiotics. My theory is that when the chemicals kill the good bacteria along with the bad, your whole body feels undefended, *because it is.* I get to feel like a fragile, scared little old lady. A good dose of probiotics sets me right again. (Luckily, these episodes have been few and far between.)

But the initial blast of the panic happened before the pills could have hit my system. That was Suggestion, plus the Unknown, plus Fear.

C.B. had finally faded away – though not without doing a bit of shrubbery-lurking when I was tête-à-tête with Bindu one afternoon. (I had shrubbery-lurked myself at the Ranch, so who was I to sneer?) I can only imagine how confusing my breakdown must have been for him – yet he had not fled, but had hung in, however futilely. He's a good guy. (In 2008 I bumped into him in Poona again, and we had tea. He had meanwhile studied Shamanic healing in the Himalayas, married a Siberian woman who looked much like him, and become very successful in Russia. I was glad, and enjoyed his warmth and sweetness.)

The way the post-panic healing continued was very beautiful. Anando and I were good friends, and he invited me to go and stay at his place at Out of Africa for a few days. This was perfect – I needed to be out of the pressure-cooker of the Commune – the fried-from-within-weinie effect. I just lay on a mattress all by myself all day while A. was at the ashram, and listened to Gopal's wonderful *Relaxing the BodyMind*, where he speaks Osho's words and plays the *dilruba.* I played it on a loop, over and over and over again. It is the most softly effective meditation tape – inviting you in towards the center, beyond body, beyond mind.

Outside, birds chirped… and all was peace and quiet. Ahhh…

I said goodbye to Bindu (whose feisty girlfriend sprayed a shaken-up bottle of soda water at me in Prem's Restaurant, bless her heart!) and flew to California. Kohrogi-san had earlier told me to go back to where I'd been born and spend some time there. I'd said, "But it's a horrible place!" and he'd said, "Then, nearby."

First I went to Newport Beach, where I had two days of hypnosis with the gifted Brian Alman (who'd visited the Commune). During this mysterious, beyond-conscious-logic process I ended up laughing, just laughing, for forty-five minutes… and he recorded it all!

Then I went to Ojai, where Krishnamurti used to hang out. It's a little town in a bowl in the coastal mountains, full of fruit orchards and spiffed-up old houses. I was hungry for the oak trees, the warm earth smells, the herby scents of the vegetation. I stayed six weeks with an eccentric family friend, who lived in a beaten-up plasticky trailer and spent his evenings listening to Bob Dylan while his old cat kneaded the man's huge paunch with its paws, purring blissfully, and his little dog continued its mission to carpet the backyard with poo. I went to a Krishnamurti gathering – a circle of tall thin white men, who spent the entire hour discussing with heavy seriousity *how to decide what they ought to discuss.* I got so fed up that in a moment of recklessness I cast myself onto the floor in the middle and crawled about roaring like a tiger. The men sat frozen and severe. Then I left and went to do Kundalini meditation, feeling just *saturated* with gratefulness at what Osho has given us.

And, a shriveled, cosmopolitan old guy fell in lust with me at an open mic poetry night, and tried to kiss me; and I was able to say, "No! No! No!"

And for the whole time I was there I felt grounded, happy, and tenderly nurturing towards myself.

Later Sarita told me, lovingly, carefully, that she had, before the Panic started, advised me to stay with C. B. because *my* Guides had come to *her* in meditation, and told her that I might die. She had been told by the Guides not to tell me all this, at that time. So she thought to herself that C.B.'s Conan-the-Barbarian effect would perhaps protect me. But when I told her about my discovery, that saying No helped me to come back to my body, she seemed distressed. "I say Yes! You say No! How can we ever meet?"

The Insurgents

I had not noticed that all around the Commune, photos of Osho had been disappearing. We knew that his photos gave off magical vibes; but now they were gone – none in the bookshop, or the Multiversity booking area. Group leaders still hung their favorites in their group-room, but in public areas there was just the wall… I *did* notice, though, another loss – a great one – the musicians who'd been troubadouring in every patch of garden; were no more there. (I loved this even though a pair of Germans were apt to sit with their guitars right under my Pyramid window, practising *Eleanor Rigby* for hours!) (The musicians had been told they had to work six hours a day on top of making music; and, incensed, they had decamped.) I noticed that we no longer sang songs with words in them at night during White Robe – hymns of love to the Master. (I am told that all songs had been only instrumental since a few months prior to Osho's leaving-body. He hadn't wanted the singing any more. I had not noticed even that.) But I am in many ways a mild sort, deeply self-absorbed, and whatever the powers-that-were wanted to do was largely tangential to me, and thus uninteresting. Osho was everywhere, so if his photo vanished, I didn't pay attention.

But others did… and one day Sarita told me she wanted to stage a protest. I was shocked – such a thing would never occur to me – but who was I to interfere? She wanted my opinion. So I held her hands, tuned in, and saw that she *was* going to do this thing, whatever it might be. A fire was in her, a scintillating pathway of indignant, rebellious fire; it was as if it came from Otherwhere. (This is actually fitting with her Human Design, but of course I didn't know that then.) It was unstoppable. I told her this. She took heart.

So a few weeks later, Sarjano, a colorful Italian, incited by my sister, stood up before White Robe and said a lot of protesty things, reading from a sheet of paper.

He was kicked out of the Commune.

Then, so was she.

The people in charge said that the cessation of devotion was what Osho had wanted: he didn't want to become a dead god to be worshiped. He wanted people to find their way fresh and alive, without being stuck on his memory. They said he'd left instructions that after a certain number of years, his photo was to be taken down; and so on.

There was no way to check if this was true.

But my sister is a devotee – a Lover. Osho was her Door, her Master, and she wanted to love him out loud, in song, and looking at his face.

I can understand this too.

People gabbled and gossiped and took sides.

This separation in our Commune was all quite horrible for me. I didn't like any of it – the protests, and the banishments. For me, all nourishment was still here in these vast little acres. The details didn't concern me much. (Sarita now thinks of this time as her 'graduation.') My tummy was churning. But I had no sides in me to take. I simply had not noticed anything was amiss. To me, we were all in this soup together – all of us – no matter what we thought or didn't. Why divide things artificially? Each of us was his own bunch of letters in the alphabet soup. All in one big pot.

It was sad, my sister going. So sad. She and her handsome French boyfriend went off to France, to begin their long and successful career as Tantra teachers. Now, of course, she is the Tantra Goddess and teaches almost everywhere… Delhi, Dharmsala, Thailand, Lithuania, California, Sweden, Norway, France, England, etc… I recently participated in a group with her called Abundance, at Osho Leela in England; and found it wonderful – clear, cosmic, funny, and relaxed; if also full-on and relentless. She is a woman with a mission, to enlighten the world through Tantra; and she wears it bravely.

An Interesting Session

My travels continued. I overworked in Japan – though at a much nicer venue now, with a different organizer, in a little town where cicadas whirred loud as anything and a lady-voiced loudspeaker announced waking and mealtimes for the entire village! (While I was there, my old nemesis Sagarpriya was sending reams of rattling faxes all day long, berating her absconding boyfriend, who was staying at this particular healing center, with his new Japanese girlfriend. Ha ha, I thought, she *is* human – and jealous! This was mean of me, I know.)

In Switzerland I stayed in Devika's chalet and welcomed Kohrogi-san and Sarita and her boyfriend, and Champaka and his French girlfriend, and we hiked and played in a high, remote waterfall together. In Maui I visited my niece and her two kids.

In Sedona I went on hovering at the edge of the Mystery School; Kaveesha had previously agreed that it wasn't needed for me to do any groups. But people looked at me oddly because of this. I went to White Robe, and enjoyed myself greatly. I danced with funky joy to Sammy Davis's Soul Band, in which Kaveesha's daughter Shaeri played drums. I was happy…

Someone I knew from the Ranch, Patipada, now known as Mary Ann, wanted a psychic palmreading from me. She wanted to give me in exchange a session of something called Human Design. I demurred, saying I had had enough of systems for the while and didn't want to take on any more. But she insisted, and finally, because she really wanted my session – and that moved me – I agreed.

We sat at her kitchen table, and her delight in what she was explaining to me was manifest. She's a chunky woman with short hair and a warm laugh, brimming with energy. She showed me a diagram on a piece of paper; a sort of pyramid shape with a stylized figure of a person in it, and nine chakras mapped out in this, connected by lines. This was my personal chart. It seemed that she thought my Design was absolutely wonderful! (I suspect she thinks everyone's is!) That was what charmed me, reassured me. And, the information itself just made things so… simple. I was glad that I had done all that ass-kicking of myself for such a long time; it was needed – but now it was wonderful to hear that I am really a very cool and light sort of person, just full of private, individualistic creativity, a 'friendly hermit,' as Mary Ann said – not here to schlep and heft and work too hard. That nothing is broken and nothing needs fixing – it's just about letting go of what I am not: emotional drama, red-hot sexual machinations, striving, willpower, stress, attempts to make things happen.

I walked out two hours later feeling just… happy. So light.

You mean, it's *okay just to be myself?*

Epiphany in a Night-Train

I lay swaying in a sleeper-train carriage in the night, Zurich to Copenhagen. And as I looked inside my body (a friend's recent health scare having activated my own hypochondria) I saw this: for so many years I had, with my Will, been peering and staring about inside my body. I thought that was the right thing to do. I had turned my focus Inwards. But now I perceived that I was harassing all my workings in there – laying a burden on them with my attention.

In that moment the attention all turned over and began to look, quite normally and mundanely, at the outside instead. This felt like a crazily dangerous thing to do – I was abandoning my seeker-hood, it seemed. But it was also a huge relief as my body sighed with appreciation and let go.

I felt more… ordinary. Some ego I'd had about being a great spiritual in-looker went away.

When I got to Copenhagen it was as if the body had always felt like this – relaxed, normal, looking about itself at the ordinary world.

Osho speaks about the difference between active and passive awareness. It would be a long time still before I understood this.

My Career Falters

At this time there was a great fashion in the seeker-world: it seemed that it was possible to get enlightened just by sitting with an enlightened person. Poonja-ji in Lucknow had started it, and other people, finding themselves feeling Realized one day, took it up; so that soon you could go to nearly any city in Europe and Sit with somebody and, if you didn't experience something great, it was just the luck of the draw.

Once Bindu and I went to a Satsang in Copenhagen, with a good-looking young man with brown wavy hair – a sannyasin who felt that something great had happened to him.

The place was packed. We were sat all over each other's feet like Indians. I felt like I was in an economy-class airplane. People asked questions and the young man answered them. It was like a very faint xerox copy of a Satsang. As soon as it was over, Bindu and I dashed out of there as fast as we possibly could, and, as we rushed off down the street, holding hands, Bindu said, "You mean enlightenment has come to *this?*"

And then we threw back our heads and laughed!

But one thing wasn't so funny: people felt that if you could have a great leap of consciousness so easily, why bother with pokey, time-consuming old therapy? Why get your palm read, why look at past lives, when you could just sit there and go *Whhheeeeee?*

Why indeed? I don't blame them. I don't know what they were experiencing. But it meant that people weren't feeling the need of my sessions. I worked in Hamburg again and things were moribund – people dashing off to Satsangs right and left while I sat in the Center's restaurant nursing a cup of herbal tea.

Hmmmm.

A Warning

One summer towards the end of the 90's, Devadasi and I and Sarita all met in Provence, where Sarita and Geho were leading a group. Kohrogi-san and Champaka and Champaka's rather querulous French wife were also there. It was not a comfortable visit, and I can't say exactly why. Devadasi and I shared a room. At night there were mosquitoes. I put fresh lavender boughs on the bed by my face to discourage them, which didn't work at all. Devadasi kept getting up in the night, again and again, to busily re-pack her suitcase – she was always trying, and not succeeding, to minimize her stuff. This was very disturbing of my sleep. The dynamic among us three was also awkward for me – I kept feeling like an odd elbow sticking out, treading water (to mix metaphors!) (And then, there was an embarrassing trip into town where I found in a shop some cute little sneakers I just loved, and bought six pairs in different colors. Then I said enthusiastically to the proprietress, *"Je t'aime! Je t'aime!"* I'd meant to say "I love them!" but I'd said instead, "I love you!" She drew back with a hiss of horror. I only realized my gaffe when I was out on the street, halfway down the block!)

One afternoon I received a session from Kohrogi-san. We were in an outbuilding all hung with flowering honeysuckle; bees buzzed in the perfumed little furled cream-and-gold trumpets and in the shaggy, fecund garden just outside.

Kohrogi-san held my feet as I lay on the sheet-covered massage table. Champaka translated: "You have a brain tumor. It is very small, and it isn't cancer; but you should see about it."

I was, at this time, feeling just fine; the only odd thing was that I had once or twice had a headache when there was thunder in the air. I had assumed that I had 'caught' this from Anando, who suffered terribly from atmospherically-triggered migraines. But it had really only been once or twice, when the day was very hot, and I was in a train.

What Kohrogi-san said to me brought up this instantaneous denial: "What? *ME, brain tumor?* That is ridiculous! I don't have a brain tumor! These psychics are full of nonsense!"

And I forgot all about it. I did, of course, tell Sarita and Mom; but they forgot all about it too.

What a thing to forget all about!

Decline

Back in Poona, mostly I felt fine. I went on giving sessions, designing jewelry; and for a while I worked in the Communications department, sorting mail and faxes; putting the faxes into envelopes to stick into alphabetized boxes on a table outside, so that people could go through and claim theirs. (I won't say that I didn't read any of the faxes. Every morning there was such a nice long river of them spilt down from the machine. It was irresistible.) I really liked this job. On New Year's Day I decorated all the fax-envelopes with colored drawings. One of these was for Bindu's girlfriend. I drew a long-stemmed rose lying horizontally across the bottom of the envelope, with a sufficiency of thorns on it; and on the stem was a little kitten with its back arched, hissing. It was a very nice drawing. Bindu told me later that she had loved it and said, "But this is just me! This is *me!*" He did not tell her who had done it. Later she had it framed and put it on the wall.

I entered a contest for the best costume for an Osho joke character, and I won as Olga Kowalski, in frumpy curlers and shower cap, all bulging with pillows I wore under a muumuu. (This character is a strident housewife who gets into all sorts of dumb jams.) The prize was a group... and I knew already which one I wanted to do: Satori.

It was one of the best things I'd ever done. Satori was an eight-day Koan group, where you work in twos, asking each other a particular question. The questionee then allows whatever arises in her to come forth. This goes on for five minutes, the question being repeated; then you change over. All kinds of stuff comes up, and as the layers peel away you are faced more and more with your own mindless mystery. It was exhilarating to stay so alert for so many long days.

The first time I'd done this kind of work, in Who Am I? (later changed to Who Is In?) in early Poona One, I had suffered a lot – just being *present* was a suffering. This time it was easy, like flying. I loved every day of it, as things kept on getting deeper and deeper. At one point, on about day seven, I uncovered a past life: I'd been a Catholic nun, in a convent, where one was supposed to abase and efface oneself; I was cleaning a big flagged hall on my hands and knees, while a huge, bloated, and petulant God looked down, into the smallest details of my activities, and my mind.

It was shocking to see this broad stripe of sediment in the unconscious strata of my psyche. I Saw, clearly and succinctly, that I had lived my current life dramatically, colorfully, wildly – as a reaction. It wasn't real… just a reaction.

But I was not, after all, well. I lay in my room in the Pyramid listening to a strange ringing in my ears. I got headaches and dizzy spells. My vision seemed to be greying. I thought perhaps I just had really bad candida.

9

Chaos

Chaos

2000 – 2003

Hong Kong

A beautiful friend, Deva Vibha, had arranged that she and I would go to Hong Kong for a month of work; I would do jewelry shows, and Vibha would help me – she had a lot of contacts there. I designed like mad for a month, making a glorious collection of sparkly crystals and stones with gleaming silver or warm gold settings. Doing it on this scale was tiring though, and I saw with dismay that my creative joy was diminished by the sense of something almost like mass-production – though of course it wasn't; most pieces were unique. But I stole time from Commune work for this; and felt divided and ill-at-ease.

In Hong Kong, with its skyscraper apartment towers and many leisure-rich expat wives, I worked much too hard, going from venue to venue, setting up shows, doing psychic tune-ins with people and their chosen pieces. A reporter came from an expat newspaper and was impressed with her reading. All went well… except that my lips swelled from (I presume) the ubiquitous MSG; and fainting spells became an almost-daily occurrence. I grew very weak. What was wrong with me?

At the end of that month I decided not to return to Poona.

This was such a complete reversal that I was surprised at myself. But the decision was clear. I knew that Bindu would be off to Goa with his Main Squeeze as soon as I got back; we'd had all sorts of fun, in Poona and in Denmark; but I had after a few years become annoyed at the six-week Goa stints without me. At first I'd liked the freedom of the triangle arrangement, but now I didn't. Bindu and I were still cooking along; but now I also felt too discouraged and ill to manage all that India body-stress. (For example, a year or two earlier, I'd landed in Bombay, gone to the Sun-n-Sand Hotel in Juhu, which was considered quite a good one; and for breakfast had requested half a papaya. The fruit had arrived all cut into chunks in a bowl. I looked at it dubiously – all those raw surfaces for something to have gotten at! – then ate it anyway. By the time, five or so hours later, the taxi had deposited me at the ashram gates, I knew I had amoebas.)

A Long Grey Time

It was November 2000. G.W. Bush had just been elected President. I landed in San Francisco, and spent a few days with my friend Lotus, ordering at her behest an expensive poo test from a lab in North Carolina, to see if it knew what was wrong with me. I spent almost $500 on a Tachyon* blanket, hoping it would make me feel better. Then I took a Greyhound bus all the long way up the coast to my mother's house in Gold Beach, Oregon.

Devadasi was grieving the death of Vedant Prem, who had one morning some weeks before, told her he loved her; then in the afternoon, sat down in his big favorite chair in the living room, closed his eyes, and left his body. He'd had a heart attack.

The family thought it was good that I was there with her.

It was a nice little house, much-improved by her and V.P./Bob. One block from the cold Oregon sea, and the beautiful sea-light came in through every window – a soft light, full of piney shadings too from the woods round about. I had one of the two bedrooms (and on the beds were the quilts and sheets I'd rescued at the end of the Ranch).

But soon I noticed a different mother than the one I thought I knew – a determined, self-starting, self-absorbed mother, not absolutely thrilled to have her fifty-year-old daughter back at home again. It was as if this mama felt she still had some living to do, and the daughter might cramp her style. She had loved Bob deeply, but she wasn't on the shelf yet, oh, no! One day, in an expression of fed-up-ness with me I had not seen since I was a child – and rarely then – she came out with: "Why – you're nothing but a *pretty little man-trap!*"

* Tachyon is a wonderful beyond-frequency, white-lightish sort of process a physical object can be put through, via a certain machine; whereupon it becomes a healing force in your life. I'd been into it for years.

Mostly I felt okay. The bad spells came about every five weeks, when I'd faint and throw up a lot. But then I'd be okay again. I was trying to live and enjoy as usual, surviving on sales of what jewelry I had left.

I went back to Sedona.

A year or so before, I'd begun to feel I was falling for my dancing partner there. His name was Keene – a mobile-hipped, sweet, full-lipped young man who worked as a graphic designer at a Native-American-run casino. He and I just danced so well together! Bellies close but not touching – moving in time – all over the floor, sassy, sexy, indefatigable. He was a private, sensitive, very cautious man, and it took a couple more visits to Sedona before we were both ready to enter an affair. When it happened, I tried to steer it towards Tantra, without, I'm sorry to say, having the slightest idea what that meant. I was going for pleasure all the way – coitus interruptus, really. And there was a basic lack of communication; a dearth of shared experiences. But he was lovely – I loved petting his springy hair, like a mass of Norwegian arctic moss. His dark skin seemed to me poignant, tender, beautiful. So Other. (He reminded me of a quiet, studious little boy I had admired when I was ten; who had liked me too, but we had known that we could only look at each other – that connecting was out of the question. Society's attitude to Race divided us, and it was a concrete divide.)

Dancing with Keene was beyond heaven. But I couldn't afford to live in Sedona, and nor was it a committed relationship – though I had longings in that direction. I felt a need to be cared for, and Keene had enough on his plate without that. I think too that he was rightly wary of my complicated life. In this grey time I struggled with a sense that things were spiraling downwards, out of my hands.

The poo tests I'd had done said I had hugely bad and remedy-resistant candida; plus hookworm eggshell bits, and various other unhelpful intestinal inhabitants. So, back in Oregon, I went on a strict candida diet. But the vomiting attacks were getting longer – now often forty-eight hours would be spent vomiting in terrible pain and then falling unconscious. But somehow this only happened when nobody was around.

Mama had eventually put an ad in the local Electricity Board newsletter. Twelve old gentlemen wrote to her. The winner was a little bald man who appeared at her door clutching a fistful of wildflowers. They started an off-again, on-again, rather fraught romance. Mama was in her early eighties; Al rather younger. She started spending quite a lot of time at his house, five hours away by car.

I was now in a strange, foggy state. Grey shadows lurked at the corners of my vision. But, right after 9/11, I flew to Switzerland, and then to Poona. (I'd been booked to fly on 9/11 itself, and ended up stranded in somebody's ancient gutted trailer in a back yard in Cottonwood, Arizona, waiting for the planes to start flying again. It was then such a relief to leave the hysterical, angry, grieving States!) I spent five weeks in Poona – it was amazing to see everyone happy and laughing when the rest of the world was so gloomy and morose. And, too, it was strange to have a Poona visit where I kept everything together successfully while I was there, instead of the previous inevitable it-all-falls-apart thing. (I was rather disappointed!) A German sannyasin, for reasons of his own, decided to become my literary agent. This never came to anything, but he bought me a computer, and we did spend a month in Switzerland working on my teenage memoirs. I felt quite well during the Poona and Switzerland times, but afterwards the malaise returned worse than ever.

Back in Oregon, I'd also, at someone's suggestion, gone onto a dating website for people with herpes; I thought those guys might be more honest and humble than the usual fellows out there, since they'd already had to own up to the deeply embarrassing fact of the Big H. I liked exchanging emails with people, and I met Graham, a very nice Mozart pianist from Portland; and soon too a fellow in Canada, Forbes, was carrying on a lively correspondence with me. But by now, wherever I went, really puzzling and terrible things were happening: in Sedona, I fell down in front of Whole Foods, vomiting into the dry verge of grass. Nobody stopped to help. Another time, I was lying in bed talking on the phone to Arjuna, the Nostradamus writer, and then abruptly started projectile vomiting. Another time, I was riding in a Greyhound bus on winding mountain roads from Trinity, California to Gold Beach, Oregon, I was heavily carsick all over the dark, swaying little toilet. Later I sat gazing out the window and noted, with a kind of sad ennui, that there were two moons in the sky. They followed us all the way to Gold Beach.

Weird meetings happened, as if my inner compass was skewed and allowed unlikely strangers in. I was walking down a shady street in Ashland,

Oregon one hot afternoon (I'd moved there for a job that never materialized), dressed in a slim skirt and white t-shirt, sunglasses, and a scarf tied under my chin. A man came out of a house and asked me, "Do you need money?"

I stopped and considered. "Yes!" I said. (I think I had $60 left to my name just then.) He said, "Come with me." Nervously I followed him past a lunging dog into an ordinary wooden bungalow. He wrote a check for $200 and gave it to me. "All I want in return," he said, "is that you *write me a letter,* thanking me, and send it to me later. Can you do that?"

I said that I could. Then he walked me out to the sidewalk. As we passed a car by the curb he said, "Do you want some tuna fish? My whole trunk is full of cans of tuna." And he opened the trunk and showed me. I declined, as somehow I wanted to get out of there. (I wrote him a nice thank-you letter later.) Another time, I got closer than I should have to a Vietnam vet with a perm and shoulderpads who turned out to have (or told me he had) a room full of guns and knives. I escaped next day to England.

One New Year's Day, amongst all these comings and goings, I was back in Oregon; alone at Mom's house in Gold Beach, while she was far away with Al. I had the idea that it is good to deep-clean on that day, to prepare for the year ahead. I started dusting high up in the corners, with a fluffy duster on a stick; but somehow the project defeated me – it was simply impossible; the energy just wasn't there. *What is wrong with me?* I wondered again. I'd been on that strict candida diet now for two years – yet my health was getting worse.

In fact, I could no longer bring myself to cut my toenails, or scrub my feet. Washing dishes was almost impossible – they sat in the sink for days until I could somehow manage to wash them.

I was working on a book – my twenty-eight volumes of teenage diaries had been typed by an Indian girl and I was editing – but my sense of day and night was all topsy-turvy; I'd stay at the computer till 5 a.m., then go for a bleak little walk while the sun was rising. Once I saw an angry-looking three-legged raccoon rushing across a woodsy road, and I felt… akin to him. Or I would walk through fog down to the deserted beach where someone had built shelters for two dozen feral cats, which stared basilisk at me as I passed. Then I'd go to bed and sleep till 5 p.m. – so that I missed all but half an hour of daylight.

The slightest thing made me throw up – a ride in a van, the smell of burritos. Increasingly, I was having seizures – train-track visuals, then headache, then thrashing about in excruciating pain, vomiting till I was dry, then fainting, waking up next day wrapped around the toilet, unable to recall the pain.

A curious symptom of the disease was that I felt sort of secretive about it. Private. I didn't want anyone to meddle. I didn't seriously consider going to a 'normal' doctor; they cost too much, and were somehow just not in my world. I had no insurance; in Poona it was so easy and cheap to see a doctor, there'd been no need. (Nor did I seem to be an insurancey type of person.) I did see a few different sannyasin healers, but none could figure out what was going on. Finally I asked Rinzai, a gifted Mystic Ring kinesiologist who now operated a health food shop in Sedona, if he could tune in. He held my hand, then said he was being blocked from seeing what the problem was.

Later I was grateful for this – for if I'd known then, what could I have done without insurance?

But occasionally I'd feel communicative and would send bewildered, complaining emails to friends and family, about my desperate financial straits as much as my health. I was again in Sedona; jewelry-purveying psychics were a dime a dozen there. My sister, always helpful, suggested an idea she thought I could try for making money; the suggestion felt unrealistic to me; I told her so, and she felt very much slighted. She decided that it would be healthiest for both of us if we didn't communicate any more! This was a huge shock to me, which fed into all the uncertainty and general ghastliness. (In retrospect, she was right: each of us needed to find our separate threads in this life, without reaction or reference or holding back because of the other. The separation would last three years.)

I was still trying to dance, but Keene said I'd lost my spunk. In despair about money, I got a job cleaning time-share condos. I lasted two exacting, punctilious days under a hefty lady boss before another seizure laid me low, and I didn't show up for work (and received a scathing scolding). I never went back.

Eventually I rode to Canada on the train to meet Forbes, the man I'd been corresponding with. We felt like friends, not lovers (in fact, my libido had shut down with the disease; I *just couldn't* any more). He watched me through a two-day seizure. I told him I thought it was a migraine. "That is no migraine," he said, gazing at me with a sort of pitying, considering stillness where I'd just come to on the bathroom floor. Then: "You keep talking about India. I think that's where you really want to be. I'm going to buy you a ticket."

I've lost count of the number of tickets I've been bought in my life (maybe people are trying to get me off their hands?) Then my affable piano-playing Portland lover Graham gave me a little pile of cash. He drove me to the Portland airport, and said to me: "If you ever need anything, just ask."

Then he kissed me, and I flew away.

Back in Poona

Once I was ensconced in my room in the Pyramid again, my health deteriorated with frightening speed. India cracks you open, brings out what's inside. And what was inside me was pretty dire. I'd be walking along the Zen Walk with somebody – that main promenade between the front, Gateless Gate and Lao Tzu Gate – and my body would simply veer to the left and crash into them. Or I'd be gossiping with someone at Lao Tzu Gate, and simply fall to the ground.

It was winter, high season. People were there from all over, exploring meditations, groups, sessions. I went to see a neurologist at Jehangir Hospital: Dr. Ichiporia, a Parsee with a very long nose and a hugely cynical line of chat. He gave me a prescription for heavy migraine pills; I took one, which made me feel so impossibly peculiar I didn't take another. Right after that pill wore off I gave a chakra reading to a Swedish policewoman. Giving sessions seemed to exacerbate the symptoms – my third eye was exercising strenuously, and it was right beside the tumor-I-didn't-know-I-had.

I liked to read with the person lying on a mattress on the floor; I kneeling or standing beside them. In this case, when the reading was over I got up from sitting beside the woman, and the room spun around. I crashed to the floor, unconscious. I came to briefly while the woman carried me in her arms towards the Pyramids. She kept asking me which was the door to my room; but I couldn't remember. Finally I recognized No. 5, and the client carried me in and put me to bed. (Thank you, Swedish policewoman!) Then she went to the health center and notified Chintana, the nurse – an Irish ex-nun of ample build, practicality, heart, and blunt realism.

I woke briefly on the stretcher on the way to the ambulance – it was night, and a street light shone overhead. The stretcher swayed like a palanquin. I woke again on a mattress-covered floor in a strange room. Vibhavan (now

Ramana) was there, and Pankaja, a British writer; and a few other people, gazing at me in consternation and concern. I was nude, and my body was twisting, turning, an endless tableau of movement; rolling, all over the floor. But for two days I was mostly unconscious.

I recovered from the seizure and went back to my apartment. I didn't know what was wrong, or what to do. So I sat down and wrote emails to everybody I could think of, describing my symptoms and asking if they had any idea what might be going on. I received a reply from my younger brother Andy: "Get an MRI scan." I did not know what this was, but it sounded like a plan.

Andy had had that pituitary tumor when he was twelve, and at that time the diagnosis could only be accomplished by doing a lumbar puncture – an experience so painful and horrible that Andy had been inspired to keep abreast of new diagnostic methodologies.

So I went to Dr. Ichiporia and requested an MRI. He agreed, gave me a chit, and told me to go to Ruby Hall, another hospital down a busy, polluted road a quarter of a mile away. So there I trudged.

The MRI, it turned out, would cost the equivalent of $105. I had precisely that much in my locked money-drawer back in my room (a recent gift from Devadasi). So I had to take a herky-jerky rickshaw ride home through the crazy rush-hour traffic, then return to Ruby Hall. The afternoon was nearly over. I lay in the MRI tube, an extremely claustrophobic space, listening to the clicks, clunks, and whirrs, as if I was in some odd spacecraft... for about twenty minutes. The way not to panic in there was to crawl down deep inside my own belly, into the *hara,* more or less; and stay there, which I did. I was proud of myself.

Then the conveyor-belt issued me forth out of the machine, like a great white metal beast sticking out its tongue, and I on it, like a fly. I saw the window, the trees outside, dusty in the grey air. The technician sat in a chair with his back to me, gazing at a screen. "Something is there!" he said, sounding concerned. A few minutes later he gave me a huge flat thick plastic carry-bag containing a lot of images on big sheets, to take back to Dr. Ichiporia.

And so I trudged back up the dirty, noisy road towards Jehangir Hospital, feeling sad. "Oh, well," I thought. "I have a brain tumor. I will die. People with brain tumors die... This is sad; I want to live some more, really. But at least it *explains* everything that's been going on. That's a relief."

It was after 5 p.m., but the doctor had waited for me. He sat now behind his desk, holding up film after film and staring at it. Then he looked over at me. "Ninety-five percent chance it's not cancer," he said. "And the tumor is completely enclosed in the dura – the membrane around the brain. But I cannot let you go home. This is dangerous, urgent – it is swelling very large. We must operate tomorrow." And he explained that, for unknown reasons, such a tumor – a benign, but cytotoxic, meningioma – periodically swells up and sends out poisons into the blood, inciting seizures. The tumor was pressing on the left frontal lobe of the brain – the seat of well-being, pleasure, cognition, the superconscious, and other good things. That's why my life had felt so grey and suppressed the past three years… I had not, for all that time, dreamt, or laughed, or cried.

My vision was affected as the tumor was pressing on the optic nerve. If the thing was not removed, it would suppress various bodily functions and I would die.

I felt a sense of complete relief. Just wonderful. It wasn't cancer. I would live. And now… there was nothing to do but let go.

Dr. Ichiporia ushered me out of his office to sit on a chair while he made phone calls. Fifteen or twenty minutes later I looked up and saw, striding towards me down the hall, faces set like a posse of rescuing vigilantes, eyes glowing with compassion – Vibhavan, Chintana, Dr. Pragitam, and Vibhavan's girlfriend. Nurse Chintana said later that that was when she knew something was really wrong with me – when she saw me sitting there completely oblivious to the smell from the nearby toilets! My olfactory sense was affected by the tumor.

From the moment I had heard that I didn't have cancer, I'd entered a state of bliss. I had not realized how much responsibility, for a fate I seemed unable to control, had been weighing heavily on me. I'd been fretting about survival, a place to live, getting from here to there – in my ill and befuddled state. Now, not only was there nothing I *had* to do, but nothing I *could* do: I could not remove my own tumor! I had to simply let go into whatever was going on. My whole being did this almost instantly, as if I had sprung into the arms of the Goddess and could at long last lie in her elastic, trampoline grip, bouncing gently up and down.

Though, when a wheelchair was brought, I protested – "I can walk!"

But I was made to sit in the wheelchair. It wasn't so bad. I felt a bit silly to be made special, is all.

One thing I was asked to do: tell the hospital how I would pay for the operation. They estimated it would cost about $2,000.

My friend Graham, in Portland, had said: "If you ever need anything… "

Vibhavan was from Portland – he was a big, bluff, kindly-yet-canny businessman-turned-devotee. His accountant had an office there.

I had Graham's phone number in the address book in my purse. I gave it to Vibhavan. Within an hour the money was on its way – $2,500; and, in the end, that was the bill, almost to the penny or paise; including every surgical glove, breath-mint for the surgeons, drill-bit for my skull; eleven days in hospital. All of it.

In any Indian hospital, as I've said, relatives are not only expected, but required, to stay with the patient and help with her care. Back in the Commune, a search went out for anyone who could come and help. In the end, with much complication and backing-and-forthing of emails, and help from Devika in Switzerland, it was arranged that Rudra would fly from England (after a rush-through of his visa facilitated by ace ashram fixer Dhyanesh). Rudra had been working at Osho Leela in Dorset for a few years. However, it would still take a week for him to get here, so meanwhile the Commune, stretched to its capacities already with the winter season influx of seekers, had to supply people to sit with me in six-hour shifts. (There was apparently some discussion as to whether this much care was appropriate to give to one old resident; the new people arriving needed all of everyone's attention. But Dr. Amrito was asked and he said yes, give the care. Thank you, Dr. Amrito!) For I would not be admitted until somebody was pledged to be with me.

I was very happy with the caretakers who kept appearing at intervals. I was by now on a drip, which made me woozy and cloudy; steroids were added to whatever feel-good stuff they dripped into my vein, to try to shrink the tumor before the surgery; it was dangerous to operate if it was engorged.

It was, in any case, generally expected, in the ashram, that I would die. Nobody outside medical circles knew what a 'benign meningioma' was; but a brain tumor is a brain tumor, and we all knew people who'd died of them. And whenever you cut somebody's skull open, anything could happen; and it might very well not be good. The anesthetic alone was dangerous.

Dr. Ichiporia would not do the surgery himself, but assist; he now had to find the best brain surgeon he could, on very short notice. And he did – he found a sort of rock-star brain surgeon, Dr. Sushil Patkar, who, among other professional positions, commanded a laboratory in Poona which was devoted to microscope brain surgery; funded by the USA.

Dr. Patkar was available only the day after Christmas, which meant another day with the tumor in me; but he told me later that this extra day had saved my life – the swelling wouldn't otherwise have decreased sufficiently, and to have operated would have been disastrous. In any case, most of the hospital staff were Christians from Madras, and would not have worked on Christmas. (Hindus consider nursing a very low-class job. Only Untouchables will deal with bodily fluids. So Christians man, and woman, the hospitals.)

I was put into a good-sized private room with basic furnishings. Jehangir is a huge, modern hospital, and I was on an upper floor, with a nice big window looking out into the dusty tree-tops and tall rough-looking buildings. As I lay there in my floaty state, I was very aware that my toenails and fingernails badly needed tending. As I've said, I had found myself quite unable to cut them; and now I could not bear the idea of going to my unknown fate all taloned and claw-y. I'd met Dr. Patkar by that time and I simply adored the man. He was big and glowy and caramel-satiny. He roared in an overbearing way at the interns and other doctors; they hated it, though they scurried to do his bidding; but I could see his heart of gold shining through every bossy roar. I was so *glad* that this was the man who was going to ferret around inside my head. He was in the best tradition of magnificent daddies; yet he was a scientist too. I still feel lucky when I think of him.

I asked a nurse if she knew of someone I could pay to cut and file my nails. (I had 185 rupees left, in my bag in the nightstand.) She said she knew one nurse who was also a manicurist. And so the thing was duly done... claws, fore and aft, pared and buffed down to civilized shape and size. Whew.

But that was not the end of it. Next morning, 26th December 2003, I was being prepped for surgery by a different little nurse, the dark dark brown of the Madrassi, where the sun is strong. This nurse was shaving my pubic area – a strange thing to do when it is one's head that will be cut open – but apparently it had to do with catheters. In any case I was too goofy with meds to resist. The young woman sploshed soapy water from a dish onto the fur, then took her razor and began to scrape. Her voice came, low, menacing:

"You paid for manicure," she said. *Scrape, scrape.* "You *paid,* no?"

"Uh – yesssss… " I replied.

The razor came closer to the cleft between the lips. *Scrape, scrape.*

"You paid *hundrrred rrrupees,* no?" *Scrape, scrape*… closer to the little bud, the pearl.

I understood, even in my gluey state, that she was jealous. That many other nurses were jealous. That I had done something unforgivable – one of them had made some extra money! But the others hadn't!

Scrape, scrape…

Luckily, that was the end of my punishment – except for the fact that my bag, with its remaining rupees, and cheap watch, and comb, was stolen out of the bedside stand while I was in surgery. But no matter. By the time I found out, I barely cared at all.

Deliverance

I didn't know that five people – including Prartho Sereno, the poet, singer, and artist – were sitting in meditation in a room right below the operating theater. Nor that others were meditating, in other countries. I didn't know that my head was strapped to the table so that it could not move even a millimeter. I did not know that a four-inch-wide strip of hair had been shaved from my hairline. (Dr. Patkar later told me he likes a bare skull to work with, but my below-the-waist-length hair seemed to him worth saving.)

Yet, when I was emerging from the anesthetic after the six and a half hours the operation took; groggy, confused, all undone, all over and all through – I *knew* – because I had heard the surgeon talking, even while I was unconscious – that he was very pleased with the way things had gone; very proud of himself; entirely optimistic. The entire growth had been removed.

Prartho was sitting with me when I emerged. "How are you feeling?" she asked.

"I dunno. Maybe – bored. Maybe – *American,*" I said, apparently. And then – "Oh *boy oh boy oh boy.*"

But very soon, Prartho and I were reciting poetry to each other. I spoke Garcia Lorca's *La Luna Asoma (The Moon Rises)* in the Spanish. Then, Prartho told me later, she knew that I was going to be all right.

It was funny, that… I'd written very little during my three years of illness. But as soon as the bulging bin-bag had been whisked out from behind my skull, the area of the brain it had been depressing bounced back again like a sponge, and the poems began to gush like a geyser. They never stopped again, and eventually began to branch out into short-stories too. (I felt as if it was a toxic, rotting black bag of garbage that was gone, all-at-once – but Chintana told me that the growth had been healthily pink and veined, and from that they knew that it was benign.) (Meningiomas have the same chemistry as uterine fibroids.)

I was filled with joy and gratefulness. I lay in my bed with tears of blissful astonishment pouring down my swollen face. I dreamt again, after all that time; richly colorful shopping dreams, full of velvety purple sweaters and satin dresses and mysterious dancing-Shiva rugs and glowing ivory face creams. The dreams told me I was here for beauty, beauty…

I was thrilled to welcome Rudra on New Year's Day, and, once I'd moved back to my place in the Pyramid, he trotted my meals from the canteen and took the empties back again. Ill-advisedly, I got up and danced once, when Rudra played some jivey music – but I could feel things rattling in my skull, and had to stop. But oh, how I could *hear* the music, newly, like I had never heard music before!

I began to furiously write and assemble a little book about this new adventure I'd gone through. Rudra took me out into Osho Teerth Park behind the ashram and I lay on an assan, my head swathed in a maroon silk shawl, a gift from Pankaja; while Rudra read Walt Whitman aloud to me in his beautiful, oh-so-deep, radio-announcer voice. How I loved my brother, blood of my blood!

I was still very fragile and weak and thin, and it exhausted me to talk. So, just as at the hospital I'd asked my various sannyasin minders to tell me their life stories, to prevent my talking (and a beautiful and touching thing it was, to hear them!) I now asked Rudra to tell me about *every love affair he'd ever had.* He did so – it took days – and I no longer felt like such a freak. His exploits rivaled my own.

A psychic from the Mystery School visited me – I often had visitors – and he told me I would have another relationship; and that it would be completely different from any I had had before. Gopal, the Vipassana teacher who had made the life-saving *Relaxing the BodyMind* tape, visited. He brought his dilruba, and played music just for me, just for *now.*

My aura heard it – it was as if the dilruba saw me, really *saw* me, and played, so exquisitely, accurately, right into my aura. And my aura was so happy – just what it needed to hear! This was a revelation… what sound *could* be! Thank you, Gopal!

Devageet visited. He asked me a question: "Where were you when you were under the anesthetic?"

"Hmmm!" I replied. "I don't know. Let me check… " I closed my eyes and went back to the operating theater, where I was strapped to the table and my skull was hinged open like a hatchback car door. People fiddling around in my head.

And I saw this: my soul was like a mountain stream, flowing over round stones, pouring and rippling along, all clear and fresh – and it was just in joy, so much joy, *because I was utterly helpless and could not do anything.* And I was told, by Those who hover nearby, "You will never forget this lesson."

And I have not forgotten.

One of the things that gave me a buoyant satisfaction during this time – besides the fact that I'd survived, and was all cleared out – was that *nobody could ask me to do a damned thing for quite a while!*

But what has all this to do with my search – with Doing vs. non-Doing?

…A very great deal, as it happens.

A couple of days after I came out of surgery, I remembered suddenly that Kohrogi-san had diagnosed the brain tumor, during that session I'd had with him in France!

Oh. My. God.

So I sent a message to him through Champaka, who often came in to give me Ito-thermie sessions (running the heated, relaxing-smoky instruments along the place where, during surgery, a tube had been inserted under the skin from temple to jaw, and the jaw unhinged… Then he moved the heated metal tubes along my legs, where the chemicals of the meds had finally released themselves in aches and twitches – and onto my back and sides, where a rash caused by an allergy to one of the meds had briefly broken out and was now healing. Thank you, Champaka. You are great, and a wonderful friend.)

I asked Kohrogi-san, "Did this happen because of the way I was working?"

The message came back: "Yes. If this had not happened, you would not have stopped." Then – "Try looking from *outside.*"

I pondered this. Look from outside? Instead of empathing, taking on a client's life from within… ? How would that work? But I wasn't thinking of clients now. I was saving my own life. I just let the words in, and let them percolate around in there.

It began to feel like a whole new way of being – not just working – was starting now; though how it would unfold I had no idea. And certainly I had the sense that listening to Kohrogi-san was a damned good idea! I was embarrassed that I had treated his diagnosis with contempt and then forgetting.

The stakes were high. Meningiomas can recur.

Much later I found this quote from Shamanic psychic healer Kay Cordell Whitaker:

There are two major indigenous traditions for psychic-hands-on healing around the world: there is the Win-Win type and there is the Warrior type. Warrior-type healers literally go to war with the disorder. They go into the patient's system, confront the disease, wrestle it, overpower it, and force it out of the person's body. Usually the way they force it out is to take at least some of the condition into themselves; they then wrestle it within themselves and expel it. This is not an easy way to do healing and warrior healers typically don't have long lives.

The other tradition is [...] based on a win-win philosophy, its approach is one of peace… approaching a disorder with respect and gratitude, providing some element of gain and win for everything involved in the process of healing. [...] In a win-win scenario, the disease willingly gives its message, its information, to the healer and the client and leaves the body. Sometimes it just downright rushes out of the body. No-one has to use an excessive amount of energy, so there's no danger and no harming.

In my work, I didn't exactly wrestle – I 'became' – actually a surrender to whatever the person's disorder was. But I did take it all in; and use all my available energy. And I often took stuff out of people. In any case, it had harmed me.

I had other theories for possible causes of the tumor:

1) For unknown reasons, these tumors are much more common in India than in the West, typically attacking women over sixty. (Indian surgeons,

therefore, are much better at dealing with them than are Western ones. Too, it is apparently well-known that Indian surgeons are defter and more delicate-handed generally.) So perhaps there is some environmental factor.

2) In my forties I had used for some considerable time a popular progesterone cream. This is used to balance the two female hormones estrogen and progesterone; but I am not very estrogenic, so I probably didn't need it. Dr. Ichiporia had said the tumor had been there for at least ten years.

3) Osho might have been radiated by the CIA during those strange episodes where he shouted from the podium that rays were being directed at him. The rays would have passed right over our heads where we sat before him.

But I could clearly sense that my over-worked, bloated third eye was at least in part responsible.

Lao Tzu Maneesha, that gentle princess, offered to sort out my post-surgery hair. I had had a bandage round my head for sixteen days by the time the hair could be freed and washed and combed. Maneesha lovingly washed the incredibly snarled-up mass and then spent an hour untangling and snipping and sorting… until finally all the hair was unknotted and lay damp on the towel around my shoulders. It had lost half its length – instead of hitting the top of my behind, it came only to my shoulder-blades. Oh, well – it was much easier to deal with, and I was so happy I regarded all of this with huge favor.

And. The main point now was to listen to my own body. What it liked, what it didn't like.

That was all.

For certainly it had not liked doing empath work year in, year out, with great earnestness and travail. Giving my body to others, impartially, like a prostitute.

This was not necessarily going to be easy, this change. People were still pressuring me to work. Nor did I know how I would survive financially without doing those sessions. But there was no arguing with how it was – this was rebirth time.

I stayed in my room nearly all the time as I healed. A Tibetan acupuncturist had told me that such a drastic event required at least seven weeks of quiet and retreat – one week for each chakra. I ignored any requests that I resume work in the Commune (by now it was called a Resort*). I erected a psychic wall against them. I knew that this was necessary. At the time, it felt like I might never work again.

I did not know then that I would claim, for my recovery, not just seven weeks of peace; but seven years. I am so glad it happened that way. (Dr. Amrito, I later heard, asked Dr. Patkar, the golden surgeon, why I was taking such a long time to convalesce. Dr. Patkar said that he didn't know; the operation had gone so well. Then he added, "But after all, she is a *Brrritish Lady!*" The expat Yankee in me was tickled pink!)

Rudra brought me news and (smoking temple) gossip as well as food. My funny brother! Once I gave him 400 rupees and asked him to go to the Blue Diamond and buy an imported glossy fashion magazine for me. I could not read yet, and I wanted to gaze at pictures of goddesses, and enjoy the shiny luxury of *Vogue* or *Bazaar* or *Marie-Claire*... the sense of utter self-indulgence. He returned with a terrible old manky second-hand Indian one instead, gotten for fifty rupees from a wallah who had them spread out on a blanket on the pavement. My brother had been *simply unable to bring himself* to spend that kind of money on a magazine!

He organized a poetry reading with some smoking-temple friends. It was in someone's room, like a 50's beatnik cave; candles in wine-bottles. I recited my signature poem, *The Crows.* People pressed wads of rupees on me afterwards. I used some of it for Rudra to see the dentist (oh, badly needed!)

I had a general feeling that any words I spoke were coming directly out of the very source, the well of my being, with no time-lapse or diversions. I had never felt like that before. It was incredibly delicious.

In the early mornings, though, I was alone. And soon I began to meditate, sitting in a legless canvas meditation chair (called a Backjack), under my light-blue mosquito net. I was so happy... a pillow would cushion my lower back; and a pillow under each knee kept me comfortable yet straight-spined. And I would feel the way energy had loosed and opened and flown all about me like a whole *herd* of birds. And how my heart just never stopped opening its mouth in surprise.

* I'm not sure why, except that the new breed of seeker was young and well-traveled and tended to stay a much shorter time; and could go swimming in the pool instead of washing dishes. For the daily labor of cooking and cleaning and path-tending was now done by local Indian workers wearing shiny passes on lanyards round their necks.

I tried an experiment. Fixing my physical position in my inner sight, I'd get out from under the net, step over to the side of the room, turn; and look back at the person sitting under the net.

I could *see* her – what her preoccupations were; her atmosphere. A valuable objectivity, a kind of *wholeness of sight,* would happen.

Then I'd get back under the net and re-enter 'me.'

Somehow, this segued into something else: I started listening, as if to something coming from that watcher's perspective outside. I knew that Human Design said it was good, when you're on the phone, to listen with your right ear; you'll hear what you need to hear. When I listened like that, I heard… words. Not audible – not actual sound – but, in a kind of silence, words nevertheless. Loving ones; astute. I found that I could open my heart and ask questions, and from that right side I'd hear pithy, ungrammatical, beautiful and true answers. I knew their truth because my body resonated with the precise intimations.

This became one of my tools – and my joys. Later, in the Swiss mountains too I would sit on a rock or a stump, on a mountainside or in the woods… close my eyes… and embark on such a conversation. I'd emerge from it later slightly drunk with bliss and love. This kind of meditation, as time went on, always lifted me up and set my mind at rest.

10

Healing

Healing

2004 – 2012

In the Alps

For two months I was simply blissed out. After that I was merely full of joy! I flew to Oregon on 28th February 2004, all scrawny and turbaned and over-sensitive; and I was so happy during the visits to Mama in Oregon and family in Maui; and then the whole nine months I spent convalescing at Devika's chalet in the Alps, watching the seasons change. Rudra eventually came and took up residence in the studio apartment downstairs. I cooked for him – practising, I knew, for the man whom the psychic in Poona had promised would arrive. Rudra helped me with editing a book I was working on about that ill-fated trip into the Himalayas with Anando, all those years before. It was something to play with, really, while I rested in my soul. I wasn't giving sessions, so didn't have to worry how I might proceed in that in a healthy way. I was meditating, receiving guidance from Those. And I was looking at this question: *what does my energy really want to do now?*

When I asked myself this, I immediately saw a picture: I was bending over, making envelopes – just like I had as a teenager. In fact, the vision echoed the creativity of my teenage time: complete freedom to make whatever I liked. No spiritual mandate saying that getting enlightened (somehow) was much more important than just fiddling around making stuff out of paper and paints and glue! Freedom to alter clothes by hand, peacefully; and lose myself in the joy of fashion. Freedom to write and illustrate my incidental, personal, quite possibly worthless little poems and stories. Even if nobody else ever cared, even if it never did a damned bit of good for anyone – that was what my being wanted to do. If it meant I was some sort of lower incarnation, so be it. *It was what I found in myself to be.*

When, in Poona, after my surgery, I'd written fervently about the experience, and then had gone to the ashram stationery office to try to get the resulting pamphlet copied so I could send it to some friends – I'd been told by the person behind the window: "No, we won't do that here. It's *personal.*" The tone of voice implied that this was a stupid, worthless and unspiritual thing; outside the oh-so-vital running of the place-that-would-save-so-many-souls.

I had replied, lightly, "I am a very *personal* person." It had felt like the calm rebel eye of a storm.

I am not going to argue though; what do I know? Spiritual discourses and writings are all about selflessness, the merging of the small self into the Infinite; the melting into the Whole, the Divine. A commune is a way to do this too – you merge your small self into the larger celebration, the larger lake or ocean. At night, when we all sat together, sang together, listened to the Master in reverent silence – it was surely like that – something enormous, something blissfully melting. In meditations, one melted, flowed, expanded past one's boundaries. All so true.

Osho had said contradictory-seeming things on this subject, as on all other subjects; seeking to trick us out of our dualistic minds. On the one hand, he spoke in tones of tenderness and awe on the beauty of the dissolution of the small self. The non-being of the ego, the great vanishment into the All. Every day we heard him speak on this with the vast authority of one who Knows; who lives in that place-beyond-place. And we were nourished by this in ways words cannot describe. We were part, then, of that vastness, even as our minds could not comprehend the notion.

On the other hand, he said that every enlightened man is a rebel – leaving behind the Known, the society's dictates; and becoming truly himself – an iconoclast, standing against the world. There is no Humanity, he said – only individuals. The Search is always individual. Each being is unique, and it is up to each of us to find that uniqueness, no matter what anyone says.

Human Design says – and I also say – artistic people are individualists. Art must be original, or it is boring; and that originality arrives in the individual's cosmic in-box from some mysterious place. It is not logical at all. Osho spoke with joy and appreciation of Samuel Taylor Coleridge, who wrote two thousand poems and only completed six of them, because the last lines for the others had simply never arrived.

Now, obviously there are different sorts of poets – as many sorts as there are poets themselves. But to write poetry – or to paint – or create music – you need to hunker down and spend time on it, in a determined, individualistic way; you cannot simultaneously be cooking for a crowd, or digging holes for building-foundations (though, of course, anything can inspire you – anything at all. Still, you will need to take a few minutes or hours off your work to write it down or paint it.)

And that separates you from the Tribe, and takes you away from productiveness. And yet, it must be done; there *are* people like that, who are guided by some muse-ful forces that insist that they do these self-absorbed, possibly-useless things. And if the person does not do them, she is miserable, twitchy, restless – and might become addictive or depressed or both. Her soul will go hungry. She will not be living the life she was designed to live.

So it is a *personal* thing – a me-me-I-I sort of thing. A creator is often a hermit too, and just not cut out to take much care of others.

It is this Individual inspiration (whether beatific or wacky) that cuts like a sharp wedge through the status quo, keeping it from stagnation. Evolution requires this shake-up. Therefore the eccentric musician or designer or poet is necessary to existence.

There are people who understand the meaning of 'the small self melting into the vaster self.' My beautiful, miraculous, peach-glowing sister is one of those. And then there are people to whom such an idea would never occur. Who have no idea what it means. Who really only get me-me-I-I. I am one of those people. (Although I've experienced something like dissolution of the 'me,' with just consciousness remaining, during out-of-body trips. And it was *incredible.)*

Once, during the 90's, I was complaining to Sarita about some lover who wasn't there for me, and Sarita advised me to go lie under a tree and 'make love with the whole Universe.' Jeezus, I thought, I don't *want* to do that! What's *that* about? Some rubbishy emptiness, is all! Not a hot man between my legs, in my arms… ! (Though much later, too, I have experienced this vaster Universe-loving; when I did exactly what my own non-tactile-by-that-time energy was dictating, during an experiment in a Tantra group; and ended up in sighing, wave-lapping communion with the sky – .)

In my explorations in the inner world, I have looked hard, and with some heartache, at this issue of the microcosm vs. the macrocosm. And what I have seen is this: the way a person is made, is her personal Door. It doesn't matter what judgments anyone might have about any of it. There are infinite varieties of people. But whatever is your case, is what you are here to live. Not what you've been conditioned to be, to persuade you away from your nature; but what the gods assigned you to. It doesn't need fixing or therapizing – therapy is for getting rid of our parents, not changing our natures.

And when you live *your* nature – you have on the hat that exactly fits you – you emerge from imprisonment, and then whatever miracle awaits the truly free, can happen to you.

I cannot tell you what that is. I can only say that being 'myself' – whatever that means – is bliss, pleasure, rightness; a resounding emplacement at just the right location in the universe.

What this has to do with others, I also cannot say; nor, really, am I especially interested. It is enough – it *must* be enough – just to do the stuff I want to do. Everyone else is free – they need not be interested too; even if at times I might really long for them to be.

I think that some people are more macrocosmic and some are more microcosmic. I think too that these two things can turn themselves inside out and become each other, at some unspecified point in the roilings and moilings of the cosmos – that at some deep level they are not really different at all. We're all bathed in both, all the time; partake of both. Personal leads to vast; vast rests in, or expresses through, personal. And I am absolutely certain that Doing isn't in it. That switching, that transformation, just happens. Maybe it's always happening.

It is Osho's genius that he effortlessly contains all these seeming opposites. And in the Human Design of his body, it was like that too. Lots of people have both.

In our spiritual boot-camp, the personal was both supported as never before in our lives: through therapy and meditation – and submerged rigorously for the good of the whole – in work. For many of us, the branching out into Individual endeavor came later, after we had detached ourselves and gone away. And we were all the better – oh, so much immeasurably the better – for the great gulp of light we had taken, which could then help us see our way in our own studios and living rooms, and in the world.

In August I took a train from Les Jeannettes, where the chalet was, to France, where Kohrogi-san was leading a group at a healing center in the lush green summer countryside. There I re-united with my sister. It was quite a traumatic visit for me, as I was still holding myself very gingerly, very preciously. Sarita and I had not met for three years, and the microcosmic and macrocosmic met with some splashing and consternation.

A French psychic there told Sarita, all unbidden, that if I didn't 'drop my ego,' something terrible would happen to me. (This same man, when I'd first met him, in Poona, had abruptly blurted to me that my spiritual growth was very lacking in some way I don't exactly remember. He had unfortunate delivery – he'd importuned, offended. I'd blocked him out thenceforth.)

This was too much. After all I'd been through! What kind of shit was this, 'drop your ego?' What did it *mean?* And who the fuck did he think he was?

I ROARED at him! "As one professional to another," I yelled, "I DON'T LIKE YOUR STYLE!" (I am particularly averse to predictions, as I hope I've said – though I have also valued them, and as much as I try not to give them, I have done so… and always, I hope, only positive ones. Such damage can be done with arrogant pronouncements; we are all so vulnerable!)

After that, the French psychic began to tremble, and then started bringing me little tidbits to eat, and flapping about. Sometimes it's good to yell at importuning souls. (That was fourteen years ago, and, so far, lots of magical, and only a few awful, things have happened. Is there a statute of limitations on bad predictions? As to the ego – whatever that means, I still can't say. I think the things need to be loved and cuddled, not bitched at. Grrrr!)

Kohrogi-san was in the room. He gave me an Ito-thermie session. I saw pictures of pine trees, and told him this.

"I also see pine trees," he said. Then he added, "You need *quiet… quiet… quiet.*"

I went back to the chalet, and spent much time falling into my inner world; finding out what was true there… what resonated with my wise and sensate body. What it *knew.*

One night there was a tiny miracle: a tonsil had become swollen and was hurting. I lay in bed in my wood-walled room, sound asleep in the dark… and was woken by a sound – a chime, or bell – and it was if it was *pointed directly into* the tonsil. I felt the presence of Those… sweet, hovering. Next morning my throat was just fine.

Nisarg came to visit me. We had a great time, catching up on all that had happened, also in her ever-eventful life. When she found out that I was channeling for myself, she got very interested, and asked if I'd do it for her. So I did; and she loved it. And so a new kind of session was born.

I was corresponding with a few men on the herpes dating site. Eventually a sweet, practical, good-looking young man flew from Springfield, Missouri to Switzerland to take me out to dinner. (That's the way he put it.) It was a very good dinner. We spent a week hiking all over the high, wintry valley in the snow, with me talking and him listening – and often laughing loudly at something I'd said. Neil behaved like a perfect gentleman, staying in a hotel, never trying even to kiss me. I didn't take him seriously at all… to me he looked like a college boy, and I was, by this time, fifty-three.

In the Placid Hills of Missouri

We spent the next seven and a half years together.

This relating was, from the beginning, truly Tantric. Not because I imposed some ideal on it – but because my whole system was simply finished with all the ways I had done things before.

It was a heart connection, deeply and vulnerably and sweetly, oh so sweetly. And we began meditating together before we ever attempted anything more physically intimate. I invited him to this meditating; and he, an innocent, having never heard of meditation or Tantra, came with me, staunch and honest and willing.

So as well as heart, there was Light between us – that thing that happens when you take a few steps towards the sacred, and it comes rushing towards you with its arms open. We meditated at first twice a week, then, after a year or so, once a week; it was enough. The rest of the time was lit up by it. I designed the meditations to fit the mood of the day, and we went into them decorously, respectfully, quietly – never missing a one. We did Goddess Gazing, and Barry-Long-style, and Candle Gazing, and Zen Walking, and Happy Star, and Dolphin Dancing, and so many more. Generally each session had three stages – ending with some silent integration time, and then sharing.

During these meditations I could finally experience and honor the subtle nuances of my feminine energy – its hesitations, its gaps, its restfulness – without any sort of badgering or goal-orientation from either Neil or myself. There was simply no need for anything to 'happen.' I could *just be,* and yet in connection, in union! Again and again I could hardly believe my luck. …I felt completely finished with the pursuit of pleasure, which turns both men and women, it seemed to me, into trained monkeys. Instead, I had finally said Yes to the Above – and it showered on us mysteries of levity, gravity, and delight. Our household was radiant and soft and orderly and sweet with happiness.

Soon, menopause came along. I lay in bed at night in my own room. (I had insisted on separate rooms as being simply humane… everybody on earth should have his or her own room. We'd cuddle or meditate in his bed and then fall asleep together, and I'd later get up and go to my own space to be alone.) I would sweat and toss and turn, but along with this discomfort a new verve was coming into my body and soul. Over months, everything changed… a creative power began to pour through me, I felt healthier than I'd ever been, and sex lost any allure it still had had. I just didn't care about it any more; it seemed outré, silly, unnecessary. Not only that, it *hurt* all of a sudden! Dr. Patkar, the Indian surgeon, had forbade any use of supplementary hormones, ever; these could bring back the tumor. And I didn't want to take them anyway. I was so happy with the new way I felt! Sex, the whole game of chasing, and focusing on sensations, and using so much energy for those attempts at relating – just felt like some wild old storm that I had battled through for forty years, and now it was gone; and the silence was wonderful.

My romantic passion for Neil flourished as bright as ever, even as I felt freed of the old need to try to please and be pleasured. This was never our focus, Neil and I… Now our meditations no longer included penetration; everything else was in them, though, that had been there – resonant quietude, expansion, caring, discovery. The Unknown.

Neil said that he didn't mind the celibacy (I did not entirely believe him, but he was by nature a mild man in bed, not in the least demanding or driven).

During this halcyon time, I had a dream: *I am on a bus. Osho is there. We look in each other's faces. I become all transparent; as he is. His eyes widen. He is smiling, aglow with an appreciation of all that has happened to me, of some new maturity in me, since we last met. He tells me I can ask three questions.*

This seems very simple, but when I awake I don't remember the questions or the answers; only a transmission that came with them: I'm being taken back into myself, layer on layer. I'm seeing that I am responsible – not in a Doing way but in a Being sense. I am what I am; therefore I become what I am. The presentness of my being is the whole story; all that needs to be told. At this true level there is no cause and effect. There is only this-stuff-ness.

In spite of the lovely peace and order of our lives, I began to crave adventure, travel, and… an audience for the poems that were pouring through me. Sometimes I visited Nisarg, and that was wonderful; sometimes my old friend Lotus in Mill Valley, California; and that was great again.

The houses Neil and I lived in were beautiful – the first was in two acres of thick-growing oak trees. I got to stay home all day and write, paint, cook. I made beautiful feasts for us and for friends. The meditations were so beautiful, and the American Midwest such a challenging place for me to live in in other ways, that I ended up writing a book about this time.

We were prosperous, comfortable – too comfortable. The American way was too dull for my blood. The locals found me too exotic and in self-defense more or less blocked my existence. So my joy-life took place in the house and on my walks; or when I meditated under a tree on a nearby hillside. Whenever other humans came into it, I would feel in the end gaspingly lonely. We moved near to Kansas City when Neil got a promotion; but that was even worse… without the cover and nourishment of the blessed oaks, my oddity and isolation stuck out even more. Once or twice a year we'd travel, and in Europe I would briefly rejoin my friends, my sister; and feel the liveliness and spontaneity of things again – so different from the predictable order of our lives at home. I'd get to skinny-dip in woodsy waterfalls with Tantrikas, and would then wonder what the *hell* I was doing in Missouri – where the very idea of skinny-dipping filled women with shame – for obesity was the norm.

And Neil himself – untraveled before he met me, in love with his native Ozarks, in all their rolling non-dramaticKness – could not help me. He was pained that I began to pine for the far-away. He grew quiet, and began to drink more and more beer at weekends. This made him jolly and affectionate, but I still found it sad. I thought it must be that he missed making full physical love. I felt worried and responsible.

Five Weeks in Poona

In 2008, after saving up for ages (I'd started doing sessions on Skype: tarot, channeling; and Human Design was slowly creeping into them too; and I sold my artwork, and whatever jewels I had left) I went to Poona for a complete dental overhaul (at one-sixth Western prices). I led a Tantra group in the Resort, did many Voice Dialogue sessions, went to the tailor a lot, enjoyed the Samadhi. All went smoothly – and, though I was not in the mood for tumult, I was again almost disappointed that nothing fell apart! I had a follow-up MRI scan, and all was well. "You are one of our success stories," said Dr. Ichiporia, and I could tell by his tone that not all of them were like that.

Garimo told me before I left that 'they' were very happy with my contribution. I was much relieved – it was nice for once not to have to see myself as an always-ill, skive-off-ing person.

While I was there I received an email from a niece who lived in Maui. Her little daughter had finally described in detail how her father had been sexually abusing her for years. I had stayed with the family a couple of years earlier and I loved the grave, intelligent, fluff-haired little sprite; the evil news sent my stomach churning. I felt that I wanted to get some sort of session, so at lunch I sat with Canadian Gandha and Vibhavan and asked them their advice on what sort of session would be best. Vibhavan offered to do a meditation with me, that afternoon; it was called *Hara Burn.*

In his large Pyramid apartment, we stood facing each other with a little distance between us, feet about shoulder-width apart, hands in a curious position: above the head but laid flat, fingertips touching those of the other hand; not touching the head; forming a sort of hand-awning. The hands were to stay like this through the entire first stage – forty minutes.

While Techno music played, I was to spend a few minutes *cooking up* the issue inside myself – thinking about it, letting it arise. Then, at a signal from Vibhavan, I was to start *pushing the whole issue down into my hara* – and go on doing this with all my might and attention, for forty minutes. We kept eye contact the entire time.

It was an epic forty minutes, and I gave it my best. What happened was that not only did I feel the outrage and helplessness of being abused; I also then found myself *entering the psyche and body of the abuser* – the child's father, but also I found myself entering the psyche of Taffy's dad who had touched me invasively when I was eleven; and then I went on to some nameless Mongol warrior who snatched women at will and bore them away, established them in his own camp, and controlled them. I experienced the joy of possession of another human being, the sense of entitlement and expansion it gave to my feeling about myself. I had to fully inhabit this, with joy… Power surged through me, and my usual wimpy ways seemed absurd and mistaken.

In this method, the body trembles and shakes, often, but you are not to yell – just go on pushing the energy into the hara. (This all might seem strange and alarming. No, I am not advocating abuse! I am advocating transcendence. Let me explain: humans, says Osho, contain all the animals. I would add that all the archetypes are in us too, somewhere. In other words, the whole human condition is accessible to us. We fear that which we don't know; that which is repressed. We are controlled by what is repressed – look at all the pedophile priests with their vows of celibacy. The great hope, the only hope, for us all is to be able to *consciously experience* an archetype, or an animalistic energy, in a safe space – in other words, in therapy or meditation. Only when something is experienced, owned, allowed, can it become conscious and freed – it is no longer bound to exert pressure on your life. This means owning it *fully* – not an iota of horror or avoidance. Only then can it take its place in the right order of things. For example, that same gross conquering Will of the molester can, if it is realized and allowed in a safe space, turn back around into a protective and yet allowing lovingness. Courage is needed to face these demons, trust is needed to let them find their freed state.

(Application is needed to do the sweaty work. And the resulting freedom is a gift. Once you know the parameters of the energies within you, only then are you free to choose your actions. Otherwise you're being controlled by the unconscious. …As it happens, consciousness tends to choose love, and 'goodness'; in its empathy, it just does.*)

When the time was up we each backed up to a separate divan across the room from each other and lay down on our backs for twenty minutes. I was trembling all over, and it felt so wonderful to let my arms relax, hear the silence instead of the hard, driving music, and just recline with closed eyes…

Afterwards I felt that I had done my bit for the family, albeit on some etheric plane. I had made my contribution, by widening the general consciousness as

* The child's parents divorced, eventually the mother got custody, and the father died of a heart attack in 2016. The child is growing up to be a gifted cellist.

much as I was able to do. That is how love, and the freedom to choose to be non-abusive, can come in. (Vibhavan remarked, I can't resist saying, that I was a true Warrior – this is a technique from men's groups, and I had acquitted myself better than many of the men he had seen do it! …Just a little braggadocio here.)*

I also had a Family Constellation session with a talented, intuitive German therapist I'd not met before. She spent three hours with me – and we did the session in Lao Tzu house, so all the clout of the Master was in the air. I used pillows to represent different members of my extended family, while the therapist guided me.

It was a mercilessly intense session, and in it I discovered that since my mother had wanted to follow her beloved father when he died when she was seven; and my father had not wanted children, and had himself been denied a real childhood – neither one of them was *really there* as parents. And so we kids were orphans.

I surveyed the devastation of this, and there was no cure. It looked like a battlefield after the battle is over – torn-up soil, engine oil, makeshift crosses, hands sticking out of the earth –. The therapist tried her best to bring a healing, but it was not to be. Sometimes all you can do is survey the devastation; and it is curiously freeing to do so. It just is like this; nothing to be done.

And I could see why my brave and stubborn little sister had felt the need to become the spiritual mother of us all: for the practical thing – re-parenting us with enough material resources – had been beyond her, but at least she could do *this* – try to enlighten us. What a burden!

* Recently, in meditation, I was seeking illumination about sexual importuning; it is something now much in the news; a thing that has been done to me and that I have done: the foisting of oneself on a reluctant Other. What I discovered (and it took a long time of falling down through the layers): it's a question between Will – third chakra – and Heart – fourth chakra. Will says, "I *will* have this person. I *will* do what I want with them." Will is insensitive because it is yang: Doing. Day by day I often use Will on myself: "I *will* finish this task so that I can relax." The "will" and "I" are connected. That's the hardness. And the blindness; yang things are insensitive because all the energy is flowing out – forward – the molecules are naturally pouring towards the tip of the phallus. So it is not receptive or reflective. It doesn't have time or space for that.

Heart is completely different. It is empathic – it sees the Other, hears the Other, when she says, "I'm just young. I'm not ready for this." "I'm tired and I need to sleep." The Heart replies, "Oh, of course! I understand! Have your space, dear person!" instead of insinuating or forcing itself into the person's space.

Seeing all this – I felt forgiving of those men who'd done that sort of thing to me. Because that same blind overriding I have done; and to myself too. And Society actually tells us that this Will is good, in other applications. You are supposed to rely on Will.

This meditation session made me want to teach heart-groups to the world.

On my return to the States, I met Nisarg in New Jersey and participated in a Human Design training she was teaching. Nisarg is a brilliant teacher – she manages to set up situations where people can make their own discoveries.

One day while she'd been teaching I'd been waving my hand around as so often, wanting to share something. Nisarg had told me sharply that it wasn't the right time. I'd felt hurt and outraged – she is my *friend!* She has to let me speak!

Early next morning I did a very thorough semi-silent Dynamic in my room. It greatly helped me understand, love, and have compassion for the attention-seeker that had been shadowing my creativity – the painful longing, in the Midwest, I'd felt for someone to see me, see what I was offering – jewels, poems, sessions, paintings. (The Midwest I knew was much more about tractors. I am sure there is poetry in tractors – many people seem to think so. But my sessions were not wanted there; people had Jesus. Generally speaking, I felt like a Christmas tree nobody wanted the presents off of.) In the Dynamic I howled… and asked, "If nobody wants what I have to offer, *why was I born?*" God (a blue mountain) said he didn't care; but he told me offhandedly to ask the Goddess. The Goddess (who lived in my belly) said that she sees and loves each thing I make, as if it is her own child.

This all happened in a deep and powerfully broken-open space, and I have never forgotten the lesson: individual creativity is a matter between the artist and her muse, and nobody else is relevant to it. One cannot *ask* for anyone to pay attention to one's offerings. People are free; they need not see you. But the Goddess sees.

I wrote three poems that day, and Nisarg, seeing a great change in my face, invited me to share; and then to read the poems aloud. And, for that little time, I was heard after all.

Thank you, beloved genius Nisarg.

Neil drove out and collected us and we three drove back across the country together to Missouri. This was a magical few days – my most amazing friend, so empathic, compassionate, gifted – communing with my best-beloved man. I sat in the back for hours listening to them talk, resonating with the way he was… *opened up* by her. In a way I'd by now almost given up on his being with me… He was a practical, quiet man – without easy words for his feelings.

Nisarg stayed a week with us and then flew home to Italy.

Steps to a Breakthrough

But it was during this settled, richly repetitive time that I finally broke through my web, my membrane, of Doing. It was one of the most significant things that ever happened to me, and is, in a way, the whole point of this story (though of course the point of the story too is to sing to you about the Soul Garden).

My trouble, my Mistake had always been Doing: manipulating my own energy. Trying to steer and control things inside. Fear of surrender to the ways of the gods and goddesses. Fear of let-go. At first, I'd thought let-go would make me fat, or lazy. Then, I thought it would mean I wouldn't get laid; and I would thus somehow miss meaning in my life. Like all addicts, I was terrified of the Gap – the place where nothing happens, and something deathlike looms near.

And the difficulty is, you cannot Do Non-Doing. You cannot control non-controlling. But I didn't know anything else. *I couldn't get there.*

Finally though, the thing happened.

It started like this: I used to go to the Unitarian Universalist Church in Springfield, because it was a place to dress up and go out to; where I could have a bit of meditation-in-company, with nobody trying to sell Jesus to me. I taught Osho's active meditations on Sunday afternoons in the church basement. There I met a beautiful dark-haired woman named Dalayna, who had experienced Osho's meditations in Japan, and was thrilled to find them here. She and I used to exchange sessions; I taught her how to give me trance journeys. I wanted to go deep; and with someone helping me it was possible in ways that it wasn't possible alone.

While I was 'under,' in that deep space, in the flowing, Knowing bliss of it – I would get the feeling that here was a Force, belonging not to me at all but to some Others, benign and beneficent – and while I was down there, they could heal... so many things. I felt they were only waiting to be asked.

It was such a beautiful place to go to... I would emerge radiant with bliss, floating and awed.

But although I meditated regularly, spoke with Guides – I could not get to this deeper subterranean reservoir on my own.

One day I gave a talk at the Unitarian Church, and someone made a video of it and later gave it to me. This was in 2007, and I had never yet seen a video of myself talking – only dancing. You know how that is – seeing yourself on film – how strange and sometimes dreadful and sometimes eye-opening?

I saw this character, this woman, up behind the podium. She seemed nimble, innocent, refined – she gestured a lot, her voice was soft and clear; she lisped a little.

And there was something else I could see – something that I could tell she didn't know: there was a sort of power in her, behind everything, that did not belong to 'her.' It was accessible, but not a servant of anything. It was some Other Whatsit, some Clear Cool Something… perhaps as if some Buddhistic transparency was standing back there – yet, without anybody's name, even Buddha's, on it. And, as I've said, unknown to the speaker. It simply stood behind her, vibrating.

This struck me, and I felt sad to be cut off from greater acquaintanceship with it.

Then, Deva Leena, the Danish woman with whom I'd worked in Japan, sent me for feedback a paper she had written, a thesis for her graduation in Cranio-Sacral therapy. I read it, and was blown away by it! It was *sooo* sensitive, deep, beautifully expressed. I just caught a feeling then that I wanted some of that too.

Leena is special in her earthy acceptance of life, her non-grandiosity, her compassion, her support of ordinariness as the material of our search. She is red-headed and quiet, a venerable sannyasin of mature years. I have seen her grow into herself over decades and I am so gratified to see in her how sinking into one's own being can make a soft glow which needs no trumpeting; a depth which becomes more and more precious as it seeks its privacy. I was also so delighted when she wrote to me of her own self-healing: while we were in Japan I had witnessed her awful suffering with migraines. Two years before she wrote the paper, a practitioner friend of hers described to her the location of just the bone in her neck which must have been displaced at birth. Then, it happened once that Leena was alone, suffering from migraine, and had no one to give her a session. So she did it herself. She lay down with hands on her neck, and finally felt the bone click back to where it was supposed to be. And, she had had no headache since then at all. Not one.

And so I felt that I wanted to go to the Isle of Mull, in Scotland, and get sessions from Leena.

A Miraculous Healing

From a letter I wrote afterwards to friends:

During my convalescence in Poona, as I'd come to terms with the various factors that might have instigated the tumor, I had seen that night and day, year in and year out, life had to twist herself and flatten herself to get round obstacles – the deviated septum, the wonky teeth – in the front of my head. Life then became a matter of pushing and compulsion; sideways pursuits ongoing. For does not life imitate anatomy?

Leena had visited me in the Pyramid and when I discussed the matter with her, she cautioned me that there might be a simpler, less invasive way of working with the matter; for example Rolfing could do a great deal… I did not really believe her, but remembered that she had said this.

And then there was that other difficulty I've long been prey to: nervousness. Most healers I've consulted have expressed concern about this. I have worked with it the best I could; and have lately been so grateful for Neil's stolid presence and the comfortable life he gives me, so that I have really no excuse to be nervous; but I have managed just the same to struggle with this scary discomfort on and off. In the house, for example, there always seems to be too much to do and I try to do it all. Sometimes, god help me, I even manage. Often I even manage to do **almost** *everything. But I'm nervous about it. And I get exhausted.*

Sitting meditation had also remained an issue: I just wasn't comfortable; lots of glitchy pressures would be there, and it was as if my energy got snagged on craggy bits of rock somewhere between my ribs and my crown. I felt I could not fall deep enough inside of myself, where the ocean is; I just could not Will myself there, and some high-strung pinchy obstacles were always in view.

Leena and I kept in touch and when I learned that she and her man Prasad had settled joyfully on the island of Mull, managing a holiday cottage place, I was much intrigued, since I love the North.

And so I asked her finally if she would work on me; help me get back into myself.

Eventually it was all arranged. I would work in Holland at Nirav's (a Dutchman who had participated in the first Mouth of the Dragon) Tantra Temple for a month to get the money, and then go to Mull for two weeks and receive ten sessions – I just knew I wanted ten.

First Neil and I had a holiday in Europe for two weeks (lots of dashing about on trains) and then Neil (rather reluctantly) left me in Holland and went back to Missouri to his job.

My work and money happened nicely and I flew on the thirtieth of April to Edinburgh, stayed overnight in a hotel, and next day stocked up at a health food store and sat on the train for four hours to Oban, where I took the ferry to Mull.

Leena and I greeted each other with glad shrieks! We went for a meal and talked and talked.

I took up residence in a little stone cottage on a wild windy headland. It had a wood stove, eco-painted walls, all mod cons, and a view of misty hills. Leena had prepared it so lovingly – food, non-feather bedding, a fire laid in the stove.

And so next day we began. I would walk half an hour on a rocky road up and down the hillocks and over peaty burns to her cottage, an old schoolhouse; where she had her session room.

Cranio-Sacral – and there are different types; I know only of Osteo and Bio-Dynamic – works on a principle incredible in its simplicity. The practitioner studies for many years in order to learn so much anatomy (Leena showed me gorgeous diagrams in which colored bones in amazing variety and profusion fit together in a breathing, flexible way in the head. You would not suppose that the skull is a country of fields and roads, plains and towns, rivers and fault-lines; above fluid magmas and fluid cores where emptiness trades oxygen with water, on and on.) When she is working with someone, she can stow all that knowledge behind a curtain and allow the client, by her particular circumstance, to tug out just the right piece of it.

Cranio-Sacral is a silence-and-stillness-based work. The assumption is that there is a core of health in each of us which just needs acknowledgment. That if the practitioner sits very still and is very still inside herself, and waits, and waits – just the hands placed here or there – eventually the health of the client's inner being will throw off (even with just an infinitesimal shift of a joint) what it does not need; will adjust what is askew.

Birth is accorded great importance in this work. (Leena says that all newborns should receive Cranio just to undo the damage and prevent much worse in the way of accrued consequences.)

My mother was so happy that I was a girl that every detail of my birth was told me again and again; as if it all was some great accomplishment I had done! But it was a very long and difficult one: I had been breech, sideways-on, unable to exit; the lady doctor, a friend of Mom's, finally had to reach in and turn me around and bring me out. I had a red splotch between my brows and another on the back of my neck; my mother called them 'birthmarks' and seemed to feel that these too were some great accomplishment of mine! They faded gradually but never altogether disappeared.

So – while Leena picked up right away that there was a great gnarled-up focus of stuck energy between my brows, she did not touch my head until session No. 6. First much else had to unfold and find its way out of me. This all happened through the merest long-sustained touch while I lay supine on a massage table in the cozy session room. I was thrown deep into the sadness of my parents the first day. I felt it as if I were in the womb, perceiving it; I felt as if my whole childhood was soaked in it. The surroundings of ancestral territories underlined this... some of my forbears came from Scotland.

I had, at that stage in the treatment, to allow the weight of my parents' enormous disappointment, unspoken grief. I had to allow myself to weigh 800 lbs without flinching and running away – I had to sink into apathy and awful stuck morose banality. I had to live a life without the joy of male/female love, without dance, without money; a world of grey old broken things and no way out visible.

After each session – which lasted two to three hours – I would walk home on the rocky track, imbibing the space and peace of air, light, and water, stone and wind.

One day it suddenly felt boring to be paying attention to my childhood like that! And Leena instantly concurred! This was after she had already lifted from me a cloak of sorrow – for that sorrow was not my own – and I had been complete in its passing; meaning, I had **paid attention** *to every morsel.*

We did a lot of paying attention – for me, always a challenging subject because my gnarled head energy wants to grab hold and interfere. I did not know how to rest back into myself and allow the observed to be separate; I could not rest in the observer. I knew this but felt powerless about it.

There was another thing I was not good at: containing energy. I had some old-sannyas idea that I had to always throw out everything; express, get rid of. I am sure Osho never told us to throw out and nothing but throw out! In fact I have a beautiful quote from him saying just the opposite: that contained energy, not thrown, takes one deeper and deeper inside. And so now I got to practise just watching twitches and furls and streams and widgetty tributaries inside, without feeding their habit of exiting right away. My mind kept protesting that I might be suppressing, though I could clearly feel the difference between suppressing and observing/resting. I began to feel a new robustness at my center.

Leena had opined that my nervousness had origin in prenatal time and my nose/forehead issue had origins in birth. She described it as a little almond-shaped gland called the amygdala on either side of the brain deep in the head. It is in charge of nerve impulses, detecting fear and preparing for emergency events; storage of emotional events and emotional learning. And whatever emotion the mother is feeling when that part of the brain is forming will be programmed into the gland forever as its default state. (That might be, I'm thinking, why Osho again and again told pregnant women that for nine months they should not be angry, ever – they should live in a way that was completely peaceful and placid and relaxed.)

Leena said that my amygdala was programmed into an adrenalized, fight-or-flight mode. This did not mean a great deal to me until I myself went down into my womb-time (not deliberately – somehow I just found myself there, lying on that table with closed eyes, with Leena standing by). And then I understood... There was my mother, in a quiet rage at my father for his various idiocies and lacks. A boiling, ongoing rage... And there, by the way, was my father's cigarette smoke – another godawful insult to my wee system – assaulting me with a different kind of toxin. Leena asked me how my cells coped with these things. Well, they ***shrank.*** *Curdled up to try to keep the painful stuff at bay. And it was not mine, that stuff; not mine at all. (Does any woman ever have a pregnancy free of anger? I doubt it – but maybe some do!) Mom, don't feel bad about this – can you imagine the beauty of uncovering this consciously; of giving myself back to myself through this challenge? If it had not been this trouble it would have been some other; for we get born through these challenges.*

One day Leena put a hand on my right knee (the bad one) and one on a foot. And peace flowed through me and I saw that the knee very lovingly had got screwed up to keep me from some of the excesses I would otherwise have pursued on the current of my wonky forehead meanderings. And she stayed there, and then went to my feet. And at a certain point a sigh went through me and I was able to fall down In for a long, long time, looking ***between*** *the molecules of the tension into its empty center.*

And she said then that my amygdala had let go and learnt a new thing – how to be something other than wound up.

This was the breakthrough. I could finally locate myself other than in the tension. Somewhere deeper. Somewhere true.

This might not sound like much – but it changed me forever. It was as if a simple fact of light was suddenly allowed in. I had been ***still*** *enough that I had fallen through* *the floorboards of myself, and found myself in silence. I had slipped down between the cells into the emptiness.*

I was invited by Leena to live through a normal birth. She put her belly at my crown and a hand here and another someplace else, and she invited me to ***push*** *with my head against her belly. And at a certain point she felt some movement in my legs, and told me to push with them, and suddenly a pulsing wave poured through me as my legs pushed exactly as if I were swimming, and the wave went up through my whole body as my head pushed and pushed. It was marvelous. My head-top kept crying out for more contact, and I could* ***feel*** *how the waves of vaginal squeezing activate the lymph, and thus the immune system is kick-started. Apparently the baby, with its own pushing, also is supposed to work to get born.*

After a bit she just kept a hand on my head exactly where it felt right to me, and I kept saying, "I feel ***included!*** *I feel* ***included!"*** *I saw that I had never before felt that I really was allowed to be alive on this earth. To be one of us, welcomed head to toe.*

Leena told me, joyfully, that when a sperm and egg meet and join, a very interesting thing occurs: nothing. For twenty-four hours or so the combo remains silent and still. Only then do the cells begin to divide. So, she concludes, we are born out of silence.

In another session this happened: Leena had her hands on my forehead, fingertips between my eyes. All of a sudden, my mouth came open and words came out as strong as strong, a statement of indubitable truth; not nasty, not heavy, but a roar of intense ***knowing:*** *"Mom, this is the* ***last time I will carry this for you!"*** *And I saw in that moment how I have been carrying a burden of my mother's rage for her, carefully, like a chalice; because that is all I* ***could*** *do. I felt the huge force of it pour up the right side of my body in a torrent unleashed, my mouth came open as wide as a lake, a howl came over the sky, my teeth vibrated; and suddenly –* ***weird!!!*** *– the whole mass of energy abruptly shifted to the middle of my body, and for the first time I was in my mid-line! It was no longer anger, it was no longer my mother's; this was my own real center column, and inside it I could perceive that the left and right sides of my body each presented a strand of being that wound about each other like the Staff of Hippocrates. And the staff itself poked out of the top of my head upwards, and dead leaves burned in a pile before my third eye.*

When I went home that day I was so agog I could navigate only very gingerly. My top of head had an open trapdoor on it and, by the way, had become about two inches taller. Or so it felt; and when I tried cooking some food and burnt the pot handle and squirted grapefruit juice all over my sweater, I knew I had better just go to bed.

There I napped and woke and felt still so odd that I went for a walk and felt my shod feet on the tilty road and came home and then lay down. My body made up its own yoga positions to stretch out what it was experiencing; aches and toxins released; and the Cranio somehow went on with my own fingers being placed here or there while I fell inside myself and things made little cricking sounds and shifted back into place.

Leena and I, on a day where the session had had a certain levity, drove afterwards to the ridiculously picturesque village of Tobermory an hour away. I shopped for prezzies for kids in my family and we ate the best, freshest salmon I've ever had, and then had tea and chocolates at a tearoom; and afterwards drove across the island, got out, and went into a windswept sheepy field near the sea and gazed at a Standing Stone.

And next day the work resumed its gravity.

Somewhere in here, too, I told my father that I just plain love him and that's that! I kissed his face all over.

That last session with my head changed my forehead. A big chunk of rock was out of it. It could now let energy move through it without grasping on. Such a relief! One of my biggest unhappinesses was gone. It took a day or two to get adjusted to the new freedom!

I was by now drawing a quick self-portrait after each session when I got home, and that one is funny! A person with astonished eyes and a very tall head!

Then it was the last day. Before the session, we discussed what we might do. Leena felt so much had been accomplished; she told me a little list of what my gifts are, and what keys I had gained in the work we had done.

Gifts: ***Clear knowing.*** *About my inner world. When asked I simply see/feel/know what is going on in a particular place. I have always had this, in spades, but hearing that my Human Design shows it, has allowed me to trust it even more completely.*

Absolute alignment with my own inner Pole, my inner North *as we called it.*

A really wide and living heart.

Ability to transform things: *the alchemical touch, where one thing, seen, becomes another thing at a higher level.*

Keys gotten:

Trust in my innate health at the center.

How to not get caught in thought-forms (but just to allow the energy underneath them instead).

How to let gravity do the work.

How to go to stillness (it takes time).

"You have your feet back."

I would add: ***Containing energy.***

How to find a safe place inside me *(one of the techniques we used).*

How to notice when my nervous system is beginning to rev up. *Leena had said at one point, "Can't you just notice when your nerves are beginning to get tense, and remind yourself, Ah, there's my nervous system! And indeed this has been one of the most helpful keys – because it's true, I just notice it's beginning to happen, and the whole shitteree (to employ a Neil-ism) just sighs and relaxes and lets go.*

And she added something I found wonderful: "This is just the beginning – the sessions work long after they are over. Yes, it's fine to give yourself Cranio. Here's the technique: wherever the energy is, contact it and find the stillness in it. Just that – and wait. Things move by themselves – just find the stillness."

What I'm still grappling with:

How to say no to things that are not mine and are not good for me. *During one session I had discovered that my being was trying to throw off every single person I had ever known! Every influence! So wonderful! Leena really stressed the value of this and said I should pay great attention to the fact that I have a right to say No – she said my face changed wonderfully, and my energy did too, each time the magic two letters escaped my lips!*

So: on this the last day; we both felt it would be good if she worked on my palate.

She had shown me wonderful diagrams of how the thin, thin bone of the palate is hinged severally, to other paper-thin bones; how it is connected with a certain very porous, delicate butterfly-shaped bone up behind the nose and at the top of it. She thought that during my birth the butterfly-shaped bone had been compressed and that the discomfort I felt was that compression.

She donned a latex glove and placed a single finger on my palate at a certain place. After a while I heard a tiny click in the back of my neck and something relaxed and my mouth seemed to become wider.

She always knew everything that happened, immediately; she said Mmmm! approvingly. Then she told me she was going to put the finger further back on the roof of my mouth, where a certain delicate bone was. I lay and rested and didn't interfere – I was getting much better at that. And then Leena began to exclaim something but I didn't hear what it was because right then

allofasuddenmyheadsnappedbackandalightningrockettoreupthroughme

and my mouth was so open and pried apart that it had never felt like that before, and my teeth became a chimpanzee's, strong and bare and fierce as anything, and a hissing gargling roar slammed into my front teeth, and this snorting jet plane scream was as percussive as a drumbeat on a huge drum in the jungle. Then I heard Leena saying, "Your nose! Your nose! It's in the nose!" and so I shifted attention and oh my god, my nose felt taller, and I said the first thing that came out which was, "My nose feels prettier!" Then – "It feels more like my mother's!" (It seemed right then that a high-bridged nose was a very strong and attractive thing.) And I sat up in astonishment and she said, "You can breathe better!" and I tried that and sure enough, there was more space in my upper nose. I realized that the blast of the roar had, from underneath, pushed the porous bedrock under my nasal structure upwards and so the nose-bone, like the pole from which a circus tent hangs, had lifted too and thus my septum had been lifted just that little bit higher. And now the whole front of my head, and my mouth as well, felt roomy and free, open and easy.

I felt as if my whole life had hung from the wonky structure of my between-brows as if from a coat-hanger, and it had had no choice but to be wonky too. I felt like I had been wearing a shoe that was too tight, all my life (only the shoe was on my head); and now it was removed. I walked home beaming and bobbing and resting inside in pure astonishment.

Then, at home, when I drank water my nose bumped the glass in a new way. When I washed my face my hand encountered a new landscape. The skin on the bridge felt stretched. The view from underneath the nose was a little more symmetrical. When I rested in the afternoon I suddenly heard a tiny **crack** *on the left side of my nose and something shifted tinily towards comfort, as if raising, weensily yet surely, new ground.*

The night before I left I gave her a channeling session, which she loved. We'd set the alarm clock wrong in our ga-ga-ness, and I barely made the ferry next early morning. Onboard I sat joyously in the café eating fried eggs and drinking tea, with the added indulgence of a piece of organic chocolate… all the way to Oban! Gazing out at the misty isles!

When I got to Holland a friend didn't recognize me in the airport! And everybody kept exclaiming things like, "You are ***here!*** *You had been kind of ghostly!" and "Your whole face looks so different!" and "You have feet!" I felt as if I had been hiding in sideways-land and suddenly could beam at the world face-on, more or less.*

It was disconcerting to give sessions, at first. I found I did not want to tune in to people's energy. I didn't want to receive anything. Then, for a bit it felt as if something wanted to come out of me rather than go in – some power; and my mind thought this was suspect. But then it all settled into this new thing: after listening to the client share her issues I would have her lie down on the mattress as usual; I would drift my hand in her aura and check it out, just a little; but then I'd sit down and hold her feet or place a hand on her belly and just be – patiently, peacefully, long and long, I'd simply go into myself, almost as if forgetting about her completely. But somehow in all of that I would come to know what was going on in her energy. And then I'd move on to the next part of the session.

And the client, I found, would be much more open to the next thing – whether my words or her own; depending on the sort of session it was. And clients would report great phenomena occurring to them whilst they lay there. And whereas before they tended to be ***very happy*** *with their sessions, they were now* ***extremely delighted.****

Being at home in Missouri is sooo lovely. The house is beautiful, the man is so sweet and good. His simplicity continues to bewilder me. My heart loves him and our clean, stately, quiet ménage. Falling into meditation is so much easier. (Though when I go outside the house I still feel squashed by the restless, shallow Midwestern vibe.) There is always far too much to do but that is not the stuff's fault: there is, as Neil has wisely pointed out before, always too much to do; one can never do it all; so why get all tensed up?

N.B.: Leena cautioned me that if I tell anyone about my experiences I should tell them not to expect the results I had! Mine was the culmination of mountains of preparation!

I wrote this soon after I got home:

* Over time, this sitting-quietly at the beginning of a session morphed into something else – a whole new kind of work. I'd sit, then by and by invite angelic presences to do whatever they liked, while I observed and described. This is the most sublime work I have ever known. Each session is a unique, ascendant rapture. I feel privileged each and every time.

Transformation

I am in Missouri but the North is in me.
There are pines and lochs around me.
An eagle sits in a tree.

I am lying down where all things
Must go to die.
But there is living in it –
Leaves touch the face of the air
And the air pats them in return.
Things grow up and fall down
And a bear comes to drink –
A big one –
At a stream unseen by man.

Just one woman
Lies here
Bathed in the peaty brew.
Just one cool brow.
Bears come to drink
But she is not bothered.
Now she is allowed.
What once was Missouri
Is now the Arctic
On a high summer softness
Of slanting light.
The air's been swept
Like a temple
By the wind.

A Peculiar Healer

When Neil and I moved to the Kansas City area we terribly missed our beautiful thick-growing forest of oak trees. I planted twenty-three new trees of several sorts, but they were babies and would take years to grow. The pretty little town, Heskia, was insular and ossified-feeling. But I somehow discovered a goofy, wild, high-powered healer in Kansas City, a sort of psychic chiropractor who diagnosed by waving his fingers in the air whilst stroking a strange amber disc he wore for a belt-buckle. He was a tall, gangling, rather tortured man (Bible-Belt conditioning can do weird things to a born rebel) who strode along at a steep forward tilt. We discovered a deep affinity… when I walked into his office the first time I felt the whole floor was raised above the ground, hovering in some rapid vibration that thrilled me.

With a few touches of his finger on acupressure points, Dr. Satterwhite would send me spinning off into depths of forgotten emotion. I'd go home and have to lie down and go Inside. Scenes from the deep past would be pushing upwards in me. I needed desperately to have a way to effectively metabolize, process, and release what was coming up. Dynamic has always been my favorite method; but the spaces I was hurled into were so poignant, so paralyzing, that it seemed that only stillness would do.

After my time on Mull I had a much better orientation to that stillness, and more openness to the possibilities it might contain.

My mother had married Al, the man with the wildflower posey, in a Buddhist ceremony, and they had roamed the countryside together taking photographs. He was in poor health, and in late June 2010 was taken to hospital; and then sent home to die. I had a long phone conversation with him just after he'd been given the prognosis. It was so touching, so heartful… this grumpy, jolly, wounded, defensive old guy was suddenly completely vulnerable and undone. Kindly hospice carers came to the house and prepared Devadasi and Al both for what was to come.

I had just returned from seeing Dr. Satterwhite when I got the news that Al had died. I immediately went and lay down… everything was swimming around. I wanted then to go with him a little way, and make sure that he was okay.

And I went, as far as I was allowed; saw Al young again, in a sharp suit and fedora, sitting on the crescent moon, insouciant and melancholic-sassy. Yes, he was okay… And at a certain point I was told to go back again, and not travel further with him. But I had communicated my love and caring; and he had heard.

Dr. Satterwhite told me I was supposed to spend lots of time in these inward-swimmings.

Gradually a new way of healing myself was born; and I am so joyful about it, so thrilled that this has come through, that I want to share it. It is a clear and succinct method, with definite steps; the unconscious, when evoked, loves a safe structure in which to reveal itself. When something painful is to be encountered, it likes the objectivity of a structure which will signal 'beginning' and 'end' for that meeting... It loves a deft, and yet respectful, hand on the reins. And the superconscious, when evoked, loves a clear question to draw its luminosity out.

I call this method Self-Healing. Ever since I discovered it, it is one of the wings of my practice; and Dynamic is the other wing. One is done in stillness; one is active. And both of them *work*.

I often spent two or three hours in-swimming, usually in the morning, after Neil had gone to work. And every session was ground-breaking, healing, and seemed... miraculous. Every time, I'd fall through the floorboards of myself into the stillness.

A full description of the method can be found in the back of this book, in the *Appendix of Treasures*.

A Visit from Sarita and Devadasi

In December 2010 Sarita took a break from her busy teaching schedule and brought our mother out to Missouri to stay ten days with Neil and me. Sarita loved the clean, huge house, and the civilization in it – regular meals, clean linen, and the little treats I'd bought for them, such as bed-hats and sleeping socks for the freezing winter. Sarita and Neil got on well, and we all watched funny movies together (Sarita enjoys good movies with a religious glee). Devadasi had begun to enter the dementia that bewildered her for the rest of her life – but it was not so very bad yet.

On one walk we took, into the tiny town, to look at the few shops, Sarita said to me, "I wouldn't be able to do this." Meaning, this much isolation and dullness all about. And I felt again that just two things made my living here possible: my love for Neil; and my self-entertaining capacities. I was always painting or sketching or cooking or writing or making the house nice.

But the thing that really made the visit worthwhile, besides the simple nourishment of family time, was this: each day Sarita and I spent an hour looking into her Human Design, while she sat at her laptop making rapid-fire notes. And we got the beginnings of a grounding in this Fact: *we are very different people. She need not be like me. I need not be like her.* And so, we don't have to blame the other as being inexplicable, horrible, strange, wrong-footed.

She felt seen… and I felt gratified that I could make some helpful contribution to things.

This lesson continues to deepen – that it really is okay to be different, and that *comparing* is not the point at all. (This is a work in progress. But, the more I am allowing myself to be myself – just this, just me, with all my foibles and hermetical focusings – the easier it is for me to let my sister be herself – public-spirited, wide-gestured, gorgeous, cosmic, inventive to the max, and *incredibly good at organizing things.)*

A Whack on the Head

Neil, through his company, managed to fix up a trip to Sweden so that he could observe robots at work in a Swedish grocery warehouse. I was thrilled! We had a beautiful meditation in a huge warm old hotel in Saltsjöbaden, outside Stockholm. And then we rocketed around on trains, making our way south again to a flight home from Amsterdam.

We spent a night at an expensive hotel in Hamburg, and I was grateful to have a memory to lay over the old one: in this same city I'd learnt of my father's passing. But it was a strange new memory: Neil and I sitting in the huge, empty hotel dining room, waiting for our meal, while he fiddled with his phone, in his endless efficiency at micro-managing our travels. A waiter brought a bread basket and set it down on the table. I noticed movement… and realized that a very small cockroach was circumambulating the rim of the basket! In *Germany!* And what I felt was, huge relief that now Neil and I *had something to talk about!*

We ended up for a couple of days in Bruges, a picturesque little tourist town in Belgium full of canals and bridges, winding cobbled streets. We stayed at the Hotel de Orangerie, a 'luxury boutique' hotel on a canal. One night we had dinner and then, wandering off towards home, got lost. We went down a narrow side street and heard music… *blues!*

We entered the wine bar, made our way up narrow winding stairs; and in a tiny loft space full of people sipping wine there was a young man singing. He was dynamite! Diffident, muscular, powerful in his movements, with a rich raunchy voice, making people laugh. He played mouth harp, several guitars in turn, thumped a thumper on an old suitcase with the motion of his foot. He sang *Pick a Bale of Cotton, There is a River, Alabama, Georgia On My Mind.* Neil and I gave each other a look, for once in perfect accord, and we stayed, though there were no chairs left and we stood right at the top of the stairs. Song after song was belted out, and we swayed and jiggled. Neil had drunk most of a carafe of wine at dinner, as was, I had discovered, his holiday habit. And now he ordered beer… and more beer. I had sparkling water.

Neil is a shy man, not given to spontaneity. He keeps his cards close to his chest, and is private and retiring by nature. But now, suddenly, he took my glass and carefully placed it atop an enormously thick, very low dark wooden beam that cut across the ancient ceiling just above our heads. The proprietor came up the stairs and, seeing the glasses, moved them to the top rung of a nearby ladder.

Neil pulled me into a dance! Nobody else was dancing yet. We had just about two square feet to move in; but he jived me and swung me, and of course I was happy – this was exactly what I always longed for! He was celebrating! Mr. Solid-Taciturn-Adorable-Stuck-to-the-Floor was moving! So I danced with happy abandon. The proprietor kept arriving with more beers while we swooped and swayed and jived. Neil would pause, drink some, put the glass down, and go on dancing.

He really got carried away. His face pursed up in his special ecstatic-cool expression, and he kept hissing at me, "Nobody else is dancing! They're all just *sitting* there!" That, I thought, was always *my* line! What was going on? All my dreams come true?

But now a very cute middle-aged couple got up and began to dance, and an older guy got up and *really* moved it! Yay! The place was sweaty and steamy and liquid in the best tradition of good times! This is what a holiday is *for!* This is what *life* is for! Time stops when the music grooves!

Neil hoisted me up into his arms and wrapped my legs around his waist! He swung me around! Wow! I had waited *six years* for this! He was cutting loose!

He tossed me up into the air.

CRACK!!!! My *head!* OUCH! On that heavy low wooden beam!

Owwwww...!!! Erk. Somewhat dampened, I nevertheless carried on. Everyone was singing by now and I sang too. Neil kept apologizing.

The top of my head *hurt!*

Back at the hotel I applied to the ouchy place some Aura Soma Physical Rescue – a few drops of deep-blue liquid out of a little squeeze-bottle – and took a shower.

I knew I would have to do Self-Healing.

My head still hurt but not too badly. I didn't think anything serious had happened; but I didn't like it. No, I *didn't like it at all.* It felt all wrong up there.

So I lay down and placed my hands on the top of my head and closed my eyes and went inside myself in the dark. Passed through various layers – a small childhood accident where my forehead was hit by a swing – past-life images of cudgels... given and received. I was shown that I should wear a hat for a few days (which I was doing anyway). But now, I had to just *stay with* the uncomfortable feelings... for as long as it took.

A lot of the impact was taken out by the skillful ministrations of Those – the Helpers. My body jerked, sighed, and released the trauma.

Then I looked for what was my responsibility in the accident.

It was this: Because I was so desperately keen to enjoy Neil celebrating, I was in denial about the fact that it was *very sad* that he could only let go when drunk! In Poona we all had danced ourselves silly every night of the week, and not a drop of booze nor an iota of any drug was imbibed or needed! We danced to abandon for the sheer love of life and the wild mystery of the Beyond that Osho gave us, or rather, gave back to us... it was our birthright, as it is everyone's.

Therefore I too was drunk: on denial, on not seeing what was right under my nose: that it showed a tragic level of fear of life – a terrible grip of miserable conditioning – to be unable to celebrate to music unless you were sozzled! I didn't want to see this because I wanted that celebration energy! Wanted a celebrating man! I was ignoring the fact that he was drunk.

So we were *both* drunk and forgot all about the big beam over our heads.

WHACK!

My head felt just about fine in the morning. In a few days I'd forgotten the impact almost completely – but I have not forgotten the lesson. *Stay awake – even if you are drunk on not noticing someone else's drunkenness!*

A Summer of Movement

Neil was an executive in a huge grocery-warehousing cooperative that covered five states. He had first two, then three, then four weeks' holiday per year, as his seniority advanced. To me, this weensy bit of me-time he got was just unthinkably paltry. But he was hanging in for more promotions and an eventual pension, and was a diligent and brilliant worker – he had great tech skills. ("Computers are *afraid* of me," he once said.) So we'd take our little bit of time and go to Maui or Europe, and he'd put it on his credit card to be paid back later month by month in an organized way. Then he'd have to fly home and go back to work, and I'd stay on for a bit, to rattle about in funky-land – sleeping on friends' couches, bopping about with Nisarg in her car with our stuff piled up to its eaves, and so on.

In the summer of 2011, a lot happened.

First of all, my oldest brother, Rudra, who lived in Vancouver, became ill. He was seventy-four, and had smoked since he was sixteen. He drank a bottle of wine every night. He was doggedly independent, and never went to doctors. Finally one of his sons had become worried about him and dragged him kicking and screaming to a doctor. The diagnosis was cancer of the vocal cord, well-advanced. Rudra refused radiation therapy.

I had loved visiting him and his grown-up children, my nephews and their families, in that pretty city by the quiet, island-sheltered sea. Now, my brother Andy and I collected our mother and drove north to Vancouver on a sadder mission. Sarita was to fly in from abroad in a few days' time. We were gathering to say good-bye.

Rudra was by now staying in a little room in the flat of his son and the son's family, and being nursed by my nephew's wonderful wife and a pair of visiting nurses. More family gathered, and we all got to say goodbye to him. He left his body the day after I went back to Missouri. Two days after that, Neil and I left for Ireland with his sister's family. I did my best to meditate with my grief en route, staying in bed for long self-healings.

Neil and I spent two weeks in Ireland with his sister and her young family, driving around to B&B's. The sister's family had never been out of the States, and their culture shock was only softened by insisting on hamburgers, fries, and vanilla ice cream at every meal. In the Midwest, as far as I can see, all the excitement that exists is couched in four things: Tornadoes, cars, movies, and high-school sports. It was the sports that got discussed at meals. All of this was *claustrophobic* for me. I did enjoy the Cliffs of Moher, because I felt my brother's wild Celtic soul in the winds and cold waves of the Atlantic – my beautiful tall hazel-eyed brother… all his slender unkempt elegance vanished into… somewhere.

I was happy to strike out on my own when the two weeks was done.

I spent a month in England, staying with, and giving sessions to, Cyril Montkestrel-Foxmaigne, a scruffy aristocrat with trodden-on trouser hems and an ancient station wagon with mud in the foot-wells. Then he gamely fired up this rackety car, and we swooped by his ex-wife's house, scooped up his three kids and their dreadlocked nanny, and we all went up to Glasgow to see Mr. Kohrogi.

I had not seen Mr. Kohrogi for seven years. Champaka had told me that you were not supposed to ask the Sensei a lot of questions; rather, you should just ask him what was really really important; and then go away and ponder it for a long time before presenting another query. Kohrogi-san had told me, in France in 2004, "You need quiet, quiet, quiet," and I had pondered that for seven years. He seemed pleased when I told him this.

Sarita had told me that she had given Kohrogi-san the Colorpuncture Transmitter Relays – that series of treatments shining colors into points on the skull – and she had realized then that he was enlightened. (Kohrogi-san calls it "remembering the original face.") He just didn't go around making noise about it.

The ten days that I now spent with him was… well, *everything.* We were all sitting in a circle in a large room in a Buddhist center in an old wooden building; there was a kitchen in the basement, where we took our meals. I sat as close to him as I reasonably could, and just drank up the vibes. Watched my mind assiduously, easily; helped oh-so-much by his presence.

The group was called Natsukashi, or the Original Face. It wasn't a linear, Western-minded sort of group, where you are going from A to Z. Rather, it reminded me of one of those soft-serve ice cream cones where a machine dispenses the soft cold confection, and your cone is held under the nozzle, and the goop piles on itself in the vertical, making a nice point when you draw it away. This is how it felt – like time was resting on top of itself, piling up in its Now-ness.

There were simple exercises, alone or with a partner, to facilitate this meeting with ourselves. I had done this group before, in France in 2004, but at the time, in my convalescence, I had really just wanted to escape and be alone. Now, with seven Midwestern years under my belt, I was hungry as never before for the sacred. I went into the group with all I had of awareness and openness.

I asked Kohrogi-san a question: "In the Midwest I feel lonely, and I find the place terrible, with its huge box stores with giant people in them pushing huge carts around and picking out huge plastic things to buy. I want to leave it!"

He said, "Loneliness is the greatest freedom." And he added, "The plastic in the stores is strange to you, because it is in between states. It is strange to itself… " and there was a bit more I don't recall; but the sense was that he supported my being there and facing myself there.

And so I let slide away from me the idea of leaving that place; and as the next day and the next opened before us I felt myself come into a huge Askingness: Okay, if I don't ask *that* question, still, I feel like Asking! My very being became an Asking: *What is going on?*

He was about to give me an Ito-thermie treatment, and first I showed him my Asking state by standing with my arms above my head, reaching towards the sky; head thrown back, body shaking all over.

"That," he boomed, "is *GRACE!*" And his fathomless eyes, and his beautiful features, and his workmanly body, and all his wrinkles – gleamed with a dark abyssal light.

This was astonishing to hear, and yet it felt true: not-knowing, and being open, is how we are in the path of blessings from the sky.

And I asked about my forehead, and all that had gone on there, and he said, "That situation is stable! That situation is stable!" And then he gave me the blessed hot-dragon treatment, that quiets everything and opens it up and warms and heals it. And Sees it too.

At lunchtimes he took his guitar out to the street and busked. (He was a rock'n'roll singer before he was a Buddha; and after too. He writes poetic ballads and protest songs as well.) Some of us would join him and dance on the grassy verge or in the street. When people threw coins in his guitar case he thought it very funny!

But the most amazing little event – for me – happened on the last day. We were all sitting in a big circle, facing him. He was finishing up the group by having eye contact with each one of us in turn. When he came to me, and his eyes settled on mine from across the room, the most extraordinary thing happened. I might have supposed that I would feel love from him, but it wasn't like that. Instead, a huge bolt of purest love started in my own feet and traveled upwards through my body and out my eyes, to him. My face split in a huge grin. My mind tried to tell me that this grin must look very stupid; but I didn't listen to it; I just grinned fit to bust. I had never felt such love in my life – no limits, no holding back, just huge grinning bliss-love, to him, shooting out of me.

He then nodded, just infinitesimally; and moved to the next person.

After the group eight of us piled into a big rental van and took off into the Highlands. I got to sit next to Kohrogi-san for hours, ascending on the vibes. Awareness kept catching the bird of a thought in its hands and holding it – and the thought would then fly away, and I'd fall deeper In. Poems would come and assail me and I'd have to scribble them down. And I was busy with another reductive thought-transcending query: one day, during the group, I'd been brooding on how Recognized my sister had become; while I languished in a backwater. Kohrogi-san had suddenly said to us, apropos of nothing: "Whenever somebody is comparing himself with someone else, and then he realizes that it is *all within himself,* he stops doing it immediately."

Sometimes we stopped at a view-point, and once the updraft of wind was so strong we spread our arms out and lay on it, held up by the wind. Kohrogi-san enjoyed this. He liked good whiskey, too, so we'd stop at a pub sometimes.

We stayed at a youth hostel in the far north. One rainy morning I was eating breakfast and happened to look out the window. There was Kohrogi-san, walking through the garden in the rain, his hoodie up over his head. He didn't know anyone was watching; he was looking down at where he was going, and his face was creased with beaming joy. He had such a rubber face, and it was showing all the inside of him, smiling and shining like anything.

And I thought, "So – it isn't that all men *have to have poker faces.* Here is one who doesn't – who isn't afraid to let his whole nature show." For I had read a book about the female brain which said that girl children are very responsive to facial expressions from birth, and will try and try to elicit expressions from people they talk to; and if the person is staying poker-faced, as men are socialized to do to prevent other men seeing their vulnerability – the little girl will try, and try, and try, with indefatigable persistence, to get some expression going. If at long last it is clear that the man is not going to show anything, the child will finally give up and go do something else.

Neil had a very good poker face on him.

At the airport in Glasgow, Kohrogi-san and I hugged goodbye. In his arms, I saw only sky… All that sky hit my heart and my eyes opened wide. And not only did I see the clear sky of him, but I saw that all around me was a sort of mist – composed of a zillion tiny thought-forms; and each thought-form was *identified.* This mist was the thing called 'me.'

I stared at him, all agog. He looked into my eyes and nodded.

In a Bog

In September of 2011, at Sarita's invitation, I spent time at Devika's chalet in the French-Swiss Alps with a group of Tantra teachers; we were going to help each other disrobe our psyches. This was wonderful, if sometimes very painful indeed as the onion was peeled. And it was wild and crazy! Many of the teachers were from the maverick-minded Antipodes, others from Hawaii or California or Scotland – and boy did those wooden walls resound with Kiwi and Aussie imprecations, pillow-beatings in many dialects, heartfelt male sobs, and so forth! And we had great hikes, up into the summer-flowery mountains – I will never forget the sight of half a dozen beautiful female Tantrikas, wearing long drapey goddess-gowns and hiking boots, all squatted under a tree side-by-side having a pee, lovely moons of bottoms showing. …And we bathed in a forest waterfall together and swam about in its huge rocky pool. And what great veggie food was produced by our French cook, the radically gorgeous Niten! (who also participated).

For me it was all manna from heaven. In my repressive little Midwestern town, people *really* never did anything like this.

While deep in a certain process, the image arose of myself as a sacrificial victim, interred in a bog for 5,000 years; and next to this bog sat my father, in his upholstered, cigarette-burned chair. The long wait, all those years of it, was for him to finally speak, and say *something that made sense to me.* He was not going to do that; I saw that he had been *willing* to sacrifice me, let me wait forever. And I would wait for Neil too… forever. This scalding vision shocked me – was this really how I wanted to spend this precious life? Waiting for one dumb male, however lovable, to speak?

There had been a day when my honeymoon with Neil had abruptly ended; his rapt, sweet, oh-so-vulnerable openness had closed. We'd been in some huge airport in Texas, jetlagged; and I'd foolishly asked him, just babbling really: "So, if you were going to have a holiday *all by yourself*, what would you most want to do?" And he'd replied, "Ummm… I guess I'd go elk-hunting in Montana." I'd felt like some big beast had kicked me in the guts, and I said, "What did the elk ever do to *you?*" It was the first time I'd criticized him.*

And he'd closed. It reminds me of the time in Women's Lib when I was a man and the princessy woman had told me to take out my shoulderpads and remove my cowboy hat. That had been it – finished. Neil never opened to the same degree again; and I was always waiting for him to. There was so much love between us that we hung in for another seven years – but it was never as it had been in the beginning.

I saw now, from the bog, that I had pushed Neil away, that day I had criticized his sacred tribal ritual. I unconsciously created the rift because in his initial openness – so poignant and raw – he was not like my father; and my father was what I knew – and so I shut Neil down, to make him known.

Before the gathering disbanded, Sarita taught me a ten-minute meditation called Shakti Empowerment, where I could observe my positively-charged chakras: belly, heart, third eye – and then invite them to blend. This releases the Shakti, the essential female power; it's lots of fun, and you can then consult wise, playful, *seeing* Shakti about your daily life. I took to it with zeal, and ended up doing it twice a day for the next six months. I was finding out my own real needs and affinities within my golden, lonesome situation in the Midwest; and identifying the things up with which I could not put.

24 Days of Desire

After I'd been back in Heskia, Missouri, for a couple of months, and my pining to be out of that place wouldn't leave me, I decided to meditate on my

* And so I did Dynamic meditation, and in it I discovered that the universe is so efficient it hires its assassins from within its own ranks. Every creature has to die; and often other creatures do the killing. This is yin and yang forces at work – the universe hangs from them – and it doesn't matter if I don't approve.

desire to leave. I was not going to Do something – try to somehow engineer my leaving – for that would have felt violent, and I still loved Neil so much. (Nor did I have money of my own, or a place to go.) But I could at least embrace what I *did* have, and that was *desire to be elsewhere.*

For twenty-four days I devoted an hour to this each day. I sat and watched sensations in my body, of this desire to leave; or I danced my desire to leave; or, on Thanksgiving Day at Neil's parents' house (always a hugely trying place for me to find myself – there's only so much I want to listen to regarding deer-hunting), I walked outside and yelled it to the sky. And I learned so much: that desire is life calling to itself; and that if you cannot have the thing you want, you can at least have Desire – and to dance it, own it, celebrate it; is a kind of gorgeous freedom.

On the twenty-fourth day I lay deep in Self-Healing, wearing my Osho robe and lungi. I was at the very bottom of my inner space, Watching in great stillness. And I saw that I had, somewhere in the layers of my mind, a Spiritual Idea that I *should* be able to be happy anywhere – that if I was a really spiritual person, as I certainly *ought* to be by now – there was no excuse if I wasn't – I would be in some goggle-eyed LSD-like ecstasy, gazing at the whorls on the bark of a tree, completely immersed in being Here.

That was what I truly believed.

The minute I saw this, just witnessed it without interfering – the Idea shook all over and left me, climbing up out of my head and rushing off into the ether. And many other spiritual ideas got up and went with it, like a mud-slide going up.

When I rose from the bed after the meditation and looked about me, everything was different. The walls seemed made out of paper; everything had become two-dimensional. It was as if it wasn't really there any more; it wasn't really real. "I've already left!" I said aloud. "I'm not here any more! I've left!"

I went for a walk and the trees and the town and the sky looked like that too – just partial, just transparent, hovering close to non-existence, like a subtly-colored cartoon.

I came home and opened my computer. There was an email from Cyril Montkestrel-Foxmaigne, the fourth son of a Marquess; the same client with the moldy car I'd driven to Glasgow in. He was asking if I would like to move to England and become his teacher.

I closed my eyes and observed the precise impact in my body. A germ of energy rose from my belly to my heart. There it exploded, in a sort of orgasm of expanding vapor; and all around the edges of the explosion were little bubbles that contained… adventure. The Unknown. There was a Knowing that this was not an invitation to any sort of real security. But even if it didn't last, didn't work out in the long run, I would at least have been released into Adventure. Adventure was sure to happen.

And that was what I really wanted.

Over the next few days, as the emails went back and forth, it turned out that Neil was also invited. Cyril wanted to start a Healing Center, and he wanted me to be the resident oracle. Practical guys like Neil would be needed too.

I had to pass the invitation on to Neil. I chose my time carefully, inviting him to a large, beautiful park where we sat on a blanket (and were bitten by invisible chiggers, unfortunately). I told him about the invitation, and said I knew he would need plenty of time to think about it. He took this in… and then never said another word about it. Six months went by.

I was quite happy not knowing… because I knew I would go (I'd also asked Kohrogi-san, who had immediately approved the idea), and I both did and didn't want Neil to come.

Meanwhile, our life together continued, with weekly meditations, and beautiful, decorous dinners I cooked each night, and once in a while a movie (when we saw *Slum Dog Millionaire,* Neil cried afterwards in the car. "How can people *treat* each other like that?" he asked, regarding the Mumbai slums and all the human exploitation therein. I loved him then so achingly.)

Natsukashi in Kyoto

In April 2012, I flew from Kansas City to Los Angeles, collected Devadasi, and flew with her to Kyoto. We stayed with my nephew Liam, his Japanese wife, and their little kids, just for a few days. The flat was small and we were cramped, but it was lovely to see them. On the second day Mama announced, "I'm going home! I'm going tomorrow." Five minutes later she said, "Where are we, China?" It went on like that… The Japanese custom with toilet slippers defeated her, and again and again she had to be told that you do NOT wear "toyo sirippu" in the rest of the flat; they are only to be worn in the toilet cubicle itself. Again and again poor Mama was horribly embarrassed as she realized she'd committed a gaffe. Also she had developed a huge disinclination to bathe. One had to bully and chivvy, both of which Sarita did much better than I. It was heart-rending to see Mama grimly clinging to her right to stay unwashed; her expression was hunted, stubborn, lonely as hell. She seemed to feel she was being persecuted in a truly evil and callous way.

The Natsukashi group took place in a beautiful Zen temple, where we all slept in rooms with paper walls, arranged around a raked gravel courtyard where there were huge rocks and carefully-placed bushes. Huge stands of bamboo surrounded the temple, along with trees. There were about forty of us, going through the same stately exercises as before; and, as always, Kohrogi-san gave two concerts – and this time his young sidekick Takamu was there, a reedy tall youth in a porkpie hat doing great 50's rock'n'roll.

One lunchtime I had a little sleep in my room, and had a dream – about a field of daisies. Back in the group room, a participant shared something about a field of daisies. I got very excited, and at tea break I went up to Kohrogi-san and said, "I had a dream! About the same thing that woman was talking about!"

This action, I perceived immediately, was a great faux pas on my part. First of all, the dear man was tired – he'd been teaching most of the day, and needed a break. Second, I had *accosted him.* So gross and ungraceful! Third, So what if I dreamt something that somebody then spoke about? This isn't strange or noteworthy! (In fact, since then I've noticed this *usually* happens in his groups!) But what he said was, rather drily, "That's *wonderful.*" And I heard, "That isn't anything to barge in about!"

After the break I apologized for being a Sharing Monster. Everybody laughed, and Kohrogi-san nodded and gleamed at me, accepting my apology.

One day towards the end of the group, we were doing an exercise involving sitting opposite someone and gazing into their eyes. (This is a very un-Japanese thing to do; Kohrogi-san is a real rebel.) I was working with my mother. As I sat looking into her brown eyes, and as I relaxed, minute after minute... I saw... apple boughs, full of quivering, sprightly white blossom. The sight of these boughs made my heart overflow with the beauty of them – of transient Spring – . I saw my mother, behind her hundred wrinkles, as a romantic young girl. And I saw the gift she had given me: the affirmation of poetry, of romance; the affirmation that Beauty is a sacred and vital value – perhaps the greatest value. Tears were brimming… those apple boughs, apple blossoms. So *beautiful.*

Kohrogi-san was roaming through the room, stopping at each pair of participants, sitting beside them for a little while. He knelt beside me and put his chin lightly on my shoulder, his warm cheek touching mine. Felicity swelled through me. I asked him, "Does Romance have anything to do with spirituality?"

"Romance is the beginning… " he replied. "And the end."

(This reminds me of one of my favorite stories Osho told: A hiker is walking alongside a farm where there are two fields separated by a fence. The farmer stands leaning against a gate. The hiker asks him, "Why do you have the bull in one field by himself, and all the cows in the other field? Wouldn't the bull be happier in with the cows?"

(Growls the farmer, "Yah – but I don't want him to think that *life is just romance!*"

(Then Osho added, "But I say to you – life *is* just romance!")

The walls in the temple were thin, and one morning Kohrogi-san was demonstrating Ito-thermie techniques to students – always a thrilling thing to watch, as you never knew what he would say, and the atmosphere was so conducive to meditation. Mama was in the room she shared with Sarita, quite nearby, complaining loudly about all sorts of things. I knew she would be very embarrassed to know that everyone could hear… yet her condition was getting past the point where embarrassment had any meaning.

Kohrogi-san gave her a session. (Her ancient, bowed, crêpey, scarred, lopsided body covered by sheets that he lifted and shifted to reach the part he was working on – .) And he told us, we students watching the Master work, and learning – that she was amazing, magnificent.

She adored him – always had done.

I think she did enjoy the Zen temple – when the *toyo sirippu* weren't haunting her – and she enjoyed walks around the many other temples we visited. She'd be holding hands with Sarita, who gave us loving, instructive little discourses about our surroundings, while I took pictures. Kyoto seems to be mostly temples. Mama would say, confidently, "I've been here before." And we would say, "But Mama, this is your first time in Japan!" And she would say, "No, I was here with Bob, of *course* I was." And she would glare at us.

I flew back to Los Angles with her, which was a very taxing undertaking. When we were changing planes in San Francisco, she started ferreting through her purse, a stern expression on her face.

"What are you looking for, Mom?"

"I'm looking for some money. I'm going to take a taxi home."

"Well, okay, Mom, but it's almost five hundred miles!" (She now lived in Lake Arrowhead, in the mountains above L.A.)

I don't think it was especially kind of us to take her traveling at this stage. But there would be many more travels for her before the end. She could not be left alone – she had already almost burnt the house down, forgetting the teakettle on the stove – so if her caretaker, my brother Jack, had to go someplace, she had to go too. And sometimes he needed a break; and the replacement caring sibling would often cart her off on some adventure. She used to love travel so much… but now she did not; always refusing to go at the last minute, and then being bullied and persuaded into the car.

Leaving the Country

Six months after the initial invitation, I asked Neil again if he would like to move to England. He had taken part in one skype with Lord Cyril, after which that worthy had declared, "Neil was *so taciturn* that I couldn't stop fidgeting around and babbling!" (Neil is part Blackfoot Sioux and part Irish. I think it is the Indian part that took to meditation and Tantra.)

Now Neil said, "I dunno. But if I had to answer *right now,* I would say no. Because I want to stay and get my pension. And you don't know what will happen with Cyril. There's no security. I don't want to be dependent on him, or anybody. And I don't want to be *poor* and *old.*"

Okay.

I had my answer.

We went on, steeped in sadness yet enjoying our time together, as I packed and sorted and tossed possessions. I sold my Commune-time archives (dream journals, group journals, and hundreds of letters) to a university – ten boxes – and had enough for my ticket to England.

But first, we flew to San Francisco for a family wedding and had a session with Prabha – the highly-respected therapist who'd worked in Center for Transformation in Poona. (I am sure it was the only session Neil has ever had, before or since.) Prabha was wonderful. Neil felt seen. He asked her what he ought to do when I wanted to know what was going on with him, and, as he put it, "Nothin' is going on! There isn't anything to tell!"

She told me not to badger him to tell me his feelings. She said he'd feel invaded, like I was his mother. And she remarked, "We get attracted to the ways someone is different from us; and then we end up blaming them for those same differences." (And, yes, I must say I'm attracted to silent men, and haven't got any patience at all with talky ones!)

She also indicated (without exactly telling me what to do), that yes, just as I was feeling myself, I'd be much better off in Europe. And, she said, "Just because you love somebody doesn't mean they are necessarily the right life partner for you."

Then Neil and I strolled off down the road and ate an absurdly delicious lunch at a raw food café, and later went back to our absurdly dirty, British-run B&B in Mill Valley. He was glowing.

So I didn't ask Neil about his feelings… for, oh lord, about two months. It was really hard. I had no real friends in Heskia, and he was my only confidante there. And he wasn't talking. Only I shared (I'd always ask him if he was in the mood to listen. Sometimes he would say, "Can you give me the Readers' Digest Condensed version?") We went on meditating together; and that was beautiful.

To be perfectly fair, there were times when, on a long drive with him, I deliberately kept my mouth shut; and after an hour or two he might say, "You're *awful quiet* over there!" (I had long perceived my job with him to be *entertainer* – like New Zealand and Norway, the Midwest seemed to me to be terribly wanting in stimulation.)

We went kayaking in the Everglades together (a side-trip to a business convention), then on to the Florida Keys. Driving south on the gorgeous route, Neil in his habitual silence, with the clear sea on either side of the long raised road, I munching organic potato chips out of a bag… suddenly it all got too much for me. He had been unforthcoming as the grave for *months* now, and I just couldn't stand it any more. I mourned aloud, swore and expostulated: "I just can't stand it! I *can't!* I'm not supposed to bug you, but I can't stand not knowing what the hell is going on with you!"

He was quietly angry. His brows lowered, his mouth thinned. Nervous about a presentation he was going to give at the convention – unable to handle pressure from me too. We spent a miserable night in Key West, in a picturesque hotel near the furthest point of land; then drove back north to a dolphin sanctuary (my idea, of course). As we approached it along the coast he was saying. "I'm not goin' in! I'm not! It's gonna be cold!"

And then… the droll dolphins, lying on their sides and looking up at us, right *into* us, with a merry eye… Neil got in the water; and stroked a dolphin, and grinned, and was as infected as I was by their Zen-master insouciance. Afterwards we walked along a boardwalk and a people-watching dolphin gazed up at us roguishly. Neil went over and looked down at it. "You're a very *pretty* dolphin!" he crooned. "Yes you are!"

One day I was sitting sewing on the couch in my big office/sitting room, and he was in his TV room, some distance away in the big house. Something made me stop what I was doing and just sit with closed eyes for a moment, feeling the vibe… And then I saw it: in our beautiful living room, with its fine eco-bamboo flooring and bay windows and gold velvet furniture and bounteous pot-plants and fireplace – that room which we almost never used – there was a butterfly. It was as big as a car; and its wings moved gently up and down. It was palpable, if ghostly; it was rich and beautiful beyond describing. It was Neil's wordless emotional being. I knew in that moment that I was usually rather oblivious to it; that it would never have a language I could easily understand; that I was tragically missing him because I didn't see it; and that I did not, and would not, have the patience to try to learn its language-less language.

Later I told him about it. He nodded definitely; just once; said, "Mmp," in a way that told me he knew exactly what I meant.

We drove to Chicago, through the terrifyingly boring flat cornfields, where I kept trying to see if there was something to love; and enjoyed Miten and Deva Premal in concert; and Neil loved it and sang mantras off-key with the best of them. And as we strolled beside Lake Michigan, it was disclosed in passing that he had some time before switched from being a Republican to being a Democrat; thus betraying his entire Midwestern Conservative Family and their whole history. He hadn't felt the need to tell me this momentous thing.

But he wasn't coming with me.

At the last we went canoeing together in a beautiful, pristine state park, and in the rented cabin I wept and wept in his arms, missing him already more than I could bear. He stayed quiet and calm.

My sixtieth birthday was doleful. We trudged around a huge art museum in Kansas City, seeing, for some reason, the exhibits *he* wanted to see, even though it was *my* birthday. It was very hot; and all my friends and family were far away.

A local woman came to our house to buy, for ten dollars, my whole collection of exuberant, healthy, luxuriant houseplants. I asked her if she would like a gift of a bag of peaches from my tree. (Three years before, I had planted six ridgy pits from delicious organic peaches. One had come up, and was now a tall, wide, thriving green tree, weighted down with huge gold-red fruit that were as sweet and tasty as the best peach you've ever had… with juice dripping down to your elbows.) "Naaaanh… " she drawled. "Ah don't lak 'em *raw?* Ah only lak 'em *canned?*"

On 22nd August 2012, Neil took me to the airport in Kansas City. He helped me with my bags to the check-in, then said, "I'm gonna go. Otherwise I'll start crying." And he turned around, and went…

View from Devika's chalet, Switaerland

Zurich, 2004

With Neil, Switzerland 2004

With Neil in Missouri

Neil with dolphin, 2012

With Nisarg in Italy, 2010

With Jacques' cat, California 2009

In the Geisha quarter, Kyoto 2012

In front of Kwan Yin statue, Kyoto 2012

Kyoto, 2012

Switzerland, 2009

Dancing with Kohrogi-san, Provence 2013

With Sarita in Thailand, 2018

Devadasi, Sarita, me; Kyoto 2012

Sarita and me, Lake Arrowhead 2015

Devadasi, Delphi 2014

Me with Kohrogi-san, Provence 2017

11

Not I, but the Wind

Not I, but the Wind

2012 – 2017

In the Pennines

For the next three and a half years I worked as a private psychic, a sort of Metaphysical Personal Trainer, for Cyril Montkestrel-Foxmaigne, living alone in a house that he paid for. (Nisarg had flown in from Italy right away – my perky, empathic, loving blonde friend – charmed him, and instructed him on how to treat me. That's how the house, and a modest salary, happened.) The work went well – he was very sincere – though there did seem to be an intrinsic awkwardness between us.

I missed Neil terribly at first, wondering how I could have swapped my own huge, clean house and loving man for an insecure, cramped, damp-as-hell place all full of grit and grime and dripping noses wiped on hands (the Brits see hygiene-concern as an unhealthy fetish). But the sense of adventure prevailed.

Neil and I had two skypes. In the first one we cried so hard we didn't want to have another. In the second, six months after I left, he announced solemnly that he was now going to start looking for a girlfriend.

"I *love* you!" I told him, tears overflowing. "I only want you to be happy!" And it was true.

Soon he met someone, and he notified me of this. A year after that he was married, very happily. I saw it on Facebook – that he was happy; that they were well-matched. That he was Settled; which was what he wanted to be.

It was hard, though, when there was a picture of her holding up a ripe strawberry – the delicious berries *I* had planted – saying, "Look what I found in Neil's garden!"

And all my well-wishing for him – and it would have been intolerable, horrible, if he had stayed lonely – didn't stop the dreams.

I often had – and still have – dreams that I am with him, and he is almost turning to me, but does not; that his wife is waiting; or that his wife has lent him to me for two weeks, but he will then go back to her… that sort of thing; and I wake from them gasping with anguish that I have lost him.

And yet there is a knowing, as deep as any I have ever had – that the love between us, born in meditation, in space and Mystery, is as alive as ever; and leaps across the sea, effortlessly, to join us in gratefulness for what we accomplished together. We made a bridge, out of grace and Nothing; and it unites us still, no matter whom else we might love. This kind of love is a freedom, it asks nothing; it is just grateful to love, to feel the magic of what can be done with a man and a woman in an empty room; not necessarily even touching. There are a few people I love like this – that just loving is a privilege.

I knew nothing of this when I was young.

Wild Geese

I loved a man
with sable hair
a v-shaped mouth
and shoulders square.

He loved me too,
and all was good
in that roomy house
in a Midwest wood.

But every year
the wild geese flew
in an arrowhead
of birds and blue

And I looked up
when I heard them call
and my heart it woke
and I tiptoed tall.

My man bent down
to shoe the car
to earn the bread
to open the jar.

Sometimes we went
across some sea
where I felt at home
much more than he.

Till then one day
I left for good
that tidy man
in his house of wood

And though I've gone
I love him still
and I call to him
over vale and hill

When I fly so high
with neck outstretched
my strong wings wide
above Earth's deck –

I cry my heart
to the wild Fall
and the cold bright air
and my brethrens' call

But that good strong man
is married fast
and his house is warm
and I fly on past

Around the world
on a river of air
while the land is cold
and the trees are bare.

Working and Traveling

I traveled a lot, seeing Mr. Kohrogi every year in France, going to groups with Nisarg in Kiev or Warsaw or Corfu; and occasionally leading a group under Sarita's umbrella, in Latvia or Kazakhstan. Cyril traveled too, going to retreats and groups all over the world; but we did a lot of work together. He was a serious young man with a pale, ascetic complexion and a froth of black curls; his eyes were the color of half-hid olive leaves. He was very tall and slender, and as languid as an eel in a moat – yet he carried himself with a certain unimpeachable aplomb. His glance was cool – you could see the knights and courtiers, the statesmen and rulers of fiefdoms, buried in him like Lords and Ladies under stones before the altar of some country church. But he was a Seeker; struggled with all his will and passion to free himself; and I helped as best I could.

The casual relationship of the Brit to hygiene was to astonish me again and again. One day I was sitting in Cyril's very basic, grubby-with-the-grime-of-the-ages kitchen with him, having a snack. A slice of cucumber flew, at the prod of my fork, off my plate and onto the floor. Cyril leant over and, with perfect, graceful courtesy, scooped up the escaped veggie in his long fingers and deposited it back on my plate, where it sat next to the tofu – all shaggy in a new coating of hair.

Once, Cyril, his three kids and I, all went to the Ally Pally – the Alexandra Palace, a huge venue outside London – to see Amma-ji, the Hugging Guru. Amma-ji is a woman of comfortable girth, with a long braid down her back, who sits in her white sari hugging whomsoever. We waited in an endless queue until finally each of us could stand in front of her and get our hug. When it was my turn, and she enveloped me in her arms, she murmured into my ear: *Madhur madhur madhur madhur madhur madhur*... and I felt the consciousness penetrate all in a flash into my roots, as if I were a rosebush from my childhood garden, and she could see to the depths of it. She could not have known my name: she was saying, *Sweet sweet sweet sweet sweet*... I staggered away drunk, and danced in my white dress all over the empty side of the hall.

I loved the wild, craggy landscape of the Pennines where we lived, and enjoyed poetry classes and open mics. And all of it – snows, floods, bitter winters, winds... *was* adventure.

It was always wonderful in August to go to hot, breezy Provence for a Natsukashi group. Some deepening or breakthrough would always occur, when Kohrogi-san gave me an Ito-thermie session; and I loved both the relaxed, loving socializing, all lit-up by his nearness; and my solitary walks. In the 2013 group I went for a walk on a warm windy day, and, as so often happens, I came back with a poem. When I later showed it to Kohrogi-san he said, enthusiastically, "This is exactly your chalacter! Exactly your chalacter!"

I didn't really know what he meant… but it seems to me now that the Wind is what fills one's empty sails and takes one here or there. The empty wind, which nevertheless moves.

Lunchtime Walk: Briande

I was two-thirds down the mountain
Before I realized I was allowed
To listen to the wind.
It took up residence in my body
Like a man moving into an Alpine palace.
There were clouds on the ground
And hills in the sky.
Trees waggled and bopped
Stiff as courtiers,
Fresh as giraffes.
The air had been scrubbed with a sharp elbow.
A million sunny leaves swung crisp
Against dark-deep shade.
My light coat and long dress
Swished around my hurrying form –
Hurrying with the wind –

Another time, I was sitting in the group while he was teaching, fretting to myself about how poets don't get the perks and recognitions that Tantra teachers do. Suddenly Kohrogi-san announced, apropos of nothing: "Everybody is famous to himself."

Another time, he looked up at the beautiful view out the big window of the group room: purple Provençal mountains receding into the distance, forested and silent… and he said a thing I puzzle over often, even now: "When you die, the scenery comes rushing towards you and into you."

During a retreat in the Pyrenees, when it was my turn I lay on a pallet at the front of the room. Kohrogi-san placed his hands on my belly, then turned his eyes to mine and held eye-contact. And held… and held… and held.

I saw myself swinging up high in my favorite swing, in a park on the moors up above the valley town where I live. In this swinging I was joyful, at home in this moment, my heart flying into the sky. And Mr. Kohrogi *met me there* – right inside my joy, there he was; accompanying me. The greatest joy – the greatest meeting – a recognition of my spirit's bird-flight, my very home of joy. I don't know if such a thing had ever happened to me before… maybe, when I was dancing with Osho, that time outside Jesus Grove, at the Ranch; but then I was not relaxed into myself, I was jumping, shrieking and giggling, freaked out as well as bounding up and down in ecstasy! I was young…

I loved just hanging out with Kohrogi-san as well. Often we'd go, a group of us, to cafés or to an outdoor market, and just be normal; yet I was (we all were) acutely aware of the presence of something More among us.

At the end of one of these expeditions I was saying goodbye to Kohrogi-san in Montpellier Station. We hugged, and I saw the most amazing thing: from the place where our two bodies met, a bird flew up – but it was completely empty; just the outline of a bird was there, yet the bird wasn't there at all. It flew up into the high rafters above us.

Then I went for my train.

In 2014 I flew to Greece to meet up with Sarita, Devadasi, and a young friend of the family, who'd brought Devadasi from California (getting a free trip out of it). We all stayed in Sarita's large rented house outside a mainland town. We took wonderful expeditions – to Delphi, to hot springs, to Mt. Olympus – but Devadasi suffered constant confusion, and someone had to sleep in the same room with her (which she hated), as she would yell loudly, and roam about in the night, and do strange things, like hide bananas in her bed, and take off her nightclothes and stuff them into her pillowcase. The on-duty carer wouldn't get much sleep. Mama refused every expedition (though she had to go anyway), would not get into any hot springs, and generally was hydrophobic, carefully skirting any puddle on a pavement, and resisting bathing with even more piteous fervor than before. Looking at a hot springs pool, in a nice tiled bath-house, she would hiss, "I'm not going in there! I'm *not ready to die!*" And nothing Sarita or I said or did could persuade her – there's nothing like an enraged, cornered old lady for obduracy.

On the day I was leaving, I sat down and held her hand. I told her all the things I appreciated about the way she had mothered me: her supportiveness about poetry, her reading aloud to us, her praising us, her joy in nature… the list was long.

She was lucid suddenly. "This is very *important,*" she said. "I want you to write it down and send it to me."

And so I flew home, and did just that.

Mama Visits

One winter dawn early in 2016, in my quiet row house in the Pennines, I had a dream – but it was the kind of dream which feels factual and real: *I went into a room that had mysteriously appeared next to my bedroom. In it was a large bed, with very fresh white sheets, and there lay Devadasi.*

"Mama!" I cried, and went up to her and sat down, clasping her hands in mine. "You've come to visit! I'm so glad! I'm so happy to see you!"

She looked up at me. "My house exploded," she said, a bit dry, a bit surprised.

I woke up. Uh-oh, I thought, something has happened to Mama! I sent emails to family, asking what was going on.

Yes, she had just fallen and broken her hip. She was in hospital, family were with her, she was being taken care of very well.

I felt reassured by the crisp white sheets in my dream. And she did recover, for the time being…

Destitution

The healing center never happened; a promised inheritance took three years to materialize, and by the time it did, Cyril had moved on from the idea.

In early 2016 he announced that he wished to continue working with me, but no longer wanted to pay my rent. (I think that Inheriting had made him more prudent.) I had two months' warning that I'd have to move; but there was approaching me one of those troughs the stars get up to, and nothing presented itself – no place to move to, nothing else to do (for it did not feel right to work with him any more). Exhausted and distraught from both fear, and schlepping Stuff up and down three flights of stairs for many weeks, I was decanted onto the pavement with my houseful of belongings and a broken rib (gotten while, utterly exhausted, I was riding with massive pot-plants in the back of a van on a steep cobbled hill. I had bounced on a wheel-well while plant-dirt cascaded over me.)

There followed eighteen months of destitution and wandering, as the stars inched their inexorable way through their changes. I had puzzlingly few sessions to do, and only the occasional house-sit in somebody's cluttered dwelling; I ended up in Devon, in Corfu, in Mexico (a wonderful client imported me for two lifesaving, jacaranda-blossom-strewn weeks), in Bristol, and all over the damp, heroic (because it sometimes floods, and has to rally itself and survive willy-nilly) Ivybridge Mills. I put most of my stuff in storage, but too much came with me wherever I went; it just seemed needed. I was working on books regardless, and that is a papery business, with piles and strewings, as well as various bits of technology required. People did not like this (nor, in fact, did I like *their* stuff any better than they liked mine; and often fantasized sweeping it all out the door – but of course I couldn't say that) – and in fact the most difficult thing about that whole time was not the insecurity, or the hunger, or the discomfort; but the *scoldings* I got from almost everybody I encountered. When you don't have a roof of your own over your head, it seems, you become fair game. Like a weakened gazelle driven to the edge of the herd for the lions to pick off, you are prey to people's Tribal need to scorn the outsider. I can think of only a couple of people who did not let loose with scoldings during that time. I was, it seemed, to be shamed; that was one of my punishments – the other was being at the mercy of those same people. And, of course, most likely they were themselves afraid – I know I cringe away from people with, for example, amputations; for their fate could so easily be visited on any of us. Homelessness must be a fear bred in the human bone.

But I did not want to meddle with what life was doing. I was desperate, and I told everyone so; but I didn't know what to Do, and no Doing felt right. My mind, of course, leafed through possibilities endlessly – work in a grocery store? Clean houses? Go stay with a stranger in Rhode Island who had invited me, in a rather forbidding and conditional way?

But not only did I not *want* to meddle, I found that I *could not* – my body would not let me "try hard to somehow make things change." It flowed, it drifted, it went here and there – in response to invitations or evictions. People gave me money, or charged me small rents for temporary tenancies in uncomfortable niches. I ate at a soup kitchen, I spread my meager session-fees or donations out to cover food for the widest possible time.

One night, about six months into the travail, I was back in Ivybridge Mills, lying in someone's upstairs box room in the dark. The person's possessions were stacked about me, but the narrow bed in which I lay was soft and warm. It was late; everything was quiet. One small window was open onto the deserted cobbled street.

I had been thinking about what avenues might be open to me. How to get a room in someone's house, when there was no guarantee I could pay the rent? (The dream of a house of my own was beyond me… all sorts of proofs of income and deposits and things are needed.) How to get any money? I knew that working in a grocery store was not going to happen; my body would object to the fluorescent lights, and my boredom would send me out within a few days. I had no degrees the world would recognize, nor did anything interest me except the things I really wanted to do: writing, sessions, art. I hadn't the stamina or the knees for cleaning houses. And when you can make £120 giving a session, it seems crazy to work for minimum wage.

It seemed I could not *be myself* and coherently survive. Everywhere I looked there were only walls.

I lay in the dark, at my wits' end. I had been criticized so much, and had traipsed about everywhere, and now there was no other thing I knew to do. I would have to leave this house soon, and then what?

Then something curious occurred. I felt a Presence… someone was in the room with me, and very near to my body where I lay. This presence was extraordinary – it radiated a sort of silent love and joy. It was a very big sort of presence, not in size but in beingness – a potent force of love that was full of command as well. It Knew.

It leant over and kissed my belly, just once.

And I understood its essence… it was *nearness.*

God is *nearness.*

I lay then floating in soft and undone bliss and heart-tears, oh so soft.

This went on and on.

Next evening my hostess took me to a Sufi concert in a neighboring town. Turkish musicians played music which had been composed to accompany Rumi's poetry, back when Rumi was still alive. His poems were read aloud in their original language. I was astonished to feel that the frequency of that music was exactly what I had experienced the night before – that heart-vibrant nearness. Tears poured down my face.

Rumi was a refugee – his whole family had to flee some evil war. I had not known that.

On the way home in the car, a local go-getter woman wanted to hear my story. I told her how I came to be couch-surfing, and she declared that she would help me get some sort of government assistance (I had already looked into this, albeit reluctantly, and had, on encountering impossible conditions and walls, given up). As often happens, though, I was swayed by someone's powerful personality, and agreed to let her help.

At that moment something closed inside my body. My wonder vanished, my awe and bliss and gratitude. It all just folded itself up and went away. (And, after some kerfuffle, the woman's offer came to naught.)

Mama Goes on Her Way

In January 2017 my mother, Devadasi, left her body. She had been living in California with her granddaughter's family. Her dementia was well advanced, and it was a great stretch for everyone to care for her; she'd suffered broken bones and had had several operations in the recent years. But she was never put in a 'home.' She was ninety-nine.

Two months later there was a beautiful memorial for her, at a large venue in a shady state park in the Back Bay. All the family and many friends arrived from up and down the West Coast, from Canada to Mexico; and some from abroad. Many people spoke. I enjoyed telling this little anecdote:

After Al, Mama's third husband, died, my brother Andy and I went to Oregon to keep her company and help sort things out. There was much to do – their affairs were in disarray, and Al particularly had packratted a great deal of stuff that needed selling and giving away.

One day I came upon Mama in the kitchen, in a typical pose: standing still, hands clasped one in the other, brow furrowed with worry; a grim and independent air around her.

I said brightly, "So, Mama, isn't it great that Andy and I are taking care of *so many things*, so that you really don't have to worry about *anything?*"

Her head turned towards me sharply. "You mean," she said, "I don't have to worry about getting *pregnant?*"

Everybody laughed – Mama was famous for her wit. Two people played guitars and sang – including my old school friend Taffy, who, like all my friends, felt that she had always been treated with love and welcome by my mother.

Later that day Sarita and I scattered a third of the ashes on a woodsy hill-top in Marin County my mother had loved when she was young. There was a view to Mt. Tamalpais and the sea. The rest of the ashes would be scattered later, in other places, by other family members.

I did not grieve in the helpless way I had – and still do – for my father. That is, I think, because I spent much more time with my mother, and always said everything that was in my heart. We had long conversations about our lives; and though she often veered off into riffs of rage against my father, still enough got said to make things feel *au courant.* I kept, from her possessions, a ring I had had made for her: gold, with a large turquoise set in it – and I sometimes wear it if I am going someplace she might specially have liked.

California was glorious that spring, after a rainy winter – wildflowers lush and colorful everywhere. I relished the entire visit (made possible, in my penury, by a generous niece. Thank you, Shushannah).

Transits

My beloved little sister (whom I had begun to gaze upon with that same surprised generosity of heart that had lately been occurring in me; a mild, intermittent sort of lovingness – just sometimes – and this rather confounded me! For I can be mean, and this meanness is not unexpected, when I see it in myself) harassed not one but two Indian astrologers to look into my stars. Both acknowledged the current famine, and both predicted that things would change in the approaching December (which did occur). In fact, they said, things would become very positive. December was still a long time away… but it was reassuring to hear. As when I'd had the panic attack, back in the late 90's, it was relaxing to know the stars were behind it.

Kohrogi-san had told me, in this floating time, "Don't plan. Just do what you feel today, and your life will meet you in the middle of the bridge." (This, I feel, is for me; everybody is different. But didn't Osho say to me, back in 1975, "Now you drop all effort. You just float like a cloud."?)

It keeps me sane to tell myself, every day, "One day at a time. Just today. Only this day."

And then, when the time came, the tide rose and work began cascading in; and finally, after staying in thirty-two different places altogether, I found a room in a quiet, clean and congenial row-house up on the moors, with a wise and prudent psychotherapist with a bookcaseful of esoterica. I also found, for very cheap rent, a studio down by the river where I could write and paint.

On another front, after months of my own inner NLP work with Compulsive Thinking (that old theme. These days it tends to come as Health Anxiety: "Oh my god! What if I have xxx disease?") one day my being was so fed up with *working on things* that it began to simply send the dark, catchy thoughts right up out the back-of-the-top of my head as light! This was a huge relief.

Meanwhile, due to an inadvertent loan and the odd session-fee, I was able to see Kohrogi-san in France during a beautiful August. I asked him, "Since I have been homeless, and staying in many people's houses, I am not meditating very much, and I feel like an idiot."

I was lying on the treatment table as I said this, draped in a sheet. He was about to give me a session whilst the group watched and learned. So now he directed his comments to the small, rapt audience.

Mr. Kohrogi is, as I've said, a beautiful man, grave and laughing, loving and warm, with eyes as deep as the night skies of all the planets. He has smoke and whiskey in his voice, and he said, "Do not misunderstand. These things happen for a reason. Madhuri is a poet. Many times the wind is coming in her poetry, and this is beautiful. Madhuri is becoming more and more like the wind." And then he added, cryptically: "Sooner or later all of you have to become poets."

And then he began tracing the hot metal sticks with their burning loquat incense up and down my back, my legs – expertly, seeingly, quickly, penetratingly;

pressing sometimes on a point atop the shoulder or on the scapula or near the navel. And I thought of how the heated stripes he was making were meant to be the opposite of the cooler stripes that remain between them – for you are not supposed to cover the whole body with heat; the difference between hot and cool is what makes the Wind – the invitation for the Chi to move and take up its liveliness and healing.

His remarks gave me, once again, the feeling that it was okay to be me:
small
singing
and, completely outside my grasp or my ken,
subject to the (often scary) Great Waves of life.
Surprised.
Allowing.
Enjoying the view.
One day at a time.
Just today.
Only today.

Appendix of Treasures

Self-Healing: a Neat, Deep, and Miraculous Technique

The beauty of this method is that you can do it alone, wherever you are. If you find yourself in a place where there are no friends to exchange sessions with, or therapists you want to go to (and/or no money to pay them with either), you have everything you need anyway, in your own two hands.

The technique works for physical ailments, emotional discomforts, spiritual aches. I've healed myself of a beginning flu, just by following the steps laid out below; I've uncovered, and brought finally into soft joy, innumerable sorrows, questions, confusions. Would you like to try it?

What you will need:

2 small pillows
A rolled towel
A blindfold or scarf
Blankets or shawl for warmth
Plenty of uninterrupted time – allow two hours, just in case.
Your own two hands
The willingness to relax deeply and allow great stillness

The Method

Lie down in bed on your back with the rolled towel under your neck. Let the thickness of the roll be what is most comfortable for you. The small pillows are placed under your elbows. The scarf or blindfold goes over your eyes. Adjust the bedclothes so that you are as comfortable as possible – neither too warm nor too cold, with no uncomfortable pressure anywhere. I like to do this work in the morning when I first wake up; but sometimes too I do it in the middle of the night when sleep is not arriving and I feel restless and wakeful. Your timing will be your own.

Place your hands on your body wherever they want to go – where the pain is, the ache, the difficulty. (If the sorrow is emotional or spiritual, I often end up with both hands on my heart.) Take some time now to just relax. Let the body be exactly as it is. Let your mind wander and do whatever it wants. When you feel that it has roamed about as much as it wanted, commenting on this and that; and you are ready to settle, begin to notice the sensations in your body where the difficulty is. Just allow them. There is nothing that your mind has to do – so you can just keep coming back to the feelings. Let them be as they are, not trying to change a thing. It is important to just let things be exactly as they are.

If you find that you want to avoid the feelings, just take note of that and let the avoidance be part of all that is going on.

Eventually you will reach a sort of plateau, or gap, where you have faced the feelings/sensations, and are ready to begin exploring. Don't rush it – this gap will arrive in its own time.

The Ten Questions

Now you can begin with the questions. You will need to peek at the list of them at first, but will soon memorize them as your body joyfully recognizes the steps. (If you have someone to exchange with, you could try having them ask the questions at first, to help you get aligned with the process and remember the steps.)

1. Show me a safe place in my body.

Just trust whatever arises in response to this question. It might be a picture, a feeling, a sound. This is a place you can come back to if you become frightened or worried. For example, I often see a stout tree-trunk in my right thigh, or my abdomen. If the place is off the body, in the aura, accept it just as it is.

The image can change, either subtly or drastically, each time you ask the question.

2. Show me the Core of Health.

The Core of Health is a Cranio concept which I find very beautiful; it means that each of us has a healthy interior somewhere, or we could not be alive. By connecting with this healthy core we begin with Health, with the affirmative acknowledgment of our center. You can come back to this, too, at any point during the Self-Healing. When you ask this question, just trust whatever arises in response. I often see a skeleton in me made of emerald… or fire… or white crystal. It can be anything. If you are not particularly visual, it might be a feeling in a certain place.

3. Where is the Silence in this?

This is an interesting question. Most often when I ask it I do not see Silence at all; I see all that is *not* Silence: the noise, the difficulty; more explicitly, more outlined. I usually ask this question over and over again for a while, so that I can give the best chance to the Silence and also to the problem to show itself.

Here you will be feeling the pain of your issue. As far as possible, face it. You don't have to *do* anything with it – please don't – but you will have to allow it to be there, in all its awfulness/pain/wincing dread. These are emotions and feelings you have wanted to avoid. But now is your chance to face them, squarely and cleanly, as best you can. Just… face what you have not faced. The finer the nuances of your noticing, the better. The real prize is when you notice an energy that has been right under your nose all along and you had never recognized it before. That is freeing! Energy often then will rush wholesale up to the crown and out the top of your head. Sometimes the body will jerk or adjust itself or sigh when this occurs.

The Silence might also be felt as a mysterious background to the pain. Life is complicated, paradoxical, ornate… you can encompass both.

If you cannot find the Silence after much asking and experiencing whatever comes up, you can acknowledge, "I can't find the Silence in this." It's really relaxing to just acknowledge this – there's no judgment on it. This helps make space to move to the next step. …Or, you might find the Silence right away. Many people I've worked with seem to.

4. Take me to the Root.

Allow whatever comes. Just trust what arises, and then face it, experience it, without Doing anything. I often see a picture from my childhood here;

something that reminds my unconscious in some way of the current situation. No need to question what the unconscious comes up with – just allow it. Just be with the pain of whatever scene is before you, that you find yourself part of. Just be with it as it is, not escaping. Notice minutely. Eventually you will feel satisfied with your deep awareness of the scene, and a gap appears. Then you are ready to move to the next layer. (If you try to move prematurely it will not work – you'll be pulled back to go on facing till the scene/energy/sensation is faced!)

5. Take me to the Real Root.

Allow whatever arises. If you see a picture from some time or place you don't recognize from this life, don't stand in its way – let it be. Face it exactly like you would something from this life. It's no different… Face the feelings, allow the story to be seen, don't Do anything. Rest and allow… Take note in yourself of the understandings which arise.

It is the mind's nature to doubt; it might say, *Oh, this can't be a past life, I am full of B.S., what rubbish is this? A picture of a haystack on fire, and me, a little boy, running away, and the barn catching too – no, how absurd!* Let the mind doubt, but stay with the living energy of the picture/feeling. It has reality in your inner world, and that is enough. Let it unfold, unroll. Face the pain of it. The more raptly still you are, the more complete the experience and the comprehension.

You might then ask yourself, *What did I learn from that life?*

6. Take me to the Deepest Root.

Here I often find myself in cave-man times, involved in a drama of survival or some such. These are our roots. It is at this level, often in a very simple scene, that I find the deepest understanding of the nature of my difficulty. When the saber-tooth tiger had me backed up against the wall of the cave, what was my overpowering emotion? What did I learn? What was my decision? Just observe what's happening. But sometimes I'll be in an incident from this life, or a recent past one. Whatever comes… Allow the Knowings which will arise as you see yourself trying to survive, or whatever is going on.

When you feel complete with this – when you have seen and allowed and learned from the Deepest Root, when releasings have occurred in your body, and you are relieved, and you feel ready to go on:

7. Show me the Key.

Here you have no idea what will come. Something will show itself – a key to what is the best thing to do here, with this symptom. In the case of a cold or flu, you might see a picture of some forgotten herbal remedy you have in the fridge. Or you might be told to rest. In the case of an emotional difficulty, you might see that the only key is to face the feelings, allow them. (To avoid pain is to avoid the joy that would come after as well.) Or, you might see a glass of water – drink more water! Or who knows what... The resourcefulness of the Knowing deep within you is amazing. Trust whatever shows itself. Often what I see here is just that I am to do what I am already doing: experience, to the best of my ability, the full breadth and depth of the dis-ease.

When you feel that you have seen the Key (for me this happens very fast), there will come a gap.

8. Show me the Healing.

This will bring you a picture/feeling/knowing of the Healed State. You might find big breaths releasing as peace comes in. As you see what the healed state looks like, you see a flash of what the dis-ease was; now that it is gone... and now the healing takes over, soft and sure. It arises from the work you have just done, it is a consummation, a wholeness, a living flow. Enjoy...

9. Show me the Light.

Who knows what will arise? Transcendence suffusing the state of Health – illuminated and uplifted. The cosmos can bring down its joy and levity to you. You lie in grace... Ahhhh... And you have earned it, and you have not Done anything. You've just used a small excavation tool – the question; and Faced what Is, and watched it transform.

Bathe in this beauty...

10. Show me the integration of this into my daily life.

As always, just relax and allow the question to do the work; allowing whatever comes in response from the Mysterious Forces. My experience is that this question brings a solid empowerment, integrated and centered; the realizations from the healing become a sort of fuel for the day, propelling me centered into life.*

* Thank you, Sarita, for the addition of this final question. It really rounds things off!

Thank you, Guides.

Say that, or Thank you, Invisibles, or whatever… You can find your own Whoever to thank. I always namaste, from my lying-down position.
And you are ready to rise.

A word, here, about your hands: They are neutral – you are not doing anything with them. You may move them about if you feel to – if one place feels finished you may start over at a new place – or change the position for more comfort or energetic relevance. The reason I've used the word 'miraculous' in my title is because these neutral hands can become something truly astonishing and full of grace: a conduit, a channel, for the healing to pass from the cosmos to you; or from you to you – who knows which? The hands then are finally the loving and cherishing you are giving yourself – so lightly, yet with such tender power coming through that you have neither 'done' nor intended. This process is a way of loving yourself so dearly. This is delicious. You love you, by being passive and paying close and rigorous attention – yet somehow something bigger is loving you.

This love acknowledges, too, that you will take the time and space out of this busy world to observe in minutest detail the merest breathings of your inner landscape/seascape/skyscape. Love comes out of this; and a feeling of empowerment: I can do all this alone, with just my own two hands!

And, a further note on Intention: when you lie down to work, do not expect or project a result: "Oh, if I do this I'll feel better." If you are carrying expectation, your presence will be diminished. Do not hope – just "be with." Then full magic is yours.

Meditation While You Are on a Walk

On one trip to France I wrote down this meditation that Kohrogi-san had spoken of:

Scenery Meditation

You know how, when you are walking in some beautiful place – in woods, or by the sea, or up on moors, or through a park... sometimes a certain view will catch you? You have just put your foot out to step forward, when a precise viewing-angle shows you a certain picture: light slanting through trees just so; a ray of sun, come down through clouds, shines on a shifting sea, just so. A tree at your right frames the path ahead of you; or you see green grass with a filled-up look about it, as if it is so green it is stuffed with green-ness, a particular rich glowing sort of color... but framed by trees darker and more solemn and old. Or perhaps you see a house and the roof slants just so, the colors of the paint lifting out warmly from a backing of forest. Or maybe there is a stream, and the light and the angle of your view shows you a slice of its burbling life, in a painterly way that delights you, reaches out to you somehow. Or a huge panorama from a hillside, where you stand lifted up above a valley, throws open a door in you where the melancholic light from the grey sky suddenly has access to your inner body.

But it is always a certain angle – a lift of the foot onwards and the special view is lost.

I first really noticed this 'precise angle' phenomenon when I was working in the far north of Norway in the summer. I walked a lot between sessions, and found myself stopping to take in certain things: somebody's duvet being aired over a second-floor balcony rail, a swath of color down the dark wood siding. And I just had to stop and stare.

Kohrogi-san says that those precise-angle views are your Higher Self, showing itself to you.

He says that painters and photographers paint those visions, or take their pictures.

So now when I walk and I am stopped in my tracks by a slant of light on a river, I stop. Stop completely, right where I am, just this position. And gaze. I feel as if I am looking at something mysterious, ineffable; some alchemy my Higher Self wants for me and I would be churlish to refuse.

If I stay long enough, things happen. I feel the view entering my body. It works in there. This working has no mind in it. No gears and reasonings are needed. Some communion is taking place between me and that exact framing. And I am washed through then, upwards, by everything at once: waves of a sort of neutral beatitude, pushing out the mind and filling me with space and affirmation: You are this. *You are just this mood you see here, just this place among the trees.*

And I walk on finally, breathing in that new space, feeling as if I'd just come out of Kundalini meditation or something like that; yet this was a random meditation, unplanned, unconstructed.

I love the simple elegance of that.

The Human Design System

"The Human Design system is a revolutionary system. [...] It is based on the understanding that the true nature of any individual can be revealed through a genetic imprint that originates from the date, time, and place of birth. Even though this might sound like traditional astrology, the Human Design system offers a much more precise and detailed reading of the uniqueness of each and any one of us."

– *From a brochure for Nisarg's groups*

And from a brochure for the work of Christine Spicer, a New Zealander and Human Design analyst and teacher:

"Have you ever wondered where your inner truth resides: Your gut? Your intuition? Your emotions? Your heart? Or something else entirely?

Human Design provides you with your own unique map called a Bodygraph. It's a synergy of ancient wisdoms and modern science including: Chinese I Ching, Hindu-Brahmin chakra system, Jewish Tree of Life, Astrology, Genetics/DNA, Quantum Physics."

I'll just say: Human Design is uncanny. It works. It helps. The internet has a great deal of information on it. The system was channeled in strange circumstances by Ra Uru Hu, a Canadian, in Ibiza in 1986; and slowly/quickly spread. It's given me the courage to be myself, in my own flow; and let others be themselves. This is great!

Poetry in Stones

(I wrote this when I still lived in the Pyramid and was still working with stones.)

Aldous Huxley has said that people are attracted to jewels because jewels can mimic a mystic experience. The jewel has that quality a person wants to discover in himself – the stone is a mirror.

I will never forget "entering into" the largest blue topaz I have ever seen. It was like walking through a doorway into a secret chamber of transparent, aqua-blue joy. I felt like a princess re-entering the innermost sanctum of her castle – treading lightly, in awe at the purity of her own heart.

A stone is also very generous. Though beautiful stones should not be considered a substitute for meditation, they can and do give of themselves without reservation: their individuality, their richness, their particular healing quality.

Stones are so different from each other! An amethyst is completely different from an agate, which is so different from a diamond, or a garnet. Each has a quality, a lovely job to do. A person who is nervous might be attracted by a string of agates. Holding the agates, suddenly there is peace... a cool, placid freshness. A person with some energetic disturbance around the head might be attracted to a clear crystal. Holding it, a sudden, magnetic clarity, shooting upwards from the crown. A pre-menstrual woman might reach for garnets – nourishment for the female organs – soothing, relaxing. A person who is nearing a big change in her life – who really, deeply, wants a change – might be immensely attracted to moldavite. Holding a diamond, closing your eyes, you get a seventh-chakra blast of pure, concentrated light, like from the sun – after all, diamonds are plant-carbons compressed and compressed until they crystallize; a long-advanced outcome of photosynthesis. Energy from the sun.

It often amazes me how so many people can feel the effect of stones. Our sensitivity is so available; the knack is just to *notice* what we are feeling. For example, rosequartz is soft and loving. Just hold it and notice; feel the heart-opening that it gives you.

Rubies have a special beauty. When I first started exploring stones I conceived a passionate desire for some of this deep-soft-red jewel. When I 'entered' the desire, with my eyes closed, at lunch one day in the canteen, I was transported to a past life where dastardly deeds were done for rubies!

My greed for them then disappeared, but what emerged was an exploration: I discovered that for past-life regressions, there is nothing like a ruby. It has the ability to transport the person deep into the past, into their issue. In that depth, a useful, freeing contact with the past can happen.

During sessions I have used stones whose color fits with a chakra (for example, amethyst is for the third eye). I lay the stone gently on the chakra. A ruby I might place in the person's hand for energetic penetration. Garnet would be for the first chakra, but the person could also hold it. Black tourmaline is fabulously grounded, and a huge one will have a marvelously calming effect and create trust. One just goes by intuition.

Each stone is an individual – each person is an individual. The interaction will be unique – and for *this* moment. Here's how I tune in: I hold the hands of a person, tune in for a moment. Then I put the stone in their hands, and tune in again. What has changed? How does the stone affect them? It's like looking at a series of little energy-vignettes, but in each lies much depth. People, listening to me describe what I'm seeing, begin to glow. And when they walk away with *their* piece – or pieces – they have a funny little smile around their faces. It's so different than buying from a shop; you've been *cared into,* and your treasure is special, for *you.*

The pieces are always given in a little velvet or silk or lace bag. (I have fun choosing the cloth for these; scraps of hand-embroidered silk, or antique kimono silk from Japan, or a fine brocade from India.) You choose the bag you like best.

I also help people choose gifts for friends. If they can bring a photo, great – we try different pieces on the photo and I 'tune in' with each one. Amazingly easy. Or, I can tune in without a photo; by hearing the person's name and location. Always good results so far!

Sometimes people pick up a piece of jewelry which doesn't suit them at all. It blocks energy somewhere – or overheats it somewhere else – or provokes melancholy (as labradorite, a beautiful, chatoyant stone with blue fires in it, can do with someone whose emotions aren't flowing). Then they aren't allowed to buy it.

Now, I want to share with you how the jewelry pieces come to be.

My first piece, a bracelet of malachite and pearls, was shown me in a dream. I found an excellent jeweler and stones-supplier I could work with and trust, and I had the piece made up, and a necklace to go with it. And I never looked back. Here's how I design:

I spend many hours in Shree Jewellers' little shop going through piles, mounds, boxes, folded papers, of lapis lazuli, faceted clear crystal from Brazil in many sizes, gorgeous, multi-colored tourmalines, faceted or cabochon; bumpy chunks of moldavite, smooth carnelians, super-intense diamonds. Whatever he's got, the jeweler, I sit with, paw through, weigh in my hand, close my eyes, feel the energy of. Out of many thousands of stones, I choose just a few from each packet. A few which are *right* – which have the essence of their kind; which are pure, which make me laugh, or bring me awe, or blow the top of my head off with their strength. I don't usually want stones with inclusions – little bits of grey rock in them – for example, rainbow moonstones often have little bits of grit in them. These little bits are also felt when I feel the stone, and they feel like what they are – in the way. (Even amber with an insect in it – more valuable monetarily than plain amber – doesn't feel good to me. Amber has a glowing, light, warm presence and the insect interferes.)

After many hours I have hundreds of stones of all sorts: chrysocolla, chrysoprase, larimar, fluorite, green onyx, and so on... each one a beauty.

I take them home. When I'm ready to design, I put a *Do Not Disturb* sign on the door – which will stay there for a few days. Once I start designing I lose interest in food, company, or anything else!

I prepare my materials: little squares of paper to draw the designs on; magic markers, pens, crayons, little ziploc plastic bags. Tweezers; a pad of paper, to list and illustrate the designs as I go. A large tray lined with white paper.

On the white spread of the large bed I start dumping out little piles of the beautiful stones. I usually have some cached from previous sorties, or other design sessions, and these come out too.

In an almost random, haphazard fashion, guided by a place I visit often but cannot account for – I start to put the stones together.

I don't draw a design first; the stones themselves tell me what to do. The design is there for the stone and not the other way around. That's why no two designs can be the same, that's why my inclinations don't run to any kind of mass production. For me, the integrity of the stone comes first. The silver or gold is a way to frame it, hold the stones together, allow them to be worn; but I order very little extra metalwork. And the silver or goldwork needs to be very good – so good it doesn't intrude on the stones.

The revelry of designing is the sense of utter freedom. Here I am so close to flying! I let things put themselves together out of some almost reckless, quirkish, spontaneous spring of the universe, reveling in their beauty as they tell me where to put them. Yes – tremendous care, in that the *feeling* has to be just right. But it is not a *serious* thing; it's the treat of the unexpected. I love to combine things which may not often have been combined before. It's like a blank paper and dozens of rich paints in many colors. It's like deciding what to wear to a special party – bouquets of colors and shapes to play with.

Each year I make something I call a "Tree of Life"– each year, of course, different. The trunk and branches of the tree are of moss-green moldavite, and the fruits and leaves are of every other stone I can find! Carnelian, sunstone, citrine, moonstone, tourmaline, lapis, turquoise, and so on. This feels like my heart when I dance!

After the designs are made, drawn on the little bits of paper and on my list, sealed with the chosen stones in the ziploc bags, they go to the jeweler. I sit for hours with him, going over each design in turn. Sometimes he makes suggestions about the silver or gold-work; the great thing is, he *understands* what I am doing. He is happy with all of it too.

When the pieces are in progress I check them; and again when they are done. When, finally, all are ready – sixty, ninety, one hundred and fifty pieces – I put them through a three-day cleaning process.

This is so very important. The stones which you see in any jeweler's shop or market stall are not clean. Stones soak up vibrations, in varying degrees depending on the stone. Even stones which don't soak stuff up – rosequartz – moldavite – Osho marble – often have dusty auras from handling, and can be refreshed with a rosewater bath plus washing and polishing with a cloth, or a treating with Serapis Bey Aurasoma Quintessence.

You've probably heard about certain famous stones which carry a 'curse.' Precious stones such as rubies, emeralds, and diamonds are often re-cut between owners to try to reduce this possibility. As I see it, these stones in particular "soak up" vibrations (crystals and opals do too) and desperately need cleaning at intervals. Re-cutting the stone might help, but not very much. The "memory" needs to be taken out of the stone.

There is a very simple way to clean any stone; it works so well. I bury them for forty-eight hours in dry magnesium sulfate: epsom salts. Yes, it's the same stuff nannies used to give kids – perhaps still do – to keep them "reglar". It's the stuff athletes use in their baths to relax and soothe sore muscles. It's a marvelous detoxifier and all-round purifier. It can be set out in bowls in rooms where therapy is done – just sitting in the corner it helps clean the vibes. It's great mixed with a little honey and warm water and scrubbed all over your (dry) body (hair too), then rinsed off. Such a clean, smooth, baby-skinned feeling; and uncomfortable vibes you've been laboring under will vanish.

After their dry bath in the salts, I take the stones out and bathe them quickly in rose-and-lavender water. Then I wash them in warm water with a little natural soap liquid in it, rinse well, and dry and polish with a soft cloth. The salts are then discarded.

After dark, I take the pieces up onto the white-tiled flat rooftop of Jesus House, lay them out on a cloth in the starlight or moonlight, and sit with them while they bathe in this cool, soft, night-feeling.

Then they are ready. Each piece is sealed into a cellophane bag (these keep silver from going dark; plastic bags encourage oxidation) until such time as they are to be displayed, in some faraway land, on white velvet, with candle-light or daylight, and perhaps soft music; with tea and cakes offered. (When there is time, and I'm in a country long enough, I like sending hand-painted invitations to the people who are invited to the party.) Electric light is to be avoided if possible; and especially fluorescent light – horrors! Both steal the subtlety of the stones' colors, and fluorescents have a disturbing vibration which cuts across the nature-vibrations of the stones – and the people who hold them.

I will never forget a show in Lugano: white velvet laid out on long tables, candle-light, and the hundred fabulous huge sparkly clean pieces of creative whimsy crystallized in timeless geology. A man walked in, stopped, looked around. He took a breath. *"Porca Madonna!"* he exclaimed, with full Italianate intonation. (Which means, *"Pig Madonna!"*)

Not all rocks are absolutely rocks, and not all rocks are equally asleep. Rocks have their respective individuality too. [...]

Also, don't be under the wrong impression, normally created by applying the law of economics, that certain things become valuable because of their rarity. This is not how these stones are valued.

[...] Precious stones are a great discovery of man. Those who were able to read the stones in depth, able to go deep in their research, to connect with them, found out that even with stones, there are some which are awake. Certain stones are more awake; certain others, more asleep. People also came to know that certain stones are awake in a particular direction. [...]

- Osho, *And Now, And Here*, Ch. 10, Q. 1 - 1970

A stone is beautiful because it is beautiful *intrinsically* – not because it is compared with other stones, or because it is relatively scarce. A pure amethyst for example will go straight to the third eye of the wearer and vibrate there in immense beauty and clarity, relaxing and opening the person's visionary space. This is its value. Amethysts, in the 1800's, were more valuable economically than diamonds, because they were more scarce. Then a large deposit of the purple crystals was found in South America and the price went down.

The value of diamonds, economically, is a contrivance. New diamond mines go on being discovered all the time. These are quickly bought up by the diamond cartel and the diamonds are warehoused, so that not too many will be on the market at once. Thus the "value" stays up. But in fact there are so many diamonds on this earth that every man, woman, and child could have a handful of them. They wouldn't have to cost much at all. Everybody could enjoy the sparkly, intense light of these lovely stones. Nature has not been miserly with them.

There's a kind of session I do with stones. People bring their entire collection, and we go through it piece by piece – tuning in, seeing which pieces fit, which should be given away, which need cleaning. If, for example, you inherited an opal ring from your granny, it will have her whole life stuffed into it, and you might want to clean it so that it has a new life as your own – so that you don't carry her sorrows each time you wear it ...This type of session quickly becomes an in-depth reading of the person.

A tip – If you have extra unset stones, your houseplants or garden plants will be very pleased to receive them.

Tip No. 2: Put lots of big unset stones around your computer. Not crystals; but rosequartz, agate, dense ruby, garnet, black tourmaline... they help protect you from EMF pollution.

After working as a therapist for many years, it was at first difficult for me to accept that it was okay to work with something – stones – which were just pure fun! Luxury! Beauty! Delight! (I had thought that human suffering was more *meaningful.)* Yes – stones can be medicinal – they are profoundly healing – but in such an aesthetic spirit! I feel privileged to work with them. Their beauty reflects the beauty in us… a thing beyond struggle.

Grateful in the Night

A while ago someone sent me a YouTube vid where a young Indian man rapped about gratefulness, interspersed with footage of all sorts of people singing and dancing their joy at being alive.

Somehow it was the right moment for me to see it. I've never liked New-Agey gratefulness manifestos – they seem to me to be escaping the gritty, gnarly inner and outer city streets of life – and my own experience is, I need the dark as mulch and loam and fodder; I need the dark too as beauty, as love, as sensibility, as courage, as wholeness. I embrace it, as best I can, and without rancor – as best I can. What else is Dynamic meditation for? Dark and light are not to be segregated; I like the lake I swim in to be deep.

But the mind has habits: to complain and doubt and worry; especially in the middle of the night, when there are no distractions. And it was the right moment for me to try something new, on the nights when I woke and felt to do something other than my Self-Healing meditation; something shorter and more immediately soothing.

So I'd lie between the sheets, under the lovely cozy weighty covers, and say to myself, *"I'm grateful that I've got green juice already in the fridge for the morning! I'm grateful I cleaned the floors in three rooms today! I'm grateful I found that teal cardigan in the charity shop! I'm grateful I gave them a pile of clothes and two books and thus got rid of that stuff! I'm grateful the bathroom is just across the hall and I don't have to go up or down stairs! I'm grateful for my wonderful bed! I'm sooo grateful for this house! I'm grateful I went food shopping today! I'm grateful for my friend Nisarg in my life! I'm sooo grateful I got that !@#$%^&* plane ticket booked today! I'm grateful there's a movie on Sunday that looks good! I'm grateful I wrote a poem today, that was fun! I'm grateful I got those audio books from the library. I'm grateful I finally got that pesky email done, that I was dreading. I'm grateful for the silence around right now! I'm grateful for my comfy warm boots!"*

Sometimes I'd add a codicil: *"I'm grateful for my comfy warm boots even if they are muddy and the zipper is gone on one so I have to tie them up with twine!"* The qualification seemed not to take away from the thankfulness – just pinpointed its accuracy.

And I found that each homely item I noted, and acknowledged, brought a sort of sigh of let-go and relaxation; as if these mundane, or not-so-mundane blessings had been waiting for me to notice and acknowledge them and, now noticed, they could expand into something even simpler – a happy out-breath. The very idea of my Gratefuls, in fact, warms and soothes me all over and makes me feel happy and sleepy. Surprising to observe just how glad I am about so many things!

It's really just that: a noticing of what is already the case. And that doesn't feel so New-Agey… instead, it's a private observingness in the dark as I lie in the arms of my room. It doesn't belong to anybody else, New-Age or Zen or whatever. It is just lovely to have each item suggest itself and feel so neatly true. The mind is also successfully steered away from its doleful predictings and grumps.

And I get so relaxed I fall asleep.

Or, you can ask, "*Who* is grateful… for (whatever blessings you are noticing)?" This however does not lead to any answers; or to a happy sleep; but to a kind of vivid wakefulness – a silent humming all over – a deepening; with colors playing over it like Northern Lights.

Thank You

Henrietta Bond, for grappling with the first edit of a messy, every-which-way manuscript. I would not have had the courage to continue if you hadn't helped make sense out of it.

Punya, for that heroic week in which you gave unstintingly of your precious time and energy in the service of this book. I am still astonished, and so very grateful, for your gimlet eye and allowing heart. Thank you too for being a cheering section, and for the final look-through to correct the bits of finer punctuation I just couldn't deal with. It is beyond my powers of expression to praise enough the help you gave in bringing the final manuscript to heel – you showed an unaccountable devotion – as well as a frightening level of expertise – and I owe you, big-time.

Roger King, dancer, wise man, and generous Innocent; for doing that first read and then showering me with encouraging praise.

Piers Cross, for your warm house, the glowing wood-stove, the great vibes; and your supportive, clear-eyed help with the tech.

Bindu, for lighting a fire under my heinie so that I'd finally get going on a project I'd long intended to get to... someday. And for your genius CD, *Plain Tales from Poona,* to which we danced before meditating, on workdays. Fly high, beloved; gone on your further journey. Most of all I remember how we laughed.

Prabha, for the encouragement.

Tracy Adams, landlady par excellence, and then calm, hospitable Rachel Tighe; for shelter while I was in the long unfolding.

Angela at Alexandros Guesthouse in Arillas Beach, Corfu; and also Maria: for the oranges and lemons and olive oil, and the roofs while I worked. And to Catherine/Sugandha, for the grand winter house-sit where I first started typing up my scribbles.

Nisarg, for Seeing, and for all the love and brilliance and supportiveness towards an oddball, for all the years.

Sarita, for old letters, bits of memory; and for the original door-opening – and so many since; and for your amazing, precious Being.

Dharmaraj, for the solidity and the supportiveness – you are a treasure and a King.

Alexander, beloved nephew, for storing old papers and photos these many years.

Chris, for holding such a warm and calm space while I was beginning the grappling with this project; it could not have been easy.

Antar, for the vote of confidence that helped keep the boat afloat.

Smaran, for finding the discourses and darshans.

...and Peggy, for your brilliant, generous, ebullient expertise and clear-eyed hard work on the cover and design. Things ran away with themselves, and you battled like a Valkyrie. You are a laughing, expostulating hero, running with all the colors of the rainbow, and white light too. I *waaaay* owe you.

The Third Angel: Srajano, whose amazing invitation to make an audio recording of this book, led to a stay in Holland replete with comfiness and great conversation. I much enjoyed your formidable, hospitable, quirky and brilliant being.

And to so many friends, for asking again and again when the book would be ready. It all helped.

...And to all the men, back then: for your goodness, your sweetness, and your accommodating of a much-clueless, butterfly soul.

L - #0383 - 170820 - C0 - 229/152/36 - PB - DID2889388